Pattern Languages of
Program Design 4

The Software Patterns Series

Series Editor: John M. Vlissides

The Software Patterns Series (SPS) comprises pattern literature of lasting significance to software developers. Software patterns document general solutions to recurring problems in all software-related spheres, from the technology itself, to the organizations that develop and distribute it, to the people who use it. Books in the series distill experience from one or more of these areas into a form that software professionals can apply immediately. *Relevance* and *impact* are the tenets of the SPS. Relevance means each book presents patterns that solve real problems. Patterns worthy of the name are intrinsically relevant; they are borne of practitioners' experiences, not theory or speculation. Patterns have impact when they change how people work for the better. A book becomes a part of the series not just because it embraces these tenets, but because it has demonstrated it fulfills them for its audience.

Titles in the series:

The Design Patterns Smalltalk Companion, Sherman Alpert/Kyle Brown/Bobby Woolf

The Pattern Almanac, Linda Rising

Pattern Hatching: Design Patterns Applied, John Vlissides

Pattern Languages of Program Design, edited by James O. Coplien/Douglas C. Schmidt

Pattern Languages of Program Design 2, edited by John M. Vlissides/James O. Coplien/
Norman L. Kerth

Pattern Languages of Program Design 3, edited by Robert Martin/Dirk Riehle/
Frank Buschmann

Pattern Languages of Program Design 4, edited by Neil Harrison/Brian Foote/
Hans Rohnert

Please see our web site at http://www.awl.com/cseng/swpatterns
for more information on these titles.

Pattern Languages of Program Design 4

Edited by

Neil Harrison

Brian Foote

Hans Rohnert

ADDISON-WESLEY

An imprint of Addison Wesley Longman, Inc.
Reading, Massachusetts • Harlow, England • Menlo Park, California
Berkeley, California • Don Mills, Ontario • Sydney
Bonn • Amsterdam • Tokyo • Mexico City

Many of the designations used by manufacturers and sellers to distinguish their products are claimed as trademarks. Where those designations appear in this book and Addison-Wesley was aware of a trademark claim, the designations have been printed in initial caps or all caps.

The authors and publisher have taken care in the preparation of this book, but make no express or implied warranty of any kind and assume no responsibility for errors or omissions. No liability is assumed for incidental or consequential damages in connection with or arising out of the use of the information or programs contained herein.

The publisher offers discounts on this book when ordered in quantity for special sales. For more information, please contact:

Corporate, Government, & Special Sales
Addison Wesley Longman, Inc.
One Jacob Way
Reading, Massachusetts 01867

Library of Congress Cataloging-in-Publication Data

Pattern languages of program design 4
     p. cm.
   Includes bibliographical references.
   ISBN 0-201-43304-4
    1. Computer software—Development.   2. Object-oriented programming (Computer science)   3. Software patterns. I. Foote, Brian.
II. Harrison, Neil.   III. Rohnert, Hans.
QA76.76.D47P36   1999
005.1'2—dc21
                                     99-37085
                                       CIP

ISBN 0-201-43304-4
Text printed on recycled and acid-free paper.
1 2 3 4 5 6 7 8 9 10—MA—0302010099
First printing, December 1999

Contents

Preface. . . . . *ix*

Introduction I. . . . . *xiii*

Introduction II . . . . *xvii*

PART 1 *Basic Object-Oriented Patterns*

   1 Abstract Class   *Bobby Woolf*   5
   2 Role Object   *Dirk Bäumer, Dirk Riehle, Wolf Siberski, and Martina Wulf*   15
   3 Essence   *Andy Carlson*   33
   4 Object Recursion   *Bobby Woolf*   41
   5 Prototype-Based Object System   *James Noble*   53
   6 Basic Relationship Patterns   *James Noble*   73

PART 2 *Object-Oriented Infrastructure Patterns*

   7 Abstract Session: An Object Structured Pattern   *Nat Pryce*   95
   8 Object Synchronizer   *António Rito Silva, João Pereira, and José Alves Marques*   111
   9 Proactor   *Irfan Pyarali, Tim Harrison, Douglas C. Schmidt, and Thomas D. Jordan*   133

PART 3 *Programming Strategies*

  10 C++ Idioms   *James O. Coplien*   167
  11 Smalltalk Scaffolding Patterns   *Jim Doble and Ken Auer*   199
  12 High-Level and Process Patterns from the Memory Preservation Society: Patterns for Managing Limited Memory   *James Noble and Charles Weir*   221

PART 4 *Time*

13 Temporal Patterns   *Andy Carlson, Sharon Estepp,*
   and Martin Fowler   241

14 A Collection of History Patterns   *Francis Anderson*   263

PART 5 *Security*

15 Architectural Patterns for Enabling Application Security
   Joseph Yoder and Jeffrey Barcalow   301

16 Tropyc: A Pattern Language for Cryptographic
   Object-Oriented Software   *Alexandre Braga, Cecilia Rubira,*
   and Ricardo Dahab   337

PART 6 *Domain-Oriented Patterns*

17 Creating Reports with Query Objects   *John Brant*
   and Joseph Yoder   375

18 Feature Extraction: A Pattern for Information Retrieval
   Dragos-Anton Manolescu   391

19 Finite State Machine Patterns   *Sherif M. Yacoub and*
   Hany H. Ammar   413

PART 7 *Patterns of Human-Computer Interaction*

20 Patterns for Designing Navigable Information Spaces
   Gustavo Rossi, Daniel Schwabe, and Fernando Lyardet   445

21 Composing Multimedia Artifacts for Reuse
   Jacob L. Cybulski and Tanya Linden   461

22 Display Maintenance: A Pattern Language   *Dwayne Towell*   489

23 An Input and Output Pattern Language: Lessons from
   Telecommunications   *Robert Hanmer and Greg Stymfal*   503

PART 8 *Reviewing*

24 Identify the Champion: An Organizational Pattern Language
   for Program Committees   *Oscar Nierstrasz*   539

25 A Pattern Language for Writers' Workshops   *James O. Coplien*
   with Bobby Woolf   557

PART 9 *Managing Software*

26 Customer Interaction Patterns   *Linda Rising*   *585*

27 Capable, Productive, and Satisfied: Some Organizational
    Patterns for Protecting Productive People   *Paul Taylor*   *611*

28 SCRUM: A Pattern Language for Hyperproductive Software
    Development   *Mike Beedle, Martine Devos, Yonat Sharon,
    Ken Schwaber, and Jeff Sutherland*   *637*

29 Big Ball of Mud   *Brian Foote and Joseph Yoder*   *653*

About the Authors *693*

Index *705*

Preface

Of Phish and Phugues

The year is 1621; the place, Plymouth, in what will eventually become Massachusetts. A group of settlers from England arrived the previous November and are now setting out to plant crops. Before long a native named Squanto stops by. Evidently a gardening enthusiast, he offers to tutor the settlers in farming techniques, first by placing fish in the ground to enrich the soil. This and other tricks of farming in the New World contribute to a bountiful harvest. The settlers survive the ensuing winter, thanks in large part to Squanto and his sage advice.

An apocryphal story, no doubt, but modern horticulturists can corroborate Squanto's fishy insights. In fact, you can buy fish fertilizers in many gardening stores. Our agricultural forebears may not have had a deep knowledge of plant physiology, but they knew what worked. And they passed it along.

Over a hundred years later and half a world away, in what is now Germany, a master of a different sort plies his trade. According to legend, Johann Sebastian Bach pays a visit to Frederick the Great, King of Prussia. After exchanging pleasantries, the king asks Bach to play something for him. Dutifully and without hesitation, Bach sits down at the organ and improvises a five-part fugue. The king, an eminent composer himself, is awed.

Bach's work is the very essence of baroque music. And he passes that mastery along—several of his children also become important musicians and composers.

Lore flows from one generation to the next. Languages are vivid examples, perpetuating and evolving through oral tradition—words and concepts passing from person to person. A case in point is English, which traces its roots to numerous languages, including German, Greek, and Latin. Herein lies a problem: the multifaceted heritage of English creates a potpourri of spelling conventions that is downright bewildering. For example, we spell the "f" sound with the letters "ph" in "physics" but with "f" in "fish" and "fugue." There are historical and linguistic reasons for such anomalies, but they don't matter much to us. We just memorize that it's "fugue," not "phugue."

In software we don't have centuries of history to draw on. We didn't learn agriculture from ancient farmers, nor can we trace our roots through the Middle English of Chaucer. But we have been around long enough to learn a few things. The most important among them is this: *We must share what we have learned.* If we keep knowledge to ourselves, hoarding it like pack rats, then our field will surely stagnate. We doom colleague and successor alike to repeat our mistakes. Gradually, reinvention displaces innovation. Progress slows. The field goes fallow.

Patterns are conduits of knowledge, capturing and conveying time-proven practices. Patterns are more than tricks or seemingly arbitrary spelling rules—they impart understanding. They teach you not just *what* and *how* but also *why* and *when*. That's where their real power lies.

What can we reasonably expect of patterns? Maybe they will help other people develop better software than we have. Maybe they'll allow people to build on what we've done right. We certainly hope patterns will help others avoid the pitfalls we've experienced.

But we can expect more. The pervasiveness of computer technology exerts a strong influence on society. Influence of such magnitude must be exercised responsibly. While patterns won't force you to act responsibly, they can ease the grind of reinvention, freeing you to consider higher purposes. Ultimately, patterns make life better for everyone—software user and developer alike.

These are ambitious and humbling goals, to be sure. We dedicate this fourth volume in the *Pattern Languages of Program Design* series to their attainment.

ACKNOWLEDGMENTS

Now for a word about the contributors to this book. A compendium of this size won't come together without many people pulling together. We are hugely grateful for their work. Specifically, we thank the authors for making this book necessary, to paraphrase Yogi Berra. We're referring not just to the authors you find here but also to the 60 percent or so of submitters whose works were not accepted. The exceptionally high quality of the submissions guaranteed the quality of the book, although it also made our job more difficult!

We recruited a veritable army of reviewers to help sift through the submissions. We owe them our sanity: Francis Anderson, Brad Appleton, Jorge Arjona, Owen Astrannen, Ken Auer, Jeff Barcalow, Kent Beck, Mike Beedle, Steve Berczuk, Manish Bhatt, Rosana Braga, John Brant, Kyle Brown, Jose Burgos, Frank Buschmann, Andy Carlson, Ian Chai, Alistair Cockburn, Jens Coldewey, James Coplien, Ward Cunningham, David Cymbala, Fonda Daniels, Dennis DeBruler, Michel DeChamplain, David Delano, Dwight Deugo, Paul Dyson, Philip Eskelin, Javier Galve, Julio Garcia, Alejandra Garrido, John Goodsen, Robert Hanmer, Kevlin Henney, Robert Hirschfeld, Ralph Johnson, Wolfgang Keller, Elizabeth Kendall, Norm Kerth, Charles Knutson, Frederick Koh, Philippe Lalanda, Manfred Lange, Doug Lea, Mary Lynn Manns, Klaus Marquardt, Paulo Masiero, Skip McCormick, Regine Meunier, Oscar Nierstrasz, James Noble, Alan O'Callaghan, Don Olson, William Opdyke, Dorina Petriu, Irfan Pyarali, Andreas Rausch, Dirk Riehle, Linda Rising,

António Rito Silva, Don Roberts, Gustavo Rossi, Cecilia Rubira, Andreas Rüping, Doug Schmidt, Ari Schoenfeld, Dietmar Schütz, Christa Schwanninger, Joe Seda, Peter Sommerlad, Michael Stal, Paul Taylor, Jenifer Tidwell, Dwayne Towell, and David Ungar.

We would like to give special thanks to John Vlissides, the managing editor of the series. He has provided us with encouragement and, occasionally, a needed prod. Neil would like to especially thank his two coeditors. Working with you has been a joy.

Finally, we would like to give special thanks to our families, friends, and coworkers who have supported us through this process. We hope that by the time you read this, we will be back to our cheery selves.

Neil Harrison, Denver, Colorado
Brian Foote, Urbana, Illinois
Hans Rohnert, Munich, Germany

Introduction I

If you are a software developer, you probably have too much to do and may not know how to do it all. You have probably heard something about patterns, since they are mentioned in sources as diverse as computer journals and the *Wall Street Journal* [Petzinger1999]. You might also think that patterns may help you find the answers to your problems quickly. However, if you are looking for a very quick answer to a specific problem, much of the material in this book is not for you. But if you are looking for proven solutions to a problem, please keep reading.

Writing computer software is different from many other disciplines. Software designers create abstract structures. Even user interfaces have only a small part of their workings visible. Hardware designers can pick up and touch their creations. Software practitioners cannot touch or see what they create. They can only see how their creation behaves. You can look at the arch in a Roman aqueduct and understand how to build one. You cannot, however, look at a computer system and understand how it works. Many intricacies will be lost to the eye. The patterns presented in this book are the product of authors who have noticed the regularities and recurring structures within a software system and can explain them, saving you from making your own mistakes.

The patterns in this book are products of the Pattern Languages of Programming (PLoP) conferences. Participants have said that PLoP conferences are among the best technical conferences they have ever attended. One reason is that PLoP conferences bring practitioners together to discuss solutions to problems. They also provide a supportive place for pattern authors to share their latest creative efforts. PLoP is about sharing experiences.

The primary goal of PLoP conferences is to improve the quality of patterns literature and patterns writing. At PLoP '97, we provided an atmosphere to support the creativity of authors. In addition to the traditional Writers' Workshops, writing workshops were held to give authors a chance to nourish their creativity. At PLoP '98, we did not categorize the pattern submissions along traditional lines. We wanted to see if workshop participants could find connections among their patterns and walk away from the conference with ideas about building new connections. A few did, and there are a number of ongoing collaborations (e.g., component design and configuration management patterns) that were inspired at this conference.

Pattern writers draw their inspiration from Christopher Alexander, an architect who, among other things, tried to capture the "Quality Without a Name" that makes buildings beautiful. The important thing for the software developer to take from Alexander's work is not, however, anything related to buildings but rather the practical value of the way beauty can improve quality. Donald Knuth said in his 1974 Turing Award lecture:

> My feeling is that when we prepare a program, the experience can be just like composing poetry or music; furthermore, when we read other people's programs, we can recognize some of them as genuine works of art. Some programs are elegant, some are exquisite, some are sparkling. My claim is that it is possible to write *grand* programs, *noble* programs, truly *magnificent* ones!

Before you dismiss this goal as too idealistic or abstract, remember that patterns are about *proven* solutions, not new and unique ones. In his biography of Alexander, *Christopher Alexander: The Search for a New Paradigm in Architecture* [Grabow 1983]. Stephen Grabow describes Alexander's distaste for simply fashionable architecture. Alexander's patterns describe "the obvious," which most of us ignore because we are so caught up in fashions and trends. New and daring works of building are often given awards despite the fact that they are often uncomfortable to live and work in. The analogies to software aren't that far off. Some software development cultures reward novel and unproven ideas over more banal proven ones. Great emphasis is often placed on inventing. But neat tricks don't always make better programs. Unless your problem is unique—and unique problems when looked at from the correct scale are rare—novelty is almost always not good. Often you'll find that the elegant, effective solution you came up with has, in fact, been used before by many others, although in isolation. Patterns are an attempt to capture these obvious solutions that are observed over time.

In some sense, software development is like traditional medicine. Unfortunately, computer programming today is where medicine was many, many generations ago: individuals attempt to solve problems, discover undesirable side effects, and make individual notes so that future generations can learn from their experiences. Patterns are an attempt to spread these notes into a community wider than just that of co-workers. They are the stories about things—things we have seen work over the recent past. They are records that we can pass along to future designers so they can avoid some of the same problems. The workshops at PLoP support this process of sharing and validating experiences. Authors submit patterns that they propose as common solutions. The participants in the workshop (and in other forums) add their stories and either validate or invalidate the solutions as patterns. Pattern authors look inside a system for the underlying structures and processes that created those structures. They then record their observations so that others can share the experience. Because of the nature of the process that the papers in this book have traveled through, you should be confident that they are not just some creative person's ideas. The difference between this book and a more traditional academic work is that nothing in here should be new. It may simply be something that a particular reader has not yet discovered.

Patterns encapsulate years of application development, observation, and experience. To find a solution is simple. To find the right solution, you need to understand the problem and the forces affecting the problem. The material in this book will help you make difficult decisions. It will expose you to some proven solutions to problems in such a way that you will be able to decide among the several approaches that, at first glance, seem to make equal sense. These patterns will help you, but they will not hand you solutions. In some sense the value and power of patterns have been obscured by the way in which they have been accepted as useful. *Design Patterns* [Gamma+1995] has been accepted as an incredibly useful book that describes ideas with which every object developer should be familiar. *Design Patterns* captures key idioms, which are accompanied by sound advice on their applicability. It is a book that should be on every developer's bookshelf; however, it only touches the surface of what patterns are about.

In one sense, then, patterns are about a quest for beauty and elegance. Patterns are also about the need to build reliable systems quickly, following the paths of other successful systems. Patterns, by giving you a chance to learn from the experiences of others, help free you from repetitive tasks, allowing you to concentrate on the innovation and invention. Pattern authors come from all aspects of the development process—from management and architects to ordinary developers. Everyone involved with the development and use of software systems has the ability to observe and document the recurring themes that work well.

People in general, and software people in particular, like to categorize. Many systems have more in common than would appear at first glance. When reading through the table of contents of this book, looking for answers, don't dismiss a particular chapter as a source of guidance simply because the title doesn't match your immediate perception of your problem. Although Coplien's C++ patterns may not be of much immediate use to you if you are programming in Smalltalk, you may find that the patterns in Hanmer and Stymfal's Chapter 23 may be useful if you have to do rather ordinary I/O. The chapters in this book could have been categorized in many ways; the categorization that you see here is the best compromise of many possibilities. The authors of the patterns in this book are sharing their wisdom and their creativity to help you learn from what they've seen in a variety of systems. Some people write to help newbies learn how to do things the right way or, at least, with fewer bloody knees. Some people thoroughly document a domain by collecting the pattern languages that span the domain's problem/solution space. Our work with patterns is just beginning. The *Pattern Languages of Program Design* volumes, along with other efforts, are an attempt to capture the wealth of software development expertise. Organizing this expertise so that it is accessible is an ongoing process; perhaps you, the reader, can help find connections and applications for these patterns that the authors, reviewers, and editors did not.

Patterns show their power when connected to other patterns. This is what patterns people call "context"—patterns that exist at a "higher level." Software systems are built from an architecture using certain tools, processes, and languages within an organization. The patterns in this book cover all these aspects. Each work stands on its own. As you read, be aware of possible connections between the patterns and the patterns' possible applications outside the domain in which the author is focused.

The ideas in these chapters may not all be new to you. If you read one of them and react knowingly with an "I knew that!" you have validated the author's work. If you find nothing new in this volume, consider yourself an expert. The truth is that no software developer can know everything. This book and those in this series that preceded it are part of a process to build a body of literature of proven techniques that you can use and build on for your own work and enjoyment.

We hope you find this book useful, enjoyable, and even inspirational.

Steve Berczuk
Bob Hanmer

Steve Berczuk is a software engineer at NetSuite Development Corporation and was program chair for PLoP '98.

Bob Hanmer is a distinguished member of the technical staff at Lucent Technologies and was program chair for PLoP '97.

REFERENCES

{Gamma+1995] E. Gamma, R. Helm, R. Johnson, and J. Vlissides. *Design Patterns: Elements of Reusable Object-Oriented Software.* Reading, MA: Addison-Wesley, 1995.

[Kernighan+1999] B. Kernighan and R. Pike. "Finding Performance Improvements." *IEEE Software*, 16(2), 1999.

[Petzinger1999] J. Petzinger Jr. "The Frontlines: To Get Machines to Talk to Each Other Two Men Write Human Language." *The Wall Street Journal*, April 14, 1999.

Introduction II

"PLoP was founded to create a new literature." With this sentence, Ralph Johnson and Ward Cunningham started the first book of this series. That was nearly six years ago. Today, several books of patterns enjoy a deserved place in the core body of computer literature. Patterns have changed the way we think about building software and have changed the way we work. When we set up project teams we follow organizational patterns; when we analyze domains, we apply groups of analysis patterns, and many of us feel naked doing design without the famous Gang of Four book on our desk. What started as a workshop at OOPSLA, in a different time, has affected the software industry as well as computer science.

So what makes a good pattern, a pattern that we constantly reach for? Jim Doble and Gerard Meszaros have written an excellent description of the elements of good patterns and pattern languages in the previous volume of this series [Doble+1998]. But even this paper describes the symptoms rather than the cause. It describes the craft the artist needs, but not the art itself. Readers often talk about the "warm and fuzzy feeling" they get when they read a good pattern or about how the pattern "resonates" with their own experience. Many computer professionals have forgotten to listen to these feelings, but pattern authors (and readers) are learning to embrace them.

There are three elements that help make a good pattern author: experience, hard work, and attitude. A good pattern discusses all the forces that lead to the solution and all the pitfalls and shortcomings that come with it. It shows the experience of the author and all those who have helped write it. It also shows the enormous amount of care put into creating the pattern—the words, the structure, and the flow. But above all, it shows a desire to engage the reader. A good pattern is written to be read; its whole structure is set up to lead readers through the paper and to give them this fuzzy feeling, this resonance with the literature and its author. Its purpose is to fascinate readers while leading them to a deep understanding of the problem and its resolution.

This humane attitude is the soul of a good pattern, and it is the deepest foundation of the pattern community. In the past the pattern movement has been compared to a religious cult and, although this is polemic, both are based on a value system and have a philosophical foundation. Patterns celebrate the humanity in software, and perhaps this accounts for the massive interest (and resultant hype) in pattern literature, as people involved with the development and use of software systems grow to realize that building software is an intensely human activity.

All of the patterns in this volume have been *improved* at a PLoP conference. PLoP (and later EuroPLoP and ChiliPLoP) were set up to nurture patterns and pattern authors, to encourage authors to write down the patterns they instinctively apply, and to contribute to Johnson and Cunningham's "new literature." We believe that PLoP is a very different kind of conference, different because we focus on the humans in the human activity of software development. The conferences make an enormous effort to generate a comfortable and welcoming environment. They are the only conferences with a naptime scheduled. EuroPLoP limits the number of attendees, not to be exclusive but to ensure the intimacy and cohesion that comes with a small group. And all PLoP conferences provide a number of social activities and services that help the attendees build a community—from collaborative games to child care for those who do not want their families to suffer for their profession. The result is a highly concentrated and productive working atmosphere.

Writers' Workshops are the main focus of the work, and all the patterns you find in this book have been through at least one such workshop. The workshops provide a supportive and safe environment in which authors get feedback from peers—other authors taking part in the workshops. Many newcomers to the PLoP conferences think they are there to present their papers but instead find that they are the only persons not allowed to speak. You have to learn to listen to your readers instead of expecting them to listen to you. And perhaps this is what makes patterns so successful—they *are* written by ordinary people, with expertise in their field, who want to improve the quality of their work and help others do the same.

Jens Coldewey
Paul Dyson

Jens Coldewey is an independent consultant in Munich, Germany, and was program chair for EuroPLoP '99.

Paul Dyson is Director of Economic Technology at Big Blue Steel Tiger Ltd., and was program chair for EuroPLoP '99.

REFERENCE

[Doble+1998] J. Doble and G. Meszaros. "A Pattern Language for Pattern Writing." In R. Martin, F. Buschmann, and D. Riehle (eds.), *Pattern Languages of Program Design 3.* Reading, MA: Addison-Wesley, 1998.

PART 1

Basic
Object-Oriented
Patterns

You might say this story began near Disney World in 1987. What story, you ask? The one about how objects and patterns became inextricably entwined. It began in a workshop at OOPSLA '87 in Orlando, where Ward Cunningham and Kent Beck first brought renegade architect Christopher Alexander's notion of patterns and pattern languages to computerdom and asked the question, why can't we have something like *that* for building software? Something like *what*?

Flash back to a decade earlier and the publication of Alexander and colleagues' *A Pattern Language*, a book that contained a collection of 253 different "patterns"—not for software, but for buildings. They described solutions to problems that arise in the siting of towns and in the design and construction of various sorts of public structures and individual dwellings. That work arose, in turn, as a response to the steel and glass orthodoxy of modern architecture during the period when Alexander and his colleagues came of age. The collected wisdom in *A Pattern Language* [Alexander+1977] was drawn not from the sketch books of the princes of modernism, but from the tested and true experience of hundreds upon hundreds of years of human building experience. Each pattern describes a problem that can occur "over and over again" and provides a solution to that problem "in such a way that you can use this solution a million times over, without doing it the same way twice."

A million times over? Never the same way twice? Traditionally, software people have had a hard time using a solution twice, let alone a million times. In hindsight, it's no surprise that patterns first found their software beachhead in the burgeoning object-oriented programming community. Objects, it seems, are a natural medium for patterns. They've proven to be an agar for architecture.

So, for most, this story really begins in late 1994, with the publication of the Gang of Four's *Design Patterns: Elements of Reusable Object-Oriented Software* [Gamma+1995], which explored this connection between patterns and objects. It described recurring motifs in object-oriented designs, and how objects can be the medium for expressing and communicating these designs as well as the building blocks for constructing them.

It is here that we begin our tale as well.

Chapter 1: Abstract Class by Bobby Woolf.   The Abstract Class pattern might be thought of as a Gang-of-Four outtake. Abstract classes are part of the underpinnings for nearly all the patterns there, and, as interfaces, can be fundamental elements in their realization in explicitly typed languages. Even in dynamically typed languages, they can function both as de facto interfaces and as template classes. Abstract classes are the seeds from which object-oriented frameworks are cultivated. Indeed, the Gang of Four recognized the importance of abstract classes, but worried that making them an explicit pattern would open a can of worms, since all the issues implicit in one pattern being built of others would be brought into an already complex tale. Better to let posterity sort this out, they reasoned, than to tackle pattern hierarchies head-on at that time. In hindsight, this was probably wise. Bobby's contribution finally brings this ubiquitous structure into the pantheon of published patterns.

Chapter 2: Role Object by Dirk Bäumer, Dirk Riehle, Wolf Siberski, and Martina Wulf. As objects mature, it is not usual for different clients, or different parts of a system, to consider different aspects of the same subject matter. The Role Object pattern shows how several objects can be used together to allow different roles, facets, or views to be attached to an object on-the-fly. The object's core identity is represented by an object, while sundry transitory concerns are modeled using dynamic Role Objects. For example, a system modeling you in your Reader role might implement `isBored()`, while an Employee role might implement `salary()`, and a core Person object might implement `name()`. Conventional object-oriented languages provide no direct support for Roles, but dynamic, collaborating objects can realize them using the Role Object pattern. It is this kind of synergy between objects and patterns that helps explain their power and enduring popularity.

Chapter 3: Essence by Andy Carlson.   Another example of the power of patterns and collaborating objects can be seen in the Essence pattern. Essence is a creational pattern for ensuring that all the vital, mandatory fields of an object will be initialized completely before allowing its creation to proceed. It uses a pair of collaborating objects to ensure this constraint is met. This pattern demonstrates once again how objects can work together to overcome the shortcomings of lone objects and the limitations of programming languages.

Chapter 4: Object Recursion by Bobby Woolf.   The Object Recursion pattern fills another gap in the literature. It elevates the hallowed recursive, polymorphic divide-and-conquer strategy that experienced object-oriented programmers have used for years to bona fide patternhood. As such, it captures an intent that falls somewhere between or beyond related Gang-of-Four patterns such as Composite, Chain-of-Responsibility, and Decorator.

Chapter 5: Prototype-Based Object System by James Noble.   At times, you might find yourself dissatisfied with the capabilities your underlying programming language provides, or you might wish to push the power and capabilities of your system onto your users. The Object System pattern shows how to do this by building one's own object system out of objects themselves. Variables, primitives, methods—even objects themselves are represented with objects in such an object system. Design patterns such as Interpreter, Visitor, Type Object, and Command all seem, at times, like steps along the road toward building domain-specific languages. Building a full Object System takes this approach to its logical conclusion. Just as objects are good for building programs, so too are they good for building programming languages.

Of course, when you build your own Object System, you can build your objects your way. You might add capabilities such as protection or constraint satisfaction to your variables or special kinds of method lookup to your class or type objects.

Chapter 6: Basic Relationship Patterns by James Noble.   James's second contribution to this section explores how objects can be used to better model *and* represent different kinds of object-to-object relationships. Many of these notions have existed heretofore only in the paper and pixel cartoon worlds of modeling notations and tools. James's patterns show how to build structures to realize these notions out of objects.

The first pattern, Relationship as Attribute, sets the stage for the others by describing the object-oriented programmer's first inclination, which is to use a field or instance variable to realize a simple, one-to-one, one-way relationship. When relationships become more complex, these concerns can be better dealt with as distinct Relationship Objects. Object-oriented programmers frequently use Collection Objects for one-to-many relationships. Situations that call for more intelligence on the part of stored values, such as, for instance, coordinating Observers, can use the Active Value pattern. Objects don't support complex bi-directional relationships directly, but you can simulate this sort of effect using paired one-way relationships. This approach is described in the Mutual Friends pattern.

Since the Gang-of-Four book's appearance, our corpus of patterns has grown to encompass software architecture, process, and a variety of domains, as the reader shall see as this volume unfolds. Yet, in many ways, the rich object-oriented design vein first tapped by the Gang of Four has remained our bread and butter. It would be premature to say we are mopping up in this area, but we are certainly filling in some of the gaps.

REFERENCES

[Alexander+1997] C. Alexander. *A Pattern Language: Towns/Buildings/Construction*. New York: Oxford University Press, 1977.

[Gamma+1995] E. Gamma, R. Helm, R. Johnson, and J. Vlissides. *Design Patterns: Elements of Reusable Object-Oriented Software*. Reading, MA: Addison-Wesley, 1995.

Chapter 1

Abstract Class

Bobby Woolf

Classification

Class Behavioral

Intent

Define the interface and general implementation for a hierarchy of classes while deferring the specific implementation details to subclasses. Abstract Class encourages polymorphic classes while allowing the subclasses to focus on how their implementations differ.

Also Known As

Template Class [Woolf1997], Base Class [Auer1995]

Motivation

Consider the need to perform simple arithmetic. Almost every application needs to use numbers like integers and floats and to perform arithmetic such as addition, subtraction, multiplication, and division.

One obvious way to perform simple math is to let the CPU do it. Any modern CPU has built-in commands to perform arithmetic with integers and floats. This is the most efficient way to perform such calculations.

The problem is that not all numerical quantities can be adequately represented as the CPU's integers and floats. Integers have a limited range. Floats have limited precision and loose precision converting between decimal and binary.

The number framework in a robust object-oriented system should take advantage of the CPU's efficiency whenever possible. However, to make the system more robust, the framework should overcome the CPU's limitations whenever possible. It should be able to represent a virtually limitless range of numbers, both really huge numbers and really minute ones. It should be able to represent a decimal number with complete precision, at least to a specified number of decimal places. It should be able to perform simple arithmetic without any loss of precision. It could even compute complex equations by simplifying them first.

A robust number library employs various classes to meet these goals: `Integer` and `Float` for CPU numbers, `LargePositiveInteger` and `LargeNegativeInteger` for huge integer values, `FixedPoint` for complete precision, `Fraction` for division without round off, and so on. The library performs as much computation as possible using the CPU, but it also uses other classes to represent numbers that the CPU cannot. Figure 1-1 shows the classes for this library.

The problem with all of these number classes is that the rest of the system does not want to be aware of them. To the rest of the system, there are just number objects and they know how to perform arithmetic. When code somewhere in the system has a statement like "x + y," it does not care whether x is a `Float` or y is a `Fraction`. The code just knows that x and y are numbers and that numbers know how to perform addition. The implication is that since some numbers know how to perform addition, all numbers must be able to.

Thus the number framework requires more than just these various number classes. It also needs to clearly show which classes are part of the library. It needs to

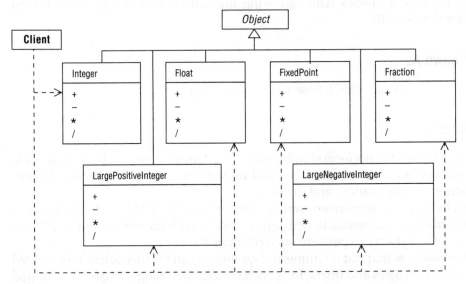

Figure 1-1 *Number framework classes before applying Abstract Class*

require that all classes in the library be able to perform a certain minimum of functionality, such as addition. And the library needs to provide all of this number functionality in a polymorphic way to hide the complexity of the various subclasses from the rest of the system.

The framework will accomplish all of this by using a generalized superclass called `Number`. A `Number` represents any kind of number, be it an integer, float, or whatever. It defines the minimal functionality that any number must provide, such as addition. It does not define a number's structure, nor does it define the implementation of the functionality. Those details are deferred to subclasses like `Integer`, `Float`, and so on. Applying `Number` as a superclass, and implementing `Integer` in a similar manner, leads to the library of classes shown in Figure 1-2.

All number classes are now subclasses of `Number`. They are defined to provide basic arithmetic. A client using a couple of number objects knows that numbers can perform basic arithmetic regardless of which subclasses the objects belong to. Also, as `negated` shows, methods that subclasses would implement the same can be implemented once in the superclass rather than implemented repeatedly in all of the subclasses. Thus even though the class is abstract, it can still contain concrete method implementations.

`Number` is an example of the Abstract Class pattern. `Number` is a superclass that gathers all of the number classes into a hierarchy and defines the interface that all of them must support. It implements general class behavior while deferring details to subclasses. Each subclass decides how to implement the interface, decides what

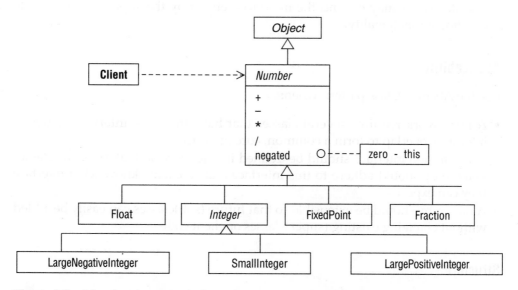

Figure 1-2   *Number framework class after applying Abstract Class*

structure it needs to support that implementation, and uses the inherited implementations as necessary. Subclasses are free to extend the basic interface to provide additional functionality, but they must support the basic interface they inherit from their abstract class.

The keys to the Abstract Class pattern are a superclass that defines the type (also called the interface, protocol, or signature) for its hierarchy, and subclasses that implement the interface in various ways. The superclass is called "abstract" because clients do not create instances of it. The subclasses that a client can create instances of are referred to as "concrete."

Keys

A framework that incorporates the Abstract Class pattern has the following features:

- A superclass that defines a type.
- One or more subclasses that implement the type.
- Polymorphism between the subclasses because they share the core interface defined by the superclass.

The framework may also include these variations on the pattern:

- The superclass may provide a partial but incomplete implementation.
- The superclass may provide a complete implementation that is a default or minimal implementation.
- The superclass may define state as well as interface.
- The subclasses may expand the interface defined by the superclass to include additional functionality.

Applicability

Use the Abstract Class pattern when:

- A framework requires several classes that have the same interface or whose interfaces overlap to form a common, core interface.
- The common interface should be defined in one place so that all of the classes know they should adhere to this interface and so clients know what interface they can expect.
- A hierarchy should be extensible so that future (sub)classes can easily be added without changing existing (super)classes or client code.

Structure

Figure 1-3 shows the structure of the Abstract Class pattern.

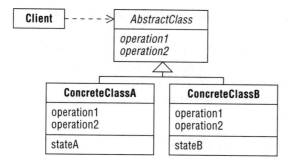

Figure 1-3   *Structure diagram*

Participants

- *AbstractClass* (Number, Integer)
  –Defines the interface that all ConcreteClasses share.
  –Does not define state unless it is common to all subclasses, including future ones.
  –Implements behavior subclasses are likely to implement identically.
  –Defers implementation of remaining behavior to subclasses.
  –May itself be a subclass of another AbstractClass.
- *ConcreteClass* (FixedPoint, Float, Fraction, LargeNegativeInteger, LargePositiveInteger, SmallInteger)
  –Is a direct or indirect subclass of its AbstractClass.
  –Implements the behavior deferred by AbstractClass.
  –Overrides behavior AbstractClass implements inappropriately.
  –Declares state necessary to implement behavior.
- *Client*
  –Collaborates with objects conforming to the AbstractClass interface.
  –Treats the objects as if they're instances of AbstractClass.

Collaborations

- Clients use the AbstractClass interface to interact with objects of any Concrete-Class.
- ConcreteClass relies on AbstractClass to provide the default implementations common to all ConcreteClasses.

Consequences

The following are advantages of the Abstract Class pattern:

- *Class polymorphism.*   The ConcreteClasses are polymorphic with each other because they all support the common interface defined by the AbstractClass.

This means that a client can use any of the ConcreteClasses without regard for which ConcreteClass it is using.

- *Algorithm reuse.* The implementation that the AbstractClass does contain is usually in the form of Template Methods [Gamma+1995, p. 325]. This is implementation (and in some cases even state) that all of the ConcreteClasses, present and future, are likely to duplicate; the implementation can be reused by implementing it once in the AbstractClass.

The following are disadvantages of the Abstract Class pattern:

- *Abstract vs. concrete.* Clients should not attempt to instantiate instances of abstract classes, only concrete ones. The superclass is said to be "abstract" because it has an incomplete implementation, so the client cannot or should not create instances of it. Each subclass is said to be "concrete" because its implementation is complete, so the client can create instances of it.
- *Single hierarchy.* The pattern forces all of the ConcreteClasses to be gathered into a single class hierarchy with a common superclass, the AbstractClass. Sometimes a class seems to belong in one hierarchy because of its type but in another hierarchy because it needs to inherit some of its implementation. In such a case, it is better to implement the class in its type hierarchy and let it delegate to an instance from its implementation hierarchy.

  Another way this problem can occur is when disparate classes need to implement the same operation. The default implementation for this operation is usually defined in the first superclass they all have in common. This in effect makes that superclass an AbstractClass for those subclasses. However, it also makes the class an AbstractClass for all of the other subclasses, even though they don't need the operation. Thus it becomes clear that inheritance is not the best way to define this operation and reuse its implementation. The classes that need the operation would probably be better off delegating to an object that has the operation.
- *Overly specific interface.* Sometimes a ConcreteClass is not prepared to implement all of the operations that an AbstractClass specifies. For example, the `Collection` abstract class in Smalltalk specifies `add` and `remove` operations, but the `Array` subclass cannot implement them. When possible, the AbstractClass should not specify an operation unless all of its ConcreteClasses will be able to implement it. When this cannot be avoided, the ConcreteClass must implement the operation anyway, usually to issue an error.

Implementation

There are several issues to consider when implementing the Abstract Class pattern:

1. *Separate classes.* An object is often implemented using a single class that defines both the object's interface and its implementation. This makes the

abstraction that the class represents difficult to reuse. The Abstract Class pattern suggests that the object should be implemented with two classes, an abstract one that defines its interface and a concrete one that implements the interface.

2. *No state.* The AbstractClass usually does not declare any state variables. If it did, all of its ConcreteClasses would be forced to inherit those variables. This would be inefficient for a ConcreteClass whose implementation did not require those variables. However, if all of the ConcreteClasses require a variable, and if future ConcreteClasses would also probably require that variable, then it can be declared in the AbstractClass.

3. *Implementation through Template Methods.* An AbstractClass is usually implemented as a collection of Template Methods [Gamma+1995, p. 325]. An AbstractClass is said to define an interface but leave its implementation to the ConcreteClasses. However, when a message has a default implementation that is appropriate for all ConcreteClasses, that implementation can be made in the AbstractClass. Such an implementation is often either a template method or a primitive operation method.

4. *No private messages.* The AbstractClass defines the hierarchy's interface. These are the public messages that the subclasses will implement. The Abstract-Class does not need to define private messages and usually does not do so. However, it may define private messages that are primitive operations of the class' template methods.

Sample Code

The `Magnitude` class in Smalltalk is an excellent example of the Abstract Class pattern. It includes the `Number` hierarchy discussed in the Motivation because numbers are magnitudes.

A `Magnitude` understands six main messages: equal-to (=), not-equal-to (~=), less-than (<), greater-than (>), less-than-or-equal-to (<=), and greater-than-or-equal-to (>=). Some examples of `Magnitudes` include `Number`, `Timestamp`, and `Character`. All of these are subclasses of `Magnitude` and understand the `Magnitude` messages, as shown in Figure 1-4.

Four of the messages are implemented as Template Methods: not-equal-to, greater-than, less-than-or-equal-to, and greater-than-or-equal-to. They are implemented in terms of two primitive operations: equal-to and less-than. The primitive operations are deferred to subclasses.

```
"Declare the class."

Object subclass: Magnitude

"Declare the methods in Magnitude."
```

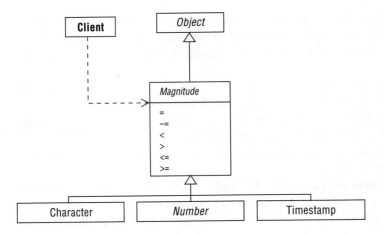

Figure 1-4 *Sample code diagram*

```
= aMagnitude
    "Make the method abstract."
    ^self subclassResponsibility


~= aMagnitude
    ^(self = aMagnitude) not


< aMagnitude
    "Make the method abstract."
    ^self subclassResponsibility


> aMagnitude
    ^(self <= aMagnitude) not


<= aMagnitude
    ^(self = aMagnitude) or: [self < aMagnitude]


>= aMagnitude
    ^(self < aMagnitude) not
```

So a subclass of `Magnitude` need only implement the two primitive operations, and it gets the other four operations for free. For example, `Character` assumes that characters are ASCII, and so it sorts them into ASCII order. To do this, it uses a message that returns a character's ASCII value, such as `asciiValue`.

```
"Declare the class."

Magnitude subclass: Character
```

```
"Declare the methods in Character."

= aCharacter
   ...
   ^(self asciiValue) = (aCharacter asciiValue)

< aCharacter
   ^(self asciiValue) < (aCharacter asciiValue)
```

Thus the AbstractClass, `Magnitude`, greatly simplifies the implementation of the various ConcreteClasses. In the sample operations shown here, implementing two messages gives the class four more messages for free.

The AbstractClass also simplifies the interface that client code must understand. The client must know that it is comparing two objects of the same subtype: two `Characters` or two `Numbers`, and so on. However, it need not care which subtype they are, because they all behave the same. They all understand the same six comparison messages.

One example of why this is useful is the way `SortedCollection` works. A `SortedCollection` is a `Collection` that sorts its elements. By default, it assumes that its elements are `Magnitudes` (of the same subtype) and it uses `<=` to put them in order. Thus it does not care whether the elements are `Characters`, `Numbers`, or `Timestamps`; since they are all `Magnitudes`, they will all work correctly.

Known Uses

Abstract classes are so fundamental that they can be found in almost any multi-level class hierarchy. In such a hierarchy, the superclasses are usually abstract; the leaf classes must be concrete. `Object` and `java.lang.Object`, the root classes for the entire Smalltalk and Java hierarchies, are the ultimate abstract classes in those languages. When a class hierarchy is named after the class at the root of the hierarchy (such as `Number`, `Collection`, `Stream`, `Window`, etc.), that class is almost always an abstract class.

Almost every documented design pattern, such as those in *Design Patterns* [Gamma+1995], features one or more abstract classes. Often the pattern suggests the creation of an abstract class if there isn't one already. For example, Composite [Gamma+1995, p. 163] uses the Component AbstractClass to define the interface for both the Leaf and Composite classes. To apply Proxy [Gamma+1995, p. 207] to a RealSubject class, the developer should use the abstract class Subject to define the interface that the RealSubject and its Proxy will share. When a pattern talks about a participant that "defines an interface" [Gamma+1995, p. 306] or "declares an interface" [Gamma+1995, p. 317] for several subclasses, it is describing an abstract class.

Auer discusses how to develop class hierarchies that are reusable and extensible [Auer1995]. He suggests using a base class to define an interface and subclasses to implement state.

Related Patterns

Most patterns employ abstract classes.

An AbstractClass is often implemented using Template Methods [Gamma+1995, p. 325].

REFERENCES

[Auer1995] K. Auer. "Reusability Through Self-Encapsulation." In [PLoPD1995].

[Gamma+1995] E. Gamma, R. Helm, R. Johnson, and J. Vlissides. *Design Patterns: Elements of Reusable Object-Oriented Software*. Reading, MA: Addison-Wesley, 1995.

[PLoPD1995] J.O. Coplien, and D.C. Schmidt, eds., *Pattern Languages of Program Design*. Reading, MA: Addison-Wesley, 1995.

[Woolf1997] B. Woolf. "Polymorphic Hierarchy." *The Smalltalk Report*. January 1997. 6(4).

Bobby Woolf can be reached at woolf@acm.org.

Chapter 2

Role Object

Dirk Bäumer, Dirk Riehle,
Wolf Siberski, and Martina Wulf

Intent

The intent of the Role Object pattern is to adapt an object to different clients' needs through transparently attached role objects, each one representing a role the object has to play in that client's context. Each context may be its own application, which therefore gets decoupled from the other applications.

Motivation

An object-oriented system is typically based on a set of key abstractions. Each key abstraction is modeled by a corresponding class in terms of abstract state and behavior. This usually works fine for the design of smaller applications. However, once we want to scale up the system into an integrated suite of applications, we have to deal with different clients that need context-specific views on our key abstractions.

Suppose we are developing software support for the bank's investment department. One of the key abstractions to be expressed is the concept of *customer*. Thus, our design model will include a Customer class. The class interface provides operations to manage properties like the customer's name, address, and savings and deposit accounts.

Let's assume that the bank's loan department also needs software support. It seems our class design is inadequate to deal with a customer acting as a borrower. Obviously, we must provide additional object state and operations to manage the customer's loan accounts, credits, and securities.

Integrating several context-specific views in the same class will most likely lead to key abstractions with bloated interfaces. Such interfaces are difficult to understand

and hard to maintain. Unanticipated changes cannot be handled gracefully and will trigger lots of re-compilation. Changes to a client-specific part of the class interface are likely to affect clients in other subsystems or applications as well.

A simple solution might be to extend the Customer class by adding new Borrower and Investor subclasses that capture respectively the borrower-specific and investor-specific aspects. From an object identity point of view, subclassing implies that two objects of different subclasses are not identical. Thus, a customer acting both as an investor and as a borrower is represented by two different objects with distinct identities. Identity can only be simulated by an additional mechanism. If two objects are meant to be identical, their inherited attributes must constantly be checked for consistency. However, we will inevitably run into problems in the case of polymorphic searches, for example, when we want to make up the list of all customers in the system. The same Customer object will appear repeatedly unless we take care of eliminating "duplicates."

The Role Object pattern models context-specific views of an object as separate *role objects* that are dynamically attached to and removed from the *core object*. The resulting object aggregate represents one logical object, even though it consists of several physically distinct objects. (See Figure 2-1.)

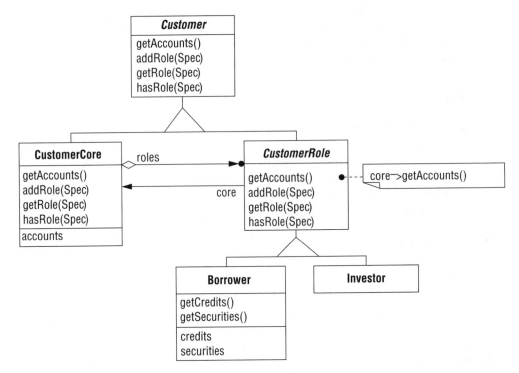

Figure 2-1 *Customer hierarchy in a banking environment*

A key abstraction such as Customer is defined as an abstract superclass. It serves as an interface without any implementation state. The Customer class specifies operations to handle a customer's address and accounts and defines a minimal protocol for managing roles. The CustomerCore subclass implements the Customer interface.

The common superclass for customer-specific roles is provided by CustomerRole, which also supports the Customer interface. The CustomerRole class is abstract and not meant to be instantiated. Concrete subclasses of CustomerRole (for example, Borrower or Investor) define and implement the interface for specific roles. Only these subclasses are instantiated at runtime. The Borrower class defines the context-specific view of Customer objects as needed by the loan department. It defines additional operations to manage the customer's credits and securities. Similarly, the Investor class adds operations specific to the investment department's view of customers. (See Figure 2-2.)

A client, like the loan application, may either work with objects of the CustomerCore class, using the interface class Customer, or with objects of concrete CustomerRole subclasses. Suppose the loan application knows a particular Customer instance through its Customer interface. The loan application may want to check whether the Customer object plays the role of Borrower. To this end it calls hasRole( ) with a suitable role specification. For the purpose of our example, let's assume we can name roles with a simple string. If the Customer object can play the role named Borrower, the loan application will ask it to return a reference to the corresponding object. The loan application may now use this reference to call Borrower-specific operations.

In a similar fashion, the Investor role is handled by its application. If the two applications do not need to know about each other, the use of role objects decouples them. The loan application does not need to load the Investor role, and the

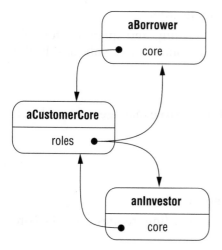

Figure 2-2 *An object diagram of the Role Object pattern*

investor application does not need to load the Borrower role, with all its associated state.

Applicability

Use the Role Object pattern if

- You want to handle a key abstraction in different contexts, each of which might be its own application, and you do not want to put the resulting context-specific interfaces into the same class interface.
- You want to handle the available roles dynamically so that they can be attached and removed on demand (that is, at runtime) rather than fixing them statically at compile-time.
- You want to keep role/client pairs independent from each other so that changes to a role do not affect clients that are not interested in that role.

Don't use this pattern if

- Your potential roles have strong interdependencies.

There are several design variations on using roles. Fowler presents a guide on these variations and shows when to use which pattern [Fowler1997].

Structure

Figure 2-3 shows the structure diagram of the Role Object pattern.

Participants

- *Component* (`Customer`)

  –Models a particular key abstraction by defining its interface.

  –Specifies the protocol for adding, removing, testing, and querying for role objects. A Client supplies a specification for a ConcreteRole subclass. In the simplest case, the subclass is identified by a string.

- *ComponentCore* (`CustomerCore`)

  –Implements the Component interface including the role management protocol.

  –Creates ConcreteRole instances.

  –Manages its role objects.

- *ComponentRole* (`CustomerRole`)

  –Stores a reference to the decorated ComponentCore.

  –Implements the Component interface by forwarding requests to its core attribute.

- *ConcreteRole* (`Investor, Borrower`)

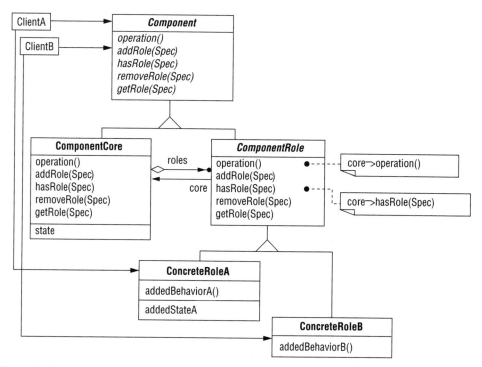

Figure 2-3 *Structure diagram of the Role Object pattern*

–Models and implements a context-specific extension of the Component interface.

–Can be instantiated with a ComponentCore as argument.

Collaborations

Core and role objects collaborate as follows:

- ComponentRole forwards requests to its ComponentCore object.
- ComponentCore instantiates and manages ConcreteRoles.

A client interacts with roles and core objects in the following ways:

- A client can add new roles to the core object. To this end, it describes the desired roles with specification objects.
- Whenever the client wants to work on a core object in a role-specific way, he asks the core object for this role. If the core object is currently playing the requested role, it is returned to the client.
- If the core object does not know about a specific requested role, an exception is thrown or an error is reported.

Consequences

The Role Object pattern has the following advantages and consequences:

- *The key abstraction can be defined concisely.* The Component interface is well focused on the essential state and behavior of the modeled key abstraction and is not bloated by context-specific role interfaces.
- *Roles can be evolved easily and independently of each other.* Extending the Component interface is very easy because you will not have to change the ComponentCore class. A ConcreteRole class lets you add new roles and role implementations while preserving the key abstraction itself.
- *Roles objects can be added and removed dynamically.* A role object can be added and removed at runtime simply by attaching it to and detaching it from the core object. Thus, only those objects that are needed in a given situation are actually created.
- *Applications are better decoupled.* By explicitly separating the Component interface from its roles, the coupling of applications based on different role extensions is reduced. An application (ClientA) using the Component interface and some context-specific ConcreteRole classes does not need to know the ConcreteRole classes used in other applications (ClientB).
- *Combinatorial explosion of classes through multiple inheritance is avoided.* The pattern avoids the combinatorial explosion of classes that would result from using multiple inheritance to compose the different roles in a single class.

The Role Object pattern has the following disadvantages and liabilities:

- *Clients are likely to get more complex.* Working with an object through one of its ConcreteRole interfaces implies slight coding overhead compared to using the interface provided by the Component interface itself. A client has to check whether the object plays the role in question. If it does, the client needs to query for the role. If it does not, the client is responsible for extending the core object in its specific use-context provided that the core object actually can play the role.
- *Maintaining constraints between roles becomes difficult.* Since the logical object consists of several objects that are mutually dependent, maintaining constraints and preserving the overall consistency might become difficult. In the implementation section we discuss several of the arising issues.
- *Constraints on roles cannot be enforced by the type system.* You might want to exclude certain roles from being attached to the same core object in combination. Or, certain roles may depend on the existence of others. With the Role Object pattern, you can't rely on the type system to enforce these constraints for you. You will have to use runtime checks instead.
- *More complex object identity exists.* Role objects introduce a logical identity over and above the physical identity of an object. The physical identity is the identity of each individual object. The logical identity is the identity of the logical object consisting of the core and its roles. For each role, you need to be able

to ask whether it is physically identical with another role (same object), and whether it is logically identical with another role (which may be another role of the same logical object). In object-oriented programming, you can implement the physical identity check using the underlying programming language, but to implement the logical identity check, you have to introduce a dedicated operation. The logical identity check can be implemented by comparing the core objects of two role objects for physical identity.

Implementation

An implementation of the Role Object pattern must address two critical issues: transparently extending key abstractions with roles and dynamically managing these roles. For transparent extension, we use the Decorator pattern [Gamma+1995]. For creating and managing roles, we apply the Product Trader pattern [Bäumer+ 1998]. Thus, the Role Object pattern combines two well-known patterns and thereby adds new semantics.

- *Providing interface conformance.* Since we want role objects to be used transparently wherever the core object can be used, they must support a common interface. From a class-based modeling point of view, a role class is considered a specialization of its core (i.e., an Investor *is-a* Customer). From a role modeling point of view (which makes roles first-class concepts of modeling), Borrower and Investor are roles of the Customer class [Riehle+1998].

  First, we factor out a common interface for all objects that can have roles added to them dynamically. This interface is provided by the Component class in the structure diagram. The class ComponentCore implements this interface. For all context-specific roles that might extend the Component's functionality, we introduce the abstract superclass ComponentRole. ComponentRole implements the Component's interface too, but only by forwarding operation invocations to the core object. Thus, roles transparently wrap the core. ConcreteRole classes must inherit from ComponentRole.

  At first glance, this looks similar to the Decorator pattern. But there are two differences:

  1. Multiple roles are not chained together; each role wraps its core directly.
  2. Roles typically do not extend the implementation of the component operations; they just forward the request to the core.

- *Creating role objects.* Role instances are used to decorate a core object at runtime. A key issue is how a ConcreteRole instance is actually created and attached to the core object. Notice that ConcreteRoles are not meant to be created by clients. Rather, the role creation process should be initiated by ComponentCore, thereby guaranteeing that role objects cannot exist on their own (i.e., independently of a core object). This also prevents clients from knowing how to instantiate role objects.

- *Deleting role objects.*   Role objects are safely attached to their core object once they have been created. They may stick around as long as the core object exists, even if all Clients are long gone. This is a typical garbage collection problem that may be addressed by known garbage collection techniques. Typically, we just leave a role object with its core object hoping that it may be reused in the future. A Client should never delete a Role object, because it never knows whether other Clients are using it.

- *Decoupling role classes from the core.*   Creating and managing roles should be done in a generic fashion. Otherwise, it becomes hard if not impossible to extend a ComponentCore with new and unforeseen roles without changing its implementation. Therefore, both the creation and the management process must be independent of concrete role classes; the ComponentCore code must not statically reference any of them.

    This can be achieved by using specification objects. To request a role, the clients pass a specification object to the core. The simplest solution is to use the type name as the specification (see Sample Code section). The core returns the role object that matches the specification. More elaborate specification mechanisms are discussed in [Riehle1995] and [Evans1997].

    The same specification objects can be used for creation. To achieve this, the Product Trader pattern can be used [Bäumer+1998]. The role object trader maintains a container of specification objects with associated creator objects—for example, class objects, prototypes, or exemplars. When a client wants to add a new role, it passes a specification object to the core. The core delegates the creation to the role object trader.

- *Choosing appropriate specification objects.*   In many cases it is sufficient to use the type name as a specification object. But sometimes it is worthwhile to use more complex specifications. .

    Suppose you have modeled Person as a core object class. Some persons may be employees, so there is a role type Employee. Because there are different kinds of employees, you will want to make Employee an interface class and model concrete roles as subclasses of Employee—for example, Salesman, Developer, and Manager. When a Client needs information about the salary of a person, it will request the role "Employee" from the core. This cannot be done using the type name, because the concrete role objects will have "Salesman," etc., as type names. In such situations you can use Type Objects [Johnson+1998] as specifications. The core can then retrieve the requested role object by evaluating sub/super-type relations.

- *Managing role objects.*   To let a core object manage its roles, the Component interface declares a role management protocol that includes operations for adding, removing, testing, and querying role objects. To support the role management protocol, the core object maintains a dictionary that maps role specifications to concrete role instances. Whenever a role object is attached to the core, the new role object is registered in the role dictionary together with its role specification.

Please note that a core object manages its role objects through references of type ComponentRole, thereby excluding ComponentCore instances from acting as roles! Because the core owns its roles, it must take care of them. In particular, it must delete them when it gets deleted itself.

- *Maintaining consistent core and role object state.* Changes to the core object or to role objects may require updates to other role objects. As an example, consider changing the name of a Person that is also a Borrower. Whenever the Person receives a new name, a flag must be raised in the Borrower role to indicate that the Borrower had a name change. The flag indicates to the system that a name change must be reported to a national institute that collects and passes on information on the creditworthiness of borrowers. Notification is mandatory for the bank. There are several possible solutions to ensure these constraints, all of which come with a price; usually the dependencies are hard-coded. We discuss a more elaborate solution in the item that follows.

- *Maintaining role attribute constraints by using Property and Observer.* If state integration becomes complex due to many interdependencies, the implementation state of the core object (or parts thereof) might be represented using a Property List ([Riehle1997], also called Variable State [Beck1997]). A property list is a list of key/value pairs that represent attribute names and values, respectively. It is usually implemented as a dictionary, which maps the attribute name on the attribute value (object).

  A role object may then register interest in a particular attribute defined as part of the core object's state and be notified if a state-changing operation is called on it. To enable this, every role object that changes an attribute must inform the core object about this change so that it can notify dependent role objects about the change. Because the Property List pattern lets the core object handle attributes generically, it does not become dependent on specific role objects and their attributes.

  Property lists are usually perceived as being a bad thing because they break encapsulation by exposing implementation state. Changes in attribute names may require all role classes depending on them to change accordingly. Moreover, bad code might cause unwanted side effects. However, when carefully handled, these problems can be avoided. Perhaps the best known example of this pattern's extensive use are the decorated nodes in abstract syntax trees, which are the key abstraction in many compilers and software development environments.

- *Maintaining conceptual identity.* The Role Object pattern lets you manage the core and its roles as a single conceptual object with integrated state. Therefore, it should be possible for clients to find out whether two distinct physical objects are actually part of the same logical object, that is, if they are conceptually identical. Different role objects share a single conceptual object identity whenever they have the same core.

For example, consider a client application that works directly with the core object through the Component interface and refers to its single role instance using a concrete role interface. From a physical point of view, the two references do not point to the same object because they reference two physically distinct objects. Thus, to find out that the two references actually denote the same conceptual object, the client must use special identity comparison operations provided by the Component interface. Usually this will be implemented as a direct comparison of two core object references.

- *Maintaining constraints among roles.* Between roles themselves (not just their state), there might be a number of constraints. A common case is that a role B requires a role A to be already played by the object. For example, if Customer and Borrower are both roles of Person, then the existence of a Customer role object is a precondition for allowing a Person to play the Borrower role. These are role-level constraints. The ability of an object to play a particular role B is restricted to those objects that already play a role A. Without that role A, role B must not be played. These constraints emerge from the application domain.

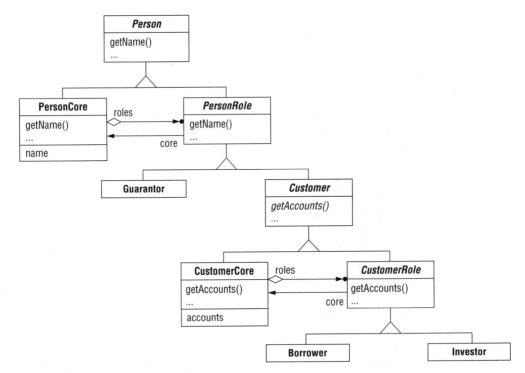

Figure 2-4 *The Role Object pattern applied recursively*

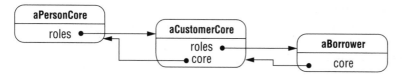

Figure 2-5   *Dynamic object diagram with roles being attached to roles*

Generally speaking, role B might not just depend on role A but also on role A being in a particular state. For the most complex cases, you won't be able to avoid using a constraint solving system. Fortunately, in practice, the situation almost never scales up to full complexity, and more pragmatic solutions are sufficient. Typical cases can be solved by using a two-phase commit protocol—that is, asking all roles first before finally executing a request, for example, to remove a role object.

• *Maintaining constraints among roles by recursively applying the Role Object pattern.*   Many problem cases of role-level constraints can be solved by applying the Role Object pattern recursively. If role A is a precondition for a number of roles B, C, D, etc., then role A can be understood as a key abstraction for these roles. Borrower and Investor can be viewed as roles of Customer, and Customer and Guarantor can be viewed as roles of Person. Since being a Guarantor does not require being a Customer, it need not be modeled as a role of Customer.

Figure 2-4 shows a recursive application of the Role Object pattern. At runtime, this leads to a chain of role and core objects. Figure 2-5 depicts the situation. The role-level constraints are simply enforced by role objects for Borrower or Investor that do not come into existence unless the Customer role already exists. Thus, modeling Customer as another key abstraction for further roles serves to ensure a vital role-playing constraint on the more general Person key abstraction.

Sample Code

The following C++ code shows how to implement the customer example discussed in the Motivation section. We'll assume that there is a Component class called `Customer`.

```
class CustomerRole;

class Customer {
public:
    // Customer specific operations
    virtual list<Account *> getAccounts() = 0;
```

```
   // Role management
   virtual CustomerRole * getRole(string aSpec) = 0;
   virtual void addRole(string aSpec) = 0;
   virtual void removeRole(string aSpec) = 0;
   virtual bool hasRole(string aSpec) = 0;
};
```

The implementation of class `CustomerCore` might look like this:

```
class CustomerCore : public Customer {
public:
   CustomerRole * getRole(string aSpec) {
      return roles[aSpec];
   }

   void addRole(string aSpec) {
      CustomerRole * role = getRole(aSpec);
      if (role == NULL) {
         role = CustomerRole::createFor(aSpec, this);
         if (role != NULL)
            roles[Spec] = role;
      }
   }

   list<Account *> getAccounts() { ... }

private:
   map<string, CustomerRole *> roles;
};
```

The specification of a role is implemented as a string that equals the class name of the ConcreteRole class. The mapping between the role's specification and the role object itself is implemented by a dictionary.

Next, we define a subclass of `Customer` called `CustomerRole`, which we will subclass to obtain different concrete roles. `CustomerRole` decorates the `CustomerCore` referenced by the `core` instance variable. For each operation in `Customer`'s interface, `CustomerRole` forwards the request to `core`. Notice that the core instance variable is typed as `CustomerCore`, thereby ensuring that customer roles are not used as core objects. The mapping between a role's specification and an appropriate creator object that is able to instantiate the specified role is implemented as a lookup table. For a detailed discussion of how to implement and manage creator objects, see [Bäumer1998].

```
class CustomerRole : public Customer {
public:

   list<Account *> getAccounts() {
      return core->getAccounts();
   }

   CustomerRole * addRole(string aSpec) {
      return core->addRole(aSpec);
   }

   static CustomerRole * createFor(
      string aSpec, CustomerCore * aCore
   ) {
      Creator * roleCreator = lookup(aSpec);
      if (roleCreator == NULL)
         return NULL;

      CustomerRole * newRole = roleCreator->create();
      if (newRole != NULL)
         newRole->core = aCore;
      return newRole;
   }

private:
   CustomerCore * core;
};
```

Subclasses of `CustomerRole` define specific roles. For example, the class `Borrower` adds operations to handle securities and credit accounts. Subclasses should not override the inherited role management operations.

```
class Borrower : public CustomerRole {
public:
   list<Security *> getSecurities() {
      return securities;
   }

private:
   list<Security *> securities;
};
```

Notice that clients must downcast the role reference returned by the core component before they can invoke role-specific operations on the role instance:

```
Foo()
{
   ...
   Customer * aCustomer = Database::load("John Doe");
   Borrower * aBorrower = dynamic_cast<Borrower *>
      aCustomer->getRole("Borrower"));

   if (aBorrower != NULL) {
      // access securities
      list<Security *> securities =
         aBorrower->getSecurities();
   }
   ...
}
```

Known Uses

The GEBOS series of object-oriented banking projects makes extensive use of this pattern [Bäumer+1997]. It provides software support for a number of banking business sections including the teller, loan, and investment departments as well as self-service and account management. The GEBOS system is based on a common business domain layer modeling the bank's core concepts. Concrete workplace applications extend these core concepts using the Role Object pattern.

The Tools and Materials framework described in [Riehle+1995b] and [Riehle+1995c] explores the role modeling design space, applying protocol copy and paste, multiple inheritance, decorators, and wrappers to achieve the effects of the Role Object pattern. These variations are more concisely described by [Fowler1997].

Kristensen and Østerbye report on using the Decorator pattern to introduce roles into programming languages [Kristensen+1996]. However, they do not address issues of creating and managing role objects in detail.

We have used a domain-specific example, Person and its roles, for illustration purposes. This example is so common that it actually represents a pattern of its own. Since a Person abstraction is needed in many contexts, there are any number of different roles that it may play. Schoenfeld discusses several examples, for example, Person and its roles in document-centered business processes [Schoenfeld1996]. We picked Person and its roles in the context of banking businesses with customers. Yet another example is Person and its roles in a bureaucratic hierarchy and the related payroll management problems.

An unrelated use of the Role Object pattern is the decoration of nodes in abstract syntax trees (ASTs). ASTs are the primary abstraction in most software development environments. They are viewed and used from many different tools, for example, syntax-directed editors, symbol browsers, cross referencers, compilers, dependency analyzers, and change impact tools. Every tool needs to annotate the AST nodes with its specific information yet is usually interested only in small aspects of the whole tree. The Role Object pattern works well to provide these tools with tool-specific interfaces on the nodes. Mitsui et al. discuss the use of the pattern in the context of a C++ programming environment [Mitsui+1993], for the specific use just discussed as well as for more general purposes.

Related Patterns

The Decorator pattern [Gamma+1995] has a similar structure but different behavior. The Decorator pattern lets developers wrap Decorators around one core, while the Role Object pattern does not allow this. In addition, Decorators typically do not extend the core functionality, while Role Objects introduce new operations.

The Product Trader pattern [Bäumer+1998] is used to dynamically create role objects based on specifications. The Product Trader pattern lets us flexibly specify which types of role objects are made available in a specific application, how they are configured, and how they are dynamically instantiated. The Product Trader pattern decouples the creation of role objects from their core so that they are not tightly coupled with it.

The Extension Object pattern [Gamma1998] addresses the same issue: A component is extended by means of extension objects in such a way that they satisfy context-specific requirements. The pattern, however, does not show how Component and ComponentRole objects can be treated transparently, which we consider a key aspect of applying the Role Object pattern. Moreover, the Extension Object pattern only touches on the issue of extension object (role object) creation and management. We view the integration of the Decorator pattern with the Product Trader pattern to be a key part of the Role Object pattern.

The Extension Object pattern has been used for role-modeling purposes by Zhao and Foster [Zhao+1998] and Schoenfeld [Schoenfeld1996]. Zhao and Foster discuss role objects as extension objects; that is, they do not transparently wrap the core object. Their key example is the notion of Point (and its roles) as it is a key in transport software systems. Schoenfeld chose the same primary example as we did, Person and its roles, but he also used the Extension Object pattern rather than transparently wrapping the core with a Decorator.

The Post pattern [Fowler1996] describes an interesting variant of this pattern. Similar to the Extension Object pattern, it describes the responsibilities of a core object in the context of a particular application. However, a Post object exists independently of the core and can live on without being assigned to a core.

ACKNOWLEDGMENTS

We would like to thank our shepherd Ari Schoenfeld for help improving the pattern in presentation and content.

REFERENCES

[Bäumer+1998] D. Bäumer and D. Riehle. "Product Trader." In R.C. Martin, D. Riehle, and F. Buschmann (eds.), *Pattern Languages of Program Design 3*. Reading, MA: Addison-Wesley, 1998.

[Bäumer+1997b] D. Bäumer, G. Gryczan, R. Knoll, C. Lilienthal, D. Riehle, and H. Züllighoven. "Framework Development for Large Systems." *Communications of the ACM*, 40 (10) ixx, pp. 52–59.

[Beck1997] K. Beck. *Smalltalk Best Practice Patterns*. Prentice-Hall, 1997.

[Coplien+1995] J.O. Coplien and D.C. Schmidt (eds.). *Pattern Languages of Program Design*. Reading, MA: Addison-Wesley, 1995.

[Evans+1997] E. Evans and M. Fowler. "Specification Patterns." In *Proceedings of the 1997 Conference on Pattern Languages of Programs* (PLoP '97). Washington University Department of Computer Science, Technical Report WUCS-97-34, 1997.

[Fowler1996] M. Fowler. *Analysis Patterns*. Reading, MA: Addison-Wesley, 1996.

[Fowler1997] M. Fowler. "Role Patterns." In *Proceedings of the 1997 Conference on Pattern Languages of Programs* (PLoP '97). Washington University Department of Computer Science, Technical Report WUCS-97-34, 1997.

[Gamma+1995] E. Gamma, R. Helm, R. Johnson, and J. Vlissides. *Design Patterns: Elements of Reusable Object-Oriented Software*. Reading, MA: Addison-Wesley, 1995.

[Gamma1998] E. Gamma. "Extension Object." In R.C. Martin, D. Riehle, and F. Buschmann (eds.), *Pattern Languages of Program Design 3*. Reading MA: Addison-Wesley, 1998.

[Johnson+1998] R. Johnson and B. Woolf. "Type Object." In R.C. Martin, D. Riehle, and F. Buschmann (eds.), *Pattern Languages of Program Design 3*. Reading MA: Addison-Wesley, 1998.

[Kristensen+1996] B.B. Kristensen and K. Østerbye. "Roles: Conceptual Abstraction Theory and Practical Language Issues." *Theory and Practice of Object System* 2 (3): 143–160, 1996.

[Martin+1998] R.C. Martin, D. Riehle, and F. Buschmann (eds.), *Pattern Languages of Program Design 3*. Reading, MA: Addison-Wesley, 1998.

[Mitsui+1993] K. Mitsui, H. Nakamura, T.C. Law, and S. Javey. "Design of an Integrated and Extensible C++ Programming Environment." In Shojiro Nishio and Akinori Yonezawa (eds.), *Object Technology for Advanced Software* (ISOTAS-93, LNCS-742), pp. 95–109. New York: Springer-Verlag, 1993.

[Riehle1997] D. Riehle. "A Role-Based Design Pattern Catalog of Atomic and Composite Patterns Structured by Pattern Purpose." *Ubilab Technical Report* 97.1.1. Zurich, Switzerland: Union Bank of Switzerland, 1997.

[Riehle+1995a] D. Riehle. "How and Why to Encapsulate Class Trees." In *Proceedings of the 1995 Conference on Object-Oriented Programming Systems: Languages and Applications* (OOPSLA '95), pp. 251–264. ACM Press, 1995.

[Riehle+1995b] D. Riehle and H. Züllighoven. "A Pattern Language for Tool Construction and Integration Based on the Tools and Materials Metaphor." In J.O. Coplien and D.C. Schmidt (eds.), *Pattern Languages of Program Design*. Reading, MA: Addison-Wesley, 1995.

[Riehle+1995c] D. Riehle and M. Schnyder. "Design and Implementation of a Smalltalk Framework for the Tools and Materials Metaphor." *Ubilab Technical Report* 95.7.1. Zurich, Switzerland: Union Bank of Switzerland, 1995.

[Riehle+1998] D. Riehle and T. Gross. "Role Model Based Framework Design and Integration." In *Proceedings of the 1998 Conference on Object-Oriented Programming Systems: Languages and Applications* (OOPSLA '98), pp. 117–133. ACM Press, 1998.

[Schoenfeld1996] A. Schoenfeld. "Domain Specific Patterns: Conversions, Persons and Roles, and Documents and Roles." In *Proceedings of the 1996 Conference on Pattern Languages of Programs* (PLoP '96). Washington University Department of Computer Science, Technical Report WUCS-97-07, 1997.

[Zhao1998] Liping Zhao and Ted Foster. "A Pattern Language of Transport Systems (Point and Route)." In R.C. Martin, D. Riehle, and F. Buschmann (eds.), *Pattern Languages of Program Design 3*. Reading MA: Addison-Wesley, 1998.

Dirk Bäumer may be reached at Dirk_Baeumer@oti.com or dbaeumer@datacomm.ch.

Dirk Riehle may be reached at Dirk.Riehle@credit-suisse.ch or riehle@acm.org.

Wolf Siberski may be reached at siberski@acm.org.

Martina Wulf may be reached at Martina.Wulf@ubs.com.

Chapter 3

Essence

Andy Carlson

Many classes, particularly persistent ones, require that a certain subset of their attributes be valid before a given instance can be considered valid. How can this be guaranteed in component-based or distributed environments where the client that creates the instances is outside our design control?

Traditional solutions involve obtaining long lists of parameters from the client at creation time or allowing an invalid object to be created and using a separate validation step. This chapter examines situations in which these solutions are not desirable or acceptable and presents an alternative solution that can be more generally applied.

Context

You are building an information system in which objects have a known set of properties (attributes and/or relationships) each of which can have a meaningful value or not (e.g., can be in an uninitialized state, be absent altogether, have a null value, or refer to a *null object* [Woolf1997]). For some classes there is a subset of properties that must always have a valid value (compulsory properties). You are considering how to support creation of instances of these classes by clients that may not be under your design control (e.g., CORBA [OMG] or ActiveX clients).

Problem

Many classes have "compulsory" properties that must be specified in order for an instance to be in a valid state, for example, before having attributes used as keys in a dictionary or database index. We would therefore like to force the clients of such classes to specify valid compulsory properties when creating new instances.

Sometimes we also need to ensure that these properties cannot be altered at any time after creation. For an example of this, consider the model in Figure 3-1.

When a Contract is created, both a Supplier and a Customer must be specified, and these cannot be changed after creation. Start time must also be specified at the moment of creation, although this can later be delayed or brought forward. End time is completely optional since the contract may be open-ended.

Typical solutions to this problem are the following:

- Avoid the issue at object creation time by using a zero argument constructor and by providing public "set" methods for all properties. Pick some later moment at which a separate validation step can be performed.

  This solution does not really solve the problem at all. It does not allow the creation process to provide feedback to the client on whether the object is legal (unless we rely on the client to call a validation method on the object, which is placing even more faith in the client). It also assumes that we know when the object should be valid so that we can check it before we try to use it. This is not always possible (e.g., when writing persistent objects to an ODMG93 [ODMG] database, no "save" operation identifiable to the application code exists). It also requires us to open up all properties to change at any time, which is unacceptable in the case of the Customer and Supplier relationships.

- If the implementation environment permits it, use only constructors (or Factory objects) that require all compulsory properties to be specified.

  This solution is better, but it can result in cumbersome constructor parameter lists. This is particularly a problem when several different permutations of parameters are valid. We may, for example, wish to allow clients to specify Customers and Suppliers either by name or by passing an object reference. This solution also forces us into questionable techniques like throwing exceptions from constructors if we want to reject any invalid values.

- If the compulsory property is a relationship to another preexisting object, force the client to ask the related object to perform the creation.

  This solution is perfectly acceptable, but it is only applicable in a limited set of circumstances, mainly those in which the related object can in some way be considered the "owner" of the object being created. In the example in Figure 3-1, we would be forced to choose either the Customer or Supplier to be the creator of the contract, neither of which may be obvious or desirable.

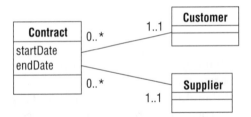

Figure 3-1 *Contract class with optional and compulsory information*

Forces

- *Object integrity and future proofing.* If clients are not under your design control (or have yet to be built), you cannot rely on them to specify valid properties or to validate the object after creation. Sooner or later such clients will attempt to create an invalid object.
- *Property immutability.* There are many situations in which immutable properties are required, either because of design decisions or implementation constraints (e.g., indexing mechanisms).
- *Validity expectations.* Some solution domains (e.g., some persistence frameworks) typically expect the object to be "valid" once the constructor completes.
- *Language limitations.* The syntax of many common object-oriented languages is limited in the ways in which they can support different permutations of constructor parameters without needing to specify every possibility separately.
- *Flexibility vs. complexity.* If every permutation of constructor parameters is specified, a cluttered interface may result.
- *Elegance.* Throwing exceptions from constructors may not be considered elegant (or even legal) in some implementation environments.
- *Interface coherence.* Classes are easier to understand and to use if the methods for manipulating and validating their properties are part of the same class.

Solution

Use a separate object (the Essence object) to receive the compulsory properties of the object being created (the CreationTarget) as shown in Figure 3-2.

There should be an Essence class for each CreationTarget class. The Essence class should have a constructor that does not require the client to supply any parameters. Assign a separate method for each property in the Essence class and have the method store the parameter value in the Essence. For properties that should not be changed after object creation, provide set methods only in the Essence class (i.e., do not provide them in the CreationTarget class).

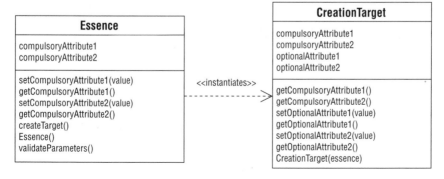

Figure 3-2 *Structure of the Essence pattern*

Force clients to obtain new instances of the CreationTarget class via a method of the Essence class. Have this method validate the properties supplied and then either create the new object or report a failure to the client. When creating the CreationTarget, the Essence object should pass a reference to itself to the CreationTarget constructor to allow it to retrieve the parameter values and initialize its own properties.

The client must first create an instance of an Essence object as shown in Figure 3-3. No extra information is required to do this. He must then call methods

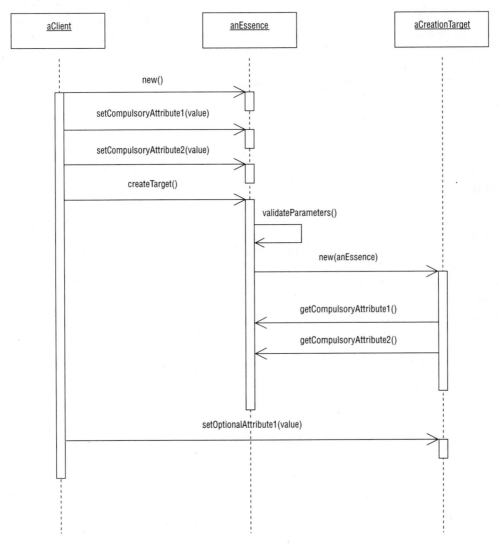

Figure 3-3 *A client creating a CreationTarget using the Essence pattern*

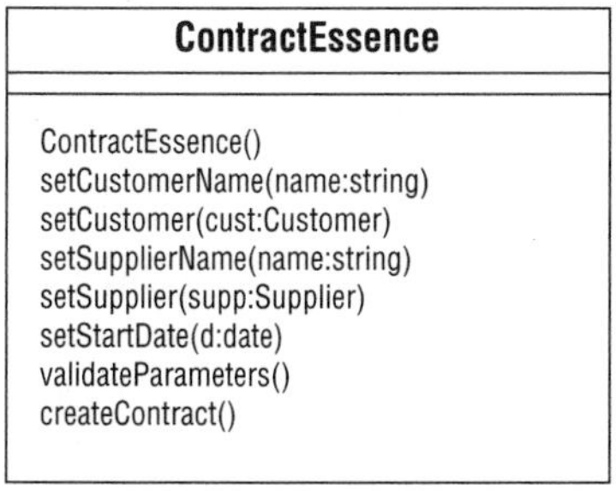

```
┌─────────────────────────────────────┐
│           ContractEssence           │
├─────────────────────────────────────┤
│ ContractEssence()                   │
│ setCustomerName(name:string)        │
│ setCustomer(cust:Customer)          │
│ setSupplierName(name:string)        │
│ setSupplier(supp:Supplier)          │
│ setStartDate(d:date)                │
│ validateParameters()                │
│ createContract()                    │
│                                     │
└─────────────────────────────────────┘
```

Figure 3-4 *ContractEssence interface*

on the Essence object to specify each of the compulsory parameters. Once this has been done, the client can call the `createTarget` method. At this stage, the Essence must validate the supplied parameters and either reject them or create a new CreationTarget as requested, passing itself to the new object's constructor. The values can then be retrieved by the CreationTarget from the Essence. Finally, the fully constructed CreationTarget is passed back to the client.

As an optional addition, the client can call the `validateParameters` method of the Essence object one or more times during specification of parameters, for example, to provide an interactive user with feedback on whether the object's fields have been completed satisfactorily.

To return to our original example, the methods for the ContractEssence class might be as shown in Figure 3-4. Note that we are now able to support alternative ways to specify Customer and Supplier without needing to include all possible permutations in the interface design.

Consequences

The advantages of the Essence pattern are listed here:

- Clients are forced to supply valid property values.
- The object is not created until valid property values are supplied by the client.
- The CreationTarget object is valid at the end of its constructor's execution.
- There is no need to provide set methods for properties that must not be changed after creation.
- Using a method per parameter allows the client more flexibility in using different permutations of parameters as there is no need to decide on these before the interface design is fixed.
- If multiple instances of the same CreationTarget class are being created with parameters that differ only slightly from each other, a single Essence can be used to create several targets, saving the client from repeatedly specifying identical property values.
- The Essence object also can be used as a Builder [Gamma1995] if the desired end result is a number of related objects rather than a single object.

Disadvantages of the Essence pattern are the following:

- Adding the Essence class introduces another class to the design, possibly causing confusion to client developers who must now decide which class to call when setting property values.
- Responsibility for validation of attribute values for CreationTarget is in two places instead of one.
- A circular dependency exists between the Essence class and the CreationTarget class.
- This pattern requires that the CreationTarget class be modified and is therefore not applicable to situations in which the CreationTarget implementation cannot be changed for some reason.

Implementation

Several issues should be considered when applying the Essence pattern:

- *Prevention of direct target creation.* The main problem to be solved in implementing this pattern is how to prevent clients from directly creating instances of the CreationTarget object while still allowing the Essence objects to do so.

  In C++ this can be achieved by making all of the CreationTarget constructors private and making the Essence class a friend of the CreationTarget class.

  In Java the CreationTarget constructors can be declared protected. The Essence class can be granted access to the constructors by placing the Essence and CreationTarget classes in the same package. This assumes that the clients are in a different package; otherwise, they too would be able to use the protected constructors.

  In distributed environments (e.g., CORBA) this job is typically much easier because the object creation process is often forced by the distribution architecture to go through some indirect mechanism (e.g., a Factory Object). Clients are therefore unable to use constructors directly.

  In environments that lack the ability to restrict method accessibility to specific clients, some protection can be obtained by the requirement that an Essence object is passed when creating the CreationTarget object. In these situations the CreationTarget constructor should call the `validateParameters` method on the Essence class. In the event that a client creates an "incomplete" Essence and then directly creates a CreationTarget (i.e., without going via the `create-Target` method on the Essence), the CreationTarget constructor at least has the opportunity to flag an error by whatever means are available.
- *Failure reporting.* Another question is how to report creation failure back to clients. This can be done either by returning a null value (or null object) or by throwing an exception.
- *Location of validation.* The designer has three choices of location for validation: 1. Validation of attribute values that cannot be changed after location

should be placed in the Essence class. 2. Validation of attributes that are not involved in the creation process should obviously be in the CreationTarget class. 3. Parameters that can be changed after creation are more difficult to deal with, as they require validation in both the Essence and CreationTarget classes. In this situation, a class-level method on CreationTarget should be considered to avoid code duplication.

The following optional enhancements also may be considered:

- *Chainable set methods.* Depending on the nature of the client, it may be useful to use Bjarne Stroustrup's [Stroustrup1994] suggestion of having all of the "set" methods on the Essence return a reference to the Essence. This allows the full set of parameters to be specified by the client in a single line if desired. Although suggested for C++, this approach will work in other languages (e.g., Java). For example:

```
(new WindowEssence()).
    textColor(black).font(courier).bckColor(grey)
```

- *Overloaded constructors.* Although it is no longer necessary, overloaded constructors can still be provided for common parameter combinations.

Known Uses

The AT&T Rialto system provides a component called the *Rialto Repository*. The Repository is implemented as a CORBA server that provides an interface on top of which data management tools can be built. Underlying this is an ODMG93 database, and it is the responsibility of the CORBA server to ensure that only valid data reaches the database. The Essence pattern has been used in several situations to solve the problem of compulsory and/or immutable properties. For example:

- Corporate Legal Entities must have a Company Name and at least a minimal set of contact information.
- Contracts must have both a supplier and a customer.
- Domains must have a domain name.

The Java class library [Java1998] includes two classes in the java.net package called URL and URLConnection. To obtain an instance of URLConnection a client must first set up a valid instance of URL and ask it to create a URLConnection. The validation mechanism is a little different from that described here. URL provides overloaded constructors that throw exceptions if invalid parameters are supplied. The implementors of this library have also chosen to provide a limited set of methods in the URL class, which provides some of the URLConnection functionality without requiring the client to explicitly create an instance of URLConnection.

The Rogue Wave DBTools.h++ class library [RW] requires the developer to obtain an instance of RWDBCursor (through which the database can be read) by first creating an instance of RWDBSelector and supplying the query parameters to it. Once the query is fully specified to the RWDBSelector, a method call is made to obtain an RWDBCursor object.

Related Patterns

This pattern was inspired by a section in Stroustrup's *Design and Evolution of C++* [Stroustrup1994] discussing the case for an argument naming syntax in C++ and alternatives in light of his decision not to build one into the language. The motivation for this pattern is, however, somewhat different from Stroustrup's.

Abstract Factory [Gamma1995] is typically used in distributed environments to create new instances of objects and can be used as the source of Essence objects.

ACKNOWLEDGMENTS

I would like to thank my PLoP shepherd, Wolf Siberski, for his helpful comments on this paper. I would also like to thank the participants in the writers workshop at PLoP '98 for their efforts that also resulted in numerous improvements. Thanks also to Trevor Hayward for his patient work to reformat this paper for the PLoP book.

REFERENCES

[Gamma1995] E. Gamma, R. Helm, R. Johnson, J. Vlissides. *Design Patterns: Elements of Reusable Object-Oriented Software*. Reading, MA: Addison-Wesley, 1995.

[Java] Sun Microsystems. *Java Platform 1.1 Core API Specification*. Palo Alto, CA: Sun Microsystems, 1998.

[ODMG] R. Cattell and D. Barry (eds.). *The Object Database Standard: ODMG 2.0*. San Francisco: Morgan Kaufmann, 1997.

[OMG] Object Management Group. *The Common Object Request Broker: Architecture and Specification*. Framingham, MA: Object Management Group, 1995.

[RW] Rogue Wave Software. *DBTools.h++ Class Reference Manual Version 2*. Corvallis, OR: Rogue Wave Software, 1996.

[Stroustrup1994] B. Stroustrup. *The Design and Evolution of C++*. Reading, MA: Addison-Wesley, 1994.

[Woolf1997] B Woolf. "Null Object." In R. Martin, D. Riehle, and F. Buschmann (eds.), *Pattern Languages of Program Design 3*. Reading, MA: Addison-Wesley, 1998.

Andy Carlson may be reached at andycarlson@acm.org.

Chapter 4

Object Recursion

Bobby Woolf

Classification

Object Behavioral

Intent

Distribute processing of a request over a structure by delegating polymorphically. Object Recursion transparently enables a request to be repeatedly broken into smaller parts that are easier to handle.

Also Known As

Recursive Delegation

Motivation

Sometimes the easiest way for an object to accomplish a task is for it to tell one or more of its parts to accomplish the same task and merge those results as necessary. Each part keeps passing the responsibility to its subparts until the responsibility finally falls on simple objects. The simple objects merely perform the task for themselves without passing the responsibility any further. In this way, the task is distributed throughout a structure as lots of smaller versions of the same task.

For example, consider the need to determine whether two objects are equivalent. Simple objects and primitives are easy to compare: just use native operations. The difficulty lies in comparing arbitrarily complex objects.

One approach is to employ a Comparer object that accepts any two arbitrarily complex objects and answers whether the subjects are equivalent. The Comparer takes the subjects, breaks each one into pieces, and compares the pieces to determine whether they're equivalent. If any of the pieces are too complex to compare, the Comparer repeats the process by breaking it into pieces, and so on, until all of the pieces are simple enough to compare.

This Comparer approach has several undesirable consequences. The Comparer must recognize what kind of object the subjects are and know how to decompose those kinds of objects into simple parts that can be compared. The more complex a subject is, the more complex the code for comparing it needs to be. Every time a developer implements a new class whose instances might need to be compared, he also needs to add code to Comparer (or a subclass) to handle the new class. The decomposition code in Comparer depends heavily on the class's implementation, so whenever that implementation changes, the code in Comparer must be changed accordingly. The subjects need to provide extra protocol for decomposing, protocol that exposes the objects' implementation. All in all, the Comparer requires lots of complex code that is difficult to develop and maintain.

Instead, the Comparer should tell the subjects to compare themselves and let them decide how to do that. The Comparer tells the subjects *what* to do, but not *how* to do it. With this approach, the Comparer object isn't even needed, because any Client can simply ask one subject to compare itself to another.

How do the subjects compare themselves? One determines if the other is equivalent to itself. It considers which parts of its state must be equivalent, then compares those. Each of those parts considers which of its parts must be equivalent and compares those, and so on until all of the parts are simple objects. At each step, the comparison process is relatively simple. Even a highly complex object doesn't need to know how to compare itself entirely; it just needs to know what its parts are, and those parts need to know how to compare themselves.

For example, consider an `Engine` object that knows its internal displacement and total horsepower. To compare it to another engine, a client must verify that both engines are the same size and same power. Figure 4-1 shows the classes involved and how to implement =.

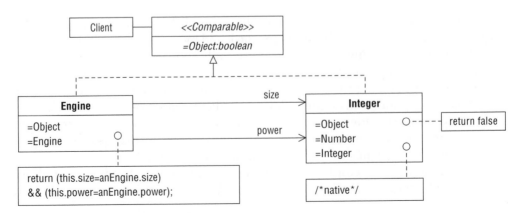

Figure 4-1 *Motivation class diagram*

The `Client` sends = to the first `Engine` with the second `Engine` as an argument. The first `Engine` compares itself to the second one by comparing their `size` and `power`. The parts are `Integers`, simple objects that the native system can compare. If the parts were complex objects, they would continue the comparison process by comparing their parts. Eventually, the simplest parts are either equal or they're not. (See Figure 4-2.)

This comparison algorithm, where an object compares itself to another by telling their parts to compare themselves, and so on, is an example of Object Recursion. An implementation of a recursive message sends the same message to one or more of its related objects, and so on. The message surfs through the parts of the structure until reaching objects, that can simply implement the message and return the result.

Keys

A system that incorporates the Object Recursion pattern has the following features:

- Two polymorphic classes, one of which handles a request recursively and another that simply handles the request without recursing.
- A separate message, usually in a third class that is not polymorphic with the first two, to initiate the request.

Applicability

Use the Object Recursion pattern when

- Passing a message through a linked structure where the ultimate destination is unknown.
- Broadcasting a message to all nodes in part of a linked structure.
- Distributing a behavior's responsibility throughout a linked structure.

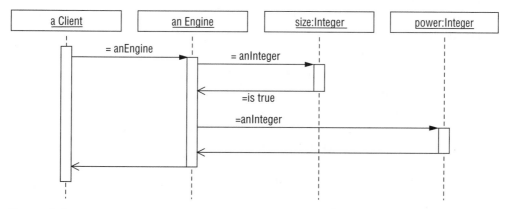

Figure 4-2 *Motivation interaction diagram*

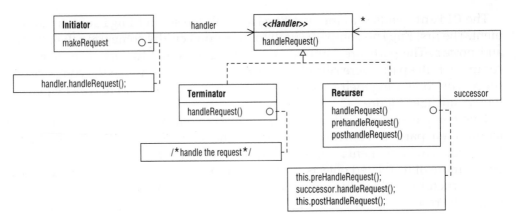

Figure 4-3 *Structure class diagram*

Structure

Figure 4-3 shows the roles of the participants.
   A typical object structure might look like Figure 4-4.

Figure 4-4 *Structure instance diagram*

Participants

- *Initiator* (`Client`)
   –Initiates the request.
   –Usually not a subtype of Handler; makeRequest is a separate message from HandleRequest.
- *Handler* (`Comparable`)
   –Defines a type that can handle requests from initiators.
- *Recurser* (`Engine`)
   –Defines the successor link.
   –Handles a request by delegating it to its successors.
   –Successors relevant to a request can vary by request.
   –Can perform extra behavior before or after delegating the request.
   –May be a terminator for a different request.

- *Terminator* (`Integer`)
  - –Finishes the request by implementing it completely and not delegating any of its implementation.
  - –May be a recurser for a different request.

Collaborations

- The Initiator needs to make a request. It asks its Handler to handle the request.
- When the Handler is a Recurser, it does whatever work it needs to do, asks its successor—another Handler—to handle the request, and returns a result based on the successor's result. The extra work can be done before and/or after delegating to the successor. If the Recurser has multiple successors, it delegates to each of them in turn, perhaps asynchronously.
- When the Handler is a Terminator, it handles the request without delegating the request to any other successors and returns the result (if any).

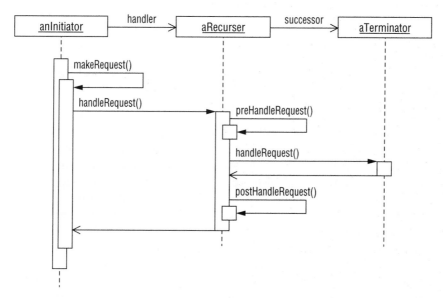

Figure 4-5 *Collaboration interaction diagram*

Consequences

The advantages of the Object Recursion pattern are:

- *Decentralized processing.* The processing of the request is distributed across a structure of handlers that can be as numerous and complex as necessary to best complete the task.

- *Responsibility flexibility.* The Initiator does not need to know how many Handlers there are, how they're arranged, or how the processing is distributed. It simply makes the request of its Handler and lets the Handlers do the rest. The Handler arrangement can change at runtime to dynamically reconfigure the handling responsibilities.
- *Role flexibility.* A Handler that acts like a Recurser for one request may act as a Terminator for another kind of request, and visa versa. For example, a leaf node acts as a Recurser for requests that are passed up the list (towards the beginning), but acts as a Terminator for requests that are passed down the list (towards the end).
- *Implementation hiding.* Encapsulates the decisions for how to handle a request within the object doing the handling.

The disadvantages of the Object Recursion pattern are:

- *Programming complexity.* Recursion, procedural or object-oriented, is a difficult concept to grasp. Proper use can make a system simpler, but overuse can make a system more difficult to understand and maintain.

Implementation

There are a couple of issues to consider when implementing the Object Recursion pattern:

1. *Separate Initiator type.* The Initiator.makeRequest( ) message must not be polymorphic with the Recursor.handleRequest( ) message. If the message that sends handleRequest() is another implementor of handleRequest( ), then the sender is still part of the recursion; there must be an implementor of makeRequest( ) that sends handleRequest( ) and starts the recursion. That makeRequest( ) message cannot be the same polymorphic message as handleRequest( ). If there is no such makeRequest( ) message, then the recursion can never be initiated, so even though the implementors of handleRequest( ) send each other, they'll never get run and they can all be deleted.
2. *Defining the successor.* The Recurser needs one or more successors, but the Terminator does not. If the Terminator implements the successor link (usually by inheriting it from the Handler), it ignores the link when implementing the handleRequest( ) messages. If all of the Terminator's messages ignore the successor link, then its value can always be null and the link is not needed.

Sample Code

Let's look at how to implement `equals` recursively.

All objects, no matter how complex, are ultimately composed of simple objects (i.e., primitives) such as integers, floats, booleans, and characters. Determining the equality of two simple objects (of the same type) is a trivial task performed natively by the operating system or CPU. Here are some examples in Java:

```
5 == 5           // integer comparison (true)
5.25 == 5.15     // float comparison (false)
true == false    // boolean comparison (false)
'a' == 'b'       // character comparison (false)
```

There's no recursion here, but these simple comparisons form the terminating case for recursion.

Comparing two ordered collections is nearly as simple: Are each of the elements equal? Thus two strings are equal if each of their characters are equal. For example, look at the implementation of `java.lang.String.equals(String)`:[1]

```java
public class String {
    private char value[];
    private int count;

    public boolean equals(String anotherString) {
        int n = count;
        if (n == anotherString.count) {
            char v1[] = value;
            char v2[] = anotherString.value;
            int i = 0;
            int j = 0;
            while (n-- != 0) {
                if (v1[i++] != v2[j++]) {
                    return false;
                }
            }
            return true;
        }
        return false;
    }
}
```

Thus if each of the characters in the strings are equal, the strings are equal. For the purposes of implementing equality recursively, a string is a terminating object.

---

[1] The standard `java.lang` method is actually `String.equals(Object)`, but we'll ignore the nasty `Object` → `String` downcast here.

Now consider a name object that stores the first name and last name separately. Two names are equal if their first and last names are equal:

```
public class PersonName {
    private String firstName, lastName;

    public boolean equals (PersonName anotherName) {
        return firstName.equals(anotherName.firstName)
            && (lastName.equals(anotherName.lastName));
    }
}
```

This contains one level of recursion—`PersonName.equals()` calls `String.equals()`—plus the primitive operation.

Now consider a phone directory object that stores a person's name and phone number. Two entries are considered duplicates if their names are equal:

```
public class DirectoryEntry {
    private PersonName name;
    private PhoneNumber number;

    public boolean equals (DirectoryEntry anotherEntry) {
        return name.equals(anotherEntry.name);
    }
}
```

Here we have two levels of recursion—`DirectoryEntry.equals()` calls `PersonName.equals()`, which calls `String.equals()`. (See Figure 4-6.)

The client doesn't really care which implementor of `equals()` it's calling; it just knows that it has two objects of the same type, and so it compares them using `equals()`. If the two objects were simple ones, no recursion would be necessary. When the two objects are complex, `equals()` is implemented recursively using other implementors of `equals()`.

Known Uses

The equality example described in the Motivation uses one-step recursion: The recursive implementation of the message sends the same message to its successor directly. If the class library includes hash table collections classes like `Set` or `Dictionary`, each implementor of `equal` also needs a corresponding implementor of `hash`; `hash` is implemented recursively just like `equal`.

A `copy` or `clone` message is often implemented using two-step recursion: The recursive implementation sends a second message to the receiver, which in turn sends the original message to its successor. Thus the two messages together implement the recursion. In the case of `copy`, the two messages are `simpleCopy`

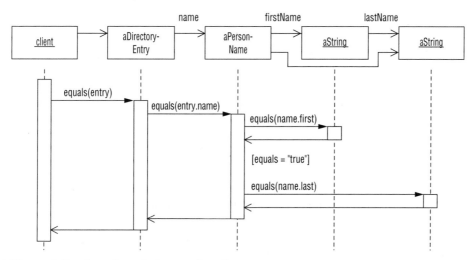

Figure 4-6 *Sample code interaction diagram*

(which only copies the root of the object) and `postCopy` (which copies the object's parts as necessary). `copy` sends `simpleCopy`, and `postCopy` in turn sends the parts `copy`, propagating the recursion.

Serialization algorithms, whether they produce text or binary output, usually use recursion. The algorithm serializes an object by serializing the root and then recursively serializing its (persistent) parts. Each branch of the recursion ends when a simple object serializes itself and is finished.

An algorithm to display an object as a string (e.g., Java's `toString()` and Smalltalk's `printString`) is usually recursive. The algorithm displays the root as a string, then recursively tells the interesting parts to display themselves.

Most linked-list, tree, and graph structures use recursion to broadcast messages through the nodes. For example, a tree structure can use recursion to pass a message from any one of its leaves up to its root. Each node in the path recursively passes the message to its parent, doing any extra work along the way as necessary. The tree can similarly use recursion to broadcast a message from its root through all of its nodes to its leaves. These recursive techniques are frequently used in graphics trees, for example, to register invalidation requests and broadcast redisplay opportunities.

Several established design patterns use Object Recursion; see the Related Patterns section for more known uses.

Related Patterns

Object Recursion vs. Composite and Decorator. When a Decorator [Gamma+1995, p. 175] delegates to its component or a Composite [Gamma+1995, p. 163] delegates to its children, this might be considered an example of Object Recursion. However, Composite and Decorator are structural (data structure) patterns, whereas Object

Recursion is a behavioral (algorithm) pattern. If the structural patterns do embody recursion, it is only explicitly one level deep (a composite or decorator delegating to its component), whereas recursion's depth is unlimited. At best, Object Recursion is a pattern that both Composite and Decorator use, but that can also be used independently of Composite or Decorator.

Object Recursion vs. Chain of Responsibility.   Chain of Responsibility [Gamma+1995, p. 223] uses the Object Recursion pattern. Chain of Responsibility uses a linked-list or tree organized by specialization or priority. When a request is made, the structure uses Object Recursion to find an appropriate Handler.

Object Recursion and Adapter.   A chain of Adapters [Gamma+1995, p. 139] can seem to use a non-polymorphic form of Object Recursion, where the behavior is recursive even though the messages aren't, as each adapter delegates to the next until the delegation terminates at the adaptee and unwinds. However, the lack of polymorphism goes against the spirit of Object Recursion.

Object Recursion and Interpreter.   In Interpreter [Gamma+1995, p. 243], the `interpret` message traverses the abstract syntax tree using Object Recursion. Client is the Initiator, AbstractExpression is the Handler, NonterminalExpression is the Recurser, and TerminalExpression is the Terminator.

Object Recursion and Iterator.   Some implementations of Iterator [Gamma+1995, p. 257] use Object Recursion. External iterators on any structure are not recursive; they use while loops instead. Internal iterators on array structures also use while loops.

An internal iterator on a linked-list structure is recursive. If the end of the list is marked by null, then the recursion is procedural. However, the terminating node of the list can work better as a null object [PLoPD3], an actual object whose type is the same as other list nodes but that never has a successor. This allows the `next` and `isDone` messages to be private and makes the algorithm Object Recursion.

An internal iterator on a branching structure (i.e., a tree or graph) must be implemented recursively. If the terminating points—the leaves and/or root—are objects, then the recursion is Object Recursion.

Object Recursion and Delegation.   Other patterns contain an object that implements a message by delegating the same message to a collaborator of the same type: Proxy is a good example. Any such example is a one-level-deep example of Object Recursion [Gamma+1995].

ACKNOWLEDGMENTS

Thanks to Eugene Wallingford for his help in writing this paper. I would also like to thank the members of my PLoP '98 writers' workshop, including: Ken Auer, David DeLano, Owen Astrachan, and Kinh Nguyen.

REFERENCES

[Gamma+1995] E. Gamma, R. Helm, R. Johnson, and J. Vlissides, *Design Patterns: Elements of Reusable Object-Oriented Software*. Reading, MA: Addison-Wesley, 1995.

[PLoPD3] B. Woolf, "Null Object." In R. Martin, D. Riehle, and F. Buschmann (eds.), *Pattern Languages of Program Design 3*. Reading, MA: Addison-Wesley, 1998.

Bobby Woolf may be reached at woolf@acm.org.

Chapter 5

Prototype-Based Object System

James Noble

Classical object-oriented systems require every object to be an instance of a class, and all classes to be written before the program is deployed. Some programs need flexible, configurable, dynamically extensible representations of objects, which cannot be determined in advance. The Prototype-Based Object System pattern describes how you can build your own object system from scratch. Using the Prototype-Based Object System pattern, you can build precisely the kind of objects you need for your application, but these objects will require more memory space and execution time than the more rigid objects supported by programming languages.

Intent

Some programs need flexible, configurable, dynamically extensible representations of objects. The Prototype-Based Object System pattern lets you build precisely the kind of objects you need for your application.

Also Known As

Frame System, Object System, Prototype-Based System, Prototype-Instance System.

Motivation

Some systems need to represent flexible, dynamic objects. This may be to support end-user tailorable or programmable systems, rapid prototyping or evolutionary development, or to model domains in which the structure and content of information are constantly changing.

Consider a system to support the initial development and analysis of civil engineering designs. This system needs to allow users (civil engineers with some computing experience) to describe their designs, and then use the information about the designs to compute properties of the designs. The system needs to allow engineers to edit all aspects of their designs—adding objects to the design (such as beams, walls, floors, and so on), deleting them, changing objects' properties (such as the cross-section, length, or composition of a beam), adding new properties to objects (such as giving one particular beam a new `color` property with the value `gray`), and changing objects' classes (such as replacing a `concrete-beam` with a `reinforced-steel-girder`). Engineers also might need to make new kinds of objects in the middle of producing their designs. For example, they might want to create a particular kind of beam and then use it repeatedly throughout the design. So that designs can be analyzed, engineers need to be able to add procedural code to the objects in their design, run the code to analyze the design, or export the design to existing analysis software. For example, a beam should be able to calculate its volume based on its length, width, thickness, and cross-section.

There are a number of possible approaches to produce this kind of system. The most traditional approach is to write a program (typically in FORTRAN or C) to model the design. While this program will undoubtedly execute efficiently, and can handle complex analysis calculations, such programs require skilled programmers to construct, and once built are typically quite difficult to modify. More modern programmers will choose an object-oriented language, but most object-oriented languages do not support arbitrary dynamic modification and extension of the objects in the program.

Alternatively, the design could be modeled using a tool designed for end-user programming, such as a spreadsheet or scripting language. Both spreadsheets and scripting languages provide a large amount of flexibility, and they are designed to support programming on-the-fly. Unfortunately, these types of tools do not provide much support for modeling. Spreadsheets can be (and, all too frequently, are) used to model anything, but they do not provide much support for modeling data other than numbers. Most scripting languages provide simple textual lists and associative arrays, but these are not really first-class objects in the language, as they do not support linked data structures.

The Prototype-Based Object System pattern describes how these requirements can best be met. Rather than fighting to add flexibility to an existing programming language or to impose structure onto a spreadsheet or scripting language, you can construct your own implementation of an object system. By implementing the objects yourself, you can ensure that new objects and new kinds of objects can be created at runtime and that the objects can be modified and extended directly. An object system can be extended to provide extra system-wide features (like persistence or constraints), to interface with external systems, and to provide good error checking and debugging support to the programmer.

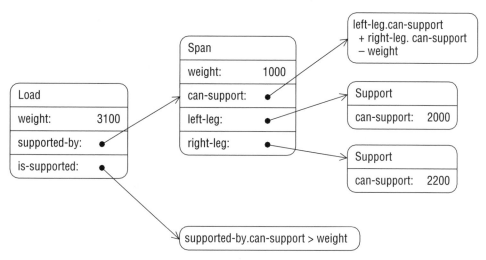

Figure 5-1 *A design for a bridge*

Consider once again the problem of modeling engineering designs. At a high level of abstraction, everything an engineer needs to manipulate when constructing a design—beams, walls, floors, and even intangible considerations like traffic flow, loaded weight, and ambient lighting—can be seen as a single kind of object, a *design element*. Each design element has a number of properties, such as its weight, height, composition, or the other design elements that are supporting it (see Figure 5-1). Because each design element is treated individually, its precise properties can depend on what it is modeling and how it is used. Using the object system, engineers can describe a design by configuring design elements, linking them to one another, and adding, removing, and adjusting their properties. Engineers can analyze a design by attaching procedural code—methods—to design elements and then executing the methods to analyze the design.

Figure 5-1 shows how a very simple design for a bridge can be represented using an object system. A main `Span` design element is supported by two `Support` design elements. The `Span` itself has to support a given `Load`, also modeled as a design element. The designer has described each design element by attaching properties to them—describing their width, length, composition, and so on—noting that every design element has a different set of properties. The designer has attached methods to the `Span` and `Load` elements to calculate how much weight the load `can-support` and whether or not the load `is-supported`.

Figure 5-2 shows how this is implemented. Each design element and each element property is modeled as an individual instance of the `DesignElement` or `Element-Property` class. A `DesignElement` stores a list of its `ElementPropertie`s and provides protocol for adding, removing, and modifying properties. The system has two kinds of `DesignElement` objects, which share a superclass to define a common interface. Most design elements are `UserDesignElement`s that can be manipu-

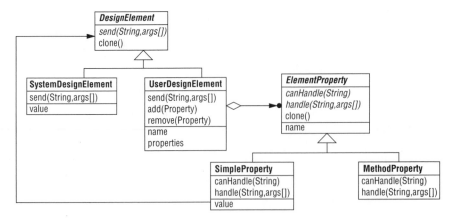

Figure 5-2 *Design elements*

lated by the user, but the system also has `SystemDesignElements` so that properties can store primitive values like integers and weights. Similarly, there are two kinds of `ElementProperties` in the system: `SimpleProperties` (like a `Slab`'s `weight` or `construction` properties) that store a reference to another `DesignElement`, and `MethodProperties` that store methods like the `Slab`'s `can-support` property and the `Load`'s `is-supported` property. Note that both `DesignElement` and `ElementProperty` have a `clone` method that produces a copy of the respective element or slot (a `DesignElement` copies all its slots when it is cloned), so that any `DesignElement` can act as a prototype to create other design elements.

Object systems are useful in any system that needs to represent or analyze designs flexibly. Besides straight design domains, object systems are also useful in CASE tools and user interface design systems. This flexibility comes at a cost, because object systems require more memory, execute more slowly, and provide less static safety than the objects provided by most programming languages.

Applicability

Use a Prototype-Based Object System when

- You need objects that can be flexibly created and modified at runtime.
- You can afford to pay significant time and space costs to buy this flexibility.
- You wish to avoid building a hierarchy of very similar classes.
- You don't need the security of a static type system.
- You need to incorporate system-wide extensions to objects' behavior, such as persistence, change detection, or constraints.
- You've tried (or considered) using simpler patterns, such as Prototype [Gamma+1995], Type Object [Johnson+1998], Property List [Sommerlad+1998b,

Riehle1997], Anything [Sommerlad+1998b], Extension Object [Gamma1998], Interpreter [Gamma+1995], and Reflection [Buschmann+1996], and they are insufficient.

Structure

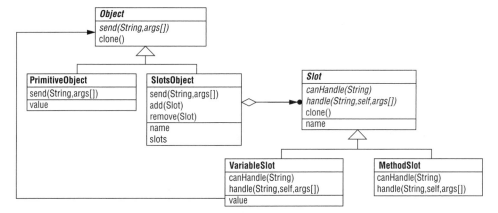

Figure 5-3 *Class structure*

Participants

- *Object* (`DesignElement`)

  –Provides an interface for all objects in the system.

  –Allows objects to handle messages.

- *SlotsObject* (`UserDesignElement`)

  –Represents the user's objects.

  –Delegates messages to its slots.

  –Allows the user to add, remove, inspect, and modify the slots comprising the object.

- *PrimitiveObject* (`SystemDesignElement`)

  –Wraps a primitive object from outside the object system, such as an object provided by the implementation language, a library, or an external resource such as a window system.

  –Delegates messages as appropriate.

  –Allows external objects to be used seamlessly from within the object system.

- *Slot* (`ElementProperty`)

  –Describes a property of an `Object`.

  –Responds to messages as appropriate.

- *VariableSlot* (`SimpleProperty`)

  –Records a single name variable local to an `Object`.

  –Assigns and returns this value in response to messages.

- *MethodSlot* (`MethodProperty`)

  –Holds procedural code for a method attached to an `Object`.

  –Executes the method in response to messages.

Collaborations

A client sends a message to an object. The object searches for a slot that can handle the message, then delegates the message to the slot.

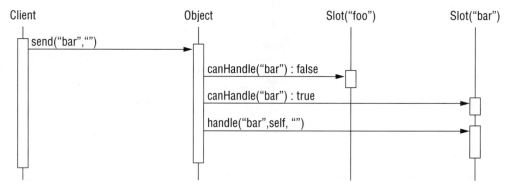

Figure 5-4 *Message lookup collaborations*

Consequences

The Prototype-Based Object System pattern has the following benefits:

- *Dynamic configuration.* The objects in an object system can be constructed and modified at runtime, whatever the underlying implementation language. Empty objects can be created from scratch and then filled with slots, or existing objects can be treated as prototypes, creating new objects by cloning.
- *Flexibility.* An object system can provide as much flexibility as is needed by the application. Any kind of object can be built simply by adding properties to an object, without reference to pre-existing objects or rigid classes.
- *Integration.* Because of its flexibility, an object system can sit at the center of a system's architecture and can integrate diverse external components. The components can either be linked directly into the object system (as `Primitive-Objects`), or the object system can provide facilities to read and write its objects so that they can be understood indirectly by completely separate components.

- *System-wide extensions.* Because you've implemented the whole object system yourself, it is easy to add features such as persistence, change detection, or constraints to every object in the system.
- *User support.* It is easy to add features to the system purely to support the user. For example, every object can be given a human-readable name to support debugging. Type errors can be checked dynamically and error messages produced at runtime. Every individual object or object property can record the date it was last edited and the programmer who made the change.
- *Portability.* With care, your object system (or at least the objects supported by the system) can be portable across different underlying languages, operating systems, and architectures. If you have made little use of platform-specific primitive objects, you can write out objects from one version of the system and read them into another.

The Prototype-Based Object System pattern also has the following liabilities:

- *Efficiency.* An object system will execute much more slowly (up to a thousand times slower) and will require more space (perhaps a hundred times as much space) as objects provided directly within a programming language. The degree of degradation depends greatly upon the sophistication of the implementation techniques used.
- *Flexibility.* An object system's flexibility is both a benefit and a liability—it is a benefit when the flexibility is required, but if it is used carelessly it can result in a large number of badly designed objects—a maze of twisty little objects, all slightly different.
- *Static checking.* Although an object system can do a lot of dynamic checking and provide a lot of information to the programmer at runtime, it cannot generally provide much compile-time support. In particular, while object systems may be dynamically type-safe (so the program will never crash if an object receives a message it does not understand), type checks probably cannot be performed statically at compile-time.
- *Method syntax.* An object system can require convoluted syntax for the methods attached to objects. If the methods are embedded within another programming language (typically the language implementing the object system), sending a message to an object system object can require many extra macro or function calls compared with sending a message to an implementation language object. If the methods are implemented using a parser and interpreter, programmers have to learn the syntax of a whole new language.
- *Complexity.* Introducing an additional object system makes the overall programming model more complex. Programmers must decide what should be supported directly by the infrastructure of the object system, what should be programmed using the object system, and what should be left to the underlying implementation language.

- *Standardization.* Your object system won't be a standard, unless you are Microsoft or a strategic group in a large company. This may make it more difficult to find users for your object system, since they may be unwilling to expend effort in developing for a narrow base. This may also make it difficult to reuse code developed for other systems, unless the object system can be interfaced to them directly. Although you can extend your object system to provide features like persistence, it will be difficult to buy or reuse existing products to provide these features.
- *Maintenance.* You must maintain and support the object system as well as the applications that are built within it, because all the applications will depend on the continued operation of the object system. This means you will need programmers who understand the implementation of the object system, as distinct from how to use the object system to support actual applications.
- *Emotional attachment.* You will build up a strong emotional attachment to your object system, and your organization may make large investments in developing and maintaining it. This can make it difficult for you and your organization to move to more modern, standard, third-party products, rather than continuing with your own object system.
- *Overuse.* Object systems are often overused. Because object systems are flexible, they can be used to solve almost any problem, but because they have many liabilities, they should be used only where other less expensive approaches (such as Prototype [Gamma+1995], Type Object [Johnson+1998], Property List [Sommerlad+1998b, Riehle1997], Anything [Sommerlad+1998b], Extension Object [Gamma1998], Interpreter [Gamma+1995], and Reflection [Buschmann+1996], or an appropriate object-oriented programming language) are not applicable.

Implementation

Consider the following implementation issues when applying the Prototype-Based Object System pattern:

1. *Implementing slots.* Slots can be implemented in two main ways in an object system. Either each slot can be implemented by an individual slot object (as shown in the Structure and Collaboration diagrams and the Motivation), or all the slots in an object can be stored directly in a hash table or array. Individual slot objects are more flexible because the slot lookup algorithm is distributed between the object (which asks slots which messages they canHandle) and the slots (which accept and handle messages); thus, for example, objects do not need to know whether a slot is a method or variable slot. Storing all slots together in a single array or hash table is more efficient but less flexible, as objects need to implement the entire lookup algorithm and to distinguish between different types of slots.

2. *Optimizing message lookup.*   Looking up slots in response to message sends is a major source of inefficiency in object systems. Using a linear search is quite slow, but it may be acceptable if most objects contain only a few slots, and testing whether a particular slot implements a particular message is quick. Hash tables can be used for more efficient slot lookup. Slot names also can be represented as symbols or instances of enumerated types, rather than strings, so that they can be compared or hashed quickly. Using an enumerated type to represent slot names makes adding new slot names more complex, but can also protect the programmer against misspellings [McDaniel+1995].

3. *Creating new kinds of slots.*   If you choose to implement individual slot objects, you can extend an object system by creating new kinds of slots. For example, you could create typed slots that can be assigned only restricted kinds of objects, slots that are not copied into any clone of their enclosing object, slots that can contain more than one object, or slots that execute a method (a demon [Raymond+1993]) whenever they are assigned.

4. *Implementing methods.*   Methods can be implemented in an object system in two ways—either by using an Interpreter or by incorporating methods directly from the programming language. Using an Interpreter is more flexible and will make it much easier for the user to extend the system's methods at runtime. Methods implemented in the underlying programming language (perhaps using macros, functions, or blocks) will execute more quickly than interpreted methods, but they will be harder to change at runtime and more difficult to write. An object system can easily incorporate both kinds of methods by providing two MethodSlot subclasses, one for interpreted methods and one for primitive methods. This can provide the best of both worlds—interpreted methods can be written on the fly, implementation language methods can be written where speed is essential, and the choice can be made on a per-method basis without affecting the rest of the object system's framework. Some object systems do not support methods; that is, objects and slots are used solely to provide flexible and extensible data representation, and computation can be carried out elsewhere.

5. *Accessing primitive objects.*   You need to provide access to objects outside the object system itself. In simple cases, these are things like integers and floats, but they can be more complex, like windows, widgets, files, and so on. A primitive object is an Adapter [Gamma+1995] that links these programming language level objects into the object system. In most languages (including C++ and Java) you will have to implement a specific primitive object for every class of object you wish to incorporate. In reflexive languages (like Smalltalk) you can build generic adapters that can incorporate any implementation language object into the object system [Gamma+1995]. Primitive objects also can be used to extend the facilities of the object system itself or to make it more efficient. For example, many object systems provide arrays implemented as primitive objects, so that

common array operations will be executed rapidly and collections of objects will not occupy too much space.

6. *Using structure descriptors and virtual copying to represent clone families.* Most objects in object systems will be structurally identical to many other objects in the system. In particular, every object created by cloning a given prototype and not subsequently changed (the prototype's *clone family*) will have the same structure. Naïve implementations of object systems require large amounts of memory to store the structure of every object in the system. To reduce memory use, you can eliminate this duplication by applying the Type Object [Johnson+1998] pattern, using structure descriptors and virtual copying. Make a read-only descriptor for each object structure, and share the descriptor between all objects with a clone family. The individual objects then need only store a pointer to the descriptor and the contents of their variable slots. Slot descriptors can provide the memory-conservation benefits of class-based systems while preserving the flexibility and user-level simplicity of a prototype-based system.

7. *Propagating structural changes.* You may want to propagate structural changes made from an object used as a prototype to all objects cloned from it. This can keep the structures of the objects in the system more consistent. This can be implemented by keeping a record of each clone family. Whenever a family's prototype's structure is changed, that is, when slots are added to or removed from it, the same change can be made to each object in the clone family. A structure descriptor can act as a Manager [Sommerlad+1998a] to record the objects in a clone family and manage the propagation.

8. *Providing inheritance.* Object systems can support inheritance between objects so that objects can share structure and behavior. For example, one way to add single inheritance between objects is to add a new kind of slot (a `ParentSlot`) that is a subclass of `VariableSlot`. When a `SlotsObject` receives a message, and the object does not contain a slot that implements the message, the message should be sent on to the object contained in the `ParentSlot`. To support true inheritance (avoiding the *self problem* [Lieberman1986]) the message should be re-sent by a variant of the basic `send` operation, which ensures that self-references in the inherited message are bound to the object that originally received the message. Object systems can be extended to support multiple inheritance by using multiple parent slots and more sophisticated method lookup algorithms.

9. *Providing classes.* If your object system makes heavy use of clone families, inheritance, and change propagation, you might prefer to implement a class-based system rather than a classless prototype-based system. Essentially, the Type Object [Johnson+1998] structure descriptors are turned into classes by making them visible to the object system's users. A class-based system makes managing groups of objects easier than managing objects individually and makes optimizations like using structure descriptors and optimized slot lookups

much easier. Using explicit classes, however, will make an object system more complex and less flexible.

10. *Adding system-wide features.*   Object systems make it easy to extend the system as a whole. For example, all the objects in the system can be made persistent simply by making the implementation of `Object` persistent, typically by adding methods that allow an object, its slots, and the objects reachable from it to be written into a file. Similarly, constraint systems (which need to detect when objects change) can be integrated into an object system by changing the implementation of `VariableSlots` so that they generate change notifications whenever they are assigned to.

Sample Code

This example is a simple object system written in Java called Ego, after Brian Foote's Ego written in CLOS [Foote1991], and inspired by Self [Ungar+1991] and Kevo [Taivalsaari1993]. A Java interface called `Ego` defines the main interface to the object system. The main method in the `Ego` interface is `send`, which sends a message and its arguments to an object. To work around Java's limited polymorphism, this interface also defines some convenience functions that send messages with no arguments, one argument, or a single integer argument.

```
interface Ego {
  public Ego send(String message, Ego args[]);

  // convenience functions
  public Ego send(String message);
  public Ego send(String message, Ego arg);
  public Ego send(String message, int i);
}
```

Objects containing slots are instances of the `EgoSlotsObject` class. Every `EgoSlotsObject` has a name, a collection of `EgoSlots`, and methods to add new slots into the collection.

```
class EgoSlotsObject implements Ego, Cloneable {
  private String name;
  private Vector slots;

  public EgoSlotsObject(String name_) {
    name = name_;
    slots = new Vector();
  }
```

```
    public EgoSlotsObject add(EgoSlot slot) {
      slots.addElement(slot);
      return this;
    }

    String objectName() {return name;}

    //...
```

`EgoSlotsObject` must understand `send`, because they implement the Ego interface. In this very simple implementation, an `EgoSlotsObject` processes a message with a linear search of its slots to find one that can handle the message and then delegates the message to the slot. Finally, `EgoSlotsObject` must implement the convenience functions from the Ego interface—these are quite straightforward so we omit them for brevity.

```
    //...

    public Ego send(String message, Ego args[]) {
      for (int i=0; i<slots.size(); i++)
        {
          if (slotAt(i).canHandle(message))
            return slotAt(i).handle(message, this, args);
        }
      throw new Error("DoesNotUnderstand: "+message);
    }

    protected EgoSlot slotAt(int i) {
      return (EgoSlot)slots.elementAt(i);
    }

}
```

Ego slots are defined by the abstract class `EgoSlot`. All slots have a name, methods for querying whether they can handle a particular message, and methods for actually handling a message.

```
abstract class EgoSlot implements Cloneable {
  protected String name;

  public boolean canHandle(String message) {
    return name.equals(message);
  }

  public Ego handle(String message, Ego self, Ego args[]) {
```

```
      return null;
   }
}
```

An `EgoVariableSlot` is a slot that holds a variable. A variable slot named "name" understands two messages—"name", which returns the value stored in the slot, and "name:" (with a trailing colon), which assigns a value to the slot. As with `send`, for convenience `EgoVariableSlot` has a number of overloaded constructors that initialize its value with different Java types.

```
class EgoVariableSlot extends EgoSlot {
  private Ego value;

  public EgoVariableSlot(String name_, Ego value_) {
    name = name_;
    value = value_;
  }

  public boolean canHandle(String message) {
    return name.equals(message) || (name+":").equals(message);
  }

  public Ego handle(String message, Ego self, Ego args[]) {
    if (name.equals(message)) {
      return value;
    }
    if ((name+":").equals(message)) {
      value = args[0];
      return value;
    }
    throw new Error("InternalErrorWrongVariableSlot: "+name+
                    " message: " +message);
  }
}
```

Methods are defined by `EgoMethodSlot` objects. An `EgoMethodSlot` simply calls its body method when it handles a message. For simplicity, Ego doesn't have an interpreter, so its methods are written in its implementation language, Java.

```
class EgoMethodSlot extends EgoSlot {
  public EgoMethodSlot(String name_) {name = name_;}

  public Ego handle(String message, Ego self, Ego args[]) {
    if (name.equals(message)) {
      return body(message, self, args);
```

```
      }
    throw new Error("InternalErrorWrongVariableSlot: "+message);
    }

  public Ego body(String message, Ego self, Ego args[]) {
    throw new Error("Undefined Message: "+message);}
}
```

To write a useful method, you make an anonymous subclass of EgoMethodSlot—here's a method that returns 42.

```
EgoMethodSlot m = new EgoMethodSlot("fortyTwo") {
  public Ego body(String message, Ego self, Ego args[])
    {return new EgoValue(42);}
};
```

The last class, EgoValue, supports primitive objects by wrapping Java objects or values. EgoValue implements the Ego interface but is not an extension of the EgoSlotsObject class, and it implements send using a series of if statements. EgoValue will throw an exception if an EgoValue holding one type is accessed as another type—for example, if an EgoValue holding an integer is sent the message booleanValue.

```
class EgoValue implements Ego {
  private Object value;
  EgoValue(Object value_) {value = value_;}
  public Object value() {return value;}

  // convenience functions
  EgoValue(int value_) {value = new Integer(value_);}
  EgoValue(boolean value_) {value = new Boolean(value_);}
  public int intValue() {return ((Integer)value).intValue();}
  public boolean booleanValue() {
    return ((Boolean)value).booleanValue();
  }

  public Ego send(String message, Ego args[]) {
    if (message.equals("+")) {
      return new EgoValue(new Integer(
        (((Integer)value).intValue()) +
        (((EgoValue)args[0]).intValue())));
    }
    if (message.equals("-")) {
```

```
        return new EgoValue(new Integer(
          (((Integer)value).intValue()) -
          (((EgoValue)args[0]).intValue())));
  }
  // and so on
}
```

Finally, here's how the Load object from the Motivation section can be defined in Ego:

```
    EgoSlotsObject load = new EgoSlotsObject("Load")
      .add(new EgoVariableSlot("supported-by",span))
      .add(new EgoVariableSlot("weight",3100))
      .add(new EgoMethodSlot("is-supported") {
        public Ego body(String message, Ego self, Ego args[]) {
          return self
            .send("supported-by").send("can-support")
            .send(">",self.send("weight"));
      }
    });
```

Known Uses

Prototype-based object systems are derived from the frame systems used ubiquitously for knowledge modeling in artificial intelligence and which contributed to the development of conventional object-oriented programming [Bobrow+1977] and eventually evolved into CLOS [Keene1989]. More recently, object systems have been used to model complex technical domains. The engineering example at the start of this pattern was inspired by an object system for supporting civil engineering developed at the University of Strathclyde [Tulloch+1996]. The Cystic Fibrosis Society uses a language based on an object system to record information about clinical surveys [Johnson1996]. Intellicorp, among others, sells modeling environments based on dynamic object systems.

Prototype-based object systems have also been used to provide powerful scripting languages for application extensions. The Basic Object System (BOS) [Dutoit+1996] and Lua [Ierusalimschy+1996] link object systems to applications written in C and C++ and provide good examples of techniques for seamless integration between object systems and implementation languages. Obliq [Cardelli1994] uses an object system to support distributed (or migratory) applications. More whimsically, many adventure games and Muds are based on object systems [Bartle1985, Lebling+1979].

A number of object systems have been implemented as part of graphical user interface toolkits. Perhaps the best known is NewtonScript [Smith1995], which is the main programming environment for the Newton MessagePad. Garnet [Myers+1990] and Amulet [McDaniel+1995], implemented in Common Lisp and C++ respectively, are user interface systems for more conventional machines. They use object systems to support user-defined constraints between objects. VisualObliq [Bahrat+1994] extends Obliq to support user interface construction.

Prototype-based object systems can be used to store and manage application-specific data. The Any framework [Mätzel+1996] has been used to provide application- and machine-independent data integration for the Beyond-Sniff development environment. Although the Any framework does not allow behavior to be attached directly to objects, it is programmable via the Python scripting language.

A recent book on prototype-based programming provides further information about prototype-based object systems [Noble+1999].

Related Patterns

The Prototype-Based Object System pattern is the structural complement of the Interpreter behavioral pattern and the Prototype creational pattern. Where an Object System supports flexible structural modeling, Interpreter supports flexible behavioral modeling, and Prototype allows objects to be constructed easily. Together, Object System, Interpreter, and Prototype can implement the architecture of a prototype-based object-oriented programming language.

The Prototype-Based Object System pattern is related to the Reflection pattern [Buschmann+1996] in the sense that the implementation of the object system itself (and any associated interpreter) is the meta-level for the object system. Whether an object system is meta-reflexive depends on whether it can compute about its own structure and behavior [Maes1987]. In practice, this means whether the implementation-level operations such as `send` and `add(slot)` are available to programs within the object system itself, so that these programs can modify their own structure and behavior. In a meta-reflexive system, for example, you can `send` an object-system-level message to an object system object and have it invoke the implementation-level message `add(slot)`.

The Prototype-Based Object System pattern also relies on other patterns. `PrimitiveObjects` are examples of the Adapter pattern [Gamma+1995]—they adapt the underlying primitive objects to the interface expected by the Object System. Using separate structure descriptors is an example of the Type Object [Johnson+1998] pattern, because the descriptors describe a clone family of objects with the same type. Because the descriptors are shared and are read-only, they are also Flyweights. The Dynamic Template [Lyardet1997] pattern describes a complex class-based Object System as an extension of Type Object. The Serializer [Riehle+1998] pattern can be used to make Object Systems persistent or distributed by storing objects on disk or sending them around a distributed system.

An object model must be defined as part of the implementation of the `Broker` [Buschmann+1996] pattern, and the Prototype-Based Object System pattern can be used to implement this object model.

The Prototype-Based Object System pattern is one of the most complex patterns in a sequence of patterns for making programs more flexible. The simpler patterns in this sequence are smaller-scale patterns, describing how to increase the flexibility of single objects, while the more complex patterns have a larger-scale impact and describe flexible architectures for whole programs. The patterns in this sequence are Prototype [Gamma+1995], to create objects without knowing their class; Property List [Sommerlad+1998b, Riehle1997] or Variable State [Beck1997], to represent a flat list of attributes; Anything [Sommerlad+1998b], to represent a nested tree of objects and attributes; Extension Object [Gamma1998], to add dynamically behavior to objects; Interpreter [Gamma+1995], to implement that behavior at runtime; Prototype-Based Object System, to implement user-defined objects with user-defined behavior; and Reflection [Buschmann+1996] to implement an entire reflexive system.

ACKNOWLEDGMENTS

Thanks to Peter Sommerlad, this paper's EuroPLoP '98 shepherd, for his interesting and useful comments, especially on the uses and dangers of Object Systems within large organizations. Thanks also to Charles Weir, Ralph Johnson, Brian Foote, the EuroPLoP '98 writers workshop members, and the PLoPD4 anonymous reviewers for their comments.

REFERENCES

[Bartle1985] R. Bartle. *Artificial Intelligence and Computer Games*. London: Century Communications, 1985.

[Beck1997] K. Beck. *Smalltalk Best Practice Patterns*. Englewood Cliffs, NJ: Prentice-Hall, 1997.

[Bahrat+1994] K. Bahrat and M.H. Brown. "Building Distributed Multi-User Applications by Direct Manipulation." In *Proc. ACM Symposium on User Interface Software and Technology (UIST)*, New York: ACM Press, pages 71–82, 1994.

[Bobrow+1977] D.G. Bobrow and T. Winograd. "An Overview of KRL: A Knowledge Representation Language." *Cognitive Science*, 1(1):3–46, 1977.

[Buschmann+1996] F. Buschmann, R. Meunier, H. Rohnert, P. Sommerlad, and M. Stal. *Pattern-Oriented Software Architecture*. New York: John Wiley & Sons, 1996.

[Cardelli1994] L. Cardelli. "Obliq: A Language with Distributed Scope." *Technical Report Research Report 122*, Palo Alto: CA, Digital Equipment Corporation Systems Research Center, 1994.

[Dutoit+1996] A. Dutoit, S. Levy, D. Cunningham, and R. Patrick. "The Basic Object System: Supporting a Spectrum from Prototypes to Hardened Code." In *OOPSLA Proceedings,* New York: ACM Press, 1996.

[Foote1991] B. Foote. "Objects, Reflection, and Open Languages." *OOPSLA'91 Workshop on Reflection and Metalevel Architectures,* 1991. http://www.laputan.org/foote/openlang.html.

[Gamma+1995] E. Gamma, R. Helm, R.E. Johnson, and J. Vlissides. *Design Patterns.* Reading, MA: Addison-Wesley, 1995.

[Gamma1998] E. Gamma. "Extension Object." In R.C. Martin, D. Riehle, and F. Buschmann (eds.), *Pattern Languages of Program Design 3.* Reading, MA: Addison-Wesley, 1998.

[Ierusalimschy+1996] R. Ierusalimschy, L. Henrique de Figueiredo, and W. Celes Filho. "Lua—An Extensible Extension Language." *Software—Practice and Experience,* 26(6): 635–652, 1996.

[Johnson1996] M. Johnson. "PreQL: A Prototype-Based Object-Oriented Epidemiology Study Description Language. In *ECOOP'96 Workshop on Prototype-Based Programming,* 1996. http://www.mri.mq.edu.au/wkjx/proto96.html.

[Johnson+1998] R.E. Johnson and B. Woolf. "Type Object." In R.C. Martin, D. Riehle, and F. Buschmann (eds.), *Pattern Languages of Program Design 3.* Reading, MA: Addison-Wesley, 1998.

[Keene1989] S.E. Keene. *Object-Oriented Programming in Common Lisp: A Programmer's Guide to CLOS.* Reading, MA: Addison-Wesley, 1989.

[Lebling+1979] P.D. Lebling, M.S. Blank, and T.A. Anderson. "Lebling+79: A Computerized Fantasy Simulation Game." *IEEE Computer,* 12(4):51–59, 1979.

[Lieberman1986] H. Lieberman. "Using Prototypical Objects to Implement Shared Behavior in Object-Oriented Systems." In *OOPSLA Proceedings,* New York: ACM Press, November 1986.

[Lyardet1997] F.D. Lyardet. "The Dynamic Template Pattern." In *PLoP Proceedings,* St. Louis, MO: Washington University Technical Report, 1997.

[Maes1987] P. Maes. "Concepts and Experiments in Computational Reflection." In *OOPSLA Proceedings,* New York: ACM Press, 1987.

[Mätzel+1996] K.-U. Mätzel and W. Bischofberger. "The Any Framework." In *COOTS Proceedings,* USENIX, Berkeley, CA, p. 179–190, 1996.

[McDaniel+1995] R. McDaniel and B.A. Myers. "Amulet's Dynamic and Flexible Prototype-Instance Object and Constraint System in C++." Technical Report CMU-HCII-95-104, Human-Computer Interaction Institute, Carnegie Mellon University, 1995.

[Myers+1990] B.A. Myers, D.A. Guise, R.B. Dannenberg, B. VanderZanden, D.S. Kosbie, E. Pervin, A. Mickish, and P. Marchal. "Garnet: Comprehensive Support for Graphical, Highly Interactive User Interfaces. *IEEE Computer,* 23(11): 71–85, 1990.

[Noble+1999] J. Noble, A. Taivalsaari, and I. Moore. *Prototype-Based Programming: Concepts, Languages, and Applications.* New York: Springer-Verlag, 1999.

[Raymond+1993] E. Raymond and G.L. Steele. *The New Hacker's Dictionary* (2nd ed.). Cambridge, MA: MIT Press, 1993.

[Riehle1997] D. Riehle. "A Role-Based Design Pattern Catalog of Atomic and Composite Patterns Structured by Pattern Purpose. *Technical Report 97-1-1,* Zurich, Switzerland: UbiLabs, 1997.

[Riehle+1998] D. Riehle, W. Siberski, D. Bäumer, D. Megert, and H. Züllighoven. "Serializer." In R.C. Martin, D. Riehle, and F. Buschmann (eds.), *Pattern Languages of Program Design 3*. Reading, MA: Addison-Wesley, 1998.

[Smith1995] W.R. Smith. "Using a Prototype-Based Language for User Interface: The Newton Project's Experience. In *OOPSLA Proceedings*, New York: ACM Press, 1995.

[Sommerlad+1998a] P. Sommerlad. "Manager." In R.C. Martin, D. Riehle, and F. Buschmann (eds.), *Pattern Languages of Program Design 3*. Reading, MA: Addison-Wesley, 1998.

[Sommerlad+1998b] P. Sommerlad and M. Rüedi. "Do-It-Yourself Reflection." In *Proceedings of 3rd European Conference on Pattern Languages of Programming*, Kloster Irsee: Germany, 1998.

[Taivalsaari1993] A. Taivalsaari. *A Critical View of Inheritance and Reusability in Object-Oriented Programming*. Ph.D. thesis, University of Jyväskylä, 1993.

[Tulloch+1996] I. Tulloch and D. McGregor. "Using Prototypes to Model Engineering Designs. In *ECOOP '96 Workshop on Prototype-Based Programming*, 1996. http://www.mri.mq.edu.au/wkjx/proto96.html.

[Ungar+1991] D. Ungar and R.B. Smith. "SELF: The Power of Simplicity." *Lisp and Symbolic Computation*, 4(3): 187–205, 1991.

James Noble may be reached at kjx@mri.mq.edu.au.

Chapter 6

Basic Relationship Patterns

James Noble

Relationships, also known as collaborations or associations, are very important in object-oriented design. For example, collaborations make up one-third of the CRC (Class Responsibility Collaboration) design technique [Wilkerson1995], and Rumbaugh has claimed that relationships are complementary to (and as important as) objects themselves [Rumbaugh1987]. Unfortunately, most object-oriented programming languages do not support relationships well. For example, designs may use one-way or two-way relationships between objects; they may associate one object with one other object, one object with many other objects, or many objects with many others; they may be complete—always relating objects—or partial, sometimes relating objects and sometimes not. Programming languages support relationships mainly through attributes (also known as variables, slots, or data members), which are one-way links from one object to one other object. This means that programmers must somehow build up other relationships using the raw materials the languages provide—objects, messages, and attributes [Rumbaugh1996].

In this chapter I present five basic patterns for implementing relationships between objects. The patterns address the most basic kind of relationships in which one object needs to be able to refer to another object at runtime. These relationships are often called *associations* or *collaborations* to distinguish them from the more complex relationships of aggregation and inheritance. The first two patterns (Relationship As Attribute and Relationship Object) describe the fundamental ways to model relationships—either using attributes or using objects. The following two patterns (Collection Object and Active Value) describe the more specialized kinds of Relationship Object that model one-to-one or one-to-many relationships. The last pattern, Mutual Friends, describes how two-way relationships can be modeled.

The elementary content of these patterns should not surprise any object-oriented software practitioner, and they can all be found in the general OO literature [Wilkerson1995, Booch+1994, Rumbaugh+1991, Rumbaugh1996]. Rather, these patterns attempt to record well-known design and programming folklore, describing techniques to new programmers and, for more experienced programmers, illustrating when particular techniques are appropriate. The patterns are mostly language independent; however, they will work best in languages like Smalltalk or Java in which (almost) everything is an object, as they do not address explicit memory management or object ownership. The patterns were motivated by the experience of teaching object-oriented design and programming to students who had backgrounds in data modeling, or who had attended a course on object oriented analysis techniques, but otherwise had no practice in object-oriented design.

Table 6-1 summarizes the problems addressed by this collection of patterns and the solutions they provide. Although these patterns do not form a complete pattern language, there is some structure to these patterns, which is illustrated in Figure 6-1. This diagram illustrates three relationships between patterns in the language. One pattern can *use* (or *contain*) another pattern—that is, the first pattern exposes a subproblem that can be solved by the second pattern. Two or more patterns can *conflict*; that is, they can provide alternative solutions to similar problems. One pattern can *specialize* (or *refine*) another pattern, that is, provide a more

Table 6-1 *Summary of the Patterns*

Pattern	Problem	Solution
Relationship As Attribute	How do you design a small, simple, one-to-one relationship?	Make an Attribute to represent the relationship.
Relationship Object	How do you design a large, complex relationship?	Make a Relationship Object to represent the relationship.
Collection Object	How do you design a one-to-many relationship?	Make a Collection Object to model the relationship.
Active Value	How do you design a globally important one-to-one relationship?	Make an Active Value to model this relationship.
Mutual Friends	How can you represent a two-way relationship?	Make a consistent set of one-way relationships.

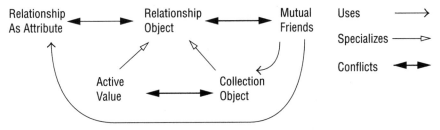

Figure 6-1 *Structure of the patterns*

specific version of the second pattern's solution to suit a more specific problem [Noble1998].

Forces

Each of the patterns in Table 6-1 resolves a number of different forces, and some conflicting patterns (such as Relationship As Attribute and Active Value) resolve similar problems in different ways. Many of the patterns consider the complexity and ease of reading or writing a particular solution—generally, solutions that are easy to write are more likely to be chosen by programmers, and solutions that are easy to read are likely to be easier to maintain. Several patterns also address the cohesion and coupling of the resulting designs, because designs with high cohesion within objects and low coupling between them are more flexible, understandable, and easier to maintain. This is often related to whether a relationship is represented explicitly by a single element of a design, or whether it is dispersed across several objects, attributes, and methods; and whether a change of state in a relationship is local, affecting only those objects participating in the relationship, or global, affecting other objects in the program. Representing a relationship explicitly makes it easier to identify the relationship within the design, to change the implementation of the relationship if necessary, to maintain consistency in two-way relationships, and to reuse both the relationship and other participating objects elsewhere. The patterns are marginally concerned with efficiency—the time and space cost of a design, and the number of objects it requires.

Example

The patterns in this chapter use examples drawn from a simple system for an insurance office (see Figure 6-2). The most important object in the system is Policy, which represents an insurance policy. Each Policy belongs to a Client (although a single client can have many policies), and a policy can also have a number of Endorsements to change its wording. When a policy is issued, it is associated with

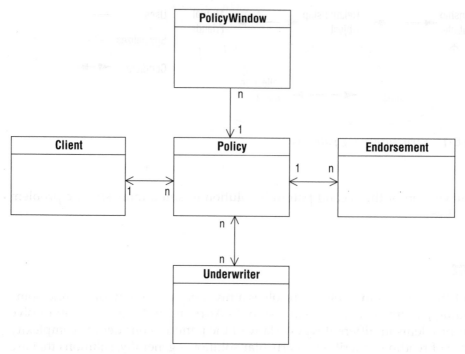

Figure 6-2 *Insurance analysis model*

one or more Underwriters, who receive a share of the premium in return for meeting a share of the costs of any claims. Finally, a PolicyWindow provides a GUI interface for the system.

Form

The patterns are written in a modified Portland form. Each begins with a question (in italics) describing a problem, followed by one paragraph describing the pattern's context and a second paragraph describing the forces the pattern resolves. A boldface **Therefore:** introduces the solution (italicized) followed by the consequences of using the pattern (the positive benefits first, then the liabilities, separated by a boldface **But:**, an example of its use, and some known uses and related patterns. The important forces are italicized throughout.

Relationship As Attribute

How do you design a small, simple, one-to-one relationship?

Simple, one-way, one-to-one relationships are very common in object-oriented models. For example, an insurance Policy object must record the date and time the policy was issued, and an Client object must record the name and address of the client it represents. Such relationships generally carry very little weight in the application domain—the objects themselves are important, but the fact that these particular objects are related is coincidental. Often, the fact that the objects are related is important to only one of the related objects (the date is important to the policy, but the policy isn't important to the date). Changes in the relationship—for example, a client changing her address—are only important *locally*, insofar as they record the changing circumstances of that object in the program domain, and don't have far-reaching effects within the program.

Because these kinds of relationships arise so often, they need to be *simple* to represent in a program, so that they are *easy to write* and can be immediately understood by later programmers *reading* the program. For similar reasons, they must be implemented so that they impose minimal overhead on the program—both in terms of the *space* required to represent the relationship and the *time* taken to manipulate it.

Therefore: *Make an attribute to represent the relationship.*

Object-oriented programming languages provide attributes (instance variables, slots, data members) that are local to each object instance. These attributes are ideal for modeling one-to-one relationships. Add accessor messages if the relationship should be publicly available and mutator messages if the relationship should be publicly changeable.

Example

Consider modeling an insurance policy. Each Policy object must record the date and time it was issued, the sum insured, and any excess. The Policy object's behavior doesn't depend upon the precise values of any of these objects, and they can be changed as necessary without consequent effects on the program's model of the domain. Because the relationships are very simple, all this information can be stored as attributes of the Policy object.

Comments

Setting and accessing attributes is *easy* and *efficient* in every object-oriented programming language, and code using attributes is easy to *read* and *write*. The attributes' scope is typically *local* to the object or class in which they are defined. **But:** this pattern *couples* the object with the attribute to the object referred to by the attribute. Attributes occupy *space* in objects even if they are not needed in a particular case; for example, if a policy has no excess, an attribute to store the excess will still be allocated in the Policy object.

This pattern is fundamental to object-oriented design, just as object's attributes (i.e., state) are fundamental to object-oriented programming. Although this pattern is simple, it is not necessarily trivial and in my experience needs to be learned, especially by programmers with a predilection for modeling relationships as tuples using collections. More importantly, it provides alternatives to the other patterns in this language that deal with more complex relationships.

Known Uses

Every object-oriented program represents simple relationships as attributes.

See Also

The *Smalltalk Best Practice Patterns* [Beck1997] contain a number of patterns that describe how to name and use attributes. As alternatives to this pattern, Relationship Object describes how to represent a complex relationship with extra objects—an Active Value for a globally important one-to-one relationship and a Collection Object for a one-to-many relationship. Mutual Friends describes how to represent two-way relationships. (Refer to Table 6-1.)

Relationship Object

Also Known As

Association Object

How do you design a large, complex relationship?

Relationships between objects can be very complex, involving two-way communication between many participating objects that are essentially peers. For example, the risks (and premiums) of all the policies issued in an insurance office must be distributed carefully to underwriters and reinsurers. This distribution does not depend solely on the details of a single policy. Rather it must take into account contracts with underwriters, reinsurance treaties, and arrangements made for other policies. These kinds of relationships embody important concepts and constraints from the programs' domain and can require complex state or behavior to implement.

Complex relationships can be implemented directly using features of programming languages such as attributes (see Relationship As Attribute (Table 6-1)), but this has several disadvantages [Booch+1994, Rumbaugh+1991]. The relationship is *dispersed* among its participating objects—it cannot be *identified* easily within the program, and thus cannot be *maintained*. Participating objects are *tightly coupled,* so a change to the relationship necessitates changing several participating objects. Participating objects' *cohesion is reduced,* because they must model a portion of the relationship as well as the abstractions they represent. If individual developers or teams "own" each object, they will need to *cooperate* to implement the relationship.

Therefore: *Make a Relationship Object to represent the relationship.*

Move any methods or variables associated with the relationship from the participating objects and place them in the Relationship Object. Change the implementations of the participating objects so that they refer to each other via the Relationship Object. The Relationship Object may need to use internal subordinate objects to implement the relationship, but these should not be visible through the Relationship Object's interface.

Example

Consider designing a system to support an insurance underwriting office. The core of such a system is a relationship between policies and underwriters that records the business written by the office. This relationship is many-to-many (a policy can be underwritten by many underwriters, and a underwriter can underwrite many policies) and partial (each policy is underwritten by a few underwriters, and each underwriter underwrites a small fraction of the policies). The relationship is subject to a large number of business rules. Distributing the implementation of this relationship over the Policy and Underwriter objects would unnecessarily complicate both these objects.

Introducing a Relationship Object—a Portfolio—simplifies the design (see Figure 6-3). All the details of the relationship are collected into the Portfolio. The Portfolio Object can use whatever internal structures are needed for an efficient implementation, and these can be changed as necessary without affecting the Policy or Underwriter Objects. The Portfolio can implement the business constraints and behavior required by the relationship.

Comments

A Relationship Object *explicitly* represents a relationship in the program. The other objects involved in the relationship are independent of it (*coupling is reduced*), so

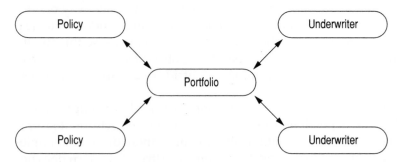

Figure 6-3 *Relationship Object*

the relationship object can be *changed* more easily and may be able to be *reused* in other contexts. An explicit Relationship Object also *increases cohesion,* since the other participating objects do not need to model part of the relationship. **But:** introducing Relationship Objects increases the *number of objects* in the program, which can increase *memory footprint,* and accessing objects indirectly via Relationship Objects can reduce *execution efficiency.*

Known Uses

ParcPlace Smalltalk provides several examples of Relationship Objects. Collections and ValueHolders are specialized kinds of Relationship Objects (Active Value and Collection Object, respectively). ObjectWorks introduced DependentsCollection objects to record and manage the relationship between an object and its dependents [ParcPlace1994], whereas the earlier Smalltalk-80 implemented this relationship using a global dictionary [Goldberg+1983].

See Also

An Active Value is a specialized Relationship Object that models a one-to-one relationship, and a Collection Object is a specialized Relationship Object that models a one-to-many relationship. Relationship As Attribute is a complementary pattern that describes how to represent simple one-to-one relationships efficiently. Observer [Gamma+1995], Mediator [Gamma+1995], and Director [Coldewey1997] describe how Relationship Objects can coordinate or control the behavior of their participating objects. Relationship Objects also can record supplementary information, such as the time span of the relationship [Boyd1998]. Martin Fowler has described Relationship Objects in detail [Fowler1997].

Collection Object

How do you design a one-to-many relationship?

One-way one-to-many relationships are almost as common as one-way one-to-one relationships. For example, a standard insurance policy can be endorsed to deal with special situations. One policy can have multiple endorsements, so this should be modeled as a many-to-one relationship between Policy Objects and Endorsement Objects. Since Endorsements are meaningless outside their particular policies, this is a one-way relationship.

Because they are so common, one-to-many relationships need to be implemented as *easily* and as *efficiently* as possible. Unfortunately, in most object-oriented programming languages, one-to-many relationships are much more difficult to implement than one-to-one relationships. The Relationship As Attribute pattern does not extend cleanly to relationships where one object is linked to more than one object, because the number of attributes in each object is fixed, and each attribute must be accessed individually. One-to-many relationships can be implemented by hard-coding the relationship into *every* participating object, but this *disperses* the relationship across all participating objects, *couples* them very tightly, and cannot be *reused* across similar relationships in a design.

Therefore: *Make a Collection Object to model the relationship.*

Most object-oriented libraries provide a variety of container or collection objects that can be used to represent one-to-many relationships. The "one" object simply stores a collection that holds the "many" objects participating in the relationship. You will need to choose an appropriate collection object from those available—for example, the *Smalltalk Best Practice Patterns* [Beck1997] contains a number of patterns on choosing Smalltalk collections.

Example

Consider modeling an insurance policy that can have one or more endorsements attached. This relationship can be represented by a List Collection Object. The Policy class simply keeps a List of all its Endorsements (see Figure 6-4). If necessary the List can be replaced with a specialized collection object (perhaps an EndorsementList) to implement any additional constraints or behavior required by the relationship.

Comments

Using a Collection Object to represent a one-to-many relationship *explicitly* simplifies a program, especially as in most object-oriented languages, collections are almost as *easy to use* as attributes. The Collection Object and the objects stored inside it are very *weakly coupled*, and so each can be *reused* in different contexts. **But:** a Collection Object introduces one or more *extra objects* at runtime, depending on its implementation, and the extra level of indirection *reduces execution speed*.

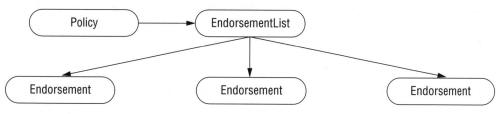

Figure 6-4 *Collection Object*

Known Uses

Collections are ubiquitous. They are the most common kind of Relationship Object, and form the core of many class libraries [Booch+1994, Goldberg+1983, Meyer1994]. Most collections implement one-to-many one-way relationships, but some, such as Smalltalk's Dictionaries, can implement many-to-many relationships.

See Also

Collection Object specializes Relationship Object, so the two patterns' benefits are similar. The *Smalltalk Best Practice Patterns* [Beck1997] includes a number of patterns that describe how to choose among Smalltalk's various Collection Objects and then how to use the collection you've chosen. *Pattern-Oriented Software Architecture* [Buschmann+1996] describes the Collection-Members variant of the Whole-Part pattern.

Active Value

Also Known As

Variable Object, Reified Variable, Value Holder

How do you design a globally important one-to-one relationship?

Some one-to-one relationships are globally important to the program, rather than merely connecting two objects. For example, a PolicyWindow object (a GUI entry window for a Policy) needs to store the values entered by the user. The Policy-Window object has a one-to-one relationship with the value of each of its entry fields. If one of these values (such as the sum insured) is changed, external code embodying business rules must be run to validate the entered value.

These kinds of one-to-one relationships are important because of their position in the program's architecture. That is, *global* objects in the program that do not participate directly in the relationship may be affected if the state of the relationship changes—changing a Policy's sum insured means that business rules must be called to verify the entered values.

A one-to-one relationship can be implemented using Relationship As Attribute. This requires programmers to *write* code to detect and signal changes individually for each attribute, reducing the *cohesion* of the class containing the attributes and increasing its *complexity*.

Therefore: *Make an Active Value to model this relationship.*

An Active Value is essentially an object that reifies a single variable. It should have an attribute to hold the variable's value and should understand two messages—an

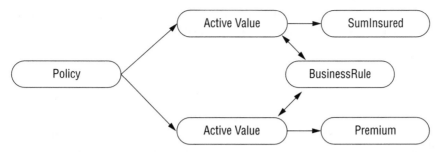

Figure 6-5   *Active Value*

accessor to retrieve the value of the variable and a *setter* to change the value. To use an Active Value, make it an attribute of the source object of the relationship, and access the relationship by sending messages to the Active Value rather than to the source object. The Active Value can detect when its value changes, and then act as the Subject in the Observer pattern [Gamma+1995] to update any dependent objects.

Example

The PolicyWindow can use Active Values to store the values of the entry fields—see Figure 6-5. Business rules for data validation can access the Active Values directly rather than via the PolicyWindow. Each Active Value can detect when it has changed and then notify interested BusinessRules. The PolicyWindow needs no specialized code to signal updates, provided all accesses to its fields are directed via the Active Values. Similarly, a BusinessRule does not need to access the Policy-Window because it can access the information it needs via the ActiveValues.

Comments

Like Relationship Object, this pattern *reduces coupling* and *increases cohesion* of the objects involved. Code to detect and signal updates in the relationship can be written and *reused* for all Active Values because it is *not dispersed* within the participating objects. **But:** Active Values *complicate* the program's structure by introducing *many small objects,* with the indirection involved increasing the *time* and *space* costs of the program. Active Values also reduce the *readability* of program text, since otherwise simple variable accesses and assignment statements must be replaced by messages sent to Active Values.

Known Uses

Active values were first provided as part of the language in LOOPS [Stefik+1986]. VisualWorks's ValueModel framework is based on this pattern [ParcPlace1994]. In particular, the ValueHolder object is a generic Active Value. The Cooldraw [Freeman-

Benson1993], Unidraw [Vlissides+1990], and QOCA [Helm+1992] constraint solvers all use Active Values to represent variables explicitly: the last two uses are mentioned in *Design Patterns* [Gamma+1995].

See Also

Active Value specializes Relationship Object, so their benefits and liabilities are similar. *Understanding and Using the ValueModel Framework in VisualWorks Smalltalk* [Woolf1994] describes how to use Active Values in VisualWorks. The Observer pattern is often used to link Active Values to the objects that depend on the relationship. Several Active Values can form a Connected Group [Li+1996].

Mutual Friends

Also Known As

Synchronized Relationship, Symmetrical Relationship

How do you design a two-way relationship?

You have a two-way relationship (also known as a bidirectional or mutual relationship) where all participating objects are equally important. For example, in the insurance system a Client object needs a two-way relationship with its Policy objects—clients need to be able to enumerate their policies to compute the total premium due, and policies need to know their clients in the event of a claim.

In a two-way relationship, each participating object needs to be *easily accessible* from every other object. A *change* in any one participating object may affect all other objects in the relationship. If an object joins or leaves the relationship, the other objects must be informed so the relationship remains *consistent*. Note that a two-way relationship may be a one-to-one, a one-to-many, or even a many-to-many relationship.

Unfortunately object-oriented programming languages' support for two-way relationships is even more limited than their support for one-way relationships. While one-way one-to-one relationships can be modeled with attributes (Relationship As Attribute) and one-way one-to-many relationships modeled with collections (Collection Object), there are no obvious language or library constructs that can model two-way relationships.

Therefore: *Make a consistent set of one-way relationships.*

Implementing Mutual Friends has two steps. First, the two-way relationship should be split into a pair of one-way relationships. Second, the one-way relationships must be kept consistent.

1. *Splitting the relationship.* The simplest kind of Mutual Friends involves a one-to-one two-way relationship. This can be split into a pair of one-to-one one-way relationships, typically implemented using Relationship As Attribute. A one-to-many two-way relationship can be split very similarly, except that one object will need a one-way one-to-many relationship, such as a Collection Object. A two-way many-to-many relationship can be split using two collections.

2. *Keeping the split relationship consistent.* Choose one of the Mutual Friends as a *leader* and have it manage the other objects as its *followers*. The leader object should provide an interface to manage the whole relationship. The followers' implementation of the relationship can be made much simpler, because they should only be invoked by the leader. Language mechanisms (such as C++'s `friend` or Eiffel's selective export) can be used to enforce this restriction. In a one-to-many relationship, the "one" object is usually the better choice for the leader, since this centralizes the responsibility for maintaining the relationship in a single object. If one object in the relationship creates the other participating objects, this object should be the leader. If a follower needs to make a change to the relationship, it should delegate the change to its leader. Note that although this pattern is called Mutual Friends, it does not have to be implemented using C++'s `friend` construct any more than the Template Method pattern [Gamma+1995] has to be implemented using C++'s `template` construct.

Example

Consider the relationship between Policies and Clients. This is a two-way, one-to-many relationship, and it can be implemented by making clients and policies Mutual Friends. The relationship can be broken down into two one-way relationships—a one-to-many relationship from Clients to Policies and a one-to-one relationship from a Policy to its Client (see Figure 6-6). A Client uses a `List` Collection

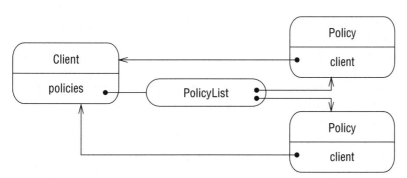

Figure 6-6 *Mutual Friends*

Object to record its Policies. The Policy object's one-way relationship can be implemented using a `client` attribute, as described in Relationship As Attribute.

The Client objects are the leaders of their Mutual Friends, because they are the "one" objects in the relationship. Client provides `addPolicy:` and `remove-Policy:` messages to acquire and dispose of Policies. These messages set the Policy's `client` attribute via a `privateSetClient` message.

In Smalltalk, the relationship could be implemented in Client as

```
addPolicy: aPolicy
    policies add: aPolicy.
    aPolicy privateSetClient: self.
removePolicy: aPolicy
    policies remove: aPolicy.
    aPolicy privateSetClient: nil.
```

and in Policy as

```
privateSetClient: aClient
        client := aClient.
```

although a real, robust implementation should check for errors in the parameters. If a Policy needs to change its own Client, it should not change its `client` variable directly; rather, it should delegate this to its leader, that is, to Client:

```
setClient: aClient
    aClient addPolicy: self
```

In Java the relevant parts of the Client would be implemented as:

```
class Client {
  PolicyList policies = new PolicyList();

  public synchronized void addPolicy(Policy aPolicy) {
    policies.addElement(aPolicy);
    aPolicy.client = this;
  }
  public synchronized void removePolicy(Policy aPolicy) {
    policies.removeElement(aPolicy);
    aPolicy.client = null;
  }
}
```

and of the Policy as:

```
class Policy {
  Client client; // visible to package, including Client class
}
```

Comments

This pattern maintains the *consistency* of a two-way relationship and introduces a minimum of *extra objects* into the design. **But:** this pattern *disperses* the implementation of a two-way relationship among all the objects participating in the relationship. This increases the *coupling* between objects, because each participating object depends on the details of the other object's implementation. It similarly decreases their *cohesion,* because each object must include part of the relationship. This pattern can be difficult to *write* correctly, because both ends of the relationship must be kept synchronized to maintain overall *consistency,* and the resulting control flow can make the program difficult to *read* and *maintain.*

Known Uses

The Smalltalk class hierarchy uses a two-way relationship between subclasses and superclasses. A class and its subclasses are Mutual Friends, with the superclass as the leader. Each class keeps a collection of it subclasses, and each subclass has a pointer to its class [Goldberg+1983]. Similarly, Smalltalk views and controllers are Mutual Friends, as are VisualWorks' VisualPart and CompositePart [ParcPlace1994].

See Also

This pattern typically uses Relationship As Attribute and Collection Object to implement the subsidiary one-way relationships. Alternatively, a Relationship Object can model an entire complex relationship. If the control flow across a relationship is primarily in one direction, you may be able to model the relationship as if it were a one-way relationship and use Self Delegation [Beck1997] for access in the other direction. The Composite and Decorator patterns often use Mutual Friends to maintain two-way relationships between containers and leaves [Gamma+1995].

James Rumbaugh [Rumbaugh1996] and Martin Fowler [Fowler1997], among others, have described how two-way relationships can be split into mutual one-way relationships. Ward Cunningham wrote a version of Mutual Friends on the Wiki-Wiki-Web, and it was discussed by Ralph Johnson and Steve Metsker [Metsker+1998]. Steve Metsker subsequently described how concurrent two-way relationships can be managed by a Judge [Metsker1998]. Databases often provide support for two-way relationships. For example, all relationships in relational databases can be traversed in either direction, and ODMG-93 object-oriented databases automatically maintain the consistency of inverse relationships [Graham+1997].

ACKNOWLEDGMENTS

This chapter is a revised version of a paper presented at TOOLS Pacific 1996 [Noble1996] and workshopped at EuroPLoP '97. Thanks are due to Wolfgang Keller, the EuroPLoP '97 shepherd for this paper, to the various members of the *"flamefest"* Writers Workshop, to John Grundy for his collaboration on *Explicit Relationships in Object Oriented Design* [Noble+1995], and to Michael Richmond, Jonathan Tidswell, John Potter, David Holmes, and the PLoPD4 anonymous referees for their comments on various drafts.

REFERENCES

[Beck1997] K. Beck. *Smalltalk Best Practice Patterns*. Englewood Cliffs, NJ: Prentice-Hall, 1997.

[Booch+1994] G. Booch. *Object-Oriented Analysis and Design with Applications* (2nd ed.). Santa Clara, CA: Benjamin Cummings, 1994.

[Boyd1997] L. Boyd. "Patterns of Association Objects in Large Scale Business Systems." In R.C. Martin, D. Riehle, and F. Buschmann (eds.), *Pattern Languages of Program Design 3*. Reading, MA: Addison-Wesley, 1998.

[Buschmann+1996] F. Buschmann, R. Meunier, H. Rohnert, P. Sommerlad, and M. Stal. *Pattern-Oriented Software Architecture*. New York: John Wiley & Sons, 1996.

[Coldewey1997] J. Coldewey. "Decoupling of Object-Oriented Systems: A Collection of Patterns." Technical report, sd&m—software design & management GmbH, April 1997.

[Fowler1997] M. Fowler. *Analysis Patterns*. Reading, MA: Addison-Wesley, 1997.

[Freeman-Benson1993] B.N. Freeman-Benson. "Converting an Existing User Interface to Use Constraints." In *Proceedings of the ACM Symposium on User Interface Software and Technology (UIST)*, New York: ACM Press, 1993.

[Gamma+1995] E. Gamma, R. Helm, R.E. Johnson, and J. Vlissides. *Design Patterns*. Reading, MA: Addison-Wesley, 1995.

[Goldberg+1983] A. Goldberg and D. Robson. *Smalltalk-80: The Language and Its Implementation*. Reading, MA: Addison-Wesley, 1983.

[Graham+1997] I. Graham, J. Bischof, and B. Henderson-Sellers. "Associations Considered a Bad Thing." *Journal of Object-Oriented Programming*, 9(9): 41–48, 1997.

[Helm+1993] R. Helm, T. Huynh, K. Marriott, and J. Vlissides. "An Object-Oriented Architecture for Constraint-Based Graphical Editing. In *Advances in Object-Oriented Graphics II*, Springer-Verlag, 1993.

[Li+1996] J. Li. "Connected Group, 1996." Reviewed at EuroPLoP '96. http://www.nada.kth.se/wli/.

[Metsker1998] S.J. Metsker. "The Judge Pattern: Ensuring the Relational Integrity of Objects." *Journal of Object Oriented Programming,* 7(11): 49–59, 1998.

[Metsker+1998] S. Metsker, W. Cunningham, and R. Johnson. "Symmetrical Reference." http://c2.com/cgi/wiki?SymmetricalReference.

[Meyer1994] B. Meyer. *Reusable Software: The Base Object-Oriented Component Libraries.* Englewood Cliffs, NJ: Prentice-Hall, 1994.

[Noble+1995] J. Noble and J. Grundy. "Explicit Relationships in Object-Oriented Development." In C. Mingins, R. Dube, and B. Meyer (eds.), *TOOLS 18,* Melbourne: Prentice-Hall, 1995.

[Noble1996] J. Noble. "Some Patterns for Relationships." In C. Mingins, R. Dube, and B. Meyer (eds.), *TOOLS 21,* Melbourne: Prentice-Hall, 1996.

[Noble1998] J. Noble. "Classifying Relationships between Object-Oriented Design Patterns." In P.D. Grant (ed.), 1998 Australian Software Engineering Conference (ASWEC '98), Adelaide, 1998.

[ParcPlace1994] "ParcPlace Systems." *VisualWorks Smalltalk User's Guide* (2nd ed.). Santa Clara, CA: 1994.

[Rumbaugh1987] J. Rumbaugh. "Relations as Semantic Constructs in an Object-Oriented Language. In *OOPSLA '87 Proceedings,* New York: ACM Press, 1987.

[Rumbaugh+1991] J. Rumbaugh, M. Blaha, W. Premerlani, F. Eddy, and W. Lorensen. *Object-Oriented Modeling and Design.* Englewood Cliffs, NJ: Prentice-Hall, 1991.

[Rumbaugh1996] J. Rumbaugh. "Models for Design: Generating Code for Associations." *Journal of Object-Oriented Programming,* 8(9): 13–17, 1996.

[Stefik+1986] M.J. Stefik, D.G. Bobrow, and K.M. Kahn. "Integrating Access-Oriented Programming into a Multiparadigm Environment." *IEEE Software,* 3(1): 10–18, 1986.

[Vlissides+1990] J.M. Vlissides and M.A. Linton. "Unidraw: A Framework for Building Domain-Specific Graphical Editors. *ACM Transactions on Information Systems,* 8(3): 237–268, 1990.

[Wilkerson1995] N.M. Wilkerson. *Using CRC Cards: An Informal Approach to Object-Oriented Design.* New York: SIGS Books, 1995.

[Woolf1994] B. Woolf. "Understanding and Using the ValueModel Framework in VisualWorks Smalltalk." In J.O. Coplien and D.C. Schmidt (eds.), *Pattern Languages of Program Design.* Reading, MA: Addison-Wesley, 1994.

James Noble may be reached at klx@mri.mq.edu.au.

PART 2

Object-Oriented Infrastructure Patterns

As our story continues, we move from mud to structure. While the adobe bricks of basic object-oriented patterns gives us solid material with which to build, we need patterns to help us lay the foundations of object-oriented systems. Thus we continue to follow Alexander, for not only do his patterns cover basic building components, they also encompass how those blocks should be fitted together to create living structures. As we move to larger-scale patterns, we find that they can't be used quite as universally as the very basic patterns. Some patterns become more appropriate for distributed systems, others for database applications. This is natural: patterns for a single-family dwelling shouldn't be used to construct an office building. In each case, though, constraining the scope of a pattern strengthens it. Just as a pattern for a private home helps satisfy the domestic needs of a family, patterns for distributed systems help programmers deal with the sticky issues of synchronization, reliability, and performance across networks.

Although these patterns are becoming more specialized, they share some object-oriented design principles. One such principle is separation of concerns. A key point of any object-oriented design is to separate the aspects of the problem so that aspects that may change separately are also independent of each other in the software design. Indeed, separation of concerns is central to these patterns. In each case, the pattern separates the application-dependent logic from the application-independent infrastructure, allowing them to vary independently.

Given the rich heritage of object-oriented design patterns, it is hardly surprising that these patterns are related to previous patterns in this series. Each of these patterns builds on other patterns, and each contains copious references to those patterns. To fully appreciate these patterns, you must appreciate their predecessors. That's how languages grow. Perhaps these are the beginnings of infrastructural pattern languages.

Chapter 7: Abstract Session by Nat Pryce. The first pattern in this section deals with client-server relationships between objects. Such relationships are usually bounded by sessions. Abstract Session creates sessions that can manage the information about clients in an efficient and type-safe manner. Furthermore, by separating the session from the application itself, it is possible to vary the type of session without changing the application code. Abstract Sessions are especially useful in implementing communications protocols.

Chapter 8: Object Synchronizer by António Rito Silva, João Pereira, and José Alves Marques. A common challenge of managing many objects is that many need to be kept in synch with one another. For example, graphical objects may require synchronization when they are displayed or modified. The Object Synchronizer pattern makes this synchronization easy.

This pattern is elegant in its simplicity: each object that is synchronized is put behind a synchronization interface object. The interface object receives the method invocation and invokes the synchronization policy before and after calling the method on the object itself.

Depending on the needs of the data and the system, there are various ways to keep objects synchronized. The Object Synchronizer pattern separates the synchronization actions from the application itself. Not only does this make the application code easier to understand; it allows the synchronization policy to vary independently of the application. In fact, if different parts of the system need to have different synchronization policies, you can do it with the Object Synchronizer pattern.

Chapter 9: Proactor by Irfan Pyarali, Tim Harrison, Douglas C. Schmidt, and Thomas D. Jordan. One of the tasks that computer programs often perform is handling multiple asynchronous events at the same time. This has become common; for example, Web servers must process multiple requests in a short time. Traditional approaches are often complicated, inefficient, or nonportable. The Proactor pattern takes a new approach: it anticipates the completion of an asynchronous operation and prepares the proper completion handler to run when the operation completes.

Like the previous two patterns, a key benefit of this pattern is the separation of concerns. It separates the software that implements the asynchrony mechanisms from the application-specific code. In addition, the policy for handling concurrent processing is separated from the threading policy of the operating system. Thus decoupled, the policies may vary without affecting each other or the application itself, and the software becomes more portable.

Abstract Session:
An Object Structural Pattern

Nat Pryce

Object-oriented frameworks are structured in terms of client/server relationships between objects; an object's services are invoked by client objects through the operations of its interface. A common design requirement is for a server object to maintain state for each client that it is serving. Typically this is implemented by returning handles or untyped pointers to the client that are used to identify the per-client data structure holding its state. The lack of strong typing can lead to obscure errors that complicate debugging and maintenance. The Abstract Session pattern allows objects to maintain per-client state with full type safety and no loss of efficiency.

Intent

The intent of this pattern is to allow a server object with many client objects to maintain per-client state and maintain type-safety.

Also Known As

Service Access Point (SAP), Context, Service Handler

Motivation

Object-oriented frameworks are structured in terms of client/server[1] relationships between objects; an object's services are invoked by client objects through

---

[1]In the context of this pattern, the term *server* is used to denote an object that provides a service to "client" objects within the framework and in no way implies any notion of distribution between clients and servers.

the operations of its interface. Typically, object interactions are defined in terms of abstract interfaces, which increase the reusability and extensibility of the framework because the set of client and server types that can be used together is not bounded and can easily be extended by framework users.

A common design requirement is for a server object to maintain state for each client that it is serving. When the interactions between the server and client objects are defined in terms of abstract interfaces, per-client state cannot be stored in the client objects themselves because different server implementations will have to store different information. This problem is usually solved by using the Session pattern [Lea1995], which imposes a three-phase protocol on the interactions between the client and the server:

1. Clients make an initial "request" call to the server when they begin to use its services. The server responds by allocating a per-client data structure for the new client and returns an identifier of that data structure to the client.
2. The client passes the identifier it received as an argument to subsequent operations on the server. The server uses that identifier to find the per-client information it holds about the caller.
3. When the client has finished using the server, it makes a final "release" call to the server, passing in the identifier that the server uses to find and deallocate the appropriate per-client data structure.

Implementing the Session pattern involves resolving the following forces:

- *Per-client state.* The server object must be able to store state about each client that is using its services.
- *Efficiency.* Invocation of service operations should involve minimum runtime overhead.
- *Safety.* The implementation should catch the use of incorrect session identifiers. Ideally, such errors should be caught at compile-time.

Implementations of the Session pattern typically use one of two methods to map from identifiers to the data structures used internally to store per-client state.

- *Untyped pointers.* Identifiers are defined to be untyped pointers that the server object initializes to point to an implementation-specific data structure and casts to the appropriate type on each invocation. For example, the 16-bit Windows API [Petzold1990] uses untyped pointers to identify windows and other system resources allocated for an application.
- *Handles.* Identifiers are defined to be values of simple types, such as integers, or opaque values. The server uses a private associative container to map between identifiers and implementation-specific data structures and must perform a lookup each time a client makes a request. For example, the UNIX file API [Lewine1991] uses integer handles to identify open files.

The choice of whether to use untyped pointers or handles is one of safety versus runtime efficiency. Untyped pointers are efficient, but passing an incorrect pointer to a server could cause the program to corrupt memory or crash. Using handles as indices to an associative container allows incorrect identifiers to be detected at runtime but at the expense of performing a lookup on each invocation, which can be costly if many invocations are made during a time-critical part of a program. Both approaches are unsafe; a client can pass an incorrect identifier to the server without the error being caught at compile-time.

Example: Network Communication

Consider a communication protocol service that provides reliable transmission of data streams, such as the TCP/IP or Novell SPX protocols provide. The protocol manager itself is implemented as an object that provides services to connect to remote endpoints and accept incoming connections. Client objects wanting to connect to a remote endpoint must request a connection from the protocol object before being able to transmit and receive data. The protocol object must maintain state information, such as unacknowledged packets and flow-control information, for each connection, and thus clients must have some way to identify the connection that they are using to transmit or receive data. When the client has finished transmitting data, it must close the session to release any resources held for the session by the protocol manager.

The following code demonstrates a possible error when using untyped handles. The code uses the UNIX Sockets API [Stevens1990] to open a TCP/IP network connection to a remote endpoint and receive or transmit integer values. The code is incorrect; the first argument to the write function in line 14 should be the socket identifier `sock`, but the loop counter is erroneously used instead. Because UNIX uses integer handles to identify sockets, the bug cannot be caught by the compiler and only manifests itself as errors at runtime.

```
1   // Select a protocol and get a socket - i.e. request
2   // a session from the selected protocol
3
4   int sock = socket( SelectProtocol(), SOCK_STREAM, 0 );
5
6   // Connect to a remote endpoint
7
8   connect( sock, ... );
9
10  // Send 10 integers to the remote endpoint
11
12  for( int i = 0; i < 10; i++ ) {
```

```
13    int number = GetANumberFromSomewhere(i);
14    write( i, &number, sizeof(number) );
15 }
16 cerr << "Transmitted 10 numbers" << endl;
17
18 // Release the protocol session
19
20 close(sock);
```

Solution

The Abstract Session pattern provides a way for an object to store per-client state without sacrificing type safety or efficiency. A protocol service object, rather than providing a client with a handle to be passed as an argument to the operations of its abstract interface, instead creates an intermediate "session" object and returns a pointer to the session object to the client. The session object encapsulates the state information for the client that owns the session and is only exposed to the client as an abstract interface through which the client can access the protocol's functionality with full type safety. When the client invokes operations of the session, the session cooperates with the service object to complete the operation. When the client has finished using the protocol, it "releases" the session, after which any pointers to the session object are invalid.

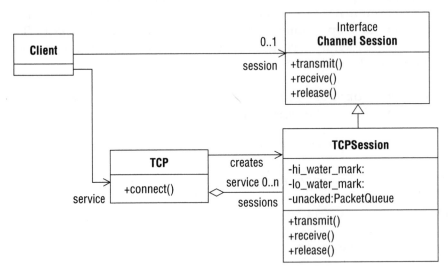

Figure 7-1 *Service and Session classes for the TCP protocol and an example Client class*

The class diagram in Figure 7-1 shows how the Abstract Session pattern can be used in an implementation of the TCP protocol. The TCP class represents the TCP protocol service and provides an operation, `connect`, with which client objects can request a connection to a remote endpoint. The TCP service then creates a new TCPSession object, initiates the handshaking protocol with the remote endpoint, and returns a pointer to the session's ChannelSession interface to the caller. The client object can call operations of the ChannelSession interface to transmit data over the connection.

As shown in Figure 7-2, the TCP object keeps track of the sessions it has created. It demultiplexes each packet received from the IP layer by passing it to the session identified in the packet's header. The session performs protocol processing and then queues the data for reading by the client object that owns it.

When the client object wants to close the connection, it calls the `release` operation of its session, after which all pointers to the session are invalid.

The Abstract Session pattern successfully resolves the forces outlined above:

- **Per-client state.**   The server object stores state about each client in the session object associated with that client.
- **Efficiency.**   Calling operations of a session object imposes no performance penalty compared to passing untyped pointers to operations of the service object and is more efficient than mapping handles to data structures using some hidden table.
- **Safety.**   The client object invokes operations on the abstract interface of the session object and so never needs to manipulate untyped handles. The session object knows the full type of the service object that created it, and vice versa, so the inter-

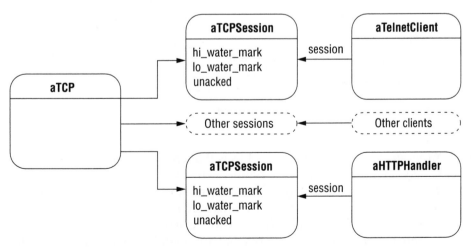

Figure 7-2 *Dynamic structure of objects implementing the TCP protocol*

actions between them are completely type-safe. When the client invokes an operation on the session, the session can call private operations of the service object, passing the manager a fully typed pointer to itself. The manager does not have to perform unsafe casts to access the state it stores within the session objects.

Applicability

Use the Abstract Session pattern when

- Interactions between server objects and client objects are defined in terms of abstract interfaces.
- Server objects must maintain state for each client object that makes use of their services.

Structure and Participants

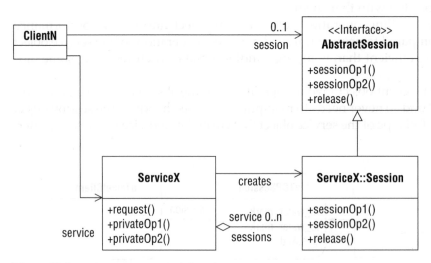

Figure 7-3 *Class structure of the Abstract Session pattern*

- *ServiceX* (Service).   Classes of server objects that create session objects (of type ServiceX::Session) for clients that are bound to them.
- *Abstract Session* (ChannelSession).   The interface through which clients bound to a server object make use of the service provided by that object.
- *ServiceX::Session* (TCPSession).   The session classes used by the ServiceX classes to store information about clients that are bound to them. Clients invoke the AbstractSession interfaces of these objects to interact with the server objects to which they are bound.

- *ClientN* (HttpHandler, TelnetClient). Objects that are making use of ServiceX through the AbstractSession interface.

Collaborations

Figure 7-4 illustrates the collaborations between objects in the Abstract Session pattern.

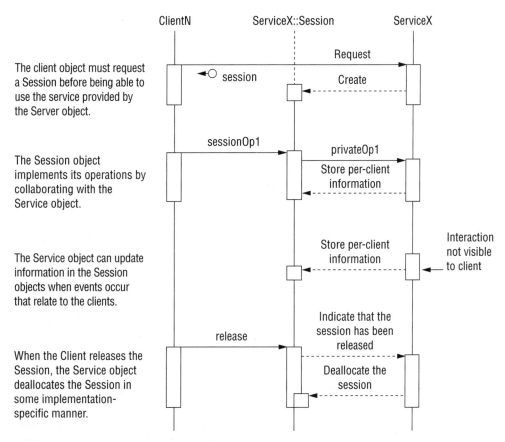

Figure 7-4 *Object interactions in the Abstract Session pattern*

- A client object that wants to use a server object requests a session from the server. The server object creates a session object (which conforms to the Abstract-Session interface), initializes the session with information about the client, and returns a pointer to the session back to the client.

- The client uses the service provided by the server object by invoking the operations of its session object's AbstractSession interface. The session object cooperates with the server object to complete the invocation.
- The server object uses information stored in the session object to process requests from its clients and can update the per-client information when events occur behind the scenes that relate to the client.
- When a client object has finished using the service provided by the server object, it calls the `release` operation of its session. Forcing clients to release sessions by calling `release` allows a service to hide the way it allocates session objects from its clients. A service could allocate sessions on the heap, in which case the `release` operation would free the session object, or a service could have a fixed number of sessions in an array, in which case `release` would update a record in the service object of the sessions that were unused and could be handed out to new clients.

Consequences

The Abstract Session pattern has the following advantages:

- *Type safety.* Interactions between clients and sessions and between sessions and servers are completely type-safe. This reduces the likelihood of obscure errors, making the code easier to debug and maintain.
- *Performance.* The interactions between clients and sessions are as fast as or faster than those using unsafe methods such as untyped pointers or handles.
- *Flexibility.* The use of abstract interfaces and encapsulation of per-client state within each Server class reduces coupling between client and server classes. A client can use any server that creates sessions that implement the AbstractSession interface.
- *Extensibility.* The pattern makes it easy to add server classes to the system; such extensions do not require existing client and server classes to change.

The Abstract Session pattern has the following disadvantages:

- *Dangling pointers.* It is possible that a session might be referenced and used after it has been released.
- *Distribution.* It is difficult to pass a session object from the server to the client if the client and server exist in different address spaces. When creating a session, the server must send information to the client to allow the client to create a Proxy [Gamma+1995] session in its local address space. Distributed object brokers, such as CORBA [OMG1995] or DCOM [Rogerson1997], can implement this functionality.
- *Multiple languages.* It is difficult to call Abstract Sessions from another language, especially from languages that are not object-oriented. This can be solved

by writing an Adapter [Gamma+1995] layer that hides session objects behind a set of procedures callable from the other languages and that uses one of the unsafe implementations of the Session pattern to identify session objects.

Implementation

The following implementation issues are worth noting:

1. *Use of the heap.* Allocating and deallocating memory from the heap is an expensive operation. Forcing clients to discard sessions via the `release` method in the AbstractSession interface, rather than an explicit deallocation of the session object, gives server objects more flexibility in the allocation of session objects. For instance, if the server allocated the session from the heap, the `release` operation would delete the session object. However, a server might preallocate sessions in a cache; when a client invokes the `release` operation of a session, it need only mark that the session is unused rather than perform a heap deallocation. If a server object does not need to store any information about its clients, it can implement the AbstractSession interface itself, perhaps using private inheritance; in this case, the `release` operation would do nothing.

2. *C++ smart pointers.* A C++ implementation of this pattern can automate the management of session lifetimes by using smart pointer classes. A smart pointer object would store a pointer to a session interface and release the interface in its destructor. A smart pointer on the stack would automatically release the session when it goes out of scope. A smart pointer held as a member of an object would automatically release the session when the object gets destroyed.

3. *Object finalization.* In a language with automatic garbage collection and object finalization, the act of releasing a session can be made synonymous with releasing the last reference to the Session object. The functionality of releasing a session can be performed by the finalization method of the Session object and so will be called automatically by the garbage collector.

4. *Java outer/inner classes.* A Java implementation of this pattern can be simplified using inner classes. The concrete Service class would be implemented as an outer class, and the concrete Session classes would be defined as inner classes. An inner class is associated with an instance of the outer class in which it is defined and can refer directly to the fields and methods of that instance. Thus, inner classes remove the need for explicit delegation from session to service and reduce the possibility of programming errors.

5. *Defining server interfaces.* If clients are always bound to servers by some third party that knows the complete type of all servers it is using, then server objects do not need to conform to an abstract interface. However, in some systems clients will bind themselves to servers by finding a suitable server object

in something like a trader or namespace and then request a session from it; in this case servers will need to conform to some abstract interface that can be used polymorphically.

Sample Code: Communication Protocols

The following source code expands on the networking example described above in which the program opens a network connection to a remote endpoint and transmits ten integers. The example is taken from an existing object-oriented protocol framework that allows programmers to construct communication protocol software by composing simple components to form protocols with rich functionality tightly tailored to the needs of the application.

The framework defines a number of abstract interfaces and base classes, which are used by protocol implementors, as well as useful abstract data types. The sessions of a protocol layer are accessed through the `ChannelSession` interface, by which client objects transmit data. Clients of a protocol layer implement the `ReceiveCallback` interface, to which their session calls back when data is received. Messages are held in `Buffer` objects that perform memory management and segmentation and reassembly of blocks of raw data. Addressing information is encapsulated as `Reference` objects.

Unlike the example code above, an individual protocol can provide multiple service interfaces. For example, our TCP implementation provides an interface named "connect" of type `ConnectService` through which objects can connect to remote endpoints, and an interface named "listen" of type `ListenService` through which objects can request endpoints that listen for incoming connection requests. Service interfaces are abstract, allowing objects to dynamically select the communication protocol to be used at runtime and to acquire the appropriate interface from a factory. For this example, we will consider only the `ConnectService` interface.

```
class ChannelSession {
public:
    virtual bool transmit( Buffer &buf ) = 0;
    virtual void release() = 0;
};

class ReceiveCallback {
public:
    virtual void receive( Buffer &buf ) = 0;
};

class ConnectService {
public:
```

```
    virtual ChannelSession *request( ReceiveCallback&,
                                     const Reference& ) = 0;
};
```

Application-layer communication abstractions (such as distributed object invocation, queued message ports, or event dissemination) communicate by marshaling typed data into and out of `Buffer` objects that are transmitted by these protocol interfaces. It is useful to encapsulate the code to manage the ownership of a protocol session within a reusable base class. For instance, the `ClientEndpoint` class below is the base class for objects that can be connected to a remote endpoint and communicate with that endpoint over a channel through a `ChannelSession` interface. The `bind` method is used to hand ownership of a session that has been acquired by some third party over to the endpoint object. The interaction abstraction derived from `ClientEndpoint` uses the session to transmit and receive data and releases the session when it is destroyed.

```
class ClientEndpoint : public ReceiveCallback {
public:
    /* Receive callback interface: implement in derived classes
     */
    virtual void receive( Buffer & ) = 0;
    /* Binding interface: attach the session object of the channel
     * used by this endpoint
     */
    bool bound() const { return _transport != 0; }
    void bind( ChannelSession *transport ) { _transport = transport; }

protected:
    ClientEndpoint() : _transport(0) {}
    /* Allow derived classes access to the private _transport session
     */
    bool transmit( Buffer& ) { return _transport- >transmit(); }
    void releaseTransport() { if(_transport) _transport- release(); }

    ~ClientEndpoint() { releaseTransport(); }

    private:
    ChannelSession *_transport;
};
```

The programmer can define appropriate interaction abstractions by deriving from the `ClientEndpoint` class. Here we assume that they have already implemented the classes `Port<T>`, encapsulating queued message ports, and `PortClient<T>`, by which a client can transmit values to a remote message port over a transport channel. We will not describe the implementation in any detail since it involves marshaling and the use of thread synchronization libraries that are not germane to the issue.

```
template <class T>
class PortClient : public ClientEndpoint {
public:
    bool out( T &message ) {
        Buffer buf;
        ... marshal message into the buffer...
        return transmit(buf);
    }
};
```

The main application code then looks as follows:

```
1    PortClient<int> send;
2    Reference remote_server = GetReferenceFromSomewhere();
3
4    // Select a protocol and get the interface of its
5    // connect service
6
7    ConnectService &connect = SelectProtocol ();
8
9    // Acquire a ChannelSession connecting the PortClient to a
10   // remote Port and pass ownership of it to the PortClient.
11
12   ChannelSession *session =
13       connect.request( sender,  remote_server );
14   send.bind(session);
15
16   // Send 10 integers
17
18   for( int i = 0; i < 10; i++ ) {
19       int number = GetANumberFromSomewhere(i);
20       send.out(number);
21   }
22
23   // Ending the program will cause the PortClient object
24   // to be destroyed, which will automatically release
25   // the protocol session.
26
27   cerr << "Transmitted 10 integers" << endl;
```

Lines 12 to 14 show the use of the Abstract Session pattern. The program selects a protocol service and requests that the service connect the PortClient object to a remote Port. The connect service returns a ChannelSession that manages the state of the connection, and the program hands ownership of the session to the PortClient. When the program calls the send operation of the PortClient in line 20, the PortClient object marshals the integer into a buffer and transmits it over the `ChannelSession`. When the `PortClient` goes out of scope at the end of the program, its destructor releases the session, closing the connection.

Known Uses

The Abstract Session pattern is widely used in the implementation of object-oriented communication protocol software. The x-kernel framework [Hutchinson+1991] and the ACE communications toolkit [Schmidt1994] both use this pattern.

Microsoft's Object Linking and Embedding (OLE) framework [Microsoft1993] uses the Abstract Session pattern for managing the size and location of embedded objects. An object such as a word-processing document that can contain embedded objects is known as a "container" and stores pointers to the `IOle-Object` interfaces of its embedded objects. Through this interface the container can, among other things, query the required size of the embedded object and set the size and position of the object. When a new `IOleObject` is embedded in the container, the container creates a Session object, known as a "client-site," in which it stores information about the actual position and size of the embedded object. The client-site object implements the `IOleClientSite` interface that the container passes to the embedded object and through which the embedded object can request to be resized. When an embedded object makes a resize request through its `IOleClientSite` interface, the container updates the size and position of all its embedded objects based on the information stored in the client-site session objects.

The Java Abstract Windowing Toolkit (AWT) [Gosling+1996] uses the Abstract Session pattern in several places. An example is the `Graphics` interface, which provides a common interface for drawing graphics on a variety of devices, such as windows, bitmaps, and printers. An object that wants to draw onto a device asks the device to create a graphics context object and receives a reference to the object's `Graphics` interface. The graphics context stores the current drawing state, such as the current font, background and foreground colors, and other state required to render drawing operations onto the associated device.

Related Patterns

The Abstract Session pattern is one way of implementing the Session pattern [Lea1995].

It is also related to the Facade, Factory Method, and Mediator patterns from the GoF book [Gamma+1995]:

- The Facade pattern uses a single intermediate object to hide the complexities of a framework of cooperating objects from the users of that framework. In contrast, the Session pattern uses multiple intermediate objects to decouple objects that provide a service from the objects that use that service and to provide type-safe interaction between objects that interact only through abstract interfaces.

- The Server object uses the Factory Method to create sessions for a client. This ensures that sessions can be initialized correctly by the server object.
- A Mediator object controls the interaction of multiple cooperating objects. The Server object of the Abstract Session pattern can be viewed as a form of Mediator controlling the interaction of all of its clients. The session objects can be viewed as simple Mediators controlling the interaction of the server and a single client.

The Acceptor and Connector patterns [Schmidt1995] are both examples of higher-level patterns that make use of the Abstract Session pattern.

The Abstract Session pattern can be used to implement an Adapter [Gamma+ 1995] around objects or non-OO libraries that use an unsafe implementation of the Session pattern.

ACKNOWLEDGMENTS

The author acknowledges many stimulating discussions with members of the Department of Computing, Imperial College, during the crystallization of this pattern and the writing of this chapter, in particular Steve Crane, Naranker Dulay, and Hal Fosså. The author also would like to thank Doug Schmidt, who shepherded this chapter through its submission to EuroPLoP '97 and suggested many improvements. Last but not least, many thanks to those who gave comments on the paper at EuroPLoP '97 and all who made the workshop such an enjoyable and rewarding experience.

We acknowledge the financial support of British Telecommunications plc through the Management of Multiservice Networks project.

REFERENCES

[Gamma+1995] E. Gamma, R. Helm, R. Johnson, and J. Vlissides. *Design Patterns: Elements of Reusable Object-Oriented Software*. Reading, MA: Addison-Wesley, 1995.

[Gosling+1996] J. Gosling, F. Yellin, and The Java Team. *The Java Application Programming Interface. Volume 2: Window Toolkit and Applets*. Reading, MA: Addison-Wesley. 1996.

[Hutchinson+1991] N.C. Hutchinson and L.L. Peterson. "The x-kernel: An Architecture for Implementing Network Protocols." *IEEE Transactions on Software Engineering*, 17(1): 64–76, 1991.

[Lea1995] D. Lea. *Sessions*. Paper presented at ECOOP '95, Aarhus, Denmark, 1995.

[Lewine1991] D. Lewine. *POSIX Programmer's Guide: Writing Portable Unix Applications*. Sebastopol, CA: O'Reilly & Associates, 1991.

[Microsoft1993] Microsoft Corporation (ed.). *Object Linking and Embedding Version 2 (OLE2) Programmer's Reference*, volumes 1 and 2. Redmond, WA: Microsoft Press, 1993.

[OMG1995] The Object Management Group. *The Common Object Request Broker: Architecture and Specification, Version 2.0*. The Object Management Group, OMG Headquarters, 492 Old Connecticut Path, Framingham, MA 01701, 1995.

[Petzold1990] C. Petzold. *Programming Windows*. Redmond, WA: Microsoft Press, 1990.

[Rogerson1997] D. Rogerson. *Inside COM—Microsoft's Component Object Model*. Redmond, WA: Microsoft Press, 1997.

[Schmidt1994] D.C. Schmidt. "ACE: An Object-Oriented Framework for Developing Distributed Applications." In *Proceedings of the 6th USENIX C++ Technical Conference*, Cambridge, MA, USENIX Association, April 1994.

[Schmidt1995] D.C. Schmidt. "Acceptor and Connector: Design Patterns for Actively and Passively Initializing Network Services." In J.O. Coplien and D.C. Schmidt (eds.), *Pattern Languages of Program Design*, Reading, MA: Addison-Wesley, 1995.

[Stevens1990] W.R. Stevens. *Unix Network Programming*. Englewood Cliffs, NJ: Prentice-Hall, 1990.

Nat Pryce may be reached at np2@doc.ic.ac.uk.

Chapter 8

Object Synchronizer

*António Rito Silva, João Pereira,
and José Alves Marques*

In this chapter a design pattern for object synchronization is described. The Object Synchronizer pattern decouples object synchronization from object functionality. This pattern supports several synchronization policies and their customization. This pattern is used when invocations to an object need to be controlled in order to preserve its consistency. The solution provides encapsulation, modularity, expressiveness, and reuse of synchronization policies.

Intent

The Object Synchronizer pattern abstracts several object synchronization policies. It decouples object synchronization from object functionality.

Also Known As

Object Concurrency Control, Object Serialization

Example

Consider the design of a Cooperative Drawing Application allowing cooperative manipulation of graphical documents. Users at different terminals can simultaneously access the same graphical document, and changes made to a local view are immediately propagated to other local views. Due to the cooperative characteristics of the application a shape can be made private, publicly readable, or publicly writable. A shape is private when it is visible only to the user who created it, that

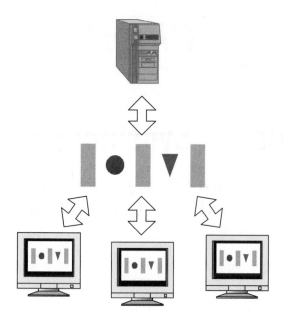

Figure 8-1 *Cooperative Drawing Application*

is, its owner. A shape is publicly readable when it is visible to all users but can only be updated by its owner. A shape is publicly writable when any user can see and modify it.

A possible architecture (Figure 8-1) for such an application contains several client applications that have their own objects (application space) and share a set of domain objects (domain space) that may be kept in a data store (persistent space). The application space has interface objects, for example, scroll bars and shapes; the domain space has shared objects, for example, shapes data; and the persistent space stores documents, for example, a graphical document including its shapes' data.

Problem

Client applications execute operations that invoke methods on shape objects. Invocations on a non-private shape object must be controlled either because it is a publicly readable shape where update invocations from non-owners should return an error, or because it is a publicly writable shape where simultaneous invocations by different client applications are liable to result in corruption of the shared shape's state.

Traditional solutions for object synchronization use the following:

• The persistent space's locking mechanisms synchronize invocations to shared resources. However, a shared object may be volatile, and the effort to make it persistent may result in unacceptable overhead. Another issue is that the locking mechanisms may not be suitable for the synchronization needs of the application.

• Synchronization mechanisms, such as semaphores [Dijkstra1968] and monitors [Hoare1974], synchronize accesses. However, this results in code tangling that prevents both functionality and synchronization-independent reuse. For instance, a shape's code should be the same for private, publicly readable, or publicly writable shapes.

Forces

An object-oriented solution for the object synchronization problem must resolve the following forces:

• *Expressiveness* requires abstraction of synchronization policies. It is not possible to find an optimal policy for all situations: policies should be customizable. The most suitable policy depends on the domain object and its operations' semantics. For instance, some domain objects are frequently accessed, thus requiring a pessimistic policy, whereas others are not, making an optimistic policy more efficient.

• *Modularity* requires separation of object synchronization from object functionality. This orthogonality allows synchronization policy switching with no repercussions on other components, as well as incremental introduction of synchronization.

• *Encapsulation* requires the synchronization part of an object to be placed within the object itself rather than spread out among its clients. This places synchronization responsibility within the object, thereby avoiding client negligence.

• *Reusability* requires separate reuse of functionality and synchronization code. It should be possible to independently reuse both synchronization code and functionality code. For instance, a shape's functionality code is reused for private, publicly readable, and publicly writable shape classes.

Solution

Figure 8-2 sketches a solution for the synchronization of a Shape object.

Invocations on a Shape are intercepted by a Shape Synchronization Interface that either can let them proceed or delay or reject them. The Shape Synchronization Interface synchronizes invocations by delegating to Synchronization Abstraction. Operations preControl and postControl of the Synchronization Abstraction control the order of invocations according to a given synchronization policy.

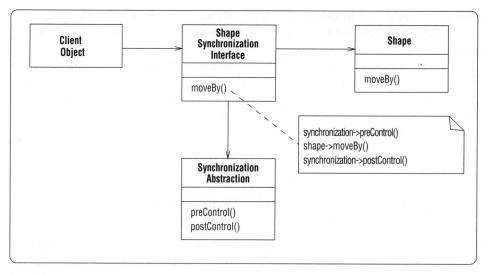

Figure 8-2 *Synchronized Shape*

- *Expressiveness* is achieved by providing different specializations of the `Synchro-nization Abstraction`. Each specialization provides specific synchronization semantics. Actually, due to synchronization complexity, `Synchronization Abstraction` represents several objects that are not represented in Figure 8-2.
- *Modularity* is achieved through the implementation of synchronization in `Synchronization Abstraction`, and so it is decoupled from `Shape`.
- *Encapsulation* is achieved because the `Shape Synchronization Interface` isolates synchronization from the `Client Object`.
- *Reusability* is achieved because `Shape` objects can be associated with different `Synchronization Abstraction` objects. This allows independent reuse of `Shape` and `Synchronization Abstraction` classes.

Applicability

Use the Object Synchronizer pattern when

- *Invocations to an object must be controlled to preserve its consistency.*   Invocations must be controlled according to a synchronization policy.
- *It is premature to decide on which object synchronization policy to use.*   At initial stages of the development process it may be too early to choose a specific policy. Moreover, it should be possible to test several policies before choosing.
- *Different synchronization policies may be used by different objects of a class.* Different synchronization and sharing semantics, for objects of the same or different classes, are often required by applications, for example, groupware systems.

Structure and Participants

The UML [Fowler+1997] class diagram in Figure 8-3 illustrates the structure of the Object Synchronizer pattern.

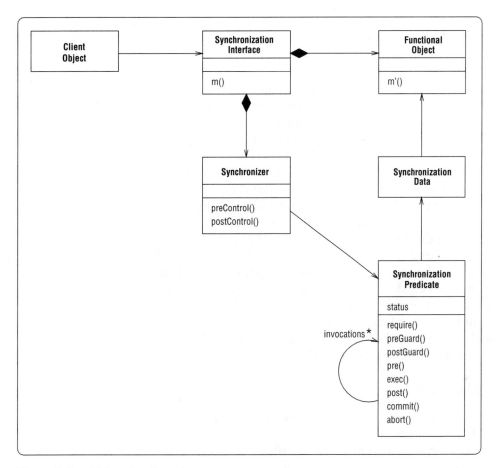

Figure 8-3   *Object Synchronizer pattern structure*

The main participants in the Object Synchronizer pattern are:

- `Client Object` (Client Object) requests a service from `Functional Object` by invoking one of its operations through `Synchronization Interface`.
- `Functional Object` (Shape) contains the functionality code and data. Accesses to it should be synchronized.
- `Synchronization Interface` (Shape Synchronization Interface) is responsible for the synchronization of invocations to the `Functional Object`

using the services provided by the `Synchronizer`. It creates a `Synchronization Predicate` object for each invocation. It invokes `preControl` before invocation proceeds on the `Functional Object` and `postControl` after.

- `Synchronizer` (**Synchronization Abstraction**) decides whether an invocation may continue or whether it should stop or be delayed (returns values CONTINUE, ERROR, and DELAY). Operations `preControl` and `postControl` control the order of invocations. The former enforces pessimistic synchronization policies, while the latter enforces optimistic synchronization policies.

- `Synchronization Predicate` (**Synchronization Abstraction**) identifies the invocation and contains its current status, which can be pre-pending, before executing; executing, when in execution; post-pending, after execution; committed, when terminated with success; and aborted, when terminated without success. In these situations, attribute `status` holds, respectively, values PRE, EXEC, POST, COMMIT, and ABORT. It also contains a queue of predicates: `invocations`. The synchronization predicate also defines the synchronization semantics of an invocation through operations `require`, `preGuard`, and `postGuard`. For validation purposes, these operations may use their local synchronization data, the synchronization data of other invocations (contained in other `Synchronization Predicate` objects), and the object synchronization data (contained in object `Synchronization Data`). Operations `preGuard` and `postGuard` verify whether an invocation is compatible with other concurrent invocations while operation `require` controls access according to the object state. Operations `pre`, `exec`, `post`, `commit`, and `abort` update synchronization data.

- `Synchronization Data` (**Synchronization Abstraction**) provides global object synchronization data, for instance, the number of items in a buffer. It may use the `Functional Object` to get synchronization data.

Collaborations

The UML sequence diagram in Figure 8-4 illustrates collaborations between objects involved in the Object Synchronizer pattern.

Four collaboration phases are described:

1. *CREATE.* This phase creates a `Synchronization Predicate` object. Its status is initialized to PRE. Operation `pre` may update policy-specific synchronization data with information about the invocation category and its argument values.

2. *PRE-CONTROL.* This phase synchronizes the invocation before accessing the `Functional Object` (operations `require` and `preGuard`). An ERROR value may be returned, preventing the execution of the client invocation; otherwise execution is delayed or resumed. If CONTINUE or ERROR values are returned, the `Synchronization Predicate` status is updated to, respectively, EXEC or ERROR by operations `exec` and `abort`. These operations may also update policy-specific synchronization data in `Synchronization Data`

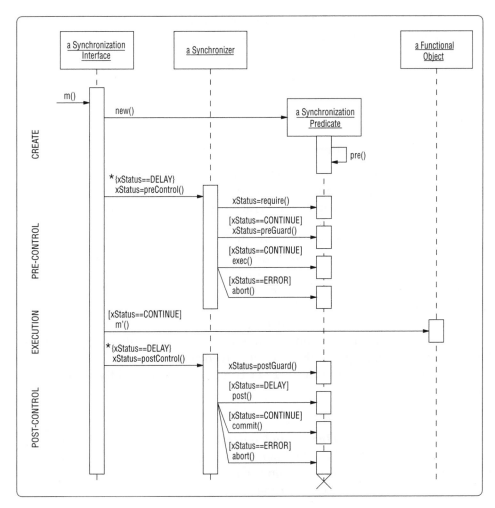

Figure 8-4   *Object Synchronizer pattern collaborations*

and `Synchronization Predicate` objects. This phase is repeated while `preControl` returns `DELAY`.

3. *EXECUTION.*   The invocation executes on the `Functional Object`. This phase occurs only if the previous phase returned `CONTINUE`.

4. *POST-CONTROL.*   This phase verifies that an invocation already done (in state `EXEC` or `POST`) is correctly synchronized with other concurrent invocations. The verification protocol (operation `postGuard`) is similar to that of the previous phase. Operations `post`, `commit`, and `abort`, on the `Synchronization Predicate` object set the status value to `POST`, `COMMIT`, and `ABORT`, respectively. Additionally, they may update policy-specific synchronization

data in `Synchronization Data` and other `Synchronization Predicate` objects. This phase is repeated while `postControl` returns DELAY.

Operations `pre`, `preControl`, and `postControl` must be executed in mutual exclusion since any interference may result in synchronization data corruption.

Consequences

The Object Synchronizer pattern has the following advantages:

- *Isolates synchronization code from client objects.* A shared object can enforce a consistent synchronization policy. Clients, by ignoring whether an object is shared or not, become simpler. Encapsulation is achieved by placing the synchronization code within the synchronized object such that client objects can invoke the `Synchronization Interface` and ignore how synchronization is achieved.
- *Separates functionality code from synchronization code.* The pattern avoids code tangling and allows separate development, test, and reuse. Synchronization code is encapsulated by classes `Synchronizer`, `Synchronization Predicate`, and `Synchronization Data`.
- *Abstracts several synchronization policies.* Examples of such policies are readers/writers, synchronization counters, or dynamic priority. The policies can be either optimistic or pessimistic. Expressiveness is achieved by specializing classes `Synchronizer`, `Synchronization Predicate`, and `Synchronization Data`.

The Object Synchronizer pattern has the following disadvantage:

- *Increases the number of classes and objects.* More classes and objects are needed than in a solution based on synchronization mechanisms such as semaphores. However, due to code tangling, synchronization based on these mechanisms is more complex and error prone.

Implementation

There are several ways to implement the Object Synchronizer pattern. This section discusses major issues and possibilities.

Customized Policies. Programmers customize synchronization policies by defining specific subclasses of `Synchronizer`, `Synchronization Predicate`, and `Synchronization Data`.

Pessimistic and Optimistic Policies. Synchronization policies can use two different generic algorithms: *pessimistic,* when the object is expected to have high contention, and *optimistic,* when the level of contention is expected to be low. Pessimistic policies synchronize object invocations before they execute, while optimistic policies

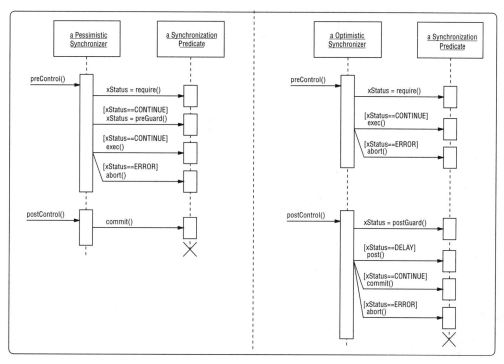

Figure 8-5 *Pessimistic and optimistic synchronizers*

only control them after their execution. These two perspectives are coded in subclasses of `Synchronizer` as illustrated in Figure 8-5.

Pessimistic policies control invocations during the PRE-CONTROL phase by verifying compatibility with other `Synchronization Predicate` objects (operations `require` and `preGuard`). During POST-CONTROL, pessimistic policies do not verify compatibility, since synchronizations were already verified (thus operation `postGuard` is not invoked). Optimistic policies do not control invocations during the PRE-CONTROL phase. Nevertheless, operation `require` must be invoked to verify whether an object's state allows invocation execution; for example, it may not be possible to get a value from an empty buffer. Afterwards, during the POST-CONTROL phase it is necessary to verify that the invocation is compatible with other executing and terminated invocations (operation `postGuard`).

Pessimistic Readers/Writers.   The readers/writers policy synchronizes each invocation taking into account the state of the other invocations. In this policy, two categories of functional object operations are considered: read and write. The policy allows concurrent execution of read operations but prevents concurrent execution of a write operation when other read or write operations are being executed.

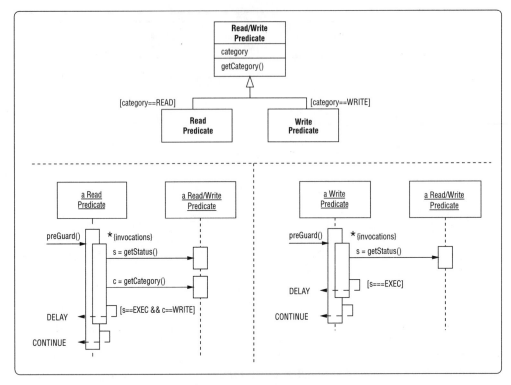

Figure 8-6 *Pessimistic readers/writers policy*

Class and sequence diagrams presented in Figure 8-6 show the specialization of `Synchronization Predicate` for a pessimistic readers/writers synchronization policy.

This solution distinguishes between read and write invocations. A generic synchronization predicate `Read/Write Predicate` defines the invocation categories, for example, `READ` and `WRITE`.

Operation `preGuard` of `Read Predicate` returns DELAY if one of the invocations' predicates is a `Write Predicate` with status value EXEC; in other words, there is another client invocation that is accessing the shared object in write mode. Operation `preGuard` of `Write Predicate` returns DELAY if there is an invocation's predicate with status value EXEC.

Optimistic Readers/Writers. Class and sequence diagrams described in Figure 8-7 show the specialization of `Synchronization Predicate` for an optimistic readers/writers synchronization policy.

Operation `postGuard` of `Read/Write Predicate` objects returns ABORT if the `abort` attribute has the value TRUE. Operation commit of `Read Predicate` sets the attribute `abort` of all `Write Predicate` objects whose status is EXEC to

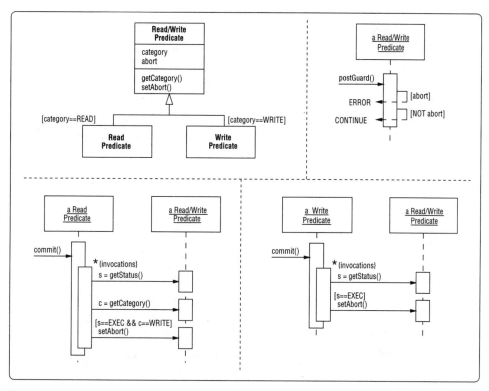

Figure 8-7 *Optimistic readers/writers policy*

TRUE. Operation `commit` of `Write Predicate` sets the attribute `abort` of all predicate objects whose status is EXEC to TRUE. We assume that each access to the shared object is done in a private copy. If afterwards the invocations terminates with success, we actualize the shared object. This corresponds to the deferred-update recovery policy of the Object Recovery pattern [Silva+1997].

Dynamic Priority Readers/Writers.   The pessimistic readers/writers policy allows starvation of writers. To solve this problem, a readers/writers policy is defined in which priorities are dynamically associated with invocations. Write invocations have associated priorities that dynamically increase with the execution of read operations. A read operation must be delayed if there is, pending execution, a write operation with maximum priority.

Class and sequence diagrams presented in Figure 8-8 show the specialization of `Synchronization Predicate` for a dynamic priority readers/writers synchronization policy.

Operation `preGuard` of `Read Predicate` returns DELAY if there is a `Write Predicate` with MAX priority. Operation `exec` of `Read Predicate` increments the priority of `Write Predicate`.

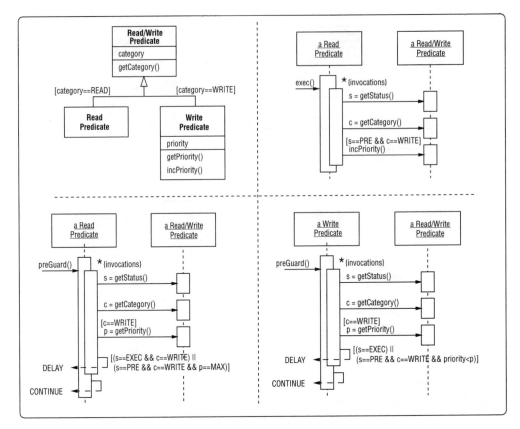

Figure 8-8 *Dynamic priority readers/writers policy*

Producer/Consumer. The producer/consumer policy synchronizes invocations, taking into account the functional object's state. Two operation categories are considered: *produce* and *consume.* The policy delays the execution of consume operations if there are no available items, and it delays the execution of produce operations when the functional object does not have enough space available for storing new items.

Class and sequence diagrams presented in Figure 8-9 show the specialization of Synchronization Predicate and Synchronization Data for a producer/consumer synchronization policy.

Class Buffer Synchronization Data contains information about the number of items in the buffer. Operation require of Produce Predicate returns DELAY if the synchronization information contained in Buffer Synchronization Data indicates that the buffer is full. Operation require of Consume Predicate returns DELAY if the synchronization information contained in Buffer Synchronization Data indicates that the buffer is empty.

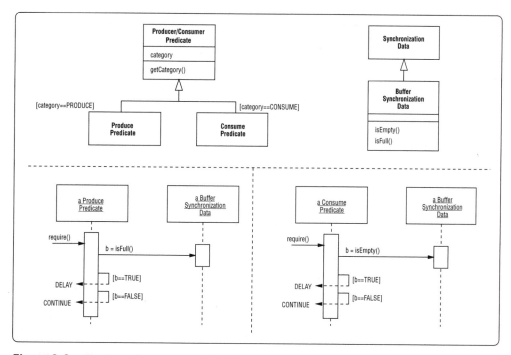

Figure 8-9   *Producer/consumer policy*

Note that operations `preGuard` and `postGuard` should be redefined if state corruption can result from the concurrent execution of `produce` or `consume` operations.

Synchronization Counters.   Several concurrent object-oriented languages, for example, Guide [Decouchant+1991], provide synchronization counters that count, for each type of invocation, the number of pending, executing, and finished invocations.

Specializations of class `Synchronization Data` can implement synchronization counters using an attribute for each counter. Moreover, it is necessary that operations `pre`, `exec`, `post`, `commit`, and `abort` of class `Synchronization Predicate` invoke the `Synchronization Data` to update the attribute values accordingly.

Note that the previously described readers/writers policies could have been written using synchronization counters.

Separation of Functional and Synchronization Variables.   Producer/consumer policies can have different specializations of class `Buffer Synchronization Data`: this class either accesses the functional object to obtain synchronization information or holds and manages its own synchronization variables. Upper and lower sequence

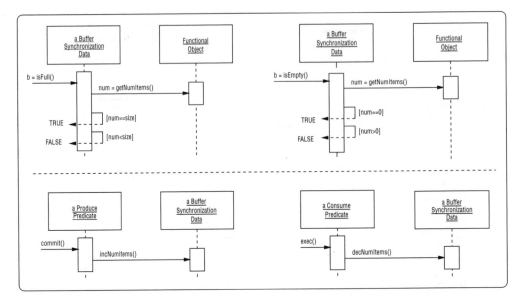

Figure 8-10 *Synchronization variables*

diagrams presented in Figure 8-10 show two possible specializations. In the upper part of Figure 8-10, the information on the number of items is contained within the functional object. In the lower part of Figure 8-10, class `Buffer Synchronization Data` has an attribute that counts the number of items in the functional object. In this case, synchronization information is not in the functional object.

The upper solution reduces concurrency, because synchronization verification conflicts with invocation execution; for example, a variable written during an invocation execution is read during the PRE-CONTROL phase of another invocation. The lower solution completely separates the functional variables from the synchronization variables.

Besides the increment in concurrency, the lower solution allows the independent reuse of the synchronization policy because it does not depend on the functional object interface. For instance, if programmers only distinguish among consume and produce invocations, they can use the presented synchronization classes for producer/consumer policies. By using customized synchronization classes, programmers of the functional class do not need to be aware of the structure and collaborations of the Object Synchronizer pattern.

Transparency. Transparency can be achieved if the `Functional Object` and the `Synchronization Interface` have the same interface. In that situation the `Client Object` can ignore whether the object is synchronized or not.

Nevertheless, there are situations when the `Client Object` must be aware of synchronization. For instance, the `Client Object` can receive an error if the invocation is rejected. In this situation, transparency can be relaxed by enriching the `Synchronization Interface` according to the `Client Object`'s synchronization requirements. Although there is transparency loss, this does not imply breaking encapsulation: synchronization is still not the client's responsibility.

Object Concurrency. Two policies of object concurrency are considered: active object and concurrent object. Active objects have an internal activity that selects and executes invocations, while invocations to concurrent objects can execute concurrently, for instance, using the caller's activity.

A synchronized object can either be active or concurrent. If it is an active object, its `Synchronization Interface` encapsulates a single internal activity that accesses the synchronization objects and the functional object. On the other hand, if it is a concurrent object the synchronization objects and the functional object can be concurrently accessed by several activities. Therefore, because of object concurrency policies, object synchronization requires different implementations of mutual exclusion and activity delay/resume services. Both implementations are orthogonal to synchronization code.

1. *Active object.* The design of an active object is described by [Lavender+1996]. It contains a queue of method objects representing pending invocations. A method object has the code associated with an invocation. Active objects use a scheduler object to select and execute pending method objects. Mutual exclusion of synchronization code is provided by the internal scheduler thread. Activity delay is implemented by moving the invocation to the end of the queue.
2. *Concurrent object.* A mutex object is used to support mutual exclusion of synchronization code. A condition object is used to block the activity associated with an invocation if DELAY is returned.

Sample Code

This section presents the implementation, in C++, of shape objects belonging to the Cooperative Drawing Application.

In the Cooperative Drawing Application, accesses to shared shapes need to be synchronized. The implementation of private, publicly readable, and publicly writable shapes is described for pessimistic policies.

Class `Shape` represents a shape. It knows its data and how to update it when the shape is moved (operation `moveBy`). The interface definition is as follows:

```
class Shape {
  public:
    Shape(Data data);
    ~Shape();
    // Move - update data
    void moveBy(Point delta);
    // Read data
    Data getData();
  private:
    // Shape data
    Data data;
};
```

Class **Shape** implements a private shape since its objects are not shared. To support public shapes the class **ShapeSynchronizationInterface**, a subclass of **SynchronizationInterface**, is defined. The synchronization associated with operation **moveBy** follows. This class uses a concurrent object policy and so **Mutex** and **Condition** objects are used to support both mutual exclusion in the synchronization code and invocation delays and resumes.

```
void ShapeSynchronizationInterface::moveBy(Point delta) {
  X_Status status;
  // creates a predicate MoveByPred
  SynchronizationPredicate* pred = new MoveByPredicate();

  // pre-control
  do {
    // begin mutual exclusion
    mutex_.acquire();
    // verify compatibility
    status = synchronizer_->preControl(pred);
    // end mutual exclusion mutex_.release();
    // if there are incompatibilities wait
    if (status == DELAY)
      condition_.wait();
  }
  while (status == DELAY);

  if (status == CONTINUE)
    // invocation proceeds on functional object shape_
    shape_->moveBy(delta);
  else return;

  // post-control
  do {
```

```
    // begin mutual exclusion
    mutex_.acquire();
    // verify compatibility
    status = synchronizer_->postControl(pred);
    // end mutual exclusion
    mutex_.release();
    if (status == DELAY)
      condition_.wait();
    else
      // only if CONTINUE or ERROR
      // awake pending invocations
      condition_.broadcast();
  }
  while (status == DELAY);
}
```

Note that since PRE-CONTROL and POST-CONTROL code fragments are independent of a particular invocation they could be defined as two protected operations of class `SynchronizationInterface`. For each synchronized operation, these generic operations could be invoked with a `SynchronizationPredicate` object as an argument.

Particular synchronization policies are defined by classes `MoveByPredicate` and `GetDataPredicate`, which are subclasses of `ShapePredicate`. `ShapePredicate` inherits from `SynchronizationPredicate` and defines two invocation categories: MOVE and GET.

```
// Generic shape predicate
class ShapePredicate : public SynchronizationPredicate {
  public:
    ShapePredicate(int cat) : cat_(cat) {}
    ~ShapePredicate() {}
    // returns category
    int getCat() { return cat_; }
    // other operations to be redefined
    // ...
  private:
    // Invocation categories: MOVE and GET
    CAT cat_;
};
```

A publicly readable shape defines `GetDataPredicate` to allow concurrent execution of `getData` invocations. Class `MoveByPredicate` restricts invocations of `moveBy` to the shape's owner and forbids concurrent execution of `moveBy` invocations. Operation `getData` is a read operation, while `moveBy` is a *private* write operation.

```
// prevents conflicts with executing moveBy
X_Status GetDataPredicate::preGuard() {
  // iterator for predicates
  PIterator iter(sync_);
  SynchronizationPredicate *pred;
  while (pred = iter.next(), pred != 0)
    // there are moveBy invocations executing
    if ((pred->getStatus() == EXEC) &&
      (((ShapePredicate*)pred)->getCat() == MOVE))
      // conflict
      return DELAY;
  // no conflict
  return CONTINUE;
}


// prevents conflicts with executing getData and moveBy
X_Status MoveByPredicate::preGuard() {
  // iterator for predicates
  PIterator iter(sync_);
  SynchronizationPredicate *pred;
  while (pred = iter.next(), pred != 0)
    // there are invocations executing
    if ((pred->getStatus() == EXEC))
      // conflict
      return DELAY;
  // no conflict
  return CONTINUE;
}


// requires that invoker is shape's owner
X_Status MoveByPredicate::require() {
  // InvOwner global function returns invoker id
  // sd_ is an instance of a Synchronization Data
  // subclass which contains the shape's owner
  if (InvOwner() == sd_->owner())
    return CONTINUE;
  return ERROR;
}
```

A publicly writable shape allows any user to move the shape. The synchronization predicates are identical to publicly readable shape's synchronization predicates except for predicate `MoveByPredicate`, which has to relax the `require` operation.

```
// publicly writable moveBy require
// any user can move the shape
X_Status MoveByPredicate::require() {
  return CONTINUE;
}
```

Known Uses

The need for object synchronization is widely recognized in concurrent programming languages, object-oriented databases, and distributed object systems. Most solutions to this problem restrict the supported number of policies and do not decouple synchronization from concurrency.

Distributed systems, for example, Arjuna [Shrivastava+1991] and Hermes/ST [Fazzolare+1993], use the Object Synchronizer pattern encapsulated by platform mechanisms. Arjuna defines two classes, `Lock` and `LockManager`: class `Lock-Manager` supports a pessimistic synchronization policy, while class `Lock` contains object-specific information. Programmers only need to redefine `Lock` operations. In Hermes there are two kinds of synchronization: implicit and explicit. Implicit synchronization offers a transparent pessimistic policy to synchronize invocations with attribute granularity; explicit synchronization uses the object's state. Explicit synchronization defines class `ProgrammableLock`, which has two operations: `isScheduable` and `isCompatibleWith`. The former uses the object's state while the latter defines the compatibility between operations.

Scheduling predicates were defined by [McHale+1991] in the context of a concurrent object-oriented language. That language contains the identical abstractions and synchronization expressiveness as the Object Synchronizer pattern.

The Object Synchronizer pattern is integrated with other design patterns: Object Concurrency [Silva1999] and Object Recovery [Silva+1997]. It is implemented as part of an object-oriented framework that supports object concurrency, synchronization, and recovery [Silva1998]. This framework is publicly available from http://www.esw.inesc.pt/~ars/dasco.

Related Patterns

The Active Object pattern [Lavender+1996] decouples operation execution from operation invocation to simplify synchronized accesses to a shared resource. The active object has an internal thread that dispatches pending operations. The internal thread can do some synchronization when selecting the next operation to dispatch. The Object Synchronizer abstracts synchronization policies independently of a particular implementation of object concurrency such as active object.

The Object Recovery pattern [Silva+1997] abstracts several policies for object recovery. Combined with the Object Synchronizer pattern it allows specialization of synchronization policies that need to recover the object's state, for example, optimistic policies. However, some combinations of synchronization and recovery policies are not possible or, though possible, penalize performance. It has been proven that some compatibility relations between invocations require a particular kind of recovery policy [Weihl1993]; for example, forward commutativity requires an update-in-place recovery policy. Common combinations are optimistic policies and deferred-update recovery policies, in which simultaneous invocations proceed on a copy of the object (optimized abort), and pessimistic policies with update-in-place recovery policies (optimized commit), in which invocations proceed on the same object.

The Proxy pattern [Gamma+1995] is used to control accesses to the `Functional Object`. `Functional Object` corresponds to `RealSubject`, while `Synchronization Interface` corresponds to `Proxy`. The `Functional Object` does not know anything about the `Synchronization Interface`.

The Strategy pattern [Gamma+1995] is used between the `Synchronization Interface` and the `Synchronizer`. It provides the configuration of `Synchronization Interface` with synchronization policies.

ACKNOWLEDGMENTS

Thanks to our colleagues Pedro Sousa, David Matos, Luís Gil, and João Martins. We also thank the participants of the EuroPLoP '96 writers workshop on Distribution.

REFERENCES

[Decouchant+1991] D. Decouchant, P. Le Dot, M. Riveill, C. Roisin, and X. Pina. "A Synchronization Mechanism for an Object-Oriented Distributed System. In *Proceedings of the 11th International Conference on Distributed Computing Systems,* Arlington, TX, May 1991, pp. 152–159.

[Dijkstra1968] E.W. Dijkstra. "Cooperating Sequential Processes." In F. Genuys (ed.), *Programming Languages,* pp. 43–112. New York: Academic Press, 1968.

[Fazzolare+1993] M. Fazzolare, B.G. Humm, and R.D. Ranson. "Concurrency Control for Distributed Nested Transactions in Hermes." International Conference on Parallel and Distributed Systems, Taipei, Taiwan, 1993.

[Fowler+1997] M. Fowler and K. Scott. *UML Distilled: Applying the Standard Object Modeling Language.* Reading, MA: Addison-Wesley, 1997.

[Gamma+1995] E. Gamma, R. Helm, R. Johnson, and J. Vlissides. *Design Patterns: Elements of Reusable Object-Oriented Software.* Reading, MA: Addison-Wesley, 1994.

[Hoare1974] C.A.R. Hoare. "Monitors: An Operating System Structuring Concept." *Communications of the ACM,* 17(10), pp. 549–557, 1974.

[Lavender+1996] R. Lavender and D.C. Schmidt. "Active Object: An Object Behavioral Pattern for Concurrent Programming." In J.M. Vlissides, J.O. Coplien, and N.L. Kerth (eds.), *Pattern Languages of Program Design 2*, pp. 483–499. Reading, MA: Addison-Wesley, 1996.

[McHale+1991] C. McHale, B. Walsh, S. Baker, and A. Donnelly. "Scheduling Predicates." In M. Tokoro, O. Nierstrasz, and P. Wegner (eds.), *Proceedings of the ECOOP '91 Workshop on Object-Based Concurrent Computing*, Vol. 612, pp. 177–193. New York: Springer-Verlag, 1991.

[Shrivastava+1991] S.K. Shrivastava, G.N. Dixon, and G.D. Parrington. "An Overview of the Arjuna Distributed Programming System." *IEEE Software*, January 1991, pp. 66–33.

[Silva1999] A.R. Silva. *Concurrent Object-Oriented Programming: Separation and Composition of Concerns Using Design Patterns, Pattern Languages, and Object-Oriented Frameworks*. PhD thesis, Instituto Superior Técnico—Technical University of Lisbon, March 1999.

[Silva1998] A.R. Silva. "Development and Extension of a Three-Layered Framework. In Saba Zamir (ed.), *Handbook of Object Technology*. New York: CRC Press, 1998.

[Silva+1997] A.R. Silva, J. Pereira, and J.A. Marques. "Object Recovery." In R. Martin, D. Riehle, and F. Buschman (eds.), *Pattern Languages of Program Design 3*, pp. 261–276. Reading, MA: Addison-Wesley, 1997.

[Weihl1993] W. Weihl. "The Impact of Recovery in Concurrency Control." *Journal of Computer and System Sciences*, 47(1):157–184, 1993.

António Rito Silva may be reached at Rito.Silva@acm.org.

João Pereira may be reached at Jao.Pereira@irria.fr.

José Alves Marques may be reached at jam@inesc.pt.

Chapter 9

Proactor

Irfan Pyarali, Tim Harrison,
Douglas C. Schmidt, and Thomas D. Jordan

Modern operating systems provide multiple mechanisms for developing concurrent applications. Synchronous multi-threading is a popular mechanism for developing applications that perform multiple operations simultaneously. However, threads often have high performance overhead and require deep knowledge of synchronization patterns and principles. Therefore, an increasing number of operating systems support asynchronous mechanisms that provide the benefits of concurrency while alleviating much of the overhead and complexity of multi-threading.

The Proactor pattern presented in this chapter describes how to structure applications and systems that effectively utilize asynchronous mechanisms supported by operating systems. When an application invokes an asynchronous operation, the OS performs the operation on behalf of the application. This allows the application to have multiple operations running simultaneously without requiring the application to have a corresponding number of threads. Proactor simplifies concurrent programming and improves performance by requiring fewer threads and leveraging OS support for asynchronous operations.

Intent

The Proactor pattern supports the demultiplexing and dispatching of multiple event handlers, which are triggered by the *completion* of asynchronous events. This pattern simplifies asynchronous application development by integrating the demultiplexing of completion events and the dispatching of their corresponding event handlers.

Context and Forces

The Proactor pattern should be applied when applications require the performance benefits of executing operations concurrently, without incurring the drawbacks of synchronous multi-threaded or reactive programming. To illustrate this pattern, consider a networking application that needs to perform multiple operations concurrently. For example, a high-performance Web server must concurrently process HTTP requests sent from multiple clients [Hu+1977, 1978]. Figure 9-1 shows a typical interaction between Web browsers and a Web server. When a user instructs a browser to open a URL, the browser sends an HTTP GET request to the Web server. Upon receipt, the server parses and validates the request and sends the specified file(s) back to the browser.

Developing high-performance Web servers requires the resolution of the following forces:

- *Concurrency.* The server must perform multiple client requests simultaneously.
- *Efficiency.* The server must minimize latency, maximize throughput, and avoid utilizing the CPU(s) unnecessarily.
- *Programming simplicity.* The design of the server should simplify the use of efficient concurrency strategies.
- *Adaptability.* Integrating new or improved transport protocols, such as HTTP 1.1 [Mogul1995], should incur minimal maintenance costs.

A Web server can be implemented using several concurrency strategies, including multiple synchronous threads, reactive synchronous event dispatching, and proactive asynchronous event dispatching. Below, we examine the drawbacks of

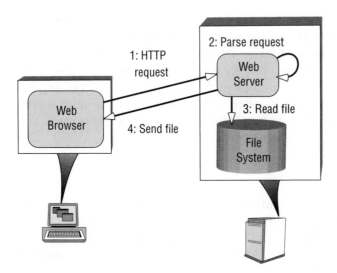

Figure 9-1 *Typical Web server communication software architecture*

conventional approaches and explain how the Proactor pattern provides a powerful architecture that supports an efficient and flexible asynchronous event dispatching strategy for high-performance concurrent applications.

Common Traps and Pitfalls of Conventional Concurrency Models

Synchronous multi-threading and reactive programming are common techniques for achieving concurrency. This section describes the shortcomings of these programming models.

Concurrency through Multiple Synchronous Threads.   Perhaps the most intuitive way to implement a concurrent Web server is to use *synchronous multi-threading*. In this model, multiple server threads process HTTP GET requests from multiple clients simultaneously. Each thread performs connection establishment, HTTP request reading, request parsing, and file transfer operations synchronously. As a result, each operation blocks until it completes.

The primary advantage of synchronous threading is the simplification of application code. In particular, operations performed by a Web server to service client A's request are largely independent of the operations required to service client B's request. It is easy to service different requests in separate threads because the amount of state shared between the threads is low, which minimizes the need for synchronization. Moreover, executing application logic in separate threads allows developers to utilize intuitive sequential commands and blocking I/O operations.

Figure 9-2 shows how a Web server designed using synchronous threads can process multiple clients concurrently. This figure shows a Sync Acceptor object that encapsulates the server-side mechanism for accepting network connections synchronously. The sequence of steps that each thread executes to service an HTTP GET request using a thread-per-connection concurrency model can be summarized as follows:

1. Each thread blocks synchronously in the Accept socket call waiting for a client connection request.
2. A client connects to the server, and the connection is accepted.
3. The new client's HTTP request is read synchronously from the network connection.
4. The request is parsed.
5. The requested file is read synchronously.
6. The file is sent synchronously to the client.

A C++ code example that applies the synchronous threading model to a Web server appears in Appendix A.1.

As described earlier, each concurrently connected client is serviced by a dedicated server thread. The thread completes a requested operation synchronously before

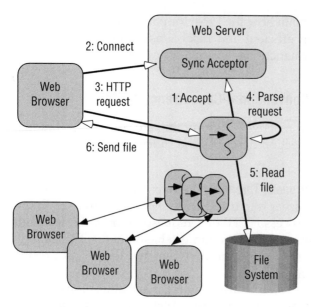

Figure 9-2 *Multi-threaded Web server model*

servicing other HTTP requests. Therefore, to perform synchronous I/O while servicing multiple clients, the Web server must spawn multiple threads. Although this synchronous multi-threaded model is intuitive and maps relatively efficiently onto multi-CPU platforms, it has the following drawbacks:

- *Threading policy is tightly coupled to the concurrency policy.* The synchronous threading model requires a dedicated thread for each connected client. A concurrent application may be better optimized by aligning its threading strategy to available resources, such as the number of CPUs via a thread pool, rather than to the number of clients being serviced concurrently.
- *Increased synchronization complexity.* Threading can increase the complexity of synchronization mechanisms necessary to serialize access to a server's shared resources, such as cached files and logging of Web page hits.
- *Increased performance overhead.* Threading can perform poorly due to context switching, synchronization, and data movement among CPUs [Schmidt1994].
- *Nonportability.* Threading may not be available on all OS platforms. Moreover, OS platforms differ widely in terms of their support for preemptive and non-preemptive threads. Consequently, it is hard to build multi-threaded servers that behave uniformly across OS platforms.

As a result of these drawbacks, synchronous threading models can lead to inefficient and complex concurrent Web servers.

Concurrency through Reactive Synchronous Event Dispatching.   Another common way to implement a synchronous Web server is to use a *reactive event dispatching model*. The Reactor pattern [Schmidt1995] describes how applications can register Event Handlers with an Initiation Dispatcher. The Initiation Dispatcher notifies the Event Handler when it is possible to initiate an operation without blocking.

A single-threaded concurrent Web server can use a reactive event dispatching model that waits in an event loop for a Reactor to notify it to initiate appropriate operations. An example of a reactive operation in the Web server is the registration of an Acceptor [Schmidt1997] with the Initiation Dispatcher. When a client establishes a new connection with the Web server, the dispatcher calls back the Acceptor. The Acceptor accepts the network connection and creates an HTTP Handler. This HTTP Handler then registers with the Reactor to process the incoming URL request on that connection in the Web server's single thread of control.

Figures 9-3 and 9-4 show how a Web server designed using reactive event dispatching handles multiple clients. Figure 9-3 shows the steps taken when a client connects to the Web server. Figure 9-4 shows how the Web server processes a client request. The sequence of steps for Figure 9-3 can be summarized as follows:

1. The Web server registers an Acceptor with the Initiation Dispatcher to accept new connections.
2. The Web server invokes the Initiation Dispatcher's event loop.

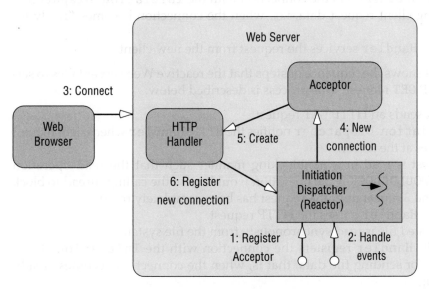

Figure 9-3   *Client connects to reactive Web server*

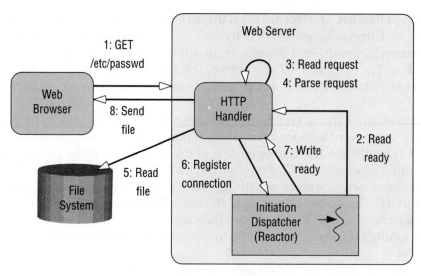

Figure 9-4 *Client sends HTTP request to reactive Web server*

3. A client connects to the Web server.
4. The **Acceptor** is notified by the **Initiation Dispatcher** of the new connection request, and the **Acceptor** accepts the new connection.
5. The **Acceptor** creates an **HTTP Handler** to service the new client.
6. **HTTP Handler** registers the connection with the **Initiation Dispatcher** for reading client request data, i.e., when the connection becomes "ready for reading."
7. The **HTTP Handler** services the request from the new client.

Figure 9-4 shows the sequence of steps that the reactive Web server takes to service an HTTP GET request. This process is described below:

1. The client sends an HTTP GET request.
2. The **Initiation Dispatcher** notifies the **HTTP Handler** when client request data arrives at the server.
3. The request is read in a nonblocking manner such that the read operation returns **EWOULDBLOCK** if the operation would cause the calling thread to block (steps 2 and 3 repeat until the request has been completely read).
4. The **HTTP Handler** parses the HTTP request.
5. The requested file is read synchronously from the file system.
6. The **HTTP Handler** registers the connection with the **Initiation Dispatcher** for sending file data, that is, when the connection becomes "ready for writing."
7. The **Initiation Dispatcher** notifies the **HTTP Handler** when the TCP connection is ready for writing.

8. The HTTP Handler sends the requested file to the client in a nonblocking manner such that the write operation returns EWOULDBLOCK if the operation would cause the calling thread to block (steps 7 and 8 will repeat until the data has been delivered completely).

A C++ code example that applies the reactive event dispatching model to a Web server appears in Appendix A.2.

Since the Initiation Dispatcher runs in a single thread, network I/O operations are run under the control of the Reactor in a nonblocking manner. If forward progress is stalled on the current operation, the operation is handed off to the Initiation Dispatcher, which monitors the status of the system operation. When the operation can make forward progress again, the appropriate Event Handler is notified.

The main advantages of the reactive model are (1) portability, (2) low overhead due to coarse-grained concurrency control (i.e., single-threading requires no synchronization or context switching), and (3) modularity due to decoupling of application logic from dispatching mechanism. However, this approach has the following drawbacks:

- *Complex programming.* As seen in Appendix A.2, programmers must write complicated logic to ensure the server does not block while servicing a particular client.
- *Lack of OS support for multi-threading.* Many operating systems implement the reactive dispatching model through the select system call [McKusick+ 1996]. However, select does not allow more than one thread to wait in the event loop on the same descriptor set. This makes the reactive model unsuitable for high-performance applications since it does not utilize hardware parallelism effectively.
- *Scheduling of runnable tasks.* In synchronous multi-threading architectures that support preemptive threads, it is the operating system's responsibility to schedule and time-slice the runnable threads onto the available CPUs. This scheduling support is not available in reactive architectures since there is only one thread in the application. Therefore, developers of the system must carefully time-share the thread between all the clients connected to the Web server. This can be accomplished by only performing short duration, nonblocking operations.

As a result of these drawbacks, reactive event dispatching is not the most efficient model when hardware parallelism is available. Moreover, this model has a relatively high level of programming complexity in order to avoid blocking I/O operations.

Solution: Concurrency through Proactive Operations

When the OS platform supports asynchronous operations, an efficient and convenient way to implement a high-performance Web server is to use *proactive event dispatching*. Web servers designed using a proactive event dispatching model handle the *completion* of asynchronous operations with one or more threads of control. Thus, the Proactor pattern *simplifies asynchronous Web servers by integrating completion event demultiplexing and event handler dispatching.*

An asynchronous Web server can apply the Proactor pattern by first having the Web server issue an asynchronous operation to the OS and registering a callback with a `Completion Dispatcher` that will notify the Web server when the operation completes. The OS then performs the operation on behalf of the Web server and subsequently queues the result in a well-known location. The `Completion Dispatcher` is responsible for dequeueing completion notifications and executing the appropriate callback that contains application-specific Web server code.

Figures 9-5 and 9-6 show how a Web server designed using proactive event dispatching handles multiple clients concurrently within one or more threads. Figure 9-5 shows the sequence of steps taken when a client connects to the Web server.

1. The Web server instructs the `Acceptor` to initiate an asynchronous accept.
2. The Acceptor initiates an asynchronous accept with the OS and passes itself as a `Completion Handler` and a reference to the `Completion Dispatcher` that will be used to notify the `Acceptor` upon completion of the asynchronous accept.
3. The Web server invokes the event loop of the `Completion Dispatcher`.
4. The client connects to the Web server.
5. When the asynchronous accept operation completes, the `Operating System` notifies the `Completion Dispatcher`.

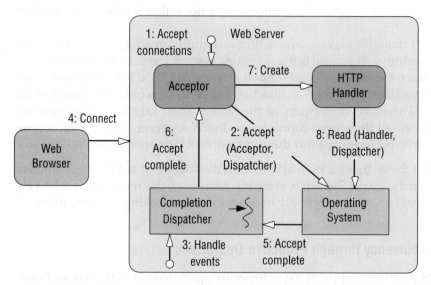

Figure 9-5 *Client connects to a Proactor-based Web server*

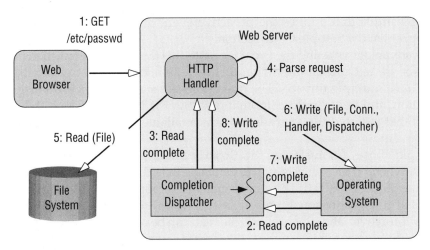

Figure 9-6 *Client sends requests to a proactor-based Web server*

6. The `Completion Dispatcher` notifies the `Acceptor`.
7. The `Acceptor` creates an `HTTP Handler`.
8. The `HTTP Handler` initiates an asynchronous operation to read the request data from the client and passes itself as a `Completion Handler` and a reference to the `Completion Dispatcher` that will be used to notify the `HTTP Handler` upon completion of the asynchronous read.

Figure 9-6 shows the sequence of steps that the proactive Web server takes to service an HTTP GET request. These steps are explained below:

1. The client sends an HTTP GET request.
2. The read operation completes and the `Operating System` notifies the `Completion Dispatcher`.
3. The `Completion Dispatcher` notifies the `HTTP Handler`.
4. The `HTTP Handler` parses the request (steps 2 through 4 will repeat until the entire request has been received).
5. The `HTTP Handler` reads the requested file synchronously.
6. The `HTTP Handler` initiates an asynchronous operation to write the file data to the client connection and passes itself as a `Completion Handler` and a reference to the `Completion Dispatcher` that will be used to notify the `HTTP Handler` upon completion of the asynchronous write.
7. When the write operation completes, the Operating System notifies the `Completion Dispatcher`.
8. The `Completion Dispatcher` then notifies the `Completion Handler` (steps 6 through 8 continue until the file has been delivered completely).

A C++ code example that applies the proactive event dispatching model to a Web server appears in the Sample Code section.

The primary advantage of using the Proactor pattern is that multiple concurrent operations can be started and can run in parallel without necessarily requiring the application to have multiple threads. The operations are started asynchronously by the application, and they run to completion within the I/O subsystem of the OS. The thread that initiated the operation is now available to service additional requests.

In the example above, for instance, the `Completion Dispatcher` can be single-threaded. When HTTP requests arrive, the single `Completion Dispatcher` thread parses the request, reads the file, and sends the response to the client. Since the response is sent asynchronously, multiple responses can potentially be sent simultaneously. Moreover, the synchronous file read can be replaced with an asynchronous file read to further increase the potential for concurrency. If the file read is performed asynchronously, the only synchronous operation performed by an `HTTP Handler` is the HTTP protocol request parsing.

The primary drawback with the Proactive model is that the programming logic is at least as complicated as the Reactive model. Moreover, the Proactor pattern can be difficult to debug since asynchronous operations often have a nonpredictable and nonrepeatable execution sequence, which complicates analysis and debugging. The Implementation section describes how to apply other patterns, such as the Asynchronous Completion Token [Pyarali+1997], to simplify the programming model for asynchronous applications.

Applicability

Use the Proactor pattern when one or more of the following conditions hold:

- An application needs to perform one or more asynchronous operations without blocking the calling thread.
- The application must be notified when asynchronous operations *complete*.
- The application needs to vary its concurrency strategy independent of its I/O model.
- The application will benefit by decoupling the application-dependent logic from the application-independent infrastructure.
- An application will perform poorly or fail to meet its performance requirements when utilizing either the multi-threaded approach or the reactive dispatching approach.

Structure and Participants

The structure of the Proactor pattern is illustrated in Figure 9-7 using UML notation. The key participants in the Proactor pattern include the following:

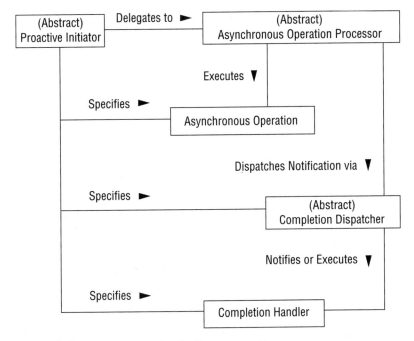

Figure 9-7 *Participants in the Proactor pattern*

- *Proactive Initiator* (Web server application's main thread).   A `Proactive Initiator` can be any entity in the application that initiates an `Asynchronous Operation`. The `Proactive Initiator` registers a `Completion Handler` and a `Completion Dispatcher` with an `Asynchronous Operation Processor`, which notifies it when the operation completes.
- *Completion Handler* (the `Acceptor` and `HTTP Handler`).   The Proactor pattern uses `Completion Handler` interfaces that are implemented by the application for `Asynchronous Operation` completion notification.
- *Asynchronous Operation* (the methods `Async_Read`, `Async_Write`, and `Async_Accept`).   `Asynchronous Operations` are used to execute requests, such as I/O and timer operations, on behalf of applications. When applications invoke `Asynchronous Operations`, the operations are performed *without* borrowing the application's thread of control.[1] Therefore, from the application's perspective, the operations are performed *asynchronously*. When `Asynchronous Operations` complete, the `Asynchronous Operation Processor` delegates application notifications to a `Completion Dispatcher`.

---

[1] In contrast, the reactive event dispatching model [Schmidt1995] steals the application's thread of control to perform the operation synchronously.

- *Asynchronous Operation Processor* (the Operating System). `Asynchronous Operations` are run to completion by the `Asynchronous Operation Processor`. This component is typically implemented by the OS.
- *Completion Dispatcher* (the Notification Queue). The `Completion Dispatcher` is responsible for calling back to the application's `Completion Handlers` when `Asynchronous Operations` complete. When the `Asynchronous Operation Processor` completes an operation initiated asynchronously, the `Completion Dispatcher` performs an application callback on its behalf.

Collaborations

There are several well-defined steps that occur for all `Asynchronous Operations`. At a high level of abstraction, applications initiate operations asynchronously and are notified when the operations complete. Figure 9-8 shows the interactions that must occur between the pattern participants:

1. *Proactive Initiator initiates operation.* To perform asynchronous operations, the application initiates the operation on the `Asynchronous Operation Processor`. For instance, a Web server might instruct the OS to transmit a file over the network using a particular socket connection. To request such an operation, the Web server must specify which file and network connection to use. Moreover, the Web server must specify (1) which `Completion Handler` to notify when the operation completes and (2) which `Completion Dispatcher` should perform the callback once the file is transmitted.
2. *Asynchronous Operation Processor performs operation.* When the application invokes operations on the `Asynchronous Operation Processor`, it runs them asynchronously with respect to other application operations. Modern operating systems, such as Solaris and Windows NT, provide asynchronous I/O subsystems within the kernel.
3. *The Asynchronous Operation Processor notifies the Completion Dispatcher.* When operations complete, the `Asynchronous Operation Processor` retrieves the `Completion Handler` and `Completion Dispatcher` that were specified when the operation was initiated. The `Asynchronous Operation Processor` then passes the `Completion Dispatcher` the result of the `Asynchronous Operation` and the `Completion Handler` to call back. For instance, if a file was transmitted asynchronously, the `Asynchronous Operation Processor` may report the completion status, such as success or failure, as well as the number of bytes written to the network connection.
4. *Completion Dispatcher notifies the application.* The `Completion Dispatcher` calls the completion hook on the `Completion Handler`, passing it any completion data specified by the application. For instance, if an asynchronous read completes, the `Completion Handler` will typically be passed a pointer to the newly arrived data.

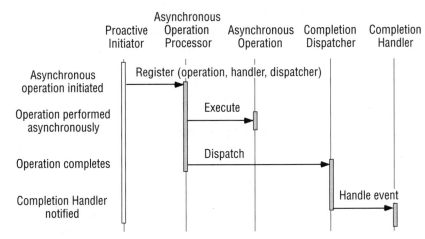

Figure 9-8 *Interaction diagram for the Proactor pattern*

Consequences

The Proactor pattern offers the following benefits:

- *Increased separation of concerns.* Proactor decouples application-independent asynchrony mechanisms from application-specific functionality. The application-independent mechanisms become reusable components that know how to demultiplex the completion events associated with `Asynchronous Operations` and dispatch the appropriate callback methods defined by the `Completion Handlers`. Likewise, the application-specific functionality knows how to perform a particular type of service, such as HTTP processing.

- *Improved application logic portability.* Proactor improves application portability by allowing its interface to be reused independently of the underlying OS calls that perform event demultiplexing. These system calls detect and report the events that may occur simultaneously on multiple event sources. Event sources may include I/O ports, timers, synchronization objects, signals, etc. For instance, on real-time POSIX platforms, the asynchronous I/O functions are provided by the `aio` family of APIs [Information Technology1995]. Likewise, on Windows NT, I/O completion ports and overlapped I/O are used to implement asynchronous I/O [Microsoft1996].

- *The Completion Dispatcher encapsulates the concurrency mechanism.* A benefit of decoupling the `Completion Dispatcher` from the `Asynchronous Operation Processor` is that applications can configure `Completion Dispatchers` with various concurrency strategies without affecting other participants. As discussed in the section on Implementation, the `Completion Dispatcher` can be configured to use several concurrency strategies including single-threaded and thread pool solutions.

- *Threading policy is decoupled from the concurrency policy.* Since the Asynchronous Operation Processor completes potentially long-running operations on behalf of Proactive Initiators, applications are not forced to spawn threads to increase concurrency. This allows an application to vary its concurrency policy independently of its threading policy. For instance, a Web server may only want to have one thread per CPU but may want to service a higher number of clients simultaneously.

- *Increased performance.* Multi-threaded operating systems perform context switches to cycle through multiple threads of control. While the time to perform a context switch remains fairly constant, the total time to cycle through a large number of threads can degrade application performance significantly if the OS context switches to an idle thread.[2] For instance, threads may poll the OS for completion status, which is inefficient. Proactor can avoid the cost of context switching by activating only those logical threads of control that have events to process. For instance, a Web server need not activate an HTTP Handler if no GET request is pending.

- *Simplification of application synchronization.* As long as Completion Handlers do not spawn additional threads of control, application logic can be written with little or no regard to synchronization issues. Completion Handlers can be written as if they existed in a conventional single-threaded environment. For instance, a Web server's HTTP GET Handler can access the disk through an Async_Read operation, such as the Windows NT TransmitFile function [Hu+1997], and hence no additional threads need be spawned.

The Proactor pattern has the following liabilities:

- *Hard to debug.* Applications written with the Proactor pattern can be hard to debug since the inverted flow of control oscillates between the framework infrastructure and the method callbacks on application-specific handlers. This increases the difficulty of "single-stepping" through the runtime behavior of a framework within a debugger because application developers may not understand or have access to the framework code. This is similar to the problems encountered trying to debug a compiler's lexical analyzer and parser written with lex and yacc. In these applications, debugging is straightforward when the thread of control is within the user-defined action routines. Once the thread of control returns to the generated Deterministic Finite Automata (DFA) skeleton, however, it is hard to follow the program logic.

- *Scheduling and controlling outstanding operations.* The Proactive Initiators may not be able to control the order in which Asynchronous Operations are executed by an Asynchronous Operation Processor. Therefore, an Asynchronous Operation Processor should be designed to support prioritization and cancellation of Asynchronous Operations.

---

[2] Some older operating systems exhibit this behavior, but most modern operating systems do not.

Implementation

This section discusses the steps involved in implementing the Proactor pattern. The implementation described below is influenced by the reusable components provided in the ACE communication software framework [Schmidt1994].

Implement the Asynchronous Operation Processor. The first step in implementing the Proactor pattern is building the `Asynchronous Operation Processor`. The `Asynchronous Operation Processor` is responsible for executing operations asynchronously on behalf of applications. As a result, its two primary responsibilities are exporting `Asynchronous Operation` APIs and implementing an `Asynchronous Operation Engine` to do the work.

Define the Asynchronous Operation APIs. The `Asynchronous Operation Processor` must provide an API that allows applications to request `Asynchronous Operations`. There are several forces to be considered when designing these APIs:

Portability. The APIs should not tie an application or its `Proactive Initiators` to a particular platform.

Flexibility. Often, asynchronous APIs can be shared for many types of operations. For instance, asynchronous I/O operations can often be used to perform I/O on multiple mediums, such as network and files. It may be beneficial to design APIs that support such reuse.

Callbacks. The `Proactive Initiators` must register a callback when the operation is invoked. A common callback implementation is to have the calling objects (clients) export an interface known by the caller (server). Therefore, `Proactive Initiators` must inform the `Asynchronous Operation Processor` which `Completion Handler` should be called back when an operation completes.

Completion Dispatcher. Since an application may use multiple `Completion Dispatchers`, the `Proactive Initiator` also must indicate which `Completion Dispatcher` should perform the callback.

Given all of these concerns, consider the following API for asynchronous reads and writes. The `Asynch_Stream` class is a factory for initiating asynchronous reads and writes. Once constructed, multiple asynchronous reads and writes can be started using this class. An `Asynch_Stream::Read_Result` will be passed back to the `handler` when the asynchronous read completes via the `handle_read` callback on the `Completion_Handler`. Similarly, an `Asynch_Stream::Write_Result` will be passed back to the `handler` when the asynchronous write completes via the `handle_write` callback on the `Completion_Handler`.

```
class Asynch_Stream
  // = TITLE
  // A Factory for initiating reads
  // and writes asynchronously.
{
  // Initializes the factory with information
  // which will be used with each asynchronous
  // call. <handler> is notified when the
  // operation completes. The asynchronous
  // operations are performed on the <handle>
  // and the results of the operations are
  // sent to the <Completion_Dispatcher>.
  Asynch_Stream (Completion_Handler &handler,
                 HANDLE handle,
                 Completion_Dispatcher *);

  // This starts off an asynchronous read.
  // Up to <bytes_to_read> will be read and
  // stored in the <message_block>.
  int read (Message_Block &message_block,
            u_long bytes_to_read,
            const void *act = 0);

  // This starts off an asynchronous write.
  // Up to <bytes_to_write> will be written
  // from the <message_block>.
  int write (Message_Block &message_block,
             u_long bytes_to_write,
             const void *act = 0);
  ...
};
```

Implement the Asynchronous Operation Engine. The Asynchronous Operation Processor must contain a mechanism that performs the operations asynchronously. In other words, when an application thread invokes an Asynchronous Operation, the operation must be performed without borrowing the application's thread of control. Fortunately, modern operating systems provide mechanisms for Asynchronous Operations, for example, POSIX asynchronous I/O and WinNT overlapped I/O. When this is the case, implementing this part of the pattern simply requires mapping the platform APIs to the Asynchronous Operation APIs described above.

If the OS platform does not provide support for Asynchronous Operations, there are several implementation techniques that can be used to build an Asynchronous Operation Engine. Perhaps the most intuitive solution is to use dedicated threads to perform the Asynchronous Operations for applications. To implement a threaded Asynchronous Operation Engine, there are three primary steps:

1. *Operation invocation.* Because the operation will be performed in a different thread of control from the invoking application thread, some type of thread synchronization must occur. One approach would be to spawn a thread for each operation. A more common approach is for the Asynchronous Operation Processor to control a pool of dedicated threads. This approach would require that the application thread queue the operation request before continuing with other application computations.

2. *Operation execution.* Since the operation will be performed in a dedicated thread, it can perform "blocking" operations without directly impeding progress of the application. For instance, when providing a mechanism for asynchronous I/O reads, the dedicated thread can block while reading from socket or file handles.

3. *Operation completion.* When the operation completes, the application must be notified. In particular, the dedicated thread must delegate application-specific notifications to the Completion Dispatcher. This will require additional synchronization between threads.

Implement the Completion Dispatcher. The Completion Dispatcher calls back to the Completion Handler that is associated with the application objects when it receives operation completions from the Asynchronous Operation Processor. There are two issues involved with implementing the Completion Dispatcher: (1) implementing callbacks and (2) defining completion dispatcher concurrency strategies.

Implementing Callbacks. The Completion Dispatcher must implement a mechanism through which Completion Handlers are invoked. This requires Proactive Initiators to specify a callback when initiating operations. The following are common callback alternatives:

Callback class. The Completion Handler exports an interface known by the Completion Dispatcher. The Completion Dispatcher calls back on a method in this interface when the operation completes and passes it information about the completed operation, such as the number of bytes read from the network connection.

Function pointer. The Completion Dispatcher invokes the Completion Handler via a callback function pointer. This approach reduces the dependency between the Completion Dispatcher and the Completion Handler to a function prototype rather than an interface. The primary benefit is that the Completion Handler is not forced to export a specific interface.

Rendezvous. The Proactive Initiator can establish an event object or a condition variable, which serves as a rendezvous between the Completion Dispatcher and the Completion Handler. This is most common when the Completion Handler is the Proactive Initiator. While the Asynchronous Operation runs to completion, the Completion Handler processes other activity. Periodically, the Completion Handler will check at the rendezvous point for completion status.

Defining Completion Dispatcher Concurrency Strategies. A Completion Dispatcher will be notified by the Asynchronous Operation Processor when operations complete. At this point, the Completion Dispatcher can use one of the following concurrency strategies to perform the application callback:

Dynamic-thread dispatching. A thread can be dynamically allocated for each Completion Handler by the Completion Dispatcher. Dynamic-thread dispatching can be implemented with most multi-threaded operating systems. On some platforms, this may be the least efficient technique of those listed for Completion Dispatcher implementations due to the overhead of creating and destroying thread resources.

Postreactive dispatching. An event object or condition variable established by the Proactive Initiator can be signaled by the Completion Dispatcher. Although polling and spawning a child thread that blocks on the event object are options, the most efficient method for post-reactive dispatching is to register the event with a Reactor. Post-reactive dispatching can be implemented with aio_suspend in POSIX real-time environments and with WaitForMultipleObjects in Win32 environments.

Call-through dispatching. In this model, the thread of control blocked in a synchronous operation is borrowed by the Asynchronous Operation Processor to execute a Completion Handler via the Completion Dispatcher. This "cycle stealing" strategy can increase performance by decreasing the incidence of idle threads. This is particularly useful when a single-threaded application wants to perform proactive I/O while still occasionally executing synchronous operations.

One way to implement call-through dispatching in Windows NT is via the Win32 functions ReadFileEx and WaitForSingleObjectEx. A thread of control can initiate an asynchronous read operation via ReadFileEx passing a Completion Handler as a parameter. After the read operation is initiated, the same thread might call the WaitForSingleObjectEx function to wait synchronously for an unrelated event to be signaled. When WaitForSingleObjectEx is called, the thread informs the OS that it is entering into a special state known as an "alertable wait state." Therefore, when the read operation completes, the OS can borrow the thread blocked in `WaitForSingleObjectEx` to dispatch the `Completion Handler` registered when `ReadFileEx` was called. In this case, the Windows NT operating system is both the `Asynchronous Operation Processor` and the `Completion Dispatcher`.

Thread pool dispatching. A pool of threads owned by the `Completion Dispatcher` can be used for `Completion Handler` execution. Each thread of control in the pool has been dynamically allocated to an available CPU. Thread pool dispatching can be implemented with Windows NT's I/O Completion Ports.

When considering the applicability of the `Completion Dispatcher` techniques described above, consider the possible combinations of OS environments and physical hardware shown in Table 9-1.

If your OS only supports synchronous I/O, then refer to the Reactor pattern [Schmidt1995]. However, most modern operating systems support some form of asynchronous I/O.

For single-threaded applications (combination A and B from Table 9-1), the correct concurrency strategy depends on the type of operations that will be performed. If an application will only be performing proactive asynchronous operations, then a thread pool of size one can be used. If an application will be performing reactive synchronous operations as well as proactive asynchronous operations, then post-reactive dispatching should be used. Lastly, if the single-threaded application needs to occasionally perform long-blocking synchronous operations, call-through dispatching should be used.

For multi-threaded applications (combinations C and D) any of the dispatching techniques can be appropriate. Oftentimes, systematic empirical measurements are the only way to make the best selection. For instance, multi-threaded solutions running on single-processor systems can decrease performance for compute-bound applications by increasing context switching overhead. In contrast, a single-processor, multi-threaded solution can sometimes increase performance for I/O-bound applications by allowing the OS and threading package to overlap computation and communication.

Table 9-1   `Completion Dispatcher` *Concurrency Strategies*

Threading Model	System Type	
	Single-processor	Multi-processor
Single-threaded	A	B
Multi-threaded	C	D

Implement Completion Handlers. The implementation of `Completion Handlers` raises the following concerns.

- *State integrity.* A `Completion Handler` may need to maintain state information concerning a specific request. For instance, the OS may notify the Web server that only part of a file was written to the network communication port. As a result, a `Completion Handler` may need to reissue the request until the file is fully written or the connection becomes invalid. Therefore, it must know the file that was originally specified, how many bytes are left to write, and what was the file pointer position at the start of the previous request.

   There is no implicit limitation that prevents `Proactive Initiators` from assigning multiple `Asynchronous Operation` requests to a single `Completion Handler`. As a result, the `Completion Handler` must tie request-specific state information throughout the chain of completion notifications. To do this, `Completion Handlers` can utilize the Asynchronous Completion Token pattern [Pyarali+1997].

- *Resource management.* As with any multi-threaded environment, the Proactor pattern does not absolve `Completion Handlers` from ensuring that access to shared resources is thread-safe. However, a `Completion Handler` should not hold onto a shared resource across multiple completion notifications. If it does, it risks inducing the dining philosopher's problem [Dijkstra1971].

   This problem is the deadlock that results when a logical thread of control waits forever for a semaphore to become signaled. This is illustrated by imagining a dinner party attended by a group of philosophers. The diners are seated around a circular table with exactly one chop stick between each philosopher. When a philosopher becomes hungry, he must obtained the chop stick to his left and to his right in order to eat. Once philosophers obtain a chop stick, they will not release it until their hunger is satisfied. If all philosophers pick up the chop stick on their right, a deadlock occurs because the chop stick on the left will never become available.

- *Preemptive policy.* The `Completion Dispatcher` type determines if a `Completion Handler` can be preempted while executing. When attached to dynamic-thread and thread-pool dispatchers, `Completion Handlers` are naturally preemptive. However, when tied to a post-reactive `Completion Dispatcher`, `Completion Handlers` are not preemptive with respect to each other. When driven by a call-through dispatcher, the `Completion Handlers` are not preemptive with respect to the thread-of-control that is in the alertable wait state.

   In general, a handler should not perform long-duration synchronous operations unless multiple completion threads are used since this will significantly decrease the overall responsiveness of the application. This risk can be alleviated by increased programming discipline. For instance, all `Completion Handlers` are required to act as `Proactive Initiators` instead of executing synchronous operations.

Sample Code

This section shows how to use the Proactor pattern to develop a Web server. The example is based on the Proactor pattern implementation in the ACE framework [Schmidt1994].

When a client connects to the Web server, the `HTTP_Handler`'s open method is called. The server then initializes the asynchronous I/O object with the callback object when the `Asynchronous Operation` completes (which in this case is `this`), the network connection for transferring the data, and the `Completion Dispatcher` to be used once the operation completes (`proactor_`). The read operation is then started asynchronously, and the server returns to the event loop.

The `HTTP_Handler::handle_read_stream` is called back by the dispatcher when the `Async_read` operation completes. If there is enough data, the client request is then parsed. If the entire client request has not arrived yet, another read operation is initiated asynchronously.

In response to a `GET` request, the server memory-maps the requested file and writes the file data asynchronously to the client. The dispatcher calls back on `HTTP_Handler::handle_write_stream` when the write operation completes, which frees up dynamically allocated resources.

The Appendix contains two other code examples for implementing the Web server using a synchronous threaded model and a synchronous (nonblocking) reactive model.

```
class HTTP_Handler
  : public Proactor::Event_Handler
  // = TITLE
  //    Implements the HTTP protocol
  //    (asynchronous version).
  //
  // = PATTERN PARTICIPANTS
  //    Proactive Initiator    = HTTP_Handler
  //    Asynch Op              = Network I/O
  //    Asynch Op Processor    = OS
  //    Completion Dispatcher  = Proactor
  //    Completion Handler     = HTPP_Handler
  {
public:
  void open (Socket_Stream *client) {
    // Initialize state for request
    request_.state_ = INCOMPLETE;
```

```cpp
  // Store reference to client.
  client_ = client;

  // Initialize asynch read stream.
  stream_.open (*this,
                client_->handle (),
                proactor_);

  // Start read asynchronously.
  stream_.read (request_.buffer (),
                request_.buffer_size ());
}

// This is called by the Proactor
// when the asynch read completes.
void handle_read_stream (u_long bytes_transferred) {
  if (request_.enough_data (bytes_transferred))
    parse_request ();
  else
    // Start reading asynchronously
    stream_.read (request_.buffer (),
                  request_.buffer_size ());
}

void parse_request (void) {
  // Switch on the HTTP command type.
  switch (request_.command ()) {
  // Client is requesting a file.
  case HTTP_Request::GET:
    // Memory map the requested file.
    file_.map (request_.filename ());

    // Start writing asynchronously.
    stream_.write (file_.buffer (),
                   file_.buffer_size ());
    break;

  // Client is storing a file
  // at the server.
  case HTTP_Request::PUT:
    // ...
  }
}
```

```
   void handle_write_stream (u_long bytes_transferred) {
     if (file_.enough_data
          (bytes_transferred))
       // Success....
     else
       // Start another asynchronous write.
       stream_.write (file_.buffer (),
                        file_.buffer_size ());
   }

private:
  // Set at initialization.
  Proactor *proactor_;

  // Memory-mapped file_.
  Mem_Map file_;

  // Socket endpoint.
  Socket_Stream *client_;

  // HTTP Request holder.
  HTTP_Request request_;

  // Used for Asynch I/O.
  Asynch_Stream stream_;
};
```

Known Uses

The following are some widely documented uses of the Proactor pattern:

- *I/O completion ports in Windows NT.* The Windows NT operating system implements the Proactor pattern. Various `Asynchronous Operations` such as accepting new network connections, reading and writing to files and sockets, and transmission of files across a network connection are supported by Windows NT. The operating system is the `Asynchronous Operation Processor`. Results of the operations are queued up at the I/O completion port, which plays the role of the `Completion Dispatcher`.
- *The UNIX AIO family of asynchronous I/O operations.* On some real-time POSIX platforms, the Proactor pattern is implemented by the `aio` family of APIs [Information Technology1995]. These OS features are very similar to the ones described above for Windows NT. One difference is that UNIX signals can be

used to implement a truly asynchronous `Completion Dispatcher`, but the Windows NT API is not truly asynchronous.

- *ACE Proactor.* The Adaptive Communications Environment (ACE) [Schmidt 1994] implements a Proactor component that encapsulates I/O Completion Ports on Windows NT and the `aio` APIs on POSIX platforms. The ACE Proactor abstraction provides an OO interface to the standard C APIs supported by Windows NT and POSIX platforms. The source code for this implementation can be acquired from the ACE Web site at www.cs.wustl.edu/~schmidt/ACE.html.

- *Asynchronous procedure calls in Windows NT.* Some systems, such as Windows NT, support Asynchronous Procedure Calls (APC)s. An APC is a function that executes asynchronously in the context of a particular thread. When an APC is queued to a thread, the system issues a software interrupt. The next time the thread is scheduled, it will run the APC. APCs made by operating system are called *kernel-mode APCs*. APCs made by an application are called *user-mode APCs*.

Related Patterns

Figure 9-9 illustrates patterns that are related to the Proactor.

The Asynchronous Completion Token (ACT) pattern [Pyarali+1997] is generally used in conjunction with the Proactor pattern. When `Asynchronous Operations`

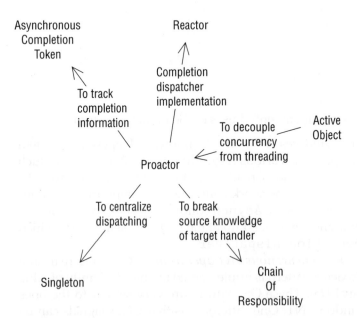

Figure 9-9 *Proactor pattern's related patterns*

complete, applications may need more information than simply the notification itself to properly handle the event. The Asynchronous Completion Token pattern allows applications to efficiently associate state with the completion of `Asynchronous Operations`.

The Proactor pattern is related to the Observer pattern [Gamma+1995], where dependents are updated automatically when a single subject changes. In the Proactor pattern, handlers are informed automatically when events from multiple sources occur. In general, the Proactor pattern is used to asynchronously demultiplex multiple sources of input to their associated event handlers, whereas an Observer is usually associated with only a single source of events.

The Proactor pattern can be considered an *asynchronous* variant of the synchronous Reactor pattern [Schmidt1995]. The Reactor pattern is responsible for demultiplexing and dispatching of multiple event handlers that are triggered when it is possible to *initiate* an operation *synchronously* without blocking. In contrast, Proactor supports the demultiplexing and dispatching of multiple event handlers that are triggered by the *completion* of *asynchronous* events.

The Active Object pattern [Lavender+1995] decouples method execution from method invocation. Proactor is similar because `Asynchronous Operation Processors` perform operations on behalf of application `Proactive Initiators`. That is, both patterns can be used to implement `Asynchronous Operations.` The Proactor pattern is often used in place of the Active Object pattern to decouple the system's concurrency policy from the threading model.

A Proactor may be implemented as a Singleton [Gamma+1995]. This is useful for centralizing event demultiplexing and completion dispatching into a single location within an asynchronous application.

The Chain of Responsibility (COR) pattern [Gamma+1995] decouples event handlers from event sources. Proactor is similar in its segregation of `Proactive Initiators` and `Completion Handlers`. However, in COR, the event source has no prior knowledge of which handler will be executed, if any. In Proactor, `Proactive Initiators` have full disclosure of the target handler. However, the two patterns can be combined by establishing a `Completion Handler` that is the entry point into a responsibility chain dynamically configured by an external factory.

CONCLUSION

The Proactor pattern embodies a powerful design paradigm that supports efficient and flexible event dispatching strategies for high-performance concurrent applications. Proactor provides the performance benefits of executing operations concurrently, without constraining the developer to synchronous multi-threaded or reactive programming.

ACKNOWLEDGMENTS

This research is supported in part by a grant from Siemens MED.

REFERENCES

[Dijkstra1971] E.W. Dijkstra. "Hierarchical Ordering of Sequential Processes," *Acta Informatica*, 1 (2): 115–138, 1971.

[Gamma+1995] E. Gamma, R. Helm, R. Johnson, and J. Vlissides. *Design Patterns: Elements of Reusable Object-Oriented Software*. Reading, MA: Addison-Wesley, 1995.

[Hu+1997] J. Hu, I. Pyarali, and D.C. Schmidt. "Measuring the Impact of Event Dispatching and Concurrency Models on Web Server Performance Over High-speed Networks," in *Proceedings of the 2nd Global Internet Conference*, IEEE, November 1997.

[Hu+1998] J. Hu, I. Pyarali, and D.C. Schmidt. "Applying the Proactor Pattern to High-Performance Web Servers," in *Proceedings of the 10th International Conference on Parallel and Distributed Computing and Systems*, IASTED, October 1998.

[Information Technology1995] "Information Technology—Portable Operating System Interface (POSIX)—Part 1: System Application: Program Interface (API) [C Language]," 1995.

[Lavender+1995] R.G. Lavender and D.C. Schmidt. "Active Object: An Object Behavioral Pattern for Concurrent Programming," in *Proceedings of the 2nd Annual Conference on the Pattern Languages of Programs* (Monticello, Illinois), pp. 1–7, September 1995.

[McKusick1996] M.K. McKusick, K. Bostic, M.J. Karels, and J.S. Quarterman. *The Design and Implementation of the 4.4BSD Operating System*. Reading, MA: Addison-Wesley, 1996.

[Microsoft1996] *Microsoft Developers Studio, Version 4.2—Software Development Kit*, 1996.

[Mogul1995] J.C. Mogul. "The Case for Persistent-Connection HTTP," in *Proceedings of ACM-SIGCOMM '95 Conference in Computer Communication Review*. Boston: ACM Press, August 1995, pp. 299–314.

[Pyarali+1998] I. Pyarali, T.H. Harrison, and D.C. Schmidt, "Asynchronous Completion Token: An Object Behavioral Pattern for Efficient Asynchronous Event Handling," in R. Martin, F. Buschmann, and D. Riehle (eds.), *Pattern Languages of Program Design 3*. Reading, MA: Addison-Wesley, 1998.

[Schmidt1994] D.C. Schmidt. "ACE: An Object-Oriented Framework for Developing Distributed Applications," in *Proceedings of the 6th USENIX C++ Technical Conference*. Cambridge, MA: USENIX Association, April 1994.

[Schmidt1995] D.C. Schmidt. "Reactor: An Object Behavioral Pattern for Concurrent Event Demultiplexing and Event Handler Dispatching," in J.O. Coplien and D.C. Schmidt (eds.), *Pattern Languages of Program Design*, pp. 529–545. Reading, MA: Addison-Wesley, 1995.

[Schmidt1998] D.C. Schmidt. "Acceptor and Connector: Design Patterns for Initializing Communication Services," in R. Martin, F. Buschmann, and D. Riehle (eds.), *Pattern Languages of Program Design 3*. Reading, MA: Addison-Wesley, 1998.

Irfan Pyarali, Tim Harrison, and Douglas Schmidt may be reached at {irfan,harrison,schmidt}@cs.wustl.edu.

Thomas Jordan may be reached at ace@programmer.net.

APPENDIX A: ALTERNATIVE IMPLEMENTATIONS

This Appendix outlines the code used to develop alternatives to the Proactor pattern. We examine both synchronous I/O using multi-threading and reactive I/O using single-threading.

A.1 Multiple Synchronous Threads

The following code shows how to use synchronous I/O with a pool of threads to develop a Web server. When a client connects to the server, a thread in the pool accepts the connection and calls the open method in class HTTP_Handler. The server then synchronously reads the request from the network connection. When the read operation completes, the client request is then parsed. In response to a GET request, the server memory-maps the requested file and writes the file data synchronously to the client. Note how blocking I/O allows the Web server to follow the steps outlined in the previous section on Concurrency through Multiple Synchronous Threads.

```
class HTTP_Handler
  // = TITLE
  //     Implements the HTTP protocol
  //     (synchronous threaded version).
  //
  // = DESCRIPTION
  //     This class is called by a
  //     thread in the Thread Pool.
  {
public:
  void open (Socket_Stream *client) {
    HTTP_Request request;

    // Store reference to client.
    client_ = client;

    // Synchronously read the HTTP request
    // from the network connection and
    // parse it.
    client_->recv (request);

    parse_request (request);
  }

  void parse_request (HTTP_Request &request) {
    // Switch on the HTTP command type.
```

```
    switch (request.command ())
    {
      // Client is requesting a file.
      case HTTP_Request::GET:
        // Memory map the requested file.
        Mem_Map input_file;
        input_file.map (request.filename());

        // Synchronously send the file
        // to the client. Block until the
        // file is transferred.
        client_->send (input_file.data (),
                       input_file.size ());
        break;

        // Client is storing a file at
        // the server.
        case HTTP_Request::PUT:
          // ...
    }
  }

private:
  // Socket endpoint.
  Socket_Stream *client_;

  // ...
};
```

A.2 Single-Threaded Reactive Event Dispatching

The following code shows the use of the Reactor pattern to develop a Web server. When a client connects to the server, the `HTTP_Handler::open` method is called. The server registers the I/O handle and the object to callback (which in this case is `this`) when the network handle is "ready for reading." The server returns to the event loop.

When the request data arrives at the server, the `reactor_` calls back the `HTTP_Handler::handle_input` method. The client data is read in a non-blocking manner. If there is enough data, the client request is parsed. If the entire client request has not yet arrived, the application returns to the reactor event loop.

In response to a GET request, the server memory maps the requested file and registers with the reactor to be notified when the network connection becomes "ready for writing." The `reactor_` then calls back on

HTTP_Handler::handle_output method when writing data to the connection would not block the calling thread. When all the data has been sent to the client, the network connection is closed.

```
class HTTP_Handler :
  public Reactor::Event_Handler
  // = TITLE
  //     Implements the HTTP protocol
  //     (synchronous reactive version).
  //
  // = DESCRIPTION
  //     The Event_Handler base class
  //     defines the hooks for
  //     handle_input()/handle_output().
  //
  // = PATTERN PARTICIPANTS
  //     Reactor = Reactor
  //     Event Handler = HTTP_Handler
{
public:
  void open (Socket_Stream *client) {
    // Initialize state for request.
    request_.state_ = INCOMPLETE;

    // Store reference to client.
    client_ = client;

    // Register with the reactor for reading.
    reactor_->register_handler
      (client_->handle (),
       this,
       Reactor::READ_MASK);
  }

  // This is called by the Reactor when
  // we can read from the client handle.
  void handle_input (void) {
    int result = 0;

    // Non-blocking read from the network
    // connection.
    do
      result = request_.recv (client_->handle ());
```

```cpp
      while (result != SOCKET_ERROR
             && request_.state_ == INCOMPLETE);

      // No more progress possible;
      // blocking will occur.
      if (request_.state_ == INCOMPLETE
          && errno == EWOULDBLOCK)
        reactor_->register_handler
          (client_->handle (),
           this,
           Reactor::READ_MASK);
      else
        // We now have the entire request
        parse_request ();
  }

  void parse_request (void) {
    // Switch on the HTTP command type.
    switch (request_.command ()) {
    // Client is requesting a file.
    case HTTP_Request::GET:
      // Memory map the requested file.
      file_.map (request_.filename ());

      // Transfer the file using Reactive I/O.
      handle_output ();
      break;

      // Client is storing a file at
      // the server.
    case HTTP_Request::PUT:
      // ...
    }
  }

  void handle_output (void) {
    // Asynchronously send the file
    // to the client.
    if (client_->send (file_.data (),
                       file_.size ())
                    == SOCKET_ERROR
        && errno == EWOULDBLOCK)
      // Register with reactor...
```

```
    else
      // Close down and release resources.
      handle_close ();
  }

private:
  // Set at initialization.
  Reactor *reactor_;

  // Memory-mapped file_.
  Mem_Map file_;

  // Socket endpoint.
  Socket_Stream *client_;

  // HTTP Request holder.
  HTTP_Request request_;
};
```

```cpp
    else
      // Close down and release resources.
      handle_close ();

  private:
    // Set at initialization.
    Reactor *reactor_;

    // Memory-mapped file.
    Mem_Map file_;

    // Socket endpoint.
    Socket_Stream stream_;

    // HTTP Request holder.
    HTTP_Request request_;
```

PART 3

Programming Strategies

As with any skilled craftsperson, the journeyman programmer can be distinguished from the novice by what's in his or her bag of tricks. And what might one typically find in such a bag? Patterns perhaps?

This section explores three collections of patterns that examine some such tricks of the trade. They may be language specific, as is the case with our first two offerings, or they may offer advice on how to cope with particularly constrained resource requirements, as with the final chapter in this section.

Chapter 10: C++ Idioms by James Coplien. This chapter presents a set of 13 patterns that address advanced object-oriented programming in C++. They may strike some readers as familiar, having been drawn, as they were, from the author's seminal *Advanced C++: Programming Styles and Idioms* [Coplien1992]. Many of these idioms focused on how to emulate the style of programming seen in more dynamic languages such as LISP using C++. The notion of a catalog of such idioms anticipated, in many respects, much of what was to come with patterns. Indeed, several of these idioms, such as Handle/Body and Envelope/Letter, are now frequently cited as if they were full-blown patterns. This chapter presents brief, accessible treatments of a number of these idioms in full pattern form for the first time and, further, attempts to thread them into a pattern language.

Chapter 11: Smalltalk Scaffolding Patterns by Jim Doble and Ken Auer. This chapter presents an altogether different bag of tricks; this one uses Smalltalk's reflective facilities to get prototype and experimental applications running quickly. The Extensible Attributes pattern shows how a LISP-style property dictionary can be readily added to an existing Smalltalk object. The Artificial Accessors pattern shows how such dynamic property dictionaries can be accessed transparently using conventional getters and setters. Generated Accessors shows how getter and setter methods can readily be synthesized. Artificial Delegation explores how an object can look for other objects to which it can forward operations it does not itself understand. The Cached Extensibility pattern shows how this dynamic behavior can be made more efficient. Finally, Selector Synthesis shows how Smalltalk's reflective facilities can be used to generate event and state-specific methods on-the-fly.

Chapter 12: High-Level and Process Patterns from the Memory Preservation Society by James Noble and Charles Weir. Readers old enough to remember when memory capacities were measured in kilobytes may have used some of these techniques. However, worrying about resources is not merely an anachronistic fetish of a few fossils and fussbudgets. The authors make the point that relative plenty is no excuse for profligacy and waste. Indeed, the memory has not been made that a reckless programmer cannot exhaust. So we'd be remiss to let the ancient wisdom of the Memory Preservation Society pass into history. Even today, PDAs, set-top boxes, real-time and embedded systems, and sundry smart appliances impose memory limitations some programmers thought they'd left behind sometime during the Z80 era.

The authors suggest one begin by Thinking Small. That is, pretend the system has even less memory than it actually does. One technique is to enforce a Memory Budget and hold people to it. Provisions for a Memory Overdraft can be made, if need be, for emergencies, or as a last resort. In many cases, a strategy where you Make the User Worry about resources lets you enlist the user as your partner in keeping resource consumption down. The Partial Failure pattern advocates graceful degradation whenever possible. The unforgettably named Captain Oates pattern (we commend the reader to the chapter's first footnote) advocates a more draconian triage strategy in the face of resource limitations. Exhaustion Tests and Memory Performance Assessments can reduce the need to resort to anything so drastic as Captain Oates.

Chapter 10

C++ Idioms Patterns

James Coplien

This chapter attempts to do three things. The first is to recast the well-known idioms of *Advanced C++ Programming Styles and Idioms* [Coplien1992] in pattern form. The second is to organize these idioms, which until now have survived as independent and largely unrelated patterns, into a true pattern language. That means that the patterns form a graph and that they should be applied in an order dictated by the structure of the graph. The third goal is to show that the patterns together (as a pattern language) attack what is metaphorically, conceptually, or actually a structural problem. Structure is a central element in Alexander's theories of beauty, a perspective that pervades all his work but which has become more directly articulated in recent works such as *Nature of Order*. These patterns do piecemeal construction of the structure of an inheritance hierarchy and the structure of the classes within it. The chapter tries to explore that geometric nature.

PATTERN INTENTS

Overall, this pattern language deals with one aspect of C++ design; in particular, it deals with that aspect that focuses on algebraic types. C++ is rich in features that support algebraic types, including operator overloading and a good family of built-in numeric types. The idioms surrounding the algebraic view are strong enough that the tradition carries on in libraries for strings and other non-numeric types. There are many non-numeric and, properly, non-algebraic types to which many of these patterns may apply.

There are also many inheritance hierarchies to which the algebraic patterns in particular are irrelevant; some types just don't have algebraic properties. The same is true even for patterns like Handle/Body (which apply largely to types that behave as built-in value types) and Counted Body (which is pertinent for Handle/Body instances with dynamically allocated resources). The Context and Forces sections of each pattern guide the reader in the appropriate application of these patterns to individual problems.

The pattern language in this chapter does not focus on techniques based on templates. One can view templates largely as a macro facility that transforms an existing inheritance structure into an isomorphic structure. However, there are some idiomatic uses of templates that might be considered in later iterations of this pattern language.

Listed below are the pattern intents, a quick index of the patterns in this paper.

- *Handle/Body.*   Separating interface from implementation.
- *Counted Body.*   Manage logical sharing and proper resource deallocation of objects that use dynamically allocated resources.
- *Detached Counted Body.*   Adding reference counting to an object to which a reference count cannot directly be added.
- *Handle/Body Hierarchy.*   To separate representation inheritance from subtyping inheritance.
- *Envelope/Letter.*   To tie together common semantics of handle and body classes.
- *Virtual Constructor.*   How to build an object of known abstract type, but of unknown concrete type, without violating the encapsulation of the inheritance hierarchy.
- *Concrete Data Type.*   Determine whether to allocate an object on the heap or in the current scope.
- *Algebraic Hierarchy.*   Structuring classes whose type relationships follow classic algebraic types.
- *Homogeneous Addition.*   Simplify the implementation of operations in an Algebraic Hierarchy.
- *Promote And Add.*   How to add objects of two different types when only Homogeneous Addition is supported.
- *Promotion Ladder.*   How to assign type promotion responsibility to classes in an Algebraic Hierarchy.
- *Non-Hierarchical Addition.*   How to deal with arithmetic operations between types when neither can be promoted to the other.
- *Type Promotion.*   How to use two type conversion mechanisms—operator functions and constructors—to build a consistent type promotion structure.

PATTERN LANGUAGE STRUCTURE

The patterns are presented as a pattern language with the structure of Figure 10-1. All the patterns are contained in Handle/Body and/or Concrete Data Type. Many

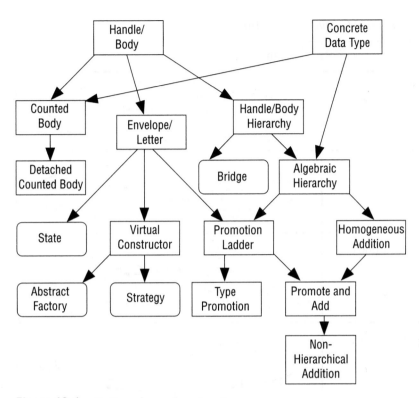

Figure 10-1 *Pattern language structure*

of the GoF patterns [Gamma+1995], indicated as rounded boxes instead of rectangles, are also in this pattern language. The GOF patterns are not reiterated here.

A Spatial Progression

One can view these patterns as a way to guide the geometry of an inheritance hierarchy in C++. Geometry is an essential consideration in patterns, a fact most contemporary software patterns fail to heed. Inheritance structures are one of the most accessible structures of object-oriented software design, though they are less evident in code than implementation hierarchies or other direct geometric properties like indentation (and what it portends for scope and other semantic properties).

Most of the crisp idioms of *Advanced C++ Programming Styles and Idioms* deal with class structures and, in particular, inheritance structures. They are the foundations of flexible object-oriented programming in C++.

Here, we both develop a pattern language based on problems, solutions, and intents, and we develop the corresponding progression of geometric structures as in Table 10-1. Only the more basic patterns are depicted here. Each shows two

Table 10-1 *Progression of Geometric Structure in the Patterns*

Pattern Name	Geometry
Handle/Body	
Counted Body	
Detached Counted Body	
Handle/Body Hierarchy	
Envelope/Letter Virtual Constructor	

ellipses, one ellipse representing the interface class, and another, the representation class. Objects (the rectangles) are members of the set defined by the class. The arrows show the relationships between objects or classes as appropriate.

THE PATTERNS

Handle/Body

Context

Advanced C++ programs using user-defined classes that should behave like built-in types as much as possible.

Problem

How do you separate interface from implementation in C++ objects?

Forces

- C++ public and private sections were designed to separate implementation from interface, but changes even to private data force recompilation.
- Changes to a class implementation cause unnecessary recompilation of client code.
- The class implementation is visible (though inaccessible) in a C++ class declaration.

Solution

Split a design class into two implementation classes. One takes on the role of an identifier and presents the class interface to the user. We call this first class the *handle*. The other class embodies the implementation and is called the *body*. The handle forwards member function invocations to the body. (See Figure 10-2.)

Example

```
class StringRep {
// this can be in a separate source file
// from class String, so it can be compiled
// separately, and made invisible to the
// client
friend class String;
   StringRep(const char *s);
   ~StringRep();
   int count; char *rep;
};
```

```
class String {
public:
    String();
    String(const String &s);
    String &operator=(const String &s);
    ~String();
    String(const char *s);
    . . . .
private:
    StringRep *rep;
};
```

Resulting Context

Data changes can now safely be made to the implementation (body) without recompiling clients of the handle.

The implementation becomes "more hidden" behind a pointer.

The extra level of indirection has a performance cost.

This pattern doesn't address the issues of deep versus shallow copy and other runtime dynamics; see the sections on Counted Body, Envelope/Letter, and their subtending patterns.

The pattern also makes inheritance less useful; see Handle/Body Hierarchy to overcome this shortcoming.

This pattern has limits in managing the dynamically allocated memory of the body class; see Counted Body. It also introduces the need for occasional redundant updates to the handle and body classes, a problem addressed in part by Envelope/Letter. To use this pattern in conjunction with inheritance, see Handle/Body Hierarchy.

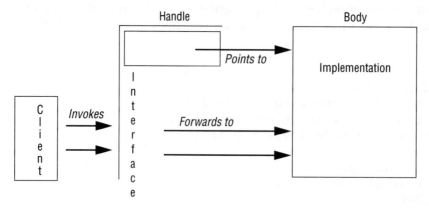

Figure 10-2

Rationale

All interesting problems in computer science reduce to what's in a name and can be solved by one more level of indirection. In high-level languages like Smalltalk, identifiers and objects are different things. An object can be associated with one or more identifiers. The loose association between identifiers and objects clarifies questions of equality and identity, for example, and lays a foundation for automatic garbage collection. The Counted Body pattern takes advantage of this property as it apes Smalltalk garbage collection in a somewhat indirect way.

Counted Body

Also Known As

Counted Handle/Body

Context

A design has been transformed using Handle/Body class pairs. The pattern may be relevant to other object-based programming languages.

Problem

Naive implementations of assignment in C++ are often inefficient or incorrect.

Forces

- Assignment in C++ is defined recursively as member-by-member assignment with copying as the termination of the recursion; it would be more efficient and more in the spirit of Smalltalk—that is, in the spirit of the benefits promised by close adherence to the object paradigm—if copying were rebinding.
- Copying of bodies is expensive.
- Copying can be avoided by using pointers and references, but these leave the problem of who is responsible for cleaning up the object and leave a user-visible distinction between built-in types and user-defined types.
- Sharing bodies on assignment is usually semantically incorrect if the shared body is modified through one of the handles.

Solution

Add a reference count to the body class to facilitate memory management; hence the name "Counted Body."

Memory management is added to the handle class, particularly to its implementation of initialization, assignment, copying, and destruction.

It is incumbent on any operation that modifies the state of the body to break the sharing of the body by making its own copy. It must decrement the reference count of the original body.

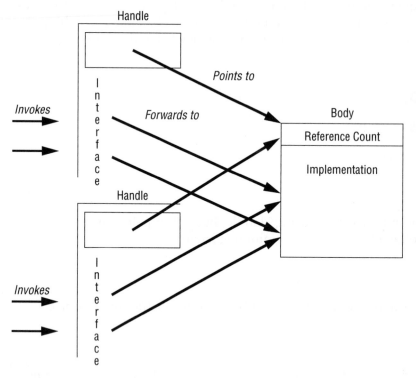

Figure 10-3

Example

```
class StringRep {
friend class String;
    StringRep(const char *s): count(1) {
        strcpy(rep=new char[strlen(s)+1],
            s);
    }
    ~StringRep() { delete [] rep; }
    int count; char *rep;
};

class String {
```

```
public:
   String():rep(new StringRep("")) { }
   String(const String &s):
     rep(s.rep) { rep->count++; }
   String &operator=(const String &s){
     s.rep->count++;
     if(--rep->count <= 0) delete rep;
     rep = s.rep;
     return *this;
   }
   ~String() {
     if(--rep->count <= 0) delete rep;
   }
   void putChar(char c) {
     // putChar does memory management so
     // it's a handle class member function
     int len = strlen(rep->rep);
     char *newrep = new char[len + 2];
     strcpy(newrep, rep->rep);
     rep->rep[len] = c;
     rep->rep[len+1] = '\0';
     if (--rep->count <= 0) delete rep;
     rep = new StringRep(newrep);
   }
   String(const char *s):
     rep(new StringRep(s)) { }
   . . . .
private:
   class StringRep *rep;
};

int main() {
   String a = "hello", b = "world";
   a = b;
   return 0;
}
```

Resulting Context

Gratuitous copying is avoided, leading to a more efficient implementation.

Sharing is broken when the body state is modified through any handle. Sharing is preserved in the more common case of parameter passing and so forth.

Special pointer and reference types are avoided.

Smalltalk semantics are approximated; garbage collection builds on this model.

This pattern presumes that the programmer can edit the source code for the abstraction of interest. When that's not possible, use Detached Counted Body.

Additional patterns are necessary to make such code thread-safe.

Rationale

Reference counting is efficient and spreads the overhead across the execution of real-time programs. This implementation is a variation of shallow copy with the semantics of deep copy and the efficiency of Smalltalk name-value pairs.

See also [Cargill1996].

Detached Counted Body

Context

Many C++ programs use types whose implementations use dynamically allocated memory. Programmers often create such types and put them in libraries without adding the machinery to make these types as well behaved as built-in types.

Problem

How do you overcome overhead of an additional level of indirection that comes when applying the Counted Body pattern to immutable classes?

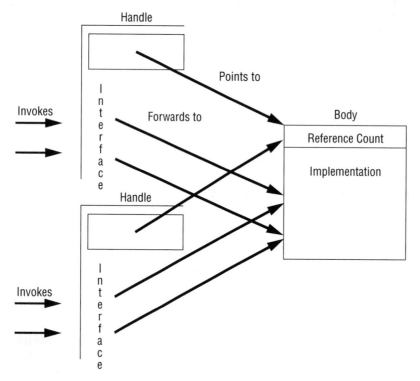

Figure 10-4

Forces

- The standard solution, Counted Body, embeds a reference count in a shared implementation that is managed by a handle class as shown in Figure 10-4.
- However, we may not add a reference count to a library abstraction, since we only have object code and a header file. We could solve this with an added level of indirection as Figure 10-5 shows, but that adds an extra level of indirection to each dereference and may be too expensive.

Solution

Associate both a shared count and a separate shared body with each instance of a common handle abstraction as shown in Figure 10-6.

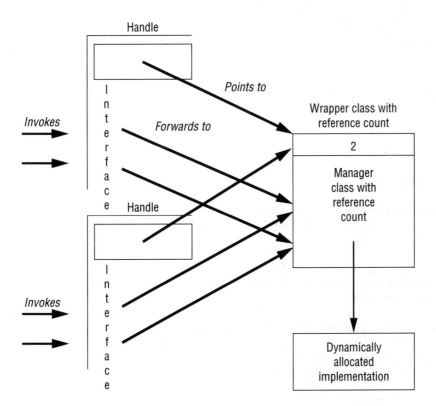

Figure 10-5

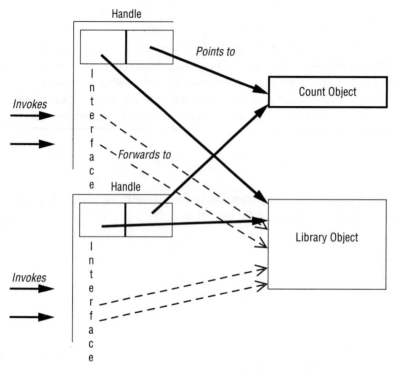

Figure 10-6

Example

```
class String {
public:
   String():rep(new char[1]),
             count(new int(1))
     rep[0] = '\0';
   }
   String(const String &s):
     rep(s.rep), count(s.count) {
       (*count)++;
   }
   String &operator=(const String &s){
     (*s.count)++;
     if(--*count <= 0) {
       delete [] rep; delete count;
     }
     rep = s.rep;
     count = s.count;
     return *this;
   }
```

```
   ~String() {
     if(--*count <= 0) {
       delete [] rep;
       delete count;
     }
   }
   String(const char *s): count(new int(1)),
     rep(new char[strlen(s)+1]) {
       strcpy(rep,s);
   }
   . . . .
private:
   char *rep;
   int *count;
};

int main() {
   String a = "hello", b = "world";
   a = b;
   return 0;
}
```

Resulting Context

Now we can access the body with a single level of indirection, while still using only a single indirection for the count.

Handles are slightly more expensive to copy than in Counted Body, memory fragmentation may increase, and initial construction overhead is higher because we are allocating multiple blocks.

The pattern source appears to be [Koenig1995]. See also [Cargill1996].

Handle/Body Hierarchy

Also Known As

Bridge

Context

A C++ program in which the Handle/Body idiom has been applied, in which some classes have subtyping relationships and implementation-sharing relationships that do not correspond with each other.

One way this shows up is when a statically typed language expresses subtyping as inheritance. The base class has an operation whose parameters correspond to degrees of freedom in its state space. The interface of the subtype is more constrained than the interface of the supertype. We want to inherit that operation in the derived class (which takes away at least one degree of freedom present in the base class; see the example that follows). Stated another way, some operations that are closed under the base class are not closed under the derived class.

Another way this shows up is when the base class has a larger state space than the derived class. A derived class should restrict the state space of the base class.

Problem

C++ ties implementation inheritance and representation inheritance together, and we may want to inherit each separately.

Forces

- You might want to inherit interface without inheriting implementation.
- In exceptional cases, you might want to inherit implementation without inheriting interface. For example, a base class member function may take one parameter for each of the degrees of freedom in its state space. Because the derived class is a subtype of the base class, it has fewer degrees of freedom than the base class. To inherit a base class operation whose parameters map onto degrees of freedom in the state space, the derived class must elide one argument (or otherwise constrain the arguments). But a base class operation inherited by the derived class should exhibit the same signature in both classes.
- If you inherit from a C++ class, you inherit its implementation.
- We usually use (public) inheritance (in the languages defined in the context) to express subtyping.

Solution

Maintain separate inheritance hierarchies for handle classes and body classes. The base interface class contains a reference to the base implementation class. (See Figure 10-7.)

Example

```
class Ellipse {
public:
    Ellipse(Pdouble majorAxis,
      Pdouble minorAxis, Point center);
    virtual void resize(Pdouble majorAxis,
                        Pdouble minorAxis);
  . . . .
private:
    // representation is in terms of two
```

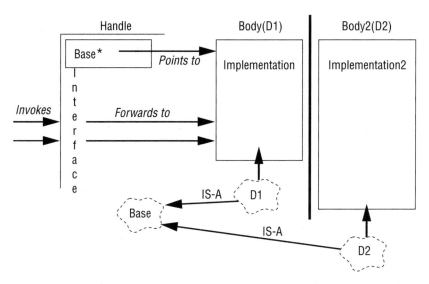

Figure 10-7

```
    // foci, the constant sum of the distance
    // between any point on the ellipse and
    // each of the two centers
    Point center1, center2, sum;
};

class Circle: public Ellipse { // because a
                               // Circle IS-A
                               // Ellipse
public:
    Circle(Pdouble radius, Point center):
        Ellipse(radius, radius, center) { }
    void resize( ? );
private:
    // can reuse sum as the radius, and one
    // of the centers as the center, but the
    // other center is wasted
};
```

Resulting Context

Interface and implementation can be separately inherited. A compact representation can be used, independent of the interface presented to the application programmer. Though this saves the memory of the extra datum inherited from the base class, it adds space for a pointer.

Rationale

Much of the power of object-oriented programming comes from separating identifiers and their semantics from objects and their semantics. In C++, objects adopt the semantics of the identifiers to which they are bound. Identifiers adopt the semantics of their compile-time type. These semantics include object size, permissible operations, and compatibility with other types. Because objects adopt the semantics of the identifiers through which they are manipulated, they carry the semantics of a compile-time type.

This chain of dependency can be broken with pointers (which relax object size restrictions) and virtual functions (which retain the semantics of a fixed set of permissible operations, but allow for variant implementations of an operation). However, no single language mechanism combines the implementation decoupling of pointers with the sharing of type semantics provided by inheritance.

In pure object-oriented languages, identifiers and objects have distinct semantics. There is a chain of dependency from type to object, but no compile-time dependency from identifier to type. Though this seriously weakens compile-time type checking, it addresses the forces described earlier.

At first glance, `resize(Pdouble,Pdouble)` seems to apply to `Ellipse`s but not to `Circle`s. It is easy to conclude this, because resize is closed under `Ellipse`, but not under `Circle`. However, resize applies equally to `Circle`s as to `Ellipse`s and is closed under `Ellipse`s in general. This means that any attempt to resize a `Circle` changes it into an `Ellipse`. Such dynamic retyping is difficult to support in the given context of statically typed languages. To overcome this restriction, use idioms (like the Envelope/Letter idiom) or design patterns (like the GoF Bridge [Gamma+1995]) that allow dynamic retyping of an object at runtime. Here, the type is a function of the number of degrees of freedom in the state. This is a subtle difference from the GoF State pattern [Gamma+1995] alone, where type depends on value.

Compare Rungs of a Dual Hierarchy from [Martin1997].

Envelope/Letter

Context

A program using Handle/Body pairs and/or Counted Body pairs.

Problem

Supporting multiple implementations of a single abstract data type (ADT) instance across its lifetime.

Forces

- Multiple implementations of an ADT share signature: we want to capture that in the design and code.
- All implementations (bodies) of a given ADT share signature with the ADT's interface (handle): we want to capture that.
- Adding a new operation to a Handle/Body pair causes redundant update to both classes.
- The handle implementation is coupled to the implementations of all possible bodies.

Solution

Derive all solution body classes from a common base class. To reflect the commonality in signature between the handle and the body, use the handle class as the common base class for alternative bodies. Make handle member functions virtual. Each alternative implementation derived from the handle class (in its role as the class defining the interface to the implementations) overrides suitable virtual functions. The base class implementation of these member functions defines the handle class functionality: it forwards requests to its associated body class instance. (See Figure 10-8.)

The solution is weakly reflexive.

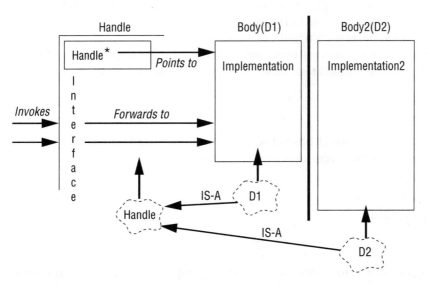

Figure 10-8

Example

Consider a Shape library with code to support Circles and Ellipses. Consider an Ellipse that is resized so it becomes a Circle. We could leave it as an Ellipse, but changing the type to Circle allows for significant optimizations. For example, rotation can now be done much more efficiently. We can implement this either through changing type in place through a function like:

```
void Shape::resize(Distance major, Distance minor);
```

which would change the type of the body object pointed to by *this; or we could have resize return a value whose type is determined at runtime:

```
Shape Shape::resize(Distance major, Distance minor) const;
```

The same is true for algebraic types.

Resulting Context

The ADT instance can now "metamorphize" between different body classes at runtime.

All bodies share a common signature and share the signature of the handle.

New signatures need be added in one less place than if the information were duplicated.

The handle class can decouple itself from the implementation of alternative body classes, if its public member functions are virtual.

This pattern is the basis for Virtual Constructors.

In Algebraic Hierarchy, this pattern forms the basis for a Promotion Ladder.

To vary the implementation at runtime, consider the State pattern [Gamma+1995].

Rationale

Others prefer to use a distinct base class for alternative implementations; this is okay, but depends on the forces one wants to resolve.

Virtual Constructor

Context

A particular client wants to create an object of an unspecified class chosen from a specified class hierarchy. Once created, any object created from the classes in the hierarchy can be used interchangeably by the client. The particular class is chosen from an arbitrary global context according to the needs of the client. The Handle/Body pattern has been applied.

Problem

How do you create an object whose general type is known by the client requesting it, but whose specific subtype characteristics must be chosen from context?

Forces

- You want to hide the implementation of the inheritance hierarchy from the user of the hierarchy's objects: only the base class interface should be published.
- Code must be written to select the most appropriate derived class. The code should be associated with the abstraction that minimizes coupling between all classes involved.
- The client must be able to use the services of any derived class object.

Solution

Just use the Envelope/Letter pattern structure. The base class is an intermediary agent that selects the appropriate derived type from context. The notion of supporting multiple implementations of an object across its lifetime generalizes to selecting the appropriate initial implementation, even in the degenerate case that the body instance doesn't change over the lifetime of the Handle/Body pair.

Example

Consider a `Message` class with a constructor:

```
Message::Message(void *ptr, short nbytes);
```

whose intent is to create a message of a suitable type according to the header information that appears in the body of an in-memory message image of length `nbytes` at address `ptr`. The concrete type of the message is unknown until run time, but it will always be some class derived from `Message`. The class `Message` can be made an envelope class, and the constructor can instantiate a body of a suitable type derived from `Message`.

Resulting Context

This pattern is the basis for Abstract Factory [Gamma+1995].

When the letter class variations are largely algorithmic, especially if the letter class contains only one member function, refine this pattern using Strategy [Gamma+1995].

Concrete Data Type

Context

Your design enumerates system classes, and you need to establish the lifetime and scope of the objects for those classes. This is particularly important for languages like C++ in which the object representation is visible to the user; that is, there are important distinctions between pointers and instances. Most of these languages lack garbage collection and other important finalization constructs.

Problem

How do you decide when to use the operator new to allocate an object instead of allocating it within some program scope?

Forces

- Unlike the procedural paradigm, where lifetime follows scope, the object paradigm leads to designs in which lifetime and scope are decoupled. Dynamic (heap) allocation is the usual mechanism to separate lifetime and scope.
- Given the context, the programming language can't make the difference between these two cases transparent.
- It's better for lifetime to follow scope, because the compiler can generate code to clean up the object when the scope closes. The programmer must clean up dynamically allocated objects.
- Yet if every object is bound to an identifier declared in some scope (whether procedure or object scope), and its lifetime is bound to some identifier in that scope, it restricts the object lifetime to being different from the corresponding real-world abstraction. Software objects should capture important real-world abstractions and must pay homage to such properties as lifetime and scope.
- On the other hand, not all classes reflect real-world objects; many are artifacts of the implementation.

Solution

Objects that represent real-world entities that live outside the program should be instantiated from the heap using the operator new. The lifetime of these objects is likely to be independent of the lifetime of any procedure or class scope, so it is unwise to declare them as objects in any scope. Window is an example of such a class.

Objects that represent abstractions that live "inside" the program, closely tied to the computational model, the implementation, or the programming language, should be declared as local (automatic or static) instances or as member instances. Collection classes (string, list, set) are examples of this kind of abstraction (though they may use heap data, they themselves are not heap objects). They are concrete data types—they aren't "abstract," but are as concrete as `int` and `double`.

Resulting Context

Objects allocated from the heap can follow the lifetimes of the application abstractions they represent. The compiler can automatically manage internal abstractions such as strings, which have no direct external world counterparts.

To deal with dynamically allocated representations, see Counted Body.

For user-defined types that behave like built-in algebraic types, see Algebraic Hierarchy.

Algebraic Hierarchy

Context

You are designing a system with user-defined types that support binary operations. Consider, for example, a number hierarchy with `Complex` as the base class. `Complex` is the most general of the number types under consideration. A `Complex` number has two scalar floating point numbers as its representation.

Problem

How do you construct the inheritance hierarchy for algebraic types?

Forces

- If we used C++ inheritance to express subtyping relationships, class `Real` would be derived from `Complex`, and `Integer` from `Real`. Each of these specific types supports all the operations of its base class.
- However, C++ inheritance also bestows all base class data on the derived class. That means that `Real` has at least two scalar floating point numbers as its representation. And likewise for `Integer`.
- We could minimize this waste by making the base class fields protected instead of private (so the derived class could "reuse" one of the base class fields). Even so, the designer would prefer to use a single integer as the representation of `Integer` rather than use a floating point number in the interest of space and computational efficiency. And `Real` still has an extra floating point number that is wasted.

Solution

Use the Bridge pattern [Gamma+1995] to separate interface from implementation. The visible part of the Bridge is called class `Number`. It contains a pointer to a representation part, which contains the representation and operations of the specific type (Complex, Real, Integer, Imaginary, etc.).

Example

```
class Number {
public:
    virtual Number add(const Number &n) {
        return rep->add(n);
    }
    virtual Number div(const Number&);
    . . . .
private:
    NumberRep *rep;
};

class Complex: public Number {
    . . . .
};

class Real: public Complex {
    . . . .
};

class NumberRep {
friend Number;
    virtual Number add(const Number&);
    virtual Number div(const Number&);
    . . . .
};

class ComplexRep: public NumberRep {
    virtual Number add(const Number &n) {
        . . . .
    }
    double rpart, ipart;
};

class RealRep: public NumberRep {
    virtual Number add(const Number &n) {
        . . . .
    }
    double rpart;
};
```

Resulting Context

Interface and implementation are now separate, and we can capture the subtyping semantics in the C++ inheritance hierarchy. Commonality between the implementation parts can be captured in a separate inheritance hierarchy if desired.

One can also combine the State pattern so given `Numbers` can change type over time:

```
class Number { . . . . };
class Complex: public Number { . . . . };
class Real: public Complex { . . . . };
class Rational: public Real { . . . . };

int main() {
    Complex i(3, -2), j(3, 2);
    i *= j; // i.e., 13
    return 0;
}
```

In fact, this use of Bridge and State and other patterns forms a small pattern language in its own right. In particular, Homogeneous Addition, Promote And Add, Promotion Ladder, Non-Hierarchical Addition, and Type Promotion fill out the structure of an Algebraic Hierarchy.

Homogeneous Addition

Context

You have built a hierarchy of classes (Algebraic Hierarchy) whose objects are to participate in binary operations. Each class is implemented using the Bridge pattern.

Problem

You need to distribute responsibilities to the objects, in other words, the addition operation. How many addition operations are there, and where do they belong?

Forces

- One of the main reasons for types in programming languages is efficiency. Good type design teaches the compiler how to generate efficient code for common operations.
- In general, efficient code must know the types of both operands involved.

- However, this leads to a combinatorial explosion in algorithms, n^2 for n types [Ingalls1986]. This violates the evolution law of continuity: it should be cheap to add a new type, not as expensive as adding code to every type that already exists!

Solution

Addition can always be expressed in terms of homogeneous operations (e.g., Promote And Add). Each type should support only homogeneous algebraic operations, unless there are substantial performance gains to be realized by doing otherwise.

The solution generalizes to other binary operations.

Example

```
class Complex: public Number {
public:
    . . . .
    // this must deal only with
    // Complex numbers
    Number add(const Number&) const;
};

class Imaginary: public Complex {
public:
    . . . .
    // this must deal only with
    // Imaginary numbers
    Number add(const Number&) const;
};
```

Resulting Context

This pattern leads to a design with a minimal number of implementations for algebraic operators. This provides a foundation for a simple implementation of Promote And Add.

Promote And Add

Context

You have an Algebraic Hierarchy. Each type knows how to add itself to an object of the same type (Homogeneous Addition). Each class knows important properties of its base class.

Problem

How do you do heterogeneous addition?

Forces

- Having Homogeneous Addition is fine, but even the most basic languages support polymorphic addition.
- The type of a result will, in general, be at least as general as the type of the more general of the two operands. For example, the result from adding a `Complex` and an `Integer` cannot be an `Integer`.
- Note that the result of multiplying two `Complex` numbers can be an integer. However, this knowledge is sophisticated enough that it belongs in `Complex`, not in `Integer`.

Solution

Using run-time type indentification (RTTI), it is straightforward to establish which of two object types is the more general. Promote And Add the object of the more specific type to the type of the more general object, using Promotion Ladder. Then, use Homogeneous Addition to satisfy the request.

C++ in particular is rich in language features that support promotions involving both user-defined types and built-in types.

The pattern generalizes beyond addition to other binary operations.

```
class Number {
public:
    virtual Number promote() const;
};
Number operator+(const Number &n1,
    const Number &n2)
{
    if (n1.isA(n2)) {
        do { n1 = n1.promote(); }
          while (n1.isA(n2) &&
            n1.type != complexExemplar);
          return n2.add(n1);
    } else if (n2.isA(n1)) {
        do { n2 = n2.promote(); }
          while (n2.isA(n1) &&
            n2.type != complexExemplar);
          return n1.add(n2);
    }
}
```

Resulting Context

This pattern fails if one of the operands is not a proper subtype of the other; to solve that, use Non-Hierarchical Addition.

Again, compare Rungs of a Dual Hierarchy from [Martin1997].

Promotion Ladder

Context

Types know how to promote themselves (Promote And Add), making heterogeneous addition possible.

Problem

Where do you put the knowledge of type promotion?

Forces

- You want to minimize cohesion and coupling between classes, even along an inheritance hierarchy. In particular, base classes shouldn't know about their derived classes.
- However, to do promotion from one type to another, each type must know something about the other.
- You might do this with casting and conversion operators, but in general the types can't be foreknown at compile time.
- Putting the knowledge of promotion in the base class might make it necessary to expose the derived class implementation if promotion is to be efficient. But putting knowledge of promotion in the derived class would likewise expose the implementation of the base class, which is even worse.
- Knowledge of promotion needn't be replicated in each pair of classes; once is sufficient. However, there must be some convention that points to the knowledge (e.g., in the more general or more derived class) to avoid ambiguity.

Solution

Each class should know how to promote itself to its own base class type. Promotions that involve more than two levels of the inheritance hierarchy can be handled by multiple successive promotions.

```
class Imaginary: public Complex {
public:
    . . . .
    Number promote(const Number& n) const {
        // always returns a Complex;
        return Number(0, n.ipart());
    }
    Number add(const Number&) const;
};

class Complex: public Number {
public:
    . . . .
    // no promote: Complex is not promoted
    // to anything else
    Number add(const Number&) const;
};
```

Compare to the pattern Intelligent Children [Martin1997].

Resulting Context

The design retains good coupling and cohesion properties; base classes needn't know about their derived classes. The work necessary to add a new type, and knowledge of how it should be promoted to other types, is kept to a minimum.

Non-Hierarchical Addition

Context

You've built a Promotion Ladder of types, each of which support Homogeneous Addition, that makes overall heterogeneous addition possible.

Problem

Sometimes, two objects are involved in a binary computation in which neither can be promoted to the type of the other. Consider the addition of an `Imaginary` and an `Integer`. Neither knows how to promote itself to the type of the other.

Forces

- You could handle such exceptions as special cases, but that would clutter the code, and it would be difficult to present a convincing case that all cases were covered.
- You could build a full promotion matrix that would map any given pair of types onto the right promotion algorithm, but that would lead to a combinatorial explosion in conversion functions.

Solution

Detect cases in which neither type can be promoted to the other. Promote both to a more general type and retry the operation.

Example

```
Number operator+(const Number &n1,
        const Number &n2) {
  if (n1.isA(n2)) {
    do { n1 = n1.promote(); }
      while (n1.isA(n2) &&
        n1.type != complexExemplar);
      return n2.add(n1);
  } else if (n2.isA(n1)) {
    do { n2 = n2.promote(); }
      while (n2.isA(n1) &&
        n2.type != complexExemplar);
      return n1.add(n2);
  } else {
    // promote both to Complex & retry
    . . . .
  }
}
```

Resulting Context

It is now possible to support the operation that called for the promotion, although the result may not be optimal, because it doesn't take into account optimizations that may be possible for specific pairs of types.

Type Promotion

Context

The pattern applies to C++ and potentially to other object-oriented programming languages.

The decision of which promotion to apply is made at compile time.

The context is inadequate for the compiler to apply built-in translation rules, as would be possible for conversion between built-in types, or between a derived class and one of its base classes. Promotion Ladder may not apply.

Problem

Promotion between objects of different but related C++ types, zero or one of which is a built-in type.

Forces

- The implementation of promotion from an object of one type to an object of another type is usually coupled to the implementation of both types.
- The C++ language lets the programmer associate such an implementation with only one of the participating types.
- The type containing the conversion implementation must be a class object type, since the programmer cannot redefine the implementation of built-in types.
- Two language mechanisms support user-defined conversions: constructors and conversion operators.
- Individually, each is an equally suitable solution in some circumstances, but use of both leads to an irreconcilable ambiguity.

Solution

A program should promote a class object type to a built-in type using a member conversion operator:

```
class RationalNumber {
public:
    operator float() const;
    . . . .
};
```

A program should use constructors (as in Promotion Ladder) for all other promotions:

```
class Complex {
public:
    Complex(const RationalNumber&);
    Complex(double);   // no double::operator
                       // Complex, so do it
                       // here

    . . . .

};
```

Resulting Context

Coupling (and, in general, friend relationships) are still necessary between types; the force is resolved only to the extent that the conversion is firmly associated with a single type. The pattern does guarantee that the type bearing the conversion is always a class object type, however.

The pattern avoids most conversion ambiguities. An additional pattern must deal with the case:

```
struct S {
        operator int() const;
        operator float() const;
};

void f( int );
void f( float );

main() {
        S s;
        f( s ); // error: ambiguous call:
                //  f ( struct S )
}
```

Rationale

A given type cannot know about every (more general) type in the universe whose instances might be created as generalizations of itself; the onus is on the type of the newly created object to understand its own initialization parameters.

Primitive types form an exceptional subpattern because their semantics are built into the compiler for efficiency, and their semantics are not as generally subject to change as those of user-defined types.

ACKNOWLEDGMENTS

Many thanks to Steve Berczuk, who was the EuroPLoP '98 shepherd for this paper.

REFERENCES

[Cargill1996] T. Cargill. "Localized Ownership: Managing Dynamic Objects in C++." In J.M. Vlissides et al. (eds.), *Pattern Languages of Program Design 2*. Reading, MA: Addison-Wesley, 1996.

[Coplien1992] J.O. Coplien. *Advanced C++ Programming Styles and Idioms*. Reading, MA: Addison-Wesley, 1992.

[Gamma+1995] E. Gamma et al. *Design Patterns: Elements of Reusable Object-Oriented Software*. Reading, MA: Addison-Wesley, 1995.

[Ingalls1986] D.H. Ingalls. "A Simple Technique for Handling Multiple Polymorphism." In *Proceedings of OOPSLA '96*, September 1986, ACM Press.

[Koenig1995] A.R. Koenig. "Variations on a Handle Theme." *JOOP* 8(5): 77–80, 1995.

[Martin1995] R. Martin. "Rungs of a Dual Hierarchy." SIGS Publications, April 1995.

[Martin1997] R. Martin. "Design Patterns for Dealing with Dual Inheritance Hierarchies in C++." *C++ Report* 9 (4), New York: SIGS Publications, April 1997.

James Coplien may be reached at cope@research.bell-labs.com.

Chapter 11

Smalltalk Scaffolding Patterns

Jim Doble and Ken Auer

Billy Joel's credo about getting "it right the first time" is compelling. Then again, it's quite possible that Billy Joel has never written a lick of software in his life! And he's probably happier for it because software is notoriously difficult to get right the first time. Any software development plan that assumes that software can be completed right the first time fails to recognize the experimental nature of software development. For a software design team, the course of a project is a learning experience. If an important bit of learning, such as discovery of requirements, misunderstandings, or design inadequacies, occurs too late in the project, the result can be project failure.

Prototyping tackles this issue head-on. The goal of prototyping is to carry out development experiments designed to allow important learning to occur earlier in the project cycle. By moving this learning forward in time, the development team has time to react to what is learned, and the risk of project failure is significantly reduced. Unfortunately, when projects are under significant schedule pressure, expenditure of time and resources on prototyping, rather than on the final product, is counter-intuitive. As a result, prototyping usually needs to be done in a hurry, or it will not be done at all.

Since the goal of prototyping is learning, the key to rapid prototyping is a ruthless focus on what you are trying to learn, at the expense of everything else. This requires designers to maintain a clear mental separation between the essence of their experiment and the scaffolding necessary to complete it. If the goal of a prototyping effort is to validate some design concepts, those design concepts need to be represented faithfully, but anything else is scaffolding[1] and should be implemented by the most expedient means available. If the only goal is to clarify requirements, the entire implementation is scaffolding, because the focus of the experiment is functionality, not how that functionality should be implemented.

Smalltalk is an ideal language for rapid prototyping due to its economy of expression and interpreted execution, which allows a rapid code/test cycle, along with its extensive available class libraries that assist with rapid creation of both design essence and scaffolding. This chapter presents a small set of patterns that have proven to be useful in the rapid development of prototypes using Smalltalk. The primary goal of these patterns is simple expedience. Expedience can be achieved in multiple ways:

- Reducing the amount of code that needs to be typed
- Automatic generation of code
- Reducing the probability of coding errors and the associated test/debug time
- Reducing the time and delays associated with communication and coordination between team members in a multiperson prototyping effort

We call these patterns "scaffolding patterns" because they are particularly well suited to the development of the scaffolding required for rapid prototyping. Some of the artifacts of these patterns may well be suited to production code. In highly dynamic systems such as reflective architectures [Foote1988] or certain black-box frameworks [Yoder1997] some of the patterns themselves are viable through production. Yet, in most software development, the negative impacts that these patterns have on clarity and maintainability (described in the Consequences section for each pattern) begin to overshadow the benefits of expediency as the focus shifts from exploration to production.

Although the patterns presented in this chapter can be applied to single-person or team prototyping projects, some of the patterns are most ideally suited to teams (indicated in the Context section for each pattern).

The patterns described in this paper include the following:

- *Extensible Attributes* adds attributes to an object without modifying the object's class.
- *Artificial Accessors* emulates accessor methods for an object's Extensible Attributes, without adding these methods to the object's class.
- *Generated Accessors* automatically generates accessor methods for attributes defined in a class.
- *Artificial Delegation* allows an object to delegate an operation to one of its attributes, without modifying the delegating object's class.
- *Cached Extensibility* automatically generates attributes, accessors, and/or delegation methods as they are used.
- *Selector Synthesis* provides an expedient means for a state-dependent object to dispatch to a specific handler method based on state and event.

The Context and Consequences sections of each pattern describe when a particular pattern is appropriate and the conditions under which one pattern might lead to another.

KNOWN USES

The authors have used one or more of these patterns in a wide variety of proto-types, including

- Switching systems
- Cellular base stations
- Billing systems
- Process modeling systems
- Table formatting subsystems
- Graphical drawing frameworks
- Various developer assistance tools

Some of these prototypes led to systems that are in production today. The authors have also come across many other Smalltalk developers who have used one or more of these patterns in their prototyping efforts. However, pointing to particular systems to direct one to these patterns is analogous to pointing to the Golden Gate Bridge to discover how one might use a ladder. When the system is done, the scaffolding has been removed, as have any real traces that it ever was present.

SMALLTALK INTRODUCTION

This chapter has been written for experienced Smalltalk developers. However, a brief introduction to some Smalltalk concepts and facilities may help those with little or no Smalltalk experience to understand the patterns.

- Smalltalk programming environments provide a common set of "collection classes," including a String class, a Symbol class, and a Dictionary class. Strings are familiar to most programmers. A symbol is essentially a string constant. Strings can be converted to symbols and symbols to strings using simple conversion methods:

```
aString asSymbol
aSymbol asString
```

The Dictionary class implements an associative memory, associating keys of any class with values of any class. For example,

```
aDictionary at: #car put: 'Toyota'
```

associates a symbol key (#car) with a string value ('Toyota').
- If a message is sent to an object whose class (including its superclasses) does not have a corresponding method, a special method, named doesNotUnderstand: is invoked. Normally, this method is provided in the Object class (which is the

ultimate superclass for all classes) but a class can override this method to provide special handling.

- Smalltalk provides facilities for accessing and modifying information about a class at runtime. For example,

```
aClass instVarNames
```

returns a list of instance variables defined for a class,

```
aClass includesSelector: aSymbol
```

determines whether or not a class contains a method corresponding to aSymbol, and

```
aClass compile: aString classified: aSymbol
```

adds a method whose code is defined by the contents of aString to a class, adding the method to the protocol specified by aSymbol.

- Smalltalk allows a message to be sent to an object directly,

```
anObject aMessage
```

or indirectly, using the perform: method:

```
anObject perform: #aMessage
```

In either case, this causes the method corresponding with aMessage to be executed.

THE PATTERNS

Extensible Attributes

Context

You are participating in a multiperson prototyping effort in which each designer has been assigned an area of focus. You are introducing a class within a prototype, and you anticipate that other designers will want to add additional attributes to your class as the prototype grows.

Problem

How can you minimize the effort required to add additional attributes to the class?

Forces

- It is easy to add an attribute to a Smalltalk class, provided that you are allowed to change the class.
- Communication and coordination effort is required to change a class if you are not the class owner.
- Requesting a coworker to change a class is no problem as long as the coworker is available at the moment you need her, and you can access the changed class immediately once the change has been completed.
- Coworkers may be unavailable when you need a change, resulting in delays or time-wasting work-arounds.

Solution

Add a dictionary attribute to your class that can be used to store additional attributes against symbol keys. Provide an accessor for the dictionary so that other classes can access additional attributes as follows:

```
anExtensibleObject attributesDictionary at: #attributeName put: value.
```

or

```
value := anExtensibleObject attributesDictionary at: #attributeName
```

Rationale

This approach allows other prototypers to add and access additional attributes without needing to change your class definition. Note that this approach is only useful in cases in which the class is required to carry the additional attributes about, but does not require additional methods, or when using a tool that allows you to partition additional methods cleanly (e.g., ENVY/Developer). Examples for which this approach is especially applicable include information records (such as database records) and protocol messages. This is also very useful when using a persistence strategy such as GemStone where adding attributes in standard fashions while maintaining existing data can be relatively time-consuming.

Consequences

It is easy to add additional attributes to an extensible class, but users of this class must access these attributes in a unique way (i.e., through the attributes dictionary). As a result, users need to know which attributes in a class are normal (i.e., accessed using normal accessors) and which attributes are extended. If an extended attribute is converted to a normal attribute, the user's code must be changed. Additionally, the performance hit taken from accessing these attributes via a dictionary versus explicit instance variables can be perceptible in contexts in which the attribute is accessed repeatedly. Since the context is one in which expediency reigns over performance, this is mostly irrelevant until the context changes. Then traditional techniques for these attributes (e.g., explicit instance variables) may be used.

As a result of these consequences, it is recommended that this pattern be used in combination with either the Artificial Accessors or Cached Extensibility pattern.

Related Patterns

This implementation of Extensible Attributes is identical to that of Variable State [Beck1996]. Kent Beck suggests Variable State as a means to deal with classes that have instance variables "whose presence varies from instance to instance." Extensible Attributes is not focused on allowing instances of the same class to have different attributes (although clearly this can be supported), but rather on the addition of attributes to all instances of a class without modifying the class itself.

Artificial Accessors

Context

You are participating in a multiperson prototyping effort in which each designer has been assigned an area of focus and are designing a class within a prototype and have applied Extensible Attributes so that other designers can dynamically add other attributes to your class as the prototype grows.

Problem

How do you make it easier for other classes to access your extended attributes?

Forces

- Extensible Attributes provide an expedient means to add attributes to another class.
- Code that accesses extended attributes can be messy due to the need to access them through the dictionary.
- If extended attributes are changed to normal attributes during the course of prototyping, code that accesses these attributes through the attribute dictionary will need to be changed.

Solution

Simulate the presence of accessors for the extended attributes by overriding the `doesNotUnderstand:` method and by using the selector that was not understood (with the ":" removed in the case of a setter method) as the key into the attributes dictionary. Thus within the `doesNotUnderstand:` method,

```
anExtensibleObject widgets: 4
```

will be converted to

```
self attributesDictionary at: #widgets put: 4
```

and

```
anExtensibleObject widgets
```

will be converted to

```
^self attributesDictionary at: #widgets
```

Rationale

This approach provides all of the advantages of Extensible Attributes, but uses the syntax of normal attributes, simplifying access to these attributes and hiding the fact that extensible attributes have been used. Over the course of the prototyping effort, the class owner can change extended attributes to normal attributes and provide normal accessors, without needing to modify the class's collaborators. The Generated Accessors or Cached Extensibility patterns can be used to facilitate this process.

Consequences

This approach effectively hides the distinction between normal and extended attributes. However, it is important to remember that the pseudo-accessor methods do not actually exist, which can lead to confusion when you are trying to trace method calls or browse implementors. If it is desired to make these accessors visible and the environment is such that the addition of methods without explicit communication is permissible, consider using Cached Extensibility. Alternatively, also consider overriding the `respondsTo:` or `canUnderstand:` method of classes that applies this pattern to further hide the fact that methods don't exist for messages that the object can handle. Note, however, that this is only useful when other classes (scaffolding or otherwise) exploit these rarely used features with respect to the class(es) that employ this pattern.

Note that the use of `doesNotUnderstand:` adds an additional performance hit to the already suspect Extensible Attributes that may sometimes be perceptible. Since the context is one in which expediency reigns over performance, this is mostly irrelevant until the context changes. Then traditional techniques for these attributes (e.g., explicit instance variables) may be used. Alternatively, if the new context allows migration to Cached Extensibility this additional overhead goes away.

Example

Here is a simple implementation of the doesNotUnderstand: method for Artificial Accessors. Note that this implementation interprets all methods that are not understood as attempts to access extended attributes, which may sometimes be too broad an interpretation.

```
doesNotUnderstand: aMessage
  | s |
  aMessage selector last = $:
    ifTrue:
      [key := aMessage selector copyFrom: 1 to: aMessage
selector size - 1.
      self attributesDictionary at: key asSymbol put: aMessage
arguments first]
    ifFalse:
      [^self attributesDictionary at: aMessage selector
asSymbol ifAbsent: [nil]].
```

Generated Accessors

Context

You are developing a prototype and are introducing a class that has a number of normal (i.e., not extended) attributes or are adding normal attributes to an existing class.

Problem

How can you minimize the effort required to make the attributes functional?

Forces

- Common practice is to have accessors (getters and setters) to attributes that may or may not be public [Auer1995].
- Certain types of attributes also typically have other simple methods that are straightforward.
- Smalltalk is untyped so there is no prescribed way to declare the types of these attributes.

- We are learning nothing from writing these simple methods, so they are basically scaffolding.
- Writing these methods is simple but take time to create and are prone to human error (typos, forgetting to return a value, etc.).
- The compiler is accessible, as are the names of attributes of a class.

Solution

Write a quick code generator that generates standard "missing" accessors for the attributes of a class. Use standard suffixes for attributes to indicate special types. Use this suffix to direct which types of accessors should be generated. For example, the instance variables named `thing`, `nameHolder`, `choicesSIL`, and `phoneNumberCollection` might indicate types of `Object`, `ValueModel`, `SelectionInList`, or `Collection`. The methods `thing`, `thing:`, `nameHolder`, `nameHolder:`, `name`, `name:`, `choicesSIL`, `choicesSIL:`, `choicesSelection`, `choicesSelection:`, `choicesList`, `choicesList:`, `phoneNumberCollection`, `phoneNumberCollection:`, `addPhoneNumber:`, and `removePhoneNumber` could all be generated automatically.

Rationale

Why spend unnecessary time typing? We don't typically spend a lot of time documenting code (especially trivial code) during prototyping so generating the defaults gets the trivial work done without losing much. If the generated code is insufficient, it can always be corrected/enhanced at least as fast as it would take to write them by hand in the first place. The bottom line is that the time it takes to write the accessor generator will probably pay for itself after being used only a handful of times.

Consequences

By automatically generating accessor methods for all of our attributes, we may generate methods that are never used. However, such methods are not really a distraction during prototyping and can be removed easily if doing so adds value. In addition, when using this approach, you should take care not to overwrite existing hand-generated methods. If care is taken in creating the accessor generator, much of the code it produces may actually be of production quality. Yet, in this context we should remember that this potentially beneficial side effect is not the main goal of creating and using the generator.

Code Example

In the interest of brevity, we only include the most basic methods for a code generation suite. This could easily be extended to detect the presumed type of the instance variable and to generate additional auxiliary accessor methods as alluded

to earlier. The example below is functional for standard VisualWorks. All methods
should be interpreted as methods for the class `ClassDescription` (or `Behavior`).
Alternatively, they could have less far-reaching effects as methods of any individual
class. This example could easily be tweaked for other dialects and/or tools.

```
createDefaultAccessors
  "Create default accessor methods for all instance
  variables that don't already have them."

  self instVarNames do: [:instVarName |
    (self includesSelector: (self getterMethodNameFor:
        instVarName) asSymbol)
      ifFalse: [self compile: (self
        createGetterMethodSourceFor: instVarName)
                classified: #accessing].
    (self includesSelector: (self setterMethodNameFor:
        instVarName) asSymbol)
      ifFalse: [self compile: (self
        createSetterMethodSourceFor: instVarName)
                classified: #accessing]].
```

```
createDefaultLazyAccessors
  "Create default accessor methods for all instance
  variables that don't already have them. Use lazy
  initialization in the getter."

  self instVarNames do: [:instVarName |
    self includesSelector: (self getterMethodNameFor:
        instVarName) asSymbol)
      ifFalse: [self compile: (self
        createLazyGetterMethodSourceFor: instVarName)
                classified: #accessing].
    (self includesSelector: (self
        defaultValueMethodNameFor: instVarName) asSymbol)
      ifFalse: [self compile: (self
        createDefaultValueMethodSourceFor: instVarName)
                classified: #defaults].
    (self includesSelector: (self
        setterMethodNameFor: instVarName) asSymbol)
      ifFalse: [self compile: (self
        createSetterMethodSourceFor: instVarName)
                classified: #'private-accessing']].
```

```smalltalk
argumentNameFor: variableName
  "Answer the name for the argument to set the variable
  Name."

  ('*Holder' match: variableName)
     ifTrue: [^'aValueModel'].
  ('*SIL' match: variableName)
     ifTrue: [^'aSelectionInList'].
  ('*Dictionary' match: variableName)
     ifTrue: [^'aDictionary'].
  ('*s' match: variableName)
     ifTrue: [^'aSequenceableCollection'].
  (#('is*' 'has*' 'use*') contains: [:pattern | pattern
        match: variableName])
     ifTrue: [^'aBoolean'].
  ^'anObject'

createDefaultValueMethodSourceFor: variableName
  "Create the source code for a simple getter method for
  the variableName"

  ^(String new: 64) writeStream
    nextPutAll: (self defaultValueMethodNameFor:
variableName); cr;
      crtab; nextPut: $^; nextPutAll: (self
        createDefaultValueStringFor: variableName);
    contents

createDefaultValueStringFor: variableName
  "Answer a string to be used to determine the default
  value of a variableName"

  ('*Holder' match: variableName)
     ifTrue: [^'nil asValue'].
  ('*SIL' match: variableName)
     ifTrue: [^'SelectionInList new'].
  ('*Dictionary' match: variableName)
     ifTrue: [^'Dictionary new'].
  ('*s' match: variableName)
     ifTrue: [^'OrderedCollection new'].
  (#('is*' 'has*' 'use*') contains: [:pattern | pattern
        match: variableName])
     ifTrue: [^'true'].
  ^'''undefined'''
```

```
createGetterMethodSourceFor: variableName
  "Create the source code for a simple getter method for
  the variableName"

  ^(String new: 64) writeStream
    nextPutAll: (self getterMethodNameFor: variableName);
    cr;
    crtab; nextPut: $^; nextPutAll: variableName;
    contents

createLazyGetterMethodSourceFor: variableName
  "Create the source code for a simple getter method for
  the variableName which uses lazy initialization."

  ^(String new: 64) writeStream
    nextPutAll: (self getterMethodNameFor: variableName);
    cr;
    crtab; nextPutAll: variableName; nextPutAll: ' == nil';
    crtab: 2; nextPutAll: 'ifTrue: ['; nextPutAll:
      variableName;
    nextPutAll: ' := self ';
    nextPutAll: (self defaultValueMethodNameFor:
      variableName);
    nextPutAll: '].';
    crtab; nextPut: $^; nextPutAll: variableName;
    contents

createSetterMethodSourceFor: variableName
  "Create the source code for a simple setter method for
  the variableName"

  | argument |
  argument := self argumentNameFor: variableName.
  ^(String new: 64) writeStream
    nextPutAll: (self setterMethodNameFor: variableName);
    space; nextPutAll: argument; cr;
    crtab; nextPutAll: variableName; nextPutAll: ' := ';
    nextPutAll: argument;
    contents

defaultValueMethodNameFor: variableName
  "Answer the string describing the name of the selector
  used to retrieve the default value of the given
  variableName."
```

```
^(String new: 32) writeStream
  nextPutAll: 'default';
  nextPut: variableName first asUppercase;
  nextPutAll: (variableName copyFrom: 2 to:
    variableName size);
  contents
```

```
getterMethodNameFor: variableName
  "Answer the string describing the name of the selector
  used to retrieve the given variableName."
```

```
  ^variableName
```

```
setterMethodNameFor: variableName
```

```
"Answer the string describing the name of the selector used
to set the given variableName."
```

```
^variableName copyWith: $:
```

Artificial Delegation

Context

You are participating in a multiperson prototyping effort in which each designer has been assigned an area of focus and are implementing a class that delegates specific operations to specific attributes. You anticipate that other designers will want to add additional attributes and delegated operations to your class as the prototype grows.

Problem

How do you prepare for additional delegated operations with minimal effort?

Forces

- Addition of a delegated operation will typically require addition of a method to the delegator as follows:

```
anOperation
  ^self delegate anOperation.
```

- Smalltalk (out of the box) does not support multiple inheritance or other mechanisms that would easily get the effect of delegation.

- We are learning little from writing these simple methods, so they are basically scaffolding.
- Writing these methods is simple but takes time and is prone to human error (typos, forgetting to return a value, etc.).
- The compiler is accessible, as are the attributes of a class and whether or not the attributes understand a particular message.
- Communication and coordination effort are required to change a class if the person needing the change is not the class owner.

Solution

Override the `doesNotUnderstand:` method of the delegator class to iterate through its attributes looking for an attribute that supports the method selector that was not understood. The first attribute found that supports the method selector is assumed to be the delegate.

Rationale

This approach allows delegated operations to be added to a class without needing to modify the class itself. In addition to its expediency with respect to normal attributes, this approach is particularly easy to use when Extensible Attributes has been applied, as the delegator can simply iterate through the values in its attribute dictionary.

Consequences

Artificial Delegation is hidden in the `doesNotUnderstand:` method, which can lead to confusion when you are trying to trace method calls or browse implementors. If you want to make this delegation visible and the environment is such that the addition of methods without explicit communication is permissible, consider using Cached Extensibility. Alternatively, as with Artificial Accessors, also consider overriding the `respondsTo:` or `canUnderstand:` method of classes that applies this pattern to further hide the fact that methods don't exist for messages that the object can handle. Note, however, that this is only useful when other classes (scaffolding or otherwise) exploit these rarely used features with respect to the class(es) that employ this pattern.

Extensive use of Artificial Delegation versus explicit delegation can add potentially noticeable performance hits due to the overhead of the `doesNotUnderstand:` mechanism. Again, we only use this pattern when expediency overrides these issues. If the context later allows migration to Cached Extensibility this additional overhead goes away.

Although it is usually not the case, Artificial Delegation and Artificial Accessors can be used in the same class at the same time as long as some means is provided for the `doesNotUnderstand:` method to distinguish between delegated operations and Artificial Accessors. One way to do this would be to prefix all accessor methods with "get" or "set." The `doesNotUnderstand:` method could then assume that the method selectors beginning with "`get`" or "`set`" are associated with Artificial Accessors, while all others are for Artificial Delegation. Alternatively, one can look for delegators first and treat not understood messages as Artificial Accessors only as a last resort.

Example

The following example demonstrates automatic delegation to attributes defined explicitly in a class. This could easily be extended to also support delegation to extended attributes.

```
doesNotUnderstand: aMessage
  "See if we can delegate to some attribute of the receiver."
  self delegateGetters do: [:getter |
    | delegate |
    delegate := self perform: getter.
    (delegate respondsTo: aMessage selector)
      ifTrue:
        [^delegate perform: aMessage selector
withArguments: aMessage arguments]].
  ^super doesNotUnderstand: aMessage

delegateGetters
  "Answer the list of unary selectors which can be used to
  delegate messages the receiver does not understand. The
  default implementation here assumes all instance
  variables have getters."

  ^self class allInstVarNames collect: [:instVar | instVar
    asSymbol]
```

Cached Extensibility

Context

You are developing a prototype and have implemented Artificial Accessors, Artificial Delegation, or other automatic functionalities via overriding `does-NotUnderstand:`. As class owner, you would now like to identify how these facilities are being used to determine what the class is actually doing (as opposed to what methods you can see).

Problem

How do you explicitly identify the implicit behavior defined by the actual use of a class or its instances and make it part of the explicit behavior of the class?

Forces

- Asking everyone (including yourself) what they've done to your class via "automatic facilities" is time-consuming and error-prone.
- If you ignore the fact that people are using the facilities you've provided, you may miss out on some essential point about the class, defeating the purpose of prototyping.
- Automatic facilities can introduce unnecessary performance problems, and it may be important to know whether perceived performance problems are due to these facilities or some fundamental flaw in the class.
- Traditional debugging techniques (like `Transcript show:`) might offer some benefit, but will be difficult to trace and are only temporary, leaving no permanent record of the virtual methods.

Solution

Again, override the `doesNotUnderstand:` method, substituting code to generate explicit methods for the virtual methods that are invoked the first time the implicit message is sent. As these facilities are used, the class will reveal how via the methods generated. One can then examine these methods and their senders to determine what is happening and what could be done better.

Rationale

Again, the time spent writing generic code to write common code patterns will quickly pay for itself. The quickly thrown-up scaffolding that gives developers "automatic" functionality can be torn down just as quickly and replaced with new scaffolding that provides a different service.

Consequences

At first glance, this pattern seems to overcome the negative consequences of patterns such as Artificial Accessors or Artificial Delegation by generating the necessary code as it is needed. However, it is important to note that this approach only generates code for methods that are executed, not for all methods that could potentially be executed. As such, the actual methods generated will depend on the extent to which the prototype is exercised during (usually informal) testing. In addition, in a configuration-controlled environment, such as ENVY, determining the home of methods desired by non-owners may not always be trivial, and Artificial Accessors postpones the necessity of addressing this issue.

Cached Extensibility cannot be used simultaneously with Artificial Accessors or Artificial Delegation because they handle the same `doesNotUnderstand:` conditions differently. However, they can be used sequentially, starting out with Artificial Accessors and Artificial Delegation and then switching to Cached Extensibility (by modifying or replacing the `doesNotUnderstand:` method) when the owner is ready to transition to explicit code.

Example

The following example illustrates how to turn Artificial Delegation into explicit delegation. It is functional for VisualWorks with ENVY/Developer, but could be easily adapted for other dialects/tools. Note that the `doesNotUnderstand:` and `delegateGetters` methods could appear in any class. The `createMethodFor:delegatingTo:from:` method need only be implemented once, in `ClassDescription`. Similar code could be written to make explicit attributes and accessors for Extensible Attributes and Artificial Accessors. Of course, the two are not mutually exclusive and many variants of the `doesNotUnderstand:` method could be created to provide appropriate solutions for specific needs.

```
doesNotUnderstand: aMessage
  "See if we can delegate to some attribute of the
  receiver."

  self delegateGetters do: [:getter |
    | delegate |
    delegate := self perform: getter.
    (delegate respondsTo: aMessage selector)
      ifTrue:
        [self class createMethodFor: aMessage
            delegatingTo: delegate from: getter.
        ^self perform: aMessage selector withArguments:
          aMessage arguments]].
      ^super doesNotUnderstand: aMessage

delegateGetters
  "Answer the list of unary selectors which can be used to
  delegate messages the receiver does not understand. The
  default implementation here assumes all instance
  variables have getters."

  ^self class allInstVarNames collect:
    [:instVar | instVar asSymbol]
```

```
createMethodFor: aMessage delegatingTo: anObject from:
      getter
| selector keywordStream argStream signatureStream
signature sourceStream targetClass category |
selector := aMessage selector.
keywordStream := selector keywords readStream.
argStream := aMessage arguments readStream.
signatureStream := (String new: 64) writeStream.
[keywordStream atEnd] whileFalse:
  [signatureStream
    nextPutAll: keywordStream next;
    space.
  argStream atEnd
    ifFalse:
        [| argClassName |
        argClassName := argStream next class name.
        signatureStream
          nextPutAll: (argClassName first isVowel ifTrue:
            ['an'] ifFalse: ['a']);
          nextPutAll: argClassName;
          space]].
signature := signatureStream contents.
sourceStream := (String new: signature size * 3)
  writeStream.
sourceStream
  nextPutAll: signature;
  cr;
  crtab;
  nextPutAll: '^self ';
  nextPutAll: getter;
  space;
  nextPutAll: signature.
targetClass := anObject class.
[category := targetClass whichCategoryIncludesSelector:
    selector.
category isNil and: [targetClass superclass notNil]]
  whileTrue: [targetClass := targetClass superclass].
self
  compile: sourceStream contents
  classified: category
  notifying: nil
  ifNewAddTo: self controller
```

Selector Synthesis

Context

You are developing a prototype and are designing a class that needs to change its behavior (i.e., how it handles particular events) based on its state. You expect that additional states and events will be added to your class as the prototype grows.

Problem

How can you implement a state-dependent object with minimal effort?

Forces

- The State pattern [Gamma+1995] provides an elegant solution for implementing state-dependent objects, but it involves defining a new class for each state, resulting in a lot of typing.
- In a prototyping effort, while the state-dependent object's overall behavior is typically important to the essence of the experiment, how this state dependence is implemented is unimportant (i.e., scaffolding).

Solution

Define states and events as symbols. For a given event/state pair synthesize a method selector by concatenating the state and event symbols, then dispatch based on the resulting selector as follows:

```
selector := 'handle', anEvent asString, 'In', aState asString.
self perform: selector asSymbol.
```

For each supported state/event combination provide an appropriately named handler method. State/event combinations that are not supported can be detected in the `doesNotUnderstand:` method and routed to a default handler.

Rationale

Once Selector Synthesis has been implemented all it takes to implement new states, events, or state/event combinations is to add appropriately named handler methods. There is no additional dispatch code to write or classes to create.

Consequences

State/event handler methods are never explicitly called (i.e., browsing senders will come up empty). On the other hand figuring out where the calls are coming from shouldn't be a big problem as long as the prototyping team is familiar with the pattern.

The combination of the use of `doesNotUnderstand:` and the runtime creation of symbols can sometimes cause a perceptible performance hit. As long as the identification of the state transitions is the focus versus the performance of those transitions, this is irrelevant.

Selector Synthesis can be used at the same time as Artificial Accessors and Artificial Delegation as long as some means is provided for the `doesNotUnderstand:` method to distinguish unimplemented state/event handlers. One way to do this would be to assume that all state/event handler method names begin with `"handle"`.

Related Patterns

A number of patterns, including State [Gamma+1995] and State Action Mapper [Palfinger1997] also address the issue of state-dependent object behavior. Selector Synthesis has the advantage of expedience, but these other patterns may be better suited to production software.

CONCLUSION

The patterns in this paper all take advantage of capabilities inherent in the Smalltalk environment to facilitate rapid prototyping. There are a number of relationships between these patterns:

- Extensible Attributes and Artificial Accessors should be used together.
- Generated Accessors is an alternative to Extensible Attributes/Artificial Accessors, which can be used in a single-person prototyping effort or when the person adding attributes is (or is authorized by) the class owner.
- Artificial Delegation and Selector Synthesis are special-purpose patterns, applicable primarily to specific design situations (e.g., responsibility delegation and state-dependent behavior).
- Cached Extensibility is essentially a "clean-up" pattern improving on Artificial Accessors, Extensible Attributes, and Artificial Delegation by generating the necessary method code as it is used.

Scaffolding patterns, like scaffolding in a building, may be used for a while, then be torn down and thrown away. Nevertheless, these patterns can play an important role in expediting prototype development, and it is in this way that they can make a meaningful contribution to the successful completion of software development projects.

ACKNOWLEDGMENTS

The authors would like to thank their PLoP '97 shepherd, Joe Yoder, for his helpful comments and suggestions.

REFERENCES

[Auer1995] K. Auer. "Reusability through Self Encapsulation." In J. Coplien and D. Schmidt (eds.), *Pattern Languages of Program Design*. Reading, MA: Addison-Wesley, 1995 (http://www.rolemodelsoft.com/patterns/self-enc.htm).

[Beck1996] K. Beck. *Smalltalk Best Practice Patterns*. Englewood Cliffs, NJ: Prentice-Hall, 1996 (http://www.phptr.com/ptrbooks/prefice/ptr_pref_013476904xp.html).

[Foote1988] B. Foote. "Designing to Facilitate Change with Object-Oriented Frameworks," Masters Thesis, Department of Computer Science, University of Illinois at Urbana-Champaign, 1988 (http://www.laputan.org/dfc/discussion.html).

[Gamma+1995] E. Gamma, R. Helm, R. Johnson, and J. Vlissides. *Design Patterns: Elements of Reusable Object-Oriented Software*. Reading, MA: Addison-Wesley, 1995 (http://hillside.net/patterns/books/ #Gamma).

[Palfinger1997] G. Palfinger. "State Action Mapper." In *PLoP '97 Proceedings,* Washington University Technical Report #wucs-97-34.

[Yoder1997] J. Yoder. "A Framework to build Financial Models." 1997 (http://www-cat.ncsa.uiuc.edu/~yoder/financial_framework/).

Jim Doble may be reached at jdoble@acm.org.

Ken Auer may be reached at kauer@rolemodelsoft.com.

Chapter 12

High-Level and Process Patterns from the Memory Preservation Society: Patterns for Managing Limited Memory

James Noble and Charles Weir

The Memory Preservation Society is an old and august body—possibly one of the oldest computer groups in existence. Ours is a virtual society, for it exists solely in the minds of programmers who find themselves challenged by the limitations of the real computers running their software, compared with the ideal systems of their imaginations. Their biggest problem is typically the dreaded shortage of memory. Over the years, our members have risen to this challenge with a variety of techniques, some traditional, others appropriate only to the object-oriented languages and sophisticated operating systems of today.

Of course, memory has become so much cheaper recently that for many environments the RAM memory use need not be a major constraint. There are very few systems, however, that can afford to ignore the issue entirely. Furthermore, the recent development of palmtop computers and intelligent mobile phones has produced an entire new type of system in which memory is limited, and users expect these systems to support much more powerful software than they would ever have contemplated in the past.

In this chapter we describe some of the patterns we've encountered in memory-challenged systems. We've been surprised at the large number of patterns we found when we started to study the subject; space does not permit us to include them all here. In this chapter, therefore, we present only the high-level and process patterns, while the remainder of the patterns are available in the full *Proceedings of the Memory Protection Society* [Noble+1998]. Included, therefore, are the following:

- Think Small
- Memory Budget
- Memory Overdraft
- Make the User Worry
- Partial Failure
- Captain Oates
- Exhaustion Test
- Memory Performance Assessment

PATTERN FORM

We've used a more condensed pattern structure than most pattern languages. As in Christopher Alexander's pattern format [Alex1977], each pattern highlights and discusses a problem, then concludes with **Therefore:**. This is followed by a specific recommendation and a discussion of how to implement this recommendation. Further sections then describe Consequences, Known Uses, and related patterns and literature (See Also). Throughout the pattern descriptions we refer to other patterns. We've illustrated many of these patterns with examples taken from a particularly memory-challenged system, the unique Strap-It-On wrist-mounted PC from the well-known company StrapItOn.

Perhaps the most vital discussion for a pattern is of the forces, or considerations and consequences, to help readers to decide when to use that pattern rather than another. In each pattern, we've identified in the Problem section at least one major force that drives each pattern—in addition to the need to restrict memory use. Then in the Consequences section, we identify the other implications, both positive and negative. Throughout, we've highlighted the significant forces in italics. To distinguish the positive from the negative consequences of each pattern, we describe the positive consequences first, the negative ones second, and partition the two with the word **However:**.

FORCES

Table 12-1 shows some of the major forces we've identified in the patterns. In each case, a "yes" answer to the question is generally good. We've described the forces in more detail in the specific patterns.

Table 12-2 shows how these forces apply to each of the patterns in the language. Each cell contains a ☺ if the pattern normally has a beneficial effect in that respect (a "yes" answer to the question in Table 12-1) or a ☹ if the pattern's effect is detrimental. A ☺ indicates that the pattern usually has an effect, but whether that effect is positive or negative depends on circumstances.

Table 12-1 *Major Forces in the Patterns*

Memory requirements	Does the pattern reduce the overall memory use of the system?
Predictability	Does the pattern make the memory requirements predictable? This is particularly important for real-time applications, where behavior must be predictable.
Fragmentation	Does the pattern reduce the amount of memory that is wasted because it is divided into fragments too small to be reallocated?
Programmer effort	Does the pattern reduce the total programmer effort to produce a given system?
Programmer discipline	Does the pattern remove restrictions on programming style so that programmers have to pay less attention to detail in all aspects of programming?
Testing cost	Does the pattern reduce the total testing effort for the application development?
Hardware and O/S cost	Does the pattern reduce hardware or operating system costs?
Local vs. global	Does the pattern tend to help encapsulate different parts of the application, keeping them independent of each other?
Design quality	Does the pattern encourage better design quality? Will it be easier to make changes to the system later on?
Usability	Will the pattern tend to make it easier for users to operate the system?

APPLICABILITY

We started writing these patterns following our work with small computer systems: palmtops and smart cards. Yet many of the patterns will be equally familiar to people working with modern mainframe systems. Such systems may have very large amounts of RAM and disk space, but they also have many—often thousands

Table 12-2 *The Patterns and the Effects of Major Forces on Each*

	Memory Reqs	Predicta-bility	Fragmen-tation	Progr. Effort	Progr. Discipline	Testing Cost	HW and OS Cost	Local vs. Global	Design Quality	Usability
Think Small	☺			☹	☹			☺		
Memory Budget	☺	☺	☺	☹	☹			☺	☺	
Memory Overdraft		☺	☹	☹	☹			☺		
Make the User Worry	☺	☺	☺	☺		☺				☹
Partial Failure	☺	☺	☹	☹	☹	☹			☹	☺
Captain Oates	☺	☺	☺	☹	☹	☹	☺	☺		☺
Exhaustion Test			☺	☹		😐				☺
Memory Assessment	☺			☹		☹				

of—simultaneous users. So the net memory available for each user is relatively small. Thus programmers of mainframe applications have similar problems to programmers of palmtops and smart cards.

Similarly, even the relatively lush memory availability of PCs and workstations can leave constraints for the programmer if the application is big enough or if the programmer must work on a large enough data set. Microsoft Windows and UNIX provide facilities to hide some of the real constraints from the programmer, but good engineering demands that systems are used up to their limits, and for every application there will be situations in which the memory demand is greater than what's available. Thus, the less memory-hungry we can make our applications, the better. Table 12-3 shows the differences and commonalties between different types of hardware.

Table 12-4 shows the importance of the different constraints on memory. This table distinguishes the total code delivered (all the code written apart from test harnesses) from the proportion of the executable code normally needed to run a typical application, that is, the Code Working Set. In each cell, three stars indicates that the constraint is usually the chief driver for a typical project architecture; two stars indicates that it is an important design consideration (but typically not the most important); one star implies something that may need some effort from programmers, but probably won't affect the architecture significantly; and no stars indicates that it's virtually irrelevant to the project.

THE PATTERNS

Think Small

How should you approach a small system?

You have to program a small system—that is, a system with *memory requirements* that will be hard to meet. The program size will be the total of the *sizes* of all the modules resident at a time, so every component of the system will add to the total size. Programmers (especially those without small system experience) *lack discipline* and will be sloppy about limiting their memory use—after all, in typical environments, it's bad engineering to spend *programmer effort* unnecessarily, and it's always more fun to add another feature than to reduce memory use. The program may suffer from *memory fragmentation,* because programmers may allocate memory but then not use it, or may dynamically allocate varying sized amounts of memory so that leftover memory cannot be allocated. For example, early versions of the Strap-It-On Wrist-Mounted PC came with fifteen different Wrist Accessory packages, but only one could run in the available memory.

Therefore: *Imagine the system is smaller than it is!*

Table 12-3 *Comparison of Different Kinds of Systems*

	Palmtop, Smart Phone Cards	Embedded System	PC, Workstation	Mainframe
Basic code	ROM	ROM	On disk, loaded to RAM	Disk, loaded to RAM
Shared code	DLLs in ROM	ROM	Shared DLLs loaded to RAM	Shared DLLs loaded to RAM
Third party code	Loaded to RAM from secondary storage	N/A	Loaded to RAM from disk or network server	Loaded to RAM from disk
UI	Graphical User Interface (GUI); libraries in ROM	Typically text-only User Interface or none	GUI, with several possible libraries as DLLs on disk	Typically text UI or none
Secondary storage	RAM disk and external cards	None	Local hard disk	Secondary disk devices
Network	Dialup via tele-communications	None	10MBps LAN	100MBps LAN
Other IO	Serial connections	As needed— often the main purpose of device	Serial and parallel ports, modem, etc.	Client terminals and work-stations, accessed via LAN
Typical applications	Diary, address book, phone, e-mail	Device control, protocol conversion	Word processing, spreadsheet, small database, accounts	Large database, accounts, stock control

Table 12-4 *Importance of Memory Constraints*

	Palmtop, Smart Phone Card	Embedded System	Microsoft Windows	Mainframe
Total code	**	**		
Code working set	ROM applications: Third party applications:**		*	
Heap and stack	**	***	*	*

Encourage every team member to keep a very tight control on the memory use. Develop a culture in which memory saving is a habit. Use design and code reviews to exorcise wasteful features, habits, and techniques.

There are many things to look out for, during specification, coding and compilation:

- Avoid unnecessary data structures.
- Choose compact data structures (e.g., atoms and enumerated types rather than strings, bytes rather than machine words, etc.).
- Avoid language features that cost memory (e.g., C++ Vtbls, exceptions).
- Avoid repeatedly allocating and releasing variable-sized data structures—allocate memory once and reuse it as necessary.
- Reduce the quality of images and sound.
- Reduce unnecessary dot point features (i.e., features that are peripheral to the program's main purpose), such as desk calculators, spell checkers, and GUIs.
- Remove hidden features, such as "gang screens" (also known as "splash screens").
- Use optional compilation techniques to remove debugging and self-checking codes from the final deliverable system.
- Use compiler flags to compress memory structures.
- Use an efficient memory allocation library, since libraries vary considerably in their memory overheads.

Consequences

You end up with a small system, which meets its *memory requirements*. **However:** you have to worry about this all the way through the development, so you need more *programmer effort* and *programmer discipline,* and programmers may trade-off *local vs. global* memory use.

Known Uses

Most development teams for small machines use these patterns to some extent. For example, the Microsoft CE versions of Windows applications cut down enormously on the features of the applications provided. Many development environments support two compilation modes, for debug and for release; the debug mode includes processing and data attributes not present in the release mode. Many C++ compilers provide flags to compress data structures rather than align data members with memory boundaries. The Psion Series 5 development used only 4-tone bitmaps (even though the hardware supported 16-tone greyscale), culled the dot-point features, and enforced strict development policies to allow a large number of applications to run simultaneously in a small memory area.

See Also

There are two alternative strategies for thinking small. If you're a pessimist, prefer to think ahead, or are facing particularly tight *memory requirements*, then you should prepare a Memory Budget so that you can plan your use of memory. If you're an optimist, prefer to fix problems only when they actually arise, or your *memory requirements* are not particularly tight, you should consider performing a Memory Performance Assessment and dealing with memory limitations once the program is running. You may need to Make the User Worry about memory, do an Exhaustion Test to be sure you support graceful degradation in the face of Partial Failures, and, where necessary, make the program do a Captain Oates, relinquishing memory to give other programs a chance to run.

Memory Budget

How do you keep control of memory in a very tight project?

Your project has very tight *memory requirements*. Unless memory constraints are a high priority it's unlikely that the system will work correctly.

Therefore: *Draw up a memory budget and worry about it a lot. Define targets for the whole system and for each component as part of the specification process.*

The most important thing about a memory budget is that people working on the project take it seriously. Some environments provide memory-use monitors or resource limits that can be used to enforce memory budgets, and these can increase the seriousness of the budgets. Sometimes it is worth defining two targets for each component—one for peak memory use, the other for the normal "idle" state.

Consequences

Having specific targets for memory use greatly increases the *predictability* of the memory use of the resulting program. Because developers face specific targets, they can make decisions *locally* where there are trade-offs between memory use and other constraints. It's easy to identify problem areas, and to see which modules are keeping their requirements reasonable, so a budget increases *programmer discipline*. Preparing memory budgets can help avoid memory *fragmentation*, because components that may cause fragmentation (by allocating memory and not using it, or allocating and releasing large numbers of small memory blocks) can also be identified early in the development process. **However:** defining, assigning, and managing the budgets requires significant *programmer effort*. Developers may achieve their *local* budgets in ways that have unwanted *global* side effects such as poor *time performance*, off-loading functionality to other modules, or breaking necessary encapsulation (see Brooks [1975]). Runtime enforcement of memory budget requires *hardware or operating system support*.

Known Uses

The OS/360 project used memory budgets [Brooks1975]. The Symbian EPOC system implements a de-facto memory budget by limiting the heap space of each application in the development environment. Even more constraining, many environments allow you to specify hard runtime limits, for example, IBM UNIX and NewMonics' PERC Real-Time Java [Nilson1995].

See Also

Memory Performance Assessment provides an alternative solution to the same problem. Memory Overdraft arrangements can help when your Memory Budget goes down the gurgler. For some kinds of programs you cannot produce a complete budget in advance, so you may need to allocate memory coarsely between the user and the system and then Make the User Worry about memory.

[Gilb1988] describes techniques for attribute specification appropriate for defining the project's targets.

Memory Overdraft

What happens when your memory budget goes wrong?

You've produced a memory budget, but *memory requirements* are *unpredictable* and hard to estimate accurately. As your development proceeds, it becomes clear that some components will need more than their budgeted amount of memory—either temporarily, to handle infrequent special conditions, or permanently.

Therefore: *Include overdraft provisions in your memory budget.*

Ensure your memory budget has some slack. When a component needs more memory, and you can't reduce its size in any other way, you can grant it more memory from the overdraft. Either the remains of this overdraft, or a separate dynamic overdraft memory allocation in the budget, can supply extra memory in emergencies at runtime.

Consequences

Your budget will be more resilient in the face of development realities, increasing the overall *predictability* of the program's memory use. **However:** Managing an overdraft takes *programmer effort*. Knowledge about the overdraft may encourage programmers to reduce their *discipline* and take it for granted, reducing the integrity of the budget. The memory allocated for overdrafts can suffer from *fragmentation* if varying amounts of memory must be allocated on demand. An overdraft is typically shared by all the modules in a program, so programmers can use an overdraft to get extra *local* memory while reducing the amount of extra *global* memory available.

Known Uses

The OS/360 project included overdrafts as part of their budgets [Brooks1975]. Prograph on the Macintosh includes a Rainy Day fund of memory that programmers can call on in an emergency [MacNeil+1995].

See Also

A Memory Overdraft may be exhausted at runtime, so Exhaustion Test to check the behavior when the overdraft is overdrawn. You can often Make the User Worry about memory as an alternative to providing a Memory Overdraft. See Captain Oates for a technique in which part of the program releases some memory if an active part of the program is making heavy use of the Memory Overdraft.

Make the User Worry

Sometimes the user is in the best position to allocate or manage the use of memory.

In many cases, especially in interactive systems, *memory requirements* cannot really be *predicted* in advance. This is because the uses for the memory will depend critically on what the user chooses to do with the system. If you try to produce a generic budget, you will overallocate the memory requirements for some parts of the program, and consequently have to underallocate others. If you allocate a large amount of space for a Memory Overdraft, you effectively postpone memory planning until runtime and are consequently more likely to run out of memory. For example, the memory requirements for a user typing small memos on the Word-O-Matic on the Strap-It-On PC will differ greatly from a user writing a Ph.D. thesis—one may require a large memory allocation for clip art and the other a large allocation for actual text.

Therefore: *Make the system's memory model explicit in its user interface, so the user can worry about memory.*

On the basis of your Memory Budget, allocate memory coarsely between the user and the program. Use a Memory Budget and other patterns from this paper to manage the system's memory. Design a model of the way user memory will be used. Expose this memory model in your program's user interface, and let the user manage the allocation of user memory directly. Note that the user in question may be an engineer configuring the system rather than a final end user.

There are number of techniques that can expose a memory model to its users:

- Constantly display the amount of free memory in the system.
- Provide tools, which allow users to query the contents of their memory, and the amount of memory remaining.
- Generate warning messages or dialogue boxes as the system runs out of memory.
- Make the user choose what data to overwrite or delete when they need more memory.

For example, Word-O-Matic allows the user to choose how much memory should be allocated to image caches and uses all the otherwise unallocated space to store the document. Word-O-Matic also displays the available memory to the user.

Consequences

The system can deliver more behavior to the user than if it had to make pessimistic assumptions about its use of memory. The user can adjust their use of the system to make the most of the available memory, reducing the *memory requirements* for performing any particular task. Although the way user memory will be allocated at runtime is unpredictable, it is quarantined within the Memory Budget, so the memory use of the system as a whole is *more predictable*. Some user interfaces can even make the user worry about *memory fragmentation*. **However:** the user now has to worry about memory, whether they want to or not, so the system is *less usable*. Given a choice, users will choose systems where they do not have to worry about memory. You have to spend *programmer effort* designing the user's memory model and making the memory model visible to the user.

Known Uses

The Macintosh and Windows systems display the amount of free disk space in every desktop disk window. Windows' Notepad has fixed limits on the size of its application data. The Acorn Archimedes can present a bar graph showing the memory use in the system, and the user can drag the bars to change memory allocations. Smalltalk-80 produces a sequence of notifier and warning messages as it runs out of memory. Music synthesizers and programmable calculators often provide a small fixed number of memory locations for programs, and users think of these systems as having just that number of memories. An early Australian laser printer required the user to store fonts into one of a fixed number of memory locations. Larger fonts required two or more contiguous locations (making the user worry about *memory fragmentation* as well as *memory requirements*). The Ensoniq Mirage sound sampler was the ultimate example of making the user worry—the user must allocate memory for sound sample storage by entering two-digit hexadecimal digits using only increment and decrement buttons. Each 64K memory bank could hold up to eight samples, provided each sample was stored in a single contiguous memory block.

See Also

The memory model exposed to the user may be the Fixed Size Data Structure or the Variable Sized Data Structure from [Noble+1998]. Functionality a la Carte [Adams1995] can be used to present the costs and benefits of memory allocations to the user. A basic Memory Budget and Memory Overdraft can provide an alternative that does not require the user to manage memory explicitly, but which will have higher *memory requirements* to provide a given amount of functionality.

Partial Failure

Also Known As

Graceful Degradation

How can you deal with unlimited demands for memory?

No matter how much we do to reduce the program's *memory requirements,* there will still be situations when the program runs out of resources.

Therefore: *Allow the program to fail partially or have its behavior degrade but not stop.*

When a program runs out of memory, it shouldn't just stop but should continue as best it can. This usually means aborting the operation that used up all the memory. It's important that this frees up enough memory to allow further operations. Alternatively, and usually better, the program may continue but in a degraded mode. For example when the Word-O-Matic fails to allocate the memory required for the voice output of a document, it continues to provide a screen-only display. More typical examples of degraded modes are as follows:

- Loading a font may fail; in this case we can use a standard system font.
- Displaying images may fail; we can leave them blank or display a message.
- A detailed calculation may fail; we can use an approximation.
- Undo information may not be saved (usually after warning the user).
- A compression process may fail; we might store the uncompressed data.

Often objects encapsulate this failure to hide it from their clients. The Word-O-Matic's voice output module still accepts commands from its clients even in its out-of-memory state, which makes programming its clients much simpler.

Consequences

This approach significantly improves the program's *usability*. With careful design, even the degraded modes can provide essential functionality. By ensuring the program can continue to operate within a given amount of memory, partial failure decreases the program's minimum *memory requirements* and increases the *predictability* of those requirements. **However:** it is hard work to program, requiring *programmer discipline* to apply consistently and *programmer effort* to actually implement, because it requires *local* mechanisms to provide a *global* effect. Supporting partial failure significantly increases the complexity of each module, increasing the *testing cost* because you must try to test all the failure modes. Partial failures can also increase memory *fragmentation*, because a module that has partially failed may not be using all the memory it has been allocated.

Known Uses

If Netscape fails to load a font due to insufficient memory, it continues with standard fonts. The Microsoft Windows application Photoshop warns the user and doesn't save undo information. Microsoft Powerpoint will use standard fonts and omit images if it runs out of memory. In UNIX, if there's insufficient memory to run a job, that job fails rather than have the whole system dying.

See Also

It's essential that this new behavior be properly tested, as described in the Exhaustion Test pattern. Whereas the Partial Failure pattern describes what a process should do when it runs out of memory itself, Captain Oates describes what a process should do when a different process runs out of memory.

Captain Oates[1]

Also Known As

Do the Decent Thing, Suicide

How do we prioritize demands for memory?

A program's *memory requirements* are not equally important. At any given time, some of a program's *memory requirements* will be more important to its clients or users than others. For example, when someone is using the Strap-It-On PC's word processor to edit a document, the user doesn't care what the fractal screen background looks like. Some programs may be exceeding their share of the Memory Budget, by holding on to a Memory Overdraft at runtime. You can increase a system's *usability* by spending scarce resources doing what the user actually wants.

Therefore: *When a system runs out of memory, surrender memory used by less vital components rather than fail the most important tasks.*

Often programs use memory to cache information that is not strictly required, in order to improve time performance. This cached information prevents the resources from being available to other processes that may need it for more vital operations. Often, too, processes running in the background may now be unnecessary and use resources needed for foreground tasks. So when the system's memory is low, indicate this condition with a signal to all the running processes. When an inactive process receives this signal it should release its inessential memory or, in more extreme situations, close down. For example, networking "IP stacks" may release some of the cached IP address map; Web browsers may release cached pages; or a word processor might delete "undo" information. Background service processes may even shut down completely.

If there is no support for signaling memory conditions, an alternative is for processes to keep track of the free memory situation by regular polling and of free inessential resources (or close down) when memory becomes short. For example when the Word-O-Matic runs out of memory its background Fizzy fractal generator automatically closes down. As a result, the word processor's *memory requirements* can be met.

---

[1] Captain Oates was a Victorian explorer whose team reached the South Pole but ran short of supplies on the way back. He sacrificed himself to give the rest of his team a chance of survival, with the celebrated last words: "I may be some time."

Consequences

This increases the system's *usability*, and by allocating memory where it is most needed, reduces the system's *memory requirements*. Programs or modules releasing large amounts of their overdrawn allocated memory also increase the *predictability* of the system's memory use, and reduce *fragmentation*. **However:** This approach requires *programmer discipline* to consider voluntarily releasing resources and *programmer effort* to implement. It introduces coupling between otherwise unrelated components, which decreases the *predictability* of the system. Releasing resources can reduce the program's *time performance*. Programs need to be *tested* to see that they do release resources and that they continue to perform successfully afterwards. Because all programs must handle the memory low signal, Captain Oates is easier with *operating system support*. This is another *global mechanism* that introduces *local complexity* to handle the signal.

Known Uses

Windows has an "about to run out of memory" signal, to which well-written Windows applications will respond. For example "ObjectPLUS," a HyperCard application by ObjectPLUS of Boston, stops playing sound and removes or compresses cached bitmaps. In Symbian's EPOC, each memory heap caches redundant blocks in case the process needs them again. When memory runs out, the system frees these blocks and retries the operation. The Apple Macintosh supports purgable memory blocks that the OS may reclaim when memory is short. These are often used for read-only caches of disk data and for resource file data.

See Also

Captain Oates allows programs to use Memory Overdrafts without affecting the overall integrity of the Memory Budget. Where Captain Oates describes what a program should do when another process in the system runs out of memory, Partial Failure describes what it should do when it runs out of memory itself.

Exhaustion Test

Also Known As

Test Small, Out-of-Memory Testing

How do you ensure that your programs work correctly in out-of-memory conditions?

Programs that deal gracefully with resource failures—say by using the Memory Overdraft or Partial Failure patterns—have a large number of extra situations to deal with because each resource failure is a different execution event. Ideally, the program should be tested in every situation that will arise in execution, but exhaustive testing will greatly increase the *testing cost*. Testing for memory exhaustion failures is particularly difficult because these events are by definition exceptional, so they will occur mostly when the system is heavily loaded or has been executing for a long period.

> **Therefore:** *Use testing techniques that simulate memory exhaustion.*

Use a version of the memory allocator that fails after a given number of allocations and verify that the program behaves sanely for values of this number. Also use another version of the allocator that inserts random failures. Test for memory fragmentation by repeatedly allocating and releasing varying amounts of memory and by verifying that the system can allocate all the nominally available memory. Verify that the program implements Partial Failure by taking alternative steps to get the job done or Makes the User Worry by reporting to the user if this is not possible.

You can combine partial failure testing with more traditional memory testing techniques such as the use of conservative garbage collectors to verify that the program does not cause resource leaks.

Consequences

Using specialized testing techniques reduces the *testing cost* for a given amount of trust in the program. **However:** being reasonably certain that the resulting program will work correctly will still have a large *testing cost*. This approach also needs *programmer effort* to build the specialized memory allocators to support the tests. Testing doesn't always detect the results of random and time-dependent behavior, for example, where two threads are both allocating independently.

Known Uses

Many development environments provide tools or libraries to allow memory failure testing. The Purify environment for C++ supports random and predictable failure of C++'s memory allocator. Symbian's EPOC provides debug versions of the allocator with similar features, and these are used in module testing of all the EPOC applications.

See Also

Exhaustion Testing is particularly important where the system has specific processing to handle low memory conditions, such as the Partial Failure and Captain Oates patterns.

Memory Performance Assessment

How do you keep memory constraints from dominating the design process to the detriment of other requirements?

Your system has to meet particular *memory requirements,* but other requirements are more important. Implementing and tracking a memory budget costs *programmer discipline* and *programmer effort* that could be better directed towards other requirements. For example, if you're developing a new operating system release for desktop PCs, then integrating a Web browser into the desktop, providing AI-based help systems, and shipping the system less than a year late, will all be more important than controlling the amount of memory the system occupies.

Therefore: *Implement the system, paying attention to memory requirements only where these have a significant effect on the design. Once the system is working, identify the most wasteful areas and optimize their memory use.*

Using this approach, development proceeds much as usual, with no special attention paid to memory use. This is fine, as long as the resulting program meets its memory requirements. If (as often happens) the program does not meet its *memory requirements* you have to perform memory optimization.

Consequences

The team develops the system effectively and faster, because they are not making unnecessary optimizations—a given amount of *programmer effort* gets you more software with better *time performance* and higher *design quality*. **However:** The *memory requirements* of the resulting program will be hard to *predict*. The program may suffer from *memory fragmentation,* especially if it does a substantial amount of dynamic memory allocation. In many cases it requires more *programmer effort* to leave memory optimization to last than performance optimization would, because memory optimization tends to require changes to object relationships that can affect large amounts of code. Memory optimization can also reduce *design quality,* require *local versus global* trade-offs, and increase the *cost of testing*.

Known Uses

This pattern occurs very frequently in projects, since it is what happens by default. Typically a team implements a system, then discovers it uses too much memory. Memory optimization follows. [Blank+1995] describe the process of taking an existing program and optimizing it to run under more constrained memory conditions.

See Also

Most of the following patterns in the language optimize a program's memory use. The patterns Lazy Optimization and Optimize the Right Place in [Auer+1995] address speed optimization, but the techniques apply equally to space optimization. Two relevant low-level patterns in the same language are Transient Reduction and Object Transformation. If you are facing particularly tight *memory requirements*, prefer to think ahead, or are a pessimist, then you should prepare a Memory Budget in advance so you can plan your use of memory.

ACKNOWLEDGMENTS

The authors wish to thank John Vlissides, EuroPLoP conference shepherd for this paper, for his valuable and exacting feedback on early drafts of this work, and the editors and anonymous reviewers for their useful comments.

REFERENCES

[Adams1995] S. Adams. "Functionality a-la-carte." In J.O. Coplien and P.C. Schmidt (eds.), *Pattern Languages of Program Design*. Reading, MA: Addison-Wesley, 1995.

[Alex1977] C. Alexander. *A Pattern Language: Towns/Buildings/Construction*. New York: Oxford University Press, 1977.

[Auer+1995] K. Auer and K. Beck. "Lazy Optimization: Patterns for Efficient Smalltalk Programming." In J.M. Vlissides, J.O. Coplien, and N.L. Kerth (eds.), *Pattern Languages of Program Design 2*. Reading, MA: Addison Wesley, 1995.

[Blank+1995] M.S. Blank and S.W. Galley. *How to Fit a Large Program Into a Small Machine*, 1995. Available as http://www.csd.uwo.ca/Infocom/Articles/small.html.

[Brooks1975] F. Brooks. *The Mythical Man Month*. Reading, MA: Addison-Wesley, 1975.

[Gilb1988] T. Gilb. *Principles of Software Engineering Management*. Reading, MA: Addison-Wesley, 1988.

[MacNeil+1995] J. MacNeil and D. Proudfoot. *The Rainy Day Fund*. Technical Note CPX_TN #30, Halifax: Pictorius Inc., 1995.

[Nilson1995] K. Nilson. *Issues in the Design and Implementation of Real-Time Java*, 1996. Available as http://www.sys-con.com/java/iss1/real.htm.

[Noble+1998] J. Noble and C. Weir. "The Proceedings of the Memory Protection Society." In the *Proceedings of the 3rd European Conference on Patterns Languages of Programming and Computing*, Kloster Irsee: Universität Verlag Konstantz, 1998.

James Noble may be reached at kjx@mri.mq.edu.au.

Charles Weir may be reached at cweir@cix.co.uk.

PART 4

Time

Programs are more like movies than paintings, more like robots than statues, more like living cells than stones. Even the simplest program doesn't just site there; it runs and returns a result. A program sends its memory on a complex multidimensional trajectory through space and time, one op code at a time. Turing's Tape whirs and inches spasmodically across its read head. All but the simplest applications operate in a constantly changing, often interactive input environment and produce a steady stream of results based on this input and their own histories.

In doing so, the programs model, record, and mimic aspects of the domain for which they were written. Hence they are not limited to what currently is. They can model what was, what might have been, or what might be someday. For that matter, they can model situations that can never be.

However, most programs are not written to allow their states to roll back to arbitrary points in their pasts, perhaps to roll forward again in a different direction. Programs that cannot remember their pasts are doomed to recompute them.

This part presents two collections of patterns that deal with objects, history, and time.

Chapter 13: Temporal Patterns by Andy Carlson, Sharon Estepp, and Martin Fowler. The Temporal Property pattern augments an attribute or relation with information specifying a time interval during which it is effective. Temporal Association addresses a more complex situation in which the association itself has a distinct identity and is cast as an intermediate object that is itself subject to time constraints. Unlike the first two patterns, the Snapshot pattern is independent of specific temporal constraints. Instead, it calls for a set of values from a number of objects to be "frozen" at a given point in time.

Chapter 14: A Collection of History Patterns by Francis Anderson.

The section concludes with patterns inspired by the intricacies of modern software change management systems and the demands of complex billing applications.

The Edition pattern associates a state change with the event that caused it. It provides the foundation for the patterns that follow, which focus on where to "hang" history information and how to manage it. Change Log can be used in simple cases where history can be tracked by logging the states of a handful of variables. History on Associations replaces a discrete variable with an object that manages a series of Editions. Its current state is the current Edition. The Posting pattern calls for a wrapper on events that tracks the history of their arrival, thereby permitting the reconstruction of sequences of events and their consequences. History on Self moves the responsibility for tracking history from variables or associations to the object itself. An object's entire state is tracked en masse. Memento Child and History on Tree deal with the complexities of managing the history of more complex aggregates.

One of the striking things about these patterns is the way they illustrate how a well-designed, well-factored object-oriented application can meet the demands of temporal facilities. Patterns like these exploit their medium, and ultimately transform it, as objects for realizing time relationships become more distinct and robust and inculcate object libraries and the languages themselves.

Chapter 13

Temporal Patterns

Andy Carlson, Sharon Estepp, and Martin Fowler

Objects do not just represent objects that exist in the real world; they often represent the memories of objects that once existed but have since disappeared or projections of how they are expected to exist in the future.

This presents a particular modeling challenge because something that appears straightforward at a point in time becomes far more complicated when the model must consider how objects change over time.

This chapter presents three patterns that show how this challenge can be addressed by elaborating the object model and by showing how the resulting model can support clients that are not concerned with the temporal aspects.

THE PATTERNS

Temporal Property

Also Known As

Historical Mapping, Time-Value Pairs

Context

You are building a complex information system in which a property of an object must be able to change over time. You need to be able to track how this property has changed or is expected to change (or both). The nature of the property is such that it holds a number of discrete values for intervals of time (as opposed to properties such as temperature that can change continuously). You may also need to implement the system using some form of database, possibly relational.

Problem

When considering how an object changes over time, we are usually concerned with how its properties are changing. These properties may be attributes, relationships, or query operations.

For example, consider the model shown in Figure 13-1.

Figure 13-1 *Basic employee model*

In this model we are concerned with two properties of the employee, namely his salary and his skill set. The resulting Employee interface would look like Figure 13-2.

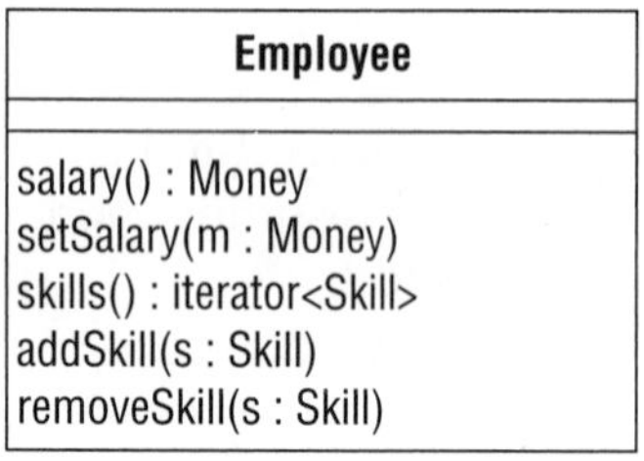

Employee
salary() : Money setSalary(m : Money) skills() : iterator<Skill> addSkill(s : Skill) removeSkill(s : Skill)

Figure 13-2 *Basic employee interface*

This does not preclude a similar interface in the Skill class if that is useful.

Now we will look at how this will need to change to allow us to record past salaries and skill sets or to represent future salaries and skill sets.

As shown in Figure 13-3, we have now attached Time Periods to the properties of Employee. In the case of Salary, we have had to create a separate class to hold the amount with an associated Time Period to indicate the period of validity. We have thus allowed for multiple salaries to be associated with the same Employee (at different points in time). In the case of Skill, this is a class whose instances may be shared by many employees, so it is necessary to introduce an intermediate object to hold the Time Period information.

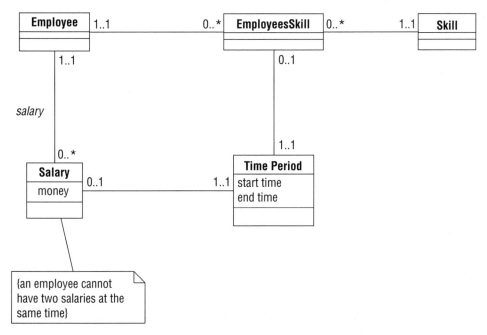

Figure 13-3 *Employee model enhanced to represent changes over time*

Using this model we can represent the following information:

- Dinsdale Piranha starts with a salary of $75,000 on January 1, 1998, and is pro-moted on April 1, 1998, which results in a salary of $85,000.
- Piranha attends an assertiveness course on March 1, 1998, and as a result, adds this to his skill set.

Now imagine that we wish to know what Piranha's salary was on February 1, 1998. We can do this by examining all of Dinsdale's Salary objects to find the one that includes the date in which we are interested. We can do something similar for the EmployeesSkill objects to find out what his skills were on February 1, 1998. In this case, we are likely to find more than one skill as a result.

We can also assign Piranha a future salary (say, for his annual pay review on January 1, 1999) simply by creating a new salary object with a time period begin-ning on January 1, 1999.

We now have the expressiveness that we need but at a cost:

- We have now gone from two classes, an association, and an attribute to five classes, five associations, and a constraint.
- To answer the question for any point in time (including "now"), we now need to retrieve and process a lot more objects.

- We have lost the clarity of the original model, particularly where cardinality is concerned: we can no longer tell at a glance whether an employee can have one or multiple salaries at a given instant.

In summary, the temporal aspects of the model have overwhelmed the other aspects. In reality, systems will have far more temporal relationships than we have shown here. We leave it as an exercise for you to decide on the number of classes, attributes, and associations required to support this.

Forces

- *Simple models are more appealing.* Developers often have a desire to keep things simple when creating a design by minimizing the number of classes and relationships and/or by not concerning themselves with the temporal aspects.
- *Simple models are sometimes not enough.* There is often a requirement for change tracking (past or future).
- *Complex models may be less clear.* The essence of the model may be hidden by the temporal aspects.
- *Future changes have an impact.* The representation of the relationship may be changed in the future, incurring a cost in changing any clients that depend on knowledge of the representation.

Solution

For properties for which you need to track changes over time, build a model (such as the one in the Problem section) that can represent the validity period of each property value. There are a number of alternative ways to implement this pattern so it is not possible to include a single abstract structure diagram without the use of a stereotype (as shown later). The Implementation section contains some alternative models.

Having chosen a model, make it easier for clients to navigate the model by hiding it behind a convenient interface of the class in whose properties we are interested. Provide support for clients that are not concerned with the temporal aspects by adding methods that do not require a time parameter and assume a default of the current time. This interface is shown in Figure 13-4.

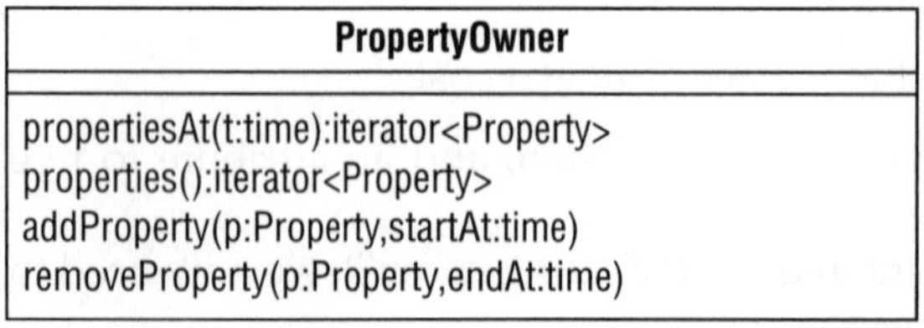

PropertyOwner
propertiesAt(t:time):iterator<Property>
properties():iterator<Property>
addProperty(p:Property,startAt:time)
removeProperty(p:Property,endAt:time)

Figure 13-4 *PropertyOwner interface*

If you are using a notation that allows it (such as UML shown here) the model structure can be made more concise by adopting a stereotype that we will call «temporal» as shown in Figure 13-5.

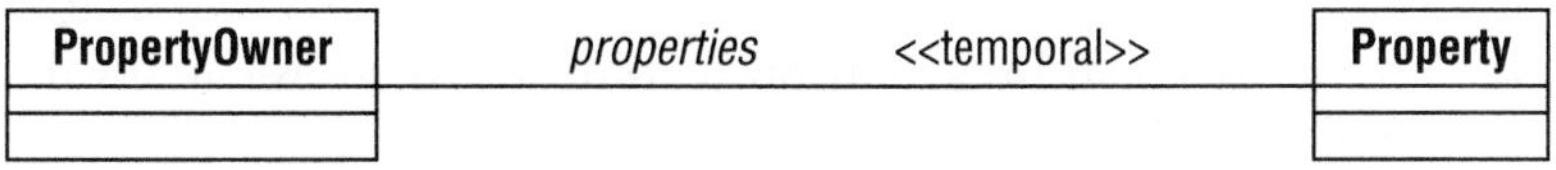

PropertyOwner	*properties*	<<temporal>>	Property

Figure 13-5 *Temporal Property structure with stereotype*

Here the salary and skills properties would be accessed through an interface like the one shown in Figure 13-6.

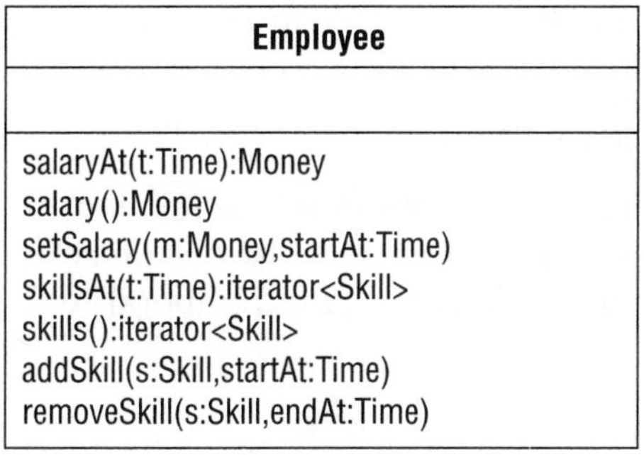

Employee
salaryAt(t:Time):Money salary():Money setSalary(m:Money,startAt:Time) skillsAt(t:Time):iterator<Skill> skills():iterator<Skill> addSkill(s:Skill,startAt:Time) removeSkill(s:Skill,endAt:Time)

Figure 13-6 *Employee interface using temporal properties*

As in the Problem section, this does not preclude a similar interface in the Skill class if that is useful.

By adopting the «temporal» stereotype, the complex diagram shown in the Problem section then becomes much simpler, as shown in Figure 13-7.

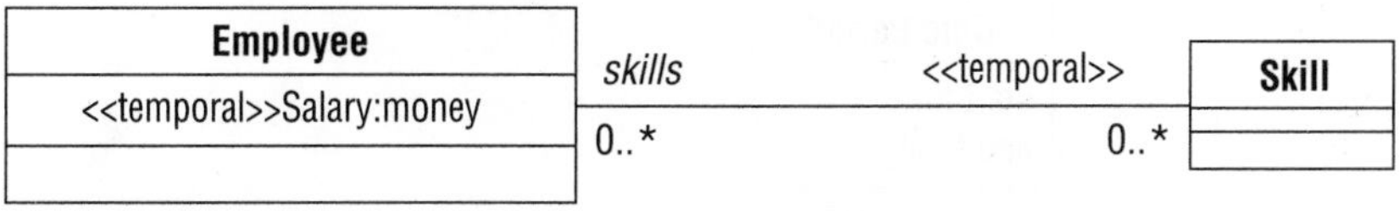

Employee	*skills*	<<temporal>>	**Skill**
<<temporal>>Salary:money	0..*	0..*	

Figure 13-7 *Employee model using stereotype*

Consequences

The advantages of using the Temporal Property pattern are the following:

- We have added the capability to represent changing properties over time to the original model.
- By using the «temporal» stereotype to express those parts of the solution that have been added to support the representation of time we have regained the simplicity of the original model.
- Along with the simplicity, we have also regained the expressiveness of the original model—we can now tell from our example model whether an employee can have more than one salary at once.
- Placing the majority of the knowledge about the relationship's representation in the PropertyOwner class ensures that other clients do not become tightly coupled to this representation.
- Using this pattern implies more regularity in the modeling of objects that have temporal properties.
- Future values will become current values and later on turn into historical values simply by the passage of time and without the need to update any stored information.

A disadvantage of using the Temporal Property pattern:

- If you need more information abut the intermediate object in the relationship (e.g., a skill level in the EmployeesSkill class), this indicates the use of a first class object for the intermediate object and would indicate using the Temporal Association pattern.

Implementation

The simplest implementation for this pattern involves creating a relationship object (PropertyAllocation) with a Time Period between the PropertyOwner and the Property as shown in Figure 13-8.

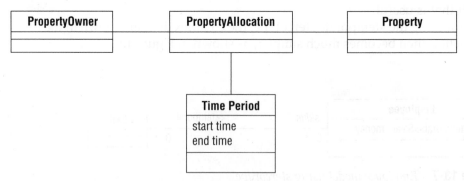

Figure 13-8 *Temporal Property implementation using the PropertyAllocation object*

Where you are sure that the instances of the Property class cannot exist without their PropertyOwner (and also that there is only one PropertyOwner class) the Time Period may be attached directly to the Property object (DedicatedProperty) as shown in Figure 13-9.

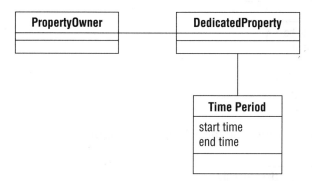

Figure 13-9 *Temporal Property implementation for DedicatedProperties*

Alternatively, you may find it useful to implement this pattern using a Temporal Collection class specially written for the purpose. This type of implementation is best suited to situations in which relational databases are not involved.

For relational database implementations you will often need to provide a class and corresponding table to hold the information required to represent the relationship. This can be avoided in situations in which dedicated property implementation can be used. In this case you can include the time fields in the property class/table. A further simplification is possible where the cardinality between an owning object and a dedicated property object at any point in time is one-to-one. In this situation you can assume the end time of one (older) property to be the start time of the next newer one and dispense with storage (and maintenance) of the end time.

Known Uses

The current implementation of the AT&T Rialto suite uses temporal patterns to represent several relationships.

The relationship between User and User Identity illustrates the dedicated form of the Temporal Property pattern as shown in Figure 13-10.

Holding User Identity in a separate class from User allows, for example, a User to change his username without the system losing track of the fact that he is still the same user and therefore that any information attached to the user (e.g., accountability or privilege information) remains unaffected. This is an example of the simplification mentioned in the Implementation section as the User Identity is assumed to have no end date until another is created with a later start date.

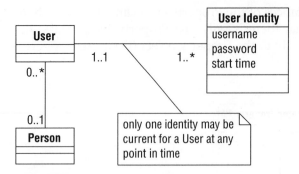

Figure 13-10   *User and identity model*

By adopting the stereotype this becomes the model shown in Figure 13-11.

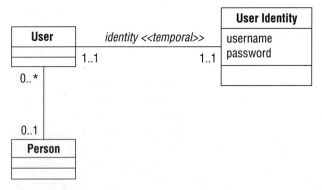

Figure 13-11   *User and identity model with stereotype*

The model is now expressing the information that required a note in the first diagram.

The representation of the validity of a particular Tariff as the current pricing information for a Price Plan also illustrates the dedicated form of this pattern as shown in Figure 13-12.

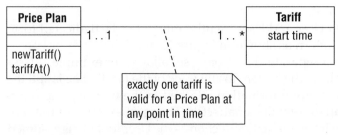

Figure 13-12   *Tariff model*

By adopting the stereotype, this becomes as shown in Figure 13-13.

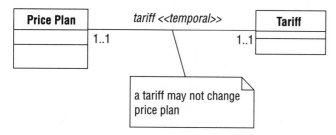

Figure 13-13 *Tariff model with stereotype*

Note that in this case, the need for a note does not go away but its contents change. We can now see the situation at any point in time by looking at the cardinality of the relationship. The need for a new note arises because of the bidirectional nature of association. Without the note, we cannot tell that the Temporal Property does not work in both directions.

Related Patterns

This pattern is a development of the Historical Mapping pattern [Fowler1997]. The Time-Value Pairs pattern [Lange1998] is also similar.

The Time Period abstraction is an example of the use of the Range pattern [Fowler1997].

This pattern is closely related to Temporal Association and when you find yourself faced with a problem of this nature you should consider carefully which is the correct one to use. Temporal Association is concerned with situations in which we are interested (from a modeling perspective) in the intermediate object in the relationship as opposed to the situation here where it is part of the implementation (if it is needed at all). Note that, as in the Employee to Skill relationship in Figure 13-3, the mere presence of an intermediate object does not preclude considering the use of Temporal Property as the intermediate object may be concerned only with implementation (e.g., representing a "cross reference" table in a relational database).

It is quite possible that you will find situations in which there are multiple relationships and/or properties that change over time. In these situations you may find that both the Temporal Association and Temporal Property patterns are needed together.

When using the Temporal Property you should consider the use of the Snapshot pattern if you wish to view one or more properties with the time and historical information removed. This may be particularly applicable if there are multiple Temporal Properties and/or mixtures of the Temporal Association and Temporal Property patterns.

Before using Temporal Property to represent future changes in the value of a property, you should ask yourself how likely it will be that the property will actually hold the indicated future values. There are (at least) two possible ways to look at the future values of a property. The first is by considering that the future values will cause the property to take a new value at the appropriate moment in time, or put another way, that the future values can be used to determine a schedule of forthcoming property changes. The second way is to consider that the future values are an estimate or plan of what will happen. In this situation, there may be several alternative plans for the same property. The Temporal Property pattern is intended for the first alternative, which is that the future values will determine how the property changes over time. If you are faced with an estimating or planning problem, you should instead consider using patterns intended for that purpose like Martin Fowler's Plan [Fowler1997].

There are several alternatives to the approach discussed here, all with their own engineering trade-offs. Francis Anderson [Anderson1999] discusses some of these. In History On Self, a copy of the whole PropertyOwner object is taken each time a property value is changed, with older copies of the object being retained and made available to clients. In Posting, the focus is more on the events that caused the change in property values. ChangeLog is probably the most similar in intent to Temporal Property but the solution is very different, as it adds an internal logging representation to the object itself to record changes in property value. Manfred Lange [Lange1998] also covers similar ground to History On Self with his Versioned Object pattern.

Temporal Association

Also Known As

Association Object, Timed Reference

Context

You are building a complex information system in which relationships between some of your objects must be able to change over time. You need to be able to track how the state of these relationships has changed or is expected to change (or both). You may also need to implement the system using some form of database, possibly relational.

Problem

The problem addressed by this pattern is similar to that addressed by Temporal Property, namely how to add the representation of time to an existing model. In this case, however, we are interested in more complex situations in which there is always an intermediate object representing the relationship. This may be either a first class object or a result of using the concepts known in OMT [Rum+1991] as 'Association as Class' and 'Link Attribute' and as 'Associative Type' in Analysis Patterns [Fowler1997].

For example, consider the model shown in Figure 13-14.

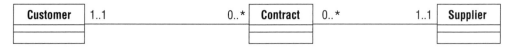

Figure 13-14 *Contract model*

If we now wish to know, for example, whether a contract has been terminated or has not yet come into force, we can achieve this by adding temporal information to the Contract itself as shown in Figure 13-15.

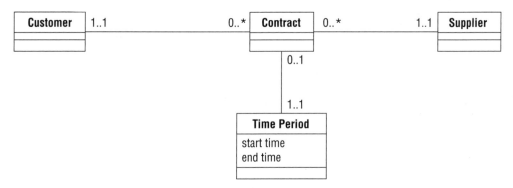

Figure 13-15 *Contract model with temporal information*

At first sight this appears identical to the Employee-EmployeesSkill-Skill relationship from the example in Temporal Property (Figure 13-3), so it would seem reasonable to ask whether that pattern can be applied here. Clearly this would not work, because it would result in the elimination of the Contract class from the model (when the stereotype is used) and its replacement by a direct relationship between Customer and Supplier. It is very likely that Contract carries other interesting information (such as billing data) and cannot reasonably be removed from the model.

The importance of the Contract class is reflected in the interface of the Supplier class as shown in Figure 13-16.

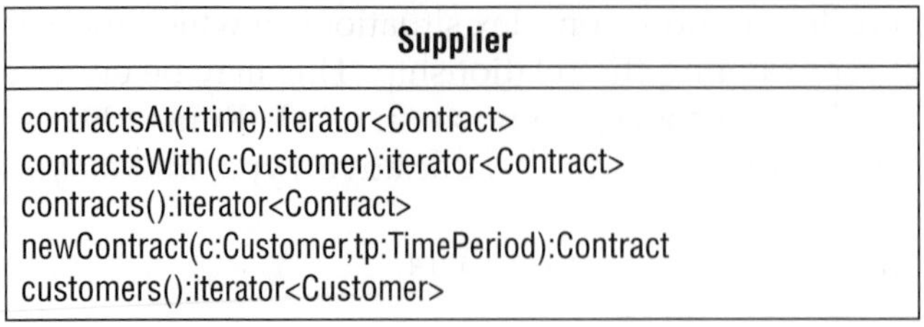

Supplier
contractsAt(t:time):iterator<Contract> contractsWith(c:Customer):iterator<Contract> contracts():iterator<Contract> newContract(c:Customer,tp:TimePeriod):Contract customers():iterator<Customer>

Figure 13-16 *Supplier interface*

Presumably the Customer class would have a similar (but possibly less capable) interface.

We have not had to complicate the model to any great extent (as we did with the Temporal Property pattern) by adding the structure necessary to represent temporal information.

Forces

- *Simple models are more appealing.*   Developers often have a desire to keep things simple when creating a design by minimizing the number of classes and relationships and/or by not concerning themselves with the temporal aspects.
- *Simple models are sometimes not enough.*   There is often a requirement for change tracking (past or future).
- *Complex models may be less clear.*   The essence of the model may be hidden by the temporal aspects
- *Future changes have an impact.*   The representation of the relationship may be changed in the future, incurring a cost in changing any clients that depends on knowledge of the representation.
- *Symmetry is attractive.*   It would be nice if there was a similar modeling convention to that adopted for Temporal Property.

Solution

In contrast with Temporal Property, there is already a preexisting intermediate object in the relationship for which we wish to track changes over time. There is, therefore, no need to introduce new classes or relationships, so add Time Period information directly to the intermediate object.

The resulting structure is shown in Figure 13-17.

As the association object has importance of its own, simplifying the model by adopting a stereotype is not useful.

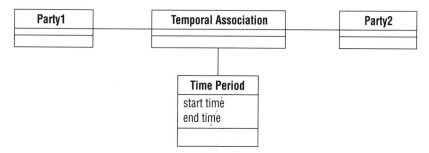

Figure 13-17 *Temporal Association structure*

Consequences

The advantages of using the Temporal Association pattern are the following:

- We have added the capability to represent changing properties over time to the original model.
- By combining the attributes of the Time Period object with the intermediate object in the relationship, the temporal aspects can be represented in a relational database.
- The ownership of the time information is kept with the object to which it relates.
- Knowledge of the relationship's representation need go no further than the objects at either end.
- The intermediate object retains its importance in the model by being exposed via the interfaces of the objects at the ends of the relationship.
- Future relationships will become current relationships and later on turn into historical relationships simply by the passage of time and without the need to update any stored information.

The following are disadvantages of using the Temporal Association pattern:

- This pattern has less implementation flexibility than Temporal Property.
- There is no parallel with the stereotype adopted for Temporal Property.

Implementation

In a relational database implementation, keeping Time Period as a separate object (and hence table) is unlikely to be useful. You can reduce the number of tables by combining the Time Period attributes with those of the intermediate class. Contract would then be as shown in Figure 13-18. This also has the effect of reducing the number of classes to that of the original model.

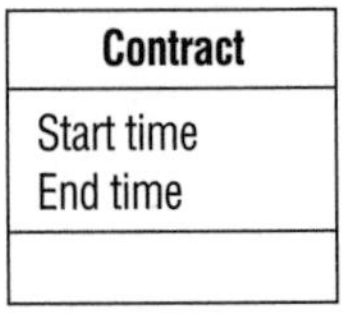

Contract
Start time End time

Figure 13-18 *Contract with time period attributes combined*

In a relational database implementation where the start time is used as part of the key information, it is likely that start time must also be introduced to any entities that are dependent on the main table (e.g., where a contract is made up of a number of items) to ensure referential integrity. An alternative approach is to provide the main table with a column populated with an identifier number unique to each (main table) row and include this column as part of the key of the subordinate tables.

Known Uses

The Contract example quoted in the Problem section is taken (in simplified form) from the current implementation of the AT&T Rialto suite.

The Premium and Client Applications within S3+, a property and casualty insurance product developed by Policy Management Systems Corporation (PMSC), uses the Temporal Association pattern for its underlying relational database. Effective date and expiration dates are included in intermediate objects such as policy, policy client association, policy insurance lines, and policy coverage.

Related Patterns

This pattern is a development of the Chronology pattern that was discussed in a writer's workshop at ChiliPLoP '98 [Carlson1998a]. It is also similar to the Association Object [Boyd1997] and Timed Reference patterns [Lange1998].

This pattern is closely related to Temporal Property, and when you find yourself faced with a problem of this nature you should consider carefully which is the correct one to use. Temporal Property is concerned with situations in which we are not interested (from a modeling perspective) in the intermediate object in the relationship either because there isn't one or because its presence merely results from considering a particular implementation.

It is quite possible that you will find situations in which there are multiple relationships and/or properties that change over time. In these situations you may find that both Temporal Association and Temporal Property are needed together.

When using Temporal Association you should consider the use of the Snapshot pattern if you wish to view one or more relationships with the time and historical information removed. This may be particularly applicable if there are multiple Temporal Associations and/or mixtures of Temporal Association and Temporal Property.

Snapshot

Context

You are building clients to make use of a complex information system in which properties of some of your objects and/or relationships between them must be able to change over time. You need to be able to track how the state of these things have changed or are expected to change (or both). Some clients are interested in how information changes over time while others are not.

Problem

There are many ways to introduce a representation of time into an object model. This may involve tracking discrete changes in properties (e.g., salary) or relationships (e.g., contracts) or continuous changes in properties (e.g., temperature). See the Related Patterns section for some examples. Having given ourselves the ability to represent time in our information model, we now wish to make use of it.

When considering how we make use of the model, it is convenient to separate those parts of the system with an interest in the information from the information storage (and representation) itself. A convenient way to do this is to consider the users of the information as "clients." These clients might be

- Complex information processing applications
- Other systems that require a periodic information feed from or interface to the model

Let us consider again the Contract example from the Temporal Association pattern as shown in Figure 13-19. That pattern allowed us to represent the validity period of a Contract and answer questions like, "What contracts did supplier X have on January 1, 1998?"

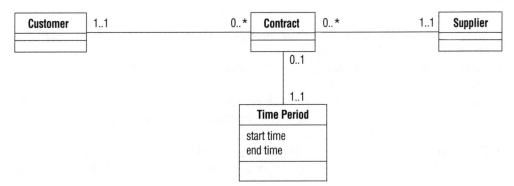

Figure 13-19 *Contract example*

Let us now consider that we are writing a billing system. Obviously, ability to obtain information about contracts is an important requirement for the implementation of such a system. Typically, a billing system will need to refer to the contract at several points in its operation for a variety of information. Another important attribute of a good billing system is that it should not continue to send invoices to customers whose contracts have ended (or have not yet begun), so we would be wise to incorporate something like Temporal Association in our design.

Now, assuming that we have implemented a rich temporal model for our Contract information and probably other properties and relationships (like the ability to change the billing address over time), we also have made life considerably more difficult for our billing system. Does the introduction of a temporal model now require our billing system to navigate through the temporal relationships to find the valid contracts for the point in time in which it is interested? Of course we can encapsulate this complexity behind convenient interfaces in our model (e.g., `Supplier.contractsAt(time)`) but the navigation processing must still be done; we have just moved the problem. If, as is often the case, different stages of the billing processing require access to the contract information, we may find ourselves repeating the same complex navigation over and over again. This is despite the fact that in a single invoicing run, we are probably only interested in the state of all relationships at the same point in time, namely the billing period end.

There are many situations in which the introduction of the time dimension complicates matters not only for the designer and developer of the model itself but also for the clients of the model. As we saw in the billing system example, one or more clients may wish to perform some complex information processing based on a particularly important point in time (e.g., billing period end or year end). Alternatively, it is possible that some clients (especially external systems) have a specific "view" that they require of the information that may not include the time dimension (e.g., requiring a periodic "feed" containing just the current information rather than a full history of changes).

Forces

- *Simple models are sometimes not enough.*   There is often a requirement for change tracking (past or future).
- *Complex models may be less clear.*   The essence of the model may become hidden by the temporal aspects.
- *Future changes have an impact.*   The representation of the relationship may be changed in the future, incurring a cost in changing any clients that depend on knowledge of the representation.
- *Performance may be a issue.*   There is a cost (that we would rather avoid) of repeatedly navigating temporal relationships to discover their state at the same time.

- *Space might be limited.*   Many solutions that give improved performance do so at the expense of increased space.
- *Clients may be unsophisticated.*   One or more clients or external systems may be unable to receive historical data.

Solution

Modify the interface normally used by clients by adding methods to allow provision of a new object called a Snapshot for a specific point in time. The Snapshot object provides a view of one or more properties or relationships with the time dimension and historical information removed. The Snapshot should provide the time to which it applies as one of its visible properties. The Snapshot object may then be used over and over again by the client or passed on to other clients.

The structure of the Snapshot pattern for a Temporal Property is shown in Figure 13-20. Note that this pattern is equally applicable to other temporal patterns (see Related Patterns).

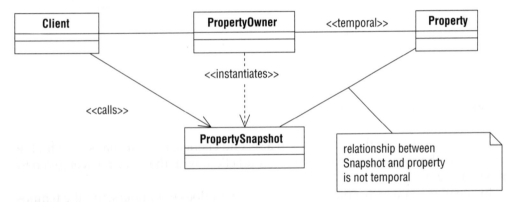

Figure 13-20   *Snapshot structure*

Normally, a Snapshot class is required for each PropertyOwner class but it would be equally valid to create a single Snapshot class to handle properties from multiple owners. If a PropertyOwner was particularly complex (i.e., had many temporal aspects), it may be desirable to create multiple Snapshot classes acting as views onto different subsets of the properties according to the requirements of the clients.

The collaborations are shown in Figure 13-21.

The client first asks the owner for a PropertySnapshot, specifying the time. If the PropertyOwner does not already have a Snapshot for the requested time, it creates a new one. The PropertySnapshot then requests the property values for the relevant time from the PropertyOwner. The PropertySnapshot object is returned to the client that can then retrieve the properties repeatedly without the implementation

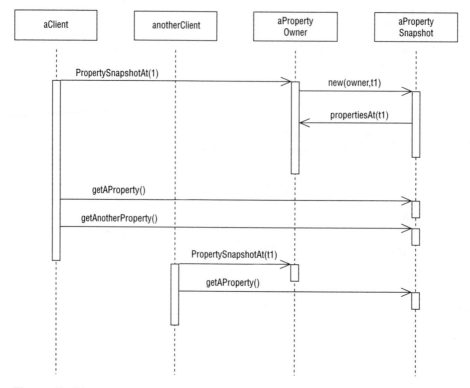

Figure 13-21 *Snapshot collaborations*

needing to recalculate the valid ones. If a second client asks for a Snapshot with the same time, the owner can provide the second client with the same answer given to the first client.

In situations in which a particular type of client does not understand the temporal aspects of the model another client can first request a PropertySnapshot for the relevant time (e.g., now) that it then passes to the temporally unaware client.

In the case of a Temporal Property, the PropertyOwner interface would be changed by the addition of the `propertySnapshotAt(t:time)` method as shown in Figure 13-22.

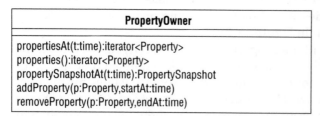

PropertyOwner
propertiesAt(t:time):iterator<Property>
properties():iterator<Property>
propertySnapshotAt(t:time):PropertySnapshot
addProperty(p:Property,startAt:time)
removeProperty(p:Property,endAt:time)

Figure 13-22 *PropertyOwner interface with Snapshot*

The PropertySnapshot interface would look like Figure 13-23.

PropertySnapshot
time
properties():iterator<Property>

Figure 13-23   *PropertySnapshot interface*

The PropertySnapshot interface is not providing any new operation signatures. There are, however, two important differences between these operations and their equivalents in the PropertyOwner class:

1. The implementation need not incur the cost of navigating the temporal information to determine the result.
2. The PropertyOwner interfaces always apply to a default time (probably the current time) whereas a PropertySnapshot can be obtained for any time specified by the client.

To use a more concrete example (from Temporal Association), the Supplier interface would become as shown in Figure 13-24.

Supplier
contractsAt(t:time):iterator<Contract>
contractsWith(c:Customer):iterator<Contract>
contracts():iterator<Contract>
newContract(c:Customer,tp:TimePeriod):Contract
customers():iterator<Customer>
contractsSnapshotAt(t:time):ContractsSnapshot

Figure 13-24   *Supplier interface with Snapshot*

And the ContractsSnapshot class might look like Figure 13-25. Note that in this case the Snapshot is supporting multiple query operations.

ContractsSnapshot
time
contracts( ): iterator<Contract> customers():iterator<Customer>

Figure 13-25   *ContractSnapshot interface*

Consequences

The following are advantages of using the Snapshot pattern:

- Snapshot eliminates the cost of repeated navigation of a temporal model.
- The temporal model can be used by clients that do not understand or have no use for historical information.
- Simple interface signatures can be used by clients without restricting the meaning of these interfaces to some default time.
- Use of Snapshots is optional—the same or other clients can still have access to the temporal information in the original model.
- If Snapshots are saved, they can provide a permanent record of the information on which a client's processing was based independent of any later change to the original temporal information.

A disadvantage of using the Snapshot pattern:
- An additional class has been introduced per PropertyOwner, partly duplicating existing functionality.

Implementation

If it is useful, you may also wish to implement some refinements or modifications to the basic Snapshot mechanism:

- Caching of snapshots may be carried out as part of the implementation of the interface that provides them to clients if it is likely that multiple independent clients will be expected to request snapshots for the same point in time.
- For properties or relationships that change in a discrete fashion, rather than having the snapshot store just its time, it may also be desirable to calculate a period of validity for the snapshot. This could dramatically improve the hit rate in the cache, depending on the typical duration between changes in the state and the chronological distribution of request for snapshots.
- If there are multiple Snapshot classes for a particular PropertyOwner, it may be better to allow clients to create instances of the required class directly (with a reference to the PropertyOwner) rather than going via the owner. This would allow introduction of new types of Snapshot without modifying the owner although the owner would then be unable to perform the caching role.

Known Uses

The AT&T Rialto Rater provides billing functionality to the Rialto suite. This uses the Snapshot pattern to "freeze" complex temporal relationships at billing period ends. The main use at present is in the Tariff subsystem, which has multiple temporal relationships that allow entire Tariffs or component parts of them to change over time.

The Rialto suite also has a real-time network user authentication component called Access Control, which is designed with speed of access as a major goal. This receives information from a repository that has a rich temporal model. The historical information in the repository is of no interest to Access Control and navigating it in real time would reduce user authentication throughput considerably, so data is fed in Snapshot form to Access Control to ensure that Access Control always has a current picture of the authorized users.

The Claims Application within S3+, a property and casualty insurance product developed by Policy Management Systems Corporation (PMSC), uses the Snapshot pattern for its underlying relational database. A snapshot of the policy-related information, such as policy coverage and insured object, is taken as of the date of the loss specified on the claim. The Claims application then uses this snapshot, thus eliminating the need to navigate via the temporal relationships to access the policy-related information that was effective at the date of the loss.

CyberLife Administration, a life insurance policy administration product developed by CYBERTEK, a PMSC company, uses the Snapshot pattern for its underlying relational database. A snapshot of policy fund value information is taken as of the monthliversary date.

Related Patterns

This pattern is a development of the Snapshot pattern that was discussed in a writer's workshop at ChiliPLoP '98 [Carlson1998b].

This pattern can be applied to most patterns that add representation of temporal information. Examples include Temporal Property, Temporal Association, and many of the patterns discussed in the papers by Francis Anderson [Anderson1999] and Manfred Lange [Lange1998].

ACKNOWLEDGMENTS

We would like to thank our PLoP shepherd, Dirk Riehle, for his helpful comments on this paper. We would also like to thank the participants in the writers workshop at PLoP '98 for their efforts, which resulted in numerous improvements. Thanks also to Trevor Hayward for his patient work to reformat this paper for the PLoP book.

REFERENCES

[Anderson1998] F. Anderson. "A Collection of History Patterns." In N. Harrison and H. Rohnert (eds.), *Pattern Languages of Program Design 4*. Reading, MA: Addison-Wesley, 1999.

[Boyd1997] L. Boyd. "Business Patterns of Association Objects." In R. Martin, D. Riehle, and F. Buschmann (eds.), *Pattern Languages of Program Design 3*. Reading, MA: Addison-Wesley, 1998.

[Carlson1998a] A. Carlson. "ChronologyPattern." Available: http://www.attlabs.att.co.uk/andyc/patterns/chronology-pattern.html.

[Carlson1998b] A. Carlson. "Snapshot Pattern." Available: http://www.attlabs.att.co.uk/andyc/patterns/snapshot-pattern.html.

[Fowler1997] M. Fowler. *Analysis Patterns: Reusable Object Models*. Menlo Park, CA: Addison Wesley Longman, 1997.

[Lange1998] M. Lange. "Time Patterns." In *Proceedings of the Patterns Language of Programming*. Monticello, IL: Allerton House, 1998.

[Rum+1991] J. Rumbaugh, M. Blaha, W. Premerlani, F. Eddy, and W. Lorensen. *Object Oriented Modeling and Design*. Englewood Cliffs, NJ: Prentice Hall, 1991.

Andy Carlson may be reached at andycarlson@acm.org.

Sharon Estepp may be reached at sharonestepp@pmsc.com.

Martin Fowler may be reached at fowler@acm.org.

Chapter 14

A Collection of History Patterns

Francis Anderson

Business systems record the state of (i.e., a subset of) the enterprise. Naturally, this state changes over time—either in response to events that originate externally to the system or that the system itself generates. Frequently, it is necessary to remember (for a significant period of time) the state of the system as it was at a particular point in time. This historical state may be read-only, for audit trail purposes, or may be updateable, for the recording of subsequent backdated transactions.

This chapter describes a series of patterns for recording the history of a domain object. First it describes some basic concepts of time (event, time interval, duration), then it describes the following patterns, whose dependencies are depicted in Figure 14-1:

- *Edition* associates a changed state with the event that caused the change.
- *Change Log* records the previous values of simple variables.
- *History On Association* records the values of a complex variable as it changes over time.
- *Posting* records the detailed changes that an event contributed to a domain object that is responsible for providing accumulated totals (e.g., balance).
- *History On Self* records the previous states of the domain object itself, as significant events cause complex changes of state.
- *Memento Child* leaves a historical copy of a domain object in the children collection of a previous aggregator in order to correctly handle backdated transactions.
- *History On Tree* recursively applies History On Self to a tree of nodes for those significant events that require the state of an entire composite structure to be saved.

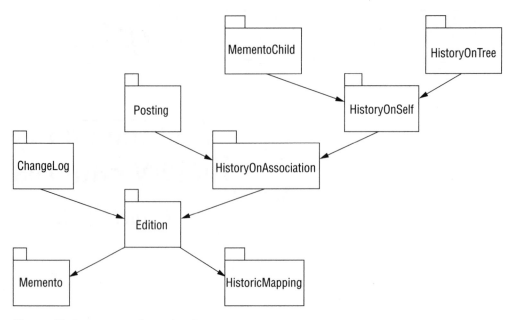

Figure 14-1 *Pattern dependencies*

Some of these patterns have been documented elsewhere [Fowler1997a], [Gamma+1995], [Johnson+1998], but are repeated since their aggregation in one place is required to tell a better story.

Jean Piaget pioneered a pattern language of time by addressing the problem of how a child is programmed. In *The Child's Conception of Time* [Piaget1946], he wrote: "the construction of time concepts are . . . operations that do not involve classes of objects, relations between invariable objects or numbers, but bear exclusively on positions, states, etc., i.e. on transformations rather than on constant states." Object-oriented techniques, however, only deal with classes of objects, their relations, and their operations. In these patterns, the transformation brought about by an action on an object is recorded by capturing the pre- or postcondition state of the object, and associating that state, via an edition, with an event representing the triggering of the action. The overall history of the domain object is maintained by adding each new edition to a chronological collection. The precise transformation caused by an event is derived by comparing the values of consecutive editions.

RELATED PATTERNS

The patterns in this chapter are fundamentally a combination of the following two patterns:

Historic Mapping [Fowler1997a]

This Analysis pattern recommends "a dictionary implementation with time period keys." A dictionary is a collection of associations (key/value pairs). The association is implemented herein by Edition, which forms the basis for the subsequent patterns in this paper.

Memento [Gamma+1995]

This Design pattern solves the problem of how to store a previous state of an object for subsequent restoration. Unlike the focus of these History patterns, which track the state of an object through multiple transactions, Memento concentrates on the ability to roll back the state within a single transaction. Many of these patterns adopt the role names of Memento:

- *Originator* is the domain object whose state is changing.
- *Memento* is the storage of the changed state. It may be an instance of the same class as (i.e., a copy of) the Originator [Alpert+1998] or some specialized mechanism. In this chapter, the main differentiation between the patterns subsequent to Edition is the way the Memento role is implemented. This depends upon the scope and complexity of the change of state brought about by the event.
- *Caretaker* holds on to the Mementos and in these patterns is played by the Originator role.

KNOWN USES

The number of potential uses for these patterns is enormous. It is frequently a requirement for most kinds of systems (business, embedded real-time, source code control systems, CAD/CAM, etc.) to be able to trace changes of state to the events that caused them. The author's experience in other than business systems is, however, limited.

All the patterns in the paper are implemented in the Objectiva Architecture, a black-box Smalltalk framework for telecommunications billing and customer care, from which the sample code is taken.

Where possible, the patterns draw parallels with source control systems and database management systems, but these systems perform configuration management at a much higher level of granularity than an individual object.

Most of the known uses are drawn from *ENVY*, a software configuration management tool for Smalltalk and Java code developed by Object Technology International (OTI). It is an integral part of IBM's Visual Age for the Java Professional.

ENVY components form a number of compositions and aggregations: Configuration Maps contain Applications, which may contain SubApplications, which may again contain SubApplications; both Applications and SubApplications may contain Classes, which are composed of a class definition and Methods. The Method is the leaf component, and a new Edition of a Method is generated for every change in code. Editions of the aggregate components are either open for work in progress, or, as work increments are completed, they are versioned and released to their containers. Versions are immutable Editions.

BASIC TIME CONCEPTS

Event

An event triggers a change of state in a system or may be raised to provide notification of a change of state. The minimum responsibility of an event is to record the timestamp at which it occurred. Events are of two kinds:

1. Ad-hoc events usually originate external to the system. Examples include Change of Customer Name and Completion of Phone Call.
2. Periodic events are usually initiated by the system itself based on an Operational Calendar [Fowler1997b]. Examples include Closure of Billing Cycle Period and Renewal of Contract.

A transaction mechanism is usually used to bring about the desired change of state. This paper is not concerned with the technical nature of the transaction itself (e.g., ACID properties), but instead concentrates on recording the resulting change of state. Transactions are entered in two basic manners:

1. An event that is entered via Online Transaction Processing (OLTP) is responsible for recording the User ID of the individual performing the transaction.
2. An event that is entered as part of a batch of transactions (e.g., a flat file) is responsible for recording the Batch ID.

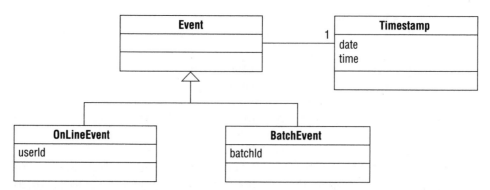

Figure 14-2 *Class diagram of Event*

Thus, events themselves become first class objects, which is essentially what happens in Command [Gamma+1995]. Frequently the event will be a naturally occurring domain class, as in the phone call example above. In the case of the customer name change being entered via an online maintenance system, there will be no naturally occurring domain class for the event (without extreme proliferation). A "generic" event is used (see Figure 14-2) to capture the timestamp and user ID, and any other information required for audit purposes.

Time Interval

A time interval has a specific start and end event; its magnitude is expressed in terms of duration (see section that follows).

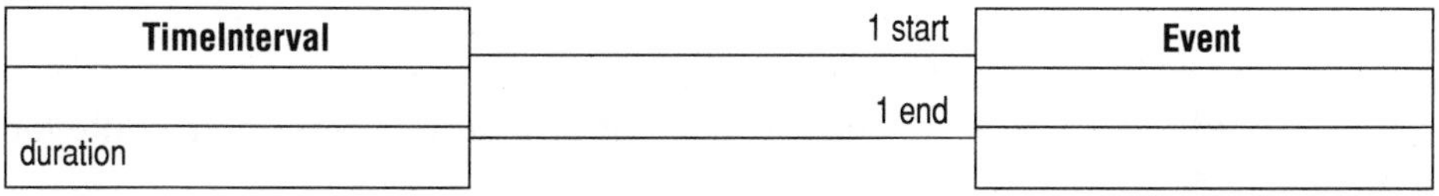

TimeInterval	1 start	Event
	1 end	
duration		

Figure 14-3 *Class diagram of a time interval*

In general, these patterns use an event as the key of the Edition—the association described by Historic Mapping [Fowler1997a]—rather than a time interval. This removes the need to store redundant start and end times when a variable with a multiplicity of "1" changes. The start or end time can be derived from the previous or subsequent Edition, as appropriate; however, the elimination of redundancy is achieved at the expense of an additional read operation.

Duration

Duration is a quantity [Fowler1997a] that expresses the difference in time between two events. The units of duration include seconds, minutes, minutes to one decimal place, etc.

THE PATTERNS

Edition

Context

An event causes a domain object to change its state; in other words, the value of one or more variables is to be changed. Audit information must be attached to the domain object to record the time and responsibility for the change.

Examples

- A developer checks out a component from a configuration management system (e.g., *ENVY*) in order to make changes to it.
- A customer changes her mailing address.
- The exchange rate for a currency changes.

Problem

How should the change of state be associated with the event that caused it?

Forces

- There should be a loose coupling between the event and the values that it affected. The event should not be responsible for knowing the values that have been changed, since the same event may affect multiple domain objects.
- A value should not know whether it is current or historical or whether it even has history recorded on it.
- Becoming a historical value of a variable should not cause a complex object to change its class.

Solution

Implement the relationship between a domain object and a historical value (as described by Historic Mapping [Fowler1997a]) by an Edition, which provides the association between an event (the key) and the changed state (the value).

Use Memento to provide the mechanism for recording the change of state, and adapt it by combining the Originator and Caretaker roles.

Provide additional interfaces on the Originator such that historical values can be accessed and changed as of a specified point in time.

The subsequent patterns in this paper all use Edition in slightly different circumstances, depending on the complexity of the change of state and the event causing it. Thus the implementation of these interfaces is not described until later.

Diagram

Figure 14-4 shows the Originator having a collection of Editions. Each Edition is an Association whose key is the Event that led to the change of state and whose value is the Memento, which is the state of one of the Originator's variables either immediately prior to the Event (precondition) or immediately after (postcondition). The subsequent patterns in this chapter optimize this structure for the different types of Event and Memento that can occur.

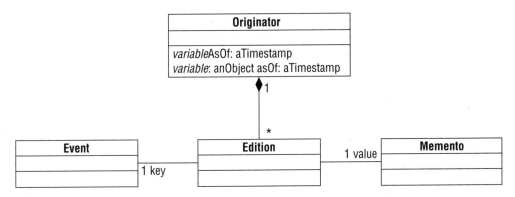

Figure 14-4 *Role diagram of Edition*

Sample Code

Edition is the basis of the following patterns, which contain most of the interesting code. The following code shows the instance creation of a default edition.

```
Edition class>>newFor: aMemento
    "A new edition is created and initialized"

    ^self new initializeFor: aMemento

Edition>>initializeFor: aMemento
    "A default event is created. This may be overridden if
    the originator is responding to an external event."

    event := Event new.
    value := aMemento

Edition>>isEffectiveAsOf: aTimestamp
    "I was effective if my event occurred before or at
    the same time as the requested timestamp"

    ^self timestamp <= aTimestamp
```

Resolution of Forces

Two new classes have been introduced—Event and Edition—thus increasing the complexity of the model and its storage requirements. Edition "wraps" the Memento nonintrusively. This is not a Decorator [Gamma+1995], because it does not replicate the interface of the Memento. Instead, the collection of Editions in the Originator is responsible for finding the appropriate Edition and returning the value of the Memento to a client.

If the value of a variable is discontinuous (i.e. there may be none or many at any point in time) the key of the Edition may be Time Interval, rather than Event. As mentioned earlier, another reason for using Time Interval as the key is to eliminate a read operation at the expense of data redundancy between the start of one time interval and the end of the previous one.

Related Patterns

- Association Class, in that the ternary relationship between client, event, and value of a variable is resolved.
- The subsequent patterns in this paper all build on Edition for handling increasing scope of the change of state.

Known Uses

As shown in Figure 14-5, saving a change to the code in a method causes a new Edition to be created. The creation of the Edition adds the timestamp and developer; the differences between editions can be browsed, identifying the actual changes that took place (see Figure 14-6).

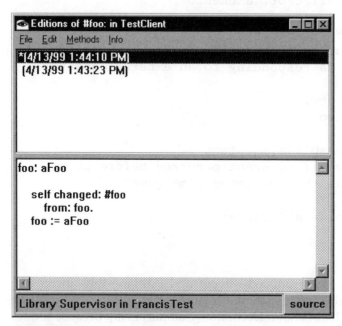

Figure 14-5 *Editions of an ENVY method*

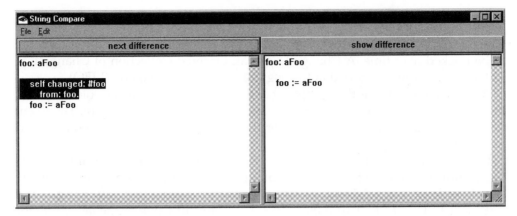

Figure 14-6 *Differences between the editions of an ENVY method*

Change Log

Context

A simple variable contains a value that can be represented as a string and whose identity is not an issue. The value of a simple variable of a domain object has changed. The previous value of the variable is to be recorded for reference/audit purposes.

Examples

- Customer changes name.
- The credit limit on an account is increased.
- The exchange rate of a currency relative to a base changes.

Problem

How to store the previous value of a changed simple variable and have the state subsequently accessible as of a previous point in time.

Forces

In most database management systems, simple variables (strings, numbers, etc.) are locally stored with the object they describe. C++ tends to refer to this situation as "has-by-value" (as opposed to "has-by-reference"). Wrapping these simple values in an Edition, and directly making this Edition persistent, could lead to a proliferation of complex objects (has-by-reference), which is not an efficient usage of persistent storage.

Solution

Assign a Change Log to those objects for whom the values of simple variables are to be tracked over time. A Change Log is an Ordered Collection of Change Log Entry. New entries are added at the beginning of the Change Log (LIFO).

A Change Log Entry is the collapsing of the Edition and Memento roles into one, in other words, both the event and the value data are stored explicitly. The Event data is stored as its timestamp and user ID; the Memento data is stored as a field name (aspect)/string value pair, as in Variable State [Beck1997].

In addition to the standard set of variable accessors, those variables of the Originator that require the accessing of a previous value also provide an accessor of the form: `variableNameAsOf: effectiveDate` (e.g., `exchangeRate AsOf: 1998/12/17`). This either returns the current value or the last value for the variable in the Change Log subsequent to the specified date.

Diagrams

Figure 14-7 shows the Originator with a simple variable (e.g., name) on which an audit trail of changes is to be kept. These are stored in the Change Log, which is an ordered collection of ChangeLogEntry. A Change Log Entry is an Event in which an aspect (name) of the Originator changed from a value.

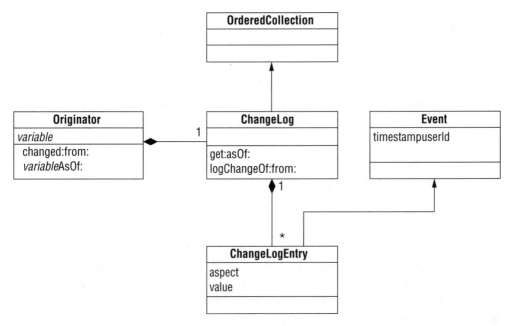

Figure 14-7 *Role diagram of Change Log*

Figures 14-8 and 14-9 demonstrate the problem of object proliferation. Change Log is specifically targeted at recording the historical values of simple variables, in other words, those in which object identity is not an issue, and can be represented as a string.

The very point of simple values is that they can be stored persistently as part of the object they describe. There is a 0-to-Many relationship between each variable of an object and Change Log Entry. If we do not want to store the value of a simple variable as a reference, we certainly do not want to store its Change Log Entries that way.

Figure 14-8 shows the transient objects for a Change Log. Figure 14-9 shows the Change Log serialized so that it can be stored locally in the Originator/Caretaker as a ByteString. A Tab character is used to separate the values of a Change Log Entry, and a carriage return is used to separate entries. A timestamp transforms into number of seconds from a fixed point in time, and a quantity transforms into unit identifier and magnitude.

In Figure 14-8, the instance of OnsEntityContext plays the role of Originator. The OnsChangeLogEntry records the fact that user FMRA changed the eye color from red at the time recorded in the timestamp.

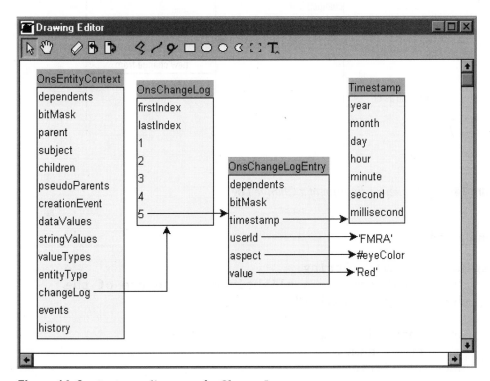

Figure 14-8 *Instance diagram of a Change Log*

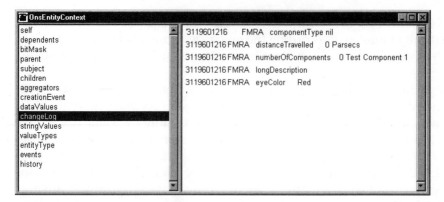

Figure 14-9   *Change Log serialized as string for persistent storage*

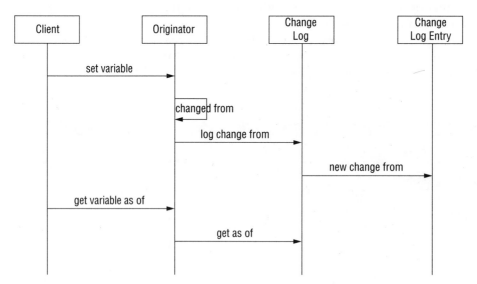

Figure 14-10   *Sequence diagram of a Change Log*

Sample Code

```
Originator>>name: aString
     "Note that this is a slightly modified use of the
     dependency mechanism"

     self changed: #name
          from: name.
     name := aString
```

```
Originator>>changed: anAspect from: previousValue
    "The previous value of the variable is logged, prior
    to invoking the standard dependency mechanism"

    self changeLog logChangeOf: anAspect
        from: previousValue.
    self changed: anAspect

ChangeLog>>logChangeOf: anAspect from: previousValue
    "A new change log entry is created and added as the
    first entry"

    self addFirst:
        (ChangeLogEntry newChangeOf: anAspect
            from: previousValue)

Currency>>exchangeRateAsOf: aTimestamp
    "If there is a change log entry that was current at
    aTimestamp, return it; else return the current value"
    | value |

    ^(value :=
        self changeLog get: #exchangeRate
            asOf: aTimestamp) isNil
            ifTrue: [ exchangeRate ]
            ifFalse: [ value asNumber ]

ChangeLog>>get: anAspect asOf: aTimestamp
    "Scan the entries backward in time, storing the value
    of the requested aspect. When a timestamp earlier than
    requested is encountered, or the end of the entries
    is reached, return the currently stored value, which
    may still be nil."

    ^self entries do:
        [ :e | | value |
        e timestamp < aTimestamp ifTrue: [ ^value ].
        e aspect == anAspect
            ifTrue: [ value := e value ].
        value ]
```

Resolution of Forces

Note that Change Log Entry is a subclass of Event rather than Edition. This means that only simple events and values may be written to the Change Log.

Since all variables in Change Log Entry can be resolved to strings, the Change Log can be serialized and stored persistently as a simple value in its Originator, or more specifically, Caretaker.

Those clients that require the current value of a variable use a regular accessor/mutator interface. On mutation, there is a slight performance hit adding the previous value to the change log. When the client requests a historical value using the "asOf:" accessor, there is a slight performance hit to find the value at the requested timestamp.

Related Patterns

- *Observer* [Gamma+1995], since in this implementation the change notification interface has been altered so that the change is logged prior to notifying any dependents.
- *Variable State* [Beck1997] is used to store the Memento value in the Change Log Entry as a field name/value pair.
- *Serializer* [Riehle+1997] enables the Change Log to be stored as a simple value rather than a collection of complex objects and occurs at three levels: the field name/value pair, the Change Log Entry, and the Change Log.

Known Uses

The PVCS software configuration management tool from INTERSOLV re-creates a previous version of a file by applying reverse deltas. In this case, the file as a whole corresponds to the Originator, and the lines of code correspond to the simple variables. Any change to a line of code is applied to the file, and its previous state is recorded in the reverse delta log.

History On Association

Also Known As

Historic Mapping [Fowler1997a] and History [Johnson+1998]

Context

The value of a variable that references a complex object has changed. The previous value of the variable is to be recorded for reference/audit purposes.

Change Log maintains historical values of simple variables (strings, numbers, etc.), but is not appropriate for complex variables that cannot be serialized.

Examples

- As an individual changes residence, the values of all previous addresses should be retained.
- As a customer changes the role it plays (lead, prospect, subscriber), the details of the previous roles should be retained.
- A piece of equipment needs to keep track of the locations at which it has been installed.

Problem

How do we maintain the historical values of a complex variable?

Forces

The same complex object may be referenced by a number of contexts, so the historical information should not reside in the referenced object (Memento). For example, a piece of equipment is moved from location to location. Since there may be a number of pieces of equipment at the same location, it is not possible to store in the location when a single piece of equipment arrived. This is in contrast to Temporal Association [Carlson+1998], in which the associated object (e.g., a contract for an organization) is compositional in nature; in other words, the multiplicity from the referenced class back to the Originator class is unary.

Solution

Replace the pointer to the complex object with an instance of History, which is a Sorted Collection (in chronological order) of Edition. When the value of the variable is changed, a new Edition is added to the History.

Historical values are obtained using `variableNameAsOf: aTimestamp`.

When the variable is multivalued at a single point in time, a Time Interval can be used as the key of the Editions in History.

Diagram

In Figure 14-11, *variable* is the name of the reference on which the Originator is required to keep history (e.g., address). In addition to the accessor and mutator methods (`address` and `address:`), the Originator's interface is extended by the "as of" accessor (`getAddressAsOf: aTimestamp`). Instead of a single valued variable (address), the Originator has a history collection of Editions sorted in

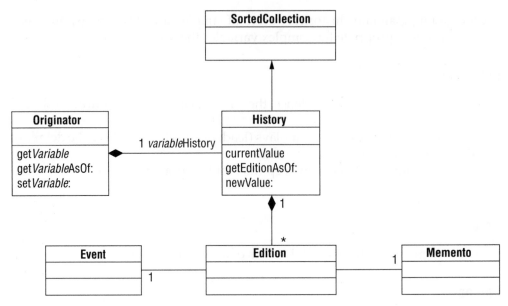

Figure 14-11 *Role diagram of History On Association*

chronological order by Event (`addressHistory`). The Event records the date at which the variable was changed to the value of the Memento (an Address). Note that, in this case, the current value also is stored as a Memento.

Sample Code

```
Individual>>address: anAddress
    "A new value is added to history."

    addressHistory newValue: anAddress

History>>newValue: anObject
    "A new edition (with timestamp defaulting to now) is
    created and added in chronological sequence."

    self add: (Edition newFor: anObject)

Individual>>address
    "The current value of history is returned."

    ^addressHistory currentValue
```

```
History>>currentValue
      "The value of the current edition is returned"

      ^self currentEdition value

History>>currentEdition
      "The edition as of the current time is returned"

      ^self getEditionAsOf: Timestamp now

History>>getEditionAsOf: aTimestamp
      "The latest edition that was effective as of the
      requested timestamp is returned"

      ^self reverse detect:
           [ :e | e isEffectiveAsOf: aTimestamp ]
           ifNone: []

Individual>>addressAsOf: aTimestamp
      "The history value as of aTimestamp is returned"

      ^addressHistory valueAsOf: aTimestamp

History>>valueAsOf: aTimestamp
      "The edition as of the current time is returned"

      ^(self getEditionAsOf: aTimestamp) value
```

Resolution of Forces

The proposed solution places all the responsibility for History on the Originator and the Edition, not on the Memento. This allows an object to be referenced in multiple historical contexts. It does, however, introduce a new persistent object—the Edition. This is a relatively trivial class, in effect, just an association, which may end up with a high number of instances, thus wasting space.

The complexity of the interface is increased by the addition of the AsOf: accessors. This is not an issue if the client only requires the current value, since the usual "get" accessor is utilized.

The performance of accessing the current value is adversely affected, since History is scanned for the appropriate Edition, which will usually be the first Edition encountered unless future values also are recorded.

When History is required on a multivalued variable (a collection), the choice of whether to use a time interval as the key of the Edition, or a collection as the value of the Edition, remains a design decision involving performance/space trade-offs.

There is a further distinction between the examples quoted earlier, in terms of the cardinalities of the relationship implemented by the variable. A contract may be owned only by one customer, whereas a piece of equipment can change location. In the former case, the edition is not required as a separate object, and its data can be denormalized into the target object (the Contract). This is the solution adopted by Temporal Association [Carlson+1998].

Related Patterns

- *History On Self* (see later section) applies this pattern, except that the Memento is the previous state of the Originator, rather than a previous value of one of the Originator's variables.
- *Temporal Association* [Carlson+1998] is a case of this pattern, where, since the multiplicity from the Memento to the Originator is unary, the edition may be denormalized into the Memento.

Known Uses

The Hartford Insurance Company User Defined Product Framework [Johnson+ 1998] uses this form of History for recording the values of attributes. In this case, although the value of the Edition may be a simple value, the key is a complex transaction, and thus the serialization used by Change Log is not possible.

Posting

Also Known As

Entry [Fowler1997a] and Item

Context

The value of an accumulated total amount has been changed via the posting of a transaction. The detail amounts that contribute to the accumulated total should be retained for audit or adjustment purposes.

This is described by

- *The Account pattern* [Fowler1997a], whose problem is "Recording a history of changes to some quantity" (e.g., balance). The solution is: "Create an account. Each change is recorded as an entry against the account." Note that the term "Account" is used here with a generic definition, not specific to bookkeeping or monetary amounts.

- *The Transaction pattern* [Fowler1997a], whose problem is "Ensuring that nothing gets lost from an account." The solution is: "Use transactions to transfer items between accounts."

The same transaction may be posted to multiple accounts (e.g., double entry bookkeeping) or even multiple times to the same account (e.g., cancellation and replacement as the result of a billing error). Although the account balance is a simple value, the Change Log is not the appropriate mechanism for tracking its history, since

- The transactions that bring about a change in the value of the balance are not simple events.
- Multiple measurements may result from the application of posting rules to a transaction. It is the amount of each individual measurement that requires recording, not just the change in balance.

Examples

A telephone subscriber makes a call, which is to be charged to the appropriate accounts. If the call is from a mobile phone to a mobile phone, the one event (the call) can result in multiple charges (e.g., airtime and landline, peak and off-peak) being posted to two accounts (the originator and the receiver of the phone call).

The closing of a contract period results in the posting of discounts and monthly recurring charges (e.g., subscription charges).

The closing of an accounting period results in the posting of federal, state, and local taxes.

The receipt of a shipment causes the stock levels of a warehouse to be increased by the number of items in the shipment.

Problem

A domain object's balance accumulator is the total of the measurements of a number of transactions. In turn, a transaction may affect multiple domain objects, with the measurement amounts being calculated by Posting Rules [Fowler1997a] specific to each. How is the contribution of each transaction to each domain object's totals recorded?

Forces

The same Event can be posted to a number of accounts. This is not only due to double entry bookkeeping—in the mobile-to-mobile phone call example the same call is to be debited to two customer accounts. Thus, the source event should not contain any information relating to its posting to an account, and any measurement of the event's posting to an account should be part of the association between the source event and the account. These measurements are frequently calculated using the Posting Rule [Fowler1997a], which depends on data from both the source event and the account.

Two distinct events have occurred: (1) the source event (e.g., the customer phone call) and (2) its posting to the appropriate account. There may be a significant delay between these two events, particularly since the posting may be performed in batch mode. This problem is documented in Two Dimensional History [Fowler1997a]. Both events must be recorded, since the domain object has the responsibility of selecting the period in which to record the totals. In accounting, this is always the current period, in other words, based on the knowledge date (date of posting); for insurance claims and other agreement-based transactions, it is frequently the date on which the source event actually occurred (applicable date).

Solution

Resolve the many-to-many relationship between Account and Transaction with a Posting subtype of Edition. This provides a "historical wrapper" around the transaction. There are therefore two events involved:

1. The Source Event (e.g., phone call or period closing), which is responsible for the source information for billing (applicable date and price determinants, such as duration of call) and is wrapped in . . .
2. The Posting, whose key is the posting event, which records when the posting was made to the account (knowledge date)

The Posting not only decorates its source event with the posting date, but also with the measurements that result from any calculations triggered by posting rules that govern the event. Unlike Edition, the value of a Posting (the Source Event) knows the Postings that it generated, and the Posting knows the account to which it was posted (the Originator).

Diagram

In Figure 14-12, Account is playing the role of Originator, and Source Event is playing the role of Memento. Account has a number of balances, which are Measurements (e.g., `onHandWidgetCount,` `backOrderedWidgetCount`). Source Events (e.g., receipt of an order) contain Measurements, which either directly, or indirectly via a Posting Rule, affect the Account balance. The Source Event is rated by the Account using the appropriate Posting Rule, which results in a new posting with calculated Measurements. The Posting is posted to the Account, whose balances are accumulated, at the time specified by the Event.

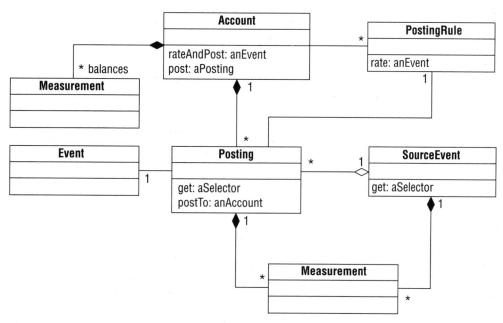

Figure 14-12   *Role diagram of Posting*

Sample Code

```
Account>>rateAndPostEvent: aSourceEvent
    "The event is rated using the appropriate posting
    rules, and each resultant posting is posted"

    ^(self rateEvent: aSourceEvent)
        do: [ :eachPosting | self post: eachPosting ]

Account>>post: aPosting
    "The posting is accumulated, added, and then told to
    post to me"

    self accumulate: aPosting.
    postings add: aPosting.
    ^aPosting postTo: self

Posting>>postTo: anAccount
    "The source event is informed of the posting, and my
    account is set"
```

```
    self sourceEvent addPosting: self.
    self account: anAccount

Posting>>get: aSelector
    "Return value of requested selector from myself or my
    source event. Implementation of Decorator"

    ^self get: aSelector
        ifNone: [ self sourceEvent get: aSelector ]
```

Resolution of Forces

The Posting provides the association between a Transaction and an Account. Except for the addition of postings to its collection, the transaction itself should remain unaltered by any posting rules applied.

The Posting provides the context upon which posting rules operate. For example, a telephone call's charges are frequently dependent on its duration, in other words, duration is an input price determinant. Posting uses Variable State [Beck1997] to store the result of previously triggered rules. If the price determinant requested by the rule is not available in the Posting, the request is forwarded to the Source Event. Posting is thus a Decorator [Gamma+1995] on the source event. The result of a calculation is stored in the Posting, and thus may itself become an input price determinant to a subsequent calculation.

The Two Dimensional History pattern [Fowler1997a] is implemented by the Posting being responsible for the "knowledge date" and the Source Event being responsible for the "applicable (or effective) date." This is why two events are necessary, to store when the transaction actually occurred and when it was posted to an account.

Related Patterns

- Many of the Analysis patterns [Fowler1997a] play a part here, including Account, Transaction, Posting Rule, and Two Dimensional History.
- The Decorator pattern [Gamma+1995] is applied since Posting must enable a Posting Rule access to its transaction's price determinants.
- The Variable State pattern [Beck1997] is an appropriate means by which Posting stores the results of the Posting Rules.

Known Uses

The Objectiva Architecture is the only known use of this pattern. There is, however, a parallel to database management systems that support forward recovery and use log files to record changes to individual records (objects, rows, or segments) within a database. If the database should become corrupt for any reason, a previous backup is restored, and the transactions are replayed up to the specified point in time.

History On Self

Context

In the patterns described earlier, the focus has been on the change of state of a single variable. History On Self handles a complex transaction that results in the change of state of a number of variables.

To continue with Piaget's analysis:

"In fact, space and time result from operations just as do concepts (classes and logical relations) and numbers, but in their case, the operations take place within the object itself."

Thus, it is not the previous state of a domain object's variable on which we need to record history; it is the state of the object itself, as the sum of its variables' states, in other words, the Smalltalk variable "self" and the Java variable "this."

Examples

- When an electric meter is changed, history of the location, state, seal number, and reading must be recorded.
- When a change is made to a method, previous versions of the class must retain their appropriate edition of the method.

Problem

How do we associate a complex change of state in which the values of multiple variables have changed with the occurrence of a single event?

Forces

- Use of History On Association and Change Log on the individual affected variables would result in a number of editions from a single event. Reconstruction of the state of the domain object prior to an event that changed numerous variables may be extremely complex.
- A new class should not be introduced for each class that requires history.
- External object references should not require updating as the result of a history snapshot.
- Queries on a unique identifier should only return a single object.

The minimum amount of additional structure should be introduced in order to track historical states.

Solution

Instead of applying history to individual variables, it is applied to the object as a whole (the sum of the values of its instance variables). An additional variable (history) is introduced. Prior to changing any state as a result of a significant event in the life cycle of the object, a new edition is written to history, with the event as the key and a copy of the object as the value. This is an example of the History On Association pattern with the roles of Originator, Memento, and Caretaker all played by instances of the same class; the relationship between the Caretaker and the Mementos is implemented by a History collection.

Since they are of the same class, both the Originator and the Memento play the role of Caretaker; that is, they have the history variable. It would be redundant for both the Originator and the Memento to be the Caretaker of all history up to the moment when the Memento was created. After taking a new history snapshot of the Originator, its Change Log and postings are initialized. When a new Memento is created, its history is initialized with its start and end Editions. Thus, a Caretaker knows whether it is a Memento by checking if its history values include itself, and a Memento can derive the time interval during which it was current.

Diagrams

Figure 14-13 shows the state of an account before the History On Self pattern was applied. In this case, the account has just been created, and therefore has no history. It has, however, had a change in a simple variable, and thus has a Change Log, and has also had a Posting (e.g., for a connection charge).

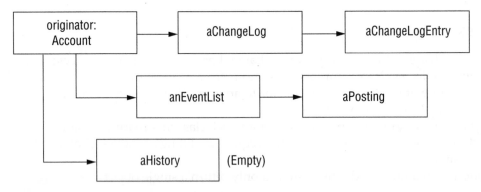

Figure 14-13 *Instance diagram before History On Self*

Figure 14-14 shows the state of the account after the closing of an accounting period, which triggers History On Self. Note that there are now two instances of Account, each representing an accounting period: the Originator is the current period, and the Memento is the previous.

- The originator's Change Log and Event List are now empty (see the method `postHistorySnapshot` in the Sample Code below).
- The Originator's history now contains an Edition, which points to the newly created Memento.
- The Memento's Change Log and Event List of postings were copied from the Originator prior to the `postHistorySnapshot`.
- A new Posting has been added to the Memento's events, representing the rating of the cycle closure event (which may include taxes or discounts).
- The Memento's history contains the same edition as the Originator's, thus indicating that it is indeed a Memento.

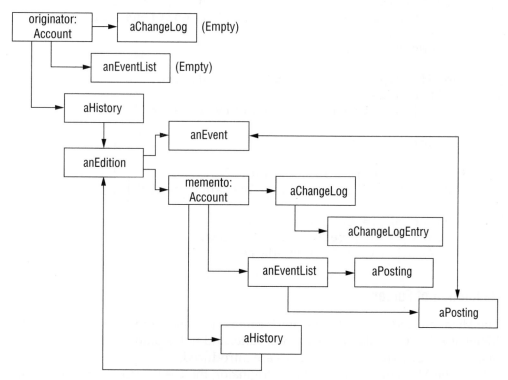

Figure 14-14 *Instance diagram after History On Self*

Sample Code

```
Originator>> historyOnSelfWithEvent: anEvent
    "Create a memento by copying myself, handle the new
    edition in history, and return the memento"
    | edition |

    edition := history newValue: self copy.
    self handleNewEdition: edition.
    ^edition value

Originator>>handleNewEdition: anEdition
    "Initialize the new memento, and reset my instance
    variables"

    anEdition value
        initializeAsMementoInEdition: anEdition.
    self postHistorySnapshot

Memento>>initializeAsMementoInEdition: anEdition
    "Reset my history to include the editions for my
    start and end events"
    | newHistory |

    newHistory := History with: anEdition.
    self hasHistory ifTrue:
        [ newHistory add: history latestEdition ].

    history := newHistory

Originator>>postHistorySnapshot
    "Reset my time-dependent instance variables"

    changeLog := ChangeLog new.
    events := OrderedCollection new.
    self initializeAccumulators
```

Resolution of Forces

The Memento and Originator are of the same class, since copy is used to create the Memento. The Caretaker is the current state, and holds onto its Mementos in the history variable. Thus no new classes are introduced.

Since the Memento is a copy of the Originator, there is no reconstruction of state involved in accessing a historical representation; the Caretaker (the latest state) either returns itself or the Memento that was current at the requested time.

One of the key decisions involved in this pattern is whether the new copy becomes the Originator or the Memento. In the approach described above, the newly created object is the Memento, which, in general, is only obtained through the Caretaker using an `AsOf:` accessor. There is no need to change external references, since they refer to the current state, in other words, the Originator/Caretaker.

The problem of only one object of a class possessing a unique key value is somewhat tricky. The following alternatives are available:

- The query mechanism could be tuned to only return the current state.
- The key could be mutated on initialization as a Memento.
- The Bridge [Gamma+1995] pattern could be used to separate the state requiring history from that (e.g., a key) that should be unchanging.
- The only additional instance variable introduced is the history collection itself; however, the complexity of object instances is increased considerably (see Figure 14-14).

Related Patterns

- Memento Child addresses the case in which a previous parent requires a reference to the Memento rather than to the Originator.
- History On Tree applies this pattern recursively to capture the history of an entire tree structure.

Known Uses

When a database backup is performed, the copy becomes the Memento.

When using a generation data group [Bodenstein1996], an IBM MVS batch job reads a previous version (generation –1) of a file and writes a new one (generation 0). In this case the copy becomes the current state. The Catalog plays the role of Caretaker.

Each time an *ENVY* method is changed, a new Edition is created. In this case, all previous editions of the containing class need to retain a previous edition of the method, so again, the copy becomes the current state.

Memento Child

Context

A parent object has children, but at any point in time, a child may only have one parent. A child may, however, move from one parent to another. The previous parent should retain the knowledge that up until a certain point in time it had that child and then lost it; the child should now be responsible for maintaining two sets of accumulated totals—those for the current and the previous parent.

Tree structures are common in business systems. In the telecommunications industry, services, agreements, and accounts are all composites, as are policies in the insurance industry. A posting to a child object rolls up to the balance of its parent. The closing of account and contract periods follow a regular cycle, but it is frequently necessary to change the structure part of the way through a period. The printing of a statement for a period should include the appropriate transactions and balances of all objects that were components during the period.

Examples

The North American Numbering Plan is composed of Numbering Plan Areas (NPAs), identified by area code, which are composed of Central Office Codes (NPA/NXX), which are assigned within Area Code. Occasionally an "NPA split" is required, in which NPA/NXXs are moved to a new NPA. Recently in Texas, the 972 area code was split off from the 214, so the phone number (214) 618-0000 is now (972) 618-0000. For a certain period of time it is necessary for the old NPA (214) to remember that it once included the moved NPA/NNX—(214) 618—even though this is now actually (972) 618.

Responsibility for an account or agreement may change part way through an accounting period due to the takeover or acquisition of an asset (e.g., a ship on which satellite service is provisioned). It must be possible for transactions prior to the transfer to appear on the invoice of the original account without having to produce a full special invoice for the partial time period.

When an electric meter is changed out at a location, not only should the meter remember where it has been installed, but the location should also remember all pieces of equipment that have been installed there over time.

Problem

The problem is twofold:

1. How to remove an object from a collection and yet retain the fact that at one point in time the reference existed.
2. How to enable transactions to post against an account that rolled up to two aggregators during the same period, while maintaining the correct balances in the context of each aggregator.

Forces

- The entire tree structure, which may be large, should not be affected, only those parents and children whose relationships are changed.
- Collections should not be allowed to grow too large.
- Proliferation of persistent collections should be avoided; preferably a collection should be stored by a value within its owning domain object.

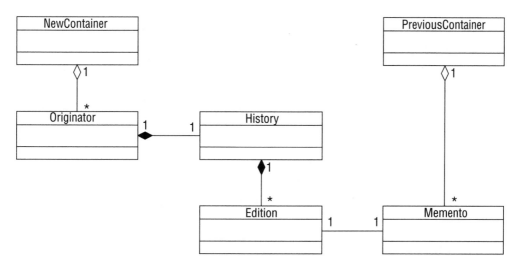

Figure 14-15 *Role diagram of Memento Child*

Solution

Apply the History On Self pattern prior to changing the Originator's parent. Instead of removing the Originator from its ex-parent's children collection, replace it with the just-created Memento. After a predetermined duration, remove Mementos from the children collection of the container.

Diagram

Figure 14-15 shows the Originator being aggregated by a NewContainer. The Memento (created by History On Self) is aggregated by the PreviousContainer. This is unusual in that external references to the object usually only reference the current state (the Originator). In this case, the responsibility is placed on the container to indicate that it holds onto Memento children (see the following Sample Code).

Sample Code

```
Originator>>container: anObject
    "Take a history snapshot on myself, remove myself from
    my previous container,
    set my new container, and add myself to it."

    container == anObject ifTrue: [ ^self ].
    self historyOnSelf.
    container notNil ifTrue:
        [ container removeChild: self ].
```

```
    container := anObject.
    anObject addChild: self.
    self changed: #container

Container>>removeChild: aChild
    "If I keep mementos of my children, do so, else remove
    my child"

    self keepsChildMementos
        ifTrue: [ self useMementoForChild: aChild]
        ifFalse: [ children remove: aChild].

    self changed: #children
    ^aChild

Container>>useMementoForChild: aChild
    "Replace the child with its latest memento"
    | index |

    (index := children indexOf: aChild) = 0 ifFalse:
        [ children at: index
            put: aChild latestMemento ]
```

Resolution of Forces

Normally for History On Self all external references are to the current state of an object, which is responsible for determining when a previous state is required. In this case, both the container and the child roles need to know that the child keeps history, thus increasing coupling; however, only the container knows that it wants to track historical children.

The parent can become cluttered with historical children. There should be some mechanism for clearing them out. This will normally be some form of aging, which is likely to occur periodically, usually when History On Self is performed on the container.

An alternative solution would be to put history on the children collection, with a new Edition created in the addChild: and removeChild: methods, but this would require multiple persistent collections, their union being all children that a parent had during a period. MementoChild seems the more elegant solution.

To correctly maintain the balances of subaccounts when a complex system of accounts changes its structure, MementoChild is normally applied after History On Tree (see section that follows) rather than History On Self.

Known Uses

When changing an *ENVY* method, the copy (in this case the new edition) replaces the original in the work in the open edition of the containing class. Other editions of the class retain a previous edition of the method.

HISTORY ON TREE

Context

Tree structures are common in business systems. In the telecommunications industry, services, agreements, and accounts are all composites, as are policies in the insurance industry. History On Self takes a snapshot of a single component object. For some major business transactions it is necessary to treat the component as the sum of its parts and to create a snapshot of an entire graph of nodes.

Examples

On close of a billing cycle of an account, the balances and invoice detail of all subaccounts must be stored. Cycle closure not only causes the historical values of the account and its subaccounts to be frozen, but this is also an event to which posting rules are applied. This occurs in numerous business examples, such as telecom products, for the calculation of discounts; and insurance, for the calculation of premiums and the historical settlements of claims.

Problem

This is an extension of a composite's lifetime responsibility for its children. In addition to cascading, copying, and deletion, some significant events may also require a composite structure to cascade the recording of history. How should the treatment of the whole as the sum of its parts be implemented for historical purposes?

Forces

* The structure of a tree at a point in time must be easy to recreate and not require the referencing of subsequent events.
* The performance and storage consequences of a historical snapshot of a complex tree are of particular concern.

Solution

Recursively apply History On Self to the descendants of the composite node that requires a complete historical snapshot. A parallel graph is created in which a

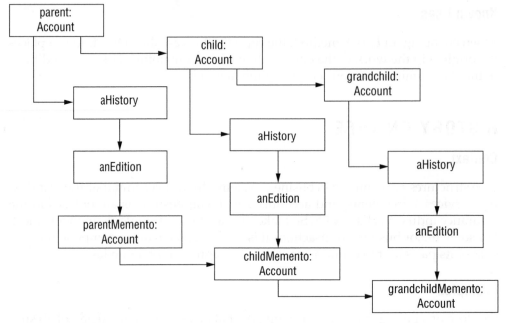

Figure 14-16 *Instance diagram of History On Tree*

historical parent node has historical children; that is, a child's memento is a memento's child.

Diagram

Figure 14-16 shows the parallel graphs created by the invocation of History On Tree. The parent, child, and grandchild each have a corresponding Memento, which themselves have the parent–child relationship. No event is shown in this diagram, but there would only be one (representing the closure of the root account). This event is the key of all the Editions and would have resulted in the appropriate postings to each of the descendant Mementos.

Sample Code

```
Account>>closePeriod
    "Create and handle the period closure event, and use
    it to trigger history on tree"

    ^self historyOnTreeWithEvent: self handlePeriodClosure
```

```
Account>>handlePeriodClosure
    "Rate and post a new period closure event"
    | closureEvent |

    self rateAndPostEvent:
        (closureEvent := self createPeriodClosureEvent).

    ^closureEvent

Originator>> historyOnTreeWithEvent: anEvent
    "Create a memento by invoking history on self, then
    tell it to propagate history on tree"
    | memento |

    memento := self historyOnSelf: anEvent.
    memento propagateHistoryOnTreeUsing:
        [ :e | e historyOnTree: anEvent ].

    ^memento

Memento>> propagateHistoryOnTreeUsing: aBlock
    "Replace my children with their latest mementos,
    obtained by evaluating the parameter block with each
    child"

    children := children collect:
        [ :eachChild |
        (aBlock value: eachChild) container: self ]
```

Resolution of Forces

This is a very expensive operation, in terms of both processing and space utilization, but requirements frequently call for it. The recursive read of the database for a deep structure can be particularly resource-consuming. Care should be taken to ensure that a snapshot of the entire composite structure is necessary before this pattern is utilized. However, when recalling historical data, only a single "as of" access is required. Once position is set within the correct temporal context for a node, only regular parent and children accesses are required for traversal.

Related Patterns

Composite [Gamma+1995] is a related pattern since in this case the whole is being treated as the sum of its parts for historical purposes.

Known Uses

In the solution above, it is assumed that all subcomponents will have activity during the current time interval. In *ENVY,* the assumption is that they will not, so editions are created in a bottom-up manner, and only those components that have changed or whose subcomponents have changed need new editions. To version an edition of a parent component, all of its subcomponent editions must be versioned.

There are times, however, during development when it is beneficial to open new editions on all the applications and subapplications in a configuration map. This allows a team of developers greater visibility to each other's changes, enabling earlier integration testing. This approach follows the History On Tree pattern, since the editions are opened selectively from the top down, although versioning occurs from the bottom up.

CONCLUSIONS

Piaget said: "the operations [of time] take place within the object itself, and by the colligations[1] of its parts, play a direct part in the transformation of that unique object which is the universe of time-space."

Thus, the patterns of time are fundamental to building accurate models that reflect the real world. They are not easy, but without them we are practicing, in the wrong sense, a timeless way of building.

ACKNOWLEDGMENTS

Ralph Johnson, for his collaboration on a previous paper, "Tree with History," and for his emphasis on examples over abstractions; Robert Martin, for his shepherding expertise to get this paper PLoP-ready and for pressing on regardless of its initial Smalltalk-centricity; The PLoP '98 Agricultural Valleys Group, for invaluable feedback, and a great PLoP experience.

REFERENCES

[Alpert+1998] S.R. Alpert, K. Brown, and B. Woolf. *The Design Patterns Smalltalk Companion.* Reading, MA: Addison-Wesley, 1998.

[Beck1997] K. Beck. *Smalltalk Best Practice Patterns.* Englewood Cliffs, NJ: Prentice Hall, 1997.

[Bodenstein1996] M. Bodenstein. "Data Rotations: Using Generation Data Groups to Manage Successive Copies of Related Data." Available: http://cornellc.cit.cornell.edu/datarot.html, 1996.

---

[1]Colligate—1. To tie together. 2. To bring (isolated observations) together by an explanation or hypothesis that applies to them all [*American Heritage Dictionary*].

[Carlson+1998] A. Carlson, S. Estepp, and M. Fowler. "Temporal Patterns." In *Proceedings of the Patterns Language of Programming*. Monticello, IL: Allerton House, 1998.

[Fowler1997a] M. Fowler. *Analysis Patterns: Reusable Object Models*. Reading, MA: Addison-Wesley, 1997.

[Fowler1997b] M. Fowler. "Recurring Events." Available: http://www2.awl.com/cseng/titles/0-201-89542-0/events2-1.html, 1997.

[Gamma+1995] E. Gamma, R. Helm, R. Johnson, and J. Vlissides. *Design Patterns: Elements of Reusable Object-Oriented Software*. Reading, MA: Addison-Wesley, 1995.

[Johnson+1998] R. Johnson and J. Oakes. "The User Defined Product Framework." Available: http://www-cat.ncsa.uiuc.edu/~yoder/Research/metadata/udp.pdf, 1998.

[Piaget1946] J. Piaget. *The Child's Conception of Time* (English translation). London: Routledge and Kegan Paul, 1969.

[Riehle+1997] D. Riehle, W. Siberski, D. Bäumer, D. Megert, and H. Züllighoven. "Serializer." In R. Martin, D. Riehle, F. Buschmann (eds.), *Pattern Languages of Program Design 3*. Reading, MA: Addison-Wesley, 1997.

Francis Anderson may be reached at francisa@altinet.net.

PART 5

Security

It wasn't so many years ago that I was in graduate school in computer science and took a course on cryptography and data security. While it was fascinating, and seemed to be potentially important, it was a fairly obscure discipline at the time. That was then, this is now. With the proliferation of PCs and the growth of email, the Internet, and electronic commerce, security is no longer waiting in the wings; it occupies center stage. Indeed, security has become an important concern for software writers across the world.

It should come as no surprise, therefore, that patterns about security are now appearing. These two offerings are particularly timely. They will not make you an expert in security and cryptography, but they do lay important groundwork that most of us should know.

Chapter 15: Architectural Patterns for Enabling Application Security by Joseph Yoder and Jeffrey Barcalow. This chapter points out that the security of the application must be considered early in the design of a system. These seven patterns affect the basic architecture of the system—adding security as an afterthought is difficult, if not impossible. Of course, given that these are patterns of software architecture, don't expect to find code snippets in them. Instead you will find design ideas to help you address security issues as you develop applications. By following these design principles during the early phases of development, application security will be much easier to integrate into your system when it is needed. This architecture is especially useful when the developer doesn't have all of the security requirements during early development.

This set of patterns begins with Single Access Point, which allows access control to be concentrated in a single place in your program. This pattern is strengthened by organizing security checks with Check Point. Roles creates common permissions and access rights for various classes of users. Session, Full View With Errors, and Limited View describe how to manage secure data in an application.

The astute observer will note that these patterns did not originate with software; indeed, these ideas have been around a long time. For example, anyone who has crossed the portal of a medieval castle will recognize Single Access Point. And the Roles pattern is somewhat reminiscent of the multiple levels of security clearance used by the U.S. Department of Defense.

Chapter 16: Tropyc: A Pattern Language for Cryptographic Object-Oriented Software by Alexandre M. Braga, Cecilia Rubira, and Ricardo Dahab.

This collection of ten patterns, which one might use in secure communications, is of a different ilk. They are especially tailored for use in creating an object-oriented cryptographic system. They focus on achieving the fundamental objectives of secure communication, namely, confidentiality, integrity, authentication, and nonrepudiation.

The patterns build on each other in the best sense of a pattern language. The foundation pattern is Generic Object-Oriented Cryptographic Architecture. This is followed by four patterns that address each of the fundamental objectives of cryptography. These, in turn, generate the five remaining patterns in the language.

Note that these patterns alone are not sufficient to make you expect, or even competent, in computer cryptography. For that you need a much more extensive treatment of the subject, such as that found in a textbook. However, if you need a basic understanding of cryptography, these are the patterns for you. These days, this is relevant for all of us.

Chapter 15

Architectural Patterns for Enabling Application Security

Joseph Yoder and Jeffrey Barcalow

Systems are often developed without security in mind. This is because the application programmer is focusing more on trying to learn the domain rather than on how to protect the system. The developer is building prototypes and learning what is needed to satisfy the needs of the users. In these cases, security is usually the last thing he or she needs or wants to worry about. When the time arrives to deploy these systems, it quickly becomes apparent that adding security is much harder than just adding a password-protected login screen. This chapter describes how to design a system so that details of security can be implemented late in development.

In corporate environments where security is a priority, detailed security documents are written describing physical, operating system, network, and application security. These security documents deal with issues such as user privileges, how secure passwords have to be and how often they might need to be changed, if data needs to be encrypted, and how secure the communication layer needs to be.

Often security is initially ignored because either the security policy is not generally available or it just seems easier to postpone security concerns. Ignoring security issues is dangerous because it can be difficult to retrofit security into an application. Although an application's design could initially be more complicated by incorporating security from the start, the design will be cleaner than the result of integrating security late in the development cycle. Also, huge code rewrites can be avoided because the corporate security policy can be integrated at any stage of the development cycle. A well-thought-out design that includes security considerations will make it simpler to adapt to changing security requirements.

The seven patterns presented in this paper can be applied when developing security for an application. They are not meant to be a complete set of security patterns.

Rather, they are meant to be the start of a collection of patterns that will help developers address security issues when developing applications. Both authors have had the experience of refactoring a system to make it meet corporate security requirements *after* the system was developed (The Caterpillar/NCSA Financial Model Framework [Yoder1997]). We both have continued with the development of industrial applications in which security is of primary importance; one dealing with security for medical applications and the other dealing with Internet financial transactions. From these experiences, we found the following patterns that can be applied while developing secure applications. In general, it can be very beneficial to structure the architecture of an application with these patterns in mind, even if you are not going to need security at a later point.

Secure applications should not allow users to get through a back door that allows them to view or edit sensitive data. Single Access Point helps solve this problem by limiting application entry to one single point. In addition, an application is only as secure as its components and its interactions with them. Therefore, any application should have a Secure Access Layer for communicating with external systems securely, and all components of an application should provide a secure way to interact with them. This layer helps keep the application's code independent of the external interfaces.

It is important to provide a place to validate users and make appropriate decisions when dealing with security breaches. Check Point encapsulates the strategies dealing with different types of security breaches while making the punishment appropriate for the security violation.

When there are many users for a system, privileges for these users can usually be categorized by the users' jobs instead of their names. In these cases, users can be assigned to certain roles that describe appropriate actions for that type of user. Groups of users will have different roles that define what they can and can not do. For example, an application might provide roles for administrating the application, creating and maintaining data in an application, and viewing the data. All users of this application will be assigned a set of roles that describe what privileges they have.

There is also common data that will be used throughout a secure system, such as who the user is, what privileges they have, and what state the system is in. For example, to access a database, the application needs the username and database location. Multiple users might be logged onto the system at the same time, and this information needs to be maintained separately for each user. Global information about the user is distributed throughout the application via a Session.

Users' views of the system will depend upon their current roles. These views can be presented as a Limited View of legal options by only showing users what they have permission to see or run. Another option is to present a Full View With Errors that allows the user to see everything. Options that the user does not have current permission to perform can be disabled, or exceptions can be fired whenever the user performs an illegal operation.

Table 15-1 *Pattern Catalog*

Pattern	Intent
Single Access Point	Providing a security module and a way to log into the system
Check Point	Organizing security checks and their repercussions
Roles	Organizing users with similar security privileges
Session	Localizing global information in a multi-user environment
Full View With Errors	Providing a full view to users, showing exceptions when needed
Limited View	Allowing users to only see what they have access to
Secure Access Layer	Integrating application security with low-level security

The pattern catalog in Table 15-1 outlines the application security patterns discussed in this chapter. It lists each pattern's name with the problem that the pattern solves. These patterns collaborate to provide the necessary security within an application. They are tied together in the Putting It All Together section presented at the end of the chapter.

This chapter does not discuss patterns or issues dealing with low-level security on which our Secure Access Layer pattern is built. These low-level security patterns deal with issues such as encryption, firewalls, Kerberos, and AFS. Many good sources of low-level security issues and techniques are available. The *International Cryptographic Software Web Pages* [ICSP1998] and *Applied Cryptography* [Schneier1995] are very good references for more details on these issues.

THE PATTERNS

Single Access Point

Also Known As

Login Window, One Way In, Guard Door, and Validation Screen

Motivation

A military base provides a prime example of a secure location. Military personnel must be allowed in while spies, saboteurs, and reporters must be kept out. If the base has many entrances, it will be much more difficult and expensive to guard each of them. Security is easier to guarantee when everyone must pass through a single guard station.

It is hard to provide security for an application that communicates with networking, operating systems, databases, and other infrastructure systems. The application will need a way to log a user into the system, to set up what the user can and can not do, and to integrate with other security modules from systems with which it will be interacting. Sometimes a user may need to be authenticated on several systems. Additionally, some of the user-supplied information may need to be kept for later processing. Single Access Point solves this by providing a secure place to validate users and to collect global information needed about users who need to start using an application.

Problem

A security model is difficult to validate when it has multiple front doors, back doors, and side doors for entering the application.

Forces

- Having multiple ways to open an application makes it easier for it to be used in different environments.
- An application may be a composite of several applications that all need to be secure.
- Different login windows or procedures could have duplicate code.
- A single entry point may need to collect all of the user information that is needed for the entire application.
- Multiple entry points to an application can be customized to collect only the information needed at that entry point. This way, a user does not have to enter unnecessary information.

Solution

Set up only one way to get into the system and, if necessary, create a mechanism for deciding which subapplications to launch.

The typical solution is to create a login screen for collecting basic information about the user, such as username, password, and possibly some configuration settings. This information is passed through some sort of Check Point that verifies the information. A Session is then created based upon the configuration settings and the user's access privileges. This Session is used to keep track of the global information that deals with the user's current interaction with the application. When opening up any subapplication, requests are forwarded through the Check Point to handle any problems and validations.

UNIX is an example of a system with multiple access points. Each network port can provide access to a separate service. These multiple access points make it difficult to secure a UNIX system as a whole. Individual applications running on a UNIX system can still be secured, however. For example, if an application has Web, e-mail, and programming interfaces, steps must be taken to ensure that each of these interfaces are forced through a shared Single Access Point before accessing the rest of the application.

The Putting It All Together section describes the initialization process in more detail. The important idea here is that Single Access Point provides a convenient place to encapsulate the initialization process, making it easier to validate that the initial security steps are performed correctly.

Example

There are many examples of Single Access Point. In order to access an NT workstation, there is a single login screen that all users must go through to access the system. This Single Access Point validates the user and ensures that only valid users access the system and also provides roles for only allowing users to see and do what they have permission to do. Most UNIX systems also have a Single Access Point for getting a console shell. Oracle applications also have many applications such as SQLPlus and the like that provide a Single Access Point as the only way to run those applications.

Consequences

Single Access Point has the following advantages:

- It provides a place where everything within the application can be set up properly. This single location can help ensure that all values are initialized correctly, that application set up is performed correctly, and that the application does not reach an invalid state.
- Control flow is simpler since everything must go through a single point of responsibility in order to allow access. Note that Single Access Point is only as secure as the steps leading up to it.

Single Access has the following disadvantage:

- The application cannot have multiple entry points to create a more flexible entrance.

Related Patterns

- Single Access Point validates the user's login information through a Check Point and uses that information to initialize the user's Roles and Session.

- A Singleton [Gamma+1995] could be used for the login class especially if you only allow the user to have one login session started or only log into the system once. A Singleton could also be used to keep track of all Sessions, and a key could be used to know which session to use.

Known Uses

- UNIX telnet and Windows NT login applications use Single Access Point for logging into the system. These systems also create the necessary Roles for the current Session.
- Most application login screens are a Single Access Point into programs because they are the only way to start up and run the given application.
- The Caterpillar/NCSA Financial Model Framework [Yoder1997] has an FMLogin class, which provides both Single Access Point and Check Point.
- The PLoP '98 registration program [Yoder+1998] provided a Single Access Point for logging into the system and entering in credit card information when users registered for PLoP '98.
- Secure Web servers, such as Java Developer's Connection, appear to have multiple access points for each URL. However, the Web server forces each user through a login window before letting them download early access software.

Nonsecurity Known Uses

- Any application that launches only one way, ensuring a correct initial state.
- Windows 95 also uses a login window that is a Single Access Point, but it is not secure because it allows any user to override the login screen.
- Single creational methods provide for only one way to create a class. For example, Points in VisualWorks Smalltalk [ObjectShare1995] helps you create valid points by providing a couple of creational methods that ensure that the object is initialized correctly. Kent Beck describes Constructor Methods as a single way to create well-formed instances of objects [Beck1997]. These are put into a single "instance creation" protocol. This becomes the Single Access Point to create new objects.
- The Constructor Parameter Method [Beck1997] initializes all instance variables through a single method, which is really a Single Access Point for that class to initialize its instance variables.
- Concurrent programs can encapsulate nonconcurrent objects inside an object designed for concurrency. Synchronization is enforced through this Single Access Point. Pass-Through Host design [Lea1997] deals with synchronization by forwarding all appropriate methods to the Helper using nonsynchronized methods. This works because the methods are stateless with respect to the Host class.

Check Point

Also Known As

Access Verification, Authentication and Authorization, Holding Off Hackers, Validation and Penalization, and Make the Punishment Fit the Crime

Motivation

Military personnel working at a base have a security badge that is checked by the guard at the front gate. They also have keys that will allow them to enter only areas in which they are authorized. No one is allowed in without a badge. Anyone who tries to enter a restricted area without clearance is dealt with severely.

The goal of application security is to keep unwanted perpetrators from gaining access to application areas where they can find confidential information or can corrupt data. Single Access Point can help solve this problem by making a single point to enter an application. At the Single Access Point, checks must be made to verify that a user is permissible. Unfortunately, these checks could make getting into the application more difficult for legitimate users. For example, a common mistake is entering the wrong password. While users may often mistype their passwords, frequent, consecutive failures without success could indicate that someone is trying to guess a password and break into the application. Application security must allow occasional mistakes while doing its best to keep a hacker out. A developer could design many checks to determine if a user is trying to break into the system or is just making common mistakes. These checks could become complicated and spread out throughout the application, making it difficult to manage and maintain the applications. Check Point helps out with this by organizing these checks.

Problem

An application needs to be secure from break-in attempts, and appropriate actions should be taken when such attempts occur. Different organizations have different security policies, and there needs to be a way to incorporate these policies into the system independently from the design of the application.

Forces

- Having a way to authenticate users and provide validation on what they can do is important.
- Users make mistakes and should not be punished too harshly for mistakes.
- If too many mistakes are made, some type of action needs to be taken.

- Different actions need to be taken depending on the severity of the mistake.
- Lots of error-checking code spread over an application can make it difficult to debug and maintain.

Solution

Create an object that encapsulates the algorithm for the company's security policy.

This object usually keeps track of how many exceptions happen and decides what action needs to be taken based on the severity of the violation. Any security check can be part of the Check Point algorithm—from password checks to time-outs to spoofing.

All organizations will have some sort of security policy that the applications developer needs to implement. The security policy may not be available when an application is designed, however. The policy also might change over the life of the application. The principal goal here is to design the application with a place to encapsulate the security policy. Early in prototyping and development, a developer might just create a dummy object that allows any user to get into the system. This dummy Check Point makes it easier to add security at a later point.

The implementation of Check Point combines several patterns. Single Access Point is used to ensure that security checks are performed correctly and that no initial security checks are skipped. A key feature of Check Point is that the security policy can be changed in a single place. In this way, the Check Point algorithm is a Strategy [Gamma+1995]. This Strategy knows what security checks are performed, the order in which checks should be performed, and how to handle failures. Different Strategy objects could be plugged in depending on the desired level of security. The authors have found the Strategy quality of Check Point to be useful because security can be turned off in a development situation and can be turned back on for testing and deployment.

In some systems, this pattern is separated into two conceptual parts: authentication and authorization. Authentication verifies who and where a user is. Authorization involves checking the privileges of an authenticated user. This distinction can be useful in a distributed system in which applications may run at different locations. Users can be authenticated from a central login application so they do not have to reenter a password for each application. Authorization can be performed on operations as needed for each application. Check Point utilizes the user's Role to provide the proper authorization to the system.

It is also useful to break this pattern into the two parts since authentication usually is done when a user starts using the system, and authorization is needed whenever a user tries to use a secured operation. Therefore, whenever a security check is needed, it can be forwarded to the authentication part of the Check Point, which in turns provides proper access according to the user's role.

A Check Point design can vary greatly because of the security policy. If a company's security policy is not yet defined or if it might change, then the Check Point algorithm should be designed carefully. Three factors should be considered in designing a Check Point component when the security policy is uncertain: failure actions, repeatability, and deferred checks.

Depending on the security violation or error, different types of failure actions may be taken. Failure actions can be broken down by level of severity. These types of failures and actions are contingent upon the security policy you are implementing. For example, the simplest action is to return a warning or error message to the user. If the error is noncritical, the security algorithm could treat it as a warning and continue. A second level of failure could force the user to start over. The third level of severity could force an abort of the login process or quit the program. The fourth, or highest, level of severity could lockout a machine or username. In this case, an administrator might have to reset the username and/or machine access. Unfortunately this could cause problems when a legitimate user tries to login later, so if the violation is not extremely critical, the username and machine disabled flags could be timestamped and automatically reenabled after an hour or so. All security failures also could be logged.

Sometimes, the level of a security violation depends on how many times the violation is repeated. A user who types a password incorrectly once or twice should not be punished too harshly. Three or four consecutive failures could indicate that a hacker is trying to guess a password. To handle this situation, the Strategy can include counters to keep track of the frequency of security violations and parameterize the algorithm.

Most security checks can be performed after the user logs in, so Single Access Point flows right into Check Point. However, security checks cannot always be performed in the Check Point as the user enters the application; they must be deferred until later. For example, it may be more efficient to defer database initialization until the database is used for the first time. In a client-server environment, an application may need to verify the user login after a server recovers from a crash. Ideally, this application could verify the user login without requiring users to retype in their passwords. For these cases, the Check Point might need a secondary interface for application components to use, or a separate authorization component might be necessary. This secondary interface is another factor to consider when designing a Check Point.

Because application security can be a tricky point in development, it may be desirable to try to make a reusable security module for use in several applications. That goal is difficult when security requirements vary between the applications. All application teams need to be involved to ensure that the framework will satisfy each application's requirements.

One approach for reusing security code is to create a library of pluggable security components and a framework for incorporating these components into applications. However, the algorithm for putting together components will almost always be overridden, making the framework difficult to generalize. Another approach is to create configuration options that allow small parts of the algorithm to be turned on and off. The Check Point can be an Achilles' heel of an application's security, so every possible branch in the logic must be carefully checked.

Example

Figure 15-1 summarizes the Check Point algorithm that was used for the Caterpillar/NCSA Financial Model. The process starts at the login window. From this Single Access Point, the Check Point algorithm begins. The password check and failure loop has three counters. One keeps track of the number of failures since the application has been loaded. The other two counters keep track of consecutive failures by that user and by someone at that terminal, which could be spread out over several application startups. When too many consecutive failures occur, the user and/or terminal is disabled for a fixed duration of time or until the administrator resets the account or terminal. These decisions were part of the Caterpillar policy and could change. Password verification is performed by the database through the Secure Access Layer. Once a correct password has been entered, several other checks are applied. The reason is that although a login might be allowed to access the database, the login might not be legal for the application. Password expiration also is implemented after these checks. Notice that while the consecutive failure error disables the account and/or machine, refusing to enter a new password simply aborts the application. When Check Point is complete, it configures the Session based on a Role. The Check Point can enter login successes and failures into a log file.

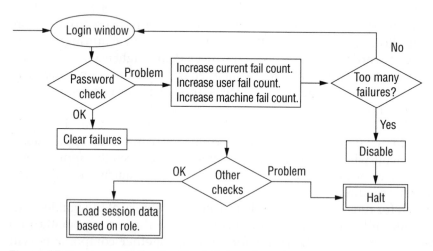

Figure 15-1 *An example of a Check Point algorithm*

Consequences

The Check Point pattern has the following advantages:

- It is a critical security location where security must be absolutely enforced. Check Point localizes the security model that needs to be certified.
- It can be a complex algorithm. While this complexity may be unavoidable, at least it is isolated in one location, making the security algorithm easier to change.

The Check Point pattern has the following disadvantage:

- Some security checks cannot be performed at startup, so Check Point must have a secondary interface for the parts of the application that need those checks. Some information needed for these security checks must be kept until needed later. This information, which could include username, password, and Roles, can be stored in a Session.

Related Patterns

- The Check Point algorithm uses a Strategy for application security.
- Single Access Point is used to ensure that Check Point gets initialized correctly and that none of the security checks are skipped.
- Roles are often used for Check Point's security checks and could be loaded by Check Point.
- Check Point usually configures a Session and stores the necessary security information in it. It can also interact with the Session to get the user's Role during the authorization process.
- Check Point often interacts with the Secure Access Layer.

Known Uses

- The login process for an ftp server uses Check Point. Depending on the server's configuration files, anonymous logins may or may not be allowed. For anonymous logins, a valid e-mail is sometimes required. This is similar for Telnet.
- The Caterpillar/NCSA Financial Model Framework [Yoder1997] uses Check Point to check passwords, Roles, and machines. The example above summarizes its implementation.
- Xauth uses a cookie to provide a Check Point that X Windows applications can use for secure communication between clients and servers.
- Java applets that need to write to a user's hard drive use the authentication/authorization process in a different way. The applet is authenticated with a certificate authority to verify who created it. Then the Web user manually authorizes to run outside the Java sandbox on the user's machine.

- The PLoP '98 registration program [Yoder+1998] has a Check Point that only allows authorized users to log onto the system and change their user information.
- The Access API, used by Reuters SSL Developer Kit—Java Edition, supports a verification flag that allows automatic relogin for applications when DACS or the Java Distributor recovers. This verification flag is supported by a secondary interface to the Check Point.

Roles

Also Known As

Actors, Groups, Projects, Profiles, Jobs, and User Types

Motivation

Every military base has a commander. This base commander gives the order if the base is to be shut down or brought to full alert status. These commands are privileges of the office of base commander, not of the particular person who holds that position. When the base commander is transferred or retires, a new person holds the position of base commander. "Base commander" is that person's role.

Security can be more complicated in multiuser applications. Users have different areas of the application that they can see, can change, and "own." When the number of users is large, the security permissions for users often fall into several categories. These categories correspond to a user's job titles, experience, or division. Meanwhile, the administrator must struggle with managing the security profiles for a large number of users. The administrator needs an easier way to manage permissions.

Problem

Users have different security profiles, and some profiles are similar. If the user base is large enough or the security profiles are complex enough, then managing user-privilege relationships can become difficult.

Forces

- With a large number of users it is hard to customize security for each person.
- Groups of users usually share similar security profiles.
- A user may need to have an individual security profile.
- Security profiles may overlap.
- A user's security profile may change over time.

Solution

Create one or more role objects that define the permissions and access rights that groups of users have.

When a user logs in, he is assigned a set of privileges that specify what data is accessible and which parts of the application can be activated. From an administrator's standpoint this user-privilege relationship (Figure 15-2) is M users to N privileges, making it difficult to manage.

Figure 15-2 *User-privilege relationship*

This pattern introduces a level of indirection (the role). This level of indirection splits the user-privilege relationship into user-role and role-privilege relationships (Figure 15-3). While these two new relationships are still M-to-N, selecting appropriate roles can reduce the total number of relationships. The primary benefit is that privileges can usually be grouped together into common categories.

Figure 15-3 *User-role-privilege relationship*

Introducing Roles creates two new relationships that must be managed: user-role and role-privilege. These new relationships can help make managing security easier. When the privileges of a job title change, that role-privilege relationship can be edited directly. When a user gets a promotion, the user-role relationship can be changed instead of checking each user-privilege relationship for accuracy.

Sometimes a subset of the original user-privilege relationship also must be maintained to allow each user to have private privileges. The easiest way to do this is to give each user an independent role that happens to be the same as their username. Roles should only be used when the extra level of indirection provides a conceptual or manageability advantage over the direct user-privilege relationship.

For the role-privilege relationship, role objects could know what privileges for which they are authorized. The converse implementation would require every privilege call to check its roles before returning a value or performing an operation. This option spreads security code throughout the application, so it should be avoided. The preferred implementation, defining privileges within the role objects, is an example of the Limited View pattern.

While creating a single role for each user may simplify organization, in reality a user could be a member of multiple roles. For example, a user might be both an accountant and a manager. An Accountant Manager role could be created but that is not a generalized solution and could require that Roles be created for every possible combination. A better solution is to make the user object's **"role"** variable store a set of Roles. This approach makes it easier to map a user to the appropriate set of Roles from an administrative standpoint. However, it makes privilege lookups more complicated inside the application. The role-privilege relationship must be checked for each of the user's roles, meaning simple comparisons must be replaced by for-loop comparisons.

Another possible implementation is to build the role-privilege relationship as described above by associating a resource with a set of privileges for a given role. This can be accomplished through the use of access control lists (ACLs) [Silberschatz+1997]. So now you have a resource-privilege-role relationship and a user-role relationship. When a user tries to access a resource at runtime, the application checks the roles for the user against ACL for that resource. Operations are only permitted when the role has privileges for that resource.

This pattern presents a simplified approach for designing with Roles. A variation of this pattern is to allow a user to have several types of roles. For example, a user object could have a set of roles describing its editing privileges and another set of roles describing its viewing privileges. If Roles overlap heavily, it may make sense to build a hierarchy of role types and subtypes. For example, the "supervisor" role would allow the supervisor to access detailed employee information for the supervisor's subordinates. Additionally, that role could be a subtype of the "employee" role because the supervisor is also an employee of the company. Also, you could think of organizing Roles in such a way that a role can contain other roles. Thus, you could also create Composite Roles for maintaining groups for Roles. Martin Fowler has written a detailed paper [Fowler1997b] that contains a good description of Roles and their implementations. While this pattern discusses Roles only in the context of security, Roles can be useful throughout the design of any application.

Example

Roles can be used with security in *many* different ways. The Caterpillar/NCSA Financial Model uses a relatively straightforward approach. After a user passes authentication and other security checks successfully (from the Check Point), the application looks up the user's roles in a protected table. Then, the user selects a single role (such as accountant, manager, or developer) from her possible roles. The application uses the selected role as the role for its database session (the database's Secure Access Layer). Since database tables can be permissioned by role, setting the database session's role automatically creates part of a Limited View. The user's login name is used for further permissioning and limiting of the view.

Consequences

Roles has the following advantages:

- Instead of managing user-privilege relationships, the administrator will manage the user-role and role-privilege relationships.
- Roles can be a convenient organizational technique for administrators.
- Roles are a good way to group together common privileges.
- Administrative tasks can be simplified by using Roles. For example, all new employees could be allowed to view and edit a training database, but only view the real database. A "training" Role could be created for these permissions. Then, any new employee account will only have to be given a training Role instead of a potentially large set of permission options.

Roles has the following disadvantages:

- Roles add an extra layer of complexity for developers.
- Even if Roles are used, each user will need a private Role to maintain private privileges and preferences.

Related Patterns

- "Dealing with Roles" [Fowler1997b] provides a whole pattern language that discusses roles with more specific implementation details.
- Check Point is used when a user tries to perform an operation without having a Role with the proper permissions.
- A user's role is needed throughout the application. The Role information can be stored in a Session object for access whenever needed.
- Roles could be used to determine the scope of a Limited View.
- When an application should behave differently depending on a user's job, the user's Roles could be used to select a Strategy for the application.

Known Uses

- UNIX uses three classifications for secure access to files and directories. The middle classification is "group," which is an example of Roles. The user-role relationship is stored in `/etc/group` and is sorted by roles. The file system stores the role-privilege relationship. Windows NT allows for descriptions of groups for allocating privileges for users in a similar way.
- Some Web servers use `.htaccess` and `.htgroups` files, which define groups of users (Roles) that can access certain areas of a Web site.
- Oracle has a Roles feature for defining security privileges. User-role and role-privilege relationships are stored in tables.
- In GemStone OODB, data is stored in a segment. GemStone treats segments analogously to the way UNIX treats files. Users in GemStone can have one or

more groups (roles), and each segment has read and write privileges defined for all users, a set of groups, and the owner. Since a segment can have a set of groups, it is a little more powerful than UNIX with respect to groups.

- The PLoP '98 registration program [Yoder+1998] has two roles: attendee and administrator.
- Java's Principal object can be to store Roles that are just strings. The Access API for Reuters SSL Developers Kit-Java Edition has an Attribute class that is analogous to Java's Principal.

Nonsecurity Known Uses

Office '97's Help system is an example of using Roles for a nonsecurity issue. The animated paperclip help character can be configured to give from no help (expert) to frequently unrequested help (beginner). This configuration is the current user's role. Windows '95 profile is also a role.

Session

Also Known As

User's Environment, Namespace, Threaded-Based Singleton, and Localized Globals

Motivation

Military personnel's activities are tracked while they are in a high-security military installation. Their entry and exit are logged. Their badges must be worn at all times to show they are only where they are supposed to be. Guards inside the base can assume personnel with a badge have been checked thoroughly at the base entrance. Therefore, they only have to perform minimal checks before allowing them into a restricted area. Many people are working in a base at the same time. Each security badge uniquely identifies who that person is and what they can do. It also tracks what the carrier of the badge has been doing.

Secure applications need to keep track of global information used throughout the application such as username, roles, and their respective privileges. When an application needs to keep one copy of some information around, it often uses the Singleton pattern [Gamma+1995]. The Singleton is usually stored in a single global location, such as a class variable. Unfortunately, a Singleton can be difficult to use when an application is multi-threaded, multiuser, or distributed. In these situations, each thread or each distributed process can be viewed as an independent application, each needing its own private Singleton. But when the applications share a common global address space, the single global Singleton cannot be shared. A mechanism is needed to allow multiple "Singletons," one for each application.

Problem

Many objects need access to shared values, but the values are not unique through-out the system.

Forces

- Referencing global variables can keep code clean and straightforward.
- Each object may only need access to some of the shared values.
- Values that are shared could change over time.
- Multiple applications that run simultaneously might not share the same values.
- Passing many shared objects throughout the application make APIs more complicated.
- While an object may not need certain values, it may later change to need those values.

Solution

Create a Session object, which holds all of the variables that need to be shared by many objects.

Each Session object defines a namespace, and each variable in a single Session shares the same namespace. The Session object is passed around to objects that need any of its values.

Certain user information is used throughout a system. Some of this information is security related, such as the user's role and privileges. A Session object is a good way for sharing this global information. This object can be passed around and used as needed.

Depending on the structure of the class hierarchy, an instance variable for the Session could be added to a superclass common to every class that needs the Session. Many times, especially when extending and building on existing frameworks, the common superclass approach will not work, unless of course you want to extend the object, which is usually not considered a good design. Therefore, an instance variable usually needs to be added to every class that needs access to the Session.

All of the objects that share the same Session have a common scope. This scope is like the environments used by a compiler to perform variable lookups. The principle differences are that the Session's scope was created by the application and that lookups are performed at runtime by the application.

Since many objects hold a reference to the Session, it is a great place to put the current State [Gamma+1995] of the application. The State pattern does not have to be implemented inside of the Session for general security purposes, however. Limited View data and Roles can also be cached in a Session. It is important to note that

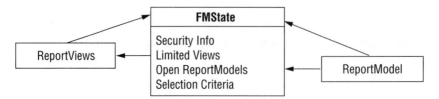

Figure 15-4 *The financial model's* FMState

the user should not be allowed to access any security data that may be held within a Session, such as passwords and privileges. It can be a good idea to structure any application with a Session object. This object holds onto any shared information that is needed while a user is interacting with the application.

Example

A Session can be used to store many different kinds of information in addition to security data. The Caterpillar/NCSA Financial Model Framework has a FMState class [Yoder1997]. An FMState object serves as a Session. It provides a single location for application components to access a Limited View of the data, the current products that can be selected, the user's Role, and the state of the system. Most of the classes in the Financial Model keep a reference to a FMState. A true Singleton could not be used because a user can open multiple sessions with different selection criteria, each yielding a different Limited View.

Figure 15-4 shows an FMState from the Financial Model. Security info includes username and role. The security information and selection criteria define the limited views. Each ReportView and ReportModel has a reference back to the FMState so it can access other data.

Consequences

Session has the following advantages:

- Its object provides a common interface for all components to access important variables.
- Instead of passing many values around the application separately, a single Session object can be passed around.
- Whenever a new shared variable or object is needed, it can be put in the Session object, and then all components that have access to the object will have access to it.
- Change propagation is simplified because each object in a thread or process is dependent on only a single, shared Session object.

Session has the following disadvantages:

- While an object may not need a Session, it may later create an object that needs the Session. When this is the case, the first object must still keep a reference to the

Session so it can pass it to the new object. Sometimes, it may seem as if every object has a Session. The proliferation of Session instance variables throughout the design is an unfortunate, but necessary, consequence of the Session pattern.

- Adding Session late in the development process can be difficult. Every reference to a Singleton must be changed. The authors have experience retrofitting Session in place of Singleton and can attest that this can very tedious when Singletons are spread among several classes. This is also true when trying to consolidate many global variables that were being passed around as parameters into a Session.
- When many values are stored in the Session, it will need some organizational structure. While some organization may make it possible to break down a Session to reduce coupling, splitting the session requires a detailed analysis of which components need which subsets of values.

Related Patterns

- Session is an alternative to a Singleton [Gamma+1995] in a multi-threaded, multiuser, or distributed environment.
- Single Access Point validates a user through Check Point. It gets a Session in return if the user validation is acceptable.
- A Session is a convenient place to implement the State pattern because the state is needed throughout the application.
- A Session can keep track of the user's role and possibly cache Limited View data.
- Lea's Sessions [Lea1995] discusses the beginning, middle, and end actions performed during resource management. This chapter's Session pattern, on the other hand, focuses on separating data that cannot go in a Singleton because of a shared environment.
- Abstract Session [Pryce1999] is a related pattern. While Abstract Session concentrates on network session, this pattern concentrates on where data is stored. In a networking environment, both patterns are typically seen and could be implemented together.
- The Thread-Specific Storage pattern [Schmidt+1997] allows multiple threads to use one logically global access point to retrieve thread-specific data without incurring locking overhead for each access
- Double-Checked Locking [Schmidt+1997] is the Singleton replacement when dealing with multitasking or parallelism.

Known Uses

- For VisualWorks, the ObjectLens framework for Oracle and GemBuilder for GemStone have `OracleSession` and `GbsSession` classes respectively. Each keeps information such as the transaction state and the database connection. The Sessions are then referenced by any object within the same database context.

- The Caterpillar/NCSA Financial Model Framework has an `FMState` class [Yoder 1997]. An FMState object serves as a Session, while keeping a Limited View of the data, the current product/family selection, and the state of the system. Most of the classes in the Financial Model keep a reference to an `FMState`.
- The PLoP '98 registration program [Yoder+1998] has a Session object that keeps track of the user's global information as they are accessing the application.
- Most databases use a Session for keeping track of user information.
- VisualWave [ObjectShare1995] has a Session for its httpd services, which keeps track of any Web requests made to it.
- UNIX ftp and Telnet services use a Session for tracking of requests and restricting user actions.
- Using Reuters SSL Developers Kit–Java Edition, clients can connect to a Java Distributor to request real-time and historical data. Since the Java Distributor simultaneously handles requests made by multiple clients, user information cannot be stored in a Singleton. Instead, a Session is created for each open network connection, and user security information for each Session is stored in a SessionPrincipal object.

Nonsecurity Known Uses

VisualWorks has projects that can be used to separate two or more change sets. While information about window placement also is stored in each project, image code is shared among all of the projects. Thus, projects could be considered nonsecured Sessions.

Full View with Errors

Also Known As

Full View with Exceptions, Reveal All and Handle Exceptions, and Notified View

Motivation

Once an officer is allowed on a military base, he or she could go to any building on the base. In effect, the officer has a full view of the buildings on the base. If the officer tries to enter a restricted area without proper clearance, either someone would stop and check them noting that they are not allowed in the restricted area, or alarms would sound and guards would show up to arrest the officer.

Graphical applications often provide many ways to view data. Users can dynamically choose which view on which data they want. When an application has these multiple views, the developer must always be concerned with which operations are legal given the current state of the application and the privileges of the user. The conditional code for determining whether an operation is legal can be very complicated and difficult to test. By giving the user a complete view to what all users have access to can make teaching how to use the system easier and can make for more generic GUIs.

Problem

Users should not be allowed to perform illegal operations.

Forces

- Users may be confused when some options are either not present or disabled.
- If options pop in and out depending upon Roles, the user may get confused about what is available.
- Users should not be able to see operations they are not allowed to do.
- Users should not view data for which they do not have permission.
- Users do not like being told what they cannot do.
- Users get annoyed with security errors, permissions denied, and illegal operation messages.

Solution

Design the application so users see everything that they might have access to. When a user tries to perform an operation, check if it is valid. Notify them with an error message when they perform illegal operations.

This pattern is very useful when a user can perform almost any operation. It is easier to show the user everything and just provide an error message when an illegal operation is attempted.

The solution for this pattern is simple when only a few error messages need to be displayed. Just display the error message to standard error or in a dialog box. If many error messages are spread throughout the application, a separate error-reporting mechanism may be useful. This mechanism also could be used for error logging.

Typically, an error-reporting framework has two principal components. The log event object has a message describing the error condition and a severity level indicating if the event is a warning, an error, or just user information. When a log event is created it can automatically register itself with the logger. The logger is a Singleton that automatically receives and processes log events. The logger can be configured to display dialogs or write to a file depending on the severity of the event.

Example

One example is an Oracle database. When you are using SQLPlus to access the data, you can execute any command. However, if you try to access data you don't have permission to see, an appropriate error message will be displayed.

Consequences

Full View with Errors has the following advantages:

- Training materials for the application are consistent for each type of user.
- Retrofitting this pattern into an existing system is straightforward. Just write a GUI that will handle all options and whenever a problem happens with an operation, simply exit the operation and open an error dialog.
- It is easier to dynamically change privileges on an operation because authorization is performed when the operation is attempted.
- It is easier to implement since you don't have to have multiple views on the data.

Full View with Errors has the following disadvantages:

- Users may get confused with a constant barrage of error dialogs.
- Operation validation can be more difficult when users can perform any operation.
- Users will get frustrated when they see options that they cannot perform.

Related Patterns

- Limited View is a competitor to this pattern. If limiting the view completely is not possible, this pattern can fill in the holes. The Putting It All Together section at the end of this paper compares these two patterns and describes when to use each.
- Checks [Cunningham1995] describes many details on implementing GUIs and on where to put the error notifications.
- Roles will be used for the error notification or validating what the user can and cannot do.

Known Uses

- Login windows inform users when they enter incorrect passwords.
- SQLPlus, used to access an Oracle database, allows you to execute any query and displays an appropriate error message if illegal access is attempted.
- Most word processors and text editors, including Microsoft Word and vi [VI1998], let the user try to save over a read-only file. The program displays an error message after the save has been attempted and has failed.
- Many unregistered shareware applications have some features disabled until the user registers. Menu choices for these disabled features are still listed, but when the user selects one, a dialog pops up that tells the user to register to activate that feature.
- Reuters SSL Developers Kit has a framework for reporting error, warning, and information events. It can be configured to report errors to standard error, a file, or a system-dependent location such as a dialog.

Nonsecurity Known Uses

- Assertions [Meyer1992] are a form of this pattern used within a programming interface. Since a class's interface cannot change, preconditions ensure that each method is used within a legal context.
- The Java programming model of throwing exceptions follows this pattern. Instead of designing methods to only be used in the proper context, exceptions are thrown forcing the rest of the application to deal with the error.

Limited View

Also Known As

Blinders, Child Proofing, Invisible Road Blocks, Hiding the Cookie Jars, and Early Authorization

Motivation

When a congresswoman visits a base in her district, she is given an escorted tour. Before her arrival a tour would be set up. Some areas of the base, such as the target range would be designed as unsafe and others might be designated top secret or need-to-know. The tour would be predesigned to give her a limited view of the base relevant to her security clearance.

Graphical applications often provide many ways to view data. Users can dynamically choose which view on which data they want. When an application has these multiple views, the developer must always be concerned with which operations are legal given the current state of the application and the privileges of the user. The conditional code for determining whether an operation is legal can be very complicated and difficult to test. By limiting the view to what the user has access to, conditional code can be avoided.

Problem

Users should not be allowed to perform illegal operations.

Forces

- Users may be confused when some options are either not present or disabled.
- If options pop in and out depending upon Roles, the user may get confused about what is available.
- Users should not be able to see operations they cannot do.

- Users should not view data they do not have permissions for.
- Users do not like being told what they cannot do.
- Users get annoyed with security and access violation messages.
- User validation is easier when you limit users to see only what they can access.

Solution

Only let the users see what they have access to. Only give them selections and menus to options that their current access-privileges permit.

When the application starts up, the user will have some role or the application will default to some view. Based upon this role, the system will only allow the user to select items that the current role allows. If the user cannot edit the data, then do not present the user with these options through menus or buttons.

A Limited View is controlled in several ways. First, a Limited View configures which selection choices are possible for the user based upon the current set of roles. This makes it so that the user only selects data they are allowed to see. Second, a Limited View takes the current Session with the user's Roles, applies the current state of the application, and dynamically builds a GUI that limits the view based upon these attributes. Null Objects [Woolf1997] can be used in the GUI for values the user does not have permission to view.

The first approach allows users to see different lists and data values depending upon their current role. This approach is primarily used when a user is presented with a selection list for choosing items to view. The GUI presented to the user is static; however, the values listed on the GUI change according to the current role of the user. An individual user may have many roles and may have to choose a role while running the application. Whenever a user changes his or her role(s), the Limited View will change.

For example, consider a financial application in which a manager has access to a limited set of products. When making a product selection inside a Limited View, the application will only present products that the manager is allowed to see. Thus, when managers go to select the desired products available, they will not get an "access denied" error.

When using the Limited View inside a Session with Role information, the view based upon the current state of the application is also limited. The actual GUI that the user sees on the screen is dynamically created. For example, a Limited View might add buttons or menus for editing, if the user's role allows for editing. Alternatively, edit options might always be disabled, but they could be dynamically enabled depending upon the role of the user and the current state of the application. The Strategy pattern could be used here to plug in different GUIs depending upon the desired results.

By limiting users to only viewing the data to which they have access and only showing them the options that are available, they know what options are currently legal. For example, in Microsoft Word, when there are no documents open, the file menu does not show the option of saving a file since there are no files to save. Similarly, when previewing an Internet document, the user does not have any options available to edit the document.

Limited View can be implemented many ways. GUIs can be dynamically created through Composites and Builders [Gamma+1995]. The Type-Object [Johnson+1998], Properties, and Metadata [Foote+1998] also are very useful in creating these dynamic GUIs. Alternatively, the State pattern can be used to represent different views with different classes. A Strategy can be used for choosing the appropriate State.

A Limited View maximizes security and usability. Unfortunately, it can be difficult to implement. You really want to consider using a Limited View when many privileges vary between users, and you don't want to frustrate your users with many error messages.

Example

One example of a Limited View can be seen in the Selection Box example in Figure 15-5. Here, the user is only provided with a list of the products they can view or edit. While other products are available in the system, those products are not shown because this user does not have access rights to them. For example, if a GUI provides a list of detailed transactions, a Limited View on this would only show a list of transactions for beans, corn, and hay for this user since that is all she is allowed to access.

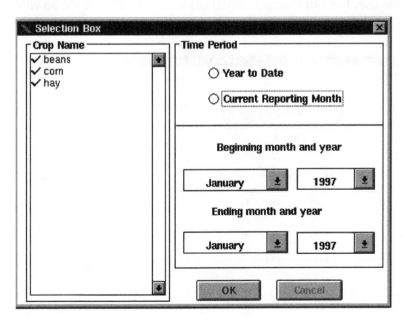

Figure 15-5 *Limited View on Selection*

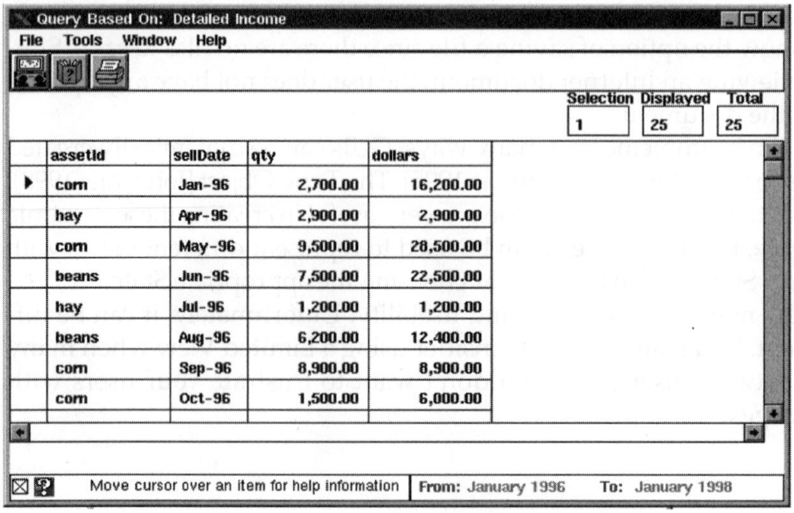

Figure 15-6 *Limited View on non-editable transactions*

Another example can be seen in Figure 15-6 and Figure 15-7. Note that Figure 15-6 does not show a button for changing the values in the database, while Figure 15-7 has that option. The view limits the ability for editing in Figure 15-6 since the user does not have the authority for editing the detailed income. In Figure 15-7, the view is limited by disabling some of the buttons. The buttons are disabled because the user has not changed any transactions and there are no values to accept or commit to the database.

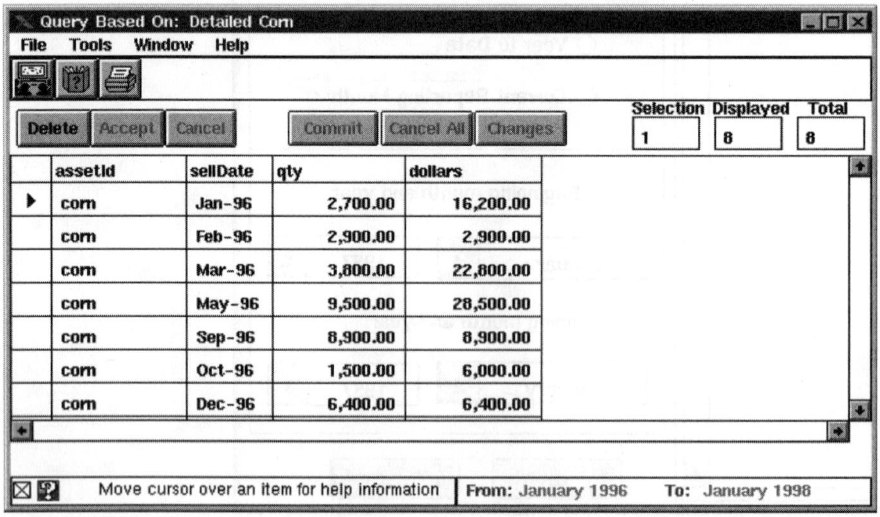

Figure 15-7 *Limited View on editable transactions*

Both the disable and the hide approaches to limiting a view have trade-offs that designers make depending upon the overall needs of the application. If the primary user will not be able to edit values, the Limited View will probably want to hide editing buttons. Whereas if the primary user will have editing functions, the Limited View will probably want to simply disable the buttons and menus as needed.

Consequences

Limited View has the following advantages:

- By only allowing users to see and edit what they can access, the developer doesn't have to worry about verifying each operation after a user selects it. The user will only be permitted to select legal items. Similarly, if the user can edit values, the editing menus and buttons will only be presented when the user has editing capabilities on the presented data.
- Security checks can be simplified by performing all of them up front.
- Users will not get frustrated with error dialogs popping up all the time telling them what they cannot do. Users will also not get frustrated by constantly seeing options to which they do not have access.

Limited View has the following disadvantages:

- Users can become frustrated when options appear and disappear on the screen. For example, if when viewing one set of data, the editing button is there and when viewing another set of data, it disappears, the user may wonder if something is wrong with the application or why the data isn't available.
- Training materials for an application must be customized for each set of users because menu operations will disappear and reappear and GUIs will change based on the Limited View.
- Retrofitting a Limited View into an existing system can be difficult because the data for the Limited View, as well as the code for selecting it, could be spread throughout the system.

Related Patterns

- Full View With Errors is a competitor to this pattern. If limiting the view completely is not possible, error messages can fill in the holes. The Putting It All Together section at the end of this chapter discusses when to use each pattern.
- A Session may have a Limited View of data that it distributes throughout the application.
- Roles are sometimes used to configure a Limited View.
- State with Strategy can be used to implement a Limited View.
- Composites and Builders can be used to implement a Limited View.
- Null Objects can be used in places where a view has been limited.

- Metadata and Active Object-Models [Foote+1998] can be used to configure what parts of a view need to be limited.
- Checks [Cunningham1995] describes many details on implementing GUIs and where to put the error notifications.

Known Uses

- The Caterpillar/NCSA Financial Model Framework [Yoder1997] presents a Limited View on the data to the user. This framework also provides Limited View in user interfaces by changing editing view screens based upon the Roles of the user.
- Firewalls provide Limited Views on data by filtering network data and making it available only to some systems.
- Web servers provide a Limited View by only allowing users to view directories in the root Web directory and in user's public_html directories.
- Most operating systems provide hidden files and directories, which are a form of a Limited View.
- Microsoft's Windows NT provides Limited Views based upon a user's role. Users are only allowed to see files they have permission to see, and they get customized menus based upon those roles.
- The PLoP '98 registration program [Yoder+1998] provides Limited Views by having a view for the administrator and a view for someone registering for PLoP. People registering for PLoP get a Limited View that allows them to view and edit only their information.
- Some shareware applications gray out features that are only enabled when the program is registered.

Nonsecurity Known Uses

- Netscape Communicator, Microsoft Office, and many other applications change their user interface depending upon what the user may be editing or viewing. This is commonly done through the use of context-sensitive menus and enabling buttons. For example, the menus available while editing a chart in Excel is quite different from those provided for editing a spreadsheet. Also, if no documents are opened, the "Save" and "Save As" menu items are not available in the "File" menu.
- Windows '95's right-click menu is context-sensitive, presenting only the options legal at the mouse pointer's target.
- Hidden files and directories, provided by most operating systems, are forms of Limited Views.
- Unlike Microsoft Word and vi [VI1998], Netscape Composer does not let the user try to save over a read-only file. The "Save" option in the file menu is grayed out for read-only files. "Save As…" is available as part of the Limited View.

- All modern GUIs really provide some sort of Limited View by enabling and disabling buttons and menus on the fly.

Secure Access Layer

Also Known As

Using Low-Level Security, Using Non-Application Security, and Only as Strong as the Weakest Link

Motivation

When secure documents are transferred from one secure area to another in the military base, it is important that the security of the documents is not violated during the transfer. If the document is being transferred via a computer disk, the data could be encrypted and then locked in a briefcase and handcuffed to the arm of the courier during transfer. This will provide an isolation layer to protect the secure information during the transfer.

Most applications tend to be integrated with many other systems. The places in which system integration occurs can be the weakest security points and the most susceptible to break-ins. If the developer is forced to put checks into the application wherever this communication with other systems happens, then the code will become very convoluted and abstraction will be difficult. An application that is built on an insecure foundation will be insecure. In other words, it doesn't do any good to bar your windows when you leave your back door wide open.

Problem

An application will be insecure if it is not properly integrated with the security of the external systems it uses.

Forces

- Application development should not have to be developed with operating system, networking, and database specifics in mind. These can change over the life of an application.
- Putting low-level security code throughout the whole application makes it difficult to debug, modify, and port to other systems.
- Even if the application is secure, a good hacker could find a way to intercept messages or go under the hood to access sensitive data.
- Interfacing with external security systems is sometimes difficult.
- An external system may not have sufficient security, and implementing the needed security may not be possible or feasible.

Solution

Build your application security around existing operating system, networking, and database security mechanisms. If they do not exist, then build your own lower-level security mechanism. On top of the lower-level security, build a secure access layer for communicating in and out of the program.

Usually an application communicates with many preexisting systems. For example, a financial application on a Windows NT client might use an Oracle database on a remote server. Given that most systems already provide a security interface, develop a layer in your application that encapsulates the interfaces for securely accessing these external systems. All communication between the application and the outside world will be routed through this secure layer.

The important point to this pattern is to build a layer to isolate the developer from change. This layer may have many different protocols depending upon the types of communication that need to be done. For example, this layer might have a protocol for accessing secure data in an Oracle database and another protocol for communicating securely with Netscape server through the Secure Sockets Layer [SSL1998]. The crux of this pattern is to separate each of these external protocols so they can be more easily secured. The architecture for different Secure Access Layers could vary greatly. However, the components' organization and integration is beyond the scope of this pattern.

By creating a Secure Access Layer with a standard set of protocols for communicating with the outside world, an application developer can localize these external interfaces and focus primarily on applications development. Communication in and out of the application will pass through the protocols provided by this layer.

This pattern assumes that a convenient abstraction is possible. For example, VisualWorks' LensSession does not support Microsoft Access, so QueryDataManager cannot be used with a Microsoft Access database. Secure Access Layer, however, provides a location for a more general database abstraction. Third-party drivers have been developed for ODBC that can communicate with Microsoft Access. By using the Secure Access Layer, it is easy to extend your application to use the ODBC protocol, thus allowing your application to communicate with any database that supports ODBC.

Example

The PLoP registration program uses a Secure Access Layer. A layer was created where all communications are processed for registering through the Web. This communications layer is positioned on top of Apache's Secure Socket Layer. This prevents any information from being sniffed during the entry of data such as credit card numbers. Also, a layer on the database side was created to provide additional security by encrypting the credit card information in the database. The secure layer uses a key for encrypting and decrypting the data when needed. Thus, even if someone was able to access the database through some back door, the credit card data is still protected.

Consequences

Secure Access Layer has the following advantages:

- It can help isolate the place at which an application communicates with external security systems. Isolating secure access points makes it easier to integrate new security components and upgrade existing ones.
- It can make an application more portable. If the application later needs to communicate with Sybase rather than Oracle, then the access to the database is localized and only needs to be changed in one place. QueryObjects [Brant+1999] uses this approach. Database accesses are routed through the QueryDataManager, which is built on top of the LensSession [ObjectShare1995]. The LensSession can map to either Oracle or Sybase. Therefore the application developer does not need to be concerned with either choice or future changes.

Secure Access Layer has the following disadvantages:

- Different systems that your application may need to integrate with use different security protocols and schemes for accessing them. This can make it difficult to develop a Secure Access Layer that works for all integrated systems, and it also may cause the developer to keep track of information that many systems do not need.
- It can be very hard to retrofit a Secure Access Layer into an application that already has security access code spread throughout.

Related Patterns

- Secure Access Layer is part of a layered architecture. Layers [Buschmann+1996] discusses the details of building layered architectures.
- Layered Architecture for Information Systems [Fowlers1997a] discusses implementation details that can be applied when developing layered systems.

Known Uses

- Secure Shell [SSH1998] includes secure protocols for communicating in X11 sessions and can use RSA encryption through TCP/IP connections.
- Netscape Server's Secure Socket Layer [SSL1998] provides a Secure Access Layer that Web clients can use for ensuring secure communication.
- Oracle provides its own Secure Access Layer that applications can use for communicating with it.

- CORBA Security Services [OMG1998] specifies how to authenticate, administer, audit, and maintain security throughout a CORBA-distributed object system. Any CORBA application's Secure Access Layer would communicate with CORBA's Security Service.
- The Caterpillar/NCSA Financial Model Framework [Yoder1997] uses a Secure Access Layer provided by the `LensSession` in ParcPlace's VisualWorks Smalltalk [ObjectShare1995].
- The PLoP '98 registration program [Yoder+1998] goes through a Secure Layer for access to the system. First the application runs on top of SSL from the Apache Server. Also, all credit card information is stored encrypted when users register for PLoP '98.
- The Access API used by the Reuters SSL Developers Kit–Java Edition uses a `DACSPrincipal` object to interact with the Data Access Control System for Reuters' Triarch data.

PUTTING IT ALL TOGETHER

Problems with Retrofitting

An important point to note is that it can be very hard to retrofit most of these patterns into an existing system. Specifically, Secure Access Layer, Session, and Limited View can be very difficult to retrofit into a system that was developed without security in mind. If a Single Access Point is created up front, it is fairly straightforward to add Check Point later. Since Roles are used to define a Session and set up during Check Point, additional Roles can easily be added later. A dummy Check Point can start out as just a placeholder, and the details of the corporate security policy can be added later. Also, if all outside requests are forwarded through some form of a Secure Access Layer, it will be easy to enhance and abstract the Secure Access Layer at a later point. Because of these problems, application developers should develop the primary architecture for implementing security from the start. It is also useful to get the security requirements as early as possible in the design process so pitfalls can be avoided.

Limited View versus Full View With Errors

Limited View and Full View With Errors are competing patterns. Limited View can simplify security checks by performing them at login and dynamically building the appropriate views to the system. The application logic will have a simpler design because it does not have to handle security exceptions throughout the code. It is also more user friendly because users do not get barraged with error dialogs. However, the application code that presents views and options to the users becomes more difficult to implement, as the system must dynamically build these views based upon the privileges of the user.

Full View With Errors is easier to implement. It is as simple as performing a security check when an operation is executed and popping open an error dialog or printing to standard error when a violation occurs. It also can be used when a security check cannot be performed up front because it is time-consuming or all necessary information is not yet known.

If an application has a small number of security checks to perform on user operations, Full View With Errors provides the easiest solution. Full View With Errors is also good when most options are the same, independent of the user's roles. If security exception handling is spread throughout the application and there are many variations of security privileges depending upon the user's Role, Limited View should be used. If some checks cannot be performed when creating the Limited View, they can still be handled individually with error messages. So while Limited View and Full View With Errors are competing patterns for individual security checks, they can both be used by an application to provide a "Limited View With Minimal Errors."

Working Together

Now that you have seen all of the patterns, you might be asking, "how do I fit it all together?" All of these patterns collaborate as an application security module and provide a mechanism for communicating with the outside world. Figure 15-8 is a map that shows how these patterns work together.

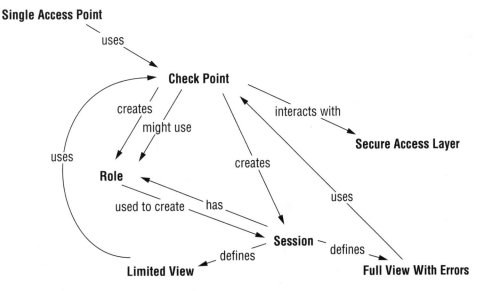

Figure 15-8 *Pattern interaction diagram*

When a user logs into the system, Single Access Point takes the user's information. Single Access Point uses Check Point, which in turn interacts with the Secure Access Layer, to validate the user's information. After validating the user's information, Check Point looks up the user's Roles and creates a Session. This Session has a reference to the Role for future use and can define the Limited View of the data along with any privileges the user has.

Check Point will be used by other application components when they need secure operations that cannot be performed at startup. Session will be referenced by any part of the system that needs global information such as Roles, State, or a Limited View of the data. User interfaces, Full View With Errors or Limited Views, will be created using the Session.

Security checks can be performed during regular program operation by calling back to the Check Point, which will use the Secure Access Layer, if necessary.

Figure 15-9 shows the steps for a typical scenario that are taken when a user successfully logs into the system. A login screen could be the Single Access Point. It initializes the system by going through Check Point. Check Point validates the user and creates a set of Roles for the user. User validation is done through the Secure Access Layer. Roles are then used to create the current Session that will be used by the application. This Session initializes itself with a Limited View based on the Roles and username passed in by Check Point. Any future requests will be forwarded through the Limited View and Check Point to the Secure Access Layer, which will return values to the Limited View, ensuring that a Limited View of the data is maintained. Full View With Errors will be used as needed to complement the Limited View.

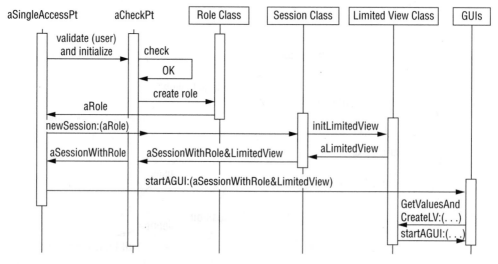

Figure 15-9 *Class collaboration diagram*

ACKNOWLEDGMENTS

We are grateful to the members of Professor Johnson's Patterns seminar: Federico Balaguer, John Brant, Ian Chai, Brian Foote, Alejandra Garrido, John (Zhijiang) Han, Peter Hatch, Ralph Johnson, Ral Lu, Lewis Muir, Dragos Manolescu, Eiji Nabika, James Overturf, Ed Peters, Chieko Shirai, Rick Kirchgesner, and Imad Zorob. Dirk Riehle and our shepherd, Eugene Wallingford, reviewed earlier drafts and provided valuable feedback. Federico Balaguer, Eric Evans, Martin Fowler, Robert Haugen, Joshua Kerievsky, Eiji Nabika, Tim Ottinger, Dirk Riehle, and Wolf Siberski provided outstanding suggestions in our PLOP '97 writers' workshop. We are also grateful to our employers and coworkers at Caterpillar, Illinois Department of Public Health, National Computational Science Alliance (NCSA), Reuters Information Technology, and the University of Illinois for providing us the support and experience to write about and develop such systems.

REFERENCES

[Barcalow1997] J. Barcalow. *Strategic Planning Support for a Financial Model Framework,* master's thesis, University of Illinois at Urbana-Champaign, Department of Computer Science, 1997. Available: http://www.joeyoder.com/papers/thesis/barcalow.html.

[Beck1997] K. Beck. *SMALLTALK Best Practice Patterns.* Upper Saddle River, NJ: Prentice Hall, 1997.

[Brant+1999] John Brant and Joseph Yoder. "Abstract Session." In N. Harrison, B. Foote, and H. Rohnert (eds.), *Pattern Languages of Program Design 4.* Reading, MA: Addison-Wesley, 1999.

[Buschmann+1996] F. Buschmann, R. Meunier, H. Rohnert, P. Sommerlad, and M. Stal. *Pattern-Oriented Software Architecture: A System of Patterns,* Chichester: John Wiley and Sons, 1996.

[Cunningham1995] W. Cunningham. "Checks." *Pattern Languages of Program Design,* In J.O. Coplien and D.C. Schmidt (eds.), Reading, MA: Addison-Wesley, 1995.

[Foote+1996] B. Foote and J. Yoder. "Evolution, Architecture, and Metamorphosis," In J.M. Vlissides, J.O. Coplien, and N.L. Kerth (eds.), *Pattern Languages of Program Design 2.* Reading, MA: Addison-Wesley, 1996.

[Foote+1998] B. Foote and J. Yoder. "Metadata and Active Object-Models." *Collected Papers from the PLoP '98 and EuroPLoP '98 Conference,* Technical Report #wucs-98-25, Department of Computer Science, Washington University Department of Computer Science, September 1998. Available: http://jerry.cs.uiuc.edu/~plop/plop98/final_submissions/.

[Fowler1997a] M. Fowler. *Analysis Patterns: Reusable Object Models.* Reading, MA: Addison-Wesley, 1997.

[Fowler1997b] M. Fowler. "Dealing with Roles." In *Collected Papers from the PLoP '97 and Euro-PLoP '97 Conference,* Technical Report #wucs-97-34, Department of Computer Science, Washington University Department of Computer Science, September 1997. Available: http://www2.awl.com/cseng/titles/0-201-89542-0/apsupp/roles2-1.html.

[Gamma+1995] E. Gamma, R. Helm, R. Johnson, and J. Vlissides. *Design Patterns: Elements of Reusable Object-Oriented Software.* Reading, MA: Addison-Wesley, 1995.

[GemStone1996] Gemstone Systems, Inc. *GemBuilder for VisualWorks, Version 5.* July 1996. Available: http://www.gemstone.com/.

[ICSP] *International Cryptographic Software Pages*. Available: http://www.cs.hut.fi/ssh/crypto/.

[Johnson+1998] R. Johnson and B. Woolf. "Type Object." In R. Martin, D. Riehle, and F. Buschmann (eds.), *Pattern Languages of Program Design 3*. Reading, MA: Addison-Wesley, 1998.

[Lea1995] D. Lea. "Sessions: A design pattern," In *ECOOP Workshop on Patterns*. August 1995.

[Lea1997] D. Lea. *Concurrent Programming in Java*. Reading, MA: Addison-Wesley, 1997.

[Meyer1992] B. Meyer. "Applying 'Design by Contract', " *IEEE Computer*. October, pp. 40–51, 1992.

[NCSA1998] NCSA HTTPd Development Team. *Mosaic User Authentication Tutorial*. Available: http://hoohoo.ncsa.uiuc.edu/docs-1.5/tutorials/user.html.

[OMG1998] Object Management Group. *Security, Transactions, . . . and More*. Available: http://www.omg.org/corba/sectrans.htm#sec.

[ObjectShare1995] ObjectShare, Inc. *VisualWorks User's Guide*. 1995. Available: http://www.objectshare.com/doc/vw/Default.htm.

[Pryce1999] N. Pryce. "Abstract Session." In N. Harrison, B. Foote, and H. Rohnert (eds.), *Pattern Languages of Program Design 4*. Reading, MA: Addison-Wesley, 1999.

[Schmidt+1997] D.C. Schmidt, N. Pryce, and T.H. Harrison. "Thread-Specific Storage for C/C++—An Object Behavioral Pattern for Accessing Per-Thread State Efficiently." In *Collected Papers from the PLoP '97 and EuroPLoP '97 Conference*, Technical Report #wucs-97-34, Dept. of Computer Science, Washington University Department of Computer Science, September 1997. Available: http://www.cs.wustl.edu/~schmidt/TSS-pattern.ps.gz.

[Schmidt+1997] D.C. Schmidt and T.H. Harrison. "Double-Checked Locking." In R. Martin, D. Riehle, and F. Buschmann (eds.), *Pattern Languages of Program Design 3*. Reading, MA: Addison-Wesley, 1997.

[Schneier1995] B. Schneier. *Applied Cryptography*, 2nd ed. New York: John Wiley & Sons, 1995.

[Silberschatz+1997] A. Silberschatz and P.B. Galvin. *Operating Systems Concepts*, 4th ed. Reading, MA: Addison-Wesley, 1994.

[SSH1998] *SSH (Secure Shell) Home Page*. Available: http://www.cs.hut.fi/ssh/.

[SSL1998] *The SSL Protocol*. Netscape Communications, Inc., Available: http://home.netscape.com/newsref/std/SSL.html.

[VI1998] *UNIX's Visual Editor (vi)*, Available: http://ECN.www.ecn.purdue.edu/ECN/Documents/VI/.

[Woolf1997] B. Woolf. "Null Object." In R. Martin, D. Riehle, and F. Buschmann (eds.), *Pattern Languages of Program Design 3*. Reading, MA: Addison-Wesley, 1997.

[Yoder1997] J. Yoder. *A Framework to Build Financial Models*. Available: http://www.joeyoder.com/financial_framework.

[Yoder+1998] J. Yoder and D. Manolescu. *The PLoP Registration Framework, 1998*. Available: http://www.joeyoder.com/Research/PLoP.

Joseph Yoder may be reached at joeyoder@joeyoder.com.

Jeffrey Barcalow may be reached at barcalow@xnet.com.

Chapter 16

Tropyc: A Pattern Language for Cryptographic Object-Oriented Software

*Alexandre Braga, Cecilia Rubira,
and Ricardo Dahab*

Historically associated to encryption, modern cryptography is a broader subject, encompassing the study and use of mathematical techniques to address information security problems. Cryptographic mechanisms are used in a wide variety of applications, such as electronic mail, database protection, and electronic commerce. The present interest in software architectures and patterns, and the existence of well-known cryptographic solutions to recurring security problems, motivate the development of cryptographic software architectures and cryptographic patterns.

In this work, we present Tropyc, a pattern language addressing four fundamental security-related services [Information Technology1998]—data confidentiality, data integrity, sender authentication, and sender nonrepudiation—organized as a pattern language for cryptographic software. Data confidentiality is the ability to keep information secret except from authorized users. Data integrity guarantees that information has not been modified without permission, which includes the ability to detect unauthorized manipulation. Sender authentication corresponds to the assurance, by the communicating parties, of the origin of information transmitted through an insecure communication channel. Nonrepudiation is the ability to prevent an entity from denying its actions or commitments in the future.

Tropyc is composed of ten patterns. The foundation pattern is Secure-Channel Communication, which expands into four basic patterns that correspond to the services just described—Information Secrecy, Message Integrity, Sender Authentication, and Signature. These, in turn, generate the five remaining patterns in the language: Secrecy with Integrity, Secrecy with Sender Authentication, Secrecy with Signature, Signature with Appendix, and Secrecy with Signature with Appendix.

The intent of this chapter is to help software developers not familiar with cryptographic techniques address the security requirements of applications. Developers looking for general software architectures for their cryptographic software or components may also be interested.

The remainder of the text is organized as follows: The next section addresses the need for cryptography-based security through an electronic payment application, PayPerClick, which is also used throughout the chapter to illustrate how our patterns can be employed. The section on A Pattern Language for Cryptographic Object-Oriented Software describes Tropyc and its ten patterns. A design of PayPerClick using Tropyc are addressed in the section on Deploying the Cryptographic Pattern Language. The final section includes conclusions and future work. Appendix A provides a brief introduction to cryptography.

PAYPERCLICK—AN ELECTRONIC PAYMENT SYSTEM

Electronic commerce applications are very good examples of systems that require cryptographic services. A simple scenario of a commercial transaction using a credit card follows:

1. Alice, a customer, asks Bob, a bookseller, for a nice book about cryptography.
2. Bob replies that he has only one copy in stock and offers it to Alice for a reasonable price.
3. Alice accepts Bob's offer.
4. Alice sends her credit card number and some further information to Bob upon his request.
5. Bob contacts the credit card's issuer to validate the card information. In case of positive validation, he accepts the payment.
6. Bob sends the book to Alice along with a receipt.

There are four security issues implicit in this scenario, which are very important when one uses an open network such as the Internet to implement the system. First, Alice requires confidentiality when sensitive information, such as credit card numbers, is sent to a seller. Second, this information should arrive uncorrupted at its destiny; that is, its integrity should be preserved so it can be correctly validated. Third, Alice and Bob need mutual assurance of each other's identity during the transaction; that is, they should authenticate the sender of the exchanged messages. The same holds for Bob and the credit card's issuer. Fourth, the payment receipt should be signed by Bob. This simple scenario becomes more complex if electronic money is used instead of credit cards. New requirements, such as anonymity and prevention of double spending, may arise.

Figure 16-1 shows the three main participants of an electronic payment transaction and the flow of money and sensitive data between them [Asokan+1997]. The Broker is usually a bank or any other kind of financial institution. The Payee can be an Internet access provider and the Payer is the customer. The Payer makes a request to the Broker for electronic cash that can be used to buy (electronic) goods over the Internet. The Payer can request a receipt issued by the Payee. The Payee requests redemption of electronic cash to the Broker. Usually real money flows from the Broker to the Payee.

Electronic payment systems are good examples of the end-to-end argument [Saltzer+1984] applied to cryptography. In fact, cryptography-based security is such an important feature of electronic payment systems that the application itself should deal with it, avoiding delegation to underlying communication subsystems. Additional information about electronic payment systems can be found in [Ferreira+1998] and [Herzberg+1997].

PayPerClick [Braga+1998] is a tool for electronic purchase and online distribution of hypertext documents based on the model shown in Figure 16-1. Hypertext documents are accessible through links to HTML pages and are visible through Web browsers. PayPerClick can be used, for instance, to sell on-line books through links in their table of contents. Therefore, customers can buy specific parts of the book by clicking on a hyperlink. The hyperdocuments are structured according to the Composite pattern [Gamma+1995], which makes the computation of the cost and fingerprint of a hypertext document an easy task. The fingerprint of a

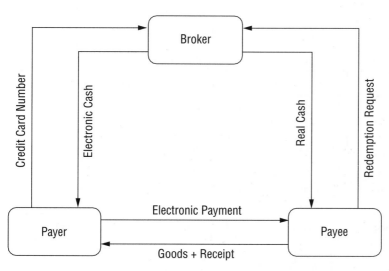

Figure 16-1 *Participants in an electronic payment transaction*

hyper-document is a Modification Detection Code (MDC) (see Appendix A) computed by traversing its tree in some order. The Payer can be implemented as Java applets, which communicate with Web servers, instances of either Payee or Broker. Payers usually have an electronic wallet. Brokers issue to Payers electronic cash, a multiple of fixed-value electronic coins.

A PATTERN LANGUAGE FOR CRYPTOGRAPHIC OBJECT-ORIENTED SOFTWARE

This section presents Tropyc, a pattern language for cryptographic software, which focuses on three goals: (1) the definition of a software architecture for cryptography-based secure communication, (2) the description of cryptographic services as patterns, and (3) the organization of these cryptographic patterns as a pattern language.

Table 16-1 summarizes the ten patterns that compose *Tropyc*. Secure-Channel Communication abstracts common aspects of both structure and behavior relative

Table 16-1 *The Cryptographic Patterns with Their Scopes and Purposes*

Pattern	Scope	Purpose
Secure-Channel Communication	Generic	Provides generic software architecture for cryptographic systems
Information Secrecy	Confidentiality	Provides secrecy of information
Message Integrity	Integrity	Detects corruption of a message
Sender Authentication	Authentication	Authenticates the origin of a message
Signature	Nonrepudiation	Provides the authorship of a message
Secrecy with Integrity	Confidentiality and Integrity	Detects corruption of a secret
Secrecy with Sender Authentication	Confidentiality and Authentication	Authenticates the origin of a secret
Secrecy with Signature	Confidentiality and Nonrepudiation	Proves the authorship of a secret
Signature with Appendix	Nonrepudiation	Separates message from signature
Secrecy with Signature with Appendix	Confidentiality and Nonrepudation	Separates secret from signature

to secure communications, regardless of the kind of cryptographic transformation performed. Information Secrecy provides confidentiality of data in transit. However, Information Secrecy alone does not prevent modification or replacement of data. Particularly in on-line communication, granting Message Integrity and Sender Authentication is also important. In other situations, it is necessary to prevent entities from denying their actions or commitments. Thus, some form of Signature is necessary. These four basic cryptographic services, in suitable combinations, generate three more patterns: Secrecy with Integrity, Secrecy with Sender Authentication, and Secrecy with Signature. For implementation efficiency purposes, two additional patterns are provided: Signature with Appendix and Secrecy with Signature with Appendix.

Figure 16-2 shows a directed acyclic graph of dependencies between patterns. An edge from pattern *a* to pattern *b* means pattern *a* generates pattern *b*. Secure-Channel Communication generates the four basic patterns. The remaining patterns

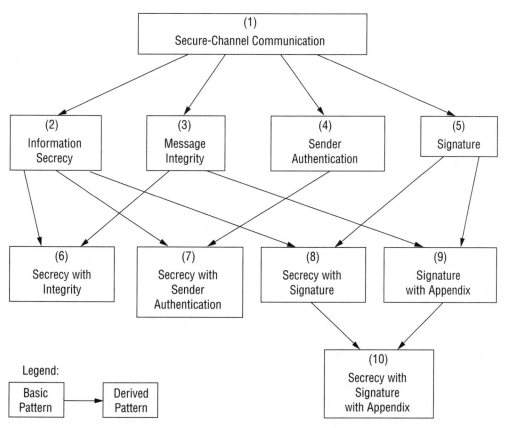

Figure 16-2 *Cryptographic design patterns and their relationships*

are derived from combinations of these. A walk on the graph is directed by two questions. First, how should the cryptographic software be structured to obtain both easy reuse and flexibility? Second, what cryptographic services should be used to address application requirements and user needs? In other words, what cryptographic services should be added to the current instantiation of Secure-Channel Communication in order to overcome its present deficiencies?

In the following patterns Alice and Bob represent two communicating participants, while Eve is an adversary eavesdropping and possibly modifying information exchanged by Alice and Bob.

THE PATTERNS

Secure-Channel Communication

Context

Alice and Bob exchange data through messages, on which they need to perform cryptographic transformations. Moreover, a flexible and reusable cryptographic software architecture is required to make cryptographic service composition easier and to separate concerns between application functionality and security requirements.

Problem

How should one structure flexible and reusable cryptographic software for secure communication?

Applicability

- When separation of concerns between functional requirements and nonfunctional security requirements should be promoted
- When the incorporation of security in software systems should be done in a structured and disciplined manner to avoid an increase in the software's complexity

Forces

- The dependencies between cryptographic features and the application's functionality should be minimized to facilitate reuse of the cryptographic components.
- Software with cryptographic code should be easy to understand, modify, and adapt.
- The increase of the systems' complexity due to the inclusion of security services should be kept under control.
- The performance of cryptographic algorithms should not be affected by the application's design.

Solution

Alice performs a cryptographic transformation $x = f(m)$ on data m before sending it to Bob. Bob receives x and performs transformation $y = g(x)$. Alice and Bob must have previously agreed on transformations f and g and either share or distribute keys, if necessary. Figure 16-3 shows a class diagram that models the cryptographic transformations. The diagram defines two template classes, Alice and Bob, and two hook classes, Codifier and Decodifier. The Codifier class has a hook method $f(\ )$, which performs a cryptographic transformation on m. The Decodifier class has a hook method $g(\ )$, which performs the transformation, $y = g(f(m))$. Figure 16-4 shows the interaction diagram between Alice and Bob. In these diagrams, a, b, c and d are the roles performed by instantiations of classes Alice, Bob, Codifier and Decodifier, respectively. The Secure-Channel Communication pattern is a high-level abstraction which is inherited by the remaining patterns of the language.

Consequences

- It separates the concerns related to the application domain from those related to the provision of cryptographic mechanisms in a structured and disciplined fashion for application developers.

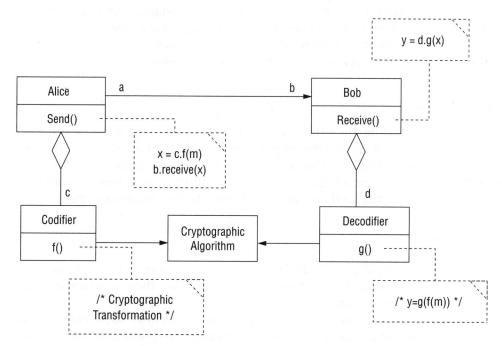

Figure 16-3 *Class diagram for the Secure-Channel Communication pattern*

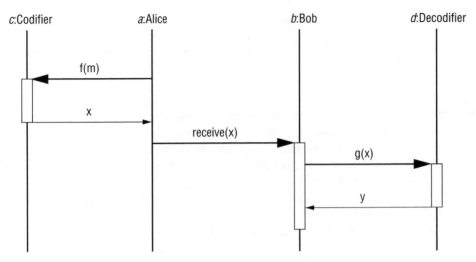

Figure 16-4 *Sequence diagram for the Secure-Channel Communication pattern*

- It promotes reusability of cryptographic mechanisms.
- It allows application developers to choose the most adequate security strategy for the system's implementation.
- It provides a system design that is easier to maintain, adapt, change, and extend than traditional approaches for developing cryptographic software.
- It may introduce inefficiencies in the cryptographic protocols, due to the references, implicit and otherwise, made in the object-oriented design.

Resulting Context

Alice and Bob can instantiate the overall architecture of cryptographic systems. However, they should choose the cryptographic patterns that are the most adequate for their application's requirements. Concrete implementations of this pattern should be based on the four basic patterns, Information Secrecy, Sender Authentication, Message Integrity, and Signature, and suitable combinations of them.

Implementation

- This pattern can be adapted to deal with file storage and recovery. In these situations, messages for storing and recovering a file replace those used for sending and receiving information.
- The reflection pattern can be used to implement the security requirements in a transparent and nonintrusive manner for application programmers, that is, without interfering in the application's original structure. The reflection mechanism

encourages modular descriptions of software systems by introducing a new dimension of modularity: the separation of base-level and meta-level computation. Reflection allows the creation of meta-objects that implement the cryptographic mechanisms and that control and extend the behavior of application objects located at the base level.

- Before secure communication begins, a negotiation step is necessary in order for the participants to agree not only on which transformation to perform but also to exchange information, such as keys and algorithm parameters.
- Eve's role depends on the concrete implementations. She can replace or modify a message in transit in the channel or insert her own messages.

Example

Electronic payment systems have high security requirements. They can be better structured when the Secure-Channel Communication pattern is used. Later sections discuss some important aspects of our case study, PayPerClick.

Known Uses

In the literature we can find various systems that use the Secure-Channel Communication pattern [Herzberg+1997, Herfert1997, Cheng+1998, Herzberg+1998, Linn1993, Zimmermann1995, Braga+1998].

Related Patterns

Several well-known patterns can be used when instantiating Secure-Channel Communication. The Strategy pattern [Gamma+1995] can be used to obtain algorithm independence. The Bridge pattern [Gamma+1995] can be applied to promote implementation independence. The Abstract Factory pattern [Gamma+ 1995] can be employed in the negotiation step to choose which cryptographic algorithm or implementation to use. The Observer [Gamma+1995], Proxy [Gamma+1995], and Client-Dispatcher-Server [Buschmann+1996] patterns can be used to obtain location transparency. The Forwarder-Receiver pattern [Buschmann+1996] can be combined with the cryptographic patterns to offer secure and transparent interprocess communication, so that Alice becomes part of the Forwarder and Bob is incorporated into the Receiver. The State pattern [Gamma+1995] can be used to provide state-dependent behavior, such as turning the security of the channel on and off. The Null Object pattern [Martin+ 1997] can be used to design a null transformation. The Reflection pattern [Buschmann+1996] can be used to separate application functionality from the security requirements. The cryptographic infrastructure, such as encryption/decryption algorithms, pseudo-random generators, hashing algorithms, and so forth, can be provided by a Security Access Layer [Yoder+1997].

Information Secrecy

Context

Alice wants to send sensitive messages to Bob. Moreover, she wants to keep these messages secret from Eve, whom Alice suspects may be trying to read their contents.

Problem

How can Alice send a message to Bob so that Eve cannot possibly read its contents?

Applicability

- When two participants need to share confidential information.
- When it is necessary to decouple encryption/decryption activity from either data communication or storage.

Forces

- Eve cannot, in any situation, gain access to the message contents.
- The cost of encryption/decryption should not be greater than the intrinsic value of the message being encrypted.
- The cost of cryptoanalysis by Eve should be much higher than that of the message itself.

Solution

This pattern supports encryption and decryption of data. Alice and Bob have previously agreed on an (assumed public) encryption function and a shared secret key (in public-key cryptography, Bob must first obtain Alice's public key). Bob encrypts the message and sends it to Alice. Alice decrypts it and recovers the original message.

Consequences

- Encryption is, in general, a slow task. The security of encrypted information relies on the secrecy of the encryption key and on the strength of the encryption algorithm. Clearly a key must be long enough to prevent an exhaustive search of the key space.
- Eve cannot read the message contents, but she still can replace or modify encrypted messages.
- Transmission or storage errors can potentially render the recovery of the original message difficult.

Resulting Context

Alice and Bob use an encrypted channel for their communication. However, this channel does not provide data integrity, sender authentication, or nonrepudiation. To achieve integrity without loss of secrecy, Alice and Bob should instantiate Secrecy with Integrity. If they want to add Sender Authentication to Information Secrecy, they should instantiate Secrecy with Sender Authentication. Furthermore, if sender nonrepudiation of secrets is desired, one should instantiate Secrecy with Signature.

Implementation

- Both private (in public-key, or asymmetric, systems) and secret (in secret-key, or symmetric, systems) keys must be kept protected from unauthorized access.
- An infrastructure to distribute public keys is required.

Example

In PayPerClick, when a Payer makes a cash request, he sends the Broker his credit card number in encrypted form. The Broker decrypts the card number with her decryption key and charges the Payer's credit card with the requested cash amount.

Known Uses

Common uses of this pattern can be found in, for example, electronic mail systems [Herfert1997, Linn1993, Zimmermann1995], automatic banking machines, and voice encryption.

Message Integrity

Context

Alice sends long messages to Bob, who wants to verify the integrity of the received messages. He suspects that they may have been corrupted accidentally, due to transmission errors. Alice and Bob do not share cryptographic keys.

Problem

How can Bob determine whether a message he received has been modified?

Applicability

- In the detection of occurrence of errors in either transmission or storage of data
- In the detection of unauthorized modification of data
- When it is necessary to generate "fingerprints" for either messages or data records

Forces

- The mechanism should be robust against unauthorized, accidental or not, modification of data.
- The mechanism should be cost-effective.

Solution

Alice and Bob agree to use an MDC (Appendix A). Alice computes the MDC of the message and sends both message and MDC to Bob. Bob computes the MDC of the message and compares it to the one received from Alice. If they match, the message has not been altered.

Consequences

- It is necessary to verify a relatively small MDC to determine whether a large amount of data has been modified.
- Eve still has the ability of substituting both message and the corresponding MDC.
- MDCs by themselves do not guarantee the authorship of a message.

Resulting Context

Alice and Bob use MDCs to detect corruption of data. However, this technique guarantees neither sender authentication nor nonrepudiation. If these are required, other patterns, such as Sender Authentication and Signature, should be used instead. Moreover, Information Secrecy can be combined with Message Integrity in the Secrecy with Integrity pattern, thus providing integrity and secrecy at the same time in the channel.

Implementation

- A message must be bound to its corresponding MDC to avoid mismatch of messages and MDCs.
- Measures should be taken to recover the original contents of corrupted data. MDCs can detect corruption, but not correct it. One standard solution is message replaying.
- When feasible, sending two or more copies of a message, with the additional feature of allowing weak correction capability, is an alternative to employing MDCs for detecting corruption.
- MDCs are often implemented using cryptographic hashing algorithms [Menezes+ 1996].

Example

In PayPerClick, electronic payments must have their integrity preserved in order for the Payee verification to succeed. Thus, the payment should be sent by the Payer along with its MDC. The Payee recomputes the MDC of the received payment and checks it against the received MDC.

Known Uses

Two common uses of MDCs are (1) the detection of file modification caused by viruses and (2) the generation of pass phrases to produce cryptographic keys. Privacy-Enhanced Mail is one of the systems that [Linn1993] provides Message Integrity. MDCs also can be used as unique identifiers of electronic coins in electronic commerce applications [Ferreira+1998].

Sender Authentication

Context

Alice and Bob want to exchange messages, but they cannot distinguish their own messages from spurious ones, perhaps inserted by Eve, in the communication channel. Moreover, we assume that they have previously established a secret key using some secure channel.

Problem

How can genuine messages be distinguished from spurious ones?

Applicability

- When the occurrence of errors during transmission or storage must be detected
- When the detection of corruption or unauthorized modification of data is necessary
- When it is necessary for both Alice and Bob to certify the origin of exchanged messages

Forces

- Authentic messages must be hard to forge.
- The authentication mechanism should detect accidental data modification as well as those supposedly done by Eve.

- The authentication procedure should be cost-effective; that is, it should not imply a cost higher than the intrinsic value of the data being authenticated.

Solution

Alice and Bob agree beforehand on a shared secret key and a cryptographic algorithm for generation of MACs (Appendix A). Alice computes the MAC of the pair (message, key) and sends both the message and the MAC to Bob. Bob computes the MAC of the received message and the shared key and compares it with the MAC he received from Alice. If they match, the message is genuine and must have been sent by Alice because, other than Bob, only Alice knows the secret key and can compute the correct MAC for a given message.

Consequences

- A message is correctly authenticated if and only if the shared key is kept secret from third parties.
- The authorship of a message produced by Alice or Bob cannot be proved to a third party, since both sides can compute valid MACs.
- Eve may insert a previously seen message along with its (correct) MAC into the communication channel, thus fooling Alice and Bob. In this situation, some guarantee of message freshness should be provided. A common solution for this problem is the inclusion of timestamps or sequence numbers as part of the message contents.

Resulting Context

Alice and Bob can authenticate the origin of messages they exchange as well as detect their corruption. However, if they want to prove the authorship of messages, the Signature pattern should be used instead. If desired, encryption facilities can be added to the communication channel to apply the Secrecy with Sender Authentication pattern.

Implementation

- A secure means for exchanging and maintaining a secret key is necessary.
- Similarly to MDCs, a message must be correctly bound to its corresponding MAC.
- MAC generators can be implemented in many ways. Two common possibilities are symmetric cryptosystems and cryptographic hash functions.
- As with MDCs, additional measures should be taken if error correction is desired.

Example

In PayPerClick, Eve may try to substitute her coins for someone else's. This substitution can be prevented if MACs of the payments are computed by the Payer whenever they are sent to the Payee. Such a solution ensures that the Payee will always receive valid payments. However, a Payee can generate a fake payment and still request redemption to the Broker. Analogously, a Payer can repudiate old legitimate payments claiming that they were generated by the Payee. If the value of payments is relatively large and coin losses are frequent, the use of the Signature pattern is a better solution to this problem.

Known Uses

MACs have been used, among other applications, to authenticate IP packages over the Internet [Cheng+1998].

Signature

Context

Alice sends messages to Bob, but he cannot distinguish Alice's messages from the ones Eve may insert in the communication channel. Furthermore, Alice can later dispute the authorship of a message actually sent by her, denying Bob the ability to prove to a third party that only Alice could have sent that particular message. We assume that Alice has a public/private key pair and that her public key is widely available.

Problem

How can one correctly attribute the authorship of a message in such a way that this authorship cannot be later disputed? In other words, how can the receiver of a particular message convince himself and a third party of the identity of the sender of that message?

Applicability

- In contexts where nonrepudiation of messages must be guaranteed

Forces

- Signatures must be dependent on the data being signed. Otherwise, they could easily be copied and tied to a different message. Thus, signatures implicitly guarantee data integrity and sender authentication.

- Signatures must be hard to forge or alter.
- The cost of signing must be substantially lower than the cost of the data being signed.
- It must be possible to verify the authenticity of a signature without its author's cooperation.

Solution

Alice and Bob agree on the use of a public-key digital-signature protocol (Appendix A). In most such systems, Alice applies the decryption algorithm to a message using her private key and sends the result (her signature) to Bob. He then encrypts the signed message with Alice's public verification key. If the result makes sense to Bob, that is, if Bob recognizes in the resulting data what he expected to be the original message, then it must be true that Alice is the sender of that message. This is the case, since only the knowledge of the key used by Alice in the signature generation procedure could have produced that signature.

Consequences

- The verification of a message's signature is based on the secrecy of the author's key and the strength of the signing algorithm. Thus, Alice could presumably deny the authorship of an old message by claiming loss or theft of her private key.
- Signatures are usually as large as the data being signed, sometimes producing an intolerable overhead.

Resulting Context

Bob can now prove to a third party that a message he has received came indeed from Alice. Data integrity and sender authentication are implicit in the use of digital signatures. However, signatures are as large as the data being signed and often even larger. A more efficient approach would be to sign a much smaller fingerprint (the hash value) of a message, instead of the message itself and send the signed fingerprint along with the message. This is exactly what is provided by the Signature with Appendix pattern. Finally, encryption can be added to the signing process giving rise to the Secrecy with Signature pattern.

Implementation

- Public-key cryptographic algorithms are generally used to generate digital signatures.
- A secure means of storing the author's private key is necessary.

- An infrastructure to make public keys for signature verification broadly available is necessary.
- For efficiency purposes, it is often preferable to sign the hash value rather than the message itself.

Example

This pattern is used in PayPerClick in two situations of sender nonrepudiation: cash issuing by a Broker and receipt issuing by a Payee. In the first case, a Broker produces a cash amount, signs it and sends the signed cash to a Payer, which verifies the Broker's signature. In the second case, a Payee verifies the Broker's signature in coins received from the Payer before issuing the receipt.

Known Uses

Electronic commerce applications use digital signatures to authenticate both customers and merchants [Ferreira+1998]. Digital signatures also can be used to guarantee authenticity and nonrepudiation of information obtained over the Internet [Herzberg+1998]. Both Privacy-Enhanced Mail [Linn1993] and Pretty Good Privacy [Zimmermann1995] provide nonrepudiation of e-mail based on digital signatures.

Secrecy with Integrity

Context

Alice and Bob exchange encrypted messages, and they want to verify the integrity of the exchanged messages. Alice and Bob do not share cryptographic keys for purposes other than encryption.

Problem

How to verify the integrity of an encrypted message without loss of secrecy.

Applicability

- In the detection of occurrence of errors in either transmission or storage of secret data
- In the detection of unauthorized modification of secret data
- When it is necessary to generate "fingerprints" for either secret messages or secret data records

Forces

- It is desirable that the integrity of secret information can be verified without disclosure of the information.
- Granting secrecy and data integrity at the same time should not happen at the expense of one or the other. For instance, it should not be any easier to decipher a message in the presence of its MDC than it is without it.

Solution

Two basic patterns are combined to solve this problem: Information Secrecy and Message Integrity. The MDC is computed over the original non-encrypted message, which is then encrypted and sent, along with the MDC, to Bob. This pattern requires only one public/private key pair (or a shared secret key) used for encryption purposes.

Consequences

- Malicious replacements of messages can still garble valid data, thus rendering it useless after decryption.
- The computation and verification of MDCs may cause a noticeable decrease of performance.

Resulting Context

Alice and Bob combine MDC generation functions and encryption in such a way that they preserve the integrity of an encrypted message without loss of secrecy.

Implementation

This pattern can be implemented by computing the message's MDC either before or after encryption. In the first case, transmission errors can be detected before decryption. In the second, when the message structure is unknown, small transmission errors only can be detected after both decryption and MDC verification.

Example

If a Payer's encrypted card number arrives corrupted at the Broker, it will not be decrypted successfully. Thus, the Broker should have the ability to detect the corruption of an encrypted message to prevent the acceptance of a wrong but perhaps valid card number. So, during a PayPerClick cash request, the Payer should compute the MDC of the card number, then encrypt the card number, and send both the MDC and encrypted number to Broker.

Known Uses

Privacy-Enhanced Mail [Linn1993] protocols provide both encryption and message integrity for electronic mail.

Secrecy with Sender Authentication

Context

Alice and Bob use public-key cryptography to exchange encrypted messages. Eve may intercept messages, but she cannot read their contents. However, she may replace or modify these messages in such a way that Alice and Bob cannot detect these modifications or replacements.

Problem

How can Alice authenticate the sender of an encrypted message without loss of secrecy?

Applicability

- When the occurrence of errors during transmission or storage of a secret must be detected
- When detection of corruption or unauthorized modification of secret data is necessary
- When it is necessary for both Alice and Bob to certify the origin of exchanged messages that were encrypted using public-key algorithms

Forces

- They are similar to the Secrecy with Integrity pattern.

Solution

We combine two basic cryptographic patterns to solve this problem: Information Secrecy and Sender Authentication. The MAC should be computed over the original non-encrypted message. Both the encrypted message and the corresponding MAC are sent to Bob. The secret key used to compute the MAC must, of course, be different from the public key used for encryption.

Consequences

- Sender Authentication restricts the number of entities who can produce genuine encrypted messages but do not grant authorship.

- Sender Authentication inserts a new step in both the encryption and the decryption processes in order to compute and verify a MAC, which can affect the system's performance.

Resulting Context

Alice and Bob combine MAC generation functions and encryption in such a way that they not only preserve the integrity, but also guarantee sender authentication of an encrypted message without loss of secrecy.

Implementation

- If Alice and Bob use secret-key cryptography for encryption, then Sender Authentication is redundant and useless, except for granting an extra degree of security.
- As with Secrecy with Integrity, this pattern can be implemented by computing MAC before or after message encryption.

Example

In a PayPerClick cash request, if the public key is used for card number encryption, then the Payer can use this pattern to ensure sender authentication vis-à-vis the Broker.

Known Uses

Secrecy and authentication can be combined to secure IP packages over the Internet [Cheng+1998].

Secrecy with Signature

Context

Alice and Bob exchange encrypted messages, but they cannot prove the authorship of such messages. Moreover, Eve can modify, replace, or insert messages in the communication channel in such a way that Alice and Bob cannot detect these spurious messages. We assume that Alice and Bob already share keys for secrecy purposes.

Problem

How can Bob prove to a third party the authorship of Alice's encrypted messages without loss of secrecy?

Applicability

- When nonrepudiation of a secret is desired

Forces

- They are similar to Secrecy with Sender Authentication and Secrecy with Integrity patterns.

Solution

We combine two basic cryptographic patterns to address this problem: Information Secrecy and Signature. Alice signs a message with her signing key, encrypts the signed message with Bob's encryption key, and sends it to Bob. Bob deciphers the encrypted message with his decryption key and verifies the signed message with Alice's verification key.

Consequences

- Signatures provide a proof of authorship of encrypted messages. However, the cost of signing long messages may become intolerably high.

Resulting Context

Alice and Bob combine mechanisms of digital signatures and encryption achieving nonrepudiation of secret messages and, implicitly, sender authentication and corruption detection of such messages. However, the resulting signatures are at least as large as the data being signed. When possible, the Secrecy with Signature with Appendix pattern should be used, providing a more efficient solution, since the signing procedure is applied on the "fingerprint" of the encrypted message.

Implementation

- Different keys should be used in encryption and signing purposes.
- As before, this pattern can be implemented in two different ways, according to the order in which encryption and signature are computed on the message. When encryption is applied first, verification of the signature only can be done after decryption, since, in principle, signatures have no apparent structure. This apparent difficulty can be overcome easily by attaching to the encrypted message a known header before signing. If the signature is applied first to the non-encrypted data, then signature verification must expose the encrypted content. This may be unacceptable when different parties are responsible for decryption and signature verification. Usually, a better strategy is to use Secrecy with Signature with Appendix.

Example

When sending a credit card number over the Internet, a user wishes it to remain secret. At the vendor's side there is the need for that number to be tied to the correct user in a nonrepudiable fashion.

Known Uses

Both Privacy-Enhanced Mail [Linn1993] and Pretty Good Privacy [Zimmermann 1995] combine encryption and digital signatures for electronic mail.

Signature with Appendix

Context

Alice and Bob sign exchange signed messages. However, they not only have limited resources for both storage and processing, but the messages they exchange are very large and produce large signatures.

Problem

How can memory requirements for signatures be reduced while increasing the performance of the digital signature protocol?

Applicability

- When a message can be kept separate from its signature
- When space and time requirements for the digital signature protocol are tight

Forces

- They are similar to those of the Signature pattern.

Solution

Two patterns are combined to solve this problem: Signature and Message Integrity. The resulting pattern implements a digital signature protocol over a message hash value, which is an MDC. Alice computes a hash value of the message and signs it. Both message and signed hash value are sent to Bob. Bob decrypts the signature and recovers the hash value. He then computes a new hash value and compares it with the one recovered from the signature. If they match, the signature is true.

Consequences

- When no technique to reduce signature size is used, digital signatures are at least as large as the data being signed. However, if messages are small, the inclusion of a new computation step to reduce the signature size is not necessary.
- The combination of weak MDCs and signatures can potentially decrease the security of digital signature protocols.

Resulting Context

Alice and Bob reduce their time and memory requirements by reducing the size of the data to be signed. Encryption mechanisms can be included in the signing process to instantiate the Secrecy with Signature with Appendix pattern.

Example

In PayPerClick, nonrepudiation of a receipt could be achieved by signing it. However, using the Signature pattern by itself in each node of the hyperdocument's tree is not practical. Even if Signature with Appendix is computed for each tree node, this computation may produce a large receipt. However, signing a single fingerprint of a hyperdocument's tree, as in Signature with Appendix, is a much faster procedure. The resulting receipt is attached to the corresponding purchased hyperdocuments.

Known Uses

When the user of an Internet application must digitally sign information, small signatures should be favored [Cheng+1998]. An example of this are signed applets: JDK uses Signature with Appendix to produce small signatures for large amounts of code [Knudsen1998].

Secrecy with Signature with Appendix

Context

Alice and Bob exchange encrypted signed messages in order to achieve secrecy and nonrepudiation. They possess limited storage and processing resources, and the messages they exchange are large.

Problem

How can one reduce the amount of memory necessary to store a message's signature, while increasing system performance, without loss of secrecy?

Applicability

- When secret data may be separated from its signature
- When the digital signature protocol operates in limited resource environments

Forces

- They are similar to previous pattern combinations.

Solution

Two patterns are combined to address this problem: Information Secrecy and Signature with Appendix. Alice computes a hash value of the message and signs it with her signing key. She then encrypts the original message with Bob's encryption key. Both encrypted message and its signed hash value are sent to Bob. He deciphers the encrypted message with his decryption key and verifies the signature of the hash value using Alice's verification key. Bob then computes a new hash value of the message and compares it with that received from Alice. If they match, the original message is correctly signed.

Resulting Context

Alice and Bob not only achieve both secrecy and nonrepudiation in their communication, but also reduce the amount of time and memory required for signatures.

Consequences

The inclusion of a hash computation in a procedure that already has two processing phases may seem a difficult decision to make. However, hash computations are among the fastest in cryptographic software. Moreover, the reduction in signing/verification time and space certainly compensate for the hashing overhead.

Implementation

This pattern can be implemented either by signing the message's MDC before message encryption or by signing an encrypted message's MDC directly.

Example

Electronic forms usually contain some sensitive information that requires both confidentiality and nonrepudiation. A typical cash request form could have fields for credit card information such as number, expiration date, card type, and owner;

other fields may contain the amount of cash requested, value of coins, and so forth. The use of digital signatures to guarantee nonrepudiation of such data can potentially result in large signatures. Secrecy with Signature with Appendix solves this problem with a substantial gain in performance.

Known Uses

Digital signatures for electronic mail, alone or in combination with encryption, are provided by Privacy-Enhanced Mail [Linn1993] and Pretty Good Privacy [Zimmermann1995] using Signature with Appendix.

DEPLOYING THE CRYPTOGRAPHIC PATTERN LANGUAGE

Figure 16-5 shows the class diagram for a PayPerClick payment transaction, using Sender Authentication and Signature. The first pattern authenticates the sender of the payment; the second signs the receipt. Consider a payment scenario, which illustrates the use of these patterns.

Let a and b be two objects, instances of the **Payer** and **Payee** classes, respectively. The encoder of a has been initialized with a secret key shared with b, and its verifier has been initialized with b's public key. Likewise, b's verifier and signer

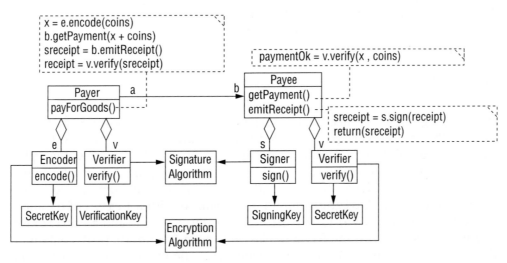

Figure 16-5 *Class diagram for the payment transaction*

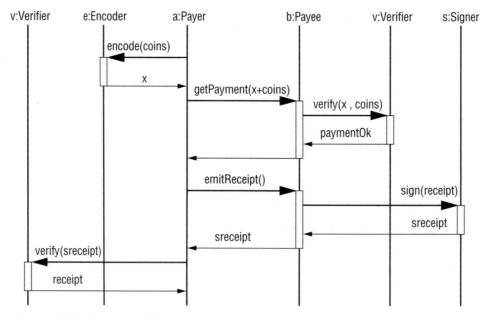

Figure 16-6 *Sequence diagram for the payment transaction*

have been previously initialized with the shared secret key and with b's private key. The following sequence of events complete the scenario (Figure 16-6):

1. a uses the `Encoder` e to compute a MAC **x** of his/her `coins`.
2. a sends the coins along with **x** as payment to b, who uses its `Verifier` v to check the validity of **x**, thus authenticating the sender of the coins, namely a.
3. a requests a receipt from b, who uses the `Signer` s to generate a signed receipt, `sreceipt`, and returns it to a.
4. a verifies `sreceipt` using the signature verifier.

The Java code in this section corresponds to a PayPerClick transaction and uses Java Cryptographic Architecture (JCA). The classes `SecureRandom`, `Signature`, `SignedObject`, `PublicKey`, and `PrivateKey` are provided by JCA. Classes `Cipher`, `SealedObject`, and `SecretKey` are supported by Java Cryptographic Extension (JCE). Information about the Java cryptographic API can be found in Knudsen (1998). Classes `Signer` and `Verifier` perform signing and verification, respectively. A `Signer` should be initialized with a `PrivateKey` and a `Signature` engine. A `Verifier` uses a `Signature` engine and a `PublicKey`. The method `sign()` in the `Signer` class returns a `SignedObject` containing the object being signed and its digital signature. The method `verify()` of the `Verifier` class takes as input a `SignedObject` and returns true if the verification succeeds.

```
class Signer {
 private Signature engine;
 private PrivateKey key;

 public Signer(Signature engine, PrivateKey key)
 { this.key = key; this.engine = engine;}

 public SignedObject sign(Serializable o)
 { return(new SignedObject(o,key,engine));}
}

class Verifier {
 private Signature engine;
 private PublicKey key;

 public Verifier(Signature engine, PublicKey key)
 { this.key = key; this.engine = engine;}

 public boolean verify(SignedObject o)
 { return(o.verify(key,engine));}
}
```

The Payer class contains a Signer s, which signs payments, an Encipher e, which encrypts credit card numbers, and two instances of Verifier: one, vPayee, verifies payment receipts issued by a Payee; the other, vBroker, verifies cash issued by a Broker. An instance of Vector is a simple electronic wallet. Payer has two methods, payForGoods(), which performs a payment to Payee and requests a signed receipt, and cashRequest(), which asks the Broker for money. Method payForGoods() returns a SignedObject containing a payment of amount coins to a Payee. The required amount of coins is removed from the wallet, and the payment is signed and sent to the Payee, from whom a receipt is requested. A payment transaction succeeds if the payment succeeds and the receipt is authentic. Method cashRequest() asks the Broker for an amount of electronic money, which should be charged to the Payer's credit card. The number of the Payer's card is sent to the Broker in a SealedObject. A SignedObject containing cash is received, verified, and credited to the Payer's wallet.

```
class Payer {
 private Verifier vPayee, vBroker;
 private Encipher e;
 private Signer s;
```

```
private SignedObject receipt;
private String myCardNumber = "0001 0002 0003 0004";
private Vector wallet;

public Payer(Signer s, Encipher e, Verifier vPayee,
            Verifier vBroker) {
this.s = s; this.e = e; this.vPayee = vPayee;
            this.vBroker =  vBroker;

public boolean payForGoods(Payee b, int price){
 boolean ok = true;
 Vector payment = new Vector();
 for(int i = 0; i < price; i++) {
  Object coin = wallet.firstElement();
  payment.addElement(coin);
  wallet.removeElement(coin);
 }
 ok &= b.getPayment(s.sign((Serializable) payment));
 receipt = b.issueReceipt();
 ok &= vPayee.verify(receipt);
 if (ok) System.out.println(receipt.getObject());
 return(ok);
}

public boolean cashRequest(Broker b, int amount){
 boolean ok;
 ok = b.getCreditCard(e.encrypt(myCardNumber));
 SignedObject o = b.issueCash(amount);
 ok &= vBroker.verify(o);
 if(ok) wallet = (Vector) o.getObject();
 return(ok);
}
}
```

Class **Payee** contains a **Signer** s, used to sign receipts and two instances of **Verifier**. One, **vPayer**, is intended for verification of payments signed by the **Payer**; the other, **vBroker**, for verification of single coins issued and signed by the **Broker**. **Payee** has two methods, **issueReceipt()**, which issues a signed receipt, and **getPayment()**, used to verify and check payments and coins. Method **issueReceipt()** returns a **SignedObject**, which contains the number of valid coins received since the issuing of the last receipt. This implementation does not consider the purchased goods for which this receipt is being issued. A better solution should contain the fingerprint of the purchased document. Method **getPayment()** takes a **SignedObject** and verifies whether it is a valid payment with valid coins in it. The `Payer` verifier checks payments; the `Broker` verifier checks coins. The method returns true if all these verifications succeed.

```
class Payee {
 private Signer s;
 private Integer coinCounter = new Integer(0);
 private Verifier vBroker, vPayer;

 public Payee(Signer s,Verifier vBroker,Verifier vPayer){
  this.s = s;
  this.vBroker = vBroker;
  this.vPayer = vPayer;
 }

 public SignedObject issueReceipt(){
  String str = (coinCounter.intValue() != 1?"s":"");
  String receipt = "I received " +
              coinCounter.toString() + " coin"+ str +
              "from you since last receipt was issued.";
  this.coinCounter = new Integer(0);
  return(s.sign(receipt));
 }

 public boolean getPayment(SignedObject payment){
  boolean ok;
  int counter = coinCounter.intValue();
  ok = vPayer.verify(payment);
  Vector coins = (Vector) payment.getObject();
  for(int i = 0; i < coins.size();i++) {
   ok &= vBroker.verify((SignedObject)coins.elementAt(i));
   if(ok) this.coinCounter = new Integer(++counter);
  }
  return(ok);
 }
}
```

The `Broker` class contains a `Decipher`, which decrypts the `Payer`'s card number, and a `Signer` s, which authenticates cash issued by `Broker`. It has two methods: `getCreditCard()`, which receives a `SealedObeject` containing the `Payer`'s encrypted card number, and `issueCash()`, used to generate an amount of coins. In method `issueCash()` an amount of cash is a `Vector` in which each coin is a `SignedObject` containing a random value. Another `SignedObject` contains the whole cash amount.

```
class Broker {
 private Decipher d;
 private Signer s;

 public Broker(Decipher d, Signer s)
 { this.d = d; this.s = s;}

public boolean getCreditCard(SealedObject o){
   System.out.println("Card Number is " + d.decrypt(o));
   return(true);
 }

 public SignedObject issueCash(int amount){
  Vector cash = new Vector(amount);
  SecureRandom sr = new SecureRandom();
  byte[] random = new byte[20];
  sr.nextBytes(random);
  for(int i = 0; i<amount; i++)
   cash.addElement(s.sign(new String(random)));
  return(s.sign(cash));
 }
}
```

CONCLUSION

Cryptography-supported security facilities are becoming a standard feature in many modern applications. To facilitate the design, implementation, and reuse of cryptographic software, the architectural aspects of cryptographic software and the patterns that emerge from them should be considered. In this work, we present a pattern language for cryptographic software. We consider our pattern language to be complete and closed into the cryptographic services domain for two reasons. First, the patterns represent not only the overall architecture of typical cryptosystems, but also all the valid combinations of the four basic cryptographic services. Second, the cryptographic patterns are widely used in many applications [Cheng+1998, Herfert+1997, Herzberg+1998, Herzberg+1997, Linn1993, Zimmermann1995] and are supported by many cryptographic APIs [CSS1997, Kaliski1995, Knudsen1998]. However, other auxiliary patterns and pattern languages, supporting infrastructure services for cryptosystems, could be possible. Tropyc documents the current usage of cryptographic techniques and the experience of cryptographic software practitioners. Therefore, it can be used to guide the decision-making process for the design of cryptographic features.

ACKNOWLEDGMENTS

This work is partially supported by PRONEX-Finep, grant 107/97 for Ricardo Dahab; Finep and CNPq, grant 7697102200 and 351592/97-0, respectively, for Cecília Mary Fischer Rubira; FAPESP, grant 97/11128-3 for Alexandre Melo Braga and 96/15329 for LSD-IC-UNICAMP. We would like to thank our shepherd Robert Orenstein and the workshop session members at the PLoP '98 conference, whose suggestions and comments were very important during the writing of the present version of this chapter.

APPENDIX A: BASIC CRYPTOGRAPHIC CONCEPTS

Modern cryptography is a broad subject, encompassing both the study and the use of mathematical techniques to address information security problems such as confidentiality, data integrity, and nonrepudiation.

It also can be defined as the discipline that embodies the principles, means, and methods for the transformation of data in order to hide its semantic content, prevent its unauthorized use, or prevent its undetected modification [Information Processing Systems1989]. Usually four objectives [Menezes1996], or services [Information Technology1998], of cryptography are considered: confidentiality, integrity, authentication, and non-repudiation. Accordingly, there are four basic cryptographic mechanisms: encryption/decryption, MDC (Modification Detection Code) generation/verification, MAC (Message Authentication Code) generation/verification, and digital signing/verification. These four services can be combined in specific and limited ways to produce more specialized services. For further information about cryptography, consult the bracketed references [Menezes+1996, Schneier1996, Stinson1995].

Confidentiality is the ability to keep information secret except from authorized users. Data integrity is the guarantee that information has not been modified without permission, which includes the ability to detect unauthorized manipulation. Sender (origin) authentication corresponds to the assurance, by the communicating parties, of the origin of an information transmitted through an insecure communication channel. Nonrepudiation is the ability to prevent an entity from denying its actions or commitments in the future.

Cryptographic Mechanisms

Cryptographic transformations are mainly based on one-way functions, which are mathematical functions for which it is computationally easy to compute an output of an input, but it is computationally difficult to determine any input corresponding to a known output. One-way functions with trapdoors are one-way functions for which it is computationally feasible to compute an input corresponding to a known output, if additional information is provided (the trapdoor). One-way functions with trapdoors are the basic construction components of reversible cryptographic transformations in which the trapdoor information works as the cryptographic key.

Secret- or symmetric-key cryptography is the set of cryptographic techniques in which a single key is used to both encrypt and decrypt data. The key is a shared secret among at least two entities. In public-key cryptography, a pair of different keys is used, one key for encryption, the other for decryption. The encryption key is publicly known and called a public key. The corresponding decryption key is a secret known only by the key-pair owner and is called a private key. In public-key cryptography, it is computationally infeasible to deduce the private key from the knowledge of the public key.

Traditionally, the two ends of a communication channel are called Alice and Bob. Eve is an adversary eavesdropping the channel. Figure 16-7 shows the overall architecture of cryptosystems. Alice wants to send an encrypted message to Bob; she encrypts message m, the plain text, with an encryption key $k1$ and sends the encrypted message c, the cipher text, to Bob, that is, $c = f(m,k1)$. Bob receives the encrypted message and deciphers it with a decryption key $k2$ to recover m, that is, $m = g(c,k2)$ and $g = f^{-1}$. If public-key cryptography is used, Alice uses Bob's public key to encrypt messages and Bob uses his private key to decrypt messages sent from anyone who used his public key. However, if symmetric-key cryptography is used, Alice and Bob share a secret key used to encrypt and decrypt messages they send to each other, that is, $k1 = k2$.

A hash function is a mathematical function that takes as input a stream of variable length and returns a stream of fixed length as a result, usually much shorter than the input. One-way hash functions are hash functions in which it is computationally easy to compute the hash value of an input stream, but it is computationally difficult to determine any input stream corresponding to a known hash value.

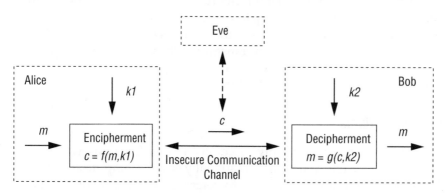

Figure 16-7 *A typical cryptosystem*

A cryptographic hash function is a one-way collision-resistant hash function; that is, it is computationally difficult to find two input streams that result in the same hash value. Hash values produced by cryptographic hash functions also are called MDCs and are used to guarantee data integrity. MACs are usually implemented as hash values generated by cryptographic hash functions that take as input a secret key as well as the usual input stream. MACs are used to provide not only authentication, but also integrity implicitly.

Digital signatures are electronic analogs of handwritten signatures, which serve both as the signer's agreement to the information a document contains and as evidence that can be shown to a third party in case of repudiation. A basic protocol of digital signatures based on public-key cryptography is: first, Alice encrypts a message with her private key to sign it; second, Alice sends the signed message to Bob; and third, Bob decrypts the received message with Alice's public key to verify the signature. Digital signatures must provide the following features: they are authentic, that is, when Bob verifies a message with Alice's public key, he knows she signed it; they are unforgeable, that is, only Alice knows her private key; they are not reusable, that is, the signature is a function of the data being signed, so it cannot be used with other data; and they cannot be repudiated, that is, Bob does not need Alice's help to prove she signed a message. The signed data is unalterable; any modification of the data invalidates the signature verification.

Common Attacks

In a brute-force attack, Eve tests all possible valid keys to decrypt a cipher text of a known plain text in order to find out the correct key. If Eve could obtain the private key of either Alice or Bob (or their secret shared key), all other attacks could be easily performed. Eve can attack a cryptosystem in four basic ways. First, she can eavesdrop the channel. Eavesdropping an open channel is easy. However, to understand eavesdropped messages of a cryptographically secured channel, the key (or keys) being used by Alice and Bob are required. Second, she can resend old messages. This attack is possible if messages do not have temporal uniqueness, which can be obtained using timestamps or by changing keys periodically. Third, she can impersonate one of the communicating ends of the channel. In such a case, Eve plays the role of Alice or Bob, either by deducing a secret key or by successfully substituting her public key for Alice's (Bob's) without Alice's (Bob's) knowledge. Fourth, she can play the role of the man-in-the-middle. To perform the man-in-the-middle attack successfully, Eve must have obtained the private keys (or the secret shared key) of both Alice and Bob, or impersonate both Alice and Bob. In such a situation, Eve can intercept encrypted messages from Alice (Bob) to Bob (Alice), decrypt them with Alice's (Bob's) decryption key and re-encrypt them with her own encryption key before re-sending them.

Auxiliary Services

An important issue of implementations of cryptographic services is whether they are supported by an infrastructure that provides a strong and secure set of auxiliary services such as generation, agreement, distribution, and storage of cryptographic keys. Usually, key generation algorithms are based on random number generators. Public keys are usually distributed together with their digital certificates, which are packages of information attesting the ownership and validity of a cryptographic key. These certificates are usually signed by a trusted third party, called a Certification Authority (CA). A private or secret key must be kept protected from unauthorized copy and modification; this can be done in two ways: it can be stored in tamper-proof hardware; it can be stored, in both encrypted and authentic forms, in general purpose hardware, such as random access memories, magnetic disks and tapes. This requires a key-encryption key which, in turn, must be protected.

REFERENCES

[Asokan+1997] N. Asokan, P.A. Janson, M. Steiner, and M. Waidner. "The State of the Art in Electronic Payment Systems." *IEEE Computer*, September 1997: 28–35.

[Buschmann+1996] F. Buschmann, R. Meunier, H. Rohnert, P. Sommerlad, and M. Stal. *Pattern-Oriented Software Architecture: A System of Patterns*. Chichester: John Wiley & Sons, 1996.

[Braga+1998] A.M. Braga, R. Dahab, and C.M.F. Rubira. PayPerClick: "Um Framework para Venda e Distribuição On-line de Publicações Baseado em Micropagamentos." In *SBRC'98— 16º Simpósio Brasileiro de Redes de Computadores*, p. 767, Rio de Janeiro, RJ, Brazil, May 1998. Extended summary.

[Cheng+1998] P-C Cheng, J.A. Garay, A. Herzberg, and H. Krawczyk. "A Security Architecture for the Internet Protocol." *IBM Systems Journal*, 37(1):42–60, 1998.

[CSS1997] Common Security Services Manager Application Programming Interface, Draft 2.0. http://www.opengroup.org/public/tech/security/pki/index.htm, June 1997.

[Ferreira+1998] L. Ferreira and R. Dahab. "A Scheme for Analyzing Electronic Payment Systems." In *14th ACSAC—Annual Computer Security Applications Conference (ACSAC'98)*, Scottsdale, AZ, December 1998.

[Gamma+1995] E. Gamma, R. Helm, R. Johnson, and J. Vlissides. *Design Patterns: Elements of Reusable Object-Oriented Software*. Reading, MA: Addison-Wesley, 1995.

[Herfert1997] M. Herfert. Security-Enhanced Mailing Lists. *IEEE Network*, 30–33, May/June 1997.

[Herzberg+1997] A. Herzberg and H. Yochai. "Minipay: Charging per Click on the Web." *Computer Networks and ISDN Systems*, vol. 29, pp. 939–951, 1997.

[Herzberg+1998] A. Herzberg and D. Naor. "Surf'N'Sign: Client Signatures on Web Documents." *IBM Systems Journal*, 37(1):61–71, 1998.

[Information Processing Systems1989] Information Processing Systems—Open Systems Interconnection—Basic Reference Model. Part 2: Security Architecture. ISO/IEC 7498-2, 1989.

[Information Technology1998] Information Technology—Vocabulary. Part 8: Security. ISO/IEC 2382-8, 1998.

[Kaliski1995] B. Kaliski. "Cryptoki: A Cryptographic Token Interface, Version 1.0." http://www.rsa.com/rsalabs/pubs/PKCS/html/pkcs-11.html, April 1995.

[Knudsen1998] J.B. Knudsen. *Java Cryptography*. Sebastopol, CA: O'Reilly and Associates, 1998.

[Linn1993] J. Linn. Privacy Enhancement for Internet Electronic Mail. Part 1: Message Encipherment and Authentication Procedures. RFC 1421, February 1993.

[Martin+1997] R.C. Martin, D. Riehle, F. Buschmann, and J. Vlissides, eds. *Pattern Languages of Program Design 3*. Reading, MA: Addison-Wesley, 1997.

[Menezes+1996] A.J. Menezes, P.C. van Orschot, and S.A. Vanstone. *Handbook of Applied Cryptography*. London, UK: CRC Press, 1996.

[Saltzer+1984] J.H. Saltzer, D.P. Reed, and D.D. Clark. "End-To-End Arguments in System Design." *ACM Transactions on Computer Science*, 2(4):277–288, 1984.

[Schneier1996] B. Schneier. *Applied Cryptography—Protocols, Algorithms, and Source Code in C*, 2nd ed. New York: John Wiley and Sons, 1996.

[Stinson1995] D.R. Stinson. *Cryptography Theory and Practice*. London, UK: CRC Press, 1995.

[Yoder+1999] J. Yoder and J. Barcalow. "Architectural Patterns for Enabling Application Security." In N. Harrison, B. Foote, and H. Rohnert (eds.), *Pattern Languages for Program Design 4*. Reading, MA: Addison-Wesley, 1999.

[Zimmermann1995] P.R. Zimmermann. *The Official PGP User's Guide*. Cambridge, MA: MIT Press, 1995.

Alexandre Braga may be reached at alexandre.braga@dcc.unicamp.br.

Cecilia Rubira may be reached at cmrubira@dcc.unicamp.br.

Ricardo Dahab may be reached at rdahab@dcc.unicamp.br.

PART 6

Domain-Oriented Patterns

Many of the patterns written to date capture basic techniques or foundations of design. A working knowledge of these patterns is critical for anyone wishing to become expert in software design. But at some point, the software must deal with the specific issues of its real-world domain; the basic design patterns take one only so far.

Fortunately, we are seeing more and more patterns that address specific problem spaces. Other sections of this book highlight certain domains, such as security and time. The patterns in this section, however, cover three pretty independent domains. The thing that ties them together is that they all have object-oriented solutions. Although these patterns are all object-oriented, notice that "OO" is not part of this section's title. That is because these patterns really transcend object-orientation and can be implemented in a number of different programming paradigms. So don't skip this section if you are object-impaired; there is much to learn here.

Not everyone is interested in the domains covered here, however. In fact, some of the domains are quite specialized. For readers with interest in these domains, the patterns should prove quite useful. For the rest, the patterns are educational.

Chapter 17: Creating Reports with Query Objects by John Brant and Joseph Yoder. We begin with patterns for the database world. One of the difficulties associated with databases is that users often want new, unanticipated types of reports at runtime. You can't know every type of report that the user will want in advance. On the other hand, providing the user with ultimate flexibility in reports requires that the user become a programmer. These patterns describe how to pull data from the database and manipulate that data after it has been extracted. This is accomplished by converting both queries and formulas into objects that can be controlled at runtime. These objects are then assembled into reports through the high-level Report Objects pattern.

Chapter 18: Feature Extraction: A Pattern for Information Retrieval by Dragos-Anton Manolescu.

Anyone who has scanned the World Wide Web knows that technology has vastly increased the amount of data available at one's fingertips. But how does one sift through all this data to find the information that is relevant to one's problem? The explosive growth of data has rendered simple searching methods and algorithms inadequate.

This pattern shows an object-oriented solution for mapping a large complex space into a small, simple feature space. Of course, it doesn't solve the whole problem; the mapping itself is the heart of the problem. This pattern provides the infrastructure to support such mappings as well as a way to process the information without actually understanding it in detail. As a bonus, it's a tutorial on the general problem.

Chapter 19: Finite State Machine Patterns by Sherif M. Yacoub and Hany H. Ammar.

Most of us learned a small amount about finite state machines in college theoretical computer science courses. Yet finite state machines are not only practical, but critical in certain domains. In fact, finite state machines lie at the heart of much of the software that controls data communication as well as many other important software functions.

Finite state machines themselves can be implemented in various software design paradigms. These patterns show ways of implementing them in the object-oriented paradigm. They build on and extend earlier pattern works in the area.

Chapter 17

Creating Reports
with Query Objects

John Brant and Joseph Yoder

The database-reporting patterns discussed in this chapter are based on our research using VisualWorks Smalltalk to generate reports dynamically that map to a relational database. We discovered these patterns while we were building a business modeling tool for Caterpillar. Although we describe the patterns from a Smalltalk perspective, we feel that they can be useful to anyone building reporting applications. Furthermore, even though our examples apply to relational database queries, these ideas could be extended to other types of queries.

The Caterpillar Business Modeling project is a pilot to demonstrate how an appropriate tool can support financial analysis and business decision-making more effectively. This project translates legacy data into a relational database format that is then mapped to and from objects. Reporting the financial aspects of the business model required building many reports based on business logic and SQL queries.

Earlier versions used predefined reports, but this solution was not dynamic enough because users kept requesting new reports. Although predefined reports initially produced fewer bugs by statically checking the queries and values, they require programmatic changes whenever a new report or query is needed. Such changes can introduce bugs and are time-consuming, because the developer must meet with the users to understand their request.

As a result, we researched making a flexible and user-configurable system. The difficulty here is to make the system both easy to understand and modify. Done incorrectly, you may push the task of programming onto end users, forcing them to specify everything the programmer would normally specify for them. Furthermore,

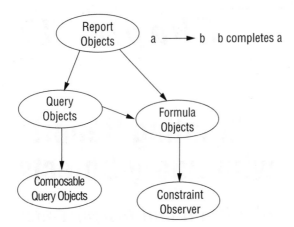

Figure 17-1 *Reporting patterns overview*

such a system is more difficult to understand because everything is created at run-time and cannot be statically analyzed. This chapter describes a collection of patterns that avoids these two extremes by defining objects such as Query and Formula that represent reports. These objects give the user reasonable defaults but can later be customized.

Our pattern language comprises five patterns (see Figure 17-1). Report Objects is the top-level pattern for defining reports. It consists of Query Objects and Formula Objects. Query Objects pull data from the database and can be composed into more complex queries by applying Composable Query Objects. Formula Objects process data returned from Query Objects and are maintained by Constraint Observers.

THE PATTERNS

Report Objects

Motivation

You are creating a reporting application that, given some input from the user, must produce a report. While most reports are known before the application is developed and released, there are many that will need to be customized after the application's deployment. For example, consider a financial application that allows users to view various aspects by selecting different input conditions. You may have designed a report to view sales by marketing areas, but the user might want to view sales by model as well. If your reporting framework is not configurable, you must program the desired changes, whereas with a configurable application, the user could define these reports at runtime. Most reporting applications will get their values from some form of formula equation based on results from a database query.

Problem

You need to create a configurable reporting application.

Forces

Most reports can be predefined with SQL code along with standard views, but these can't contain all the possibilities a user might want. Predefined reports are easier to understand since the code can be statically analyzed. However, new reports will require a programmer to modify the system, and such modifications are prone to errors.

Alternatively, you could make everything configurable, as many report writers already do, so that users can create their own reports. But giving the user the ability to define reports on-the-fly can be difficult, because you must present the options in an easy-to-understand format that is less complex than programming. Otherwise, you will have merely pushed the complexities of programming onto the users.

Solution

Define objects representing the report. These objects are made up of objects that process the data and those that view the data. A report is created by attaching processing objects to viewing objects. In this chapter we discuss only the processing objects.

The processing objects can be further split into objects that fetch data from the database and objects that manipulate the data. Thus, you can build objects that represent the queries and objects that represent formulas needed in the reports. The Query Objects pattern allows you to select data from the database, while the Formula Objects pattern lets you operate on data returned by Query Objects.

When reporting, you need to define queries and to apply functions on the results from queries. As noted in the Forces, the solution can range from predefining the SQL queries to providing the user with a report writer to dynamically generate any type of report. This pattern is more of a middle-of-the-road solution that allows you to make objects that represent queries needed for the reports along with objects for constructing complex values by composing those results. This pattern gives the user something that Works Out of the Box[1] while still allowing for customized reports [Foote+1998a].

---

[1] An artifact that Works Out of the Box is one that is immediately able to exhibit useful behavior with minimal arguments or configuration. Enough defaults are provided to get the user up and running without needing to know details of the system.

Consequences

This pattern gives you more flexibility in creating reports primarily due to the way data is processed, i.e., as an object. Data in an object can be manipulated at runtime. Unlike other implementations in which methods define the processing, this technique provides more flexibility since objects are more easily manipulated at runtime than methods [Foote+1996].

Although this pattern provides more flexibility when constructing the reports, it also makes the data processing harder to understand. If queries are built into methods, then they can be statically analyzed, but since they are built at runtime, we must reason about the configuration of objects at runtime. Determining such runtime properties can be difficult if not impossible.

Related Patterns

- The Query Objects pattern helps build objects that query relational databases.
- The Formula Objects pattern constructs objects that represent formulas.
- The Metadata and Active Object-Model patterns [Foote+1998b] can be used to describe the reports and the queries/formulas that compose them. This provides a powerful mechanism for creating and changing the reports at runtime.

Known Uses

- VisualWorks ReportWriter [ParcPlace Systems1995] separates the retrieval of data into filter objects and the report view definition into layout objects.
- The Caterpillar/NCSA Financial Model Framework [Yoder1997] was implemented using this pattern.

Query Objects

Motivation

You are defining reports for your users. Each report queries the database for the information and displays it to the user. While many queries that the user will require are known when you are developing the software, there are some that the user will want to add later. For example, you might have a sales query that returns the sales for a specific time interval, but you might want to modify the query to display only Asian sales.

Problem

You need to create new queries for reports at runtime.

Forces

If all reports are known in advance, the solution is to create the queries when you build the system. Predefined queries are easy to understand and predict since you just need to analyze the source code. However, they fall short when trying to develop dynamic mappings to the data. Furthermore, changing these queries requires program modifications that cannot be performed by the users.

Another option is to create queries at runtime by providing the user with an interface for creating them. This option would require the users to know something about your database to build the query. Although users may know what data is stored and what it is used for, they may not know how such information is stored in the database (e.g., they may not grasp the concepts of joining two tables).

Solution

Create objects that represent queries. Define the operations that will be used to manipulate the queries. For a relational database, you might have operations for selecting which rows should be returned, projecting the fields to be returned, and so forth. Next, define a method that will return the results of the query. For queries that need to dynamically add new conditions, you can use the Composable Query Objects pattern.

For query operations that take expressions such as selections and projections, you can use the Formula Objects pattern to create these expressions. Whenever the expression's value changes, you can update the query that will update the report.

This basic intent of this pattern is to convert methods that contain your queries into objects that are easier to manipulate. This is similar to the Strategy pattern [Gamma+1995], but the main purpose of this pattern is to make objects that are easily manipulated whereas the Strategy pattern is more concerned with making them interchangeable.

Although the motivation and forces of this pattern focus on creating a runtime-configurable system, Query Objects also makes it easier for the developer to program. Queries can be described with Query Objects by writing object-oriented code rather than SQL. Query Objects are similar to Smalltalk collections in which common protocol such as `project:`, `select:`, and `join:` create new Query Objects.

Example

For the Asian sales example, you would define an object that represented the sales query, which is just a mapping to retrieve the sales records. You would then add basic manipulation operations such as `project:` that picks which fields are returned, and `select:`, which selects the records to be returned. In addition to these operations, you need an operation to return the values from the query, such as a `value` method. This method converts the query into SQL code that is executed by the database and finally returns the resulting set of values. Using such a protocol, you could modify the sales query object to extract Asian sales simply by evaluating a statement like this one:

```
salesQuery select: salesQuery continent = 'Asia'
```

This statement modifies the `salesQuery` query object by adding the condition "`salesQuery continent = 'Asia'`". This condition is an object that can be modified to support different conditions. For example, the string `'Asia'` might be a variable, which can change at runtime. The = method in the "`salesQuery continent`" object has been overridden so that it is evaluated when the query is performed.

Consequences

The Query Object pattern makes it possible to manipulate queries at runtime. Since the queries are objects, they can be changed to add or remove conditions. This provides the needed flexibility to dynamically create or modify queries for new reports.

One disadvantage of this pattern is that dynamic queries can be slower than precomputed queries. The precomputed queries can be optimized for the database, whereas the dynamic queries might be translated to a slower query. Furthermore, static queries can be pre-computed in database views. If this is a major problem, then you might need to write an optimizing translator that will do a better job translating the query objects into database statements.

Related Patterns

- Formula Objects can create expressions for the select conditions.
- The Composable Query Object pattern can build new queries out of existing queries.
- The Strategy pattern [Gamma+1995] is similar since methods are being encapsulated into objects.
- The Crossing Chasms pattern language [Brown+1995] can be used to map between objects and relational databases.

Known Uses

- VisualWorks ReportWriter [ParcPlace Systems1995] created special filters for retrieving data from SQL databases. Although these are objects, they are more like strategies because they do not provide an interface for manipulation.
- Borland Database Engine [Rudraraju1995] supports query objects that can be manipulated.

- The Refactoring Browser's BrowserEnvironments [Roberts1999] allow programmers to dynamically query properties of a Smalltalk program.

Composable Query Objects

Motivation

You have decided to use the Query Objects pattern to build dynamic queries, but you have many reports with similar queries. Rather than having to define a query for each report, you would like to define one query for the common part and then create new queries based on the common query. This would let you create new queries easily in some minimalist fashion. Not only would this help during the creation of queries; it would also help during debugging because you will only need to fix the common part once, and then all of the dependent queries will be automatically fixed. Furthermore, it allows the dependent queries to dynamically update whenever the common query modifies its selection criteria.

For example, given the sales query from the previous section, you might want to look at both Asian sales and North American sales during a time interval. Whenever you update the time interval, both reports also should be updated. The only differences between these two reports would be the sales records that are selected.

Problem

You want to create different queries with simple modifications to common base queries.

Forces

You could use the previous patterns to build a query object for each sales query, but this would be hard to keep up-to-date with other selections. From the example above, imagine that the user decides to continue to look at and compare the North American sales with the Asian sales but then decides to view the fourth quarter instead of the third quarter. This would require triggers or callbacks to make sure that all open views were updated appropriately.

Another solution is to "wrap" new constraints on existing queries. Although wrappers[2] are harder to implement, they do ensure consistency with changing constraints. They also provide a nice way to build a new query from existing queries. If any query needs to be modified to fix a bug, then its wrappers will also be updated without the need for direct modification.

---

[2] We use the terms *wrappers* and *decorators* synonymously as is done in VisualWorks Smalltalk.

Solution

Build queries out of composable parts. Define one class to represent tables in the database, and for each query operation define a class that performs the operation. Additionally, define methods for each operation that will create the appropriate object for that operation on the query. For a relational database, we would define a `TableQuery` class to represent tables and define classes such as `Selection-Query` to represent the selection operations, `JoinQuery` for join operations, and so forth. Since all operations are performed on some query, we can create the abstract superclass, `WrapperQuery`, to handle wrapping these queries with the operations. Finally, you might define methods that create these operations. For example we can define a `selectWhere:` method that will create a `Selection-Query` on the query (see Figure 17-2) as opposed to the `select:` method in the previous section that modifies the existing query with the new selection.

To convert a query object into database statements, we use the Interpreter pattern [Gamma+1995]. Each type of query object will be a node for the interpreter. The table query objects are the terminal nodes for the interpreter, and the operation nodes are the nonterminals since they wrap other query objects. Instead of making an interpreter to create the complete database statements, you can make separate interpreters that will create the statement parts (e.g., you would have one interpreter for the `where` clause, another for the projected fields). The primary difference between this use and the Interpreter pattern is that the query objects can generate their output without any additional input.

Finally, each of the `WrapperQueries` should be updated whenever its wrapped query changes. This can be accomplished by using the Observer pattern [Gamma+1995]. The `WrapperQueries` will be observers, and their wrapped

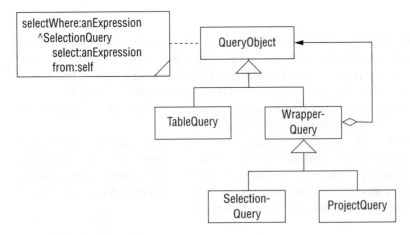

Figure 17-2 *Query Objects hierarchy*

queries will be subjects. Whenever a wrapped query changes, the `Wrapper-Query` will also change, allowing the reports to update.

Example

For the sales by continent example, we would have a base query object that retrieves all the sales records from the database for a particular time interval. To create a report for a continent, we would just need to create a new query to select those records for that continent. For example, we could create the Asian's sales query with

```
salesQuery selectWhere: salesQuery continent = 'Asia'.
```

Whenever the `salesQuery`'s date interval changes, it will notify its dependents, which are the continent sales queries. Both of the continent sales query objects will change and cause their reports to update. Figure 17-3 shows the base `salesQuery` object. Both the Asian sales query and the North American sales queries are observers of the `salesQuery`.

Consequences

This pattern makes "exploratory programming" easier because you do not need to understand all facets of the database when creating a query. For example, you can extend the sales query without understanding which tables were used, what are the date fields, and so on. You would only need to know that there is a `continent` field. Furthermore, a visual language could be constructed to more easily manipulate these queries.

While this pattern allows you to dynamically create similar queries and automatically maintain them, it also results in objects that are harder to implement.

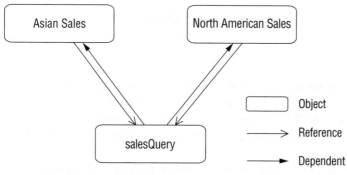

Figure 17-3 *salesQuery objects*

Since the knowledge of a query is spread among several objects, it is harder to create the database statements for the query. We must traverse all of the objects to create the database statements, whereas if all of the details of the query were in one object, then we could directly create the database statements.

Another disadvantage of this pattern is that it results in many small objects wrapping other query objects. These wrappers make it harder to debug the system, since it is more difficult to traverse the wrappers to see what the query is performing.

Related Patterns

- This pattern uses the Decorator and Composite patterns [Gamma+1995] as it wraps new responsibilities and composes new objects.
- Another view is to consider each operation as a parse node using the Interpreter pattern [Gamma+1995]. Although we could have just referenced these patterns, we felt it important to include this pattern to show the concrete usage of the design patterns to form Composable Query Objects.
- Observers [Gamma+1995] are used by Composable Query Objects to maintain consistency with the `WrapperQueries`.

Formula Objects

Motivation

You are creating a reporting application. Some values are directly available, but many are calculated. For example, `Profit` is a calculated value based on `Income` and `Expenses`. While some of these formulas might be known when the program is created, we want to allow the user to create or modify formulas at runtime.

Problem

You need to modify formulas and have them automatically maintained.

Forces

One option would be to define methods for all formulas, but that would require programmer intervention whenever adding or changing formulas. Not only might it introduce new bugs; it also will take time to complete since the change must be explained to the developers. This might require filling out paperwork, attending meetings, and so forth.

Another option would be to have the user create the formulas at runtime, but many formulas do not change. Users shouldn't have to enter these formulas; they

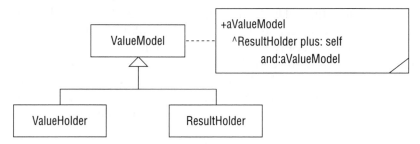

Figure 17-4 *ResultHolder example*

should already be defined. Furthermore, users are more likely to have precedence errors in entering their formulas and are less likely to fully test them.

Solution

Define an object that represents the results of a computed formula. The result object that is to be used in other formulas should be in the same hierarchy as the objects that create it. Next, define the basic formula operations to more easily create the Formula Objects. For example, you might define methods such as +, −, *, and / for performing basic arithmetic operations. To make sure that the result object is consistent with its inputs, we can use the Constraint Observer pattern.

Example

As an example, consider VisualWorks, which stores many of its values in Value-Models so that they can easily be plugged into its UI framework. To create a result object we could subclass ValueModel to create a ResultHolder[3] that would hold the result of the formula (see Figure 17-4). We could then define basic operations +, −, *, and / on ValueModel to return a new ResultHolder whenever they were executed. Now if both Income and Expenses are ValueModels, then we can create a ValueModel that represents Profit simply by executing "Income - Expenses".

Consequences

This pattern allows both users and programmers to use formulas without knowing how they are maintained. Only the person implementing the pattern needs to understand that. This reduces much of the complexity that would have been

---

[3] VisualWorks already has a BlockValue class that incorporates both the Formula Object pattern and the Constraint Observer pattern.

required when creating new formulas. Instead, the people creating formulas can concentrate on making them correct and not on how to maintain them.

Formula Objects are useful not only for generating dynamic reports but also to assist the developer with writing the code by treating these values as objects. For example, rather than getting the value from queries, calculating the resulting value based on some mathematical function, and then setting the variable to equal the value; you can just assign C := A + B where A and B can be Formula Objects or Query Objects.

One disadvantage of using Formula Objects is that it is easy to create too many objects, since an object is created for each subexpression in the formula. For example, a simple formula for computing margin percentage such as "(Income — Expenses) / Income" would create two objects: one that represents "Income — Expenses" and another for the margin percentage. The extra objects aren't generally a problem in practice, but they could cause problems in applications with many complex formulas. In these applications it may be necessary to "optimize" the formula by making the computed result responsible for the complete formula instead of just the expressions in the formula.

Related Patterns

- The Constraint Observer pattern can be used to keep the result object consistent with its inputs.
- The Interpreter pattern [Gamma+1995] can be used to create result objects from user entered formulas.
- The Composable Query Object pattern is similar. The primary difference is that Composable Query Objects operate on queries while Formula Objects operate on the results of queries.

Known Uses

- The WyCash Report Writer [Cunningham1991] has a few formulas that can add additional columns to a report. These are similar to instances of Formula Objects in that they define objects for "formula columns" that are based on other columns and/or rows. Using such a system, users are able to build their reports without having to define new types of formulas.
- VisualWorks ReportWriter [ParcPlace Systems1995] has formula objects that can take either Smalltalk blocks or formulas defined in their own macro language.
- VisualWorks [ParcPlace Systems1994] has BlockValues that can be used to create formulas for ValueModels.
- The Accounts framework [Keefer1994] defines functions of time that are used for the attributes of an account.

Constraint Observers

Motivation

You have applied the Formula Objects pattern to create formulas dynamically, but now you need to update these values whenever one of their input values change. For example, you may have created a formula "`Income — Expenses`" to calculate `Profit`. Whenever `Income` or `Expenses` change, `Profit` should change to maintain the consistency of the formula.

Problem

You need to automatically update calculated values of formulas whenever an input value changes.

Forces

A simple solution would be to create a method for each formula that updates the new values whenever an input changes. This would require a new method for every possible formula, which may not be known in advance.

Constraint systems [Benson+1992] are another solution that provide the needed flexibility to automatically maintain the formulas. However, they can limit how programs are written and can be very difficult to understand, especially when trying to follow the control flow while maintaining the formulas.

Solution

Create a constraint object that is responsible for the calculation. Use the Observer pattern [Gamma+1995] to update the constraint whenever an input to the formula changes (i.e., the inputs for the formula will be the subjects and the constraint will be the observer). Whenever the constraint is updated, it evaluates the formula and assigns the result.

The constraint object can either be a part of the result or a separate object. Representing it as separate objects is more flexible since the constraint and the result can be varied independently. Furthermore, each result object could have multiple constraints associated with it. But if the constraints are created by formulas, then the extra flexibility is not needed since every result object would have only one constraint object.

Example

For the `Profit` example, the constraint depends on both the `Income` and the `Expenses` objects (see Figure 17-5). Whenever the "–" constraint receives

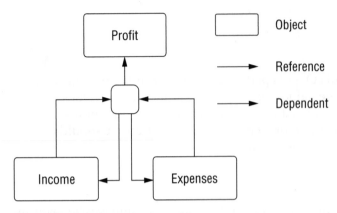

Figure 17-5 *Profit example*

the `update` message from `Income` or `Expenses`, it evaluates and assigns the result to `Profit`.

Consequences

The main advantage of this pattern is simplicity. If you were to use another constraint system, then you would be required to maintain complicated data structures so the constraints would be optimally solved.

Additionally, if you were to use methods, then you would also need other data structures that listed the methods to be executed when an event occurred. This is a maintenance nightmare primarily because you have to maintain many methods that recalculate the values.

The main disadvantage of this pattern is that it can lead to suboptimal performance. For example, in the earlier formula `Profit` will change whenever `Income` or `Expenses` change. But if every time one value changes the other also changes, then we will be updating `Profit` twice when one update is all that is required. Although these extra calculations don't have a big impact for simple arithmetic formulas, the overhead might be unacceptable for formulas that involve queries. In these cases a simple flag might be used to delay updating until all objects have changed. If the flag still does not work, you probably need a constraint system that can optimally solve the constraints.

Constraint Observer is a simple pattern for implementing a constraint system, but it will not work for many general constraint problems. For example, constraints that are circular would cause this system to get into an infinite cycle of update messages. This is not a problem though, since the constraints were created with formulas, which guarantee no circularities.

Related Patterns

The Observer pattern [Gamma+1995] can be used to update the constraints whenever an input value changes.

Known Uses

- The Constraints pattern described by [Johnson1992] is similar. It is used by Hot-Draw to update figure locations whenever a dependent figure changes its location. HotDraw only defined simple equality constraints, but it could simulate more complex formulas using `Locator` objects.
- VisualWorks has a special class that implements Constraint Observer for `ValueModels`. The `BlockValue` object [ParcPlace Systems1994] has both the result and the constraint. The result is stored in the `value` instance variable, and the action performed by the constraint is stored as a `BlockClosure` in the `block` instance variable.
- IBM VisualAge Smalltalk [IBM1997] implements a Constraint Observer for maintaining consistency between observable parts (see the connection classes). Visual parts are wired to nonvisual parts, and whenever the value of one is changed, the value of the dependent part is updated.

CONCLUSIONS

With changing business requirements, users need flexible programs that quickly adapt to their business needs. Users can't wait for programming changes that take weeks. Therefore, it is important to provide the flexibility necessary for the program to adapt to the user's needs. The patterns discussed in this chapter help provide such support. They accomplish this by transforming queries and formulas into objects by which they can be more easily manipulated.

ACKNOWLEDGMENTS

We are grateful to the members of Professor Johnson's Patterns seminar: Jeff Barcalow, Ian Chai, Brian Foote, Charles Herring, Ralph Johnson, Mark Kendrat, Don Roberts, and Susanne Schacht; our shepherd Kyle Brown; and the members of our writer's workshop who reviewed earlier drafts and provided valuable feedback.

REFERENCES

[Benson1992] B. Freeman-Benson and A. Borning. "Integrating Constraints with an Object-Oriented Language." In *Proceedings of the 1992 European Conference on Object-Oriented Programming*, pp. 268–286, June 1992.

[Brown+1996] K. Brown and B.G. Whitenack. "Crossing Chasms—A Pattern Language for Object-RDBMS Integration." In J.M. Vlissides, J.O. Coplien, and N.L. Kerth (eds.), *Pattern Languages of Program Design 2*. Reading, MA: Addison-Wesley, 1996.

[Cunningham1991] W. Cunningham. "The WyCash Report Writer." In *OOPSLA '92 Workshop, "Towards an Architecture Handbook."* Available: http://c2.com/doc/ooplsa91.html.

[Foote+1996] B. Foote and J. Yoder. "Evolution, Architecture, and Metamorphosis." In J.M. Vlissides, J.O. Coplien, and N.L. Kerth (eds.), *Pattern Languages of Program Design 2*. Reading, MA: Addison-Wesley, 1996.

[Foote+1998a] B. Foote and J. Yoder. "The Selfish Class." In R. Martin, D. Riehle, and F. Buschmann (eds.), *Pattern Languages of Program Design 3*. Reading, MA: Addison-Wesley, 1998.

[Foote+1998b] B. Foote and J. Yoder. "Metadata and Active Object-Models." *Collected Papers from the PLoP '98 and EuroPLoP '98 Conference,* Technical Report WUCS-98-25, Washington University Department of Computer Science, September 1998. Available: http://jerry.cs.uiuc.edu/~plop/plop98/final_submissions/.

[Gamma+1995] E. Gamma, R. Helm, R. Johnson, and J. Vlissides. *Design Patterns: Elements of Reusable Object-Oriented Software*. Reading, MA: Addison-Wesley, 1995.

[IBM 1997] IBM. *VisualAge for Smalltalk User's Reference*. April 1997.

[Johnson1992] R.E. Johnson. "Documenting Frameworks with Patterns," In *OOPSLA '92 Proceedings,* 27(10): 63–76, October 1992.

[Keefer1994] P.D. Keefer. *An Object Oriented Framework for Accounting Systems*. Master's Thesis, University of Illinois at Urbana-Champaign, Department of Computer Science, 1994.

[Roberts1999] D.B. Roberts. *Practical Analysis for Refactoring*. Ph.D thesis, University of Illinois at Urbana-Champaign, Department of Computer Science, 1999.

[Rudraraju1995] Pandu Rudraragu White paper for *Borland Database Engine and IDAPI.* February 1995. Available: http://www.tietovayla.fi/BORLAND/bbebde/id1ovrvw.htm.

[ParcPlace Systems1994] ParcPlace Systems, Inc. *VisualWorks Object Reference*. June 1994.

[ParcPlace Systems1995] ParcPlace Systems, Inc. *VisualWorks ReportWriter: Tutorial and User's Guide*. February 1995.

[Yoder1997] J. Yoder. *A Framework to Build Financial Models*. Available: http://www.joeyoder.com.

John Brant and Joseph Yoder may be reached at brant@cs.uiuc.edu and joeyoder@joeyoder.com.

Chapter 18

Feature Extraction: A Pattern for Information Retrieval

Dragos-Anton Manolescu

Technology determines the types and amounts of information we can access. Currently, a large fraction of information originates in silicon. Cheap, fast chips and smart algorithms are helping digital data processing take over all sorts of information processing. Consequently, the volume of digital data surrounding us increases continuously.

However, an information-driven society has additional requirements besides the availability of and ability to process digital data. We also should be able to find the pieces of information relevant to a particular problem. Having the answer to a question but not being able to find it is equivalent to not having it at all. The increased volume of information and the wide variety of data types make finding information a challenging task.

Current searching methods and algorithms are based on assumptions about technology and goals that seemed reasonable before the widespread use of computers. However, these assumptions no longer hold in the context of information retrieval systems. "Good ideas do not always scale" [Kay1986].

This chapter presents a pattern that provides a proven solution for searching large volumes of information. The pattern originated in the information retrieval domain. However, information retrieval has expanded into other fields such as office automation, genome databases, fingerprint identification, medical imaging, data mining, multimedia, and so forth. Since the pattern works with any kind of data, it applies to many other domains. You will see examples from text searching, telecommunications, stock prices, medical imaging, and trademark symbols.

The key idea of the pattern is to map from a large, complex problem space into a small, simple feature space. The mapping represents the creative part of the solution.

Every type of application uses a different kind of mapping. Mapping into the feature space is also the hard part of this pattern.

Traditional searching algorithms are not viable for problems typical to the information retrieval domain. Since they were designed for exact matching, they are cumbersome for similarity search. In contrast, Feature Extraction provides an elegant and efficient alternative. With information retrieval expanding into other fields, this pattern works in a wide range of applications.

Context

Digital libraries handle *large amounts of information*. They offer access to collections of documents represented in electronic format. According to Bruce Schatz [Schatz1997]:

> A digital library enables users to interact effectively with information distributed across a network. These network information systems support search and display of items from organized collections.

An increasing number of users are discovering online information retrieval and interactive searches. Once comfortable with the new tools, they demand that new materials be available in digital libraries. Obtaining digital representations of documents is thus required. Since the process is getting cheaper and faster, extending a digital library is easy.

This increase in the amount of information obviously has a strong impact on the supporting software. Consider, for example, the case of searching—text retrieval. One can't imagine a digital library without this basic operation. Several different algorithms are available for traditional text retrieval [Faloutsos+1995b]. However, they don't always work in the context of digital libraries. For example, full text scanning, regular expression searching, and signature files have bad response times for large amounts of information. Inversion (the method used by many Web search engines) scales well but has a large storage overhead (up to 300%) and expensive index updates.

Large volumes of data are not the only challenging characteristic typical of digital libraries. Unlike conventional database systems, digital library users usually perform *similarity searches* (i.e., approximate searches) instead of exact searches. In a traditional database system, users ask queries like "what is the title of the book with the ISBN 0201633612." (In case you're wondering, it is *Design Patterns*.) In contrast, in a digital library system, a user can ask "list in decreasing order of similarity all books that are on the same subject as the one with ISBN 0201633612." (Database systems also can answer such queries if provided appropriate manual classification.) This corresponds to a query by example. Conventional database systems can handle some approximate searches, but they were not designed for this purpose.

The emergence of multimedia content within electronic publications raises another issue. One can provide as a query a digital image and ask for all electronic documents that contain similar pictures; for example, "retrieve the documents that contain images that look like this sunset." Here the challenge is "understanding" the contents of the image. Digital images (and any other multimedia data for that matter) are *complex data*. Although computers are good at representing and manipulating digital representations of this type of information, decoding their contents remains a research issue. One possible fix for this problem is to have a person annotate each image with a set of keywords. But manual classification is time-consuming and potentially error-prone [Eakins+1998]. Therefore, it quickly runs into scalability problems.

Problem

"We generate more information that we can control. This unmanaged data tide is at toxic levels" [Kelly1994]. Many applications must search for similarities in large amounts of information that often has a complex representation. How does software keep this information under control?

Forces

- Information retrieval systems handle large amounts of data. Signature files and inversion or other "traditional" search algorithms are not viable for applications such as digital libraries.
- Similarity searching is useful in many domains. Although relational algebra handles exact queries well, it is cumbersome for similarity searches.
- Multimedia databases contain digital representations of acoustic and visual data. Current software can't "understand" the meaning of this complex information.
- Information retrieval systems require small space overhead but also low computational overhead for queries and insertions.
- Computer users want fast response times.

Solution

Work with an alternative, simpler representation of data. The representation contains some information that is unique to each data item. This computation is actually a function. It maps from the problem space into a feature space. For this reason it is also called a "feature extraction function."

A typical feature extraction function for text documents is automatic indexing. The function maps each document into a point in the k-dimensional keyword (or feature) space—k is the number of keywords. Automatic indexing consists of the following steps [Faloutsos+1995b]. First, it removes common words like "and," "at," and "the." Next, it reduces the remaining words to their stem (normalized form). For instance, it reduces both "computer" and "computation" to "comput." Then a dictionary of synonyms helps to assign each word stem to a "concept class" [Schatz1997]. (These three steps are also known as *preprocessing*. Preprocessing extracts concepts from contents.) Finally, the method builds a vector in the keyword space. Each vector element gives the coordinate in one of the k dimensions and corresponds to a concept class. Two options for computing the coordinates in the feature space are the following:

1. Binary document vectors use only two values to indicate the presence or absence of a term.
2. Vectors based on weighting functions use values corresponding to term frequency, "specificity," etc.

Figure 18-1 illustrates how document indexing maps from a document space into a three-dimensional feature space. A multidimensional index structure stores the feature space representation.

Typically, Feature Extraction maps from a *larger* problem space into a *smaller* feature space. Consider the previous example of document indexing. In the document space, each document contains a large number of words. Searching a collection of documents requires many string matching operations. However, in the keyword space, documents correspond to multidimensional vectors. When we apply this pattern, searching for documents that contain a given set of keywords involves computing some linear expressions (see the section on Implementation Notes). This is much faster than string matching. Therefore, Feature Extraction enables scalable solutions for problems that deal with large amounts of information.

In the feature space, *similarity searching* corresponds to operations on normalized vectors. A popular and intuitive choice for similarity measure is the cosine function. (Many other choices are available. For instance, people working with digital libraries prefer asymmetric functions.) In the three-dimensional space from

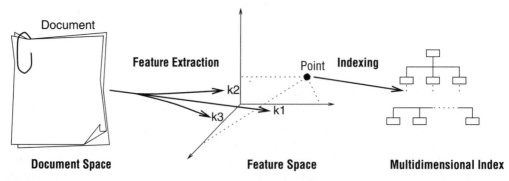

Figure 18-1 *Mapping a document into a three-dimensional feature space*

Figure 18-2, for example, $\vec{b}$ is more similar to $\vec{a}$ than $\vec{c}$. In terms of the two angles α and β, $\alpha < \beta$ and thus $\cos \alpha > \cos \beta$. We can easily compute the cosine value from the inner product—see the section on Implementation Notes. Consequently, matching a query in the feature space can be represented by linear expressions [Kantor1994]. Moreover, the answers to a query can be ranked in order of similarity. Queries return only the answers that are above a given threshold. Therefore, Feature Extraction provides a natural and low-overhead solution for similarity searches.

However, using Feature Extraction for similarity searches has its own limitations. The pattern considers that similarity in the feature space corresponds to similarity in the problem space. People do not necessarily perceive things this way. Here are two reasons:

1. The problem space may be ambiguous. Text is a notorious example. Humans handle this problem by using the surrounding text to establish a context.
2. The feature extraction function is non-injective. Distinct points from the problem space can map into the same point in the feature space. More on this issue later.

Domain mappings are a widespread technique in mathematics. Usually they map from a *complex* domain into a *simpler* one—here, complexity refers to the operations within the domain. A well-known example is the operational method for the solution of differential equations [Bronshtein+1997]. The method consists of going from a differential equation, by means of an integral transformation, to a transformed equation. The transformed equation is easier to solve than its differential counterpart. Two possible integral transformations are the Laplace transform and the z transform.

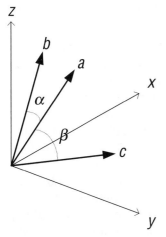

Figure 18-2 *Cosine function and vector similarity*

In a software context, mapping from the problem space into the feature space also enables computers to manipulate complex information. Digital images are one example. Current image databases employ this pattern to obtain simplified representations for images. Unlike the typical domain mappings from mathematics, these simplified representations lose information. They consider only the *most significant* image features, for example, the low-frequency coefficients of the Fourier transform. Common features for images are color histograms, textures, shapes, or a combination of these. Using these features the pattern enables applications to process different types of complex information without "understanding" the contents.

When mapping from a large problem space, Feature Extraction considers only a few significant features in the feature space, discarding the rest. This truncation yields a non-injective mapping. For example, two documents can map into the same point in keyword space. However, this does not mean they are identical. Since the mapping is not injective, there is no inverse function. Several points in the problem space can map into a single point in the feature space. This property affects all applications that employ this pattern to provide answers to queries. The solution is to add a postprocessing step that filters out the "false alarms." Since the typical number of false alarms is small, the postprocessing step usually performs a sequential search to eliminate them.

Besides postprocessing, this pattern requires two additional stages:

1. Feature Extraction works with the features of the working set of items (documents, images, etc.). Whenever a new item is added to the data store, the system computes its features (i.e., coordinates in the feature space). Therefore, each *insertion* needs this extra step.
2. *Query processing* also changes. The fundamental idea of Feature Extraction is to perform all computations in a smaller, simpler space. Processing then takes place in this space. Consequently, answering a query requires computing its representation in the feature space as well.

To summarize, Feature Extraction complicates insertion and query operations since it requires additional processing and a data store. See Figure 18-3.

Information retrieval (IR) is one of the domains that employs Feature Extraction extensively. IR has expanded into fields such as office automation, genome databases, fingerprint identification, medical image management, data mining, and multimedia [Kantor1994]. In many of these applications the objective is to minimize response times for different sorts of queries. Performance depends on how fast the system performs searches in the multidimensional feature space. Therefore, the choice of a Spatial Access Method is critical. However, this may be challenging. Good unidimensional indexing methods scale exponentially for high dimensionalities, eventually reducing to sequential scanning [Agrawal+1993]. They work only when a small number of dimensions are sufficient to differentiate between data items. The next section provides a few alternatives that work well for a larger number of dimensions.

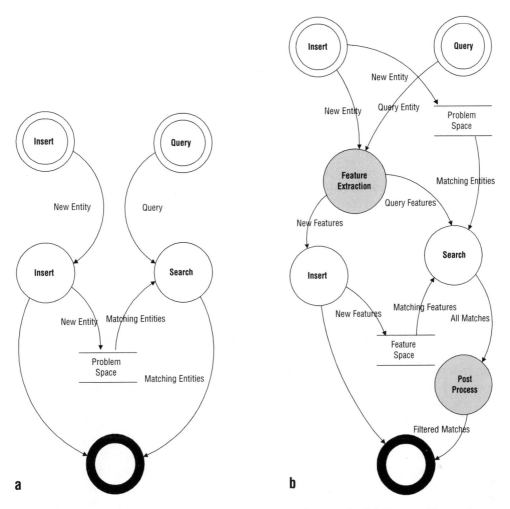

Figure 18-3a,b *Insertion and query processing without and with Feature Extraction. (The additional stages required for Feature Extraction are shaded.)*

Design Decisions. Applying the Feature Extraction pattern involves three design decisions. This section covers these decisions and discusses some potential choices.

The creative part of this pattern is obtaining a suitable feature extraction function. This is also the hard part of the pattern. Many domains emphasize correctness. A query should return all the qualifying information, without any "misses." The false alarms due to the non-injective mapping are less of a problem; postprocessing (Figure 18-3a,b) removes them. Users of this pattern need a formal proof to demonstrate the correctness of the selected feature extraction function. Alternatively, a domain-specific algorithm may automatically construct a correct feature-extraction function for a given problem. For example, Faloutsos and colleagues describe such an algorithm for indexing, data mining, and visualization of traditional and multimedia datasets [Faloutsos+1995a]. Obviously, the feature extraction function is both domain-dependent and problem-dependent.

The Discrete Fourier Transform (DFT) is an example of a feature extraction function. This function is suitable for pink noise "signals," whose energy spectrum follows $O(f^{-1})$. A wide range of data (e.g., stock prices, musical scores, etc.) fits this description. Consequently, DFT is usable in many different domains. This transformation has been successfully used for similarity searches [Agrawal+1993]. Its properties guarantee the completeness of feature extraction. Since DFT is orthonormal (i.e., distance-preserving), the distance between two data items in the problem space is the same as the distance between their corresponding points in the feature space. Therefore, we can use DFT with any similarity measure that can be expressed as the Euclidean distance between feature vectors in some feature space. The section on Known Uses provides additional examples of feature extraction functions.

After we've found a feature extraction function, we must decide which features to consider further. As explained before, the pattern discards some features. For example, systems that use DFT keep only a few low-frequency coefficients. This "lossy" part of the pattern ensures that the feature space is smaller than the problem space. Deciding on the number of features involves a trade-off between accuracy and speed. At one extreme, the system is "lossless" and keeps all features. This ensures no false alarms. However, searching a large (feature) space is what the pattern is trying to avoid. At the other extreme, we use only one feature. In this case, the degenerate search in the feature space is fast—it simply returns everything. Postprocessing takes a long time, though, since it filters all data items. Therefore, the number of features determines the balance between the searching time in the feature space and the postprocessing time in the problem space.

The third part of this pattern involves choosing a suitable spatial access method. The choice depends on the number of features—dimensions of the feature space. Many methods are available for indexing low-dimensionality domains—for example, hash tables or B-tree variants. However, as the number of dimensions grows, they degenerate into sequential scanning. R-tree variants (e.g., R*-trees [Beckmann+1990] and SS-trees [White+1996]) offer good performance for a larger number of dimensions.

To summarize, the Feature Extraction pattern involves three design decisions, not necessarily in this order:

- *Determine the feature extraction function.*   This is the most challenging part of the pattern.
- *Decide what features to consider.*   This decision determines the balance between the search time and the postprocessing time.
- *Choose a spatial access method.*   This determines how fast the system can search the feature space.

Consequences

Feature Extraction provides solutions for several important information retrieval problems. First, it enables scalable solutions for systems that deal with large amounts of information. Second, it provides a natural and low-overhead solution for similarity searches. And third, it enables software to process different types of complex information without "understanding" its contents.

The Feature Extraction pattern has the following benefits:

- It can manage large amounts of data. Compared to sequential scanning, applications using this pattern obtain an increasingly better performance as the volume of data increases [Agrawal+1993].
- Similarity searching corresponds to vector operations in feature space. These have low computational overhead, and they make ranking the results easy, if not trivial.
- Software can manipulate complex information without having to decode its semantics. This is key for implementing multimedia databases.
- Users can easily refine queries. Once they have the results, they mark only those that are relevant. The system adjusts the original query and performs a new search. If the user's feedback is consistent, such queries converge in a few iterations. This mode of operation is also known as *relevance feedback* [Salton+1988]. In the feature space, relevance feedback consists of adding the selected vectors to the query vector.

Feature Extraction has the following liabilities:

- It is hard to determine feature extraction functions. This is often the subject of doctoral dissertations or even careers.
- An efficient search in the feature space requires spatial access methods. Not all good indexing methods scale well with the number of dimensions. Obtaining an efficient and scalable multidimensional index structure is difficult.
- Inserting new items and answering queries require additional processing. The designer has to determine the right balance between the number of features and the postprocessing time.
- The features require an additional data store. Systems that use Feature Extraction use two data stores. The "problem space" data store holds the domain-specific entities, for example, documents, images, and so forth. Likewise, the "feature space" data store holds their features. Figure 18-3a,b shows this situation.

Implementation Notes

A possible implementation solution is to group all the feature extraction code into a Manager object [Sommerlad1998]. Three properties of the Manager pattern make it an excellent candidate for encapsulating Feature Extraction. First, the Manager has access to all subject instances. Consequently, it is an ideal place to implement postprocessing. Second, within a given domain, its functionality does not depend on the subject classes. Therefore, developers can change the implementation of the subject class without affecting the manager. Finally, other applications that need feature extraction can reuse the manager's code.

Therefore, the Manager object encapsulates Feature Extraction and indexing. This provides a flexible solution. For example, we can begin without a fancy spatial access method and concentrate on getting the feature extraction function right. Once we're satisfied with this part, we can experiment with different indexing algorithms, persistence mechanisms, and so forth. All of these changes are transparent to the rest of the application.

The feature extraction manager acts as a Factory [Gamma+1995] for subject objects and is responsible for their life cycle. We first use the manager to bring new subjects into the system. Afterwards, clients employ the manager's services to obtain subject objects in response to queries. When a client no longer needs the answers for a query, it asks the manager to discard the corresponding subjects.

As explained in the Solution section, queries that rely on Feature Extraction return a variable number of answers, ranked in order of similarity. Therefore, the manager needs an ordered collection to store its subjects. Since it has access to

Manager	
Create subject	Client
Dispose subject	Mapping strategy
Insert	Filtering strategy
Search	Subject
Iterate over subjects	Database
Map in feature space	

a

Mapping Strategy	
Extract features	Manager
	Subject
	Feature set

b

Filtering Strategy	
Discard false alarms	Manager
	Subject
	Feature set

c

Database	
Insert	Manager
Search	Subject
	Feature set

d

Figure 18-4a–d *Class responsibilities and collaborations*

all subjects in this collection, another useful service is iteration in increasing or decreasing order of similarity. The manager can provide this functionality to its clients by implementing the Iterator pattern [Gamma+1995].

Figures 18-4a–d and 18-5 illustrate a possible implementation. Figure 18-4a–d depicts the classes, their responsibilities, and collaborations, and Figure 18-5 shows a UML class diagram [Fowler+1997]. Separate Strategy objects [Gamma+1995] carry out the information retrieval processing. The `_mappingStrategy` object encapsulates the feature extraction function. Likewise, the `_filteringStrategy` encapsulates postprocessing. This solution provides increased flexibility, since strategy objects are easier to reuse than individual methods. We also can configure and plug them in at runtime. (Sometimes systems require dynamic configuration. Some use several feature sets to answer a query. See Known Uses for an example.) The `Database` class implements the database operations `dbInsert` and `dbSearch`—(discussed later). The manager's `next` and `dispose` methods allow clients to iterate over the results of a similarity search.

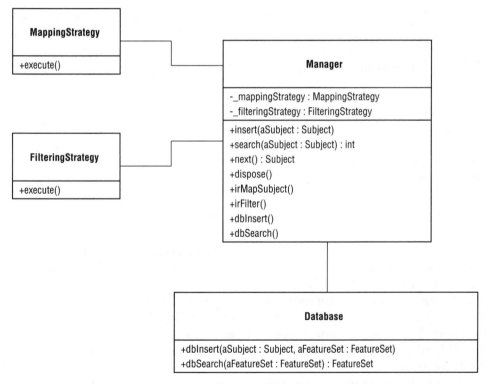

Figure 18-5 *The Manager and its collaborating objects. (The attributes for the* `Database,` `MappingStrategy,` *and* `FilteringStrategy` *classes are not shown.)*

Figure 18-6 shows a client adding a new subject to the information retrieval system:

- The `Client` sends the `insert` message to the `Manager` with the `Subject` object as the argument.
- The `Manager` object responds by sending the `irMapSubject` message. This returns the vector representation of the `subject` object in the feature space.
- Finally, the `Manager` sends the `dbInsert` message. This updates the data store index (if any) and adds the `Subject` object and its feature vector to the appropriate data stores.

Figure 18-7 provides an example for a query operation:

- A `Client` sends the `search` message to the `Manager` and passes a query as the argument.
- The `Manager` responds by sending the `irMapQuery` message. This maps the query document into the feature space and returns its corresponding feature vector.
- Next the `Manager` sends the `dbSearch` message. This message involves a similarity function that performs the search in the feature space. For example, we could use the cosine function to determine the similarity between two vectors. We obtain the value from the inner product of the two vectors—see also Figure 18-2:

$$\cos \alpha = \frac{\vec{a} \cdot \vec{b}}{\left\| \vec{a} \right\| \left\| \vec{b} \right\|}$$

where $\left\| \vec{a} \right\|$ and $\left\| \vec{b} \right\|$ are the vector norms. In Cartesian coordinates this corresponds to a linear expression, since

$$\vec{a} \cdot \vec{b} = a_x b_x + a_y b_y + a_z b_z$$

- Once we have the answers, the `irFilter` message performs postprocessing and discards all false alarms. For the sequence diagram illustrated in Figure 18-7, `irFilter` leaves three matches.
- The `Manager` creates the corresponding `Subject` objects.
- The `Client` iterates through these subjects by sending the `next` message to the `Manager`. This message returns one `Subject` object for each invocation.
- The `Client` sends the `dispose` message to the `Manager` whenever it no longer needs the subjects.
- Finally, the `Manager` retires each `Subject` by sending it the `dispose` message.

In Figures 18-6 and 18-7, all messages that implement Feature Extraction have the `ir` prefix. Similarly, messages that involve database operations have the `db` prefix. All these operations are localized within the `Manager` object. We can begin

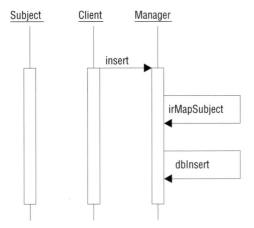

Figure 18-6 `insert` *sequence diagram*

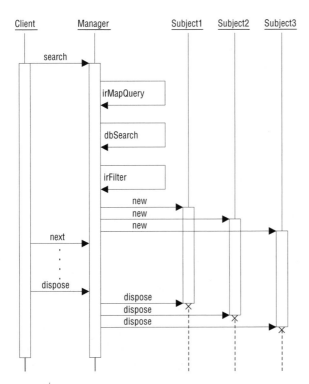

Figure 18-7 *Query sequence diagram. (The messages sent between* `next` *and* `dispose` *are not shown.)*

with a traditional database implementation (only `dbInsert` and `dbSearch`) and add Feature Extraction later, for example, when the size of the database starts to cause scalability problems. This addition will require the following changes:

1. Implement the `irMapQuery`, `irFilter` (Figure 18-7), and `irMapSubject` (Figure 18-6) methods. These delegate to the two IR strategies (Figures 18-4 and 18-5).
2. Modify `dbSearch` (Figure 18-7) to use the similarity function. For example, in SQL this could translate into replacing the `WHERE` clause with a call to a stored procedure that computes the cosine value.

Related Patterns lists other patterns that may be useful when implementing Feature Extraction.

A Scenario

This section illustrates how these pieces fit together with a simple scenario. Since digital libraries or multimedia databases may seem esoteric, this scenario considers a more familiar domain. Bulleted paragraphs in this section refer to the solution presented in the Implementation Notes.

Professional recruiters assist companies in finding matches for their openings. A company looking for new employees provides the recruiter with a wish list. The list contains some qualifications the company is looking for but is not exhaustive. Then the recruiter uses the list to query her database. This query returns all the people within the database that satisfy the search criteria. Since this type of application requires a similarity search, it is a good candidate for Feature Extraction.

To use Feature Extraction, the recruiter begins by studying several wish lists to get an idea of what companies are looking for. The objective is to decide what the key characteristics that differentiate potential candidates are, from the employer's perspective. These are the "features." For this example, let's assume that they are knowledge of three programming languages (C, Smalltalk, and Java) and a modeling language (UML). Therefore, the feature space has four dimensions. Every résumé will correspond to a point in this space.

In Figures 18-6 and 18-7 this corresponds to deciding that

- `irMapSubject` and `irMapQuery` map into a four-dimensional space.
- `dbInsert` and `dbSearch` use a four-dimensional indexing algorithm.

In this case, extracting features is easy. The recruiter scans each résumé and when she finds any of these four languages, she sets the corresponding coordinate to 1. For example, if Michael lists in his résumé Ada, C, Fortran, and Smalltalk, the corresponding vector is $\vec{v}_{Michael} = (1,1,0,0)$. The information about Ada and Fortran is lost.

- Therefore, `irMapSubject` from Figure 18-6 performs a full text search for these four keywords. Once it computes the feature vector, `dbInsert` stores it in the database along with its corresponding résumé.

After all résumés are mapped into the feature space, the recruiter is ready to use the system. Let's assume that a company has an opening for someone who knows Smalltalk (over three years' experience), Java, and UML. In the feature space, this query corresponds to the vector $\vec{v}$ = (0,1,1,1). Note that since the experience requirement does not have a corresponding feature, it is lost.

- The search message from Figure 18-7 has the supplied wish list as a parameter. Next, `irMapQuery` maps this query into the feature space and obtains $\vec{v}_{query}$.

A search computes the similarity between the query and all the other vectors in the database and returns only the ones above a given threshold. Let's assume that they are (in order) Adam with (1,1,1,1), Bob with (0,1,1,1), Clark with (0,1,1,1), and Donna with (0,1,1,0). Adam, Bob, and Clark are exact matches for the query vector and would have been found by a traditional database system as well. However, while Donna's vector does not have the UML component, the similarity function is above the threshold, and therefore she is also a match.

In a traditional database system, this sort of matching requires a complex Boolean expression. Feature Extraction provides a more elegant solution. Similarity matching is essential here, since the wish list is not carved in stone. For example, if Donna is proficient with OMT, her other credentials are better than the others, and she has an employment authorization, then logically she will get an offer.

- In Figure 18-7, this corresponds to the `dbSearch` message. `dbSearch` computes the similarity between the query vector and all the other vectors stored in the database.

Postprocessing compares the original query with the résumés of each potential candidate and returns only the ones that meet the experience requirement as well.

- The `irFilter` message from Figure 18-7 implements postprocessing. In this case, it does a full text search in the four résumés returned by `dbSearch` and discards Bob's résumé, since it does not satisfy the experience requirement. Once `irFilter` completes the processing, the `Manager` creates a `Subject` object for each match. Clients send the `next` message to iterate through these objects.

Therefore, instead of comparing *all* the résumés with the original query, Feature Extraction maps this problem into a four-dimensional space where the solution is simpler. This returns all qualifying answers plus a few false alarms. Postprocessing performs a full text scan *only* on these answers and discards the false alarms.

Sample Code

The following code fragments illustrate how an image retrieval system employs feature extraction. This code has been used in a Smalltalk implementation of the

MARS system [Ortega+1997]. (At the time of this writing, more information about MARS was available on the Web at http://www-db.ics.uci.edu/pages/.)

The addImage: method adds new images to the system. It corresponds to the situation illustrated in Figure 18-6. First addImage: computes all features of the image in the newImageFeatures variable. Next, it updates the index imageRepresentationSet with the image identifier, its file name, and the computed features.

```
ImageDatabase>>addImage: anImgFilename
| newImageId newImageFeatures newImageRepresentation |

newImageFeatures := ImageFeatures
extractFeaturesFromImageFile: anImgFilename
        withTextureNormalizer: textureNormalizer
        withDfTable: dfTable.
newImageRepresentation := ImageRepresentation
representImageWithId: newImageId
        withFilename: anImgFilename
        withFeatures: newImageFeatures.
imageRepresentationSet addLast: newImageRepresentation.
```

In this application, Feature Extraction consists of color histogram, color layout, and texture information. The code fragment that does feature extraction follows. It extracts each type of feature in one of the variables colorHistogram, color-Layout, and texture.

```
ImageFeatures>>extractFeaturesFromImageFile: aString
        withTextureNormalizer: aTextureNormalizer
        withDfTable: dfTable
| image |

image := ImageReadWriter createImageFromFileNamed: aString.
colorHistogram := ColorHistogram
        extractFromImage: image histogram: 8 by: 4.
colorLayout := ColorLayout
        extractFromImage: image grid: 5 by: 5
        histogram: 8 by: 4.
texture := image extractTexture: aTextureNormalizer.
```

Extraction of the actual features is delegated to the Image class. The following code shows the implementation for the color histograms. This type of processing is domain-dependent.

Image>>colorHistogram: aNumber1 by: aNumber2
"returns aNumber1 by aNumber2 color histogram flattened as an array, saturation being more significant and hue being less significant"

```
| length area colorhist quantizedhue quantizedsat
        histindex |

length := aNumber1 * aNumber2.
area := width * height.
colorhist := Array new: length withAll: 0.
self pixelsDo: [:x :y |
  quantizedhue := self quantizedHueAtPoint: x @ y
          levels: aNumber1.
  quantizedsat := self quantizedSaturationAtPoint: x @ y
          levels: aNumber2.
  histindex := (quantizedsat - 1) * aNumber1 + quantizedhue.
  colorhist increment: histindex.].
^(colorhist collect: [:each | (each / area) asFloat])
```

Finding answers for a query involves mapping the query in the feature space, finding all the matches, and filtering out the false alarms (see Figure 18-7). The following code fragment performs the search in the feature space using a distance function specific to image processing.

ImageDatabase>>searchForFeatures: anImageFeatures
withWeights: aWeightArray

```
| index matches |
anImageFeatures start.
searchResult initialize.
matches := OrderedCollection new.
imageRepresentationSet do: [:each |
  searchResult addSearchObject:
        (each distance: anImageFeatures
           withWeights: aWeightArray)].
index := 1.
[index <= ((searchResult size) min: 8)]
   whileTrue:
        [matches add: (searchResult at: index).
        index := index + 1.].
^matches
```

Known Uses

Feature Extraction is not new. One of its pioneers was Gerald Salton. He employed feature extraction in the SMART system [Salton1969] at Cornell a long time before the term *digital library* became a buzzword.

Since most of the information we produce currently is available in electronic form, many application domains use Feature Extraction. These include (among others) telecommunications, multimedia, medicine, and business. Table 18-1 summarizes the domains and the feature extraction functions for the examples presented in the remainder of this section.

1. Korn and colleagues use Feature Extraction to perform ad hoc queries on large datasets of time sequences [Korn+1997]. The data consists of customer calling patterns from AT&T on the order of hundreds of gigabytes. Calling patterns are stored in a matrix in which each element has a numeric value. The rows correspond to customers (on the order of hundreds of thousands), and the columns correspond to days (on the order of hundreds).

In this case, the problem is the compression of a matrix that consists of time sequences while maintaining random access. Generic compression algorithms (e.g., entropy coding, etc.) achieve good compression ratios. However, queries do not work on compressed data and require decompression. The amounts of data corresponding to calling patterns render this solution infeasible.

Table 18-1 *Examples of Feature Extraction Functions from Several Domains*

Domain	Feature Extraction Function	Sample Query
Telecommunications	Singular Value Decomposition	What was the amount of sales to Gnomovision on August 16th, 1997?
Finance	n-point Discrete Fourier Transform	Which companies have sales patterns similar to Gnomovision?
Medical imaging	Shape size, roundness, orientation, distance, and relative position	Which x-rays are similar to Bob's x-ray?
Trademark imaging	Image aspect ratio, circularity, transparency, relative area, right-angleness, sharpness, complexity, directedness, and straightness	Is Gnomovision's symbol sufficiently similar to any other trademark symbols to cause confusion?

Feature Extraction with Singular Value Decomposition (SVD) avoids the need for decompression. This truncates the original matrix by keeping only the principal components of each row and achieves a $40:1$ compression ratio. Therefore, SVD maps the large customer calling pattern matrix into a smaller matrix in the feature space. The compressed format is lossy but supports queries on specific cells of the data matrix as well as on aggregate queries. For example, a query on a specific cell is, "What was the amount of sales to Gnomovision on August 16th, 1997?" The method yields an average of less than 5 percent error in any data value.

2. The financial domain also employs large amounts of data. Feature Extraction provides a fast way for searching stock prices [Faloutsos+1994] and is useful for any other time-series databases (e.g., weather, geological, environmental, astro-physical, or DNA data).

The problem here is finding a fast method for locating subsequences in time-series databases. The system needs to answer queries like, "Which companies have sales patterns similar to Gnomovision?" Sequential scanning does not scale for large amounts of data. It also has a large space overhead since each search requires the availability of the entire time sequence.

Feature Extraction with an n-point DFT provides a fast and dynamic solution. The DFT maps each time-series into a trace in a multidimensional feature space. Since the method considers only a few low-frequency coefficients, queries return a superset of the actual results. Afterwards postprocessing eliminates all false alarms. The method requires small space overhead and provides response times orders of magnitude faster than a sequential scan.

3. Besides handling large amounts of data, Feature Extraction is also applicable for software systems that manipulate complex information. Digital images are a typical example. Computers are good at manipulating the basic image compo-nents like luminance and chrominance. However, decoding the semantics of the information contained within an image (its contents) remains a research issue.

Petrakis and Faloutsos use this pattern for similarity searching in medical image databases [Petrakis+1997]. The objective is to support queries by image content for a database of medical images. A typical query is, "Find all x-rays that are similar to Bob's x-ray." This problem has the following requirements. First, it needs to be accurate. The results of a query must return all qualifying images. Second, query formulation must be flexible and convenient. The user (a medical doctor) should be able to specify queries, by example, through a GUI. Finally, response times and scalability are important. Performance must remain consistently better than sequential scanning as the size of the database grows.

The system represents image content by attributed relational graphs holding features of objects and relationships between them. This representation relies on the (realistic) assumption that a fixed number of objects are common in many images—for example, liver, lungs, heart, and so forth—and "labels" all these common objects. For this application, the feature extraction function considers five features for each labeled object in the image: size, roundness, orientation, distance, and relative position. The last two features describe the spatial relationship between two objects.

These features are sufficient for medical purposes. However, the method can handle any other additional features that the domain expert may want to consider. This approach outperforms sequential scanning and scales well with the size of the database.

4. Trademark images are important elements of a company's industrial property. They uniquely identify the producer of a product or service. However, to gain legal protection, trademark symbols must be formally registered. The patent office has to ensure that all new trademarks are sufficiently distinctive to avoid confusion with existing marks.

Trademark image retrieval has several unique characteristics. First, trademark examiners search for images by primitive features, for example, shape. Second, trademark registries hold large collections of images in electronic format. And finally, in the trademark field, successful retrieval criteria are well defined. These characteristics make trademark image retrieval an ideal candidate for content-based image retrieval techniques.

The Artisan project (Automatic Retrieval of Trademark Images by Shape ANalysis) [Eakins+1998] is intended to replace the Trademark Image System (TRIMS) currently in use at the U.K. Patent Office. This system needs to answer only one type of query: "Given a candidate trademark, is it sufficiently similar to any existing mark to cause confusion?" After studying how trademark examiners work, the researchers concluded that shape is the most important characteristic, and they can neglect other attributes. For example, they register the images in black and white, deliberately discarding color information. Consequently, Artisan works only with shape features. The feature extraction function considers nine features organized in two vectors. The boundary shape vector consists of four features: aspect ratio, circularity, transparency, and relative area. Likewise, the family characteristics vector consists of five features: right-angleness, sharpness, complexity, directedness, and straightness.

Related Patterns

- The manager can return Proxy [Gamma+1995] objects for subjects. This may be useful in circumstances such as when subjects have large memory footprints or are available on remote databases.
- The pattern is independent from the feature extraction function. Domain experts select any function suitable for some problem, ensuring that it produces correct results. Strategy [Gamma+1995] objects can represent various feature extraction functions. This is useful for domains that consider multiple feature sets. One example is image databases for which popular feature choices are patterns, colors, and textures.

- Digital library systems are likely to use Feature Extraction for compound documents that contain text and multimedia information. In this case, components could use the Extension Object pattern [Gamma1998] to provide interfaces for information-retrieval operations.

ACKNOWLEDGMENTS

Ralph Johnson originally encouraged me to document Feature Extraction as a pattern and directed me toward the pioneering work of Gerald Salton. The members of the Software Architecture Group at the University of Illinois (John Brant, Ian Chai, Brian Foote, Peter Hatch, Ralph Johnson, Don Roberts, and Joe Yoder), Brian Marick, and James Overturf have provided substantial feedback on several drafts. My shepherd, Kyle Brown, made additional suggestions. The Smalltalk implementation of MARS was written by Michael Ortega-Binderberger, who also provided feedback and suggestions for improvement. Likewise, the members of the "Mosaic of subcultures" writer's workshop at PLoP '98 provided valuable input. Finally, additional comments came from Christos Faloutsos, some members of the CANIS group at the University of Illinois, and the anonymous PLoPD4 reviewers. I am grateful to them all.

REFERENCES

[Agrawal+1993] R. Agrawal, C. Faloutsos, and A. Swami. "Efficient similarity search in sequence databases." In D. Lomet (Ed.), *Proceedings of the Fourth International Conference on the Foundations of Data Organization and Algorithms,* Chicago, IL, USA. October 1993. Lecture Notes in Computer Science, vol. 730. New York: Springer-Verlag, 1993. Available: ftp://olympos.cs.umd.edu/pub/TechReports/fodo.ps

[Beckmann+1990] N. Beckmann, H.-P. Kriegel, R. Schneider, and B. Seeger. "The R*-tree: An efficient and robust access method for points and rectangles." In H. Garcia-Molina and H. V. Jagadish, (eds.): *Proceedings of the 1990 ACM SIGMOD International Conference on Management of Data,* pp. 322–331, Atlantic City, NJ, May 1990.

[Bronshtein+1997] I.N. Bronshtein and K.A. Semendyayev. *Handbook of Mathematics,* 3rd ed. New York: Springer-Verlag, 1997.

[Eakins+1998] J.P. Eakins, J.M. Boardman, and M.E. Graham. "Similarity retrieval for trademark images." *IEEE Multimedia,* 5(2):53–63, 1998.

[Faloutsos+1994] C. Faloutsos, M. Ranganathan, and Y. Manolopoulos. "Fast subsequence matching in time-series databases." In *Proceedings of the 1994 ACM SIGMOD International Conference on Management of Data,* pp. 419–429, Minneapolis, MN, USA, May 1994. Available: ftp://olympos.cs.umd.edu/pub/TechReports/sigmod94.ps

[Faloutsos+1995a] C. Faloutsos and K.-I. Lin. "Fastmap: A fast algorithm for indexing, data-mining and visualization of traditional and multimedia datasets. In *Proceedings of the 1995 ACM SIGMOD International Conference on Management of Data,* pp. 1163–174, San Jose, CA, USA, May

1995. Also available as Technical Report CS-TR-3383, UMIACS-TR-94-132, Institute for Systems Research TR 94-80. Available: ftp://olympos.cs.umd.edu/pub/TechReports/sigmod95.ps

[Faloutsos+1995b] C. Faloutsos and D.W. Oard. *A Survey of Information Retrieval and Filtering Methods*. Technical Report 3514, Department of Computer Science, University of Maryland, College Park, MD 20742, August 1995.

[Fowler+1997] M. Fowler and K. Scott. *UML Distilled—Applying the Standard Object Modeling Language*. Object Technology Series. Reading, MA: Addison-Wesley, June 1997.

[Gamma+1995] E. Gamma, R. Helm, R. Johnson, and J. Vlissides. *Design Patterns—Elements of Reusable Object-Oriented Software*. Reading, MA: Addison-Wesley, 1995.

[Gamma1998] E. Gamma. *"Extension Object."* In R.C. Martin, D. Riehle, and F. Buschmann (eds.), *Pattern Languages of Program Design 3*. Reading, MA: Addison-Wesley, 1998.

[Kantor+1994] P.B. Kantor. "Information Retrieval Techniques." In M.E. Williams (ed.), *Annual Review of Information Science and Technology*, vol. 29. American Society for Information Sciences, 1994.

[Kay1986] A.C. Kay. OOPSLA '86 Keynote Address.

[Kelly1994] K. Kelly. *Out of Control—The New Biology of Machines, Social Systems, and the Economic World*. Reading, MA: Addison-Wesley, 1994.

[Korn+1997] F. Korn, H.V. Jagadish, and C. Faloutsos. "Efficiently Supporting Ad Hoc Queries in Large Datasets of Time Sequences. In *Proceedings of the 1997 ACM SIGMOD International Conference on Management of Data*, pp. 289–300, Tucson, AZ, USA, May 1997. Available: ftp://olympos.cs.umd.edu/pub/TechReports/sigmod97.ps

[Martin+1998] R.C. Martin, D. Riehle, and F. Buschmann (eds.). *Pattern Languages of Program Design 3*. Reading, MA: Addison-Wesley, 1998.

[Ortega+1997] M. Ortega, Y. Rui, K. Chakrabarti, S. Mehrotra, and T.S. Huang. "Supporting Similarity Queries in MARS." In *Proceedings of the Fifth ACM International Multimedia Conference*, Seattle, WA, USA, November 1997.

[Petrakis+1997] E.G.M. Petrakis and C. Faloutsos. "Similarity Searching in Medical Image Databases. *IEEE Transactions on Knowledge and Data Engineering*, 9(3):435–447, 1997.

[Salton1969] G. Salton. *Interactive Information Retrieval*. Technical Report TR69-40, Cornell University, Computer Science Department, August 1969.

[Salton+1988] G. Salton and C. Buckley. *Improving Retrieval Performance by Relevance Feedback*. Technical Report TR88-898, Cornell University, Computer Science Department, August 1988.

[Schatz1997] B.R. Schatz. "Information Retrieval in Digital Libraries: Bringing Search to the Net." *Science*, 275:327–334, 1997.

[Sommerlad1998] P. Sommerlad. *"Manager."* In R.C. Martin, D. Riehle, and F. Buschmann (eds.), *Pattern Languages of Program Design 3*. Reading, MA: Addison-Wesley, 1998.

[White+1996] D.A. White and R. Jain. "Similarity Indexing with the SS-Tree." In *Proceedings of the Twelfth International Conference on Data Engineering*, pp. 516–523. New Orleans, LA, USA, February–March 1996. IEEE Computer Society.

Dragos-Anton Manolescu may be reached at dragos.manolescu@acm.org.

Chapter 19

Finite State Machine Patterns

Sherif M. Yacoub and Hany H. Ammar

Finite state machines (FSMs) are widely used in many reactive systems to describe the dynamic behavior of an entity. The theoretical concepts of FSMs and an entity's specification, in terms of state transition diagrams, have long been used. This chapter presents an FSM pattern language that addresses several recurring design problems in implementing a state machine in an object-oriented design. A basic design pattern for FSMs is presented; its design evolves from the general understanding of state machine functionality. Then the basic pattern is extended to support solutions to several design problems that commonly challenge system designers. These design decisions include state-transition mechanisms, design structure, state-instantiation techniques, and the machine type. Since FSMs are frequently applicable to areas of concurrent and real-time software, it is useful for the system designer to consult a catalog of classified state machine patterns. The pattern language presented in this chapter covers the three-layer FSM pattern by Robert Martin [Martin1995] and extends the set of patterns described by Paul Dyson and Bruce Anderson [Dyson+1998]. Discussion on nested and concurrent states (i.e., statecharts) can be found elsewhere [Yacoub+1998].

The following section provides an overview on the new pattern language and its relationship to other patterns of state. A pattern road map is presented to illustrate the semantic relationships between patterns—that is, how they coexist or contradict. We then describe a turnstyle coin machine example that is used throughout our discussion. The rest of the chapter describes the state machine patterns and how the example is redesigned as patterns from the language are applied.

ROAD MAP OF THE PATTERNS

The set of patterns presented here constitutes a pattern language of FSMs. Figure 19-1 shows the set of patterns and how they are related. The patterns address design issues related to the machine type (Meally, Moore, or Hybrid), the design structure (Layered or Interface Organization), exposure of an entity's internal state (Exposed or Encapsulated State), and the instantiation technique of state objects (Static or Dynamic State Instantiation).

The extend symbol (we use the inheritance symbol [UML1999]) shows that a pattern extends another by providing a solution to an additional design problem. The double-headed arrow, with the "X" label, indicates that only one of the patterns will appear in the design because they contradict each other according to their motivation or solution facets. The dotted arrow shows that one pattern motivates (leads to) the use of another; the arrowhead shows the direction of motivation. A labeled single-headed solid arrow indicates the classification according to a certain design decision.

The basic FSM pattern (Basic FSM) is an extension of the State pattern of Erich Gamma and colleagues [Gamma+1995], also referred to as State Object [Dyson+1998]. It adds implementation of the state transition diagram specifications such as actions, events, and a state transition mechanism. The Basic FSM is classified, according to the state transition mechanism, as Owner-Driven Transitions and State-Driven Transitions, which are in tension with each other.

For maintainability purposes, the Basic FSM design can be structured into Layered Organization and Interface Organization. The Layered Organization splits the behavior and the logic transitions so that the machine can be easily maintained and comprehended. The Interface Organization allows the design to be embedded into the overall application design and facilitates communication between other entities and the machine design.

According to the mechanism for producing an FSM output, that is, the machine type [Roth1975], the Basic FSM is extended into Meally, Moore, or Hybrid to describe whether the outputs are dependent only on the entity's current state or on the events as well.

The entity described by an FSM has a particular state at a given time. The current state of the entity can be exposed to other application entities to allow direct invocation of the state class methods, that is, Exposed State. It also can be encapsulated inside the entity, and no access is permitted from other application entities, that is, Encapsulated State. The designer will only use one of these two patterns by choosing either to expose the entity's current state or prevent access to it.

Basic FSM considers a state class for each state of the entity, and thus you need a mechanism to instantiate the state objects. State instantiation can be either static or dynamic. In Static State Instantiation, all the state objects are created at the initialization phase, while in Dynamic State Instantiation the states are created dynamically during runtime. Only one of the two patterns will be incorporated in

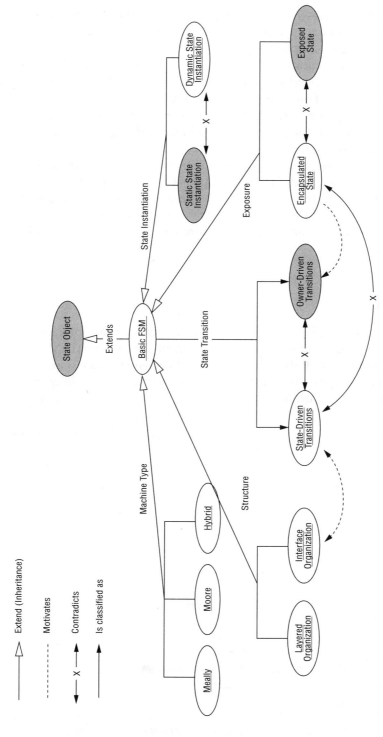

Figure 19-1 *Relationship among state machine patterns. (The underlined patterns are those addressed in this chapter.)*

your state machine design, depending on the number of states, the required response time on state transitions, and the availability of memory, which will be discussed later in this chapter.

Usage of one pattern may lead to usage of another. If you decide to use Encapsulated State, you will need to secure access to the state object; therefore, you may use an Owner-Driven Transitions. Usage of Interface Organization leads to application of the State-Driven Transitions pattern and vice versa, because moving the state transition logic to the states is a step in simplifying the entity's interface to other application entities.

The State Object, Owner-Driven Transitions, and Exposed State patterns are discussed by Paul Dyson and Anders [Anders+1998]. Robert Martin discussed the Static Instantiation pattern [Martin1995]. We will not further discuss these patterns (shaded ellipses in Figure 19-1). Appendix A summarizes the patterns as problem/solution pairs and provides references to those that are addressed in other literature.

EXAMPLE

We will consider applying the state machine pattern language to the turnstyle coin machine example described by Robert Martin in Three-Level FSM [Martin1995]. Figure 19-2 summarizes the machine specifications using a state transition diagram.

The machine starts in a locked state (Locked). When a coin is detected (Coin), the machine changes to the unlocked state (Unlocked) and opens the turnstyle gate for the person to pass. When the machine detects that a person has passed (Pass), it turns back to the locked state. If a person attempts to pass while the machine is

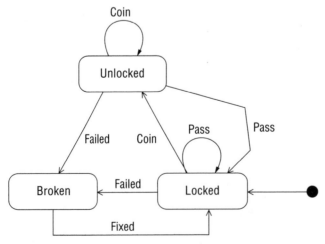

Figure 19-2 *Example: the state transitions diagram of a coin machine*

locked, an alarm is generated. If a coin is inserted while the machine is unlocked, a "Thank you" message is displayed. When the machine fails to open or close the gate, a failure event (Failed) is generated and the machine enters the broken state (Broken). When the repair person fixes the machine, the fixed event (Fixed) is generated and the machine returns to the locked state.

A direct traditional implementation of the example in an object-oriented design would use a class called `CoinMachine` and keep track of the entity's state as an attribute of the class. For each event received by the machine class, a conditional check would be implemented to act according to the current state. For example, the processing of the coin event would differ if the machine is locked or unlocked. The person would be allowed to pass (if it is locked) or the "Thank you" message would be displayed (if it is unlocked). A sample implementation would look like:

```
enum State = { Locked, Unlocked, Failed };

class Coin_Machine {
    State CurrentState;

    void coin() {
        switch(CurrentState) {
            case Broken :    // Display an "out of order" message
            case Unlocked:   // Display a "Thank you" message
            case Locked :    // Unlock the machine's gate
            // ...
        }
    }
};
```

The example above will be redesigned using the patterns presented in the rest of this chapter.

Basic FSM

Context

Your application contains an entity whose behavior depends on its state. The entity's state changes according to events in the system, and the state transitions are determined from the entity specification.

Problem

How can you implement the behavior of the entity in your design?

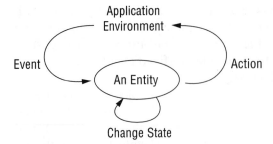

Figure 19-3 *The entity behavior in an application environment*

Forces

- *Understandability of the design.*   The traditional approach of using one class is easy to implement, but you will need to replicate state checking statements in the methods of that class because you cannot make the entity take any action unless it is in a correct state. This will make the class methods look cumbersome and will not be easily understood by other application designers.
- *Traceability from specification to implementation.*   The specification of an entity's behavior is normally described in terms of a state transition diagram such as that shown in Figure 19-2. State transition diagrams clearly distinguish the states, the events, and the actions of an entity behavior as related to the application environment. The implementation of the entity's behavior should possess the same characteristics to ease the traceability of the specification to implementation.
- *Flexibility and extensibility.*   Implementation of state machines using a single-class or tabular implementation would localize the behavior description in one implementation unit. However, this would limit the extensibility of the design. A good model would imitate the behavior of the entity as related to the application environment. Figure 19-3 shows the behavior to be mapped in the design model.

Solution

Implement the entity's behavior using a design model that distinguishes the entity and its states, events, state transitions, and actions.

Structure

Figure 19-4 illustrates the structure of the Basic FSM pattern.

- Construct an abstract state class `AState` that contains static methods implementing the actions taken by all states of the entity.

- Have all the possible concrete classes inherit from the abstract class. Create virtual methods for all possible events in the `AState` class. The concrete classes implement these methods as specified for the behavior of the entity in each state and invoke the actions that affect the application environment.
- Create a class for your entity that contains a current state of type `AState`. Delegate all events received by the entity to the current state using the `Entity_State` reference. Choose a state transition mechanism—the State-Driven or Owner-Driven Transitions patterns.

Example Resolved

How do you use the Basic FSM pattern to implement the coin machine behavior?

1. Identify and create the concrete state classes `Locked`, `Unlocked`, and `Broken`.
2. For each concrete state class, implement the event methods: `Coin` method for coin insertion, a `Pass` method for person passage, a `Failed` method for machine failure, and a `Fixed` method after being fixed. Events are specified as virtual methods in the abstract class `AState` and are implemented on each state accordingly. However, you need not implement all events in every state, only those that are identified from the state diagram; for example, the `Pass` event need not be implemented in the `Broken` state of the machine. Thus, you can provide default implementation for events in the `AState` class.
3. Implement static methods for all possible actions in the `AState` class. The specification shows that the following actions are taken by the FSM in various states: allows a person to pass (`Unlock`), prevents a person from passing (`Lock`), displays a "Thank you" message (`Thankyou`), gives an alarm (`Alarm`), displays an out-of-order message (`Outoforder`), and indicates that the machine is repaired (`Inorder`).

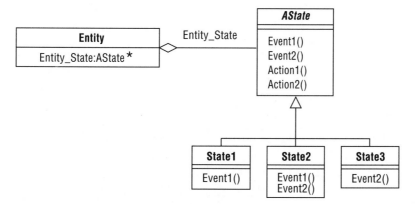

Figure 19-4 *Structure of the Basic FSM pattern*

Figure 19-5 shows the class diagram of the example using the Unified Modeling Language [UML1999].

Consequences

- The design is understandable because the pattern maps the elements thought of and described in the state transition diagram to classes and methods in an OO design and hence eases the traceability from the state transition diagram (Figure 19-2) to a design (Figure 19-4). For example, the coin insertion event is mapped to coin methods implemented in each state to give a particular implementation according to the current state.
- The model of interaction of an entity with the environment, in terms of actions and events, is mapped to method implementations in an OO design that reflects the practical model.
- The model is flexible enough to handle the addition of new states as well as other events. However, as the number of states increases, the design becomes more complex because a state class is required for each state. For such cases, Statechart patterns [Yacoub+1998] can be used to simplify the design.

Related Patterns

The Basic FSM pattern should possess a state transition mechanism that could be either the Owner-Driven Transitions [Dyson+1998] or the State-Driven Transitions pattern.

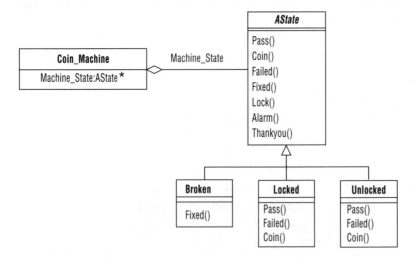

Figure 19-5 *Coin machine resolved using the Basic FSM pattern*

State-Driven Transitions

Context

You are using Basic FSM. You need to specify a state transition mechanism to complete the entity's behavior implementation of Basic FSM.

Problem

How would you implement the state transition logic but keep the entity class simple?

Forces

- *Reusability of state classes versus complexity of the entity.* Since the entity holds a reference to its current state class, you can intuitively implement the state transition inside your entity. This has the disadvantage of increasing the complexity of the entity because you would implement every condition that combines the current state and the event that causes state transitions in the entity class itself. But it has the advantage of reusing the state classes. However, you want the entity implementation to be simple, which is why you first chose to use a state machine pattern and delegate the event processing to the current active state class.
- *Concatenating the event processing.* The entity state delegates the event processing to its current state. If you implement the state transition in the entity, then you have split the processing of the event in two, one for the state transition in the entity and the other for the event processing and action activation in the state class. You would rather delegate the state transition logic to the current state and have one unified processing mechanism for events.

Solution

Delegate the state transition logic to the state classes, make each state knowledgeable of the next upcoming state, and have the concrete states of the entity initiate the transition from self to the new state.

Structure

Figure 19-6 illustrates the structure of the State-Driven Transitions pattern.

- Use the pointer to self `NextStates` in the abstract class `AState` to provide generic pointers to upcoming states.
- The concrete states have to know their entity. Thus, create a static pointer to the entity (`Entity_Ref`) in the abstract class `AState`, which can be shared by all concrete states. The state of the entity can then be changed via a static method

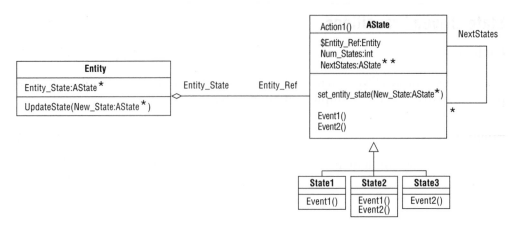

Figure 19-6 *Structure of the State-Driven Transitions pattern*

(`set_entity_state`) that can be invoked from any concrete state class. The entity's current state has to be exposed to the state change mechanism encapsulated in `AState`.

- A variation of the solution would be to modify each event method to return the state for which the entity should change or return itself in case of no transition. This would remove the circular reference between the `Entity` and `AState` classes; however, you have to update the current state of the entity after each event delegation. The first solution is assumed for the rest of the patterns.

Example Resolved

How can you use the pattern to solve the following problem: you don't want the `Coin_Machine` class to know about the transitions from one state to another; it just dispatches the events to the current state object. Make each state knowledgeable of the next coming state; for example the `Broken` class has pointers to the `Locked` class. From the specification of the problem (state transition diagram in Figure 19-2), you identify the transitions from source states to destination states, and in the implementation of the event causing the transition in the source state, you call `set_entity_state` with the destination state as an argument. For example, in the implementation of the `Fixed` event, the entity's state is changed by calling `set_entity_state(Locked)`. Figure 19-7 illustrates the coin machine example resolved using the State-Driven Transitions pattern.

Consequences

- The State-Driven Transitions pattern simplifies the coin machine class implementation as it delegates the event processing to the concrete state class. However, it puts burden on the state classes, which require more instantiation and declaration effort to ensure that each concrete state class points correctly to the next state.

• All the processing related to an event is contained in the event method implementation of state classes. This localization is important for good maintainability of event processing.

Related Patterns

State-Driven Transitions is in conflict with Owner-Driven Transitions; only one state transition mechanism should be used in the design.

Since we have chosen the implementation using an entity's reference in the state class **AState**, State-Driven Transitions is also in conflict with Encapsulated State as will be discussed later in this chapter.

The Factory Method pattern [Gamma+1995] can be used to manage the creation of the state objects.

Interface Organization

Context

You are using Basic FSM to implement the behavior of an entity.

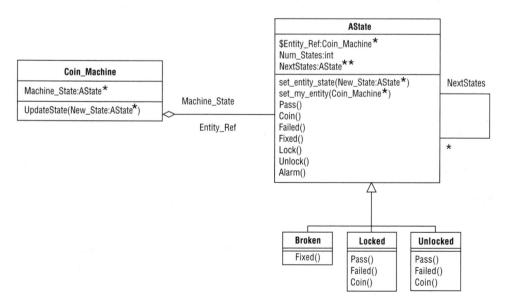

Figure 19-7 *Coin machine resolved using the State-Driven Transitions pattern*

Problem

How can other application entities communicate and interface to your entity?

Forces

- *Interface-centric design.* Your entity may not be a stand-alone design but rather one that is embedded in an application. When you embed the entity behavior design in the overall application design, you think of the way other application entities interact with the entity and whether they keep references to just the entity or they can access its state classes. Therefore, you want to define an interface for the entity.
- *Simple interfaces versus delegation and state class complexity.* To simplify the interfaces of the entity behavior design, consider decoupling the entity interface and the states transition logic and behavior. This necessitates delegating all processing to the state classes, which makes these classes more complex but on the other hand leaves the design with a simple interface with which to interact. Then the interface role is to receive events and dispatch them to its state implementation.

Solution

Encapsulate the transition logic in the states and hide it from the entity interface; that is, use a state-driven transition mechanism. Design the FSM to distinguish the

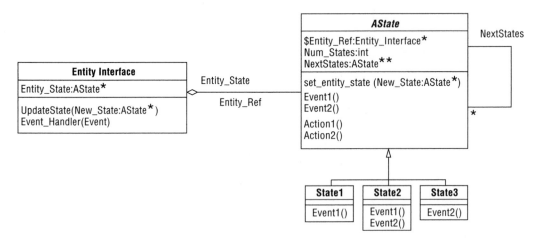

Figure 19-8 *Structure of the Interface Organization pattern*

interface that receives events and the states that handle events, invoke actions, and maintain the correct current state of the entity.

Structure

Figure 19-8 illustrates the structure of the Interface Organization pattern.

Example Resolved

Figure 19-9 illustrates the example resolved using the Interface Organization pattern.

In the example, you create a `CoinMachine_Interface` class and an `Event_Handler` method to handle and dispatch events. The `CoinMachine_Interface` class acts as an interface to the logic encapsulated in the design. The interface knows which state the entity is currently in and thus, it handles the incoming events and invokes the appropriate state event method. The `Event_Handler` receives events from the application environment and calls the state implementation of the event.

Consequences

Using the `Entity_Interface` class clarifies the interaction of the entity with the other classes of the application and hence separates the interface and the actual logic and implementation of the state machine.

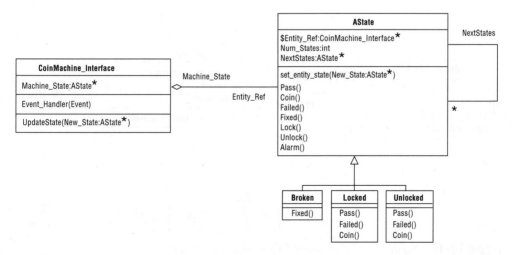

Figure 19-9 *Coin machine resolved using the Interface Organization pattern*

Related Patterns

The Interface Organization pattern motivates the designer to use State-Driven Transitions to simplify the tasks required of the interface by delegating the state transition logic to the states themselves.

Layered Organization

Context

You are using Basic FSM to implement the behavior of an entity.

Problem

How can you make your design maintainable, easily readable, and eligible for reuse?

Forces

- **Understandability of the design.** When you use Basic FSM to describe the behavior of the entity, you find that the events and the actions are all defined in the AState class. For example, the AState class in the coin machine contains a large set of methods; this often occurs when you try to simplify the entity's interface and encapsulate the actions, events, and state transitions in the state classes, which makes them more complex, even in an example as simple as the coin machine.

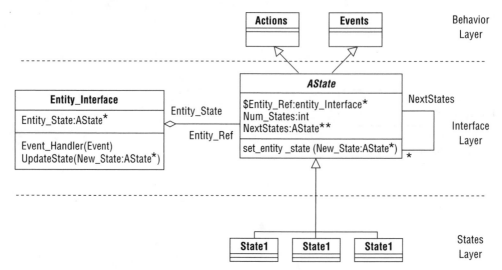

Figure 19-10 *Structure of the Layered Organization pattern*

- *Maintainability of the application.* Figure 19-3 showed that the interaction of the entity with the environment describes its behavior as events received by the entity and actions taken by it; however, you cannot clearly distinguish this behavior in the Basic FSM because both are defined in the abstract state class. This impedes the maintainability of the design because it becomes difficult to distinguish events and action methods and to add new ones. Therefore, you will want to separate the events and the actions in a different design layer, that is, the entity's behavior layer.

Solution

Organize your design in a layered structure that decouples the logic of state transitions from the entity's behavior as defined by actions and events.

Structure

The structure has three layers (Figure 19-10):

- *The behavior layer.* The behavior of the state machine is described by `Actions` and `Events`.
- *The interface layer.* This layer has the interface that reacts to external events and calls the attached state to behave accordingly.
- *The states layer.* This layer describes the concrete states of the machine.

The `Event` class contains all events that occur in the environment and to which the FSM responds. It is an abstract class; the response to each event will differ according to the current state. Thus each concrete state will implement the functionality for that particular event.

The `Actions` class contains all the methods that can be executed in the state machine and will affect the application environment or invoke another event. These actions describe the outputs of the state machine called by event methods in the concrete classes. In many cases, you will have one implementation of actions used by several classes.

Multiple inheritance from `Events` and `Actions` composes the behavior of the machine such that any concrete state class encapsulates the behavior specification.

Example Resolved

In the coin machine example, the events are distinguished as `Coin`, `Pass`, `Failed`, and `Fixed` methods. The possible actions are `Lock`, `Unlock`, and `Thankyou`. When the layered solution is used, the events and action classes will contain these methods (Figure 19-11).

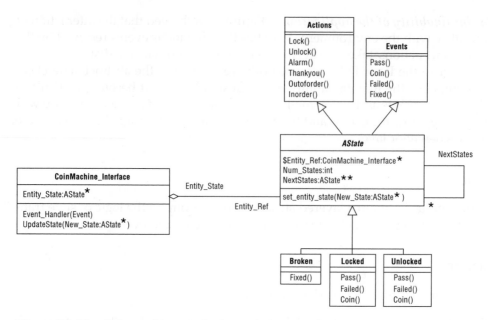

Figure 19-11   *Coin machine resolved using the Layered Organization pattern*

Consequences

- How does this structure facilitate the maintainability of the design? Assume that the designer will change the implementation of the Lock method due to installation of a new locking mechanism. Instead of getting lost in a large number of methods, he can easily consult the layered organization design for the Lock method in the `Actions` class and modify it.
- The structure of the machine separates actions, events, and state transitions, which eases its maintenance and reuse. The multiple inheritance followed by several single inheritances shows a three-layer architecture that simplifies the state machine design. Multiple inheritance is used for mixing [Gamma+1995, p. 16] the functionality of the two classes (`Actions` and `Events`) into `AState` class. This is different from the traditional "is-a" meaning of the inheritance relationship.

Mealy

Context

You are describing output actions of the machine and when to produce them. The requirements specify that the outputs should be produced only in response to specific events that occur while the entity is in a particular state.

Problem

How do you activate the FSM outputs?

Forces

• *Explicit generation of outputs on an event/state combination.*   You want the actions taken by the entity to be associated with the entity's present state and the current inputs affecting it [Roth1975]. For example, the coin machine should produce a "Thank you" message if a coin is inserted and it is in the `Unlocked` state, which is an action associated with the event `Coin` and the state `Unlocked`. In a design context, the inputs are those events occurring in the applications domain; thus you will need to associate the activation of outputs with the event handling in each state class.

Solution

Let the states produce the outputs in response to events. In each concrete state, implement the calls to the necessary action methods from the concrete method implementation of the events.

Example Resolved

In a coin machine, a "Thank you" message will appear each time the machine is unlocked and a coin is inserted, and similarly other event/output pairs are specified in the following Meally version of the specification (Figure 19-12).

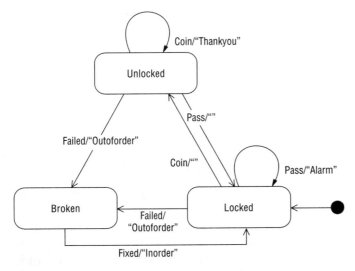

Figure 19-12   *A Meally machine example*

As an example, in the event handling of `Failed` in class `Unlocked`, a call to `Outoforder` will be implemented as follows:

```
void Unlocked::Failed() {
    Outoforder();
    // The Outputs associated with input event
    // "Failed" in state "Unlocked"
}
```

Consequences

Whenever an event is required to produce an output, the output actions can be called from inside the event method of that specific state. This associates the outputs with the event/state combination.

Related Patterns

The Moore and Hybrid patterns are the alternatives used to generate the FSM outputs.

Moore

Context

You are using an FSM. You have identified the set of outputs (actions) that the machine produces. The outputs of the FSM depend only on its current state.

Problem

How do you activate the state machine outputs?

Forces

- *Avoid code replication as the number of states increases.* You could consider applying the Mealy pattern to implement the calls to the outputs, but then you will find that you are replicating calls to these output methods. This is because you want to produce the output for the machine in a given state, and thus you will have to check all the state entry conditions from other states and add the calls to the output method in each one of them. For example, if a warning lamp is required to be turned on each time the coin machine is in the `Broken` state, you will have to call the output routine to turn the lamp on in two situations, one in the `Failed` event of the `Locked` state and the other in the `Failed` event in the `Unlocked` state. This will require many calls to the output method, which will increase as the number of state entries increases.

- *Maintainability of the design.*   You are calling outputs associated with being in a state from the event methods of other states. Therefore, you would rather associate the actions taken by the entity with the entity's present state only [Roth1975]. In a design context, this is translated as producing the outputs on entering the state, and hence you don't have to worry about calling outputs from the event methods of other states. Therefore, you can easily maintain the outputs of a particular state.

Solution

Create an output method for each concrete state, implement the calls to the required actions in the output method, and make the state transition mechanism call an output method of the next upcoming state. In State-Driven Transitions, the machine changes state by calling the `set_entity_state` method. Thus, a method called `Output()` is added to the previous design, which is *specific* for each state and is called by the `set_entity_state` routine using the new state as the caller. In Owner-Driven Transitions, the output method will be invoked from the owner after each transition condition is satisfied.

Example Resolved

In a state-driven transition design for the coin machine, consider that a lamp will be turned on whenever the machine is broken and turned off whenever it is operating in either the `Locked` or `Unlocked` state. A Moore machine version specification is shown in Figure 19-13.

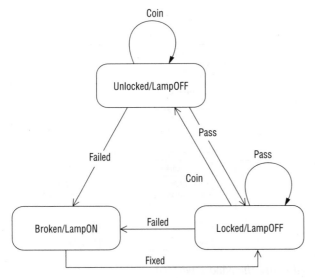

Figure 19-13   *A Moore machine example*

Thus, the Output() method of the Locked and Unlocked states will set the lamp off, and the Output() method of the Broken state will turn it on. The call to the Output() method will be invoked as follows:

```
void AState::set_entity_state(AState* New_State){
    New_State->Output();
    // Call the output of the upcoming state
}
```

Figure 19-14 shows the design using a Moore FSM.

Consequences

The output method of the state class produces all the actions associated with that particular state and hence provides a focal method for maintaining these outputs.

Related Patterns

The Meally and Hybrid patterns are the alternatives used to generate the FSM outputs.

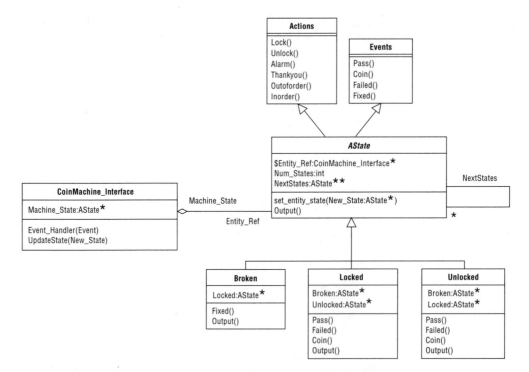

Figure 19-14 *Coin machine resolved using the Moore pattern*

Hybrid

Context

You are using an FSM pattern. The machine produces some outputs in response to events, and some other outputs are associated with the entity's state.

Problem

How do you activate the state machine outputs?

Forces

- **FSMs can be a combination of the Meally and Moore patterns.**   When you consider using a Meally pattern, you will find that some outputs are dependent on the states only; however, you cannot use a pure Moore pattern because some other outputs are dependent on the event's response. But does the implementation of a Meally contradict that of a Moore? As discussed in their Solution sections, they are not. Therefore, you can use a Hybrid machine by which some actions taken by the entity are associated with the entity's present state only (a Moore behavior), and some other actions are constricted by both the entity's state and an event in the application (a Meally behavior).

Solution

Use a combination of the Meally and Moore FSMs. The pattern solutions provided for each of these patterns do not contradict one another and, in fact, can be used together.

Example Resolved

In the coin machine example, it is desired that the activation of the Lamp output is associated with being in a particular state, while the "Thank you" message is generated only on the Coin insertion event while in the Unlocked state. Thus, in the event handling of the Coin method in class Unlocked, the call to the Thankyou method is placed as shown in the Meally pattern. You also add the Output() method that is called by the set_entity_state method using the new state as the caller. The Output() method of the Locked and Unlocked states will set the lamp off, and the Output() method of the Broken state will turn it on as explained in the Moore pattern.

Related Patterns

The Meally and Moore patterns are parts of the solution of the Hybrid pattern.

Encapsulated State

Context

You are using an FSM. The sequence of state changes is defined in the entity's specification.

Problem

How can you ensure that no state changes are forced on your entity?

Forces

- *State transitions should not be forgeable.* The Exposed State pattern allows other application entities to access and retrieve the entity's state [Dyson+1998]. This prevents the owning class from having a large number of methods that are state-specific and state-dependent, but it allows other application entities to know about the entity's state and to possibly change it. This might conflict with your desire to keep the states known to the entity only, a situation that often occurs for safety purposes. This arises when the specification of the entity's behavior necessitates that the sequence of state transitions is to follow the causes (events) only. For example, in an automated train control system, you want to open the train's door if and only if the train has stopped; thus you cannot expose the train state because an external entity can accidentally inject an event causing the doors to open.

Solution

Encapsulate the current state inside the entity itself and keep the state reference as a private attribute. In our implementation, only the entity itself can change its state by handling the events causing the state change but still delegating the behavior to the current state. Thus Owner-Driven Transitions [Dyson+1998] would be used, and the concrete state reference would be private or protected. However, you also can use State-Driven Transitions, but in this case, the implementation of the methods should return a reference to the new state instead of having the abstract state class refer to the entity interface.

Example Resolved

In the coin machine example, the `Entity_State` is declared as protected, and the event handler will not only delegate the handling to the concrete state implementation but will also change the reference to the new concrete state.

Related Patterns

The Encapsulated State pattern is in tension with Exposed State [Dyson+1998].

Dynamic State Instantiation

Context

You are using an FSM pattern to implement your entity's behavior. The application in which you are using the entity is large, and the entity has many states.

Problem

How do you instantiate the states in your application?

Forces

- *Limited availability of memory versus performance.* You can statically instantiate all the states of the entity at the initialization phase as described in Three-Level FSM [Martin1995], but since the number of states is enormous in large applications, this will consume large memory space and thus decrease the availability of free memory. Therefore, it is preferable to keep only a few state objects loaded in memory, such as the current state and the possible upcoming states. This will possibly slow down the state transition process because of the amount of time required to create and delete state objects. However, the number of states kept loaded is small, which will occupy less memory.

Solution

Upon state transitions, load the upcoming state and unload the current state, and then update the entity's state with the new one. This design decision has several implementations depending on the selected state-transition technique of the machine. As an example, when each state is knowledgeable of the next upcoming state (that is, State-Driven Transitions), let the old state create the next state object, and then the invocation of the state change method in the entity will delete the previous state.

Example Resolved

In the coin machine example, if you are required to dynamically instantiate the states,[1] you will add the two methods `CreateUpcomingStates` and `Delete-UpcomingStates`, which are called from an `UpdateState` method of the coin machine as follows:

```
void Coin_Machine::UpdateState(AState* New_State) {
    Entity_State->DeleteUpcomingStates(New_State);
    delete Entity_State;
    Entity_State = New_State;
```

---

[1] In this example, the number of states is small and hence static instantiation is more suitable. However, we used this simple example for illustration purposes only.

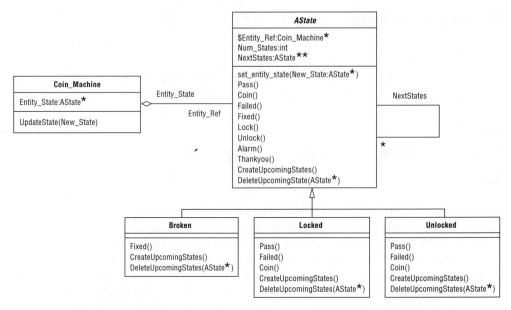

Figure 19-15 *Coin machine resolved using the Dynamic State Instantiation pattern*

```
    Entity_State->CreateUpcomingStates();
}
```

Figure 9-15 illustrates the coin machine example resolved using the Dynamic State Instantiation pattern.

These two methods are implemented for each concrete state to create and delete its `NextStates`. For example, the `Locked` state in our example can have the following implementation:

```
void Locked::DeleteUpcomingStates(AState* CurrentState) {
    for (int i = 0; i < Num_States; i++) {
        if (CurrentState != NextStates[i]) {
            delete NextStates[i]);
        }
    }
    delete NextStates;
}

void Locked::CreateUpcomingStates() {
    Num_States =0 ;
    NextStates = new AState*[2];
    NextStates[Num_States] = new Broken();   Num_States++;
    NextStates[Num_States] = new Unlocked(); Num_States++;
}
```

Consequences

The dynamic instantiation mechanism has the advantage of keeping few state objects loaded at a time; however, its disadvantage is that it slows down the state transition operation because you delete the previous states and create objects for the upcoming states. Thus, the Dynamic State Instantiation pattern is not applicable to real-time systems for which Static State Instantiation is recommended.

Related Patterns

Static State Instantiation is an alternative to Dynamic State Instantiation to instantiate the state objects during the entity initialization.

KNOWN USES

FSMs are widely used in many reactive systems, and their design represents a general problem to be addressed by system designers. They are often used in communication systems in which the status of the link between two or more communicating entities limits the behavior of the above application layers. FSMs are widely used in control systems, such as the motion control system of automated trains and elevator controls. Gamma and colleagues have identified some known uses in graphical user interfaces [Gamma+1995]. Dyson and Anderson have also addressed their usage in library applications [Dyson+1998]. Automated Teller Machines are one of the most widely known and used examples of an application whose state plays a major role in the flow of operations.

ACKNOWLEDGMENTS

We would like to thank Andreas Rueping, who was our EuroPLoP '98 shepherd, for his valuable comments and feedback that helped us to identify the exact problem/solution pairs in the work and to sharpen various sections of the patterns. We are also grateful to Wolfgang Keller for his feedback during the Euro-PLoP '98 pattern writing workshop. This work was supported by the DoD Grant No. DAAH04-96-1-0419, monitored by the Army Research Office, to West Virginia University

REFERENCES

[Gamma+1995] E. Gamma, R. Helm, R. Johnson, and J. Vlissides. *Design Patterns: Elements of Reusable Object-Oriented Software*. Reading, MA: Addison-Wesley, 1995.

[Dyson+1998] P. Dyson and B. Anderson. "State Patterns." In R. Martin, D. Riehle, and F. Buschmann (eds.), *Pattern Languages of Program Design 3*, p. 125. Reading, MA: Addison Wesley Longman, 1998.

[Roth1975] C. Roth. *Fundamentals of Logic Design,* p. 203. St. Paul: West Publishing Co., 1975.

[UML1999] *UML 1.1 Notation Guide,* UML Resource Center. Available: http://www.rational.com/uml/resources/documentation.

[Martin1995] R. Martin, "Three-Level FSM." In J. Coplien and D. Schmidt (eds.), *Pattern Languages of Program Design,* p. 383. Reading, MA: Addison-Wesley, 1995.

[Yacoub+1998] S. Yacoub and H. Ammar. "A Pattern Language of Statechart." In *Proceedings of the Fifth Annual Conference on the Pattern Languages of Programs.* PLoP '98, Technical Report WUCS-98-25. Allerton Park, IL, August 1998.

Sherif Yacoub may be reached at yacoub@csee.wvu.edu.

Hany Ammar may be reached at hammar@wvu.edu.

APPENDIX A:
SUMMARY OF FINITE STATE MACHINE PATTERNS

Pattern Name	Problem	Solution	Reference
State Object	How can you get different behavior from an entity if it differs according to the entity's state?	Create states classes for the entity, describe its behavior in each state, attach a state to the entity, and delegate the action from the entity to its current state.	[Gamma+1995] [Dyson+1998]
Basic FSM*	Your entity's state changes according to events in the system. The state transitions are determined from the entity specification. How can you implement the entity behavior in your design?	Use the State Object pattern and add state transition mechanisms in response to state transition events. FSM pattern = State Object pattern + State Transition mechanism	[Martin1995] [Dyson+1998]
State Transition			
State-Driven Transitions*	How would you implement the state transition logic but yet keep the entity class simple?	Have the states of the entity initiate the transition from self to the new state in response to the state-transition event.	[Dyson+1998]

Pattern Name	Problem	Solution	Reference
State Transition			
Owner-Driven Transitions	You want your states to be simple and shareable with other entities, and you want the entity to have control of its current state. How can you achieve this?	Make the entity respond to the events causing the state transitions and encapsulate the transition logic in the entity.	[Dyson+1998] [Martin1995]
Structure			
Layered Organization*	You are using an FSM pattern. How can you make your design maintainable, easily readable, and eligible for reuse?	Organize your design in a layered structure that decouples the logic of state transition from the entity's behavior, which is defined by actions and events.	[Martin1995]
Interface Organization*	How can other application entities communicate and interface to an entity whose behavior is described by an FSM?	Encapsulate the state classes and state transition logic inside the machine and provide a simple interface to other application entities that receive events and dispatch them to the current state.	
Machine Type			
Meally*	How do you activate the FSM outputs if they should be produced at specific events while the entity is in a particular state?	Make the concrete event method of each state call the required (output) action method in response to the event.	
Moore*	How do you activate the FSM outputs if they are produced only at the state entry and each state has a specific set of outputs?	Implement an output method in each state that calls the required actions. Make the state transition mechanism call the output method of the next upcoming state.	
Hybrid*	What do you do if some FSM outputs are activated on events and some other outputs are activated as the result of being in a particular state only?	Make the event method of each state produce the event-dependent outputs, and make the state transition mechanism call an output method of the upcoming state to produce the state-dependent output.	

(continued)

Pattern Name	Problem	Solution	Reference
Exposure			
Exposed State	You want to allow other external entities in your application to know of your entity's state and to call some of the state's methods.	Provide a method that exposes the state of the entity and allows access to the current state.	[Dyson+1998]
Encapsulated State*	Your FSM should follow a sequence of state changes that should not be changed by other application entities. How can you ensure that no state changes are forced on your entity?	Encapsulate the current state inside the entity itself and keep the state reference as a private attribute. Only the entity itself can change its state by handling the events causing the state change, but it still delegates the behavior implementation to the current state.	
State Instantiation			
Static State Instantiation	Your application is small and has few states. Speed is a critical issue in state transitions. How do you instantiate your entity's states?	Create instances of all possible states on entity instantiation. Switch from current to next state by altering the reference to the next state.	[Martin1995]
Dynamic State Instantiation*	Your application is large, and you have too many states. How do you instantiate the states in your application?	Don't initially create all states; make each state knowledgeable of upcoming states. Create instances of upcoming states on state entry and delete them on state exit.	

*Addressed in this chapter.

PART 7

Patterns of Human-Computer Interaction

In earlier years, the primary means of interacting with computers was with punched cards and fanfold printouts. By today's standards, it was exceedingly cumbersome, but it was all we had. It didn't stop us from wishing for something better, though. Thanks to visionaries such as Arthur C. Clarke, we dreamed of better things, such as conversing with computers like HAL, the computer aboard the space ship in *2001—A Space Odyssey*.

Of course, reality took a different turn. We got interactive terminals, then graphics and mice. Now we have hypertext links and the World Wide Web. And the proliferation of PCs means that far more people are interacting with computers than even the most optimistic prognosticators of the fifties and sixties imagined. Yet with all this progress, computers that are easy to use just don't happen. Careful attention must be paid to all aspects of the interface between the human and the computer. Web sites and other hyperlinked applications must be designed to help the user navigate through them. Updates of graphics can be painfully slow if they aren't done right. Unless care is taken, unimportant information may obscure critical notifications. With so many computers in the world, effective interaction with computers has become doubly important. Computers not only must be useful, they must be easy to use as well.

With the prominence of computers in our lives, it should come as no surprise that this section on human-computer interaction patterns is the largest of the book. Here we have four sets of patterns, each exploring different facets of user interface software. These areas are significantly different—from look-and-feel design to highly reliable systems. Yet there is a common theme to these patterns: the overall architecture of a system can significantly shape its interaction with users. Therefore, the software that interacts with people must be designed as an integral part of the whole system.

Chapter 20: Patterns for Designing Navigable Information Spaces by Gustavo Rossi, Daniel Schwabe, and Fernando Lyardet.

We begin our tour of human-computer interaction patterns with patterns that apply particularly to the design of hypermedia applications, especially Web information systems. The chapter points out the special problems of navigating through hypermedia and gives a tight little collection of patterns to address these problems. These patterns have a rich set of examples, but you will undoubtedly recognize many of these patterns and will have your own examples of them.

The first two patterns deal with organizing collections of nodes based on their context; these make navigating a set of related nodes easier. Two more patterns, Active Reference and Landmark, help keep the user from getting lost in the nodes. The remaining two patterns, News and Shopping Basket, deal with dynamic Web applications providing update information and collecting information such as might be used in e-commerce.

Chapter 21: Composing Multimedia Artifacts for Reuse by Jacob L. Cybulski and Tanya Linden.

This set of patterns deals with the practical problems of designing software to support a multimedia interface. How do you design your software to handle the display of multiple objects? How do you arrange them in a coherent manner? How do you deal with similar collections of objects to be displayed? And how do you present the objects to the user, particularly when objects are of different media types, such as static text, video, and audio? The five patterns presented here help answer these questions.

These are patterns of software design, as opposed to patterns of interface design. At a superficial level, they are independent of the look and feel of the interface; indeed, they focus specifically on the internal software. But the innards of the software manifest themselves to the user in the way interfaces look and perform and in how consistent they are within an application. A coherent software design behind the user interface will pay dividends in increased usability.

Chapter 22: Display Maintenance: A Pattern Language by Dwayne Towell.

These patterns move deeper into the implementation of user interface software. Updating graphical objects on a display is very complex, but accuracy and speed are necessary for display updates. Multiple overlapping objects on the screen make updating them that much more difficult and time-consuming.

Some of these patterns, such as Display List and Painter's Algorithm, address the correctness of the display. Most of the other patterns deal with improving the performance of display updates. It is interesting to see the tension between two of these patterns, Request Update and Global Update. Implementations of display software will follow one or the other, depending on the situation.

Chapter 23: An Input and Output Pattern Language: Lessons from Telecommunications by Robert Hanmer and Greg Stymfal.   Our final pattern language for input and output is somewhat different. These patterns, subtitled Lessons from Telecommunications, are not concerned with screen layout or Web pages. Their domain is highly reliable and available systems, such as telephone switching systems. The human interface is secondary to the main purpose of the system (such as switching phone calls), but the interface is critical for reporting and responding to emergencies.

The patterns in this language address four major problems. First, switching offices are physically large, so IO systems must take that into account. Second, not all input is created equal—the important interactions must have priority. Third, these systems typically generate lots of output, which must be managed. Fourth, during crises, special rules apply. These patterns provide a comprehensive map through the intricacies of input and output in highly reliable systems.

Chapter 20

Patterns for Designing Navigable Information Spaces

Gustavo Rossi, Daniel Schwabe,
and Fernando Lyardet

DESIGNING HIGH-QUALITY HYPERMEDIA APPLICATIONS

One of the key distinguishing features of hypermedia applications is the notion of navigation. While designing the navigational structure of the application we have to take into account the types of intended users and the set of tasks they are supposed to perform using the application. We describe the navigational structure of a hypermedia application by defining navigational classes that constitute a (customized) view of the application domain. This view is defined using a set of base classes such as node, link, and index. Once the navigation structure is specified, interface aspects of navigation objects can be defined. Separating navigation from interface design allows us to decouple the global navigational structure from interface details.

Nodes are described by two types of attributes: content attributes and anchors. Content attributes store the information to be presented to the user, while anchors are the origin of links. Navigational design poses many problems for the designer, such as preventing the user from getting disoriented while navigating and giving him or her a sense of location at all times. In summary, a hypermedia application will be successful if the underlying information architecture allows the user to find what he or she wants easily, without feeling overwhelmed or having to browse through dozens of pages before completing the task. Patterns in this chapter address the construction of sound navigation architectures.

Our purpose here is to show how we can apply the ideas underlying patterns to the design of well-structured hypermedia applications. This chapter focuses on some simple and powerful patterns: Navigational Context, Active Reference, Landmark, News, and Basket. They are part of a larger pattern language that also includes architectural patterns and patterns for user interface design. These patterns can be found in [Rossi1996], [Garrido1997], and [Lyardet1998].

We do not address interface or implementation issues because they depend strongly on technologies that are changing fast (like existing versions of HTML, XML, or existing hypermedia authoring environments). In fact, the implementation strategies for these design patterns themselves generate new patterns (or implementation idioms), which are not addressed in this work.

DESIGN PATTERNS FOR HYPERMEDIA

The first two Navigational Context patterns address the problem of dealing with collections of nodes; they are usually applied together, although we have observed uses of each individually.

Navigational Context: Set-Based Navigation

Intent

Provide the user with closed navigational subspaces that can be easily navigated.

Problem

Hypermedia applications usually involve dealing with collections of nodes (e.g., paintings, cities, persons, products, etc.). These collections may be explored in different ways, according to the task the user is performing. For example, we may want to explore paintings of a painter, paintings on a certain subject, and so forth, and it is desirable to let the user move easily from node to node. Since the defining relation between set members is seldom represented explicitly, hypermedia applications do not generally include explicit links between set members, and thus it is harder to explore them. The usual strategy followed by designers consists of providing an index to set members (see, for example, the results of a Netscape Search). While looking at any given set member, users must then go back to the index to navigate to the next member of the set. Therefore, the attractiveness of the hypertext navigation metaphor is lost.

Forces

- Tasks supported by hypermedia applications typically involve manipulation of collections of objects.
- Hypermedia applications involve traversing collections of similar nodes.
- Elements in a collection are not necessarily related by semantic links.
- Accessing elements in a collection using indexes is straightforward but it requires backtracking to the index for accessing the "next" member of a collection.
- Providing explicit links between set members on an individual basis is cumbersome.

Solution

Consider Set-Based Navigation a "first-class" navigation strategy. Group nodes in meaningful sets and provide intraset navigation facilities, such as indexes and links for letting the user navigate to the "next" and "previous" elements of the current one. When meaningful, provide access to the first element of the set. We call these navigable sets "navigational contexts." In Figure 20-1, we show a schematic view of a navigational context.

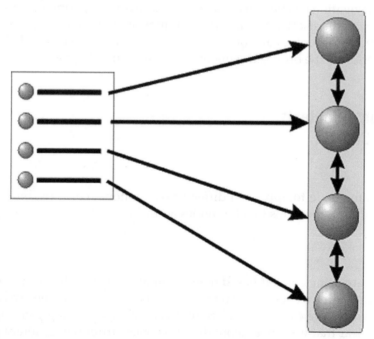

Figure 20-1 *Set-Based Navigation pattern*

Navigation inside contexts complements conventional semantic links, as, for example, those connecting a painting with its painter or painters with their biographies. In other words, the reader can browse through the set or leave it to explore other nodes (or eventually other sets). Contexts are typically defined based on user profiles and tasks and can be defined in many different ways:

- *Class-based.*   Objects in this kind of context belong to the same class C and are selected by giving a property P that must be satisfied by all its elements; for example, "all Paintings on nature."
- *Link-based.*   Objects in this kind of context are of the same class and are selected when they belong to a 1-to-n link; for example, "all Paintings by Picasso." Note that a particular case of this type is the context formed by all elements that are part of a composite object.
- *Enumerated.*   In this kind of context, elements are explicitly enumerated and may belong to different classes. A typical example is a guided tour, such as the one in a museum showing different artworks.
- *Dynamic.*   In this kind of context elements are inserted during navigation. An example of this type of context is the "history" maintained by many browsers.

Known Uses

Set-Based Navigation has been used in many successful hypermedia applications. For example, in Microsoft's Art Gallery, paintings of the London National Gallery are presented in different categories: by place, period, and subject. Paintings in these categories can be browsed sequentially as shown in Figure 20-2.

Navigational Context: Nodes in Context

Intent

Allow the same node to appear in different navigational contexts, modifying its appearance and connections to other nodes according to the current context.

Problem

Suppose we are using context-based navigation in a gallery with paintings. When we reach van Gogh we choose to navigate to his paintings, and then arrive at Sunflowers. However, we can also reach Sunflowers while exploring paintings about nature. It is clear that we will explore the same object from two different perspectives. For example, while accessing it as a work by van Gogh we would like to read some comments about its relationships with other paintings by van Gogh; we

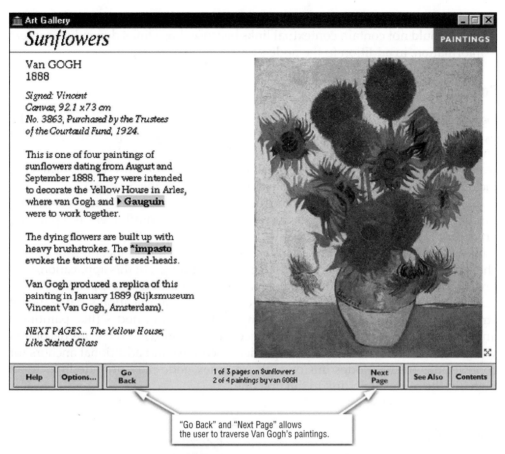

Figure 20-2 *Navigating sequentially through paintings in Art Gallery*

would also like to have easy access to other paintings he painted. Meanwhile, as a painting on nature, it would be fine to read (or see) something about that subject and be able to access other paintings on the same theme (perhaps not van Gogh's). This means that we will need not only to present the information in a different way in both cases, but also to provide different links or indexes.

Forces

- We want to access the same hypermedia component under different contexts.
- Nodes in the same set should be connected with (contextual) links; it is desirable that one can move to the "next" painting in different collections.
- It's impractical and may cause inconsistency to have different objects represent the same component in each different context.

- The current context of navigation is not a concern of the node; for example, a node should not contain contextual links because those links depend on context information, in addition to the node's data.

Solution

Decouple the navigational objects from the context in which they are to be explored and define the objects' peculiarities as Decorators [Gamma1995] that enrich the navigational interface when the object is visited in that context. In this way, Nodes in Context allows the same object to provide different information, including links, according to the context in which it is being accessed.

In Art Gallery, for example, the anchors shown in Figure 20-2 allow navigating through the current context; for example, if we accessed Sunflowers as a painting on nature the "next" button allows us to see another painting on nature. Meanwhile if we reach Sunflowers as a van Gogh painting, the meaning of "next" changes to allow us to navigate to another of his paintings. In this application, contextual information is presented to the reader in the bottom center pane.

Navigational Context shows how to organize the application's navigational structure. Navigational Contexts are composed of a set of nodes (like paintings) and context links (links that connect objects in a context). Nodes are decorated with additional information about a particular context and additional anchors for context links (using Nodes in Context). An index node may provide links to all nodes in the context or a link to the first one.

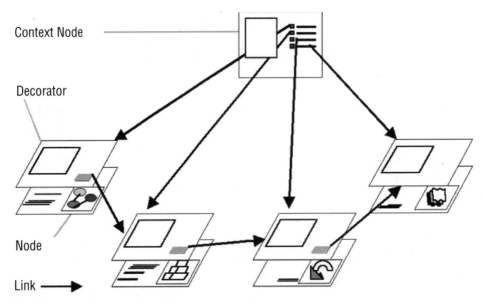

Figure 20-3 *Diagram of Nodes in Context pattern*

Getting back to the van Gogh example, we may think about "Painting" and "Author" as types of application nodes. We will have two possible navigational contexts: theme-related context and author-related context. Accordingly, we will define theme-related-context decorators and author-related-context decorators as defining the pertinent information that a painting will show in each context, and anchors for the "previous" and "next" painting in the same context. A diagram of the interacting elements is shown in Figure 20-3, where the context node has an index to the nodes and each decorator provides an anchor to the "next" node in the context.

Known Uses

As mentioned before, Microsoft's Art Gallery uses both Navigational Context patterns. Navigational Contexts also can be found in the Portinari Project [Lanzelotte 1993] and in MacAuley's "The Way Things Work" [MacAuley1997].

Active Reference

Intent

Provide a perceivable and permanent reference about the current status of navigation, combining an orientation tool with an easy way to navigate to a set of related nodes, at the same or higher level of abstraction.

Problem

In many hypermedia applications, particularly those involving spatial or time structures, we need to provide the reader with a way to understand where he is and help him decide where to go next. For example, in a digital museum, we would want the reader to see the artworks, and at the same time know where in the museum he is. The usual naive solution is to include an index (or other access structure) to the elements we intend the user to navigate. However, this solution requires the user to backtrack from the current node to the index to see where he is or to move to another node, at the same time ensuring that his current position is highlighted in the index. These navigational operations, moving backward to the index and forward to the target, may disorient the reader, especially when there are many choices at each step.

Forces

• Navigation through diverse concepts, of diversified themes, at different levels of abstraction or composition, is known to induce readers to become "lost in the cyberspace." Therefore, a reference to current state of navigation is needed.

- The solution of using an index to nodes on a certain theme or of a certain type provides a shortcut to arrive at that set of nodes, but once the reader is in one of those nodes, the reference is lost.
- The navigation history can be of some help, but it usually considers all nodes at the same level of abstraction without any guidance about composition or theme level.

Solution

Maintain an active and perceivable navigational object acting as an index for other navigational objects (either nodes or subindexes). This object remains perceivable together with target objects, letting the user either explore those objects or select another related target. In this way, we are able to interact with both the index and the target nodes. Note that we are slightly changing the usual navigation style in hypermedia (Web) applications in which departure from a node (or index) closes it, and we can only return to it by backtracking.

An example of this solution can be found at the Web site http://www.excite.com/travel/ (formerly http://www.city.net). As we can see in Figure 20-4, the readers have a permanent reference about where they are located while they explore cities in the world (see Location: South America → Argentina → Buenos Aires at the left).

Figure 20-4 *Example of Active Reference pattern in http://www.excite.com/travel/ countries/argentina/buenos_aires/*

In particular, a reader can choose to go to the region in which the city is located. The pattern is only used partially here, by showing the geographical hierarchy leading to the city (even if the user did not visit all those intermediate levels). A more sophisticated implementation would be to provide an index to all cities in the region. In http://www.excite.com/travel, an index to all cities in a region can be seen when a region is selected, although this reference is lost once one is inside a city. When we use Active Reference, the reader has a perceivable and permanent record about the status of navigation and, in this way, we not only provide an orientation tool, but also make it available while the reader is navigating the target nodes.

Another interesting example can be seen in Le Louvre CD-ROM, in which the user can explore different rooms in the museum from a visual spacial index as shown in Figure 20-5.

Notice that the strategy in this use of Active Reference is somewhat different from the one in www.excite. In this case, the user can see the whole navigational space: both rooms in Région Sully and the whole museum, and can select a new region or a new room in the current region, and explore it. Though this is only one possible way to navigate through rooms and regions, it provides the user with a

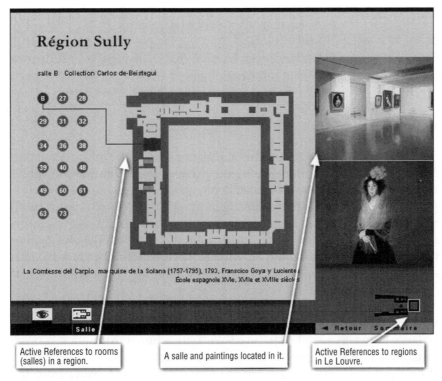

Figure 20-5 *Active Reference in Le Louvre*

complete sense of where each room is located. In this example the user could even get more information about a region (using the Interface on Demand pattern [Garrido 1997]) as well as information about a painting, navigating to that painting.

This example shows an interesting rationale for applying the Active Reference pattern. In Le Louvre we want the end user to explore not only paintings, but also the whole museum building; notice that in Figure 20-5 the spatial structure has been given greater relevance than the individual painting (though this one can be further seen in the whole page).

Known Uses

Microsoft's The Ultimate Frank Lloyd Wright uses Active Reference to show his buildings in different states in the United States. In Microsoft's Multimedia Beethoven, we can access an active reference of the Ninth Symphony. In Grolier's Encyclopedia, the reader has permanent access to a dictionary and to nodes accessed from the dictionary. This pattern is used in the Web as seen in the example above.

News

Intent

Given a large and dynamic hypermedia application (for example a Web site), provide the users with easily accessible information about new items that have been added.

Problem

Most large Web sites are tree structured; this way of organizing the information provides a simple navigation metaphor. On the other hand, these information spaces tend to be large and are hardly ever completely navigated by a single user.

Suppose that we are building a site offering a great variety of computer hardware products (like hard drives, printers, scanners, etc.). In this context, new information may be frequently added. Since most users navigate a Web site neither thoroughly nor regularly, this becomes an issue to be considered because the success of a new product may be closely related to the customer's knowledge of its existence.

Clearly, vital commercial information like this cannot be left to be discovered by chance. Trying to solve this problem poses a design challenge for Web designers who must balance between a well-structured Web site where information is organized in items with subitems, and so forth, and a structure-less, one-level-deep star-shaped navigational structure where all information is reachable from the home page. The latter approach is clearly not desirable because the usability of the site is greatly reduced and may become unmanageable as it grows.

Forces

- Web sites usually grow as new information items are added.
- New information items may be added in arbitrary locations deep within the navigation structure.
- We need to allow the users to easily reach the newest additions since that may be a key to success to our site.
- Using a star-shaped design structure is not a good solution because it may not represent the hierarchical or network structure of the site.

Solution

Structure the home page in such way that a reserved space is devoted to the newest additions and presents descriptive "headlines" about them. Use those headlines as anchors to link them with their related pages. This approach allows the designer to preserve the information's good organization while giving users feedback about the changes that take place within the Web site. The News pattern implements shortcuts to information that may be located in the leaves of a tree-structured site without compromising the underlying structure. Notice that the navigational structure of the application is slightly affected by the addition of (temporary) links from one node to others.

Users also can get to the information advertised by news by browsing the site in the usual way. In fact, as new headlines appear, old ones will be replaced. In Figure 20-6 we show three Web sites where the Headlines pattern is used extensively for corporate announcements, http://www.ibm.com/, http://www.inprise.com/, and http://www.sun.com/. An additional, complementary solution is to add a "newness" indicator (a splash symbol, changing color, etc . . .) next to new or recently changed items wherever they naturally occur in the application.

Known Uses

News is used in hundreds of Web sites and applications, such as http://www.nga.gov, where it is used to announce new collections and the current tours available.

Landmark

Intent

Provide easy access to different though unrelated subsystems in a hypermedia application.

Problem

Suppose we are building a Web information system for an electronic shopping store such as www.amazon.com. By entering the site, we can buy many different

There are several ways of implementing the News pattern.

When several News items are to be presented, they are organized according to their relevance in sections like "Hot Topics" or "Today's News."

Figure 20-6 *Three examples of Web sites using the News pattern:* http://www.ibm.com/, http://www.inprise.com/, *and* http://www.sun.com/

products such as videos, books, or CDs. We can explore the products, and we can follow links to recommendations, comments on the products, news, and so on.

When we describe the navigational schema (i.e., the network of nodes and link types), we try to follow closely those relationships existing in the underlying object model; for example, we can navigate from an author to his books, from a CD to the list of songs it includes, and so forth. . . . We can go from a book to some comments previous readers made about it or read about related books. However, we may want the reader to be able to jump to the music or book (sub) stores, or to his or her shopping basket, at any given moment. If we explicitly describe a link between every navigation object (such as book, comment, news, songs, etc.) to the Music Store, the Book Store, or the Shopping Basket, we end up with a spaghetti-like and difficult-to-understand navigation topology.

Forces

- Hypermedia applications may involve different unrelated subsystems.
- Users should be able to easily navigate to each subsystem's entry point.
- There may be no semantic relationships among items in different subsystems.

Solution

Define a set of landmarks and make them accessible from every node in the network. Make the interface of links to a landmark look uniform. In this way users will have a consistent visual cue about the landmark. We may have different levels of landmarking according to the hypertext area we are visiting. In Figure 20-7 we can see an example of Landmarks in the Amazon bookstore.

Known Uses

Landmarks are found in practically all Web applications, as most have a global navigation bar that remains accessible through the site. In MacAuley's *The Way Things Work*, the reader can permanently jump to Inventions, Principles of Science, and World of Machines, [MacAuley1997].

Basket

Intent

Keep track of user selections during navigation, making these selections persistent to process them when the user decides it.

Problem

Electronic commerce is now a reality on the Web. However, users often want to navigate through the e-market to decide what they will buy and at what moment.

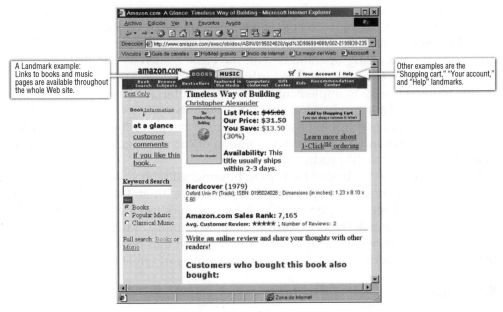

Figure 20-7 *Landmarks in Amazon.com*

In www.amazon.com for example, a user can browse through hundreds of books or CDs and choose a subset of them to buy. The naive solution would be either to ask the user to buy the product at the moment she finds it or force her to bookmark all the products she likes and buy them in another navigation session. It is clear that these approaches are not suited to cases in which we want to buy dozens of different products as it is quite burdensome for the user (and even for the shop) to require one transaction for each product. This alternative also has another drawback, namely, that we would need to navigate to the checkout page many times, thus wasting connection time.

Note that these e-commerce restrictions should not interfere with the overall Web site navigational structure.

Forces

- Selecting objects from a large set for further processing is used in many kinds of applications, such as e-commerce. It is a way to implement the "divide and conquer" problem solution strategy, where the number of elements to be processed is smaller in each successive step.
- Asking users to proceed in a one-by-one basis each time they choose an object may be cumbersome.
- Selected objects should persist from one navigation session to another.

Solution

Provide the user with a metaphor similar to bookmarking, by allowing him to select the products he wants to buy as they are traversed. Provide a "persistent" store for those items (a basket) that can be accessed as another navigation object and associate processing operations with the basket, such as eliminate an item, change quantities, check out, and so forth.

This solution is easy to implement by adding an interface object (usually a button) to every available product in a shopping site. When the user selects this product, it is added to his shopping list. Later the user can go to the shopping basket where he will find either a detailed description of each product or a summarized one plus an anchor to the product page.

In many Web sites the basket facility can be enriched with validation operations. For example, if a customer is planning her vacation with an Internet travel agent service, the travel agent may be capable of doing some checking on the arrival and departure times, on hotel reservations, and on the viability of flight connections.

The result is a very natural approach, since it resembles the way people buy at the supermarket, adding products to their shopping cart while they walk.

Known Uses

There are many examples of this pattern available on the Web. One of them is the Amazon Bookstore (http://www.amazon.com), as shown in Figure 20-8.

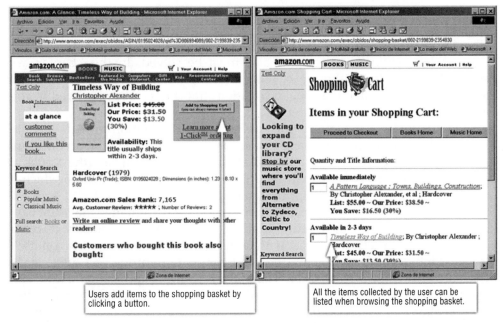

Figure 20-8 *An example of Basket in www.amazon.com. (Customers select a book by clicking on a button to add the current item to the shopping basket. All selected items are shown in the basket page.)*

Another example is business travel (http://www.biztravel.com), where the user adds different destinations to a business tour, together with car and hotel reservations. The system checks, among other things, the dates of departure and arrival from the different destinations (you can't make a hotel reservation if you are leaving before arriving).

A completely different example is PublishersDepot (http://www.publishersdepot. com/), an image bank where the users can search for different kinds of images (based on textures, backgrounds, etc.), and put them on a list, called a light table. Furthermore, the users are able to create different lists of selected pictures that are persistent; the Web site keeps those lists of selections made by a user, and every time the user logs in, additions or deletions can be made to these lists.

MAKING NAVIGATION PATTERNS WORK SYNERGISTICALLY

Defining the navigational structure of a hypermedia application requires not only defining meaningful nodes and connecting them judiciously by reflecting the semantic relationships in the application domain, but also helping the user find the desired information and making him or her feel comfortable while navigating.

Providing orientation tools like maps or shortcuts like indexes is important, but more subtle organization problems also must be solved. In this chapter, we described some patterns that go beyond the simple nodes and links hypertext model and that show that the usual navigation strategies can be improved by following the solutions in those patterns.

Navigational Context patterns such as Set-Based Navigation provide navigation paths through members of a set, thus enriching the navigation architecture in a structured way. When the same node belongs to different sets, the Nodes in Context pattern shows a way to decouple the node from the context in which it is accessed by using the Decorator design pattern.

Meanwhile, the Active Reference pattern shows a way to change the usual navigational semantics of hypermedia applications by allowing indexes or other access structures to actively coexist with target nodes. When the application itself is divided into several subsystems, the Landmark pattern provides a cue to make those subsystems readily accessible from any part of the application. News and Basket are patterns for dynamic Web information systems. While News shows how to make updates or additions easy to find, Basket lets the user keep track of selections and process them all together when he is ready.

This pattern system is complemented with a set of interface patterns that shows how to cope with the problem of designing multimedia interfaces for navigational objects in hypermedia applications.

REFERENCES

[Rossi1996] G. Rossi, A. Garrido, and S. Carvalho. "Design Patterns for Object-Oriented Hypermedia Applications." J. Vlissides, J. Coplien, and L. Kerth (eds.), *Pattern Languages of Program Design 2*, Reading, MA: Addison-Wesley, 1996.

[Garrido1997] A. Garrido, G. Rossi, and D. Schwabe. "Pattern Systems for Hypermedia." Proceedings of PLoP '97, Allerton, IL, 1997.

[Lanzelotte1993] R.S.G. Lanzelotte, M.P. Marques, M.C.G. Penna, J.C. Portinari, I.D. Ruiz, and D. Schwabe. "The Portinari Project: Science and Art Team Up Together to Help Cultural Projects." In *Proceedings of the Second International Conference on Hypermedia and Interactivity in Museums* (ICHIM '93), Cambridge, UK, September 1993.

[Lyardet1998] F. Lyardet, G. Rossi, and D. Schwabe. "Patterns for Dynamic Websites." Proceedings of PloP '98, Allerton, IL, 1997.

[MacAuley1997] D. MacAuley. "The Way things Work," 2.0, D.K. Multimedia, 1997.

Gustavo Rossi may be reached at gustavo@sol.info.unlp.edu.ar.

Daniel Schwabe may be reached at schwabe@inf.puc-rio.br.

Fernando Daniel Lyardet may be reached at fer@sol.info.unlp.edu.ar.

Chapter 21

Composing Multimedia Artifacts for Reuse

Jacob L. Cybulski and Tanya Linden

A multimedia product is a software system or an information environment that uses computer technology to integrate text, graphics, images, video, and audio to deliver information. In addition, interactive multimedia allows its user to communicate with the presentation system to control delivery of multimedia information. Recent developments in multimedia cover such issues as multimedia authoring, presentation and collaboration, approaches to structuring, representation and storage of multimedia information, hardware and software technology to support multimedia transfer and delivery, and more [Haskins1994].

Our multimedia project, Teacher's MATE (Multimedia-Assisted Teaching Environment) [Cybulski+1997], adds yet another aspect to the field of multimedia research. In our work, we focused on the construction, organization, and management of *reusable multimedia components*. We proposed new methods and techniques for handling multimedia and constructed tools that help users of multimedia authoring systems more effectively identify, represent, generalize, classify, store, search and retrieve, select, adapt, and integrate the multimedia components and the processes that manipulate them.

In our research, as this chapter will clearly show, we have adopted terminology that is a characteristic mix of multimedia and software reuse vocabulary. Therefore, we refer to reusable multimedia components and processes as *artifacts*. Some artifacts have a proprietary format inaccessible to our authoring and reuse tools, and hence, they require special software for their creation and modification. We call such artifacts *atomic*. Existing multimedia components can be aggregated with the use of our repository services into larger *composite artifacts*. Artifacts are held

Table 21-1 *Most Important Idioms for Reuse of Atomic Components*

Idioms for creation of new artifacts and alterations of existing artifacts and their parts look at the aspects of	Idioms for showing and playing audio-visual components and for querying their properties look at the aspects of
Creating an atomic artifact of a given type	Determining a set of attributes appropriate for a given atomic type
Destroying an existing atomic artifact	Modifying an attribute of an artifact or its part
Combining a number of components into a new atomic artifact	Checking for an attribute value of an artifact or its part
Combining an atomic component with the contents of another	Presenting an atomic component
Splitting an atomic artifact into a number of fragments	Controlling and interacting with an atomic component
Extracting a smaller part of a large component	
Removing a part of a large component	
Erasing a part of a component	
Rearranging component parts	

together in a composite artifact with the assistance of glue, that is, special data structures and processes that define the layout and the organization of components in their container. Reusable multimedia components can be organized into elaborate arrangements and presentations that can subsequently be delivered to the user over one or more synchronized communication channels.

ATOMIC ARTIFACTS

There are many different atomic artifact types that can be used in the construction of multimedia documents and presentations, for example:

- Text document (in Mac, PC, and UNIX text, HTML, RTF, PostScript)
- Sound (e.g., WAV, MIDI, RealAudio, AU)

- Bitmap (e.g., GIF, JPEG, TIFF)
- Picture (e.g., Windows Meta File Format or Mac PICT)
- Animation (e.g., animated GIFs, QuickTime, MPEG)
- Video (e.g., MPEG, QuickTime, RealMedia, VDO, AVI)
- Scriptlet (e.g., JavaScript, HyperCard, Tcl/Tk, Macromedia, Perl/Tk)
- Applet (written in Java or ActiveX)
- Control (e.g., buttons, sliders, options)

Because these artifacts cannot be directly created and modified by our repository services, we use special purpose software in order to do so. Although the artifacts of different types require different kinds of authoring software, certain services that these packages provide are very similar. We try to capture these similarities in multimedia authoring idioms that could be used to guide the implementation of such authoring packages (see Table 21-1).

The authoring idioms present the details of possible actions, operations, and transformations applicable to all kinds of multimedia artifacts. They provide a useful abstraction for multimedia artifacts regardless of differences in their media, representation, and function. They define the multimedia authoring terminology, and they specify a virtual machine for multimedia component construction, editing, and presentation. The idioms, however, do not offer any insight into the relationships that artifacts of different media types could form, the groups they may be part of, the approaches to their composition, and the methods of their reuse. These issues can only be addressed in respect to the composite multimedia artifacts that are described in detail in the next section.

COMPOSITE ARTIFACTS

There exists a rich selection of off-the-shelf packages that can be used to produce sophisticated graphics, sound, animation, and video, for example: Adobe Photo-Shop, Mixman Technologies' Mixman, Apple QuickTime, and Ulead Media Studio, respectively. An effective multimedia production, however, only can be achieved when the multimedia objects generated by such packages can subsequently be placed into new documents or presentations, and hence, combined into larger groups of multimedia objects. Many of the commercial software products allow their users to group and alter components of mixed media, either directly or by means of various software integration and communication utilities, for example, Microsoft OLE, OpenDoc, or CORBA. Products such as Adobe Illustrator, CorelDRAW!, or Microsoft FrontPage and PowerPoint are at the forefront of multimedia contenders; still, only a few of them consider reusability of their multimedia artifacts as an essential aspect of their functionality. Some address the issue of reuse only in a very narrow sense, for example, by the use of clip art, document templates, or search engines.

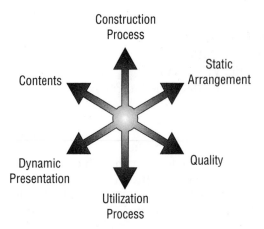

Figure 21-1 *Dimensions of multimedia authoring and reuse*

In our multimedia-reuse project, we defined a collection of multimedia-reuse patterns that address six dimensions of multimedia authoring and reuse (see Figure 21-1), that is, the contents and quality of artifacts, their arrangement and presentation, and the processes leading to their construction and utilization. The resulting Multimedia Authoring and Reuse Pattern Language (MARPL) is currently used as a guide to the definition and implementation of a multimedia-authoring environment that actively supports reuse of multimedia components.

The patterns presented in this chapter address only those issues that we considered the most urgent for the builders of a multimedia reuse tool—artifact construction, contents, arrangement, and presentation. The issues of quality and utilization of multimedia artifacts have not been fully explored at this point of time. Nevertheless, we have identified a number of concerns that must be investigated before we finalize a thorough and complete pattern language for multimedia authoring and reuse (for further discussion, see Conclusions at the end of this chapter).

MULTIMEDIA AUTHORING AND REUSE PATTERN LANGUAGE (MARPL)

In this section, we describe five patterns, which constitute a small part of MARPL, and aim to support the construction of reusable multimedia artifacts (see Table 21-2). As shown in the table, all five patterns address the construction dimension and all but one pattern are concerned with utilization issues.

The first, Glue, is concerned with defining the contents of composite artifacts, and their construction and destruction. This pattern introduces the concept of glue that enables joining subcomponents based on their physical, logical, and temporal properties. Glue can be used as a mechanism for many other operations on composites, for example, addition and removal of components (unglue, add, and glue again), union and intersection of collections (unglue, union, or intersection followed by glue), attaching semantic attributes to artifacts (by gluing these two kinds of information artifacts), and so on. Glue is not concerned with either visual arrangement of components within the composite artifact or parameterization of composites. These issues are addressed by the Components Layout and Template patterns, respectively.

Components Layout addresses the issues of arrangement, construction, and utilization of multimedia artifacts. It describes audiovisual relationships between components. It defines the order of displayed artifacts and the ordering method. Different methods of ordering artifacts will determine the look and behavior of displayed artifacts; for example, occlusion order may allow one artifact to be hidden by another; XOR, AND, and OR ordering can define bitmap operations on the overlapping artifacts; partial orders may enforce artifact collision on attempted overlay, and so forth.

The Template pattern addresses all but one dimension of multimedia reuse: contents, quality, construction, utilization, and static arrangement. It defines reusable templates containing gaps that can be filled in or replaced by other components. Templates also can be used to define controls (as collections of possible gap fillers), forms (as a template with textual gaps), hot links between documents (when the gap is filled in with components of another composite artifact), or hyperlink (a navigable hot link). Unlike Components Layout, this pattern is not concerned with the audiovisual arrangement of components.

Define and Run Presentation covers the issues of contents of a multimedia product, its construction, utilization of components, and actual presentation process. The pattern defines a notion of a delivery channel or a group of parallel channels

Table 21-2 *Multimedia Reuse Pattern Language versus Six Dimensions of Multimedia Reuse*

Pattern Language	Contents	Quality	Construction	Utilization	Arrangement	Presentation
Glue	X		X			
Components Layout			X	X	X	
Template	X	X	X	X	X	
Define and Run Presentation	X		X	X		X
Synchronize Channels			X	X		X

through which the artifacts are sent to display visual information or to play sound. If these channels are connected to the gaps of a predefined template, this pattern could be used in conjunction with Template.

Synchronize Channels is a pattern that describes temporal relationships between artifacts sent through parallel channels. The synchronization may be responsible for starting and stopping video or sound, adjusting temporal position, changing the presentation speed, and so on. Thus, the pattern addresses the issues of construction, utilization and, most of all, presentation of artifacts.

There are many other patterns that extend this subset of multimedia reuse pattern language. Some are presented by Linden and Cybulski [Linden+1999], others have been explored by other researchers in multimedia: for example, Rossi, Garrido, and Carvalho—Navigation Observer pattern [Rossi+1996], German and Cowan—Design patterns for hypermedia [German+1999], Tidwell—Interaction Design Patterns [Tidwell1998].

We opted for a customized format for pattern description. The pattern's context is covered in two sections: Problem and Precondition, whereas forces and motivation are spread over pre- and postconditions. We distinguish between the need of applying the pattern and the cases where the pattern is applicable, thus we have an additional section on applicability. We also split consequences of using a pattern into two sections: advantages and disadvantages. The reason for using this pattern format is to help the potential users of the pattern decide if this pattern is applicable to their situation. They can make this decision by reading the Problem Description and Precondition Sections only. The developer can decide if the pattern could be used in the process of the multimedia product design based on the Advantages and Disadvantages sections of the pattern alone.

We are using UML notation for sample structures.

Glue

Problem

There is a need to join a number of multimedia artifacts into a single composite artifact.

Precondition

The artifacts should be designed in such a way that their physical, logical, or temporal properties match when joined.

Postcondition

The result is a composite artifact (see Figure 21-2a, b, c). All joined artifacts become the components of the composite artifact but they can be easily decoupled.

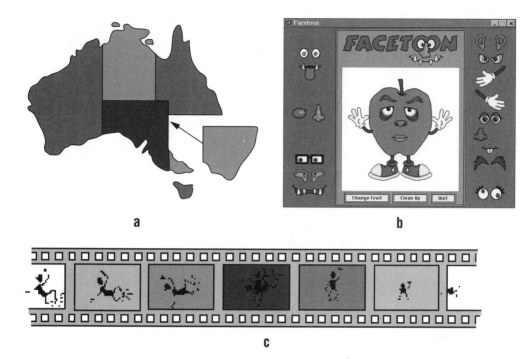

Figure 21-2 *Composite Artifacts "glued" to match their physical (a), logical (b), and temporal properties (c)*

Solution

Put the artifacts together and apply special *glue* to join them into a composite object. The glue also determines which of the artifact properties are needed to match for the components to hold together. If there is a need to extract a component out of a composite artifact, just remove the glue and the components will be available for extraction.

Applicability

Use this pattern

- To create a composite image based on the physical properties of its components (for example, a jigsaw puzzle or a map, see Figure 21-2a).
- To create a composite image based on the logical properties of its components (e.g. photo-fit, see Figure 21-2b).
- To create a synchronized composite sound or video based on the temporal properties of their components (e.g. joining video sequences with fading effect, see Figure 21-2c).

- To extract a video frame from the video sequence (see Figure 21-2c).
- To extract a component from a composite image (e.g. from a jigsaw puzzle, see Figure 21-3).

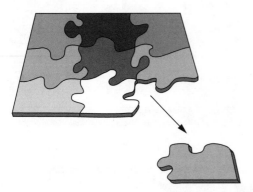

Figure 21-3 *Extracting the required component from the Composite Artifact*

Sample Structure

Glue is applied to atomic and composite components and joins them into a new Composite Artifact (see Figure 21-4).

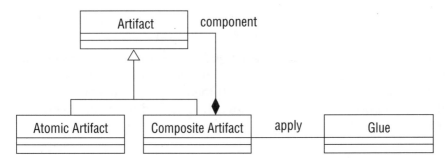

Figure 21-4

Examples

Different types of glue can be found in many existing software products. In some graphic editors, joining of artifacts can be achieved with special authoring operations, such as "Group," "Insert," "Join," "Contain," or "Link-and-Embed." Examples of these operations follow:

- *Group.* Grouping is often used in Microsoft products (e.g. PowerPoint and Word) for creating composite images. "Ungroup" operation as opposed to "group" is an act of removing glue and making components of composite images available for selection, cutting or copying.
- *Insert.* While grouping of components creates a new composite object, insertion of components into an artifact implies that the artifact itself is a composition of its parts. For example, we can insert an image into a word processing document, a header file into a C program, a video into a PowerPoint slide, etc.
- *Join.* Join can be formed with a special bonding object, for example, HTML or JavaScript, Java applet, hyperlink, or video stream. This bonding object is glue.
- *Contain.* Containment can be accomplished by placing objects in the container. Examples are drawing canvas, frame (using Java terminology), or Web browser frames. A container object is a type of glue. A container filled with components forms a composite. For example, in Java different layouts are used for positioning objects within the container, which could be a frame, applet, or panel. A Java layout is a container and glue at the same time.
- *Link-and-Embed.* In all previous examples, the component becomes dependent on the composite artifact that contains it, in the sense that, to be modified, the component should be extracted, edited, and subsequently reinserted. In linking-and-embedding the components maintain their independence. They can be part of several composites. If such a component is altered, the change is immediately effective in all composites.

As containment is of special interest to multimedia programmers, let's look at one specific implementation of glue using Java. In this example, we create an empty menu container, named File, to be filled with menu items.

Filling the menu container with the menu items such as "Load...," "Save," and "Exit" (see Figure 21-5) translates into the code shown below:

```java
public ContainerMenu()  {
   setTitle("Demonstrate container ");
   setSize(300,200);
   addWindowListener(this);
   MenuBar mbar = new MenuBar();

   //Creating empty menu container
   Menu m = new Menu("File");
   //Creating MenuItem components
   MenuItem miLoad = new MenuItem("Load...");
   MenuItem miSave = new MenuItem("Save");
   MenuItem miExit = new MenuItem("Exit");
```

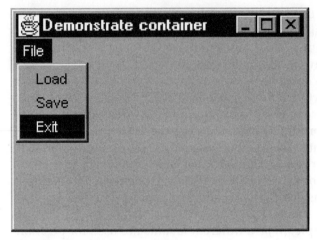

Figure 21-5 *Menu container "file" filled with the MenuItem components*

```
//Gluing statements
m.add(miLoad);
m.add(miSave);
m.add(miExit);
mbar.add(m);
setMenuBar(mbar);
}
```

In this example, we used predefined Java class Menu as an example of glue whose gluing feature is implemented as the method add(MenuItem).

Consequences

The Glue pattern has the following advantages:

- It allows the application of certain operations to the artifact as a whole, for example, resizing, deleting, and changing colors.
- It facilitates matching of components' properties.
- It provides a way of encapsulating components.

Glue's disadvantages depend on the type of glue:

- Altering the actual composition may be more difficult.
- Modifying attributes of individual components may prove to be difficult in certain cases, for example, in some packages, to change the color of an image component or to modify text within the composite artifact, glue has to be removed first (by ungrouping the artifact).

- Glue may introduce components coupling: for example, if a component is linked and embedded into several artifacts, its modification in one composite may cause unwanted changes in other composites.
- The semantics of a component in a group may differ from that of the same artifact out of context: for example, text inserted into a word processing document may change its meaning; added textual description of an image may alter its interpretation.
- Glue may make it necessary to change some of the physical properties of artifacts. For example, addition of text to a word processing document may require massive reformatting; when joining several images, the color scheme of some of the components may have to be adjusted to match the general color scheme.

Comments

Note that Glue can be responsible for a wide range of useful behavior, for example, addition and removal of subcomponents, extraction of a subset of subcomponents, and union and intersection of composites.

Extracting components is easy if a component can be selected and copied while being part of another component, which is often possible with text or image type components. Sometimes, however, to select a component from the composite artifact, the artifact has to be ungrouped first (the case of glue removal as mentioned earlier).

Various types of glue are used in different patterns. For example, Partial Order Glue is discussed in Define and Run Presentation, Arrangement Glue is discussed in Components Layout, and so forth.

Components Layout

Problem

Several artifacts need to be arranged in respect to their audiovisual properties.

Precondition

All artifacts have to be visualized or played and their relative positions can be established.

Postcondition

Multimedia artifacts are placed in their respective positions or they are moved to new positions (see Figure 21-6).

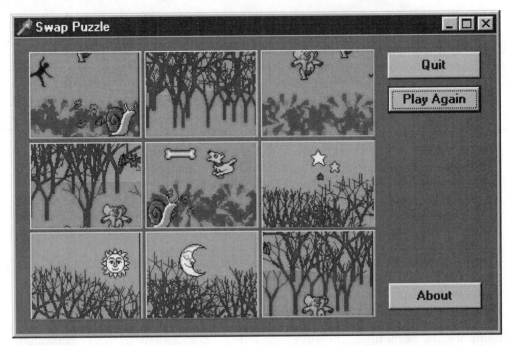

Figure 21-6 *Arranging components in a layout that defines artifacts' positions*

Solution

Compose the artifacts into a layout and arrange them with the use of arrangement glue to associate each component with its position within the layout. Artifact positions can be altered in three ways:

- Spatial properties of the artifact position may be changed, for example, x and y coordinates.
- Associations between artifacts and their respective positions may be reassigned, for example, placing an artifact in a predefined position (see Figure 21-6).
- The method of arranging artifacts in the layout may be redefined, for example, by changing the arrangement glue from the Cartesian to the polar coordinate system.

Applicability

Use this pattern

- When several artifacts, such as text, images, and animation, need to be visually arranged.

- When a template layout needs to be defined: for example, the positions of gaps within the layout are based on the positions of variable components in the template instances.
- When several presentation channels need to be arranged for simultaneous viewing.
- When resizing visual composites: for example, resizing the browser window may require repositioning of text and images.
- When the order of overlapping artifacts needs to be changed, for example, to show hidden objects.
- When the method of artifacts visual arrangement is to be altered, for example, changing from a two-dimensional to a three-dimensional presentation.

Sample Structure

A layout contains atomic and composite components, which are associated with particular positions by arrangement glue (see Figure 21-7).

Examples

- All multimedia products such as slides, Web pages, and text and graphic documents need to be arranged for viewing.
- Many existing graphical editors allow positioning and repositioning of graphic components. The components can be moved across the canvas, or they can be sent into background or foreground; some also allow changing the viewing mode (e.g., design vs. preview, or 2D vs. 3D) or the perspective (one point vs. two point).

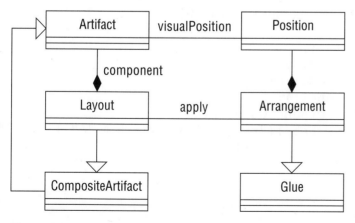

Figure 21-7

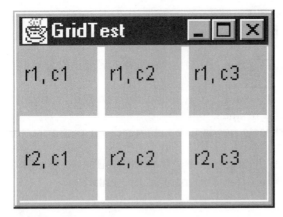

Figure 21-8 *Grid layout as a method of arranging components (panels and labels) in the container*

- Text editors and word processors also allow repositioning of textual components, changing the section's order in the outline, or changing the display mode (e.g., page view, outline, print preview).
- Environments created using Java control positioning and repositioning of components inside the container using various layouts. These layouts are various types of glue that hold components in the composite. For example, GridLayout splits the surface of the container into cells and components are positioned in those cells (see Figure 21-8). In this example, we show how panel and label components are added to the GridLayout container:

```
public static void main(String[] args) {
   GridTest f = new GridTest();
   //Defines the type of layout for the frame
   f.setLayout(new GridLayout(2,3,5,10));
   Panel[][] p;
   p = new Panel[2][3];
   for (int r=0; r<2; r++)
     for (int c = 0; c<3; c++) {
       p[r][c]= new Panel();
       p[r][c].setBackground(Color.pink);
       p[r][c].add(new Label("r" + (r+1) + ", " + "c" +
                             (c+1)));
       f.add(p[r][c]);
     }
   f.show();
}
```

Related Patterns

Template, Define and Run Presentation, Glue, Synchronize Channels

Consequences

The Components Layout pattern has the following advantages:

- The position within the layout is independent of the artifact. This means that changes to the layout do not affect the internal structure of components.
- Arrangement glue can be changed without altering the relative position of artifacts. This allows dynamic mapping of the coordinate systems, dimensions, magnification, perspective, or graphical precision.
- Positions can be defined in non-numeric terms, for example, gaps in a visual template.
- Components' visibility can be controlled either by the existence/non-existence of their layout positions, by their shared positions with occluding objects, or by the visibility property of layout positions.

The Components Layout pattern has the following disadvantage:

- Changes in the layout may force the designer to change certain properties of participating artifacts: for example, moving an image to a new place may require it to be resized, or moving text to a new position may suggest changes to its font.

Comment

Note that in this pattern an artifact's position becomes a visual attribute of the artifact, whereas in the Template pattern the location of the artifact is defined by the gap it is filling or replacing. While Define and Run Presentation also is concerned with the presentation of multimedia artifacts, it focuses on the temporal rather than the spatial arrangement of artifacts.

Note that changes to the layout of the artifacts do not affect the composition of the layout artifact, whereas the modification of the layout composition will always affect the arrangement of the remaining artifacts.

Template

Problem

There is a need to produce a collection of composite artifacts similar in structure and contents.

Precondition

There exists a class of similar composite artifacts.

Postcondition

A composite artifact representing the generalization of similar composites is constructed (see Figure 21-9). It is then used to create a set of instances, each of which includes all shared components and components specific to the instance.

Solution

Define a special kind of a composite artifact, called a *template*, which contains all shared components and gap components. A template can then be used to generate

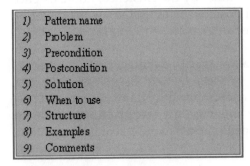

(a) Document outline

(b) Template with gaps

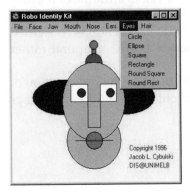

(c) Template with changeable attributes

Figure 21-9   *Different forms of document templates*

new instances by filling in or replacing the gaps with noncommon artifacts. This approach creates a template from scratch.

A template could be derived from a base composite artifact in the process of generalizing preexisting composite artifacts by replacing variable components with gaps (the opposite of creating instances). This base artifact is used as a prototype for a collection of similar artifacts.

There are three ways of creating instances from a template:

- Changing property gaps of common artifacts
- Using fill-in gaps that can be nondestructively associated with new artifacts
- Destructively replacing placeholder gaps with new artifacts

Applicability

Use this pattern

- When a collection of legacy composites is to be generalized for reuse purposes.
- When a multimedia template is to be derived from its prototype.
- When a template is designed in the participatory process that results in multiple alternatives.
- When creating a document standard for the collection of similar documents (see Figure 21-9a).
- When defining a form to be filled in with other documents and components (see Figure 21-9b).
- When creating a graphical object that could be customized by filling in missing components (see Figure 21-9b) or by setting the properties of its partially defined components (see Figure 21-9c).
- When establishing a hot link or a view between a template and another artifact. Hot links or views allow us to associate a component with the composite without hard coding it into the composite. Thus the component can be edited using the appropriate software without breaking the association with the composite— for example, OLE links in Microsoft products.
- When creating puzzles and games in which components have to match gaps in a template (see Figure 21-9b).

Sample Structure for Creating Templates

Figure 21-10 illustrates how a template is created by using a base artifact: variable artifacts are removed and replaced by gaps but common artifacts are kept.

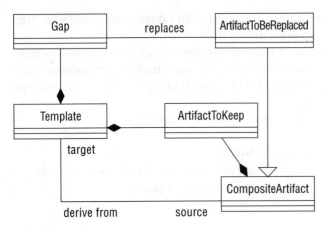

Figure 21-10

Sample Structure for Creating Instances

Gaps in the template are replaced or filled by atomic or composite artifacts, thus creating a new artifact (Figure 21-11).

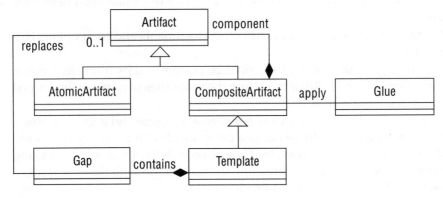

Figure 21-11

Examples

Templates are commonly used in the processing of both text and graphics. They can be used to define Web document skeletons, document outlines and masters (see Figure 21-9a), and partially defined graphic objects (see Figure 21-9b, c)—all such multimedia documents that can be easily adopted and adapted to the new multimedia application. A presentation/slide layout that proved to be effective can be turned into a reusable presentation/slide template. A reusable system documentation template may be designed by giving an example of such a document first and then generalizing it by removing the systems-specific information.

The following examples illustrate different types of gaps:

- Property gaps are used in the example given in Figure 21-9c to allow changes to a robot's face, for example, the shape of its eyes, mouth, and ears. This is implemented in Java using methods of a Graphics object that display shapes, for example, `drawOval()`, `drawPolygon()`, `fillRect()`, `fillOval()`. It's even easier in Delphi in which the shape of an object is determined by the value of its "Shape" attribute, for example, `Mouth.Shape := stRectangle`.
- Java GridLayout, as discussed in the Components Layout pattern, is an example of a template with fill-in gaps.
- BorderLayout in Java splits the container into five areas: North, South, West, East, and Center. These areas are placeholder gaps, which are replaced by the components and resized to accommodate those components (see Figure 21-12). In this example, we use placeholders (panels and labels) to preserve visual continuity.

Related Patterns

Synchronize Channels

Consequences

The Template pattern has the following advantages:

- Artifacts derived from the same template are visually consistent.
- A template generalizes a collection of composites.
- A template groups common reusable components and puts them in one location, which is a single point for future reference, modification, and reuse.
- Gap artifacts preserve the integrity of a collection of artifacts after the removal of variable components.
- Gaps allow live association (like hot links) between two components, for example, OLE links.
- Gaps allow parameterization of composite artifacts.

The Template pattern has the following disadvantages:

- Certain types of glue may require the construction of gaps that match the property of the common components.

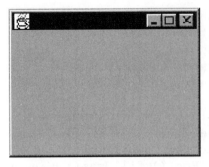

(a) Use of fill-in gaps leads to visual discontinuity (Gaps are hidden in this example.)

```
//Constructor
public BorderLayoutFrame()  {
    setSize(new Dimension(200, 150));
    setTitle("");
    setLayout(new BorderLayout());
}
```

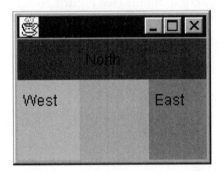

(b) Use of placeholder gaps preserves visual continuity (Gaps are visible in this example.)

```
public BorderLayoutFrame()  {
    setSize(new Dimension(200, 150));
    setTitle("");
    setLayout(new BorderLayout());
/*Creating placeholder in the North
area of the Border layout */
    Panel np = new Panel();
    np.setBackground(Color.blue);
    np.add(new Label("North"));
    add(np,"North");
/* Creating placeholder in the West
area of the Border layout */
    Panel wp = new Panel();
    wp.setBackground(Color.green);
    wp.add(new Label("West"));
    add(wp,"West");
/* Creating placeholder in the East
area of the Border layout */
    Panel ep = new Panel();
    ep.setBackground(Color.red);
    ep.add(new Label("East"));
    add(ep,"East");
}
```

Figure 21-12 *Replacing placeholders in the template with components*

(c) Replacing the placeholders (Replacement components have the same visual properties as gaps.)

```
public BorderLayoutFrame()  {
   setSize(new Dimension(200, 150));
   setTitle("");
   setLayout(new BorderLayout());
/*Replacing the placeholder in the North
area of the Border layout */
      Panel np = new Panel();
      np.setBackground(Color.blue);
      np.add(new Label
      ("Replacing placeholders"));
      add(np,"North");
/*Replacing the placeholder in the West
area of the Border layout */
      Panel wp = new Panel();
      wp.setBackground(Color.green);
      wp.add(new Label("Hello"));
      add(wp,"West");
/* Replacing the placeholder in the East
area of the Border layout */
      Panel ep = new Panel();
      ep.setBackground(Color.red);
      ep.add(new Label("There"));
      add(ep,"East");
}
```

Figure 21-12   *(Continued)*

- Some types of multimedia artifacts have built-in gaps that need to be referenced in a unique and consistent fashion, for example, Windows, XOR groups, or views.

Comments

This pattern is used to create templates for generalization and for creation of static collections of multimedia artifacts. This is in contrast with the Synchronize Channels pattern that allows the creation of artifacts synchronized in time.

This pattern describes the process of template creation and its use. These two activities pose distinct problems, each of which demands a unique solution. Some may even suggest that each of these problems should be formulated as a separate pattern. However, we believe that the tasks performed in template creation and its use are intimately related, and therefore the solutions need to be interwoven. Hence, we present one pattern to deal with these problems.

Define and Run Presentation

Problem

An organized collection of artifacts needs to be shown in sequence to the user.

Precondition

All artifacts are partially ordered, such as hierarchical or network ordering.

Postcondition

A selection of multimedia artifacts with matching logical and temporal properties is serialized so that they can be shown in sequence.

Solution

Plan the presentation of multimedia artifacts by organizing them in a partial order using a special type of glue. Define a delivery channel to carry the multimedia message as a series of artifacts. The choice of presented artifacts can be made during either the planning or the delivery stage. The artifacts may be delivered via a single channel or multiple channels.

Applicability

Use this pattern

- When a collection of multimedia artifacts needs to be shown to the user in sequence one at a time (see Figure 21-13).

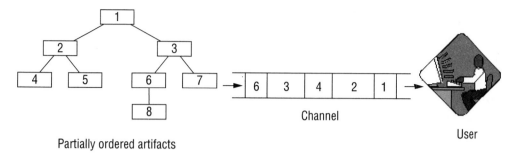

Partially ordered artifacts

Figure 21-13 *Partially ordered artifacts are serialized and sent to the user through a channel*

- When groups of multimedia artifacts need to be shown to the user simultaneously, but the multiple series are asynchronous (so that they cannot be shown in a single channel presentation of a series of composites).

Sample Structure

Each artifact contained in the presentation is numbered and, according to this partial order, artifacts are sent through delivery channels (see Figure 21-14).

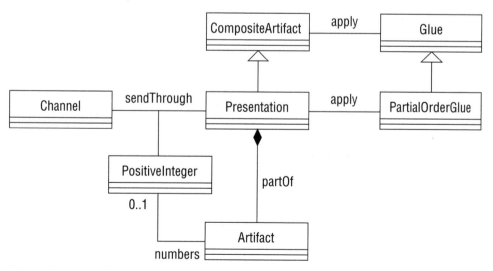

Figure 21-14

Note that in this sample structure the presentation is defined as an ordered composite artifact that is composed of atomic and composite components.

Example

A slide presentation can be given as a series of visual artifacts sent across a single presentation channel. Graphics can be overlaid with sound in a two-channel presentation. A template can be used to design a multichannel presentation of multimedia contents (one channel per gap).

Related Patterns

This pattern can be used in conjunction with the Synchronize Channels, Glue, and Template patterns, for example, to deliver a multiframe presentation of synchronized multimedia components by attaching individual channels to template gaps.

Consequences

Define and Run Presentation has the following advantages:

- These patterns allow a collection of artifacts to be presented that otherwise could not be viewed simultaneously.
- The serialization process may be controlled by either the presenter or the viewer.
- The order of artifacts can be defined either at design or presentation time.
- The pattern does not impose any restrictions on the use of multiple channels, whether they be synchronous or asynchronous.

Define and Run Presentation has the following disadvantages:

- Placing artifacts in one presentation may require changes to their properties; for example, the audio-fading affect may be needed to facilitate smooth transition between two sound artifacts.
- This pattern does not take into consideration the temporal requirements of different types of artifacts; for example, video artifacts may be played while being sent (stream), or they may start playing only after the whole artifact arrives.
- The presenter has restricted control over the viewer's side of a channel; for example, the presenter may send and play a video artifact but there is no feedback on its progress or control over it.

Comment

Note that since the presentation is defined as a composite artifact, it is also possible to parameterize presentations (in the temporal domain) with the use of temporal templates and gaps.

A partial order among artifacts may be imposed by the physical order of the artifacts, hyperlinks, or random access indices.

Multiple parallel channels may be used to deliver truly multimedia presentations, where artifacts of different media types are shown to the user at the same time. The content can be dynamically created during the presentation.

Synchronize Channels

Problem

A number of continuous artifacts (such as video or sound) and noncontinuous artifacts (such as text or images) sent through multiple channels need to be synchronized into a multichannel presentation.

Precondition

Artifacts are sent along parallel channels. Each continuous artifact defines a sequence of temporal positions. Temporal properties, such as playing speed or position within an artifact, can be modified.

Postcondition

The change to an artifact's temporal property in one channel is reflected in temporal properties of artifacts in other channels (see Figure 21-15).

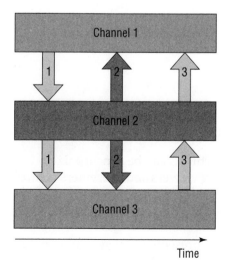

Figure 21-15 *Synchronizing a set of temporal artifacts using a position from any other artifact as a reference*

Solution

For noncontinuous artifacts define delay artifacts. Delays define the sequence of temporal positions within the composites of continuous and noncontinuous artifacts. The solution supports multiway indexing [Buford1994].

- Create indexes of sequences and store them as a synchronization glue, that is, a table of temporal cross-references. The table is used as a lookup to adjust artifacts' positions in every channel to the position of the selected artifact.
- Alternatively, mapping functions can be used to adjust artifacts' positions.
- Synchronized artifacts form a synchronization composite.

Applicability

Use this pattern

- When multichannel parallel presentations need to be synchronized, for example, text with graphics and voice with video.

Examples

- Synchronization of voice with the text to be annotated
- Synchronization of voice and graphics to allow narrative of graphical presentations

Related Patterns

Define and Run Presentation

Consequences

Synchronize Channels has the following advantages:

- In a multiple-channel presentation displayed artifacts can be synchronized.
- The presentation can be interactive by providing viewers and presenters control over channels and feedback on the presentation events; for example, one channel can be used for the interaction with the user and the remaining channels can provide feedback.
- Continuous and noncontinuous artifacts can be presented and synchronized in a uniform fashion.
- This pattern deals with temporal properties of continuous artifacts and introduces the time dimension for noncontinuous artifacts.

Synchronize Channels has the following disadvantages:

- This pattern may deal only with those continuous artifacts that allow the modification of their temporal properties. For example, if we have a continuous artifact that cannot be controlled (e.g., certain cases with sound or video), it cannot be synchronized with other artifacts.
- The introduction of a time dimension and interaction significantly increases the complexity in the planning and delivery of presentations.

Comments

Note that synchronization may be necessary in two cases:

- On the boundary of two artifacts; for example, when voice annotates images, the first image should be delayed until the first voice annotation completes and the second image is displayed simultaneously with the second voice annotation.
- Within a continuous artifact; for example, when video and sound are being sent through separate channels.

CONCLUSION

In this chapter we proposed an approach to composing multimedia products. Our approach emphasizes the reuse of multimedia artifacts created in the process. We identified a number of multimedia authoring idioms dealing with atomic artifacts and suggested several multimedia reuse patterns for handling composite artifacts. Our patterns address the issues of artifact contents, quality, arrangement and presentation, construction, and utilization. They are concerned with composition and decomposition of artifacts, their generalization through templates, their visual arrangement and presentation over communication channels, as well as the quality model dealing with the analysis, organization, and synthesis of reusable multimedia artifacts.

We are currently working on a comprehensive multimedia pattern language and the presented patterns are a small part thereof. We are also involved in the development of an authoring tool that relies on a multimedia-reuse pattern language to produce a high-quality and effective tool in multimedia design and delivery.

ACKNOWLEDGMENTS

We would like to thank our shepherd Alejandra Garrido for her help and suggestions in revising this chapter. We are very grateful to everyone at PLoP '98 and especially to Brian Foote and Don Roberts for their insightful comments and clarification of some of the technical issues in this chapter. We would also like to thank David Kemp for his comments.

REFERENCES

[Buford1994] J.F.K. Buford. "Multimedia Systems." New York: ACM Press, 1994.

[Cybulski+1997] J.L. Cybulski and M. Mackowiak. "Teacher's MATE: Multimedia Assisted Teaching Environment." In *"Doing IT at Melbourne" Symposium*, pp. 56–61. University of Melbourne, 1997.

[German+1999] D.M. German and D.D. Cowan. "Three Hypermedia Design Patterns." In *Tenth ACM Conference on Hypertext and Hypermedia*. Darmstadt, Germany, 1999.

[Haskins1994] D. Haskins. "The Complete Idiot's Guide to Multimedia." Indianapolis: Alpha Books, 1994.

[Linden+1999] T. Linden and J.L. Cybulski. "MARPL: Multimedia Authoring and Reuse Pattern Language," Research Report, University of Melbourne, Department of Information Systems, 1999.

[Rossi+1996] G. Rossi, A. Garrido, and S. Carvalho. "Design Patterns for Object-Oriented Hypermedia Applications." In J.M. Vlissides, J.O. Coplien, and N.L. Kerth (eds.), *Pattern Languages of Program Design 2*, pp. 177–191. Reading, MA: Addison-Wesley, 1996.

[Tidwell1998] J. Tidwell. (1988): "Interaction Design Patterns." Available: http://www.mit.edu/~jtidwell/interaction_ patterns.html.

Jacob Cybulski can be reached at j.cybulski@dis.unimelb.edu.au.

Tanya Linden can be reached at t.linden@dis.unimelb.edu.au/staff/tanya.

Chapter 22

Display Maintenance: A Pattern Language

Dwayne Towell

Maintaining a display involves the correct and timely rendering of a virtual environment on a physical device. Accuracy and speed are important because the extent to which the user can experience the virtual environment is limited to the interface actually presented. If the presentation fails, the user is confronted with a discontinuity in the virtual environment and the experience suffers. If the presentation lags behind the user, again the experience suffers. Speed and accuracy are not simple goals, so together they demand complex solutions.

The Display Maintenance pattern language describes proven solutions to a variety of display update problems of graphical interfaces on products from games to desktops. These patterns capture experience from many operating systems and application frameworks. Although engineers developing these types of architectures will receive the most benefit from them, understanding the display strategies that have become so common should be beneficial to everyone.

Display Maintenance contains nine patterns. Display List, Request Update or Global Update, and Painter's Algorithm form the kernel of the language as shown in Figure 22-1. Although they are independently applicable, together these patterns have a synergy that is worth more than their parts. Request Update and Global Update describe different solutions to the problem of when and what to redraw. The other patterns describe optimizations that can improve the user experience if resources such as rendering time are scarce. All improve speed or perceived speed except Double Buffer, which improves the visual effects of Painter's Algorithm. A summary of each problem-solution pair is listed in Table 22-1.

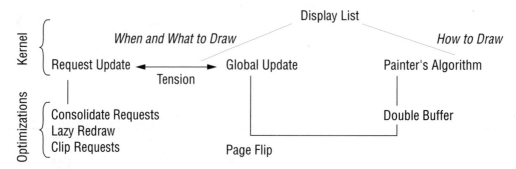

Figure 22-1 *Display Maintenance overview*

Table 22-1 *Display Maintenance Problem-Solution Pairs*

Pattern	Problem	Solution
Display List	Visible component occlusion is important, yet should not be a burden to the components.	Maintain a list of all visual components; let order dictate occlusion.
Request Update	Visual components may be occluded by others, complicating display updates.	Request display update rather than redraw directly.
Global Update	Tracking many update requests can be inefficient.	Assume the entire display should be redrawn.
Painter's Algorithm	Rendering with correct occlusion requires significant knowledge.	Draw all components, "back to front".
Consolidate Requests	Processing individual update requests from user events can be unexpected and is inefficient.	Consolidate update requests generated by a single user event.
Lazy Redraw	Multiple redraws may hinder interaction and are inefficient.	Postpone redraws until time allows.
Clip Requests	Updating hidden regions is unnecessary and inefficient.	Exclude opaque foreground regions from update requests.
Double Buffer	Updating components directly to the display causes display "flicker".	Render to a hidden display, then use a single operation to update the display.
Page Flip	Copying the entire Double Buffer is inefficient.	Swap the active display buffer.

THE PATTERNS

Display List

Visible component occlusion is important to graphical presentation, yet these components should not have to know about occlusion.

Many graphical interfaces rely on depth cues to provide feedback to the user. Important objects such as the current document, active tool set, or dialogs appear "above" other currently less important interface components. This allows efficient use of screen real estate. A common way to generate an illusion of depth is that foreground objects cover background ones. This occlusion allows work to be sorted and tools to be organized.

Adding or changing visible objects, such as a view object from a Model-View-Controller architecture [Krasner1988], may directly affect other objects. For example, when a dialog box covers an active video, the real-time video component must avoid corrupting the dialog's display real estate. This requires the video component to know how to avoid the dialog box. This could be solved by assuming that dialogs always occlude video, then a static relationship between object types could be enforced. On the other hand, if this assumption cannot be made, dynamic relationships must be established and maintained. This is the case with document windows. As the user "pulls" each window forward, it occludes any windows "behind" it to give the illusion of depth.

New collaborations between existing types or new object types exacerbate the problem even more. When these new collaborations are established object definitions must be updated. This added overhead in both the object definition and the runtime organization obfuscates the primary task.

Therefore:

Maintain a list of all visual components; let order dictate occlusion.

Require visual components to be inserted into the display list in order to be added to the interface. Items covered by another object have positions later in the list, while items covering it occur earlier in the list. Each individual component is no longer responsible for its intercomponent property of occlusion; that responsibility has been moved to the list.

As new object types are created, no existing type relationships need be updated. As new components are added at runtime, no private intercomponent relationship needs to be updated, only the public list. If depth cues change, the list can be reordered.

Consequences

Display List extracts "visual depth" from an architecture and encodes it in a data structure. This allows questions such as "am-I-in-front?" and "what-is-the-mouse-over?" to be answered. It also allows the concept of depth to be well represented within an architecture. Interobject coupling is reduced, which increases object independence. Display List requires all visible objects to be publicly acknowledged; objects are not allowed to access the display unless they are included in the list. Maintaining the list increases development cost as well as runtime costs.

Known Uses

Most desktop environments use Display List. For example, Microsoft Windows includes a system-managed list of windows (HWNDs). Many drawing programs expose Display Lists through their user interface via features like bring-forward and push-behind. Macromind's Director worksheets represent a type of two-dimensional Display List: vertical is depth and horizontal is time.

Related Patterns

Painter's Algorithm is typically used to render a Display List. Request Update can be used to decide when rendering should occur. Display List is a specialization of Collection Object [Noble1999]. Very expressive, hierarchical displays can be developed if each visible object is a component of a Composite [Gamma+1995, p. 163] object.

Request Update

Visual components may be occluded by others, complicating display updates.

If visual components overlap in predictable ways, updating the display can be relatively simple. For example, an object moving across a static background might simply redraw the background as it moves. Of course this requires the object to know about the background. Alternatively, a component moving across a background composed of several images might take a "snapshot" of the display before drawing itself. When the component moves, it restores the saved image to the display, takes a snapshot of the new location, and redraws itself. In neither case, however, is the background allowed to change.

The interactions between otherwise independent components complicate display updates. They force components to know details of their environment that they would not normally need to know.

Even worse, if components overlap in complex and unpredictable ways, updating the display can be very difficult. For example, when a component "behind" another changes, only the visible parts should be updated until the foreground component no longer occludes it.

Requiring this level of intercomponent negotiation complicates not only display updates, but design, implementation, and maintenance as well.

Therefore:

Request display update rather than redraw directly.

As time or events force a component to change, it modifies its internal state, but does not actually perform a display update. Instead, it posts a request to update the display, usually including information about the area suspected to be out of date.

For example, a moving ball might periodically update its location and then request a display update of its previous and current locations. When the system redraws the display, it can guarantee that the area once occupied by the ball will be updated with any items behind it. Likewise, the ball will be drawn in its new location.

Consequences

Request Update requires visible objects be able to redraw upon request. If "race" conditions can occur, such as state changes during redraw requests, additional state information may be required.

Request Update decouples the invoking objects from the resolving subsystem. This improves design, but can severely impact performance over a functionally equivalent (monolithic) design that requires each object to know all related objects.

Known Uses

Microsoft Windows uses `InvalidateRect()` and related functions to invoke a Request Update. Windows receive a `WM_PAINT` message when requested to redraw. HotDraw `Figures` use Request Update to invalidate the view when their state changes.

Related Patterns

Display List typically provides the context for honoring update requests. Usually, Consolidate Requests, Lazy Redraw, and Clip Requests are used to improve efficiency. Global Update is an alternative.

Global Update

Tracking many update requests is inefficient.

For many games and presentation products display requests occur regularly, and include much, if not all, of the display. In these cases applying Consolidate Updates and Clip Requests may actually hinder performance. Each update cycle includes the overhead to clip requests against opaque areas and maintain an "invalid" region. Even the effort to clip redraws against the "invalid" region can dramatically drain resources needed for the primary task—presenting a rich visual experience.

Therefore:

Update the entire display.

Instead of tracking update requests individually, force updates to rerender the entire display. Not only does this eliminate the slow maintenance algorithms from the application, it also allows rendering to more easily be optimized. Since drawing is no longer constrained by clip regions, rendering is simpler and can usually be optimized.

Consequences

Global Update trades finesse for brute force. In doing so it radically changes performance by redefining the bottlenecks. Hardware bandwidth replaces maintenance overhead, which may be appropriate if hardware is cheaper than engineering costs. It also allows a single path through the application to be fully optimized.

Known Uses

Television, Sega, Nintendo, and many other game products use Global Update to improve performance.

Related Patterns

Global Update is a requirement for Page Flip. Request Update is an alternative.

Painter's Algorithm

Rendering a single visual component with correct occlusion requires significant inter-object knowledge of boundaries.

Using depth as an interface element requires that each visual object be subject to arbitrarily complex visibility boundaries. For example, in desktop environments the desktop itself is simply another visual object and must always appear "behind" other objects. Updating an object's appearance requires determining its visibility boundaries. This, in turn, requires all objects to report their exact boundaries in some globally defined format. Although possible, this is generally not practical in light of text and other complex shapes. Assuming boundaries can be determined, all objects are then required to support complex display restrictions to prevent incorrectly occluding other objects.

If objects can be translucent, boundary information is not enough. Image data for partially occluded objects must be available for blending with the "foreground" image. This allows the background objects to appear visible "through" the foreground object.

Therefore:

Draw all components, without regard to occlusion, "back to front."

Similar to the way an oil painter might fill a canvas, Painter's Algorithm applies each object to the display from "back to front." This allows each visual object to replace any part of the image "behind" it. Because all objects are guaranteed to be drawn in order, each object need only be responsible for its own update mechanism. Update boundary management is eliminated because all occluded areas will have been correctly overwritten. Translucent objects not only replace covered images, they change them.

Consequences

Painter's Algorithm requires the display to be rewritable, and in the case of translucent drawing (blending an image with the pixels "behind" it), that it be readable. Painter's Algorithm also imposes a heavy penalty: display update cost. Completely updating all visible objects can be time-consuming and wasteful. Fortunately, several Display Maintenance patterns provide optimizations.

Known Uses

Netscape and many other Web browsers use Painter's Algorithm to ensure proper occlusion. When the background image changes, usually because it has (finally) been downloaded, the entire browser display region is redrawn. Microsoft Windows uses Painter's Algorithm when updating the display if computing an appropriate "clipping region" is too expensive. HotDraw [Johnson1992] uses Painter's Algorithm within `Drawing`.

Related Patterns

Painter's Algorithm is usually implemented on a Display List. If all visual objects are completely known at design time (unlikely, but possible in some game environments) Display List is not required.

Painter's Algorithm can be thought of as a Chain of Responsibility [Gamma+1995, p. 223] for updating the display—each visual in turn is given the "update the display" responsibility. As with all Chains of Responsibility, coupling is reduced at the expense of cooperative receipt.

Double Buffer can be used to reduce display "flicker" normally generated by Painter's Algorithm. This is especially true when objects are deeply layered, have complex boundaries, and/or are translucent.

Consolidate Requests

Processing individual update requests from user events can be unexpected and is inefficient.

User events make changes to the virtual environment represented by the display. Even though these operations are perceived as single actions, several objects may be affected. For example, changing a desktop property might affect all the desktop icons. Internally each item must be updated in turn, but they should update nearly simultaneously to allow the user to perceive them as a single operation.

When updating many items it is desirable to pay overhead costs only once. Several things contribute to high redraw overhead. A large number of objects increases iteration and caching costs. Determining each object's relevancy can expensive, as in the case of a CAD application. Certainly, re-rendering any object penalizes an application. If redraw overhead is high, performing multiple redraws can severely impact the application as a whole.

Therefore:

Consolidate update requests generated by a single user event.

As update requests are made, instead of performing each update immediately, merge the request with any previous requests. The merger produces a running "invalid" region to be updated later. After all updates have been made, redraw the display satisfying all requests at the same time. This not only results in all updates happening rapidly, but also reduces the total cost by eliminating much overhead.

For example, changing the global desktop icon size forces each icon to be resized, which in turn forces each icon to generate an update request. As each request is made, it is accumulated until processing the change request is complete. Then the entire invalid region is redrawn at once.

Consequences

Consolidate Requests postpones fulfillment of requests while the system is in transition. This can improve the user's perception of the virtual environment being modeled. On the other hand, if transition times are lengthy, it can give the appearance that the system has failed to respond.

Known Uses

Microsoft Windows, the Macintosh operating system and HotDraw use Consolidate Requests to organize and optimize redrawing.

Related Patterns

Consolidate Requests is an optimization of Request Update. Consolidate Requests is also known as Collect Damage [Beck1994].

Lazy Redraw

Consecutive, similar redraws may hinder interaction due to unreasonable performance demands.

As long as redraws can be performed as fast as requested, the virtual environment interacts well with the user. When events require redraws more frequently than possible, the illusion of a virtual environment breaks down, as the display becomes unresponsive. Performance demand is the product of frequency and size. Frequent requests occur due to user actions, such as window resizing on a desktop, or application-generated events, such as in games. The number, size, and complexity of elements directly affects the update performance. Since the virtual environment is designed for interaction a compromise must be reached.

Therefore:

Postpone redraws until time allows.

Although the display provides a view of the virtual environment, the user actually interacts not with the display but with the virtual environment. Therefore, continue to update the virtual environment, but only update the display if time is available. In most environments, this means that as long as input events are pending, no redraw is performed. Once all user input has been processed the display is brought up-to-date. This creates a smooth transition from a completely responsive system with resources to spare to an overworked system with few resources available.

Consequences

Lazy Redraw postpones fulfillment of requests until the system has resources available to perform them. This can improve performance for the experienced user, since immediate feedback is not necessary. The novice user, on the other hand, is more likely to wait for confirmation (i.e., redraw) before proceeding.

Since Lazy Redraw implements a heuristic for metering performance based on input requests it may not always be correct. Therefore, a method for programmatically forcing a redraw should also be provided. For example, regardless of how poor performance may be, a slide show program is expected to correctly display certain "key frames."

Known Uses

Microsoft Windows and HotDraw use Lazy Redraw to optimize redrawing.

Related Patterns

Lazy Redraw is an optimization of Request Update. Lazy Redraw is also known as Update at User-Speed [Beck1994].

Clip Requests

Updating hidden regions is unnecessary and inefficient.

When update requests occur for occluded regions, redrawing the foreground is inefficient and unnecessary since it will not change. Consider a background status window on a desktop as in Figure 22-2. If it updates while it is completely occluded, there is no need to perform the update request. It is not currently visible, and it will be redrawn correctly if it ever becomes visible. If the window were par-

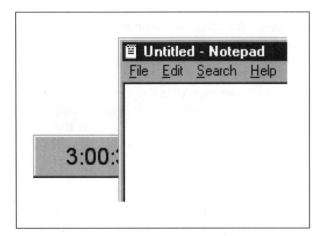

As the time is updated each second, the entire clock window may be invalidated; however, only the visible portion of the clock's window should be updated.

Figure 22-2   *Clip Requests example*

tially visible, it would be most efficient to redraw only the visible portion. However, visibility is a dynamic property of the entire environment, not information readily available to the process making changes to any particular window.

Therefore:

Exclude opaque foreground regions from update requests.

The display environment contains the needed visibility information. For example, a desktop maintaining a list of windows knows what region each window covers. When a request is made, any overlapping regions (contained later in the list) represent wasted effort. The update will be lost when later windows overwrite it. Eliminate these hidden regions by traversing that part of the list and subtracting any overlap area. Only completely opaque regions occluding the update request should be removed.

Consequences

Clip Requests eliminates wasted effort at the expense of keeping additional information. Update requests must include a source, as well as a region, to allow the system to determine which areas should be ignored. This requires slightly tighter binding between update processes and the display system.

Clip Requests works best when requests and visible components are restricted to rectangular regions and all objects are opaque. This is typically the case with desktop systems, and it is used extensively in these environments to speed redraws and give the impression of solidity.

If objects are translucent they should not be considered to occlude other objects, since the final image depends on more than one object. Also, as object boundaries become complex, managing the update region and clipping redraws to it, can easily generate more work than is being saved. To avoid this problem, consider assuming only rectangular objects are opaque.

Known Uses

Microsoft Windows, the Macintosh operating system, and other desktop environments use Clip Requests to optimize redrawing.

Related Patterns

Clip Requests is an optimization of Request Update. The Display List provides a ready-made Chain of Responsibility [Gamma+1995, p. 223] for trimming requests. Each visible component is responsible for removing any part of the request it occludes.

Double Buffer

Updating components directly to the display causes display "flicker."

When using Painter's Algorithm to update the display, undesirable side effects result. Changing components momentarily disappear before reappearing in a new state or at a new location. This effect breaks the illusion of permanence and solidity. Although this may be acceptable for desktop environments, it is generally not acceptable for games and other multimedia applications such as slide shows.

Another unwanted effect results when objects change while in "front" of several background components. Each of those components must be redrawn before the changed component is updated. This excessive redrawing produces display "flicker" as components are updated. Not only is this distracting to the user, it interferes with the illusion of depth and draws unwanted attention to otherwise simple changes.

Even worse, if a background component changes, foreground components must be redrawn even if they do not change. In cases in which the background components are completely hidden, it may only be distracting for desktops, but it is completely unacceptable for games, in which hidden objects should never be visible.

Therefore:

Render visible components to a hidden display, then use a single operation to update the visible display.

Rendering to a hidden display avoids redraw effects. "Flicker" and hidden component visibility are avoided since the user cannot observe the redraw process. Once the hidden display is complete a single operation is used to copy the new image to the visible display. This allows components to instantly change from one location to another, or from one image to another, even when partially occluded, completely hidden, translucent, or in front of complex backgrounds.

Consequences

Double Buffer trades resources for presentation quality. Display buffer memory, potentially a premium resource, and time are the most significant resources required. Considerable design and implementation changes may be required especially if objects rely on "extra" display features such as cursors, carets, or "rubber-banding" services.

Known Uses

PowerPoint, Doom, QuickTime, and many other products use Double Buffer to improve presentation quality.

Related Patterns

Page Flip is a specialization of Double Buffer that may be appropriate if large areas of the display will be updated in each frame.

Page Flip

Copying the entire Double Buffer is inefficient.

When the entire display is redrawn, typically due to Global Update, Double Buffer requires the entire display buffer to be copied. That process can represent a significant portion of the resources available. In addition, copying is not even required if the hidden display buffer will be completely regenerated during the next redraw cycle.

Therefore:

Swap the active display buffer.

Swap the hidden display buffer for the active one. Rendering will alternate between the two buffers. While the one is visible the other can be redrawn.

Consequences

Page Flip assumes Global Update is being used.

Page Flip is only available if multiple physical display buffers are supported. Usually this means the display subsystem allows the active buffer to be changed. However, if hardware "blitter" bandwidth is available it can be used to emulate selecting the active buffer by copying between display buffers.

Known Uses

DirectDraw, Sega, Nintendo, and many other game products use Page Flip to improve performance.

Related Patterns

Page Flip is an optimization of Double Buffer and assumes Global Update is in use.

ACKNOWLEDGMENTS

This chapter was prepared for presentation at PLoP '98. Thanks are due to James Noble for his great shepherding and to Roger Bonzer for his many comments on several drafts.

REFERENCES

[Beck1994] K. Beck, R.E. Johnson. "Patterns Generate Architectures." In *Proceedings of the Eighth European Conference on Object Oriented Programming*. Lecture Notes in Computer Science, 821:139–149, Bologna Italy, July 1994.

[Gamma+1995] E. Gamma, R. Helm, R. Johnson, and J. Vlissides. *Design Patterns: Elements of Object-Oriented Software Architecture*. Reading, MA: Addison-Wesley, 1995.

[Johnson1992] R.E. Johnson. "Documenting Frameworks with Patterns." In *OOPSLA '92 Proceedings, SIGPLAN Notices*, 27(10):63–76, Vancouver, BC, October 1992.

[Krasner1988] G.E. Krasner and S.T. Pope. "A Cookbook for Using the Model-View-Controller User Interface Paradigm in Smalltalk-80." *Journal of Object-Oriented Programming*, 1(3):26–49, 1988.

[Noble1999] James Noble. "Basic Relationship Patterns." In N. Harrison, B. Foote, and H. Rohnert (eds.), *Pattern Languages of Program Design 4*. Reading, MA: Addison-Wesley, 1999.

Dwayne Towell may be reached at dwayne@imagebuilder.com.

Chapter 23

An Input and Output Pattern Language: Lessons from Telecommunications

Robert Hanmer and Greg Stymfal

A specialized set of patterns for defining the human-machine interface has come into use within the world of telecommunications switching products. The patterns presented here provide an essential interface between a system and its human masters. Several of the patterns discuss concepts specific to a telecommunications system, but most are general enough to provide insight for anyone designing the input/output (IO) interface for a large system.

This chapter begins by discussing the environment within which these patterns are applicable. Two different methods of visualizing the overall structure of this language are then presented, one graphical and the other in the form of topical pattern groupings. The patterns are then introduced. Supplemental material includes thumbnail sketches of the patterns.

BACKGROUND

The environment within which telecommunications switching equipment is installed is different from that of a traditional computing center. This section describes some of the differences that constitute the common context for these patterns.

A key difference between the IO of a telecommunications system and a general computer is that the IO of a telephone switching system is purely secondary to its main purpose. A general computer might be specialized to a special function, such as processing mathematical equations quickly, but the results still must proceed through the IO channel. This is not the case in a switching system. These systems manage specialized hardware to connect (switch) different telephone lines. This function does not require CRTs, paper printers, keyboards, mice, or magnetic tape.

Another significant difference is that a telecommunications system has a multitude of workers who are responsible for system maintenance and administration. This workforce can be grouped into several different communities of interest ([Huttenhoff+1977], [Green+1977], [Giunta+1977]):

- *Those concerned with the maintenance of the machine.* This community has a work center called the Maintenance Operations Center.
- *Those concerned with administrating the machine.* Their work center is called the Maintenance Administration Center.
- *Those concerned with the telephone lines and trunks connected to the switching machine.* They have two work centers in addition to the Maintenance Administration Center, called the Trunk Operations Center and the Terminal Equipment Center.

In many computing environments a console terminal is the primary channel for the operator to communicate with the system. Most users are not authorized to send and receive administrative commands. In telecommunications systems there are many terminals within each work center that are each as powerful as a traditional console.

Telephone switching systems are large. A switching office serving a city center might occupy several thousand square feet and have tens of thousands of telephone lines and trunks connected to it. As a result, the workers are a long physical distance from the primary input/output devices when they are working inside the system. It also means that the workforce has many pieces of equipment to operate and maintain.

Reliability is a very important system capability. Reliability engineers calculate the expected availability of the system based upon some predicted Mean Time to Repair. This is the time it takes for maintenance personnel to respond to and repair a component. It is therefore very important that the maintenance people be informed quickly of any problems. Reliability, usually expressed in terms of a few minutes of downtime per office per year, also leads the designers towards using custom hardware and software especially designed to facilitate reliable systems. In order to maintain this availability, telephone switching systems are typically monitored around the clock by personnel trained and ready to respond to any emergency.

Using custom hardware and software usually results in the system being behind the leading edge of computer technology. When the systems from which these patterns were mined were being created in the 1970s their IO channels were capable of being operated at either 110 or 1200 baud [Budlong+1977, pp. 169–170].

In some cases these primitive IO devices are still used because they are well-known to the system designers and are more reliable.

Even as telephone networks get more complicated, the desire to remotely monitor and maintain them has increased. The ability to remotely monitor system operations adds an additional level of complexity. Handling this additional complexity wasn't always provided for in the initial designs.

KNOWN USES

The patterns contained here are the proven practices of a number of telephone switching systems such as the Lucent Technologies 1A ESS local switch, the 4ESS toll and tandem switch also from Lucent Technologies and the AG Communication Systems GTD-5 local switch.

LANGUAGE MAP

Figure 23-1 shows the relationships among the patterns in this language.

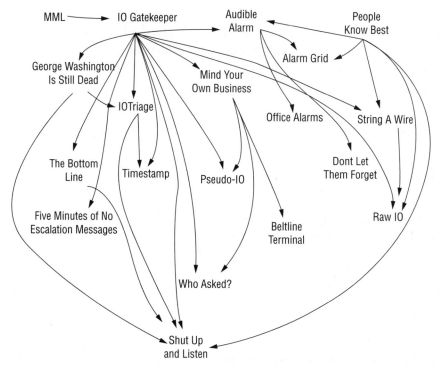

Figure 23-1

The diagram shows patterns that enhance the solutions of other patterns, resolve previously unresolved forces in a pattern, or take advantage of an earlier pattern to provide some new system capability. In Figure 23-2, pattern *B* refines pattern *A*, helping to solve unresolved forces or new problems that *A* introduced.

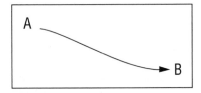

Figure 23-2

CATEGORIES OF PATTERNS

Four functional categories can be used to categorize these patterns. Both MML and IO Gatekeeper deal with all four of these topics. The categories are physical location, the relative importance of input, the quantity of messages, and periods of emergency interaction.

1. *Physical* **location.**   Switching offices are large in physical terms. These patterns present measures to be taken to mitigate the effects of large size.

   Mind Your Own Business

   Beltline Terminal

   Pseudo-10

   Audible Alarms

   Alarm Grid

   Office Alarms

   Who Asked?

2. *Relative* **importance** *of input.*   Some interactions with the system are more important than others. These patterns present the measures that need to be taken to ensure that the important interactions happen in a timely fashion.

   IO Triage

   Timestamp

   Shut Up and Listen

   Don't Let Them Forget

3. **Quantity** *of messages.*   Switching systems are large in terms of lines of code and numbers of subsystems; many will have things to say at the same time.

These patterns help to manage the sheer quantity of messages.

George Washington Is Still Dead

The Bottom Line

IO Triage

5 Minutes of No Escalation Messages

Shut Up and Listen

4. *Periods of* **emergency** *interaction.* During crisis times special rules should apply. These patterns discuss some of these special rules as they impact IO.

Audible Alarms

Alarm Grid

Office Alarms

String A Wire

Raw IO

Don't Let Them Forget

THE PATTERNS

MML

Also Known As

huMan-Machine Language

Problem

How can communications with a large and complex machine be made easier for humans and more reliable?

Context

There are many different subsystems that will need to communicate with human operators and administrators. A large volume of IO with many varied user needs and functions is expected.

Forces

- Switching system software development will be easier if each software subsystem defines and implements its own IO specifications. It is easier to develop alone than to coordinate with others.

- Development expense and system architecture will be more streamlined if the different subsystems define the system languages to a common specification.
- At least one-third of errors during system operation are due to mistakes made by the human operator. (The other two-thirds are hardware faults and software faults.) Any steps that can be taken to reduce the contribution of the human-machine interface to this statistic will be beneficial.

Solution

Use a standard messaging format. This allows the system to be consistent when reporting problems in different parts of the system. It also allows humans to become familiar with the format of messages and thus simplifies learning. This reduces the amount of documentation that is required because there can be commonality between subsystems. (See Figure 23-3.)

Without
MML

MML

Figure 23-3

Resulting Context

A large volume of IO with many varied users' needs and functions using a standard language/format will be given a consistency that helps users. Mechanisms to deal with the large volume of input and output are needed, such as Bottom Line and George Washington Is Still Dead.

In addition, since the system is quite large, there might be many different users, each trying to interact with the system. To keep things straight, patterns such as Mind Your Own Business, Who Asked?, and IO Triage are useful.

Sometimes, especially to save human resources, a computer system might be created to monitor the system. In many cases, a custom interface can be created to facilitate computer-to-computer communications. Sometimes this is too much overhead and a pattern such as Pseudo-IO helps by having the monitoring computer use the MML messages intended for humans.

Examples

MML (huMan-Machine Language, an international standard) and PDS (Program Documentation Standard) are two examples.

Rationale

Imagine if all application/user programs on a general computing system used the same standard message language. That is the scope of this pattern. This is accomplished in the world of telecommunications as described in the Background section. Doing so lowers the rate of procedural (human-caused) errors and hence increases the system availability. It also simplifies development by allowing the creation of shared, reusable command parsers.

Reference.   [Clement+1997, pp. 245–246.]

IO Gatekeeper

Problem

How can a large system support the existence of a single MML for a large community of authorized users?

Context

IO is secondary to the system's primary purpose. There may be many different subsystems that need some sort of interface with the human world.

Forces

- Allowing each subsystem to send messages to the terminals independently produces anarchy. Obtaining a cohesive view of the system's status is impossible due to the disordered presentation.
- Creating a centralized subsystem introduces a bottleneck into the IO processing.

Solution

Design a centralized point to conduct all communication between humans and the system (see Figure 23-4). Design and then use an internal interface language that supports the use of MML towards the human interfaces. This will function as a gatekeeper or doorway through which all IO must pass. Use a Singleton [Gamma+1995] to enforce a single occurrence of the Gatekeeper.

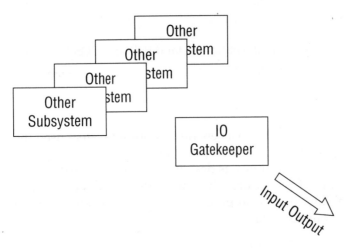

Figure 23-4

Resulting Context

By defining the interfacing language for the Gatekeeper, development and use of the system is made easier.

The Gatekeeper function allows many useful features to be created. These include timestamping, identifying important messages (IO Triage), sorting messages to internal or external recipients (Pseudo-IO and Who Asked?), throttling the output of messages (The Bottom Line and George Washington Is Still Dead). The Gatekeeper can also tie the IO system together with the alarm system (Audible Alarm), using a tag associated with the message (such as its priority tag, see IO Triage) to indicate if an alarm should be sounded. The Gatekeeper also can be made responsible for privileges and only allow privileged people or terminal groups to execute the most potentially destructive commands.

The Gatekeeper by definition will consolidate IO together into a single stream. The resulting output stream can be torrential. The patterns Mind Your Own Business and Who Asked? are employed to sort it out.

Rationale

Since IO is not essential to the primary system processing of telephone calls, the impacts of this bottleneck are mitigated.

If the IO Gatekeeper is not a Singleton [Gamma+1995], few benefits arise from having a gatekeeper at all since the result is as if every subsystem communicated directly with humans.

Mind Your Own Business

Problem

If all the output comes through the IO Gatekeeper, who should see it?

Context

There is a standard input and output messaging language (MML) defined for the whole system. This implies that there will be some framework within the system that supports all IO, consolidating messages from every part of the system into a single unified output.

Forces

- Only a few workers need to see any particular output. For example, the people in the Maintenance Operations Center don't need to see messages about the progress of a Recent Change (database update) transaction.
- The system shouldn't confuse the workers by presenting information they don't know how to use.
- The volume of messages that are possible from a large system is enormous. If it were all to be dumped to one terminal it would be impossible for workers to find the information they need.
- Access control is enhanced if the type of information a particular terminal receives is changed through simple wiring configurations rather than complicated programming changes.
- Frequently the entities watching the outputs are not human, but are other computer systems. Output stream specialization is useful because these systems are only interested in a small part of the possible output.
- Much of the information in the system is routine and not related to any particular user.
- The primary output devices in a maintenance center should always receive output, even if no one is logged on.

Solution

Define different output classifications. The IO Gatekeeper should mark different terminal/console connections to receive output only for some classifications. These are called *logical channels*. The system sends messages only to the community of users interested in them. Some example logical channels are Maintenance, Secondary Record, Recent Change, and Network Management (see Figure 23-5). A receive-only printer is used within maintenance communities to provide for a continual record of activity even if no one is logged on.

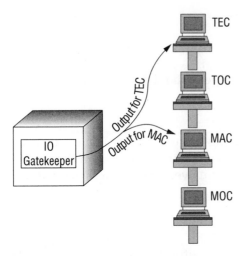

Figure 23-5

Resulting Context

The large volume of IO is reduced on any one channel when it is distributed by function. This results in labor savings—workers don't need to wade through the output to find the messages in which they are interested. And the reduction in IO helps computer systems monitoring this system by reducing the volume of output they must digest.

Some users move around within an office and might still need to see the output. Beltline Terminals addresses this by providing the ability to redirect output to a different output device.

By centralizing output processing (see IO Triage), the categories and logical channels can be used to send output to the right place as in Who Asked?

Example

In a general-purpose computing system the operator console receives some messages that user terminals do not receive. In telecommunications systems there are many different operator consoles for different communities of interest.

Reference.   [Clement+1977, pp. 245–246]

IO Triage

Problem

Important information is hidden or delayed by less important information.

Context

The IO Gatekeeper coordinates the IO message stream. A large volume of IO is still presented to the workers even after applying the message reduction patterns George Washington Is Still Dead and The Bottom Line.

Forces

- Too much information deadens the workers.
- Information about a critical situation—for example, all the telephone lines going out of service, or a critical piece of the system hardware failing, needs to be issued as soon as it is detected to allow the workers to repair it.
- Information that reports trivial things can be deferred to display after the important information is presented.
- Workers might not be looking at the screen when there is something important happening.

Solution

Tag messages with a priority classification. Design IO software to display a higher priority message on the output device before a message of a lower priority (see Figure 23-6). Use a consistent definition of the different priorities. One definition used by the 4ESS Switch is shown in Table 23-1.

Resulting Context

The most important information will be displayed first, followed by less important and possibly quite old information. This requires the IO Gatekeeper to prepare

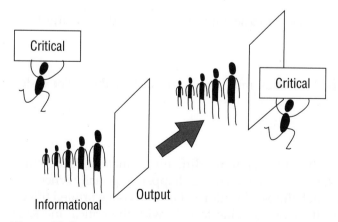

Figure 23-6

Table 23-1 *4ESS Switch Message Priorities*

Priority Tag	Meaning
Critical	The office cannot perform its required actions to process telephone calls.
Major	The system is in a state that one more failure will result in a Critical loss of service.
Minor	A small portion of the system is in trouble. The system is more than one failure away from a total lack of service.
Manual	The system is responding to a human input message.
Information	The system is behaving normally.

messages for display in the desired order. Use a message sequence tag to facilitate a complete understanding of the system state (see Timestamp).

Output messages tagged critical, major, or minor are sometimes referred to as action messages because they require some action on the part of the local workforce.

The issue of people not watching their terminal when something important is being reported will be addressed by the Audible Alarm pattern. The priority tag provided by IO Triage should be used as an input into the alarm system to sound the appropriate alarm.

Timestamp

Problem

How can workers provide some sense to a seemingly random order of output?

Context

IO Triage has been applied. Messages may not come out in the strict order requested by subsystems.

Forces

- Some problems reported in the IO stream are difficult to analyze. Little clues might be important, even the order in which things happen, especially when trying to decipher near-coincident failures. The informational message printed fifteen minutes ago might contain the essential clue to help with the critical message printed five minutes ago.

- Time within a computer system is different than time to humans. A timestamp with just the minutes and seconds hides millisecond time period details.
- The IO Gatekeeper can perform a little extra processing and tag messages with some helpful information.

Solution

Apply a sequence number to all messages when the IO Gatekeeper receives them (see Figure 23-7). That will help identify message ordering. Since humans like to work with a time base, the current time can be used as the sequence number. The current time is when the message was received by the IO subsystem and should contain meaningful time units such as seconds or milliseconds.

```
#135/0957 am/Critical: εαιϖεεαιϖε
#134/0956 am/Minor: αρειρεαιϖεα
#120/0952 am/Information: ερυερυ
#121/0953 am/Information: νϖιναστιν3
#136/0958 am/Information: εφϖειϖαλ
#140/1002 am/Major: α4εραϖα
#137/0958 am/Information: φεφιαυβε
#138/0959 am/Information: ϖϖειαυβεπ
#139/1000 am/Information: αρευιβπυαεβι
```

Figure 23-7

Resulting Context

If the message printing time also is displayed, the difference in times can provide a valuable clue to the analyst.

Who Asked?

Problem

What logical channel receives the results of a specific manual input request?

Context

A worker usually only uses one terminal at a time. Mind Your Own Business has resulted in the IO stream being divided into different logical channels. The IO Gatekeeper centralizes output with a prioritization scheme.

Forces

- Lots of terminals, lots of terminal classifications, many users—do they all see my messages?
- Broadcasting the answer to everyone would confuse the workers who have no idea about that function (i.e., maintenance workers seeing database change output). It also pollutes the output channels with extraneous information, resulting in desired information being lost in reams of paper.
- There is a class of workers that has primary responsibility for the correct functioning of the system. These workers should be kept informed, to some degree, of what the other communities of workers are doing.

Solution

The IO Gatekeeper should display the output related to a specific input request to the logical channel that made the request. Send it to all the terminals monitoring a particular logical channel. You might want to put it on additional channels to allow for logging or oversight by a superuser (see Figure 23-8). Give the message a Manual tag to indicate that it is a direct response to an input message (see IO Triage), so the message won't be misinterpreted as a spontaneous system output.

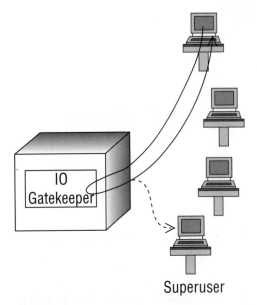

Superuser

Figure 23-8

Resulting Context

Sometimes important information is displayed at the primary maintenance terminal, so that people responsible for the correct functioning of the system see it.

Reference.   [Clement+1997, pp. 245–246]

George Washington Is Still Dead

Also Known As

Show Changes

Problem

How can the output be kept free from too many messages saying the same thing?

Context

Sometimes the system needs to output reports about the state of the machine. While a particular problem might be detected hundreds of times (as in The Bottom Line), if the state isn't changing frequently the messages might be overkill. For example, if hundreds of trunks go out of service, the office condition might change when the first trunk goes out of service, and then not change again until the 101st trunk goes out of service.

Forces

- Displaying the status of the office condition for each new trunk out of service report from the second to the hundredth trunk is too much information. There isn't really enough to require a new report.
- Too much information deadens the workers.
- The fact that the office state or condition has changed is the real information that the workers need to know.
- Just display messages that report a change in state. Don't display a message each time the alarmed state is detected.

Solution

Have the IO Gatekeeper keep track of messages and send only changed state announcements that represent a real change of state (see Figure 23-9).

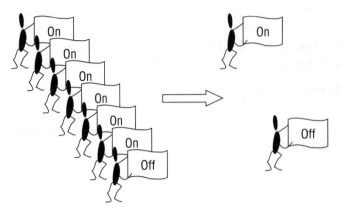

Figure 23-9

Resulting Context

Redundancies will be removed from an otherwise large volume of IO.

The reports of state changes are important, so some method of reporting them is required. IO Triage is needed to keep the important information coming out even when the output channels are flooded.

Related Patterns

Sometimes there are no actions that the workers can perform in response to a change in system state. It is in these circumstances that the Five Minutes of No Escalation Messages pattern applies.

Even given the reduction in messages that results from applying this pattern, a mechanism to ensure that humans are able to input a message against a flood of output is required. Shut Up and Listen addresses this problem.

The Bottom Line is similar to this pattern but deals with multiples of the same report. It summarizes a given report with the number of occurrences. This leads to delay in reporting the event, however, because of the need for aggregation.

The Bottom Line

Problem

Many messages are about the same type of event (such as a trunk going out of service), and they flood the output message stream.

Context

Some situations produce many, many reports. For example, if a part of the system interfacing to many trunks has just gone out of service, a message reporting that a trunk is out of service might display hundreds of reports, one for each trunk. This pattern applies to the places where a report should be generated because some condition has just been detected.

Forces

- Outputting a report whenever an event happens pollutes the output channels, diverting attention from other activities. Even with a priority output system in place (see IO Triage), the channel can become full, and important output or input (see Shut Up and Listen) can be missed.
- Sometimes reporting many events gives the workers an idea of a trend, but this information can be given many times or as a single message reporting many events. Reports are not of critical importance and can be delayed slightly during the aggregation period.

Solution

The IO Gatekeeper should group messages about a common event and only display a summary message that includes a tally of the number of occurrences (see Figure 23-10). The system should also supply a way to provide the entire output upon human request, as it may be essential to identify problems.

Trunk Out
of Service
Messages

100 Trunks
Out of Service

Figure 23-10

Resulting Context

Even with the reduction in messages from applying this pattern, a mechanism to ensure that humans are able to input a message against a flood of output is required. Shut Up and Listen addresses this problem.

Related Patterns

George Washington Is Still Dead deals with state change reports while The Bottom Line deals with aggregation of nearly identical messages.

Five Minutes of No Escalation Messages helps those cases in which aggregation delays can only partly be tolerated. It causes messages to be printed out periodically as well as in summary form.

Five Minutes of No Escalation Messages

Problem

The human-machine interface is saturated with error reports for which humans can't do much except worry.

Context

Any continuous-running, fault-tolerant system, where transient conditions may be present can produce too many messages, even with summary and priority filters (The Bottom Line, George Washington Is Still Dead, IO Triage).

Some system reports describe events that humans cannot help resolve.

Forces

- Many problems work themselves out, given time. There is no sense in wasting time or reducing level of service trying to solve a problem that will go away by itself (Riding Over Transients [Adams+1996]).
- The switch can use all of its resources displaying messages.
- Humans panic when they think the switch is out of control (Minimize Human Intervention [Adams+1996]).
- If the only human action might be detrimental to the system, the best action might be for the system to delay reporting information.

Solution

When taking the first action in a scenario that could lead to an excess number of messages, display a message. Then periodically display an update message (see Figure 23-11). If the abnormal condition ends, display a message that everything is back to normal. Do not display a message for every change in state.

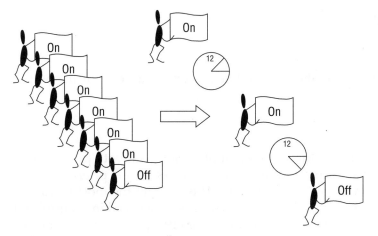

Figure 23-11

Continue nonstop machine-to-machine communication of status and actions throughout this period (see String A Wire).

If something is so important that it can't wait five minutes, an Audible Alarm should report it.

Resulting Context

This solution will keep the system operator from panicking from seeing too many messages. Machine-to-machine messages and measurements will keep a record for later evaluation as well as keep the system's actions visible to people who can deal with it. There are other computer systems monitoring the actions taken. These systems can deal with a great volume of messages.

Other messages that are not related to the escalating situation that is producing too many messages will be displayed as though the system were normal. Thus the volume of escalation messages does not adversely affect the normal functioning of the system.

Of course the five-minute time period alluded to in the title is only a suggestion. It is based upon the situations from which this pattern is mined.

Related Patterns

Note the conflict with People Know Best [Adams+1996] in which humans should be kept thoroughly informed of system progress. Five Minutes of No Escalation Messages applies when no helpful human actions are possible. This can occur when the system is reporting traffic-induced system overloads.

This pattern also applies to those cases in which the delay to aggregate messages (see The Bottom Line) is too long and some intermediate report is necessary.

Shut Up and Listen

Problem

Humans need to be heard by the system. Users need a way to shut the output stream off.

Context

The IO Gatekeeper is flooding the system output stream with both priority messages reporting abnormal events and informational messages. A priority scheme for message output is in place (see IO Triage). This will get the most important information out to the workers first. It doesn't address humans taking control and altering system behavior. People Know Best [Adams+1996] states that even when the system is designed to correct problems automatically experts will sometimes be able to help the system through stressful incidents.

Sometimes, even though George Washington Is Still Dead and The Bottom Line are applied, the output stream is still flooded.

Forces

- If the output is shut off, important information might be missed.
- If users wait until the outputting is completed, the system might be in a degraded service mode. Then again, in some circumstances the output stream may be perpetually flooded.
- Full-duplex IO might help, but makes message interpretation more difficult. If half-duplex is chosen, some way of interrupting the output is necessary.

Solution

The IO Gatekeeper should give human input a higher priority than displaying output information. Make sure that input messages are processed even when the output system is operating at full capacity.

Provide a way to interrupt the output stream long enough for a human to get a request into the system. Design this so that no output messages are lost.

Mark the output related to human input messages at priority level comparable with Critical output messages (see IO Triage) so that responses to human input are not stuck at the end of the output message queue (see Figure 23-12).

Resulting Context

Human requests (input messages) will be heard even though the output buffer is full. All human input messages are treated at the same priority level. A separate input mechanism (such as a Master Control Console [Budlong+1977]) that bypasses the IO subsystem can be provided for high priority input.

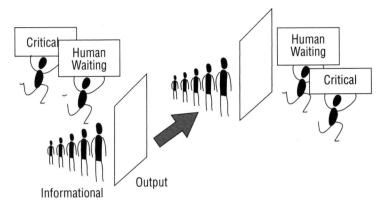

Figure 23-12

Pseudo-IO

Problem

Some subsystem provides a way for humans to access information. Now another subsystem needs this same information also.

Context

The system is large and has several subsystems. The IO Gatekeeper processes individually buffered messages and distributes them to the appropriate subsystem for handling. IO that previously went only from machine to human now must also go between subsystems inside the system.

The system has many logical IO channels (see Mind Your Own Business).

Forces

- Adding a machine-to-machine interface increases the complexity of the system.
- Adding in a powerful new interface or interface protocol is difficult once the system architecture is set.
- Perturbing a working subsystem to add a new interface to a new subsystem risks introducing new faults and breaking the working subsystem.

Solution

Allow one subsystem to insert a message into the input message stream. In other words, allow the system itself to create a message that is processed just like any other input message received from outside the system (see Figure 23-13).

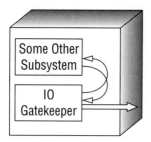

Figure 23-13

Resulting Context

This provides a system that makes it easy to add new switch feature capabilities and to connect them to already present IO services.

Beltline Terminal

Problem

The terminal isn't where the worker needs to be to do his or her work.

Context

The system produces a large volume of IO that is distributed by function (see Mind Your Own Business). Certain terminals are dedicated for specific workers. Some workers move around in the office. Because of the size of the system, they might be a long way from their maintenance terminal when they want to enter or see some messages related to what they are doing (e.g., they might be changing circuit packs).

For many years within a telephone office there have been jacks to plug in audio headsets to allow workers to talk with other workers.

Forces

- Reduced labor costs/higher productivity if the worker doesn't need to continually go for long walks to use a terminal.
- Reduced possibility of accidentally damaging something by frequent traversals of the office to reach the terminal.
- Increased system availability if workers can attend to their work quickly. Long walks to the terminal area increase the Mean Time to Repair.

Solution

Provide remote terminal connections so that workers can plug in a terminal IO device anywhere they want (see Figure 23-14). This is called a *Beltline Terminal*. Allow the worker to redirect (copy) the output of the desired logical channel to the Beltline Terminal.

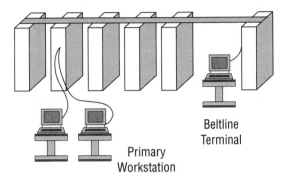

Figure 23-14

Resulting Context

Workers can move around the office and can take their terminal with them. This increases productivity and system availability and reduces Mean Time to Repair. The typical configuration of a Beltline Terminal is an ordinary display device, such as a VT100 terminal, on a cart.

Rationale

The system is already physically large, with many wires. The system is mounted in custom cabinets with custom wiring. Adding a few additional wires around the office to allow the workers to plug in a terminal (in addition to audio headsets) is a minor expense.

Reference. [Huttenhoff+1977, p. 1050]

Audible Alarm

Problem

How can the system get information to workers immediately when a significant problem has occurred?

Context

Some things are too important to wait for a potentially slow IO Gatekeeper to process and to wait for some human to notice and read. Even with messages receiving a priority tag (IO Triage) the IO Gatekeeper must still queue the message for output. People Know Best [Adams+1996] requires that the support systems and humans that monitor the system have full information about its state. Due to the complexity of the IO system the overhead to perform the standard IO cannot be afforded in all circumstances, so MML does not apply.

Forces

- In a large office a simple message on one or several terminals might be unnoticed by the office personnel who are needed to handle the problem. This can lead to service being impacted longer than is absolutely necessary.
- The IO system has a lower processing priority than the systems that ensure that the system is sane and functioning normally. We cannot count on the IO system being executed in a timely manner during times of crisis. This can delay processing for a long time in a system that is trying to recover from catastrophes.
- During crisis situations the humans may be looking elsewhere and will not see a report on a terminal.

Solution

Provide a method of reporting alarms audibly in the office. This will reach out and alert humans that there is some problem that they should identify and resolve to reduce telephone service impacts. Remote visual indicators also should be provided, such as colored lights spread throughout the office.

The audible alarm system should be driven by the IO protocol defined within the system. Messages being passed to the IO Gatekeeper should have a special tag to indicate that an alarm should be sounded and which alarm. The priority tag defined by IO Triage can be used for this. There are a multitude of sounds that can be used to indicate different alarm severities, including sirens, bells, gongs, and the like (see Figure 23-15).

Figure 23-15

Resulting Context

The time to begin the correct remedial action has a contribution towards the Mean Time to Repair, which in turn has an impact on the system's overall availability.

Priority messages will be presented to personnel in a way that stimulates several senses.

The specification of the alarmed items is usually done at design time. Since these are big systems that may vary subtly from office to office some method of customizing to a specific customer site is desirable (see Office Alarms).

The alarm system will typically sound alarms—at the local switching office and to some remote monitoring location.

A method of silencing the alarms by a manual action needs to be implemented. This allows the craft to have some peace and quiet while they try to isolate the problem. This method needs to rely upon as little software as possible, since they might want to retire the alarm while the software system is insane. A push button driving a hardware circuit is the best solution. Now that they have a method to silence the alarms, Don't Let Them Forget that the alarm happened and that there is something needing their attention.

Rationale

Audible Alarms provide an interface to the human operators that parallels the interface provided by the IO system. Since it is parallel, it will provide the operators with information that they might not get in a timely manner through the IO system.

The alarm system should have a low probability of failure. The hardware should have few failure points and use reliable components. Another consideration in the hardware design is to make the system "toothpick proof." This refers to the ease with which office personnel can disable a part of the system by inserting a toothpick into the appropriate relay contact to prevent closure.

If the alarm system itself is to fail, having it report its own failure is a desirable event. In the area of the alarms the usual principle of "failing silently" may not apply.

Reference. [Huttenhoff+1977, p. 1051]

Alarm Grid

Problem

Workers need to know where to look for the problems, especially hardware problems.

Context

Audible Alarms and IO messages report emergency situations. People Know Best [Adams+1996] requires that support systems monitoring the system have full information about the system's state. The time required to begin the correct remedial action has a contribution towards the Mean Time to Repair, which in turn has an impact on the system's overall availability. There might be many alarms asserted simultaneously. For example, when a piece of hardware that terminates the trunks fails, the system will want to report the hardware failure as well as the failures of all of the trunks that it contains.

Forces

- Simultaneous alarms confuse workers and create uncertainty on where to look first.
- The IO system has a lower processing priority than the subsystems that ensure that the system is sane and functioning normally. We cannot count on the IO system to quickly report routine messages during times of crisis. This can delay processing for a long time in a system that is trying to recover from catastrophes.
- Audible Alarms are presented by the IO Gatekeeper as soon as they are detected.

Solution

Divide the office into smaller grids that point to the location of the error. Tie alarm circuits together to report to the main office alarm panel. When an alarmable situation occurs within this alarm grid, alert all concerned personnel via Audible Alarms that there is a problem. Also provide visual indicators in the form of colored lights on the ends of frames within a grid to show that abnormal conditions exist somewhere in the grid (see Figure 23-16).

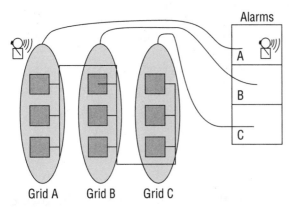

Figure 23-16

Resulting Context

Alarm grids allow problem reports to selected communities of interest. This is similar to the logical channel concept of Mind Your Own Business.

Alarm grids can be arranged hierarchically within an office. This allows refinement of reporting and the potential to tie together several grids to report larger summary events during off-hours when fewer people are watching the system.

Reference.   [Huttenhoff+1977, p. 1051]

Office Alarms

Problem

How can problems that are unique to a particular field site be integrated into the pre-defined classification of messages?

Context

Both visual and audio alarms show emergency information organized by Alarm Grid. Different sites might have custom alarming requirements, such as door locks, specialized A/C, coffeepots, related systems, and so forth.

Forces

- A separate, parallel interface for site specific alarms would introduce confusion, since its user interface would probably not be identical to the standard interface.
- The actual interface and system actions that take place when the alarm is fired could be transparent and indistinguishable from the predefined system alarms. This will help avoid user errors and potential outages based upon failure to act on stimuli.
- Humans are confused if some important things are not alarmed while seemingly less important things have predefined alarms associated with them.
- The designers and equipment manufacturers can't foresee every unique office configuration containing conditions that need to be alarmed. The switch-owning customers probably don't want to pay for such thoroughness either.
- Good user interface design requires that similar things behave in similar manners.

Solution

Design the alarm system to allow easy insertion of new office-specific alarms (see Figure 23-17). This is an example of the Decorator pattern from [Gamma+1995].

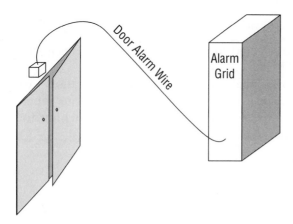

Figure 23-17

Resulting Context

Both generic priority messages and site-specific events have visual and audio alarms. This provides a measure of customer programmability to the office. Switch owners may tailor this part of the system to their own corporate operating policies.

Switch owners should be able to change the priority (IO Triage) of the messages so that they fit the situation.

Don't Let Them Forget

Problem

For how long should the system honor a human's request to silence the alarms?

Context

Audible Alarms can be very annoying, leading workers to want to silence and ignore them. A system in trouble can have many alarms asserted simultaneously. Sometimes the noise can be overwhelming and distracting to the workers, so a method of silencing, or retiring, the alarm is provided.

Forces

- The choices include reasserting alarms immediately, or keeping them quiet for some predetermined length of time.
- Some mechanism to silence the alarms is desirable to provide some quiet for thought.

- If the system is in trouble the ability to function properly may be compromised if alarms aren't reported promptly. This can lengthen Mean Time to Repair.
- Ignoring the manual action to silence alarms will be annoying and distracting to the workers. They might spend time trying to silence them, instead of resolving the problem that is trying to be reported.

Solution

Act on all requests to retire an alarm. But don't remember a request to silence alarms. The next time that the system detects an alarmed condition, sound the alarm, regardless of how recently it was retired (see Figure 23-18).

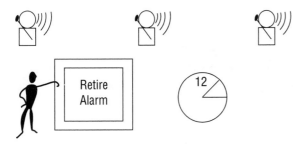

Figure 23-18

Resulting Context

The system will report alarms whenever they are appropriate. The worker will have to repeatedly silence them, until the problem is corrected and the system no longer reasserts the alarm. The worker will have until the next alarm detection period before hearing the alarms again.

Related Pattern

This pattern deals with alarmed situations, whereas George Washington Is Still Dead is about slightly less critical information.

String A Wire

Problem

Critically important information must get to other computer systems.

Context

Sometimes the IO Gatekeeper is too slow, or is in a partial capability mode, or the system can't afford the resources to send a message to a nearby system.

An interface specification document has probably been written that outlines how the two systems should communicate, or at least that the need to communicate exists and what information should be exchanged.

Forces

- Standard MML messages could be used between two systems, but both systems will have to spend resources (memory, time) to encode and decode the message in the other system's language.

Solution

Provide a hardwired messaging connection (e.g., Dynamic Overload Controls, E2A telemetry channels, etc.). Use the interface specification document to describe the interface so that both systems can be developed towards a common interface view (see Figure 23-19).

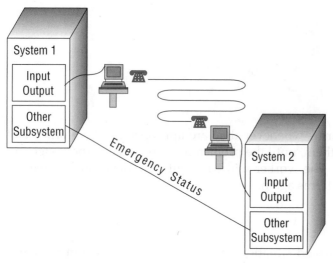

Figure 23-19

Resulting Context

The system will present information to monitoring systems even when the ordinary IO methods cannot be afforded due to emergency or resource utilization priorities.

If more information is needed than a simple hardwired messaging connection can provide, consider adding Raw IO.

Reference.   [Green+1977, pp. 1174–1175]

Raw IO

Problem

How do we provide IO during those times when the IO system is unavailable, for example, during system initialization or times of emergency?

Context

Sometimes the IO Gatekeeper is too slow, or is in a partial capability mode, or the system can't afford the resources to do IO. These might be just the situations in which people need to be informed about system state. String A Wire cannot provide enough information in these circumstances.

Forces

- Humans watching a system that has no ability to communicate are tempted to do something drastic—like manually requesting an initialization. This is rarely the right thing to do (see Minimize Human Intervention [Adams+1996]).
- If the system doesn't communicate during times of crisis, there is nothing to help an expert user help the system (see People Know Best [Adams+1996]).
- Recovery and initialization programs are in total control of the system and typically have the ability to look inside other subsystems and perform their work. In fact, this is probably safer than allowing the IO subsystem loose during periods of system recovery.
- The IO system is large with many more interfaces than the recovery system, so a large amount of code must be available during recovery for IO to work.

Solution

Display the output via brute force mechanisms such as writing directly to a logical channel and avoiding the IO system. This should be limited to recovery periods only (see Figure 23-20).

The periods during which this raw IO mechanism operates should be limited. The system should try to restore the IO system as soon as possible.

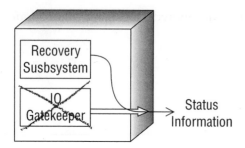

Figure 23-20

Resulting Context

During critical periods, the safe course is chosen and the recovery programs administer IO rather than rely on the IO system.

PATTERN THUMBNAILS

Table 23-2   *Input Output Patterns*

Pattern Name	Pattern Intent
Alarm Grid	Group alarms into grids to help the workers identify problems.
Audible Alarms	Sound audible alarms to alert office personnel of problems.
Beltline Terminal	Allow workers to take their terminals with them.
Don't Let Them Forget	Reassert alarms when necessary, purposely forgetting requests to retire the alarms.
Five Minutes of No Escalation Messages	Don't confuse workers with too frequent messages.
George Washington Is Still Dead	Issue state change messages only when the state changes, not to remind about the current state.
IO Triage	Add a priority tag to each output message and sort the output using them.

Pattern Name	Pattern Intent
Mind Your Own Business	Only send output to concerned terminal groups (logical channels).
MML	Use a standardized IO language.
Office Alarms	Allow the alarm system to be customizable with site-specific alarms.
Pseudo-IO	Provide for internal subsystems to add IO to the stream.
Raw IO	Provide a way for recovery systems to bypass the IO Gatekeeper.
Shut Up and Listen	Give human input/output messages a high priority.
String A Wire	Provide a system-to-system emergency information channel.
The Bottom Line	Issue messages to summarize a number of events rather than for each of many events.
Timestamp	Add a timestamp and/or a sequence number to each output message.
Who Asked?	Return output only to the logical channel/terminal that requested it.

Table 23-3 *Referenced Patterns*

Pattern Name	Pattern Intent	Page References to [Adams+ 1996]
Minimize Human Intervention	Give machine enough intelligence to not require human intervention.	551–552
People Know Best	Assume humans know more than the machine.	552–553
Riding Over Transients	Give transients time to clear up on their own.	554–555

ACKNOWLEDGMENTS

The authors would like to acknowledge the following people for their help in preparing this pattern language: Ralph Jones (1937–1998)—inventor of the Alarm Grid concept and of the concept of using message tags as the key to sound an Audible Alarm. Reviewers within Lucent Technologies: Rick Rockershousen who reviewed 1A ESS content; Glen Moore who was one of the original developers of the 4ESS Switch IO system; Chuck Borcher and Deatrice Childs who participated in a review of Alarm Grid and Office Alarms; and Juel Ulven for reviewing the alarm patterns.

David DeLano, our PLoP '98 shepherd, provided invaluable comments to improve these patterns, and the participants in a TelePLoP sponsored workshop and the Zen View Writers' Workshop group at PLoP '98 provided invaluable assistance.

Five Minutes of No Escalation Messages is co-authored by Mike Adams and a previous version was published in [Adams+1996].

REFERENCES

[Adams+1996] M. Adams, J. Coplien, R. Gamoke, R. Hanmer, F. Keeve, and K. Nicodemus. "Fault-Tolerant Telecommunication System Patterns." In J.M. Vlissides, J.O. Coplien, and N.L. Kerth (eds.), *Pattern Languages of Program Design*. Reading, MA: Addison-Wesley, 1996.

[Budlong+1977] A.H. Budlong, B.G. DeLugish, S.M. Neville, J.S. Nowak, J.L. Quinn, and F.W. Wendland. "1A Processor: Control System." *Bell System Technical Journal*, 56(2): 135–179, 1977.

[Clement+1977] G.F. Clement, P.S. Fuss, R.J. Griffith, R.C. Lee, and R.D. Royer. "1A Processor: Control, Administrative, and Utility Software." *Bell System Technical Journal*, 56(2): 237–254, 1977.

[Green+1977] T.V. Green, D.G. Haenschke, B.H. Hornbach, and C.E. Johnson. "No 4 ESS: Network Management and Traffic Administration." *Bell System Technical Journal*, 56(7): 1169–1202, 1977.

[Giunta+1977] J.A. Giunta, S.F. Heath III, J.T. Raleigh, and M.T. Smith Jr. "No 4 ESS: Data/Trunk Administration and Maintenance." *Bell System Technical Journal*, 56(7): 1203–1237, 1977.

[Gamma+1995] E. Gamma, R. Helm, R. Johnson, and J. Vlissides. *Design Patterns Elements of Reusable Object-Oriented Software*. Reading, MA: Addison-Wesley, 1995.

[Huttenhoff+1977] J.H. Huttenhoff, J. Janik Jr., G.D. Johnson, W.R. Schleicher, M.F. Slana, and F.H. Tendick Jr. "No 4 ESS: Peripheral System." *Bell System Technical Journal*, 56(7): 1029–1055, 1977.

Robert Hanmer may be reached at hanmer@lucent.com.

Greg Stymfal may be reached at stymfalg@agcs.com.

PART 8

Reviewing

There is more to being a software professional than hacking out code in the middle of the night. We all have a responsibility to share our ideas with each other. But sharing ideas means holding them up for scrutiny and evaluation by our peers, an intimidating prospect. Fortunately, there are patterns about how to make this review process most effective and helpful. Here are two sets of such patterns.

Chapter 24: Identify the Champion: An Organizational Pattern Language for Program Committees by Oscar Nierstrasz. When we started on the arduous task of picking the best pattern papers from 75 submissions for inclusion in this book one submission struck a chord from the very beginning. Not only is "Identify the Champion" a great paper, but it also gave us valuable advice on how to proceed in the selection process. This pattern language supports the program chair of a technical conference and has been used many times. The core idea is to make the program committee members champion specific papers. Being a champion for a paper means stating, "I really like this paper and am ready to fight for its acceptance."

Our job as editors of this book was slightly different from that of a program chair. We did not enjoy the luxury of a physical program committee meeting, nor did we work under a strict deadline. Nevertheless, Identify the Champion helped us be more efficient in the selection process. It turned out that each of us championed a couple of papers, partly based on the reviews we got from our formidable army of reviewers, partly based on our own opinions.

Many papers were clearly good enough to be accepted or bad enough to be rejected. The difficult decision was what to do with the borderline papers. Interestingly, it turned out that the so-called borderline papers that ended up as chapters in this book almost always had champions. A few had detractors—also a pattern in this collection—and they tended to be rejected. The papers about which we all had lukewarm feelings were generally rejected. This is appropriate, since the papers that none of us championed will probably have little reader appeal as well.

At times, we fell back into our old habits of trying to assess the papers purely objectively. As it turned out, not only was this considerably slower, but the outcome was no fairer than championing the papers we really liked, even when that was based on more subjective "gut feelings." In the future, we will use championing more extensively! Even if you do not expect to be program chair or editor sometime soon, read this chapter. It presents many insights about how to make sound decisions on many complex technical subjects under strict time pressure.

Chapter 25: A Pattern Language for Writers' Workshops by James O. Coplien with Bobby Woolf.   The other chapter in this section is, by contrast, on how to help others and yourself to improve your writing so that your papers will shine in the public. Mutual support and encouragement among a group of authors are the main concepts in A Pattern Language for Writers' Workshops. It describes how the Writers' Workshops at PLoP conferences are run.

At PLoP conferences, authors come together to review each others' patterns. Generally, the patterns are still works in progress. Each paper is reviewed during the conference in the format of a Writers' Workshop. Unlike a traditional design review, the focus is on helping the author improve the work. And since most of the attendees are authors themselves, they form a community of authors who support each other in the framework of this pattern language.

Writers' workshops are not new. Dick Gabriel, computer scientist and poet, adapted Writers' Workshops for us from the creative writing community. We have continued to modify them for our own use, but we have kept the same goals as the authors and poets—to protect the dignity of the author and to improve our writing. In fact, all the works in this book have been through at least one Writers' Workshop at a PLoP conference. This chapter describes our Writers' Workshop practice and adds eye-opening insights into the inner workings of group dynamics and human nature. Even engineers will appreciate that.

Chapter 24

Identify the Champion: An Organizational Pattern Language for Program Committees

Oscar Nierstrasz

Program committees (PCs) for many computing science conferences adhere to standards that are more common for journal publications in other domains. A great deal of time and effort is invested in reviewing submitted papers. In most cases, the PC meets physically for one or two days, thus entailing considerable expense. Occasionally "virtual meetings" are held by telephone or e-mail, but the dynamics of the meetings are essentially the same: each submission must be judged on its own merits and accepted only if there is general agreement that the paper meets the standards of the conference.

Clearly, in order for a paper to be accepted, it helps if there is some PC member who "champions" it at the meeting. Although the idea of championing seems to be central, it is seldom formally incorporated into the review process. When it is, experience shows that it has a dramatic effect in focusing attention on the key issue—that is, accepting the best papers—and making meetings much more effective. In order for this to work well, however, it is important to instill the idea of "championing" throughout the review process. We present here a small pattern language[1] that captures successful practice in several such conference review processes.

---

[1] It is a "language" (as opposed to a "catalogue") in the sense that one should combine the individual patterns to form a complete solution to the problem addressed.

Table 24-1 *Pattern Overview*

Pattern	Intent
Identify the Champion	Make the paper review and selection process for a scientific conference more efficient by focusing program committee members' attention on whether or not they will "champion" a submitted paper during the program committee meeting. (This pattern is a prerequisite for the others.)
Experts Review Papers Champions Review Papers	Distribute papers to PC members who are likely to be competent champions. (These are two competing patterns.)
Make Champions Explicit	Make PC members aware of championing before they start reviewing papers.
Identify the Conflicts	Analyze the review results and group papers into interesting categories.
Identify Missing Champions	Detect and avoid archetypical problems that arise during PC meetings.
Champions Speak First	Maintain order during the PC meeting.
Consensus on PC Papers	Handle the special case of papers submitted by PC members.

This pattern language is targeted first of all to PC chairs, who must define the review process and chair the meeting, and second of all to PC members, who need to understand the key problems and issues in the process. Finally, the language may be of interest to authors who are submitting papers to such conferences.

For an overview of the patterns, see Table 24-1.

THE PATTERNS

Identify the Champion

Context

You are the PC chair for a computing science conference with high scientific standards. You should define a review and selection process for selecting the best papers from those submitted.

Most review processes are superficially the same, but the details can be quite different from conference to conference.

The PC chair collects submissions and distributes them to individual PC members for review. PC members may return papers to the PC chair in case of conflict of interest or lack of expertise. Each submission is typically reviewed by three or four PC members. Review forms are collected and sorted, and submissions are ranked prior to a PC meeting where the papers are discussed and either accepted or rejected for presentation at the conference.

A PC meeting typically lasts one to two days, during which, for example, twenty to thirty papers are selected for presentation at a conference from a much larger number of submissions, for example, fifty to two hundred. For each paper, the PC chair invites the PC to present arguments in favor of and against acceptance. In principle all papers are discussed, but often the papers with the lowest scores are summarily rejected and are only discussed if someone explicitly requests it. Anonymous extracts of the review forms are typically returned to all authors to help them improve their papers, regardless of whether they were accepted or not.

Problem

How should you design the review process so that the PC meeting will succeed in selecting the best papers?

Forces

There are a large number of forces at play. Here we list some of the most important. Some forces that are specific to only certain phases of the review process are listed under the other patterns that follow.

- Each PC member should have roughly the same number of papers to review, and papers should be reviewed by domain experts.
- It is hard to assign an objective score to a paper, since numerical ratings or qualifications like "strong accept" or "good paper" will be interpreted differently by each reviewer.
- PC members have limited time to devote to evaluating fifteen to twenty papers.
- PC meetings are expensive to organize.
- It is hard to know in advance which papers will generate the most discussion.
- Without strong guidelines, a PC meeting can quickly degenerate into chaos.

Solution

Make the paper review and selection process for a scientific conference more efficient by focusing program committee members' attention on whether they will champion a submitted paper during the program committee meeting.

Be sure to distribute the papers to PC members who are likely to champion them. Organize the review forms, the ranking and sorting of reviews, detection of conflicts, and the review meeting itself around the identification of champions. Use rating schemes with explicit operational meaning, such as "I will champion this paper," rather than an implicit, subjective meaning, such as "strong accept," or "better than average," or "5." Group papers around the presence or absence of champions and detractors rather than by ranking them with weighted scores. Drive all discussions and decisions by identifying the champion.

Rationale

In practice, only those papers that are successfully championed by a PC member present at the meeting will be accepted. Since this happens anyway, the entire review and selection process will be much more efficient and effective if championing is made explicit in the process.

Identifying the champion forces PC members to focus on their behavior during the PC meeting rather than on their subjective impressions while reading the paper.

Examples

The notion of championing is commonly applied during PC meetings to keep discussions focused, but it is rarely made explicit in the rest of the process. Some recent PCs that have made championing explicit include ICSE '98,[2] ECOOP '98,[3] OOPSLA '98,[4] FSE 6,[5] and PLoP '98.[6]

Related Patterns

Jim Coplien [Coplien1998] describes several related patterns drawn from various OOPSLA program committees, including AssigningPapersToReviewers [Johnson1998], SortedPaperList [Beck1998], and PaperChampion [Coplien1998a]. The earlier patterns, however, do not explain how the notion of championing can really drive the whole review process.

---

[2] International Conference on Software Engineering

[3] European Conference on Object-Oriented Programming

[4] Object-Oriented Programming Systems, Languages and Applications

[5] Foundations of Software Engineering

[6] Pattern Languages of Programs

Dick Kemmerer, the PC chair of ICSE 98 [personal e-mail communication] points out a variant of Identify the Champion that has some distinct drawbacks:

> "Several weeks before the PC meeting I told the PC that we would be following a procedure close to what you described in the paper, and gave them all a pointer to the paper, asking them to read it before the meeting. I immediately got an objection from one PC member who said he did not want to use the "champion" approach. . . . I mention this because there are folks out there that have a preconceived notion of the "champion" approach. At these PC meetings a paper would not be accepted *unless someone was willing to put their name on it* (i.e., their name appeared on the paper as "recommended by"). . . . The problem seems to be that people are less likely to want their name to appear in print as being the endorser than to be a champion as per your approach."

Shepherding is a pattern of guiding a paper (or rather, its authors) through rough terrain so that it can reach ground where it can be truly championed without reservations. Some conferences (like PLoP) make heavy use of shepherding, whereas others avoid it.

A variant is Conditional Acceptance in which the PC chair exercises discretion over publication of the final version of the paper. Yet another variant is Mentoring, in which authors who seek advice in preparing a paper for submission may be assigned a "mentor," who is usually a PC member.

Write to the Program Committee [Beck1993] is a pattern that authors can apply to increase the chances that their papers will be accepted. The idea is to write in such a way as to win over a potential champion by catching her attention and providing good ammunition to argue for acceptance during the PC meeting. A good understanding of the dynamics of PC meetings helps in applying this pattern. A related tactic is to try and identify specific PC members who are likely to review the paper and write in such a way as to win them over as champions. (It almost goes without saying that this tactic can easily backfire!)

Experts Review Papers

Context

You are a PC chair and have decided to apply Identify the Champion. You are expecting one hundred to two hundred submissions, each of which should be evaluated by three to four PC members.

Problem

How do you distribute papers to the PC?

Forces

- Papers should be reviewed by someone competent to evaluate their contribution.
- It can be hard to guess who is the best person to review a paper.
- The most convincing champion for a paper is a domain expert.

Solution

Try to match papers to domain experts in the PC.

> One easy way to get a rough match is to first get all PC members to identify the domains and keywords that correspond to their main areas of expertise and their secondary areas of interest. Then, in the Call For Contributions (CFC), ask authors to explicitly state which of these apply to their submissions. When submissions arrive, use this information to match papers to PC members.
>
> It helps to scan each paper to get a feeling of who should review it. If related work by some PC member is explicitly mentioned in the paper or the references, then that may be a good person to review it *unless there is a conflict of interest* (i.e., the PC member is a co-author or colleague!).

Rationale

An expert who likes a paper is typically more willing to champion it than a non-expert.

Resulting Context

If an expert is less than enthusiastic about a paper, that is likely to kill its chances for acceptance, especially if the positive reviews are from PC members who are competent in the domain, but not experts.

Champions Review Papers

Context

You are a PC chair and have decided to apply Identify the Champion. You need to distribute submitted papers to PC members who are competent to evaluate them.

Problem

How do you distribute papers in such a way as to maximize each paper's chance that it will find its champion?

Forces

- Papers should be reviewed by someone competent enough to evaluate their contribution.
- It can be hard to guess who is the best person to review a paper.
- The most convincing champion for a paper is a domain expert.

Solution

Let PC members pick the papers they want to review.

> One (not very good) way to do this is to distribute a list of titles and authors to all PC members and have them select which papers (a) they would like to review (i.e., they think they might champion) (b) they feel competent to review, and (c) they do *not* want to review (either because they do not feel competent, or because they have a conflict of interest). There are two problems with this approach: (1) PC members will have too little information to go on, and (2) it will take at least a week to get the responses back (if you're lucky).

> A better way is to request authors in the CFC to *preregister* their intent to submit a paper, at least a week in advance of the paper deadline, by sending the PC chair an e-mail containing the title, authors, contact author's coordinates, an abstract, and keywords (see Experts Review Papers). After the preregistration deadline has passed, send the list of abstracts electronically to the entire PC, and ask them to categorize papers as above based on this information. When the paper submission deadline passes and all papers are in, papers should already be assigned to PC members and can immediately go out.

Rationale

Asking PC members to "bid" for papers to review reinforces championing.

Examples

Many conferences, ICSE in particular, traditionally use a bidding procedure.

Related Patterns

AssigningPapersToReviewers [Johnson1998] discusses some of the main ideas behind both Experts Review Papers and Champions Review Papers. The key difference is that the patterns presented here focus on giving papers the best chance of being championed.

Make Champions Explicit

Context

You are a PC chair who plans to apply Identify the Champion. You must design review forms that will help you prepare a successful meeting.

Problem

How can you make it easy to tell which papers will be championed in advance of the meeting?

Forces

- Reviews are necessarily subjective, since numerical ratings, or qualifications like "strong accept" or "good paper" will be interpreted differently by each reviewer.
- A PC member who gives a paper a high score is not always willing to champion it.
- Just as surprisingly, PC members who give mediocre scores to paper sometimes turn out to be strong champions.
- Review forms with lots of numerical grades (i.e., for originality, soundness, readability, etc.) are hard to convert into a single, meaningful score.
- Review forms that are too complex annoy reviewers, and much of the information they record is typically ignored during the PC meeting.
- PC members often delegate papers to "subreviewers," who may not be fully aware of the details of the review and selection process.

Solution

Ask PC members explicitly on the review form whether they intend to champion the paper.

> It is very tempting to introduce very fine-grained scales of appreciation on review forms, such as scales from 1 to 10 for various criteria, including originality, soundness, presentation, etc. These kinds of ratings typically have the opposite of the desired effect, namely, they waste the reviewers' time and make it more difficult to tell who is willing to champion a paper.
>
> In practice the only ratings that are really critical for the PC meeting are (1) a score indicating whether the paper should be accepted, and (2) a score indicating the reviewer's expertise. The other issues, though important, normally appear in the written commentary (if they are relevant) and are not essential to running the PC meeting.

The most important thing about the paper's score is to make the *operational* semantics of the score clear. It frequently happens that a PC member gives a paper a strong accept "because it was the best of the papers I had to review," but not because it was particularly good. There are four essential semantic categories:

A: Good paper. I will champion it at the PC meeting.

B: OK paper, but I will not champion it.

C: Weak paper, though I will not fight strongly against it.

D: Serious problems. I will argue to reject this paper.

These four positions cover the interesting ones taken by PC members during discussion. Finer gradations of appreciation are typically uninteresting. Note that it is not important how the scores are labeled—for example, they may still be numeric (i.e., from 1 to 5 or from 0 to 10), or textual (i.e., strong/weak accept/reject), but their meaning must be clear.

The most important positions are A and D, as these are, respectively, the champions and detractors. B and C are fence-sitters, but will also supply arguments for or against. The difference between a B and a C is that B is basically in favor of a paper, but is not willing to champion it, whereas C is not impressed by a paper, but could be convinced if someone else champions it.

Separate ratings of high or low confidence are not especially useful, since low confidence tends to show up anyway as a B or C position.

A separate rating for the reviewer's expertise, on the other hand, is essential to detect the *inexpert champion* situation. The following ratings are used *only* for conflict detection and *not* to rank papers:

X: I am an expert in the subject area of this paper.

Y: I am knowledgeable in the area, though not an expert.

Z: I am not an expert. My evaluation is that of an informed outsider.

Note that it is not necessarily the intention that all reviewers be experts. In conferences with broad scope, it can be useful to have some nonexpert reviews to evaluate a paper's accessibility to a general audience. Only in rare situations, however, should a nonexpert consider championing a paper.

The scores and expertise ratings would normally *not* be revealed to authors, as this information is purely procedural and has no function after the selection process is done.

The remaining parts of the review form will vary, but typically include: (1) a summary in which the reviewer briefly summaries the paper and its main contributions, (2) points in favor/against acceptance that help focus the discussion at the PC meeting, (3) additional comments for the authors, and (4) Additional comments for the PC. Other parts of the review form are used to help run the meeting or the conference itself. These include paper number, authors, titles, and date, as well as questions such as "Should the author be invited to give a demo?" and "Is this paper a candidate for our award?"

Rationale

The most important thing for a reviewer to decide is whether he thinks that the paper is worth defending at the PC meeting, not whether it is a great paper or not. Make Champions Explicit helps put reviewers in the right frame of mind.

PC members who delegate papers to subreviewers are aware that they must be prepared to play the role of champion/detractor on the basis of the review. They are warned in advance if they are the only champion of a paper.

Examples

ICSE '98, ECOOP '98, OOPSLA '98, FSE 6, and others

Identify the Conflicts

Context

You are a PC chair who has applied Make Champions Explicit in designing your review forms. It is now a week before the PC meeting and all (or most) of the reviews are in.

Problem

How should you order or group the papers in preparation for the meeting?

Forces

- It is hard to convert the results of several reviews into a single meaningful score.
- When papers are ranked numerically, there will often be high-ranking papers that are rejected and low-ranking papers that end up being accepted.
- The PC meeting runs more smoothly if "similar" papers are grouped together, that is, all those that can be quickly accepted, those that will surely be rejected, those that will generate debate.
- It is important to identify controversial papers as early as possible.
- It is hard to guess which papers will be controversial.

Solution

Group papers according to their highest and lowest scores. Take care to identify papers with both extreme high and low scores. Do not attempt to rank papers numerically.

The purpose of ranking and classifying papers is to give some structure to the PC meeting by grouping together papers that are likely to require the same kind of debate. Whereas numerical rankings typically fail to achieve this, grouping by presence or absence of champions quickly gets to the point.

A particularly simple and effective way to group papers is to assign a two-letter code to each paper, consisting of the highest and the lowest scores, and to sort the papers by this code. If we are using scores A-D, as described in Make Champions Explicit, this yields ten groups of papers, of which seven are interesting:

AA, AB.   All reviews are positive, and there is at least one champion. These papers will almost certainly be accepted.

AC.   This means that all reviews are A, B, or C. This is a likely accept, since there is at least one champion and no strong detractor. The only question is whether the reservations of the C review are serious or not.

AD.   This is a serious conflict and will certainly lead to debate. Note that this does not distinguish between cases in which, for example, we have three As and one D, or one A, one B, one C, and one D. In practice, the important positions are the extremes.

BB.   All reviewers are fence-sitters. Everyone likes the paper, but no one is willing to be a champion. The discussion should determine whether the Bs are really As or not.

BC.   These tend to be borderline papers, since no one is willing to be either a strong advocate or a detractor. Such papers are often put on a "slush pile" and resurrected or discarded after the rest of the program has been defined.

BD.   These papers are likely to be rejected. There is no strong champion, but there is a strong position against acceptance. Such a paper might still be accepted if the B decides to champion it after all.

CC, CD, DD.   These papers are almost certain rejects. Papers may be resurrected from this group only under exceptional circumstances, for instance, if it turns out that none of the reviewers were experts, but another PC member who is an expert in the domain reads the paper during the meeting and decides to champion it.

Note that this classification scheme works independently of the number of reviews each paper receives. What is significant are the high and low scores.

Rationale

Identifying the extremes highlights potential controversy. Where there is no controversy, the PC can typically come to a quick decision.

Examples

Dick Kemmerer reports:

> "As far as using the approach at ICSE98 goes, . . . I had six categories instead of four. . . . The categories were: . . . Will argue for acceptance (A); Inclined to accept (B); Not opposed to acceptance (C); Not opposed to rejection (D); Inclined to reject (E); Will argue for rejection (F).
>
> Having the two middle categories caused some problems, and I would use only four if I were to do this again.
>
> Before the meeting I separated the papers into three groups:
>
> > Group 1 (Likely Accepts): AA, AB, AC
> >
> > Group 2 (Mixed): AD, AE, AF, BB, BC, BD, BE, BF, CC, CD, CE, CF
> >
> > Group 3 (Likely Rejects): DD, DE, DF, EE, EF, FF
>
> In addition, all PC member papers were postponed until all other papers were decided.
>
> We first discussed the Group 1 papers and they were all accepted with little time devoted to them. Next we rejected all of the Group 3 papers without discussing them, although I stated that any PC member that wanted to bring one of them up was welcome to do so. This did not happen. The middle group as you predicted took the most time.
>
> I also distributed reviews for papers with conflicting reviews to the reviewers beforehand for online discussion. When reviews were changed I entered the updated review before the PC meeting. I also informed each PC member what papers they would champion before the PC meeting, so that they were prepared."

At the OOPSLA '98 PC meeting, a similar scheme was used (ratings from A–F), with very similar results.

Related Patterns

SortedPaperList [Beck1998] has a similar intent, but considers instead the total number of accepts or rejects that a paper has received.

Identify Missing Champions

Context

You are a PC chair who has applied Make Champions Explicit in designing your review forms. It is now a week before the PC meeting and all (or most) of the reviews are in.

Problem

What problems should you detect in advance of the meeting?

Forces

- PC members have limited time to devote to evaluating fifteen to twenty papers.
- PC meetings are expensive to organize.
- Not all reviewers will be experts.
- Not everybody will make it to the meeting.
- Some reviews will be late or missing.

Solution

Identify which papers are likely to be championed by whom and make sure that champions are prepared for the meeting. If a potential champion is not an expert, or for some reason cannot attend the meeting, take some compensating action (like soliciting an extra review).

> Since PC meetings are expensive to organize (think not only of the travel and hotel costs, but of the salaries paid for those attending!) and cannot be repeated, and the selection process depends so heavily on the identification of champions, it is important to detect potential problems *before* the meeting takes place. This means that reviews should be returned to the PC chair well in advance—typically at least a week before the PC meeting. To reduce delays, to facilitate analysis of the results, and to permit automatic preparation of review packages, it is a good idea to distribute review forms electronically.

The following situations are variants of "missing champions" that should be detected early to help PC members better prepare for the meeting:

Late or missing reviews. This is the most basic problem to check for. PC meetings often start with only one or two reviews received for some of the papers. In such cases it is often necessary to get someone to review papers on the fly at the meeting, which is clearly a half-measure. Each paper should receive a minimum of three reviews for a fair review process. Check which papers are missing reviews and pressure the PC members to deliver them. If you doubt that the review will arrive on time, try to solicit an extra review.

Missing champion (or detractor). The PC chair should check whether anyone who cannot be present at the meeting happens to be the only champion or detractor for a paper. An e-mail exchange in advance between the reviewers may help them come to a consensus in advance of the meeting or at least to clarify the source of disagreement.

Absent reviewers. This is a variation of the above, in which *none* of the reviewers are present to present their views of the paper. In a large conference with two hundred submitted papers and twenty or thirty PC members, it is almost inevitable that a couple of papers will fall into this category. These papers should be discussed by e-mail. If necessary, another review should be solicited by an attending PC member.

Unprepared champions. Very often a PC member is surprised to discover at the PC meeting that she is the only champion for a submission. An unprepared PC member may buckle under negative criticism of the paper and withdraw support. PC members often pass on papers for evaluation to "subreviewers." This can be an efficient way to review large numbers of papers, as long as the PC member carefully checks the papers and reviews before the meeting. If a PC member ends up being a champion for a subreviewed paper, it is essential that she be warned in advance in order to validate or overturn the review.

Inexpert champions. Sometimes during the PC meeting it turns out that the only champions for a paper have low confidence because they are not experts in the problem domain, while the experts either were not assigned the paper or are only lukewarm about acceptance. Typically, nonexperts will back down from an "accept" position if there is dissent from an expert. In such cases it can be useful to solicit an extra review from an expert in advance of the meeting.

Low overall expertise. If none of the reviewers is an expert, then the selection process can break down regardless of the scores given by the reviewers. In such cases the PC chair should solicit an expert review in advance of the meeting.

Finally, papers submitted by PC members, or for which PC members have a conflict of interest (i.e., papers submitted by close colleagues), require special treatment during the meeting, but do not constitute problems as such.

Rationale

Identifying champions in advance helps everyone to be better prepared for the PC meeting.

Champions who are unable to attend the meeting have a better chance to influence the meeting if they are identified explicitly well in advance.

Champions Speak First

Context

You are a PC chair who has applied Make Champions Explicit in designing your review forms. You have also used Identify the Conflicts and Identify Missing Champions to group the papers and identify potential problems in advance. You are now ready to run the PC meeting.

Problem

How do you focus attention at the meeting?

Forces

- Each PC member present has only reviewed a fraction of the papers.
- Meeting participants feel obliged to talk about all the papers they reviewed.
- Meandering discussion wastes time.

Solution

Discuss the papers in groups, according to Identify the Conflicts. For each paper, first invite a champion to introduce the paper and then to present reasons why it should be accepted. Then invite any detractors to explain why they think it should not be accepted. Finally, open the general discussion and try to reach a consensus. If there is no champion, *the paper should not be discussed.*

> If no conscious effort is made to quickly identify champions, much time can be wasted discussing papers that have no chance of being accepted. Very often, when a paper comes up for discussion, a PC member will start by saying, "Well, I didn't like this paper because . . ." This is not very useful, first of all because it does not tell the rest of the PC what the paper is about. Second, it does not lead to effective decision making, since the purpose of the meeting is to *accept* papers, not to reject them (i.e., it is more productive to concentrate on discussing papers that have a chance of being accepted than those that don't). Long unfocused discussions with delayed decisions may exhaust all reviewers. In the end, the decision taken may depend on who has the most stamina.
>
> It is good to set some ground rules to keep discussions focused. For each paper, the champion, if one exists, or the closest there is to a champion, should introduce the paper by briefly summarizing it and presenting the points in its favor. Then, the detractor (or whoever has the strongest negative points) should speak next. Finally the remaining reviewers can back up these arguments or fill in missing points. If there is a detractor, then the champions and detractors typically play the roles of defence and prosecution in a trial, and the rest of those present play the role of the jury. Frequently either the champions or the detractors become convinced by the arguments of the other, and a consensus is quickly reached.
>
> If no consensus is possible, it may be necessary to ask the PC to vote. In this case *all* PC members present who have participated in the discussion should vote (since they act as a jury).
>
> PC members also should be reminded of the criteria for acceptance. These may be more stringent, or more lax, depending on the nature of the conference, or may be quite specialized. Typically, an accepted paper should have a clear, original

contribution, and fulfill the usual criteria of readability, completeness, and so forth. Originality is a strong criterion and many papers fail to be accepted if they do not clearly demonstrate new results. A champion/detractor should address these specific criteria.

If there is no clear champion for a paper, the discussion should focus on checking why no one wants to champion it (i.e., to try to smoke out a reluctant champion). If no champion can be identified, the paper can be quickly rejected.

Delaying a decision on a paper is almost always a bad idea. A decision should only be delayed if something will happen in between that may change the outcome, that is, if an expert will check the paper for originality. Borderline papers (BC grouping) may be delayed until the other papers have been considered.

On the other hand, if the champion for a paper is not present, then the discussion and decision *must* be delayed until that person either arrives or can be consulted, that is, by telephone or e-mail.

It is highly recommended to supply each PC member attending the meeting with copies of all the reviews for which they do not have conflicts. This makes it easier for everyone present at the meeting to actively participate in the decision-making process, even for papers they have not personally reviewed.

The actual order in which papers are handled does not seem to matter much in practice, as long as they are handled in relatively coherent groups. It is common to start by accepting as many of the "easy" papers as possible and by rejecting all of the unchampioned papers before starting in on the controversial papers.

Rationale

Discussions tend to be shorter and more focused if they can only take place when a champion is identified. Delays only take place if there is a chance that a new champion can be identified.

Explicitly encouraging PC members to champion papers provides opportunities to draw reluctant champions out in the discussion. (Each reviewer can be explicitly asked, "Are you willing to champion this paper?")

Resulting Context

Champions Speak First can stifle debate if applied too rigorously. One must be careful not to discourage reluctant champions.

Examples

This pattern is so common that there are few PCs that do not apply it in some form. The key difference is whether the PC meeting has been prepared in advance by applying the related patterns mentioned in the Context section.

Related Patterns

PaperChampion [Coplien1998a] presents a similar idea, though without advance preparation by champions.

Consensus on PC Papers

Context

You are a PC chair running a PC meeting according to Champions Speak First.

Problem

How should PC papers be handled?

Forces

- Sometimes weak papers are accepted to conferences where one of the authors is a PC member.
- A conference will not be taken seriously if it appears that PC members can get their papers more easily accepted than other authors.
- You may want to apply more stringent requirements to PC papers than to other submissions.

Solution

PC papers should be accepted only if there is at least one champion and there are no serious (expert) detractors.

> Whenever a PC paper is discussed (and, typically, whenever a PC member has a conflict of interest with a paper being discussed), the PC member concerned leaves the meeting and is only called back when a decision has been taken.

Rationale

By making sure there are no detractors, PC papers will be accepted only if there is a consensus. This generally ensures that such papers are "at least as good as" the best papers accepted to conference.

ACKNOWLEDGMENTS

Many thanks to Serge Demeyer, Rachid Guerraoui, Dick Kemmerer, Tony Simons, and Jim Coplien, who suggested numerous improvements to the presentation and the contents. Thanks as well to the PCs and PC Chairs of ECOOP, ESEC, ICSE, and OOPSLA who have helped make this pattern explicit.

I am also indebted to Mike Beedle, the PLoP '98 shepherd for this paper, and to my PLoP '98 workshop group, who suggested numerous simplifications and encouraged me to decompose Identify the Champion into a pattern language. I especially thank Bob Hanmer and David Cymbala who helped me factor out the individual patterns.

Many thanks as well to Ian Chai and colleagues at UIUC who workshopped the paper and sent additional comments. Finally, I am grateful to the PLoP D4 reviewers who suggested several simplifications and cuts.

FURTHER READING

[Beck1993] K. Beck. OOPSLA '93 Panel. Available: http://www.acm.org/sigplan/oopsla/oopsla96/how93.html.

[Beck1998] K. Beck. "SortedPaperList." Available: http://c2.com/cgi/wiki?SortedPaperList, in Coplien "OopslaProgramChairPatterns."

[Coplien1998] J. Coplien. "OopslaProgramChairPatterns." Available: http://c2.com/cgi/wiki?OopslaPrograChairPatterns.

[Coplien1998a] J. Coplien. "PaperChampion." Available: http://c2.com/cgi/wiki?PaperChampion, in Coplien, "OopslaProgramChairPatterns."

[Johnson1998] R. Johnson, "AssigningPapersToReviewers." Available: http://c2.com/cgi/wiki?AssigningPapersToReviewers, in Coplien, "OopslaProgramChairPatterns."

Oscar Nierstrasz may be reached at oscar@iam.unibe.ch. WWW: http://www.iam.unibe.ch/~oscar/.

Chapter 25

A Pattern Language for Writers' Workshops

James O. Coplien with Bobby Woolf

Peer review is a crucial element of the quality improvement process for any document and more broadly for any intellectual work. Most intellectual disciplines rely on a peer review culture for the advancement of knowledge, and those disciplines often focus more on content than on expression. Design reviews and code walk-throughs focus on what might be broken, not on what works. Most refereed journals scrutinize works first against standards of formalism and second, if at all, for readability. These reviews have their place, and most of them should be retained in the cultures that use them. The pattern community is less interested in the advancement of knowledge than in the broad dissemination of sound practice and is equally concerned with content and expression. Its review forum, a Writers' Workshop, provides a useful supplement to the traditionally more technically focused reviews.

Writers' Workshops, which come from the creative literature community, provide an alternative to prevailing peer review practice that is well-suited to the needs of the pattern community. Writers' Workshops follow a collection of normative behaviors designed to give authors constructive feedback on their work while protecting their dignity. The following patterns document those normative behaviors and the structures that support them.

This is a "cheap" pattern language. These patterns reflect a chronological (rather than structural) progression of application. There is no single ideal medium to describe what goes on in a Writers' Workshop. I use patterns here not so much because they describe structure, but because they provide an ideal form to elaborate the forces behind these practices.

None of these patterns stands alone; they combine to make a whole larger than the sum of the parts. The patterns interact in intricate ways; I attempt to describe the interactions in the course of the presentation.

This language describes our many Writers' Workshop experiences at Bell Labs and at pattern conferences. The rationales and forces recall the initial tutoring that the Hillsiders received from Richard Gabriel back in the spring of 1994 at a retreat near Ben Lomond, California. That's the closest link we have to the creative literature community, which has a lot more experience with this format than does the pattern community. I offer this language as capturing practice that has worked well for us, in hopes that others find it useful.

OVERVIEW

There are two kinds of patterns in this pattern language: setup and process patterns. The setup patterns come first, starting with the most general and proceeding through more refined patterns. The process patterns are presented in the order they are used.

Setup Patterns

1. *Open Review.* How to provide a forum for dialogue that is more effective than anonymous refereed reviews, while preserving the interests of both the author and the reviewers.
2. *Safe Setting.* How to make feedback more open and effective by raising the comfort level, particularly for the author.
3. *Authors Are Experts.* How to balance assessment of content and expression in a work.
4. *Workshop Comprises Authors.* How to deal with feelings of mistrust for outsiders, those who aren't stake holders, who might throw stones at the work.
5. *Community of Trust.* How to help authors feel that the experience will help them, rather than tear them down.
6. *Moderator Guides the Workshop.* How to keep things moving and to ensure that the rules are followed.
7. *Sitting in a Circle.* How to build a sense of identity, community, and openness in the group.
8. *Authors' Circle.* How to recognize the peer group that builds the Community of Trust.

Process Patterns

9. *Reading Just before Reviewing.* How a reviewer should avoid overpreparing or underpreparing for the workshop.

10. *Author Reads Selection.* How to bring focus to the workshop and to recognize the humanity behind the work.
11. *Fly on the Wall.* How to keep the author in the activity without becoming a disruptive presence.
12. *Volunteer Summarizes the Work.* How to bring focus to the reviewing activity and to give the author feedback on whether the work is effective in making a crisp point.
13. *Positive Feedback First.* How to give the gathering a supportive tone and to start with feedback that will put the author in a receptive mood.
14. *Suggestions for Improvement.* How to communicate improvements to the work without attacking the author or the work.
15. *Author Asks for Clarification.* How to give the author an opportunity to solicit more refined feedback without appearing to rebut the feedback that was provided.
16. *Positive Closure.* How to leave the author with a positive feeling at the end of the feedback.
17. *Thank the Author.* How to help the author remember the workshop as a positive experience.
18. *Clearing the Palate.* How to give a sense of closure to the workshop.
19. *Selective Changes.* How the author deals with a lack of consensus in the feedback.

The patterns follow Alexander's pattern form. For those unfamiliar with Alexandrian form, it is described in an appendix to this chapter.

SETUP PATTERNS

1. Open Review

. . . a successful review process depends on cooperation between an author and a group of peers who review the work. The goal of the process is to expand the body of knowledge in a particular community while protecting the integrity of the work produced by the community. **What kind of review forum supports the most effective communication between authors and reviewers, supporting dialogue, yet limiting vulnerability and bad feelings?**

*   *   *

Because peer review is an intensely human process, it is important to consider human concerns. A painful or onerous process would discourage frequent practitioners. Yet an overly permissive and accommodating process doesn't serve the goal of sustained high quality.

Most refereeing processes use anonymous review. If your review is anonymous, you don't have to worry about how your feedback will affect the way the author perceives you as an individual. Strong reviewer feedback may not be well received by the author and may be interpreted by the author as a personal indictment or attack, particularly if the paper is rejected. The author may never know you reviewed the paper, so any relationship—personal or professional—between the author and the reviewer is unaffected by the review process. This process depends on a faceless, anonymous review agent such as an editorial board, program committee, or a pool of reviewers "hidden" behind an editor. The review agent is held to be objective, impartial, and expert. The intent is to protect the dignity of both the author and the reviewers.

Yet, in this setting, it's hard to let the author know that the reviewers care about the work or that they have the author's best interests at heart. The author may feel that the reviewers are cowards for remaining anonymous. And it's more difficult for the reviewers to benefit from the author's appreciation of their efforts. It's hard for reviewers to feel that the author knows they care. The author can't appreciate the reviewers' experience and background or the broad context that is best explored through dialogue. Dialogue is crucial to the shared understanding that leads to fundamental insights and progress in a work.

But open dialogue leaves the reviewers and authors exposed, bereft of the protection afforded by the anonymous review process.

Therefore:

Provide an open review forum whose structures protect the dignity of both the authors and reviewers, making a Safe Setting (2) and Community of Trust (5) for both. Control negative author engagement with Fly on the Wall (11) and Author Asks for Clarification (15). Make the author feel welcome with Positive Feedback First (13). Develop personal engagement with Sitting in a Circle (7) and Thank the Author (17).

* * *

A Writers' Workshop format supports the dialogue necessary to effective two-way communication. It improves on the one-way feedback in refereed forums. The feedback has a short delay, which avoids the frustration and coordination problems of long feedback delays.

This pattern distinguishes the practice of the pattern community from that of most contemporary peer review. It is practiced in reading groups, at pattern workshops, and pattern conferences. However, the process for admitting patterns into the published literature of the pattern community still employs a form of anonymous peer review.

2. Safe Setting**

. . . the pattern community strives to develop a high-quality body of literature that improves the quality of life for users, developers, managers, and others in the software community. The creative literature community uses a review format called a Writers' Workshop to improve the quality of literature that is published beyond a small circle of colleagues. Authors clearly can benefit from the feedback of their peers and colleagues. **How do you establish a Safe Setting to provide free-flowing input to authors while preserving their dignity?**

*   *   *

There are few things that satisfy authors more than seeing their work published and widely read and applied. For works published without a critical review process, authors will receive their first feedback from the market they aim to influence. This may provide a rude awakening for the author.

On the other hand, peer review can be equally frightening and demoralizing because the author is open to criticism from peers who know the material and the author well.

Familiarity with the material makes it possible for these reviewers to provide the largest volume of feedback; familiarity with the author makes it possible for them to "push the author's buttons" in the review process.

Yet such review is important.

Therefore:

Provide a Safe Setting where the author can receive useful expert feedback directed at the work rather than at the author, with the goal of preserving the dignity of the author.

*   *   *

You can help the author feel at home by using the patterns Workshop Comprises Authors (4) and Authors' Circle (8), which help provide a peer setting with opportunity for reciprocation; Moderator Guides the Workshop (6), which prevents the workshop dynamics from getting out of hand; Positive Feedback First (13), which bolsters the author's sense of contribution and self-worth; Suggestions for Improvement (14), which defines the tone of constructive feedback; and Positive Closure (16) and Thank the Author (17) through which the community formally recognizes the author's contribution.

3. Authors Are Experts

. . . the pattern community is building a body of literature to capture expertise and is particularly interested in practices and techniques that are not intuitive to inexpert practitioners. **How do you balance assessment of content and expression in the work?**

*   *   *

Any given pattern is both a process and a thing, which must be experienced to be described. Most engineering reviews focus on the technical aspects of the solution itself, rather than on its relationship to any problem, or the trade-offs or understanding that go into the solution. Even in a technical review in which all those factors are present, the opportunities for the literary, humanistic, and social impact of a pattern are lost. And these are the factors that give a pattern the Quality Without a Name.

It is too easy for engineers to degenerate into technical details and to miss the aesthetic and holistic impact of a pattern.

The nature of patterns is that they are fundamental, essential "laws of nature," which means that it's likely that many people have shared the experience and insights of a pattern. A good pattern captures an experience that is an important part of Being Alive, tapping deep shared human history and cultural ties.

The substance of these experiences transcends criticism. We are taught, as part of good communication skills, never to say "you're wrong" or even "I disagree" to any statement of the form: "I feel that . . ." People own their feelings. Feelings should not be *challenged;* to do so would violate a Safe Setting (2).

Yet authors can improve most of their patterns; they can benefit from the sensibilities and experiences of others, particularly as regards their exposition and literary qualities. If we wrote as well as we owned our feelings, there would be no need for feedback. But human review and interaction have proven themselves to improve the quality even of subjective literature.

The problem is to keep people focused on providing input on the presentation that can be heard and used, and to avoid exploring the solution in too much depth.

Therefore:

View authors as experts in the material they present. This implies that the focus of the workshop is on form more than content. Problematic feedback on the content of a pattern suggests that it may not yet be a pattern.

* * *

Technical soundness of a design, or of the principles behind it, is a staple of software community reviews. Software pattern communities should consider a separate forum, such as a Design Review (a pattern language yet to be written), that uses traditional review mechanisms to assess the technical merit of a pattern. The exercise should be separate from the Writers' Workshop, which assesses the presentation of the pattern.

Even if the author is not an expert on the topic of the work, there isn't much the Writers' Workshop can do to bridle authors or "keep them in their place."

Of course, Writers' Workshops are a good place to explore relationships between patterns and to help weave existing patterns into a broader collection of literature called a pattern language. For example, a reviewer may know of other solutions to the same problem addressed by the pattern being reviewed. By comparing related patterns, authors can refine the context and force sections of their own patterns.

4. Workshop Comprises Authors*

. . . as described in Safe Setting (2), the goals of the writing community can best be achieved only when authors are given feedback useful for evolving their work while preserving their dignity. **How should the forum deal with feelings of mistrust for outsiders, those who aren't stakeholders, who might throw stones at the work?**

*   *   *

The best feedback comes from authoritarian sources, and most review settings elicit the feedback of experts (and those with vested interests) in an authoritarian setting. This posture can contribute to a feeling that critics are not accountable for what they say and that leaves the author in a disadvantaged position. Authors feel uncomfortable while in this position.

There is no reason that an author should trust reviewers except on the basis of their reputation. Trust based on subject matter reputation creates a hierarchy in the review community, structuring "those who know" against "those who write." This breaks down the sense of community and leaves the author vulnerable to feelings of inferiority.

Jerry Weinberg notes that one of the strongest power positions is learned in our grade school years, when the teacher is in the position of power to convey ideas to the student, who is passive.

Even though expert feedback is important, pattern authors are usually the most expert at communicating the pattern they have experienced again and again. What nature of expertise can best improve the work? In the pattern community, it is best that Authors Are Experts (3) in the material they compose.

Therefore:

Assemble the workshop membership from other authors who are interested in the material, who have a stake in the material, or who the author otherwise believes will contribute to the goal of improving the work. If all the participants are authors, it contributes to an egalitarian community. Authors know and appreciate the Writers' Workshop culture and are less likely to create disruptive faux pas than a casual outsider would.

As authors, the reviewers have experience with the pattern form and its effectiveness and can contribute ideas to improve the expression of the idea.

*   *   *

This principle derives from the prevailing practice of the creative literature review community. Richard Gabriel relates that he knows only of one major review setting where this principle is violated (the Writers' Workshops at a creative literature event called Bread Loaf), but that, even there, they are explicit about putting the rule aside.

You wouldn't engage a bereavement expert to improve a poem on dying, but an accomplished poet.

The author may invite nonauthors who he or she trusts to improve the work while maintaining the sense of community.

5. Community of Trust**

. . . a group of authors and a moderator are assembled to review a literary work. The author is bringing a work for review, a work in progress, and seeks help in refining the work. This group will develop into a community of trust that can serve several authors. At a conference like PLoP, there are many papers to review. **How do you best utilize this group and give the author confidence that the group will build up the work rather than tear it down?**

*   *   *

An effective Writers' Workshop is built on a community of trust. Trust is a key ingredient in a Safe Setting (2) for reviews. One important objective of the Writers' Workshop format is to guarantee a community of trust so that the author's dignity is retained.

The author is willing to release unpolished work for review in this setting, knowing that everyone knows that it is unfinished work, which implies a different review perspective than for typical, polished, conference submissions.

However, the review of a single work rarely takes longer than an hour, which is not enough time to cement long-term relationships. A group of people can develop trust only through many shared experiences. If a Writers' Workshop is to provide a community of trust, it must be together for a period of time.

The Writers' Workshop reviewers could participate in an Outward Bound exercise to build trust; this is how the Hillsiders built their initial community of trust. However, there often is no time for such exercises, and such exotic measures are frowned upon in the mainstream corporate cultures that patterns mean to serve.

Therefore:

Organize Writers' Workshops by areas of interest that tie together the works of the authors involved. The authors/reviewers and gallery should remain with the same workshop for the duration of the reviews of all authors' works.

Manuscripts are not published outside the workshops in which they are reviewed until the author refines the works and offers them for wide publication.

*   *   *

At PLoP, we start to build trust by assigning a Pattern Shepherd (a pattern language yet to be written) to help the author prepare his or her work for the workshop. The shepherding process helps filter out the most embarrassing misfits, so that all papers enter the forum with the benefit of the shepherd's insights on what makes a good pattern.

6. Moderator Guides the Workshop**

. . . a set of well-meaning, qualified people (Workshop Comprises Authors (4)) has gathered with an author to review a work such as a pattern or pattern language. **How do you keep things moving and ensure that Writers' Workshop guidelines are appropriately followed?**

*   *   *

A diverse group of people makes only clumsy progress without guidance from an authority who might (even arbitrarily) decide on the format, the duration of phases of the workshop, and so forth.

Most groups naturally seek a leader.

Someone needs to make sure everyone is given a chance to speak and that egos are kept in check. In general, someone should act as an authority to represent the interests of the workshop as a whole for everybody, and in particular, to represent the interests of the author, especially when the author is silent (Fly on the Wall (11)).

Therefore:

Each session is led by an experienced moderator, who guides (not directs) the discussion. The moderator is responsible to see that all runs smoothly. Done well, moderation is a background task: The Writers' Workshop tradition alone is usually enough to guide the main flow of the activities.

*   *   *

The moderator has many tasks and needs many skills. There are many different moderation styles, including Active Listening Moderation (a pattern language yet to be written) where the moderator affirms (feeds back) everything that is said, particularly during suggestions for improvement. There are more passive styles of moderation.

Some moderators call on reticent participants to speak; most moderators are more hands-off.

Moderators teach the remaining patterns to the group (by example and gentle guidance) and guide their use, subject to the moderator's style. Depending on the setting, the moderator may be responsible for securing copies of the work for the reviewers. The moderator initially welcomes the author and invites the author to read a selection from the work. The moderator then thanks the author and invites him or her to become a Fly on the Wall (11). The moderator invites a volunteer to summarize the pattern. The moderator makes sure that no negative criticism leaks into Positive Feedback First (13). The moderator decides when the positive feedback has reached diminishing returns and segues into Suggestions for Improvement (14). The moderator brings that session to a close and welcomes the author back into the inner circle, encouraging him or her to ask questions of clarification. The moderator leads the Thank the Author (17) ceremony and invites a Clearing the Palate (18) speaker.

The moderator may also arrange for a scribe to help the author record major discussion points.

There should be a separate pattern language for workshop session moderation.

7. Sitting in a Circle**

. . . authors are assembled to review the work of a colleague. Just as the symmetry and geometry of office space can thwart or support "what happens there," so can the simple organization of room furniture. **How should a Writers' Workshop room be laid out to facilitate the desired patterns of communication and to create the right sense of community?**

* * *

A Writers' Workshop is a community of trust and support, and the room structure should reflect that. Most meeting rooms are set up with tables and chairs. The tables help people take notes, provide a place for beverages, and support those who sag as the meeting drags on.

However, tables also provide a shield to hide behind. While the presenter may feel vulnerable at the front of the room, the rest of the attendees feel shielded behind the sturdy ramparts of the meeting room tables, which are rarely flimsy card-table affairs, but formidable hardwood structures. It is convenient to hide behind them.

Yet, in a Writers' Workshop, we want to make the author feel comfortable, as if the reviewers are not attacking from behind defended bulwarks.

Therefore:

Seat the reviewers in a circle. Both the author and moderator form part of the circle; the structure is fully egalitarian. Don't use tables: All participants should present an equally vulnerable and supportive face to the circle as a whole. Beverages can go on the floor. Except for the author, who may wish to bring a clipboard to take notes, few of the participants should be writing during the review.

* * *

The author may stand in place for Author Reads Selection (10) or, if the author is so inclined, may move to the center of the circle.

During the review proper, when the author is a Fly on the Wall (11), it is sometimes customary for the author to move outside the circle.

Because authors form the Community of Trust (5), they might form their own Authors' Circle (8) inside a circle of observers, in fishbowl style.

See Sitting Circle [Alexander1977, ff. 857]; and Different Chairs [Alexander1977, ff. 1157]. Many other of Alexander's patterns are relevant to the setting of a Writers' Workshop, such as Pool of Light, Sequence of Sitting Spaces (for multiple Writers' Workshops at a single venue), Sunny Place, and Outdoor Room.

8. Authors' Circle*

. . . the reviewers are assembled Sitting in a Circle (7), ready for the review process. The circle brings the full community in direct contact with the author and with each other.

It has become common practice to invite observers to Writers' Workshops: Where do they sit?

* * *

Bringing nonauthors into the literal and figurative inner circle might cause discomfort for the author and can be contrary to a Safe Setting (2).

On the other hand, the Writers' Workshop is a good learning opportunity for those outside the literary community, and they should be welcome.

But just because they are in the room doesn't mean that they are part of the Community of Trust (5). If they are made part of the circle, they will feel like participating; yet they don't yet know the conventions for effective participation. Excluding them altogether is disengaging.

Therefore:

Arrange the room in two circles. The inner circle contains the authors and the moderator. The outer circle, or gallery, is for nonauthors. (See Figure 25-1.)

Authors who wish to remove themselves from active participation should also remove themselves to the outer circle, rather than sit passively in the inner circle: The author being reviewed (and the moderator, representing the author's interest) should expect participation from all members of the inner circle.

* * *

This pattern strongly recalls Workshop Comprises Authors (4).

The circle makes it easy for everyone to see the author eye-to-eye during Author Reads Selection (10), Author Asks for Clarification (15), and Thank the Author (17). All the reviewers can see each other during the dialogue of Suggestions for Improvement (14). The outer circle also provides a context for the Fly on the Wall (11) author to retire to (behind the Authors' Circle) as the work is being reviewed.

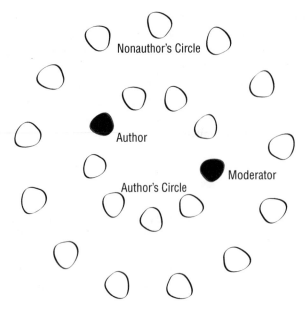

Figure 25-1

PROCESS PATTERNS

9. Reading Just before Reviewing

. . . the panel of reviewers is assembled, and their work is set before them. The goal of the Writers' Workshop is to improve the work while validating the author. But reviewer input should be validated, too. Reviewers come in good standing because the Workshop Comprises Authors (4), but reviewers should become familiar with the work so their specific feedback is credible. **How do you avoid underpreparation or overpreparation for a workshop?**

* * *

Everyone who critiques a pattern should have read it. It's possible to critique a pattern from expert knowledge of the subject matter, but here, we presume that Authors Are Experts (3) and that the presentation, the "experience" of the pattern, is the focus of the review.

A reviewer can spend many hours thoroughly reading a pattern and studying for its review. A reviewer may research references and track down every possible lead. But most of the leads will be dead ends, and most relate to technical details beyond the technical scope of the review.

On the other hand, many reviewers tend to give a paper only superficial review or may pore over the work in real time. These reviewers are not only a distraction to the review process, but they do the author a disservice.

If some reviewers prepare thoroughly, their detailed reviews are likely to swamp the input of other reviewers. The volume of well-considered input may easily mask the sublime insight produced by a spontaneous review.

Therefore:

Reviewers should read the pattern just before reviewing it. The pattern will be fresh in their minds; the pattern's emotional impact remains with the reader. This is sufficient to assess the literary and aesthetic qualities of a work.

* * *

Some reviewers may read and annotate other authors' works far in advance. If the author permits, such reviewers may provide written comments to the author, but only after the workshop is done.

10. Author Reads Selection**

. . . the reviewers have read the work (Reading Just before Reviewing (9)) and now the review process begins. **How do we get to know the authors a bit, to make them feel like valued people, more than just the vehicle for the work being discussed?**

* * *

It is hard to know what's going on inside authors' heads unless they are given an opportunity to speak. The goal of a Writers' Workshop is to improve the work while preserving the author's dignity. To appreciate the need to be sensitive to the author and his or her feelings, we want to get to know him or her a bit.

But if authors speak when they most want to during the feedback, it stifles and throttles the feedback process. And we anticipate the pattern Fly on the Wall (11) that derives from this force.

An author brings a rich constellation of insights, experiences, and stories, some subset of which have been captured in pattern form, but many of which remain in the author's head. Patterns attempt to capture that knowledge so that the reader can re-create the experience of the expert that led him or her to appreciate the pattern.

If authors extemporize while reading their patterns, we gain additional insight.

People love to hear stories, and some people love to tell stories. Most authors can tell many stories that led them to recognize the pattern they describe, though the pattern itself doesn't capture most of that folklore (for sake of compression and conciseness).

But a pattern must stand on its own. One should be able to understand and use a pattern on its own merits, without the support of author interpretation. Patterns form a broadly disseminated body of literature that helps readers develop some of the expert's insights, which relieves the expert from having to be everywhere at once. Readers shouldn't depend on first-hand interpretation from the author, because the author won't always be accessible to the reader.

Therefore:

The author stands and reads a selection of his or her choice. The author may read only the material that is available, verbatim, to the reviewers. By letting authors read their works we recognize their presence and welcome them to the forum.

Authors may read any selection they like. The section should be short enough to not bore the audience.

We can hear the voice inside the author's head, the internal dialogue, behind the pattern.

* * *

The goal is to convey what is important to and about the author; the reviewers have already read the pattern, so they know its content. If even the inflection of the author's voice conveys interpretation, the reviewers should be on guard that the pattern could be improved to capture the importance of such inflection.

By letting authors read a selection of their choice, the reviewers are afforded insight into the authors' priorities for what is important, for what is beautiful, for what they are proud of.

Author Reads Selection also serves as a formal beginning to the session to help the reviewers become mentally centered and fully present.

That the author stands here anticipates the balanced response of Thank the Author (17).

11. Fly on the Wall**

. . . after the Author Reads Selection (10), the reviewers are seated in the Authors' Circle (8), ready to give feedback on the work. What does the author do now? **How do you keep the author engaged, yet at an objective distance?**

* * *

The author should hear the comments directly, and should know who said them, so they have the fullest possible context.

Yet the comments are likely to be more frank if the author isn't present.

But too much frankness contradicts Safe Setting (2). And the discussion should not be allowed to become an argument between the author and a reviewer. The point is not what the author thinks about his or her own work or what he or she meant to say, but what the reviewers think and what they think he or she said. Authors often wonder, "What goes though my audience's heads when they read my paper?" This is their chance to find out, but they should stay out of the discussion and not influence it so that they get the audience's opinions, not their own.

Therefore:

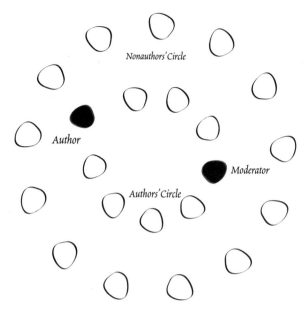

Figure 25-2

Ask the author to step out of the Authors' Circle (8) and become a Fly on the Wall (11). (See Figure 25–2.) During Volunteer Summarizes the Work (12), Positive Feedback First (13), and Suggestions for Improvement (14), the author:

- Is not referred to by name, but is instead called 'the author'
- May absolutely not speak
- Should not make eye contact with the reviewers (which is largely the responsibility of the reviewers)

*   *   *

This helps the reviewers focus on the material by putting the author out of sight and out of mind. The author can still appreciate Positive Feedback First (13), but is distanced from the personal impact of Suggestions for Improvement (14).

The author may remain in the circle, but remain silent, particularly in small (6 or fewer participants) groups.

12. Volunteer Summarizes the Work*

. . . the reviewers are Sitting in a Circle (7) and the author has become a Fly on the Wall (11). At this point, the reviewers have all the information they will get before making their assessments. **How can the group telegraph, to the author, that they're at least starting on the right track?**

* * *

A good pattern appeals to our intuition, and the author can gauge the effectiveness of a pattern in part by how well it appeals to the intuition of those who read it. A good pattern touches us deeply. After all the words have passed, we are left with a single impression, and its feelings—a gestalt that touches our own experience and recalls deep (and sometimes inarticulate) knowledge.

Yet few review processes yield to intuition; most rely on detailed, rational arguments whose detail is sometimes irrelevant if the larger point is lost. Most design review settings dissect a design into parts and then review each part on its own terms. It's more important, with a pattern, to assess the effectiveness of the whole. Understanding the forces of the whole naturally leads a designer to a suitable implementation and other details.

Therefore:

After the Author Reads Selection (10), the moderator asks a volunteer to summarize the work in his or her own words. If the summary validates the author's intent, the author has a degree of confidence that the pattern is intuitive.

If the summary is off base, the rest of the review may follow the summary and be for naught—but the author has important information about the effectiveness of the pattern. Also, a summary captures only a single viewpoint, which the author can balance with feedback from other reviewers.

* * *

It's possible to solicit multiple summaries by asking if there are dissenting summaries after the first one is given. However, this usually leads to a degenerating discussion that defers the business of Positive Feedback First (13), so many moderators ask only for a single summary.

The summary provides a jumping-off point for Positive Feedback First (13) and Suggestions for Improvement (14).

13. Positive Feedback First**

. . . the reviewers are Sitting in a Circle (7), the author is a Fly on the Wall (11), and the pattern has been summarized (Volunteer Summarizes the Work (12)). The reviewers are ready to provide feedback to the author. **How do they provide feedback so it has the best chance of being successful and of setting the proper tone?**

* * *

When we review literature, there are bits that we enjoy and bits we'd like to improve.

Yet most review settings dwell on the improvements, since the parts that we like need no work and therefore need no mention. Most engineers are trained to find and solve problems. Most engineering evaluations focus on problems, on areas for improvement, consistent with their training and practice. But, more broadly than this, we seem to be better at finding "misfits" than we are at noticing the lack of patterns or constructs that support quality. Quality is more than the lack of misfits, but Western, reductionist criticism focuses on the negatives, leaving the positives unmentioned.

The problem with this approach is that it leaves doubt in the mind of the author about the soundness of the paragraphs, or the styles, or the organization, that were left unmentioned. Did the reviewers leave them out because they ran out of time? Because they were less offensive than the problems they mentioned?

Leaving the positive side of their contribution left unrecognized leaves authors feeling insecure.

The author may also become confused and remove a well-done bit of text to address feedback that should be dealt with elsewhere.

Therefore:

Start the review process by accentuating the positives: what works, what is good, what the author should leave unchanged in the next iteration of the work. This makes it explicit what is good and should be left alone during editing. This engages the author in the process from the beginning.

* * *

Making a conscious effort to surface the positives underscores the author's contribution and makes the review a Safe Setting (2). By doing positives first, their importance is underscored, and the author starts off encouraged rather than discouraged. That means that the author is more likely to hear the rest of the feedback—much more so than if the feedback had been given in the other order.

Giving positive feedback first also puts the reviewers in a frame of mind where they are likely to give more balanced and well-considered answers than if they built momentum on the cleverness of what they believe to be a well-founded criticism.

14. Suggestions for Improvement**

Also Known As

Constructive Feedback

. . . the reviewers gave Positive Feedback First (13), but still must tell the author what can be improved on the next round of editing. The author is still sequestered as a Fly on the Wall (11). **How do you point out "problems" without attacking the author of the work?**

* * *

The main output of the Writers' Workshop is an improved piece of literature. Some improvements correct sins of omission; most authors appreciate learning about these, as they don't attack anything produced by the author (only the lack of something produced). Other improvements require that the author remove or change manuscript text. Human nature sometimes equates imperfection in a creation with the imperfection of its creator.

We can divide these criticisms into two kinds: criticism of content and criticism of presentation. Because Authors Are Experts (3), the focus of Writers' Workshops is on presentation, though content criticism is fair game. Engineers take technical criticism harder than any other. Design reviews are better than Writers' Workshops to support the detailed, reductionist analyses necessary to validate technical issues. Writers' Workshops focus more on presentation and aesthetics (Authors Are Experts (3)). But an attack on presentation, language, and aesthetics can be equally devastating, as authors may construe the criticism as applying to their personality, intelligence, or to their upbringing in a culture different from the one in which they work.

Unsupported criticism is difficult to take, particularly if the author cannot respond, as provided by Fly on the Wall (11) and Author Asks for Clarification (15).

Destructive criticism not only has the possibility of making the author uncomfortable, but provides no outlet for learning.

Therefore:

Provide constructive feedback to the author; that is, offer no criticism unless it is accompanied by a well-considered suggestion for improvement that the author can act on.

Erich Gamma suggests: Provide constructive feedback by first stating the problem, then follow with a suggestion.

Though responsibility lies with each reviewer, the moderator can help guide, remind, and support people in giving constructive feedback. Good moderators do this in an unobtrusive way.

* * *

No review is without risk, and authors take some risk of having their worldview upset by a review; that's how learning takes place. The main result of Suggestions for Improvement is that the author feels that colleagues are trying to help, that they care that the author's dignity is preserved, and that they offer their own insights to increase the knowledge of the author. The second result is that the author actually learns from constructive criticism.

Ralph Johnson adds: "Forcing all criticism to include a way to improve is limiting, because it might be that the criticism that one reviewer makes could be answered by another. But then that second reviewer would probably have come up with it anyway, so you aren't losing much by limiting criticism, and you are gaining a lot."

This pattern is a high point in the workshop, the high point of tension for the author. At the end of this section, the Author Asks for Clarification (15) on any issues that remain from the Suggestions for Improvement (and from other sections as well, but most will be from here).

Remaining angst about this section is brought to closure in Thank the Author (17) and Clearing the Palate (18).

15. Author Asks for Clarification**

. . . at the end of the formal review input of a Writers' Workshop, the author may be anxious about some of the things that were said. Until now, the author has been a Fly on the Wall (11), but we can't have a Safe Setting (2) unless the author is given a chance to speak (beyond just reading the work as in Author Reads Selection (10)). **How do we give the author a chance to speak without starting a debate?**

* * *

Not all reviewer comments stand alone. In a Writers' Workshop, reviewers are providing comments on-the-fly, comments that may not fully articulate the reviewer's rationale.

Reviewer comments can be ambiguous, confusing, or unclear in many ways.

It doesn't serve the author (and the work) well if the author leaves before the reviewers clarify their comments.

Therefore:

The Author Asks for Clarification after the moderator calls an end to the formal comments.

Note that this is not an opportunity for the author to clarify his or her position with the reviewers, since the pattern must stand on its own. The information flows from the reviewers to the author, not vice versa.

If authors harbor disagreements with any reviewer conclusions or remarks, they should take them away from the Writers' Workshop in silence. Such disagreement or remarks provide information for the author, information the author can use to clarify the pattern on the next iteration. By mutual agreement, the author and reviewer can discuss deeper issues (and, particularly, technical issues) in the afterglow of the workshop.

* * *

This brings the ceremony to closure and ties up all the formal loose ends. Further patterns, like Thank the Author (17), provide more complete emotional closure. The author can now take the feedback and iterate further on the pattern, making Selective Changes (19).

16. Positive Closure**

Also Known As

Sandwich Feedback

. . . we do Positive Feedback First (13) to keep the author from shutting down before constructive criticism is offered. However, since the constructive criticism of Suggestions for Improvement (14) is near the end of the workshop, it is more likely to linger in the author's mind than the earlier positive feedback. **How do you leave the author with a positive feeling at the end of the feedback?**

* * *

You could reverse the order of feedback, but that would make it difficult to satisfy the forces behind Positive Feedback First (13). Opening up the workshop to positive input may trigger a cascade of such comments, making it difficult to bring the workshop to a close. You could count on Thank the Author (17), but undistinguished applause might be viewed as disingenuous or hypocritical, particularly in cultures in which these are important values.

Therefore:

The moderator asks a single reviewer either to recap an important positive aspect of the work or to describe some aspect of the work that uniquely makes it shine. Make the author feel special by recognizing a unique contribution that owes to the author's unique abilities, skills, insights, or effort.

Limited discussion may ensue (up to a minute at most) but a single positive comment usually suffices.

* * *

This encouraging note can reduce or dispel the discomfort that follows a discussion—even a positive discussion—of a long suite of shortcomings in the author's work. By focusing on the author's unique talents, this pattern recalls Authors Are Experts (3). Further positive reinforcement comes from Thank the Author (17).

17. Thank the Author**

. . . authors invest much of their time and risk their reputations by putting their intellectual achievement out for criticism. By doing so, they can contribute richly to the body of literature on which practice is based, and by which the industry moves forward. The authors deserve our gratitude. **How do we convey our gratitude so that the author leaves the workshop encouraged?**

* * *

People seek and need recognition for their valuable contributions. We feel good when we help someone, particularly when we are recognized for our contribution. It is a high point in an engineer's work program when a customer thanks or recognizes them for having solved an important problem.

Most of the Writers' Workshop focuses on evaluating and scrutinizing the author's work, which elicits an emotional response that's antithetical to that engendered by gratitude. Writers' Workshops can be draining on the author; authors must be keenly alert and keep their guard up during a review, even though they have no chance to retort.

Therefore:

End the Writers' Workshop with a display of gratitude for the author. It's particularly effective if the moderator asks the author to remain seated while all reviewers stand and applaud the author. Reviewers make eye contact with the author.

This brings the ceremony to closure, helps authors let down their guard and fully recognize that the people around them are there to support and refine the work, and appreciate the author.

* * *

Broad publication, in a recognized and highly reviewed journal or book, also is good for the author's stature and self-image.

Gratitude has been called the most powerful of human emotions.

18. Clearing the Palate

. . . after the work of a Writers' Workshop is done, peoples' heads are full, and emotions run strong (perhaps both high and low). There is a sense of closure, perhaps feelings of exhaustion. Different people experience each workshop differently. **How do you clear peoples' heads, preparing them for what comes next?**

* * *

A steady stream of Writers' Workshops can be draining.

People invest much of themselves—emotionally, intellectually, even spiritually—in a Writers' Workshop. The experience can leave some participants unfocused and off center as the workshop's issues race around in their mind.

For example, reviewers yearn to start working with authors to give them more detailed feedback (which would usually not be useful, as most authors are too drained, distraught, or emotionally high to accommodate them) or to have some other outlet for their thoughts and opinions.

A distraction can bring the group back to its center. By shifting the group from left brain to right brain, or from a technical topic to a personal topic, or by focusing on something entirely irrelevant, the group can clear out the aftermath of the previous workshop and move on to what follows.

Therefore:

At the close of each review, ask for a volunteer to say something irrelevant. The subject can be a joke, an anecdote, a short story, a puzzle, or anything unrelated to the prevailing topic matter of the workshops. Clearing the Palate, analogous to the neutral foods eaten between wine tastings, readies the group for what comes next.

This also helps exercise and engage parts of the brain that would otherwise remain unused.

* * *

This is one of a family of related patterns, another one being Clearing the Room with a Bad Joke (not presented here).

This sets the stage for a break, for another Writers' Workshop, or for the end of a session.

This section also puts the session to bed and brings to closure any anxieties harbored by the author of the previous session and any worrying "about what will happen to them next."

19. Selective Changes**

Also Known As

Author's Prerogative

. . . the workshop is done, and the author has received Suggestions for Improvement (14), and is working on the next iteration of the pattern or pattern language. **How should the author incorporate workshop feedback into the work?**

* * *

Authors may receive diverse, even contradictory, feedback on their work. It's an advantage to have a diverse collection of reviewers, since chances are good that they'll think of something the author didn't think of. On the other hand, such a broad group of reviewers may not provide a consensus view. Indeed, there is nothing about the Writers' Workshop format that drives toward consensus.

This leaves the author with a dilemma: which reviewers' opinions should the author act on?

Furthermore, the author may disagree even with unambiguous opinions that come out of the Writers' Workshop. Should the author be bound to act on the advice from the workshop?

Therefore:

The author is not bound to the verbatim advice of the Writers' Workshop. Rather, the experience might help the author develop a new perspective, which in turn inspires the author to change the work. There may be simple changes that the author chooses to make if convinced they are worthwhile. But, in all cases, changes are at author discretion: the results of the Writers' Workshop are the property of the author.

* * *

Sometimes, a work has the benefit of feedback from multiple workshops. Issues ignored in one workshop may resurface in another; good writers put their prejudices aside and heed these hints.

ACKNOWLEDGMENTS

Many thanks to Linda Rising and Ralph Johnson for comments on earlier iterations of these patterns. Special thanks to Bobby Woolf who, as PLoP shepherd for these patterns, provided many particularly useful comments. The PloPD4 version benefited greatly from the comments of Joshua Kerievsky.

An earlier version of these patterns was published as "Writers' Workshops" [Coplien1997].

REFERENCES

[Alexander1977] C.A. Alexander, et al. *A Pattern Language*. New York: Oxford University Press, 1977.

[Coplien1997] J.O. Coplien. "Writers' Workshops." *C++ Report 9*(4):51–60, 1997.

James O. Coplien may be reached at cope@bell-labs.com.

APPENDIX—ALEXANDRIAN PATTERN FORM

Alexandrian Form, from Christopher Alexander's work, is the original pattern form. The sections of an Alexandrian pattern are not strongly delimited; the major syntactic structure is a "Therefore:" immediately preceding the solution. Other elements of the form are usually present: a clear statement of the problem, a discussion of the forces, the solution, and a rationale.

Each Alexandrian pattern usually follows an introductory paragraph that enumerates the patterns that must already have been applied to make the ensuing pattern meaningful. The pattern itself starts with a name and a confidence designation of zero, one, or two asterisks. Patterns with two asterisks are the ones in which the authors have the most confidence because they have empirical foundations. Patterns with fewer asterisks may have strong social significance, but are more speculative.

Here is Alexander's own description of his form [Alexander1977, pp. x–xi]:

> For convenience and clarity, each pattern has the same format. First, there is a picture, which shows an archetypal example of that pattern. Second, after the picture, each pattern has an introductory paragraph, which sets the context for the pattern, by explaining how it helps to complete certain larger patterns. Then there are three diamonds to mark the beginning of the problem. After the diamonds there is a headline, in bold type. This headline gives the essence of the problem in one or two sentences. After the headline comes the body of the problem. This is the longest section. It describes the empirical background of the pattern, the evidence for its validity, the range of different ways the pattern can be manifested in a building, and so on. Then, again in bold type, like the headline, is the solution—the heart of the pattern—which describes the field of physical and social relationships which are required to solve the stated problem, in the stated context. This solution is always stated in the form of an instruction— so that you know exactly what you need to do, to build the pattern. Then, after the solution, there is a diagram, which shows the solution in the form of a diagram, with labels to indicate its main components.
>
> After the diagram, another three diamonds, to show that the main body of the pattern is finished. And finally, after the diamonds there is a paragraph which ties the pattern to all those smaller patterns in the language, which are needed to complete this pattern, to embellish it, to fill it out.

PART 9

Managing Software

Managing software development is like herding cats. You can have the best-laid plans and the most meticulously detailed requirements, and something will still go wrong. The customer changes his mind; the software architect leaves the company; the design has some insidious bug that doesn't get uncovered until late in system test. And what is the result? The product is late, it works slightly differently than intended, and the internal design is not nearly as neat as anyone wanted. It's enough to drive one crazy. One of the problems is that software is developed by people, for people. And people are not as well behaved as bits are. Actually, most software is developed by teams of people to satisfy the requests of other groups of people. And teams are even less well behaved than individuals. In fact, with all these people involved, it's a wonder that any software gets completed at all!

Despite the difficulties of managing software, or perhaps because of them, there has been no shortage of material on how to manage software projects. This is particularly true of the patterns community. Each of the Pattern Languages of Program Design books has had some patterns on software organizations, process, or management. Why is there such fascination with such a difficult area? One reason may be that patterns are inherently people-oriented; patterns are written for human consumption. Perhaps this has tended to make us more aware of the people issues that pervade software development.

We conclude this volume of patterns with four sets of patterns about managing software. They are as follows:

Chapter 26: Customer Interaction Patterns by Linda Rising.   We begin our tour with patterns that focus on our relationships with customers. Perhaps this is appropriate, for software development begins—and ends—with customers. It is unfortunate that while we recognize this fact, far too few of us are aware that interacting with customers doesn't come naturally, but is an acquired skill. These patterns will help us acquire that skill. Many of the patterns in this pattern language are common sense: Mind Your Manners and Show Personal Integrity seem self-evident. But the problem with common sense is that it is so uncommon. A reminder is in order. Other patterns, such as Be Aware of Boundaries, are somewhat less obvious. Taken together, they form a nice primer for nurturing customer relationships.

Chapter 27: Capable, Productive, and Satisfied: Some Organizational Patterns for Protecting Productive People by Paul Taylor.   With these patterns, we move from the customers to the people that develop the software. Since software development is a creative activity, the creators must be nurtured. Furthermore, software development happens in groups; most software is developed by several people working together. These patterns help foster an environment conducive to software development. There are patterns for creating, managing, and supporting teams. These include Production Potential, which encourages recognition of team progress in terms of an ability to produce, rather than simply in terms of the state of deliverables. The final patterns, Effective Handover and Arranging the Furniture, deal with the problem of maintaining productivity as the project matures and staff turns over.

Chapter 28: SCRUM: A Pattern Language for Hyperproductive Software Development by Mike Beedle, Martine Devos, Yonat Sharon, Ken Schwaber, and Jeff Sutherland.   When you are in the heat of battle—development is underway, and deadlines are looming—what patterns might be helpful? Turn to the SCRUM patterns. There are two main themes in the SCRUM patterns. The first is Sprint—breaking the traditional software development cycle into a series of small steps (sprints) that each last about a month. The second theme is the SCRUM Meeting, very short daily status and priority-setting meetings. The rather fanciful name comes from scrums or scrummages in rugby, in which the opposing teams face each other in short, intimate skirmishes. Naturally, the SCRUM Meetings described here are a good deal more congenial!

Chapter 29: Big Ball of Mud by Brian Foote and Joseph Yoder.   Real life is not like what we read about in our Software Engineering textbooks. In spite of our best efforts to create tidy, elegant software architectures, all too often our software ends up looking like a Big Ball of Mud. Why is this? What can we do about it? These patterns explore various approaches to the problems that software professionals in the trenches face. Throwaway Code deals with writing code that might be transitory or prototypical in nature. Piecemeal Growth and Keep It Working address incremental software evolution. Shearing Layers examines the impact of differing rates of change on the structure of our systems. Sweeping It under the Rug and Reconstruction deal with the rehabilitation or replacement of systems that have undergone structural decline.

These patterns are different from the others in this section in that they have a definite architectural flavor. In fact, they might fit as well in a section on software architecture as in a section on managing software. This underscores an important, but subtle characteristic of software: The organization of the software is inextricably connected with the organization and management of the individuals who create it.

Chapter 26

Customer Interaction Patterns

Linda Rising

Most of the Customer Interaction Patterns were mined from a presentation by David Saar, senior product planning manager at AG Communication Systems. Although many developers in our company have customer interaction experience, this was the first time a product development team had been formally prepared for their first interaction with the customer, in this case, GTE.

After the presentation, I remembered a guideline from Jim McCarthy's book [McCarthy1995] that seemed to capture the intent of David's message. I converted the guideline to the pattern, It's a Relationship, Not a Sale.

Linda Leonard, product development leader at AG Communication Systems, contributed the ideas for Be Responsive and Show Personal Integrity, which contain some important, down-to-earth suggestions for improving customer interaction. The idea for Know the Customer came from Rod Veach, our on-site customer representative from GTE.

As patterns were added to this collection, a structure began to emerge. It has been a challenging task to mine these patterns from experts in customer interaction and apply what I am learning about pattern languages to coax a fledgling language from a "pile o' patterns"—to quote Kent Beck's observation at a PLoP '96 workshop session. The struggle to clearly define the relationships among the patterns was as difficult as writing the patterns themselves but just as rewarding. I continue to improve each pattern and also the language.

These patterns have many known uses (See Table 26-1). Usually David would say "Life!" when I asked him for a specific known use. Obviously, these patterns can be applied in any human interaction!

Pattern names are capitalized and part of the narrative, following patterns by Gerard Meszaros and Jim Doble [Meszaros+1998].

Table 26-1 *Customer Interaction Patterns*

Pattern	Intent
It's a Relationship, Not a Sale	This pattern is the foundation for all the customer interaction patterns. Develop a relationship with the customer. Focus on this relationship, not the current transaction. Use Know the Customer and Build Trust.
Know the Customer	Learn as much as possible about the customer. Use Listen, Listen, Listen; Be Responsive and Customer Meetings: Go Early, Stay Late.
Build Trust	Every contact with the customer is a chance to build trust. Take advantage of it. Use Listen, Listen, Listen; Be Responsive and Customer Meetings: Go Early, Stay Late.
Listen, Listen, Listen	Listen to the customer with the intent to understand. Use Show Personal Integrity; Be Aware of Boundaries; Take Your Licks; and Mind Your Manners.
Be Responsive	When you receive a request from the customer let the customer know you received it and how you plan to resolve it. If you can't get final resolution as promised, contact the customer, and say what you have done so far.
Customer Meetings: Go Early, Stay Late	Arrive at customer meetings early enough to meet other attendees and spend time socializing. After the meetng, allow a little time to talk to others with common business interests.
Show Personal Integrity	Don't withhold important information from the customer but Be Aware of Boundaries.
Take Your Licks	Don't argue. Try to understand how the customer's business is impacted. Don't try to appease the customer by making promises you can't keep. Use Be Aware of Boundaries.
Be Aware of Boundaries	Treat every conversation with the customer as part of a negotiation. Don't discuss commercial considerations, e.g., price, cost, schedule, and content that aren't part of your responsibilities. Use Mind Your Manners.
Mind Your Manners	Be polite. Dress appropriately to meet customer expectations. Show respect for everyone, including competitors. Be especially careful in interactions with others from your company in front of the customer.

Early versions of the patterns were workshopped at PLoP '97. After several internal workshops and updates, a later version was workshopped at PLoP '98. The patterns are now mature enough that I teach a class based on them at AG Communication Systems.

THE PATTERNS

It's a Relationship, Not a Sale

Problem

How should you treat customers so they'll be satisfied with your company's products?

Context

You are a product developer. You may be part of a team or a single contributor. You currently play an active role in interfacing with customers or you have been asked to take on this role.

Bruce Whitenack's Customer Rapport (develop a rapport with the customer) [Whitenack1995] and Jim Coplien's Engage Customers (closely couple the customer role to the developer) [Coplien1995] define the context for this pattern.

Forces

- Developers usually have a product focus not a customer focus.
- We want to delight our customers.
- We want to protect our own interests.

Solution

Develop a relationship with the customer. Focus on this relationship, not the current transaction.

Know the Customer and then use that understanding in your product as part of an ongoing commitment to Build Trust with the customer.

Resulting Context

Customers will feel they're buying into a relationship, not just buying a product. Your customers will feel like staying with you. Your customers will sense that you are going somewhere together.

A long-term relationship means repeat business. It's much cheaper to keep a customer than to find a new one.

Having a good relationship with a customer is not enough to ensure financial success. Innovative solutions will capture markets regardless of customer relationships. The solutions in these patterns are only part of an overall business plan that includes attractive, innovative products.

The customer can become too dependent on you. As a result of your relationship with the customer, you will be the one to whom the customer turns. You will be the one who gets all those late-night phone calls, those last-minute requests for urgent fixes.

Rationale

In his presentation, David Saar emphasized the importance of developing a relationship with the customer. On many projects, developers need a customer contact to answer questions that arise during development, and usually team members simply want to be handed a name and a phone number. David explained that just having a person to call is not enough, that a relationship with the customer will give the results developers wanted.

The relationship with the customer is like a dance. You take steps, and the customer takes steps in response, and then you take more steps. You must be focused on the flow of transactions, on the overall pattern and direction, not merely on the current product. Human relationships are fragile and not formed instantly but develop slowly and evolve over time.

The following is from *Selling with Honor* [Kohn1997]:

> In business as in life, it takes a long time to make friends.

The following is from Dan Behymer, director of quality systems at a manufacturing facility in Cincinnati [Behymer1997]:

> The quality-satisfaction gap is not about products. It is about feeling. In a culture where you are bombarded every day with advertisements, objectives and incentives, where someone is always after your hard-earned money, you just want to know that if you buy their goods, they will care once the sale is over. We want someone who cares and will take action. Caring can't come from a total quality improvement team, reengineering, just-in-time or any formula, objectives, or consultants. Customers are human; companies are collections of humans.

Known Uses

The following is from an AGCS postmortem:

> Our customer knows that this is a new product. They've been great about taking releases that are not perfect and working with us to get the product where it should be. We need this customer feedback in the iterative development approach we're taking.

The following is from another AGCS postmortem:

The customer pulled us into the SOA (service order activation) market. We didn't know much about NP (number portability), and the customer was also learning. We followed the customer and just let them lead us.

The following is from Nick Ash, senior telecommunications analyst for Caterpillar, in an interview for *Inside AGCS* [*Inside*1998]:

Now that [ROAMEO is] up and running, [AGCS] is monitoring the system and alerting me if things don't look right. . . . This wasn't a matter of installing the system, leaving, and now we're on our own. I feel like I have the support of AGCS on an ongoing basis.

I think you have a very good product and you should be proud of your company and the service employees provide. I'm impressed with AGCS as a company.

Pattern Source

Jim McCarthy, adapted by Linda Rising from *Guideline #17*, "It's a relationship, not a sale" [McCarthy1995].

Know the Customer

Also Known As

Know the Customer's World, Live with the Customer, Shadowing

Problem

What's the best way to establish a relationship with the customer?

Context

You deal with customers who use your products in their products or services. You understand It's a Relationship, Not a Sale.

Forces

- Organizations are dynamic; we are changing; our customer is changing.
- Customers have different interaction styles.
- Developers usually feel that knowing the product is enough.
- We want results quickly, so do our customers.

Solution

Learn as much as possible about the customer.

Help the customer and the customer's customers succeed. This means learning the "inside" of the customer's business and the "far side" (the users and vendors whose products must work with yours). Understand the needs and drives of all customers along the customer chain, from intermediate providers to ultimate users.

Think about the customer's needs instead of your own and the business will take care of itself. Understand how your customers make money and help them make more and your income will take care of itself. Helping your customer succeed is a sure way to success.

There is no substitute for an on-site visit. See the customer's world and the problems they face. One trip is worth hours of brainstorming about the customer's needs.

Get hands-on experience in the customer environment. Some customers will allow you to visit their site and take notes while people use your product. Customers also can provide documentation for their business processes.

Provide customer support at an appropriate level. A vice president feels more comfortable talking to someone at a higher level, while engineers want someone who knows low-level details.

If the customer does not speak your language (technical, lingual), learn at least some of the customer's language.

When you're attending a customer meeting, don't just spend time with friends. It's easier to socialize with people you know, but make an effort to meet and greet the customer. Use Listen, Listen, Listen, Be Responsive, and Customer Meetings: Go Early, Stay Late.

Resulting Context

When we understand the customers' world, our products become more useful. Understanding the world of our customers' customers helps ensure that products work well for the customer.

When we understand our customers' values, we become an extension of their enterprise.

Understanding the customer enables a better understanding of customer priorities. This can be valuable if a trade-off between schedule and functionality must be made.

Applying this solution is not as easy as it may sound. Company culture and politics may be beyond your understanding.

This is an ongoing task; our environment and that of our customer continually change. Our organization and the customers' organizations are many-headed beasts and present different views to different people at different times.

Rationale

Knowing your customer's products and services and how the customer gets these products and services to market helps you understand how the customer thinks from a business point of view.

As described by John Guaspari [Guaspari1998]:

> It's not enough to ask customers, "How are *we* doing?" We have to ask, "How are *you* doing?" We need to understand what our customer's wants and needs are. If we really understand these things we'll be able to apply our expertise to meet the needs they express and some things they may not even know they need.

The following is from an article by Rob Thomsett [Thomsett1997]:

> The question "What are your requirements?" is the wrong question. The right question is "What is your world?" Once we have begun to understand our customers' organization, their concerns, and their way of working, we can begin to get a clearer idea of them, and it becomes much easier to understand their requirements.

> To understand their needs, we must understand their culture, their hopes, and their expectations. Doing this requires you to get to know your customers as people first and customers second. Understand your customers and you'll understand their expectations.

Known Uses

This pattern can be applied in many human relationships. Members of the ARC (Administrative Resource Center) at AGCS were quick to point out that Tom Snelten, product development leader, was a good coach because he was able to see the world from the ARC viewpoint.

The following is from an AGCS team postmortem:

> Once you get to know the customers, they would ask you about anything, including other products!

The following is from another AGCS team postmortem:

> If you know someone, they'll do anything for you. You can call them in the middle of the night. If you don't have a relationship like that, you have to follow an official path and it takes longer.

Members of the ARC have said:

> There are some people you can kid with and some you can't. You have to learn how to deal with people as individuals.

The following is from ARC member Doris Freeman:

> Suppose someone brings me something to scan in. Usually they just say, "Please scan this." I try to learn more by saying, "You want me to scan this so you can put it on the web? or send it in an e-mail? or edit it?" They will then say what they have in mind and I can help determine exactly what the end result should be. Sometimes the requester hasn't thought ahead and going through this exercise saves time for both of us! It's good to ask questions. Find out what the customer *really* wants.

The following story is from Carole Boese, Fe Pati, and Ellen Lara, about the Adopt-A-Printer Process instituted by the ARC:

> The following customer satisfaction issue was noted in the 1995 ARC Customer Survey: Service of printers in Building 1, 2nd Floor, was #1 in negative rating and #6 in importance to those customers.

> Members of the ARC followed up and learned that no department was responsible for the daily maintenance of printers. As a result, the ARC formed a sub-team to implement a solution to customer printer/toner concerns. Header sheets were also collected and recycled as pads of scratch paper. There were no concerns from customers in the 1996 survey. In fact, a great improvement in this service was realized.

Pattern Source

Rod Veach, as told to Linda Rising.

Build Trust

Also Known As

Build Relationships

Problem

How can you strengthen a relationship with a customer?

Context

You understand It's a Relationship, Not a Sale and are trying to Know the Customer.

Forces

- We need to interface with the customer.
- Customers need contacts in our organization with whom they feel comfortable.
- People are reluctant to spend time with people they don't know.

Solution

Every contact with the customer is a chance to build trust. Take advantage of it.

You can't simply build relationships by phone or e-mail, no matter how sophisticated the information highway becomes. There will still be a need to meet face-to-face. People trust people they see regularly.

The following is from If I Knew Then What I Know Now [Edler1995]:

> Not calling is not caring. Staying in touch with customers means everything. Customers need to see and hear from their suppliers. They need to know how much you care. Remember to listen first. These contacts invariably lead to priceless new information.

> All things being equal people will do business with people they like. All things not being equal, they still will!

Use Listen, Listen, Listen, Be Responsive, and Customer Meetings: Go Early, Stay Late.

Resulting Context

As a trusting relationship is established, customer interaction becomes easier, questions are answered, problems are solved, and progress is made.

It's easier to build a relationship than to rebuild a relationship. Don't assume that a relationship is static. It must be supported and maintained over time.

Rationale

Stephen Covey has observed [Covey1989]:

> If I make deposits into an Emotional Bank Account with you through courtesy, kindness, honesty, and keeping my commitments to you, I build up a reserve. Your trust toward me becomes higher, and I can call upon that trust many times if I need to. I can even make mistakes and that trust level, that emotional reserve, will compensate for it. My communication may not be clear, but you'll get my meaning anyway. . . . When the trust account is high, communication is easy, instant, and effective.

Every customer encounter is a valuable opportunity to add to your Emotional Bank Account.

According to Scott Hunter [Hunter1998], clients prefer to do business with people they like, with people who seem genuinely interested in them, who deal with their concerns. The worst customer interaction mistake for some customers is to get right down to business at the first meeting with the customer, while others do not want to waste time on preliminaries. It's extremely important to Know the Customer. The most critical result produced during an initial meeting is to begin to build trust.

As Mike Reynolds, vice president of the AGCS Business and Market Development Group, has observed: "People buy products from people."

As David Saar has said: "Customers only trust those they know—in person. That is what makes my travel so essential."

Known Uses

The following is from an AGCS team postmortem:

> We had problems with our demos but we were able to assure the customer that the product would work and spent time establishing a good relationship and building trust. We talked to the customer every day. This is especially important early on.

The following is from another AGCS team postmortem:

> We continue to work closely with Rod Veach to maintain trust. We have very open discussions about problems. What works well for us is to bounce it off Rod first to find out how GTE would react.

The following story is from Kathy Kromrie-Williams:

> A customer at a remote site called up with a negative growth problem. They were getting an error message saying they hadn't deleted a device they had just deleted. I tried to reproduce the problem but everything worked fine here! We talked on the phone as I entered the commands. They swore up and down that they had followed the User's Guide. Something didn't seem right.
>
> I knew Stan Ricksecker had a good relationship with the customer, so I asked him to help me. Minutes later, Stan told me they were afraid they would have to pay for a fix if they admitted that everything they had done wasn't as documented in the User's Guide. Once he found that out, it didn't take him long to find out they had used the wrong command. The fix was easy and provided without cost to the customer.
>
> The relationship Stan had with the customer and their trust in him could not be replaced by my knowledge of growth processes or anything else. Once customers know you will work with them, together you can accomplish anything!

The following story is from Karen Grover:

> Steve Holm had been working on ATIUM View for some time when he was transferred to the Wireless project. Steve had a good working relationship with a customer who was preparing to install a distance learning network. When Steve moved to Wireless, he informed the customer about the transfer but promised to see the work through until the network was turned up (4 months in the future). Steve attended meetings and fielded calls from the customer, but then passed the requests along to me and others—the Facade pattern? The customer was happy because Steve's project

move was transparent to them. It worked nicely for me, too, because Steve passed along a lot of information to help me with the requests so I didn't have to tackle the requests cold.

According to an AGCS postmortem:

Customers usually don't want too many contacts. They just want to interact with one person.

Pattern Source

David Saar, as told to Linda Rising.

Listen, Listen, Listen

Problem

What's the most effective way to develop the customer relationship?

Context

You understand It's a Relationship, Not a Sale. You are trying to Know the Customer and working to Build Trust.

Forces

- Too many customers demand your time.
- What people say may not be what they mean.
- Your attention may be divided across multiple tasks.
- It's hard to always give 100 percent—fatigue, illness, personal problems, and so forth.

Solution

Listen to the customer. Show genuine interest. Pay attention when they're talking; don't just use the time to prepare your response. Don't interrupt. Don't go off on tangents. Follow their agenda.

If we're too anxious to please, we may speak out of turn. Let the customers talk. Give them room.

It may not be until the tenth sentence that customers says what they really want. If you cut them off too early, you'll miss their meaning.

Pick up information. Learn what the customer is thinking. Hear what *isn't* said.

Sometimes you need to push for more information. Ask probing questions. Ask them to draw a picture!

Portray an agreeable, winning attitude. Be flexible and positive. Take action items. Work with the customer.

Use Show Personal Integrity, Be Aware of Boundaries, Take Your Licks, and Mind Your Manners.

Resulting Context

The customer will feel valued and will feel that concerns are being heard and issues addressed. More than this, the customer's needs really will be heard since we are really listening.

Listening is only one part of building a trusting relationship with the customer. In isolation it will not work. It must be part of an overall customer interaction strategy.

Rationale

What people say is often open to misinterpretation. Sometimes what they say isn't what they mean. Remember, this solution is applied in the context of Know the Customer.

As Stephen Covey has said [Covey1989]:

> "Seek first to understand" involves a very deep shift in paradigm. We typically seek first to be understood. Most people do not listen with the intent to understand; they listen with the intent to reply. . . . When I say empathic listening, I mean listening with intent to understand. I mean seeking first to understand, to really understand. . . . Empathic listening gets inside another person's frame of reference. You look out through it, you see the world the way they see the world, you understand their paradigm, you understand how they feel.

From the New Revised Standard Version of the Bible, James 1:19: ". . . be quick to listen, slow to speak. . . ."

The following is from *If I Knew Then What I Know Now* [Edler1995]:

> Listening is the most difficult skill to learn and the most important to have. Learning how to listen—and really hear—what people are saying can make all the difference. When you listen well you hear:
>
> What customers say and what they really mean.
>
> What your customers are really looking to achieve, including hidden agendas.
>
> What your customers think is important.
>
> Spend twice as much time listening as talking.

Known Uses

The following story is from David Armstrong's *Managing by Storying Around* [Armstrong1992]:

> A sales manager at Armstrong International wanted to add an obsolete feature to the division's new fish finder. This approach contradicted the company's strategy of always providing the latest and greatest technological advance. The sales manager wanted to add a simple flasher to a product that already provided information on the location and size of the fish. No one could understand why the simple indicator that a fish was nearby would be useful. The sales manager pointed out that many longtime customers were not comfortable with the new, computerized technology and wanted the simple interface they were used to.

> The feature was added. Customer response was great and the product is still on the market. The moral of the story is listen, listen, listen.

The following is from *Selling with Honor* [Kohn1997]:

> How can you find out what people really need? Ask lots of questions and listen more than you talk!

> Black & Decker has a reputation for listening to consumers. In the 1970's, the company discovered that consumers wanted a portable vacuum cleaner for small spills. This led to the hugely successful Dustbuster. In 1994, hearing that consumers wanted both hands free 75% of the time they use a flashlight, the company created the SnakeLight. How does Black & Decker stumble onto these innovative products? They ask lots of questions and listen for needs.

Pattern Source

David Saar, as told to Linda Rising.

Be Responsive

Also Known As

Don't Leave Your Customer Hanging, Keep Your Customer in the Picture

Problem

What's an acceptable response time for customer requests?

Context

You understand It's a Relationship, Not a Sale. You are trying to Know the Customer and are working to Build Trust using Listen, Listen, Listen.

Forces

- We want to be attentive to our customers.
- We can't always give an immediate response. We may be away from the office or the system may be down.

Solution

Always return customer phone calls the same day, even if you know the customer will have already left the office and you will only be able to leave a voice mail. Somehow we don't feel bound by common etiquette when it comes to e-mail but a customer request via e-mail should always be acknowledged.

Never let the customer wait more than a week for a response on anything or more than a day for acknowledgment of the request. When you receive the request, contact the customer to say you received it and how you plan to resolve it. If you can't get final resolution in a week, contact the customer, and say what you have done so far.

Sometimes (as members of the ARC recommend), you must get back to customers immediately and try to complete requests in a day.

Ask customers, "What is your deadline?" to determine an appropriate response time.

Always have a message on your voice mail and autoreply on your e-mail if you are out of the office. This notifies internal as well as external customers if you're away and whom to contact in your stead.

Don't let your enthusiasm for a quick response lead you to overpromise. Show Personal Integrity.

Resulting Context

Keeping customers informed of your progress on a request lets them know you are taking the request seriously, that action is being taken. Customers will feel you have their best interests at heart.

Rationale

People don't like to be ignored and that includes customers.

Nothing annoys customers more than thinking you're not being responsive. It doesn't help to be working hard on their behalf to resolve a problem if you don't let them know you're working on it.

Known Uses

The following is from GTE Services in the annual quality survey:

My experience with working with AGCS has been outstanding. Their work/quality is excellent. They keep all necessary parties informed as to the status of all jobs. They are extremely easy to work/communicate with.

The following is from an AGCS postmortem:

Always remember to acknowledge voice mail or e-mail. Just say, "I got it!"

The following is from Marianne Davis:

Ameritech called and asked if AGCS would be interested in quoting price/delivery for TR11-88 requery. I got details on the project and within two days provided them with a quote.

Over the next week, I spent time getting to know the customer and telling them about AGCS. When I asked when they were going to make a decision, I was told they were leaning toward AGCS but had to wait for a reply from another company. They had given the other company the opportunity to bid this project two weeks prior to giving it to us. Overall, it took the other company about a month to get back to Ameritech with a quote.

Once we were awarded the business, it took about two weeks to get a signed contract. This was the start of a great relationship with Ameritech. To top things off, we delivered thirty days early with 0 defects. I agree with everything in these patterns. The main reason Ameritech went with us was because they felt comfortable with us every step of the way.

The following is from Kathy Kromrie-Williams:

A remote site was experiencing database problems that were interfering with providing certain services to the customer.

All attempts to re-create the problem using our interactive simulation tool or the prototype failed. We had an entire week's database changes shipped to us. Using the same load they had, I tried to re-create the problem by entering an entire week of the same commands. This took me several days, working day and night. During this time, the customer received no word from us.

Finally, the customer called and wanted to know what was going on. By this time, all the commands been entered and everything looked like it worked fine. We decided to do an audit of their patches and found several that were missing.

Our customers are very knowledgeable. I wish I had kept them more informed. We might have come up with the idea of the patch audit sooner. Certainly they would have felt more involved. It's too easy to be on one side of a problem and not benefit from expertise on the other side. Keeping the customer informed is only one of the many lessons I learned from this experience, but one of the most important.

Pattern Source

Linda Leonard, as told to Linda Rising.

Customer Meetings: Go Early, Stay Late

Also Known As

Perfunctory (routine) Meetings, Schmooze!, Meet to Greet

Problem

You have to attend customer meetings and find them a chore. You're not getting anywhere building good customer relationships at these meetings. Often team members arrive just as the meeting starts and leave as the last slide is presented.

Context

You understand It's a Relationship, Not a Sale. You are trying to Know the Customer and are working to Build Trust.

Forces

- We want customers to be aware of the current status of the product.
- Some people feel that social interaction (especially meetings!) is lost productivity.
- Time management strategies discourage wasting time.

Solution

Arrive at the meeting with enough time to meet other attendees and spend a little time renewing old relationships and forming new ones. After the meeting, allow a little time to talk to others with common business interests.

If we are holding the meeting we should plan for these pre- and postmeetings but keep them as short as possible.

Resulting Context

When you show up a little early, you send a message to customers that you value their time. This also allows the meeting to start on time.

The extensions before and after the meeting more than justify the routine occurrence of the meeting itself, which becomes a shared experience instead of an obligation. A perfunctory or routine meeting becomes a more positive experience that helps build trust and solve real problems.

Don't lose your sense of the time constraints of the customer and your team members. We are all under time pressure, so a fine balance is required to convey the right message to our customers.

Rationale

There are many meetings whose real purpose is to get concerned parties together. The announced purpose may be, for example, to hear status information, but the true benefit is the personal exchange that happens around the meetings.

Spending time socializing beforehand allows everyone to come to the meeting with a sense of camaraderie. As a result the meeting is more effective. That, in turn, makes the time after the meeting more worthwhile. Often a postmeeting gathering is where the real work is done.

This pattern has broader implications than customer interaction. As our company includes more and more telecommuters, there is the increasing loss of visibility to these employees. This can be harmful both to the worker and the company. The employee feels removed from team interaction, and the company loses sight of the employee's contribution.

The following is from a Fast Company online newsletter [Imperato1999]:

> There is a legitimate social component to meetings. Sure, we'd all rather spend our time on "real work" than "idle chitchat." But you should never overlook the social side of work rituals—even in meetings that are "all business." In many of the meetings I run—especially meetings that take place early in the day—I schedule 5 or 10 minutes of open time, just to encourage people to relate to one another. If you plan for such time, if you put it on your agenda, then you won't feel as if you're not doing what you ought to be doing. Instead, you can enjoy going around the room and asking people what they did last night or over the weekend.

The following story is from Kathy Kromrie-Williams:

> Our group had a "meeting rep" who volunteered to go to all possible meetings to represent the group and save valuable time for team members. It sounded like a great idea. The volunteer was well intentioned and was sincerely trying to save effort for the team.
>
> The result, however, was a real loss of visibility by the team. No one else was part of interface meetings, so they had no input to agreements and misunderstood some requirements. The real impact was to the team's visibility to the rest of the project. Team members missed valuable networking opportunities and visibility to project management.

Pattern Source

David Saar, as told to Linda Rising.

Show Personal Integrity

Problem

How much should you share with the customer?

Context

You understand It's a Relationship, Not a Sale. You are trying to Know the Customer and working to Build Trust using Listen, Listen, Listen.

Forces

- We can't tell customers every possible risk.
- Customers want to know everything.

Solution

Part of an ongoing relationship and good project management is to identify the top N risks. Share the impacts of all major risks with the customer. Be honest and straightforward in your communications and demand the same from people you deal with. Otherwise any relationship is doomed.

Honest communication means being open. Withholding important information is not honest. Customers who believe we don't lie about a situation still will not trust us if they believe we are not telling them the complete story. Be Aware of Boundaries.

Simply being honest is not the intent of this pattern. Some kinds of honest comments can be destructive. Remember the context of this pattern contains the patterns It's a Relationship, Not a Sale, Know the Customer, and Build Trust.

Resulting Context

The customer will know that you can be relied upon to convey important information, even if it is not good news. The customer will learn to trust your word.

When you have a trusting relationship with customers and Show Personal Integrity, the customers are calmer in the face of announced risks.

Once the risks have been shared, the customer will expect regular status reports. Don't just leave the customer hanging with a list of showstoppers and no updates.

Rationale

Stephen Covey has noted [Covey1989]:

Integrity includes but goes beyond honesty. Honesty is telling the truth—in other words, conforming our words to reality. Integrity is conforming reality to our words—in other words, keeping promises and fulfilling expectations. Lack of integrity can undermine almost any other effort to . . . [Build Trust]. People can seek to understand, remember the little things, keep their promises, clarify and fulfill expectations and still fail to build reserves of trust if they are [two-faced].

The following quotes are from *Selling with Honor* [Kohn1997].

Don't lie, don't deceive, and don't overpromise. Tell the truth. What you sacrifice in immediate profit will be more than made up in referrals and repeat business.

Don't hide even small defects. Always disclose something that would bother you, because it would also probably bother a potential . . . [customer]. And if they found out, they'd wonder what else you were hiding.

Known Uses

The following is from an AGCS team postmortem:

When problems come up and we tell Rod Veach, "Don't worry about it!" He believes us. We would never hide anything from Rod. We let him know immediately about any problems.

Pattern Source

Linda Leonard, as told to Linda Rising.

Take Your Licks

Problem

What's the best way to deal with an angry customer?

Context

You're in a customer meeting or get a phone call or voice mail from a customer. From time to time customers may be disappointed with some aspect of the business relationship. This disappointment may come from unmet expectations, product performance, or from simple misunderstandings. This disappointment is often manifested as anger. More often than not, this anger is directed toward any company representative who is at hand.

You understand It's a Relationship, Not a Sale. You're trying to Know the Customer and Build Trust.

Forces

- No one likes to be yelled at.
- Our natural response is to be defensive.
- Being defensive is likely to escalate the customer's anger.
- Anger can damage the relationship with the customer.
- We want to diffuse the customer's anger.
- We want to protect our own interests.

Solution

Don't argue. Mind Your Manners.

An irate customer is not a rational customer but, nonetheless, Listen, Listen, Listen and try to understand how the customer's business is impacted.

Do not try to appease the customer by making promises you cannot keep. Be Aware of Boundaries. Instead, ask questions; find out what the real concerns are. Take notes. Assure the customer that these concerns are a priority and follow up on them.

Resulting Context

The customer will calm down sooner if verbal punches are not returned. When the customer has finished venting, the problem will still be there but the customer will feel better knowing that you understand the issues and will act on them.

Trying to solve the problem on the spot has pitfalls, too. Giving concessions easily may give the customer the impression that angry outbursts are the best way to do business with us. If you promise something you cannot deliver, the customer's expectations will again be unmet and trust will be broken.

Rationale

As unpleasant as the situation may be, the customer may have good reasons for being dissatisfied. By remaining calm and allowing the customer to vent, the anger will diffuse.

Keeping your composure is especially important. You represent the company. Flying off the handle will not build trust.

Pattern Author

Michael Duell

Be Aware of Boundaries

Also Known As

Stay Within the Lines

Problem

Developers, especially engineers, love to solve problems and answer questions. It's difficult when in a problem-solving mode to step back and realize the impact of proposing a solution or giving an answer.

Context

You are interacting with a customer and may be in a position where it's easy to become engrossed in issues and/or problems. You understand It's a Relationship Not a Sale. You are trying to Know the Customer and are working to Build Trust using Listen, Listen, Listen.

Forces

- We want to delight our customers.
- Customers may have unrealistic expectations and demands.
- We don't want to make promises we can't keep.

Solution

Boundaries are different for different team members. Some can give information and make commitments. Each team member should know his role and be aware of the boundaries that are appropriate for the setting, the customer, and the point in the project.

Don't discuss commercial considerations, for example, price, cost, schedule, and content that aren't part of your responsibilities.

Treat every conversation with the customer as part of a negotiation. Don't give away data or make instant judgments. Don't say, "Oh, that's easy!" or "That's impossible!"

Take note of any questions outside your area and get back with answers. Own the action items until you find the appropriate person to take responsibility for getting back to the customer. Use Mind Your Manners.

Resulting Context

The customer will feel that concerns are being heard and issues addressed but no commitments are made that might later have to be broken. More than this, the customer's real concerns will be heard but the company's as well as the customer's interests will be protected.

It is not the intent of this pattern to allow a team member to cover up mistakes or avoid talking about risks; remember to Show Personal Integrity.

Rationale

There can be wide impacts from simple discussions that can result in broken promises or incorrect information. Especially during early discussions, your goal is to understand what the customer really wants. It's easy to get carried away in customer interaction especially when trying to Build Trust and using Listen, Listen, Listen.

Boundaries are good for people. They set limits on actions and make it easier to act.

We must be aware that everyone represents the company and can impact current, future, and even past customer interaction. Off-hand remarks can have a lasting impact on the customer and current and future negotiations. There may be commercial implications of technical issues, for example, real time memory size. Don't set the customer up for disappointment. Interactions with the customer can change not only customer perceptions but also dollar amounts in negotiations.

The following is from a book about life at Microsoft [Bick1997]:

> When a tough question comes up, "I don't know but I'll find out!" is a lot safer than bluffing. No one expects you to know everything. This answer shows you're honest, you're not panicking in the face of a challenge, and you're responsive. Be sure to follow up with the answer!

Pattern Source

David Saar, as told to Linda Rising.

Mind Your Manners

Problem

When we interact with customers, we don't always think about etiquette, dress, and behavior.

Context

You understand It's a Relationship, Not a Sale. You're trying to Know the Customer and are working to Build Trust.

Forces

- Some people think that considering etiquette, dress, and behavior are a waste of time.
- People can react strongly to etiquette, dress, and behavior they consider inappropriate. They may even take it personally.

Solution

Mind Your Manners. Be polite. Be aware of body language. The way you dress and behave influences the way the customer sees you and our company.

Dress appropriately to meet customer expectations. Sometimes "business casual" is acceptable. At other times a suit is required, while on occasion, jeans are the norm. It helps to Know the Customer.

Show respect for everyone, including competitors.

Be especially careful in your interactions with others from our company in front of the customer.

Resulting Context

Customers will feel that we are concerned about all aspects of our business interaction and are ready to share their concerns and issues with our products.

Don't be so focused on minding your manners that your behavior is stiff or overly formal.

Rationale

Common courtesy is so uncommon! Simple, thoughtful acts convey a concern for the other person's welfare that is essential in any business interaction.

Our workplace environment may be very casual. We may not always be aware of pleasantries when interacting with our team, but these are important in customer interaction.

How we treat each other is an important sign to the customer about how we treat people in general.

The following is from ARC member Mitchi Page:

> I recently placed an order with a company. I asked when the new catalog was coming out. The reply, "Oh, our brilliant marketing department decided not to issue our new catalog until the first of the year," made me feel uneasy. When a customer contact makes sarcastic remarks about the company or someone in it, I feel uncomfortable dealing with them.

As Dave Thomas, founder of Wendy's Hamburgers, said in *Selling with Honor* [Kohn1997], "Be nice to everyone. Be polite."

Known Uses

Thanks to Karen Grover for pointing out an article in the *Wall Street Journal* [Bounds+1998] that described how an applicant for the top legal position at NovaCare, Inc. was turned down because he wore a casual outfit and carried a backpack at his interview. Vice President Gerry Johnson Geckle said that even if the applicant had presented better credentials, he wouldn't have been acceptable because "he didn't look professional." The successful applicant wore a dark suit and white dress shirt.

On the other hand, the *Journal* article went on to say, applicants can be rejected because they were overdressed. One instance was reported by an applicant who wore a linen suit, pumps, with flawless hair and makeup to an interview for a teaching job in suburban Colorado schools. The school principal appeared in faded shorts and propped her bare feet on a chair. Another interviewer wore jeans. The applicant was told that she looked like a "model" or "cheerleader," and that other teachers would be put off by her appearance.

Pattern Source

David Saar, as told to Linda Rising.

ACKNOWLEDGMENTS

Thanks to David Saar for the initial inspiration for these patterns, for spending time reviewing the patterns, and for providing the quote from Mike Reynolds. Thanks to Greg Gibson for the aliases (in the sections Also Known As) and the positive feedback. Thanks to Paul Bramble for the improvements to Listen, Listen, Listen. I would like to thank Lizette Velazquez, my PLoP '97 shepherd, for helping me eliminate the recursion from this pattern language. Her comments showed me how to make the patterns stronger.

Thanks also go to Charlie Schulz, Linda Leonard, and Rod Veach for their valuable suggestions. Thanks to the members of the PLoP '97 Workshop on People and Process for their insightful comments: Brad Appleton, Mike Beedle, Steve Berczuk, Charles Crowley, David DeLano, David Dikel, David Kane, Don Olson, and Bill Opdyke. Thanks to Ralph Cabrera, Kathy Kromrie-Williams, Jim Peterson, and Oscar Villa for the valuable workshop discussion on these patterns. Thanks to Kathy for the great stories!

Thanks to Julie Kemp, Ellen Lara, Debbie Liebman, Lynn Mattila, Mitchi Page, and Chalice Webb for giving me the ARC perspective and having such fun doing it! Thanks to Carole Boese, Doris Freeman, Rita Huard, Tracy Kelty, Annette Meyer, Fe Pati, and Nancy Schulte, and special thanks to Ken Arnold for the masculine viewpoint! Thanks to Peter Sommerlad, my shepherd for PLoP '98, for all his helpful comments and to Bill Opdyke, my program committee member, for contributing valuable feedback. And finally, thanks to the members of the PLoP '98 Workshop, Zen View, for their valuable comments: Jens Coldewey, David Cymbala, Bob Hanmer, Fernando Lyardet, Bill Opdyke, Oskar Nierstrasz, Rosemary Michelle Simpson, and Jenifer Tidwell.

REFERENCES

[Armstrong1992]. D. Armstrong. *Managing by Storying Around: A New Method of Leadership*. Doubleday, 1992.

[Behymer1997] D. Behymer. Letter to the Editor, *Quality Digest*, May 1997, p. 10.

[Bick1997] J. Bick. *All I Really Need to Know in Business I Learned at Microsoft*. New York: Simon & Schuster, 1997.

[Bounds+1998] W. Bounds and J.S. Lublin. "Workplace: Will the Client Wear a Tie or a T-Shirt?" *The Wall Street Journal*, July 24, 1998.

[Coplien1995] J.O. Coplien. "A Generative Development-Process Pattern Language." in J.O. Coplien and D.C. Schmidt (eds.), *Pattern Languages of Program Design*, pp. 184–237. Reading, MA: Addison-Wesley, 1995.

[Covey1989] S.R. Covey. *The 7 Habits of Highly Effective People*. New York: Simon & Schuster, 1989.

[Edler1995] R. Edler. *If I Knew Then What I Know Now: CEOs and Other Smart Executives Share Wisdom They Wish They'd Been Told 25 Years Ago*. New York: G.P. Putnam's Sons, 1995.

[Guaspari1998] J. Guaspari. "The Hidden Costs of Customer Satisfaction," *Quality Digest*. February 1998, pp. 45–49.

[Hunter1998] S. Hunter. "Establishing and Maintaining Good Client Relations." Available: http://www.thehost.com/hunter/clientr.htm.

[Imperato1999] G. Imperato. "You Have to Start Meeting Like This." *Fast Company On-Line Magazine, 23:* 1999.

[Inside1998] "Caterpillar Communicates with ROAMEO." *Inside AGCS*. July/August 1998, pp. 10–11.

[Kohn+1997] L. Kohn and J. Saltzman. *Selling with Honor*. Berkley, NY: Berkley Books, 1997.

[McCarthy1995] J. McCarthy. "It's a Relationship, Not a Sale." *Dynamics of Software Development*, pp. 71–73. Redmond, WA: Microsoft Press, 1995.

[Meszaros+1998] G. Meszaros and J. Doble. "A Pattern Language for Pattern Writing." In R. Martin, D. Riehle, and F. Buschmann (eds.), *Pattern Languages of Program Design 3*, pp. 527–574. Reading MA: Addison-Wesley, 1998.

[Thomsett1997] R. Thomsett. "It's the Expectations, Stupid!" *American Programmer*. April 1997, pp. 30–33.

[Whitenack1995] B. Whitenack. "RAPPel: A Requirements-Analysis-Process Pattern Language for Object-Oriented Development." in J.O. Coplien and D.C. Schmidt (eds.), *Pattern Languages of Program Design*, pp. 260–291. Reading, MA: Addison-Wesley, 1995.

Linda Rising may be reached at risingl@acm.org.

Chapter 27

Capable, Productive, and Satisfied: Some Organizational Patterns for Protecting Productive People

Paul Taylor

The greatest asset of a software development organization is a productive, cohesive team. Quality software, architectures, and systems can be developed only when productive, cohesive teams operate. These patterns address team capability and productivity—ways the capability to produce and evolve software can be created and maintained.

The "growing alternative" metaphor [Brooks1995] strongly underlies these patterns; software is *grown* by a group of people who share a culture of understanding of the problem space, the domain, the system requirements, the implementation technology, and a shared perception of the potential future of the system. A productive development team therefore represents a development capability that should be seen to be of greater value to the business than architectures or other software artifacts, which can be evolved while team activity is maintained. These patterns help a culture of productivity to grow.

ABOUT THESE PATTERNS

These patterns are primarily about people, process, and understanding, rather than products, production, and artifacts. Their solutions resolve forces, creating more productive software development environments by re-interpreting or "bending" selected forces to help the people be more productive.

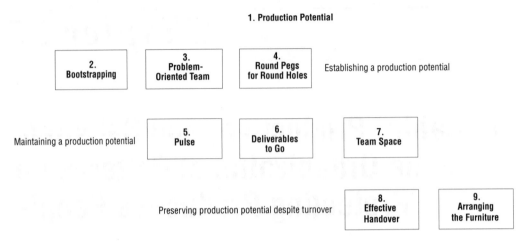

Figure 27-1 *Taking a capability-based view of a software development team*

The nine patterns shown in Figure 27-1 describe the establishment and maintenance of a productive team culture. Production Potential is the root pattern of the language fragment, addressing a capability-based view of the team. Three patterns, Bootstrapping, Problem-Oriented Team, and Round Pegs for Round Holes address establishing a productive team. Three patterns, Pulse, Deliverables to Go, and Team Space address the managing and scheduling of an established team. The remaining patterns—Effective Handover, and Arranging the Furniture—address maintaining a healthy level of productivity as the project delivers.

Many excellent organizational pattern languages have been written (for example, [Coplien1995]). By contrast, these patterns take a capability-based view of a development team and address ongoing management of this capability. In Eric Raymond's terms [Raymond1998], they pragmatically recognize the reality of cathedral-style development and address some of the inherent inflexibilities of the "bazaar" qualities.

A PATTERN FOR RECOGNIZING A TEAM'S POTENTIAL

Production Potential

A pattern for obtaining a fair and informed assessment of team capability and progress.

Context

You have a development team deeply involved in iterative development.

Problem

You observe a great deal of activity but little apparent progress on the deliverables. From this activity, you must get an accurate and fair assessment of both the team's progress and its capacity to produce.

Forces

- Teams need an infrastructure of understanding to support progress.
- Team progress cannot be solely assessed from the state of the deliverables in project directories.
- Teams often make significant progress without touching deliverables.
- Leaps in progress sometimes result in refactoring, such as the removal of source code or seemingly trivial software changes.

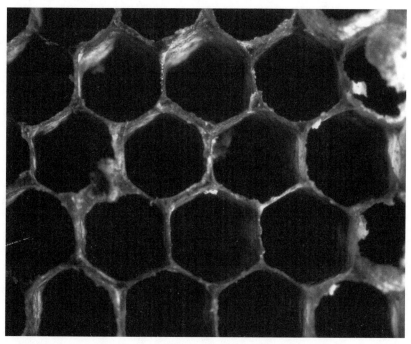

Industrial and natural infrastructures are tangible indicators of a capability to produce. In software development, the intellectual infrastructure exists in intangible forms: the experience and knowledge of the team, its key people, and their determination to deliver.

Solution

Teams are complex living, breathing, evolving, collaborating entities. Products are the concrete outcomes of their collective and individual labors. Teams corporately enact processes to deliver products.

Team managers frequently fall into the trap of managing the product rather than the process—we interpret people issues in terms of their products and measure people's capacity in product terms. This indirection can cause team managers to miss critical opportunities to create a team environment that balances productivity with the quality of work life. A concrete example of this phenomenon is the way we frequently measure team progress in terms of deliverables, rather than in terms of an increasing and maturing *capacity to progress.*

Teams make progress by learning, and learning is iterative. It can be a mistake to judge progress by the state of a team's deliverables, particularly early in the project. Learning often results in the throwing away of software artifacts—classes, designs, or microarchitectures—but these discards represent progress in the team's understanding of the problem and a growing confidence in the mechanisms that will be used as parts of the solution. Conversely, a design shortcoming discovered late in the project may represent a significant backward step that is not reflected in the software or artifacts on disk.

At any point in time, a team's progress is a function of the following quantities:

- The collective understanding and degree of confidence of the team members
- The collective degree of comfort with the solution of the team members
- The design and architecture models and documentation (although these often lose some validity as indicators of progress late in the project)
- The software architecture and modules, represented in source code

The last two measures of progress are visible, while the first two are not. Hidden progress of this kind must not be undervalued through lack of acknowledgment or recognition. Intellectual progress increases a team's *problem-solving capability* or *potential energy.* This potential energy will be converted into the kinetic energy of software production at a time when all significant preconditions have been met.

Therefore:

Measure team progress by a mix of assessed progress in all dimensions of work.

You should look for progress on many fronts and relate this progress to the project phase. You can weight your individual assessments to form an overall view of progress. It is then possible to consider where progress shortfalls are occurring.

Resulting Context

This pattern's message underlies the entire pattern language fragment, so it deserves to be stated loudly: *A software development team's most valuable attribute is its potential to produce. Production potential is a function of experience, knowledge, under-standing, established roles, and a supporting environment.*

The patterns in this language fragment interwork to generate productive teams by creating an environment where this capacity to produce is realized. Viewing progress in terms of the team's production potential helps to recognize the value of work done that contributes only indirectly to deliverables.

Known Problems

Business managers who do not understand complex software development may not condone investment in a capacity to produce. Development of intellectual infrastructure may need to produce a token piece of concrete infrastructure (e.g., process documentation, testing tools, development tools) to satisfy management.

Developers can be difficult people from whom to extract accurate progress information. It takes time to learn the right questions to ask of each individual.

Related Patterns

A team's Production Potential typically translates into high productivity at times of peak Pulse. Round Pegs for Round Holes may help you learn what kinds of questions to ask individual team members.

SOME PATTERNS FOR ESTABLISHING PRODUCTION POTENTIAL

Bootstrapping

A pattern to help a newly formed team become productive.

Context

You have a recently formed development team in which most team members are new to the problem domain, the application, and each other.

Problem

Your newly formed team must become productive *quickly.*

Forces

- An unproductive team costs the same to run as a productive one—the length of the initial phase of low productivity must be minimized.
- An unproductive team is an unstable team and is more easily driven apart by external influences.

Gearing up for the creation and manipulation of intellectual property requires disciplined planning, preparation, and execution.

- Leadership is much more difficult before team dynamics, individual abilities, interests, and roles have been established.
- There is a danger that people will start building solutions before they understand the problem.

Solution

In the early days of a team's existence, people cope with their disorientation by looking for firm ground upon which to build their understandings. If not responsibly guided, people run the risk of diverging, spending too much time on unnecessary detail, or looking for eye-catching decorations when a firm foundation is required.

The standard approach of allocating tasks and work areas to individuals addresses the mechanics of project planning but not team formation, which is best fostered by interaction and group problem solving. A useful approach is to focus on responsibilities—what has to be *known* and what has to be *done*.

Therefore:

Partition some responsibilities, and share *others.*

Your developers should understand this approach, since a responsibility-driven allocation of work reinforces one of the basic principles of object-orientation, although care should be taken not to overdo the analogy.

In order to partition responsibilities well, you must recognize that some responsibilities are best owned by individuals with specific capability and experience. You will need to draw on your experience to spot these responsibilities, and then on your experience of working with your team members to correctly allocate them (this is where Round Pegs for Round Holes comes in). Here are some candidate responsibilities that you might choose to partition:

- Abstractionist roles—senior designers who seed the business model and software architecture
- Business domain expert roles—business representatives who produce detailed domain models, investigate critical domain issues, and connect with information sources
- Development environment roles—senior developers who understand software tools and build environments
- User liaison roles—users, possibly outside the core development team, who translate business requirements to software architecture

Not all responsibilities should be partitioned. There are many responsibilities of team membership that must be evenly shared. The mechanical (but important) tasks in building software must be shouldered by the team rather than by a few individuals. Here are some candidate responsibilities that you might choose to share:

- Everyone must have an understanding of the system's high-level architecture.
- Everyone must have an understanding of the system's business or technical context.
- All developers must be fluent in the development language and basic development environment; for example, everyone must converge on naming, coding, and layout conventions.
- All developers must be comfortable with source version control, debugging techniques, and software build processes.

Resulting Context

By partitioning and sharing development responsibilities with your team, you achieve a degree of understanding, openness, and trust that can never be achieved by simply hanging names on a Gantt chart. Your people will additionally benefit from your openness and clarity in these assignments. They also should be reminded that the assignments are not fixed indefinitely.

From an external management perspective, a rapidly bootstrapped team will be perceived as more cost-effective than one that bootstraps more slowly or haphazardly.

Known Problems

If shareable responsibilities are narrowly partitioned, the individual will suffer from being excluded from the team's intellectual culture. It is a far worse mistake to share responsibilities that require critical skills or a singularly focused approach, such as object-oriented domain analysis or requirements modeling. The results of such inappropriate assignments may haunt the project for a considerable time.

Many teams have a star performer, the brilliant and personable individual who seems like the ideal candidate for every partitioned responsibility. Resist the temptation to overload this individual, first for her sake and second because you need to give other rising stars the chance to grow into expertise and leadership.

Some responsibilities may fall somewhere between being partitionable and shareable. Partition these, and observe them carefully as the Pulse begins to beat.

Related Patterns

Bootstrapping addresses the launching of a new team rather than the incremental replacement of members in an established team. Bootstrapping sets the context for a Problem-Oriented Team to operate. Team turnover is addressed by Effective Handover. Initial Bootstrapping initiates the first phase in the Pulse.

Problem-Oriented Team

A pattern for encouraging a team culture that focuses on the problem space.

Context

You have a development team with assigned responsibilities, after Bootstrapping.

Problem

You must now convert individual capabilities into team productivity.

Forces

- Teams consist of individuals, each with their own interests and agendas.
- Working relationships within the team must be allowed to establish and settle before people feel and become productive.

Undivided attention is not always so easy to achieve. Where the subject is intellectual property, team cohesion involves aligning people's motivations and interests.

- Software projects, particularly young ones, present a maze of possible activities, many of which are unproductive, futile, or harmful.
- Establishment of constraints within a project takes time and effort.

Solution

Your team's ramp-up period may be viewed as a time of *constraint discovery*, when people discover the constraints in the problem domain, the requirements, and the software architecture that will shape the delivered solutions. Learning constraints goes hand in hand with learning the nature of the problem. Once the problem space and its constraints have been probed, a foundation can be formed upon which design and construction can commence.

The problem space is only half the picture—the team forms a space of its own, held together by relationships, navigated by communication, and constrained by the members' capabilities and attitudes. Although each individual discovers the relevant problem space constraints in his own way, team member interaction establishes the team space.

Team cohesion is about balancing these dependencies and individualities. Although a balance is always achieved with time, elapsed unproductive time must be avoided. The catalyst to speed this reaction must be a common motivation. Experience suggests that *the imperative to fully understand the problem* is such a catalyst.

Therefore:

Stimulate an interest in the problem space, and use it as the common motivation to build team cohesion.

Focusing the team on the problem space gives each member an appreciation of their part, a taste of the project's vocabulary, and a base of confidence to aid communication. Team members who, for whatever reason, never grasp the problem being solved by the software system often lack vision and commitment to go beyond short-term tasks—they often want to be told what to do. While not everyone needs to lead, everyone needs to be able to find motivation.

To focus a team on the problem space, you can

- have the system's potential users visit and educate the team.
- create some nontechnical tasks that involve both users and developers.
- use excursions so that team members can experience the system's business context.
- tie architectural decisions back to the problem space during architecture and design reviews.

Learning the problem space is a means to an end (a Problem-Oriented Team), not an end in itself. Resources should be applied to this activity accordingly.

Resulting Context

Individual team members with an understanding of the problem can better understand the reasons for their tasks and work orientation, and are well placed to make the right decisions in designing their own components of the solution. A collective understanding of the problem facilitates better and more accurate team communication.

Known Problems

Some problem spaces are highly complex and cannot be mastered by all team members in a short time. In this case, choose a critical but manageable part of the problem space.

Related Patterns

An appreciation of the problem is strengthened by Deliverables to Go, which brings developers and users together around deliverables.

Round Pegs for Round Holes

A pattern for effectively assigning tasks to people.

Context

You must allocate tasks appropriately among team members during iterative software development.

Problem

By assigning a task to the wrong person, you can waste time, get inferior results, and discourage both the individual and the team.

Forces

- Developers are not interchangeable.
- Not all developers like or are good at doing the same basic tasks.
- Different business situations require different work approaches.

Suitability and motivation are co-dependent — the ideal assignment of tasks requires a deep knowledge of individuals.

- People are most productive when they are able to do what they do best.
- People don't always recognize what tasks they do best.
- People need new challenges.

Solution

Experienced managers get to know their team members well enough to allocate tasks appropriately. Software developers differ widely—some like to work quickly to provide fast turnaround on small tasks, while others prefer to take more time and deliver quality and thoroughness. These are personality characteristics—you cannot determine them from resumes or interviews. An individual's capabilities and preferred work modes must be observed over time in their current team context.

Therefore:

Discover each individual's preferences for working and allocate tasks accordingly.

This solution uses *observation,* then *action.* First, you must observe how your people work. Then you must apply these observations in your decisions about "who does what" in the mix of team tasks. You cannot shortcut this process of discovery, but you can hasten it by trying noncritical task allocations to test people's abilities and interests.

Take the demonstration of a product's user interface as an example. User interfaces are often demonstrated by the lead GUI developer, although better presenters may be available elsewhere in the team. A demonstration to users requires a smooth and focused run through the business tasks, rather than a deep knowledge of how the code is structured. By rotating the task around different team members, one can determine the right demonstrator for the prototypes' different audiences.

The "preferences for working" that you should learn are orthogonal to preferences for technologies and software layers. People with different work preferences are needed in all of the system's architectural layers and technologies. A looming software deadline illustrates this point. The known bugs that inhibit release are typically classified into those requiring simple but tedious fixes and those really difficult ones that require complex testing with debugging processes or tools. This workscape demands not only different technical abilities, but different personal work modes; some bugs need a quick resolution that will hold up in 80 percent of cases, while others require a methodical approach and thorough application of the fix—an informed selection of the individual to do these tasks is critical. You can speed up the acquisition of this knowledge by allocating different bugs to individuals as you approach the deadline.

Resulting Context

Knowledge of an individual's working preferences pays off in several ways. Obviously, you can make better assignments of tasks to people. Team members will also appreciate the personal attention evident in their assignments, and the breadth and depth of their skills may increase.

Known Problems

Observations must be made over time, in the heat of battle, as individuals learn and advance by small steps at a time. Your observation work must not become micromanaging or stand-over supervision—remember to let people know what you are doing, and periodically discuss how assignments are going.

The knowledge you gain of individuals is valuable and must be used *only* to make informed decisions about task allocation; other uses risk contravening the working relationship between you and your team.

Related Patterns

Times of lower Pulse rates may be best for testing out an individual's performance on a new task.

SOME PATTERNS FOR MAINTAINING PRODUCTION POTENTIAL

Pulse

Pulse is a pattern for managing the peaks and troughs of team activity to ensure a high average level of productivity in the long term.

Context

Your team must develop and deliver a significant amount of the project's functionality over the coming months.

Problem

Your team is capable of bursts of higher productivity to meet production demands, such as a software release—but you must handle the timing, length, and frequency of these peaks with great care.

Forces

- Increasing the delivery pressure on a team results in a short-term productivity increase.
- Teams cannot maintain peak productivity rates indefinitely.
- Teams without delivery pressure do not produce to their capability.

The Pulse rate is the basic indicator of the body's work rate; it directly correlates with physical and emotional exertion as a result of external demands. Exercise increases the body's pulse to a predetermined level for a short period of more intense work. It then relaxes to its normal level.

Solution

Teams usually operate in a cycle of increased and decreased work rates dictated by project schedules and deliverables. Over time, the period of the cycle will emerge; once the team's work rate is observably cycling, the rhythm can be used to everyone's advantage.

Therefore:

Determine the team's delivery rhythm *by putting the team through periods of higher pressure release cycles.*

To gain control of the project Pulse, you need to determine the optimum pressure and recuperation periods, then establish a project rhythm of production peaks and troughs, carefully aligned with the project plans and deliverables.

All projects experience external pressure to maintain high productivity for long periods. You can break long periods of a high Pulse rate by inserting space and time between two or more *real* releases:

- Rotate team members through activities that are amenable to changing personnel, such as software support, testing, or training.
- Provide additional support for pressured individuals within the work environment.
- Provide support outside the project environment where appropriate, such as for child care, carefully managed time away, or other assistance.

Alternatively, there may at times be long periods of lower productivity due to changing project goals or dependencies on other groups or products. Maintain project rhythm by breaking long recuperation cycles with an artificially created release (a *manufactured* pressure cycle) or with useful development work such as class and architecture generalization, framework development, or work on other nice-to-have deliverables for consumption by the project team.

Resulting Context

Regular and managed productivity peaks allow team members to plan and anticipate work peaks that can help in managing life's other commitments. Conversely, deliverables can be planned to coincide with the team's delivery peaks, so that the team exerts pressure back on the business, shaping its future schedules and the timing of deliverables.

Known Problems

Project Pulse is more evident when the team and its focus are stable; adding or removing team members can significantly affect the team's delivery capability. When the team lineup changes, the rhythm must be reestablished. Ideally, people should change at times of low project Pulse.

Projects have dependents (users being an obvious example) who need to be considered when planning a peak in project Pulse.

Related Patterns

A project's Pulse rate can be steadily increased after Bootstrapping and once a Problem-Oriented Team has formed. Peaks in Pulse rate typically produce Deliverables to Go. Levels of productivity should be assessed by Production Potential rather than the team's perceived activity levels. Periods of recuperation are best for an Effective Handover.

Deliverables to Go

A pattern for ensuring the team's deliverables are used.

Some things are best consumed here and now. When this is not possible, they lose value.

Context

Your team maintains (or will shortly maintain) released software.

Problem

You must plan the scope and timing of your team's deliverables so that their recipients will use them.

Forces

- Developers want their work to be appreciated.
- Developers want the extent of their solutions to be explored and tested.
- Users receive the best support from developers when the work is fresh in the minds of both parties.
- Unused or unwanted deliverables de-motivate developers.
- Unused deliverables open the door to a lower standard of quality.
- Requests for new functionality that are not responded to carefully and in reasonable time de-motivate users.

Solution

Synchronizing the timing and expectations between the development team and user community is critical to getting good results from both.

Therefore:

Only release when users are ready to consume.

This pattern requires an agreement between developers and users that works both ways. First, developers must treat user acceptance and requests for new or additional functionality seriously. Second, users must recognize their responsibility to explore the deliverables they have requested via the system requirements process. This can only happen when developers have access to users and can begin to integrate users into the team. You can stimulate this integration by

- Encouraging user involvement in team activities (e.g., business or domain experts can be involved in reviews).
- Encouraging the involvement of certain developers in user or business activities such as business processes, tests and trials, or system or prototype evaluations.

When this agreement matures, it should be possible for the development team to delay a planned deliverable until users are ready for it (with their agreement) and without fear of recrimination or embarrassment.

Resulting Context

The relationship between developers and users should be a *truce*—users should exert pressure on developers to motivate their work and maintain quality, and developers should exert pressure on users to test and explore their product. A healthy resolution of these forces increases communication and builds trust between developers and users.

Related Patterns

Large releases typically get delivered at the end of a peak in the Pulse rate and are followed by a carefully managed recuperation. A Production Potential measure at the time of release should show full effort focused on the deliverable.

Team Space

A pattern of physical interaction that occurs when people are free to cycle through the phases of individual and collective problem solving.

People should be able to interpret and impress upon their physical surroundings.

Context

Your team is deeply involved in iterative development.

Problem

Your physical work environment should be arranged to maximize people's productive time.

Forces

- People performing detailed, complex *thinking* work benefit from periodic short breaks from their work environment.
- Developers need to feel that relaxing their concentration for short periods is acceptable behavior.
- If not provided, team members will find or create this space themselves.
- People unintentionally distract others when their relaxation periods occur out of phase.
- In the absence of a team space, teams may splinter into smaller cliques and allegiances that meet in more inaccessible or private locations.

Solution

If productivity is to be maintained over time, a holistic, healthy work environment must recognize the natural rhythm of human work. It is widely recognized that productivity peaks interleave with nonproductive periods during an average working day. When resting or reflecting between periods of higher productivity, developers need to change their surroundings, change their posture, and casually interact.

Therefore:

Create a physical space for casual, unplanned interactions between team members.

Your team space should be small enough to feel something like a domestic lounge room, but large enough to comfortably house the entire team without individuals feeling physically constrained. It should preferably be close to the team's work space and sufficiently private to be inconspicuous to visitors. Its partitions, walls, and contents should be as movable, replaceable, and flexible as possible, to allow redefinition as the team size, its members, and its activities change.

This pattern differs from the others in this pattern language fragment because its solution involves *physical space* in which a social context welcomes people by allowing them to physically relax and mentally change gear. A social context can be created using couches, video equipment, posters, and icons collected during the team's ongoing life. Let the members decorate and arrange the space themselves.

Many of Alexander's architectural patterns for domestic living are applicable if the project has the option to design a space. For example, a team space should have Alcoves (179) and might follow Structure Follows Social Spaces (205) [Alexander 1977] so that concurrent activities can occur, and so that longer term activities, such as ongoing discussions, diagrams, white boards, or games can be left undisturbed over days, weeks, or even months.

Resulting Context

A team space exists for the team members and should be owned by the team members. The team space can be used for social events, like welcoming a new member or sending off a departing member. It can be used for discussing and making decisions in which consensus is required.

Known Problems

Activities in the team space may become a distraction at times from pressing work. This may be addressed by taking the work into the team space for a period. Most team members will understand and respect the motivation for providing the facility.

A team space is not a marketplace, a cafeteria, or a sporting complex—rather, it is a space for the team only and should be designed to be used briefly and frequently during periods of productive work. Company-sponsored gymnasiums, health centers or sporting facilities are *not* examples of this pattern, because they typically inhibit work-related interactions and usually demand a prolonged break from the team environment.

Related Patterns

Alexander's patterns for domestic spaces are directly relevant to the design of the physical team space.

SOME PATTERNS FOR PRESERVING PRODUCTION POTENTIAL

Effective Handover

A pattern that resolves the risk of lost productivity when an experienced team member is replaced.

Handovers can be designed to provide an opportunity for growth.

Context

Your team is running at peak productivity or nearing a critical delivery phase.

Problem

A critical team member is departing, so you must minimize the lost productivity that will inevitably result.

Forces

- The departing developer has the most detailed knowledge of a critical piece of the software system.
- The replacement has development skills but no application, architecture, or domain knowledge.
- The departing developer has unfinished work that must be done before departure.
- A full handover would tie up both developers for several weeks, killing the departing developer's productivity.

Solution

In software development, we do handovers notoriously badly. In development, the equivalent of a "shift" is a very long period, sometimes several years, and the depth of contextual knowledge required before useful work can be done is considerable. The knowledge of the application, its business domain, and the project's history that account for critical architecture and technology decisions may have taken months or years to accrue. In most project situations, when a key developer leaves, it is nearly impossible for the departing developer to impart a significant degree of knowledge to the replacement.

Therefore:

The departing developer should hand over to an existing developer, setting the replacement free to do new *work.*

It make much more sense to

- start the new team member on solving a different problem.
- leave the departing developer as much uninterrupted time as possible to work on resolving unfinished work, bugs, documentation, and incomplete work.
- give an existing team member the task of picking up the departing developer's software.

An effective handover preserves the team's ability to work and support a large and complex software architecture by redistributing responsibilities around the team's proven pillars. By handing over to an experienced team member, the difficult task of picking up the departing expert's area now becomes an exercise in identifying what the continuing team member *additionally* needs to know. When compared to the base level of project expertise, individual expertise often shrinks to manageable proportions.

Resulting Context

This solution recognizes that even the most expert team member builds her expertise on a common base of project experience, history, and context. It is this context that takes the time to learn and assimilate. The resolution removes a demanding and typically unachievable requirement for the new team member to "fill the expert's shoes." Instead, the newcomer can learn at a more manageable pace and be free to migrate towards the areas and work activities that he would naturally choose. This gives the newcomer freedom to succeed in his own space.

Known Problems

The continuing developer may become overloaded. If this happens, use the departure as an opportunity to shuffle and reallocate everyone's tasks and responsibilities.

There may not be a suitable or significant piece of system behavior ready for the newcomer to start work on. There are many alternative tasks that a new team member can usefully do to learn a software system while making a useful contribution—code refactoring, code reviewing, reverse engineering of design documentation, updating design or user documentation, testing, and test scripting are all practical examples.

Related Patterns

Performing effective handovers when team members are replaced preserves the current Pulse rate as much as possible. The newcomer should immediately be assessed for work preferences (Round Pegs for Round Holes). The team member picking up the departing developer's design and code may spend some initial time Arranging the Furniture.

Arranging the Furniture

Arranging the Furniture is a pattern that aids the task of learning to inhabit (settling into) someone else's software.

Placement and arrangement allow us to impose personality on a space, building a sense of ownership.

Context

Your established team is entering a time of transition as original members are replaced by newcomers.

Problem

Your newcomers must quickly come to grips with large and complex software modules.

Forces

- People are "territorial animals" and need a degree of ownership to be productive.
- A new maintainer needs to gain confidence and familiarity with someone else's code before being productive.

- For a software module to be *alive,* it must be actively inhabited on an almost daily basis.
- Familiarity and confidence are achieved incrementally—in software, one edit at a time.
- Many people feel ownership only after they have contributed to a product.
- People develop confidence and familiarity more quickly when they see they have control over their environment.

Solution

People, like cats, can be territorial. Adult male cats spray on trees, bushes, fence posts, and doors to mark their territory and then only begin to relax after they have explored and understood their immediate surroundings. To some extent, software developers need to mark their intellectual territory before a personal feeling of ownership can be established.

Source code can be changed to increase familiarity without changing its performance or behavior and without violating project coding conventions. Many small changes can be made to enhance code familiarity in the eyes of the reader.

Therefore:

An adopter should be encouraged to "move in" by cosmetically arranging code.

Taking up residence in a physical space involves arranging the furniture, hanging some new pictures on the wall, and placing frequently used things in convenient locations. Software equivalents include comments, documentation approaches, and names. Settling into someone else's source affords the opportunity to move it toward project standards that may involve anything from simple layout rearrangement (inter-symbol spacings, control block justifications, and the like) to minor rewriting.

To settle into a new software module, you may choose to

- Correct departures from project coding guidelines and conventions.
- Add comments to express your understanding of the source in your own words.
- Add tracing so that you will be able to follow control flow when the source executes.
- Add assertions within methods to test your understanding of how class attributes are used.
- Add defensive code to guard your module against bad arguments.
- Change (locally scoped) names or other symbols that are ambiguous or not meaningful.

Arranging the Furniture is intended to be an incremental activity. As each new "room" is visited, explored, and understood, the explorer leaves the room subtly rearranged, so that it is more understandable and recognizable when subsequently revisited. It is important that this task remains a background one and does not become a systematic pass through dozens of source files, unless of course the state of the software dictates this action.

Resulting Context

Arranging the Furniture is about cosmetic change, not structural or functional change. When you are very familiar with a software module, you may begin restructuring (breaking up long methods or eliminating code or attribute duplication) and refactoring (changing class boundaries and relationships to evolve the abstractions, design, and architecture).

Known Problems

Arranging the Furniture must not be used as an excuse to "trash the backyard." Habitation affords the freedom to change style, not structure or long-established project norms. The software architecture, class and module interfaces, and project coding standards must not be broken.

New graduates, full of idealism and undisciplined energy, may need their "furniture arranging" to be supervised by a team member with a few years' experience who can discern rearrangements that improve habitation from those that only stamp personality.

Related Patterns

Arranging the Furniture usually occurs after an Effective Handover. Arranging the Furniture can still be done at times of high Pulse, if the arrangements are made at the site of current work.

ACKNOWLEDGMENTS

These patterns have been mined from the author's experience of five software development projects over a 12-year period working in teams in the following application domains—distributed transaction switches, communication protocol engines, client-server middleware, legacy application gateways, and telecommunications fault management systems. The author would like to acknowledge Don Olson for shepherding the early drafts and Christine Mingins for supporting the documentation of these themes as patterns.

The images used herein were obtained from IMSI's Master Photos Collection, 1895 Francisco Blvd. East, San Rafael, CA 94901-5506, USA.

REFERENCES

[Alexander1977] C. Alexander. *A Pattern Language.* Center for Environmental Structure, Berkeley, University of California. Oxford Press, 1977.

[Brooks1995] F.P. Brooks. *The Mythical Man-Month (Anniversary Edition).* Reading, MA: Addison-Wesley, 1995.

[Coplien1995] J.O. Coplien. "A Generative Development-Process Pattern Language." In J.O. Coplien and D. C. Schmidt (eds.), *Pattern Languages of Program Design (PLoP1).* Reading, MA: Addison-Wesley, 1995.

[Raymond1998] E. Raymond. "The Cathedral and the Bazaar." Available: http://www.redhat.com/knowledgebase/otherwhitepapers/whitepaper_cathedral.html. Accessed 28 April 1998.

Paul Taylor may be reached at ptaylor@csse.monash.edu.au.

Chapter 28

SCRUM: A Pattern Language for Hyperproductive Software Development

Mike Beedle, Martine Devos,
Yonat Sharon, Ken Schwaber,
and Jeff Sutherland

Can a repeatable and defined process really exist for software development? Some think this is not only possible but necessary, for example, those who favor the CMM (Capability Maturity Model) approach to software development [Paulk+1995]. The CMM defines five stages of process maturity: initial, repeatable, defined, managed, and optimizing, and it asks its users to define the processes of 18 KPA (key process areas).

However, many of us doing work in the trenches have found over time that the *repeatable* or *defined* process approach makes many incorrect assumptions, such as the following:

- *Repeatable/defined problem.* A repeatable/defined process assumes that there is a step or steps to capture requirements, but in most cases, it is not possible to define the requirements of an application like that because they are either not well defined or they keep changing.
- *Repeatable/defined solution.* A repeatable/defined process assumes that an architecture can be fully specified, but in reality it is evolved, partly because

of missing or changing requirements (as described above), and partly because of the creative process involved in designing new software structures.

- *Repeatable/defined developers.* The capabilities of a software developer vary widely, so that a process that works for one developer may not work for another one.
- *Repeatable/defined organizational Environment.* Schedule pressure, priorities (e.g. quality vs. price vs. manpower), client behavior, and so on are never repeatable, and because they are highly subjective, they are very hard to define.

The problem with these assumptions is that these variables do have large variances. In real life projects there are always large dynamic variations that can have a great deal of impact on the overall project. For example, newly found changes in the requirements during an application implementation—a typical occurrence—may affect drastically a project's schedule that assumed that *all* the requirements would be captured up front. However, removing this uncertainty is nearly impossible because of the nearly universal sources of requirements change: business requirements driven changes, usability driven changes, re-prioritization driven changes, testing driven changes, and so forth. This issue cannot be solved through improved methods for identifying the user requirements. Instead it calls for a more complex process of generating fundamentally new operating alternatives.

In other words, once we accept that these dynamic variabilities do exist, we clearly need more adaptive ways to build software. However, what we fear is that most current methods do not allow us to build *soft enough* software; present methods and design paradigms seem to inhibit adaptability. Therefore the majority of software practitioners nowadays tend to become experts at what they can *specify in advance*, working with the unstated belief that there exists an optimal solution that can be planned a priori. Once technology is adopted by an organization, it often becomes a constraining structure that in part shapes the action space of the user. Thus we build software too much like we build hardware—as if it were difficult to change, as if it has to be difficult to change. In many organizations, "The system requires it" or the "The system does not allow it" have become accepted (and often unavoidable) justifications for human behavior before and after the system is released to production.

In contrast, SCRUM allows us to build *softer* software, so there is no need to write full requirements up front. Since the users do not know what is possible, they will ask for the pre-tech-paper solution that they perceive to be possible ("looking at the rearview mirror"). But in truth, not even the software developers know fully what can be built beforehand. Therefore, the user has no concept of what is possible before he or she can feel it or touch it. As such, the SCRUM patterns presented here offer a collection of empirical techniques that assume up front the existence of uncertainty but that provide practical and specific techniques to tame it. These techniques are rooted in complexity management, that is, in self-organization, management of empirical processes, and knowledge creation.

In that sense, SCRUM is not only a "parallel iterative and incremental" development method, it is also an "adaptive" software development method.

HOW DOES SCRUM WORK?

SCRUM's goal is to deliver as much quality software as possible within a series (three to eight) of short time boxes (fixed-time intervals) called Sprints that typically last about a month.

Each stage in the development cycle (Requirements, Analysis, Design, Evolution, and Delivery) is now mapped to a Sprint or series of Sprints. The traditional software development stages are retained primarily for convenience tracking milestones. So, for example, the Requirements stage may use one Sprint, including the delivery of a prototype. The Analysis and Design stages may take one Sprint each, while the Evolution stage may take anywhere from three to five Sprints.

Unlike a repeatable and defined process approach, in SCRUM there is no predefined process within a Sprint. Instead, SCRUM Meetings drive the completion of the allocated activities.

Each Sprint operates on a number of work items called a Backlog. As a rule, no more items are externally added into the Backlog within a Sprint. Internal items resulting from the original pre-allocated Backlog can be added to it. The goal of a Sprint is to complete as much quality software as possible, but typically less software is delivered in practice.

The end result is that there are non-perfect releases delivered every Sprint.

During a Sprint, SCRUM Meetings are held daily to determine the following:

- Items completed since the last SCRUM Meeting.
- Issues or blocks that need to be resolved. (The SCRUM Master is a team leader role responsible for resolving the blocks.)
- New assignments the team that should complete before the next SCRUM Meeting.

SCRUM Meetings allow the development team to "socialize the team members' knowledge" as well as produce a deep cultural transcendence.

This "knowledge socialization" promotes a self-organized team structure within which the development process evolves on a daily basis.

At the end of each Sprint there is a demonstration to:

- Show the customer what's going on.
- Give the developer a sense of accomplishment.
- Integrate and test a reasonable portion of the software being developed.
- Ensure *real progress,* that is, the reduction of Backlog, not just the production of more paper/hours spent.

After gathering and reprioritizing leftover and new tasks, a new Backlog is formed and a new Sprint starts. Potentially, many other org patterns (organization and process patterns) may be used in combination with the SCRUM patterns.

Figure 28-1 shows the relationships among the SCRUM patterns.

Figure 28-1 *The SCRUM pattern language*

THE PATTERNS

Sprint

Context

You are a software developer or a coach managing a software development team where there is a high percentage of discovery, creativity, or testing involved.

You are building or expanding systems, which allow partitioning of work, with clean interfacing, components, or objects.

Problem

You want to balance the needs of developers to work undisturbed and the needs of management and the customer to see real progress, as well as control the direction of that progress throughout the project.

Forces

- Developers need time to work undisturbed, but they need support for logistics; management and users need to be convinced that real progress is being made.
- Often, by the time systems are delivered, they are obsolete or require major changes. The problem is that input from the environment is collected mostly at the start of the project, while the user learns mostly by using the system or intermediate releases.
- It is often assumed that the development process is a well-understood approach that can be planned and estimated. If a project fails, that is considered proof that the development process needs more rigor. These step by step approaches, however, don't work because they do not cope with the unpredictabilities, both human and technical, in system development. Therefore, at the beginning of a

project it is impossible to make a complete, detailed specification, plan, or schedule because of the many uncertainties involved.

- Overhead is often created to prove that a process is on track. Current process automation adds administrative work for managers and developers and often results in marginally used development processes that become disk-ware. (Misfit: Activity is not synonymous with results. More often than not, a project plan shows activities but fails to ensure real progress or results.)

Solution

Divide the project in Sprints. A Sprint is a period of approximately 30 days in which an agreed amount of work will be performed to create a deliverable. Each Sprint takes a pre-allocated amount of work from the Backlog, and it is assigned to Sprints by priority and by approximation of what can be accomplished during the Sprint's length. In general, chunks of high cohesion and low coupling are selected—either horizontal or vertical "packets," that is, vertical or horizontal components.

As a rule, nothing is added externally to the allocated Sprint Backlog during a Sprint. External additions are only added to the global Backlog, but blocks (unresolved issues) resulting from the Sprint can be added to the allocated Sprint Backlog. A Sprint ends with a demonstration (Demo After Sprint) of new functionality.

This gives the developers space to be creative, to learn by exploring the design space and by doing actual work. Undisturbed by outside interruptions, they are free to adapt their ways of working using opportunities and insights. At the same time, this keeps management and other project stakeholders confident by showing real progress instead of documents and reports produced as *proof* of progress.

During the Sprint, outside chaos is not allowed in the increment. The team, as they proceed, may change course and their way of working within the Sprint.

The net result is that each Sprint produces a visible and usable deliverable that is shown to the users at the demo (Demo After Sprint). An increment can be either intermediate or shippable, but it should stand on its own. The goal of a Sprint is to complete as much quality software as possible and to ensure real progress, not paper milestones as alibis.

Rationale

- The fact that no items are added to the Backlog externally allows development to progress "full speed ahead," without needing to think about changes in direction.
- The fact that developers are not "tested" during the Sprint is empowering.

- The ability to choose a process per Sprint is empowering and enables adaptation to changing circumstances (different developers, different project phases, more knowledge, etc.).
- Sprints are short; therefore, the problem of completing a Sprint is much simpler than that of completing a project. It is easier to take up this smaller challenge.
- Developers get feedback frequently (at the end of each Sprint). The can therefore feel their successes (and failures) without compromising the whole project.
- Management has full control—it can completely change direction at the end of each Sprint.
- The end users are deeply involved throughout the development of the application through the Demos after the Sprints, but they are not allowed to interfere with the day-to-day activities. Thus ownership and direction still belong to the users but without their constant interference.
- Project status is visible since the Sprint produces working code.

Known Uses

At Argo, the Flemish department of education, we have been using Sprints since January 1997 on a large number of end-user-projects and for the development of a framework for database, document management, and workflow. The Backlog is divided in Sprints that last about a month. At the end of each Sprint, a working Smalltalk image is delivered with integration of all current applications. The team meets daily in SCRUM Meetings, and Backlog is re-prioritized after the Demo in a monthly meeting with the steering committee.

Resulting Context

The result is a high degree of "effective ownership" by the participants, including users who stay involved through the Demos and the prioritizing of the Backlog. "Effective ownership" in this case means both empowerment and the involvement of all the participants.

At the end of a Sprint, we have the best approximation of what was planned at the start. In a review session, the supervisors have the opportunity to change the planning for the future. The project is totally flexible at this point. Target, product, delivery date, and cost can be redefined.

With SCRUM we get a large amount of post-planning flexibility (for both customer and developer).

It may become clear in the daily SCRUM Meetings throughout the Sprint that some team members are losing time at non- or less productive tasks. Alternatively, it may also become clear that people need more time for their tasks than originally allocated by management. Developers may turn out to be less competent or experienced at the allocated task than assumed, or they may be involved in political or power struggles. The high visibility of SCRUM, however, allows us to deal with these problems. This is the strength of the SCRUM method manifested through the SCRUM Meetings and the Sprints.

Difficulties in grouping Backlog for a Sprint may indicate that priorities are not clear to management or to the customer.

Backlog

Context (From: Sprint)

You are connected to a software project or any other project that is chaotic in nature that needs information on what to do next.

Problem

What is the best way to organize the work to be done next and at any stage of the project?

Forces

Traditional planning methods like Pert and Gantt assume that you know in advance all the tasks, all their dependencies, all task durations, and all available resources. These assumptions are wrong if the project involves any learning, discovery, creativity, or adaptation.

Not having a repository of tasks in any shape or form simply translates into project failure. There must be some sort of project control.

Solution

Use a Backlog to organize the work of a SCRUM team.

The Backlog is a prioritized list. The highest priority Backlog item will be worked on first, the lowest priority Backlog item will be worked on last. No feature, addition, or enhancement to a product is worth fighting over; it is simply either more important or less important at any time to the success and relevance of the product.

Backlog is the work to be performed on a product. Completion of the work will transform the product from its current form into its vision. But in SCRUM, the Backlog evolves as the product and the environment in which it will be used evolves. The Backlog is dynamic, constantly changed by management to ensure that the product defined by completing the Backlog is the most appropriate, competitive, useful product possible.

There are many sources for the Backlog list. Product marketing adds work that will fulfill their vision of the product. Sales add work that will add new sales or extend the usefulness to the installed base. Technology adds work that will ensure the product uses the most innovative and productive technology. Development adds work to enhance product functions. Customer support adds work to correct underlying product defects.

Only one person prioritizes work. This person is responsible for meeting the product vision. The title usually is product manager or product marketing manager. If anyone wants the priority of work changed, they have to convince this person to change that priority. The highest priority Backlog has the most definition. It is also prioritized with an eye toward dependencies.

Depending on how quickly products are needed in the marketplace and the finances of the organization, one or more SCRUM Teams work on a product's Backlog. As a SCRUM Team is available (newly formed or just finished a Sprint) to work on the Backlog, the team meets with the product manager. Focusing on the highest priority Backlog, the team selects the one the team believes it can complete within a Sprint iteration (30 days). In doing so, the SCRUM Team may alter the Backlog priority by selecting a Backlog that is mutually supportive, that is, one that can be worked on at once more easily than by waiting. Examples are multiple work items that require developing a common module or interface and that make sense to include in one Sprint.

The team selects a cohesive group of top priority Backlog items that, once completed, will have reached an objective, or milestone. This is stated as the Sprint's objective. During the Sprint, the team is free to not do work as long as this objective is reached.

The team now decomposes the selected Backlog into tasks. These tasks are discrete pieces of work that various team members sign up to do. Tasks are performed to complete Backlog to reach the Sprint objective.

Resulting Context

Project work is identified dynamically and prioritized according to:

1. The customer's needs
2. What the team can do

SCRUM Meetings

Context (From: Backlog)

You are a software developer or a coach managing a software development team where there is a high percentage of discovery, creativity, or testing involved. An example is a first time delivery where the problem has to be specified, an object model has to be created, or new or changing technologies are being used.

Activities such as scientific research, innovation, invention, architecture, engineering and a myriad of other business situations may also exhibit this behavior.

You may also be a "knowledge worker," an engineer, a writer, a research scientist, or an artist, or a coach or manager who is overseeing the activities of a team in these environments.

Problem

What is the best way to control an empirical and unpredictable process such as software development, scientific research, artistic projects, or innovative designs where it is hard to define the artifacts to be produced and the processes to achieve them?

Forces

Estimation

- Accurate estimation for activities involving discovery, creativity or testing is difficult because it typically involves large variances, and because small differences in circumstances may cause significant differences in results. These uncertainties come in at least five flavors:
  1. Requirements are not well understood.
  2. Architectural dependencies are not easy to understand and are constantly changing.
  3. There may be unforeseen challenges with the technology. Even if the challenges are known in advance, their solutions and related effort are not known.
  4. There may be bugs that are hard to resolve in software; therefore, it is typical to see project estimates that are several orders of magnitude off. You can't "plan bugs," you can only plan bug handling and provide appropriate prevention schemes based on the possibility of unexpected bugs.

     Example: You Got The Wrong Number. In projects with new or changing requirements, a new architecture, new or changing technologies, and difficult bugs to weed out, it is typical to see project estimates that are off by several orders of magnitude.

  5. On the other hand, estimation *is* important. One must be able to determine what are the future tasks within some time horizon and prepare resources in advance.

Planning

- Planning and reprioritizing tasks takes time. Involving workers in time planning meetings decreases productivity. Moreover, if the system is chaotic, no amount of planning can reduce uncertainties.

Example: Paralysis By Planning. Some projects waste everybody's time in planning everything to an extreme detail but are never able to meet the plans.

- However, a plan that is too detailed becomes large and is hard to follow; the larger the plan is, the more errors it will contain (or at the very least the cost of verifying its correctness grows).

    Example: The Master Plan Is a Great Big Lie. Many projects that try to follow a master plan fall into the trap of actually believing their inaccuracies and often face disappointment when their expectations are not met.

- No planning at all increases uncertainty among team members and eventually damages morale.

    Example: Lost Vision. Projects that never schedule anything tend to lose control over their expectations. Without some schedule pressure no one will do anything, and worse, it will become difficult to integrate the different parts being worked on independently.

Tracking

- Too much monitoring wastes time and suffocates developers.

    Example: Measured to Death. Projects that waste everybody's time in tracking everything to an extreme detail but are never able to meet the plans. (You measured the tire pressure until all the air was out!)

- Tracking does not increase the certainty of the indicators because of the chaotic nature of the system.
- Too much data is meaningless—the Needle in a Haystack Syndrome.
- Not enough monitoring leads to blocks and possible idle time between assignments.

    Example: What Happened Here? Projects that never track anything tend to lose control over what is being done. Eventually no one really knows what has been done.

Solution

To provide for accurate estimates, plans, and appropriate tracking, meet with the team members for a short time (~15 minutes) in a daily SCRUM Meeting, where the only activity is asking each participant the following three questions:

1. What have you worked on since the last SCRUM Meeting? The SCRUM Master logs the tasks that have been completed and those that remain undone.
2. What blocks, if any, have you found in performing your tasks within the last 24 hours? The SCRUM Master logs all blocks and later finds a way to resolve the blocks.

3. What will you be working on in the next 24 hours? The SCRUM Master helps the team members choose the appropriate tasks to work on with the help of the Architect. Because the tasks are scheduled on a 24-hour basis, the tasks are typically small (Small Assignments).

This will provide you with more accurate estimates, short-term plans, appropriate tracking, and correcting mechanisms to react to changes and adapt every 24 hours.

SCRUM Meetings typically take place at the same time and place every day, so they also serve to build a strong culture. As such, SCRUM Meetings are rituals that enhance the socialization of status, issues, and plans for the team. The SCRUM-Master leads the meetings and logs all the tasks from every member of the team into a global project Backlog. He also logs every block and resolves each block while the developers work on other assignments.

SCRUM Meetings not only schedule tasks for the developers, but can and should schedule activities for everyone involved in the project, such as integration personnel dedicated to configuration management, architects, SCRUM Masters, or a QA team.

SCRUM Meetings allow knowledge workers to accomplish mid-term goals typically allocated in Sprints that last for about a month.

Scrum Meetings can also be held by self-directed teams, in that case, someone is designated as the scribe and logs the completed and planned activities of the Backlog and the existing blocks. All activities from the Backlog and the blocks are then distributed among the team members for resolution.

The format of the Backlog and the blocks can also vary, ranging from a list of items on a piece of paper, to software representations of it over the INTERNET/ INTRANET [Schwaber1997]. The SCRUM Meetings' frequency can be adjusted and typically ranges anywhere between 2 hours and 48 hours.

On C3 (described on wiki [Wiki1999]) they have these meetings standing up. This ensures that the meetings are kept short and to the point.

Rationale

It is very easy to over- or under-estimate, which leads either to idle developer time or to delays in the completion of an assignment. Therefore, it is better to frequently *sample* the status of small assignments. Processes with a high degree of unpredictability cannot use traditional project planning techniques such as Gantt or PERT charts *only*, because the rate of change of what is being analyzed, accomplished, or created is too high. Instead, constant reprioritization of tasks offers an adaptive mechanism that provides sampling of systemic knowledge over short periods of time.

SCRUM Meetings help also in the creation of an "anticipating culture" [Weinberg1997] because they encourage these productive values:

- They increase the overall sense of urgency.
- They promote the sharing of knowledge.
- They encourage dense communications.
- They facilitate honesty among developers since everyone has to give a daily status.

This same mechanism encourages team members to socialize, externalize, internalize, and combine technical knowledge on an ongoing basis, thus allowing technical expertise to become community property for the community of practice [Nonaka1995]. SCRUM Meetings are therefore rituals with deep cultural transcendence. Meeting at the same place at the same time, and with the same people, enhances a feeling of belonging and creates the habit of sharing knowledge.

Seen from the System Dynamics point of view [Senge1990], software development has a scheduling problem because the nature of programming assignments is rather probabilistic. Estimates are hard to come by because:

- Inexperienced developers, managers, and architects are involved in making the estimates.
- There are typically interlocking architectural dependencies that are hard to manage.
- There are unknown or poorly documented requirements.
- There are unforeseen technical challenges.

As a consequence, the software development becomes a chaotic *beer game,* where it is hard to estimate and control the *inventory* of available developer's time, unless increased monitoring of small assignments is implemented [Goldratt1990], [Senge1990]. In that sense the SCRUM Meeting becomes the equivalent of a *thermometer* that constantly samples the team's temperature [Schwaber1997].

From the Complexity Theory perspective [Holland1995], [Holland1998], SCRUM allows flocking by forcing a faster agent interaction, therefore accelerating the process of self-organization because it shifts resources opportunistically through the daily SCRUM Meetings.

This is understandable, because the relaxation of a self-organized multi-agent system is proportional to the average exchange among agents per unit of time. And in fact, the "interaction rate" is one of the levers one can push to control "emergent" behavior—it is like adding an enzyme or catalyst to a chemical reaction.

In SCRUM this means increasing the frequency of the SCRUM Meetings, and allowing more *hyperlinks* as described below, but up to an optimal upper-frequency bound on the SCRUM Meetings (meetings/time), and up to an optimal upper bound on the hyperlinks or the SCRUM Team members. Otherwise the organization spends too much time socializing knowledge, instead of performing tasks.

Known Uses

(Mike Beedle) At Nike Securities in Chicago we have been using SCRUM Meetings since February 1997 to run all of our projects including BPR and software development. Everyone involved in these projects receives a week of training in SCRUM techniques.

(Yonat Sharon) At Elementrix Technologies we had a project that was running way late after about five months of development. Only a small part (about 20 percent) was completed, and even this part had too many bugs. The project manager started running bi-daily short status meetings (none of us was familiar with the term SCRUM back then). In the following month, the entire project was completed and the quality had risen sharply. Two weeks later, a beta version was out. The meetings were discontinued, and the project hardly progressed since. I don't think the success of the project can be attributed to the SCRUM Meetings alone, but they did have a big part in this achievement.

One of my software team leaders at RAFAEL implemented a variation of SCRUM Meetings. He would visit each developer once a day, and ask him the three questions; he also managed a Backlog. This does not have the team building effects, but it does provide the frequent sampling.

C3 and VCaps projects (described on wiki [Wiki1999]) also do this. They call it a "standup meeting." (BTW, I adopted this name in Hebrew, since in Hebrew "meeting" is "sitting," and so we say "standup sitting".)

Resulting Context

The application of this pattern leads to

- Highly visible project status
- Highly visible individual productivity
- Less time wasted because of blocks
- Less time wasted because of waiting for someone else
- Increased team socialization

CONCLUSION

SCRUM is a knowledge creating process with a high level of information sharing during the whole cycle and work progress.

The key to SCRUM is pinning down the date at which we want completion for production or release, prioritizing functionality, identifying available resources, and making major decisions about architecture. Compared to more traditional methodologies, the planning phase is kept short since we know that events will require changes to initial plans and methods. SCRUM uses an empirical approach to development where interaction with the environment is not only allowed but encouraged. Changing scope, technology, and functionality are expected; and continuous information sharing and feedback keeps performance and trust high.

Its application also generates a strong culture with well-defined roles and relationships, with meaningful and transcending rituals.

ACKNOWLEDGMENTS

We would like to thank all of the SCRUM users and reviewers from whom we have received feedback over the years. Also, we thank all of the members of the Chicago Patterns Group that attended an early review session of the SCRUM Meeting pattern (especially Brad Appleton, Joe Seda, and Bob Haugen). Finally we thank our PLoP '98 shepherd, Linda Rising, for providing us comments and guidance to make our paper better.

(Personal acknowledgment from Mike Beedle.) I'd like to thank both Jeff Sutherland [Sutherland1997] and Ken Schwaber [Schwaber1997] for adapting the SCRUM techniques to software in the early 1990s, and for sharing their findings with me. SCRUM has made a significant contribution to the software projects in which I used the technique.

REFERENCES

[Beedle1997] M.A. Beedle. "cOOherentBPR—A Pattern Language to Build Agile Organizations." *PLoP '97 Proceedings*, Technical Report WUCS-97-34, Washington University, 1997.

[Coplien+1995] J.O. Coplien and D.C. Schmidt. *Pattern Languages of Program Design (A Generative Development-Process Pattern Language)*. Reading, MA: Addison-Wesley, 1995.

[Goldratt1990] E. Goldratt. *Theory of Constraints*, Burlington. MA: North River Press, 1990.

[Holland1995] J. Holland. *Hidden Order—How Adaptation Builds Complexity*. Reading, MA: Helix Books, Addison-Wesley, 1995.

[Holland1998] J. Holland. *Emergence—from Chaos to Order*. Reading. MA: Helix Books, Addison-Wesley, 1998.

[Nonaka1995] I. Nonaka and H. Takeuchi. *The Knowledge Creating Company*. New York: Oxford University Press, 1995.

[Paulk+1995] M.C. Paulk, C.V. Weber, and B. Curtis. *The Capability Maturity Model: Guidelines for Improving the Software Process*. Reading, MA: Addison-Wesley, 1995.

[Schwaber1997] Ken Schwaber's *SCRUM Web page:* http://www.controlchaos.com.

[Senge1990] P. Senge. *The Fifth Discipline—The Art and Practice of the Learning Organization*. New York: Doubleday/Currency, 1990.

[Sutherland1997] Jeff Sutherland's *SCRUM Web page:* http://jeffsutherland.com/scrum/index.html.

[Weinberg1997] G. Weinberg. *Quality Software Management, Vol. 4, Anticipating Change.* New York: Dorset House, 1997.

[Wiki1999] http://c2.com/cgi/wiki.

Mike Beedle may be reached at beedlem@fti-consulting.com.

Martine Devos may be reached at mdevos@argo.be.

Yonat Sharon may be reached at yonat@usa.net.

Ken Schwaber may be reached at virman@aol.com.

Jeff Sutherland may be reached at jeff.sutherland@computer.org.

Chapter 29

Big Ball of Mud

Brian Foote and Joseph Yoder

Over the last several years, a number of authors [Buschmann+1996, Garlan+1993, Meszaros1997, Shaw1996] have presented patterns that characterize high-level software architectures, such as Pipeline and Layered Architecture. In an ideal world, every system would be an exemplar of one or more such high-level patterns. Yet, this is not so. The architecture that actually predominates in practice has yet to be discussed—the Big Ball of Mud.

A Big Ball of Mud is a haphazardly structured, sprawling, sloppy, duct-tape and bailing wire, spaghetti code jungle. We've all seen them. These systems show unmistakable signs of unregulated growth and repeated *expedient* repair. Information is shared promiscuously among distant elements of the system, often to the point where nearly all the important information becomes global or duplicated. The overall structure of the system may never have been well defined. If it was, it may have eroded beyond recognition. Programmers with a shred of architectural sensibility shun these quagmires. Only those who are unconcerned about architecture and, perhaps, are comfortable with the inertia of the day-to-day chore of patching the holes in these failing dikes, are content to work on such systems.

Still, this approach endures and thrives. Why is this architecture so popular? Is it as bad as it seems, or might it serve as a way station on the road to more enduring, elegant artifacts? What forces drive good programmers to build ugly systems? Can we avoid this? Should we? How can we make such systems better?

We present the following seven patterns:

- Big Ball of Mud
- Throwaway Code
- Piecemeal Growth
- Keep It Working

- Shearing Layers
- Sweeping It under the Rug
- Reconstruction

Why does a system become a Big Ball of Mud? Sometimes, big, ugly systems emerge from Throwaway Code. Throwaway Code is quick-and-dirty code that was intended to be used only once and then discarded. However, such code often takes on a life of its own, despite casual structure and poor or nonexistent documentation. It works, so why fix it? When a related problem arises, the quickest way to address it might be to expediently modify this working code, rather than design a proper, general program from the ground up. Over time, a simple throwaway program begets a Big Ball of Mud.

Even systems with well-defined architectures are prone to structural erosion. The relentless onslaught of changing requirements that any successful system attracts can gradually undermine its structure. Systems that were once tidy become overgrown as Piecemeal Growth gradually allows elements of the system to sprawl in an uncontrolled fashion.

If such sprawl continues unabated, the structure of the system can become so badly compromised that it must be abandoned. As with a decaying neighborhood, a downward spiral ensues. Since the system becomes harder and harder to understand, maintenance becomes both more expensive and more difficult. Good programmers refuse to work there. Investors withdraw their capital. And yet, as with neighborhoods, there are ways to avoid, and even reverse, this sort of decline. As with anything else in the universe, counteracting entropic forces requires an investment of energy. Software *gentrification* is no exception. The way to arrest entropy in software is to refactor it. A sustained commitment to refactoring can keep a system from subsiding into a Big Ball of Mud.

A major flood, fire, or war may require that a city be evacuated and rebuilt from the ground up. More often, change takes place a building or block at a time, while the city as a whole continues to function. Once established, a strategy of Keeping It Working preserves a municipality's vitality as it grows.

Systems and their constituent elements evolve at different rates. As they do, things that change quickly tend to become distinct from things that change more slowly. The Shearing Layers that develop between them are like fault lines or facets that help foster the emergence of enduring abstractions.

A simple way to begin to control decline is to cordon off the blighted areas and put an attractive façade around them. We call this strategy Sweeping It under the Rug. In more advanced cases, there may be no alternative but to tear everything down and start over. When total Reconstruction becomes necessary, all that is left to salvage is the patterns that underlie the experience.

Some of these patterns might appear at first to be antipatterns [Brown+1998] or straw men, but they are not, at least in the customary sense. Instead, they seek to examine the gap between what we preach and what we practice.

Still, some of them may strike some readers as having a schizoid quality about them. So, for the record, let us put our cards on the table. We are in favor of good architecture.

Our ultimate agenda is to help drain these swamps. Where possible, architectural decline should be prevented, arrested, or reversed. We discuss ways of doing this. In severe cases, architectural abominations may even need to be demolished.

At the same time, we seek not to cast blame upon those who must wallow in these mires. In part, our attitude is to "hate the sin, but love the sinner." But it goes beyond this. Not every backyard storage shack needs marble columns. There are significant forces that can conspire to compel architecture to take a back seat to functionality, particularly early in the evolution of a software artifact. Opportunities and insights that permit architectural progress often are present later rather than earlier in the life cycle.

A certain amount of controlled chaos is natural during construction and can be tolerated, as long as you eventually clean up after yourself. More fundamentally, a complex system may accurately reflect our immature understanding of a complex problem. The class of systems that we can build at all may be larger than the class of systems we can build elegantly, at least at first. A somewhat ramshackle rat's nest might be a state-of-the-art architecture for a poorly understood domain. This should not be the end of the story though. As we gain more experience in such domains, we should increasingly direct our energies to glean more enduring architectural abstractions from them.

The patterns described in this chapter are not intended to stand alone. Instead, they are set in a context that includes a number of other patterns that we and others have described. In particular, they are set in contrast to the life cycle patterns, Prototype Phase, Expansionary Phase, and Consolidation Phase, presented in Foote and Opdyke [Foote+1995] and Coplien [Coplien1995]; the Software Tectonics pattern in Foote and Yoder [Foote+1996] and the framework development patterns in Roberts and Johnson [Roberts+1998].

Indeed, to a substantial extent, much of this chapter describes the disease, while the patterns above describe what we believe can be the cure: a flexible, adaptive, feedback-driven development process in which design and refactoring pervade the life cycle of each artifact, component, and framework, within and beyond the applications that incubate them.

FORCES

A number of forces can conspire to drive even the most architecturally conscientious organizations to produce Big Balls of Mud. These pervasive, global forces are at work in all the patterns presented. Among these forces are the following:

Time   There may not be enough time to consider the long-term architectural implications of one's design and implementation decisions. Even when systems have been well designed, architectural concerns often must yield to more pragmatic ones as a deadline starts to loom.

One reason that software architectures are so often mediocre is that architecture frequently takes a back seat to more mundane concerns such as cost, time-to-market, and programmer skill. Architecture is often seen as a luxury or a frill or the indulgent pursuit of lily-gilding compulsives who have no concern for the bottom line. Architecture is often treated with neglect, and even disdain. While such attitudes are unfortunate, they are not hard to understand. Architecture is a long-term concern. The concerns above have to be addressed if a product is not to be stillborn in the marketplace, while the benefits of good architecture are realized later in the life cycle, as frameworks mature and reusable black-box components emerge [Foote+1995].

Architecture can be looked upon as a *risk* that will consume resources better directed at meeting a fleeting market window or as an *opportunity* to lay the groundwork for a commanding advantage down the road.

Indeed, an immature architecture can be an advantage in a growing system because data and functionality can migrate to their natural places in the system unencumbered by artificial architectural constraints. Premature architecture can be more dangerous than none at all, as unproved architectural hypotheses turn into straightjackets that discourage evolution and experimentation.

Cost   Architecture is expensive, especially when a new domain is being explored. Getting the system right seems like a pointless luxury once the system is limping well enough to ship. An investment in architecture usually does not pay off immediately. Indeed, if architectural concerns delay a product's market entry for too long, then long-term concerns may be moot. Who benefits from an investment in architecture and when is a return on this investment seen? Money spent on a quick-and-dirty project that allows an immediate entry into the market may be better spent than money spent on an elaborate, speculative architectural fishing expedition. It's hard to recover the value of your architectural assets if you've long since gone bankrupt.

Programmers with the ability to discern and design quality architectures are reputed to command a premium. This expense must be weighed against the expenses of allowing an expensive system to slip into premature decline and obsolescence. If you think good architecture is expensive, try bad architecture.

Experience   Even when one has the time and inclination to take architectural concerns into account, one's experience with the domain, or lack thereof, can limit the degree of architectural sophistication that can be brought to a system, particularly early in its evolution. Some programmers flourish in environments where they can discover and develop new abstractions, while others are more comfortable in more constrained environments (for instance, Smalltalk vs. Visual Basic programmers.) Often, initial versions of a system are vehicles whereby programmers learn what pieces must be brought into play to solve a particular problem. Only after these are identified do the architectural boundaries among parts of the system start to emerge.

Inexperience can take a number of guises. There is absolute, fresh-out-of-school inexperience. A good architect may lack domain experience or a domain expert who knows the code cold may not have architectural experience.

Employee turnover can wreak havoc on an organization's institutional memory, with the perhaps dubious consolation of bringing fresh blood aboard. A succession of chefs can spoil the broth, as each seasons it to his own taste.

Skill Programmers differ in their levels of skill as well as in expertise, predisposition, and temperament. Some programmers have a passion for finding good abstractions while some are skilled at navigating the swamps of complex code left to them by others. Some programmers are particularly adept at discerning good abstractions and take pride in their ability to find them. Other programmers exhibit an almost insouciant disregard for abstraction and regard it as filigree. They take pride instead in their ability to quickly slather new code atop the old and to ride herd over the tangled kudzu thickets that are inevitably the result of this approach. Programmers differ tremendously in their degrees of experience with particular domains and their capacities for adapting to new ones. Programmers also differ in their language and tool preferences and experience.

Visibility Buildings are tangible, physical structures. You can look at a building. You can watch it being built. You can walk inside it and admire and critique its design.

A program's user interface presents the public face of a program, much as a building's exterior manifests its architecture. However, unlike buildings, only the people who build a program see how it looks inside.

Programs are made of bits. The manner in which we present these bits greatly affects our sense of how they are put together. Some designers prefer to see systems depicted using modeling languages or Microsoft PowerPoint pictures. Others prefer prose descriptions. Still others prefer to see code. The fashion in which we present our architectures affects our perceptions of whether they are good or bad, clear or muddled, or elegant or muddy.

Indeed, one of the reasons that architecture is neglected is that much of it is "under the hood," where nobody can see it. If the system works, and it can be shipped, who cares what it looks like on the inside?

Complexity One reason for a muddled architecture is that software often reflects the inherent complexity of the application domain. This is what Brooks called "essential complexity" [Brooks1995]. In other words, the software is ugly because the problem is ugly or at least is not well understood. Frequently, the organization of the system reflects the sprawl and history of the organization that built it (as per Conway's law [Coplien1995]) and the compromises that were made along the way.

Renegotiating these relationships is often difficult once the basic boundaries among system elements are drawn. These relationships can take on the immutable character of "site" boundaries that Brand [Brand1994] observed in real cities. Big problems can arise when the needs of the applications force unrestrained communication across these boundaries. The system becomes a tangled mess and what little structure is there can erode further.

Change   Architecture is a hypothesis about the future that holds that subsequent change will be confined to that part of the design space encompassed by that architecture. Of course, the world has a way of mocking our attempts to make such predictions by tossing us the totally unexpected. A problem that we might have been told was definitely ruled out of consideration for all time may turn out to be dear to the heart of a new client we never thought we'd have. Such changes may cut directly across the grain of fundamental architectural decisions made in the light of the certainty that these new contingencies could never arise. The "right" thing to do might be to redesign the system. The more likely result is that the architecture of the system will be expediently perturbed to address the new requirements, with only passing regard for the effect of these radical changes on the structure of the system.

Scale   Managing a large project is a qualitatively different problem from managing a small one, just as leading a division of infantry into battle is different from commanding a small special forces team. "Divide and conquer" is, in general, a necessary but insufficient answer to the problems posed by scale. Alan Kay, during an invited talk at OOPSLA '86 observed that "good ideas don't always scale." That observation prompted Henry Lieberman to inquire "so what do we do, just scale the bad ones?"

Big Ball of Mud

Also Known As

Shantytown, Spaghetti Code

Shantytowns are squalid, sprawling slums. Everyone seems to agree they are a bad idea, but forces conspire to promote their emergence anyway. What is it that they are doing right?

Shantytowns are usually built from common, inexpensive materials using simple tools. Shantytowns can be built using relatively unskilled labor. Even though the labor force is "unskilled" in the customary sense, the construction and maintenance of this sort of housing can be quite labor-intensive. There is little specialization.

Credit: Planned Parenthood—World Population

Each housing unit is constructed and maintained primarily by its inhabitants, and each inhabitant must be a jack of all the necessary trades. There is little concern for infrastructure, since infrastructure requires coordination and capital and specialized resources, equipment, and skills. There is little overall planning or regulation of growth. Shantytowns emerge where there is a need for housing, a surplus of unskilled labor, and a dearth of capital investment. Shantytowns fulfill an immediate, local need for housing by bringing available resources to bear on the problem. Loftier architectural goals are a luxury that has to wait.

Maintaining a shantytown is labor-intensive and requires a broad range of skills. One must be able to improvise repairs with the materials on hand and master tasks from roof repair to ad hoc sanitation. However, there is little of the sort of skilled specialization that one sees in a mature economy.

All too many of our software systems are, architecturally, little more than shantytowns. Investment in tools and infrastructure is too often inadequate. Tools are usually primitive, and infrastructure, such as libraries and frameworks, is under-capitalized. Individual portions of the system grow unchecked, and the lack of infrastructure and architecture allows problems in one part of the system to erode and pollute adjacent portions. Deadlines loom like monsoons, and architectural elegance seems unattainable.

*   *   *

As a system nears completion, its actual users may begin to work with it for the first time. This experience may inspire changes to data formats and the user interface that undermine architectural decisions that had been thought to be settled. Also, as Brooks [Brooks1995] has noted, because software is so flexible, it is often asked to bear the burden of architectural compromises late in the development cycle of hardware/software deliverables precisely because of its flexibility.

This phenomenon is not unique to software. Stewart Brand [Brand1994] has observed that the period just prior to a building's initial occupancy can be a stressful period for both architects and their clients. The money is running out, and the finishing touches are being put on just those parts of the space that will interact the most with its occupants. During this period, it can become evident that certain wish-list items are not going to make it and that exotic experiments are not going to work. Compromise becomes the order of the day.

The time and money to chase perfection are seldom available, nor should they be. To survive, we must do what it takes to get our software working and out the door on time. Indeed, if a team completes a project with time to spare, today's managers are likely to take that as a sign to provide less time and money or fewer people the next time around.

You need to deliver quality software on time and under budget.

Cost Architecture is a long-term investment. It is easy for the people who are paying the bills to dismiss it, unless there is some tangible immediate benefit such a tax write-off, or unless surplus money and time happens to be available. Such is seldom the case. More often, the customer wants something working by tomorrow. Often, the people who control and manage the development process simply do not regard architecture as a pressing concern. If programmers know that workmanship is invisible, and managers don't want to pay for it anyway, a vicious circle is born.

Skill Ralph Johnson is fond of observing the inevitability that "on average, average organizations will have average people." One reason for the popularity and success of Big Ball of Mud approaches might be that this approach doesn't require a hyperproductive virtuoso architect at every keyboard.

Organization With larger projects, cultural, process, organizational, and resource allocation issues can overwhelm technical concerns such as tools, languages, and architecture.

It may seem to a programmer that whether to don hip boots and wade into a swamp is a major quality-of-life matter, but programmer comfort is but one concern to a manager, which can conflict with many others. Architecture and code quality may strike management as frills that have only an indirect impact on their bottom lines.

Therefore:

Focus first on features and functionality, then focus on architecture and performance.

The case made here resembles Gabriel's "worse is better" arguments [Gabriel1991] in a number of respects. Why does so much software, despite the best intentions and efforts of developers, turn into Big Balls of Mud? Why do slash-and-burn tactics drive out elegance? Does bad architecture drive out good architecture?

What does this muddy code look like to the programmers in the trenches who must confront it? Data structures may be haphazardly constructed or even next to nonexistent. Everything talks to everything else. Every shred of important state data may be global. There are those who might construe this as a sort of blackboard approach [Buschmann+1996], but it more closely resembles a grab bag of undifferentiated state. Where state information is compartmentalized, it may be passed promiscuously about though Byzantine back channels that circumvent the system's original structure.

Variable and function names might be uninformative, or even misleading. Functions themselves may make extensive use of global variables as well as long lists of poorly defined parameters. The functions themselves are lengthy and convoluted and perform several unrelated tasks. Code is duplicated. The flow of control is hard to understand and difficult to follow. The programmer's intent is next to impossible to discern. The code is simply unreadable and borders on indecipherable. The code exhibits the unmistakable signs of patch after patch at the hands of multiple maintainers, each of whom barely understood the consequences of what he or she was doing. Did we mention documentation? What documentation?

Big Ball of Mud might be thought of as an antipattern, since our intention is to show how passivity in the face of forces that undermine architecture can lead to a quagmire. However, its undeniable popularity leads to the inexorable conclusion that it is a pattern in its own right. It is certainly a pervasive, recurring solution to the problem of producing a working system in the context of software development. It would seem to be the path of least resistance when one confronts the sorts of forces discussed earlier. Only by understanding the logic of its appeal can we channel or counteract the forces that lead to a Big Ball of Mud.

One thing that isn't the answer is rigid, totalitarian, top-down design. Some analysts, designers, and architects have an exaggerated sense of their ability to get things right up front, before moving into implementation. This approach can lead to inefficient use of resources, analysis paralysis, and design straightjackets and cul-de-sacs.

Kent Beck has observed that the way to build software is to: "Make it work. Make it right. Make it fast" [Beck1997]. "Make it work" means that we should focus on functionality up front and get something running. "Make it right" means that we should concern ourselves with how to structure the system only after we've figured out the pieces we need to solve the problem in the first place. "Make it fast" means that we should be concerned about optimizing performance only after we've learned how to solve the problem and after we've discerned an architecture to elegantly encompass this functionality. Once all this has been done, one can consider how to make it cheap.

When it comes to software architecture, form *follows* function. Here form "follows" not in the traditional sense of *dictating* function. Instead, we mean that the distinct identities of the system's architectural elements often don't start to emerge until *after* the code is working.

Domain experience is an essential ingredient in any framework design effort. It is hard to try to follow a front-loaded, top-down design process under the best of circumstances. Without knowing the architectural demands of the domain, such an attempt is premature, if not foolhardy. Often, the only way to get domain experience early in the life cycle is to hire someone who has worked in a domain before.

The quality of one's tools can influence a system's architecture. If a system's architectural goals are inadequately communicated among members of a team, they will be harder to take into account as the system is designed and constructed.

Finally, engineers will differ in their levels of skill and commitment to architecture. Sadly, architecture has been undervalued for so long that many engineers regard life with a Big Ball of Mud as normal. Indeed, some engineers are particularly skilled at learning to navigate these quagmires and at guiding others through them. Over time, this symbiosis between architecture and skills can change the character of the organization itself, as swamp guides become more valuable than architects. As per Conway's law [Coplien1995], architects depart in futility, while engineers who have mastered the muddy details of the system they have built in their images prevail. Foote and Yoder [Foote+1998a] went so far as to observe that inscrutable code might, in fact, have a survival advantage over good code, by virtue of being difficult to comprehend and change. This advantage can extend to those programmers who can find their ways around such code. In a land devoid of landmarks, such guides may become indispensable.

The incentives that drive the evolution of such systems can, at times, operate perversely. Just as it is easier to be verbose than concise, it is easier to build complex systems than it is to build simple ones. Skilled programmers may be able to create complexity more quickly than their peers and more quickly than they can document and explain it. This is akin to a phenomenon dubbed the *Peter Principle of Programming* by authors on the Wiki-Wiki web [Francis1999]. Complexity increases rapidly until it reaches a level of complexity just beyond that with which programmers can comfortably cope. At this point, complexity and our abilities to contain it reach an uneasy equilibrium. The blitzkrieg bogs down into a siege. We built the most complicated system that can be made to work [Francis1999]. Like an army outrunning its logistics train, complexity increases until it reaches the point where such programmers can no longer reliably cope with it.

Such code can become a personal fiefdom, since the author care barely understand it anymore, and no one else can come close. Once simple repairs become all-day affairs, as the code turns to mud. It becomes increasingly difficult for management to tell how long such repairs ought to take. Simple objectives turn into trench warfare. Everyone becomes resigned to a turgid pace. Some even come to prefer it, hiding in their cozy foxholes and making their two lines-per-day repairs.

It is interesting to ask whether some of the differences in productivity seen between hyperproductive organizations and typical shops are due not to differences in talent, but differences in terrain. Mud is hard to march through. The hacker in the trenches must engage complexity in hand-to-hand combat every day. Sometimes, complexity wins.

Status in the programmer's primate pecking order is often earned through ritual displays of cleverness, rather than through workman-like displays of simplicity and clarity. That which a culture glorifies will flourish.

Yet a case can be made that the casual, undifferentiated structure of a Big Ball of Mud is one of its secret advantages, since forces acting between two parts of the system can be directly addressed without having to worry about undermining the system's grander architectural aspirations. In the typical Big Ball of Mud, these aspirations are modest at best. Indeed, a casual approach to architecture is emblematic of the early phases of a system's evolution, as programmers, architects, and users learn their way around the domain [Foote+1995]. During the Prototype and Expansionary Phases of a system's evolution, expedient, white-box inheritance-based code borrowing and a relaxed approach to encapsulation are common. Later, as experience with the system accrues, the grain of the architectural domain becomes discernible and more durable black-box components begin to emerge. In other words, it's okay if the system looks at first like a Big Ball of Mud, at least until you know better.

*   *   *

Brian Marick first suggested "Big Ball of Mud" as a name for these sorts of architectures, and made the observation that this was, perhaps, the dominant architecture currently deployed, during a meeting of the University of Illinois Patterns Discussion Group several years ago. We have been using the term ever since. The term itself, in turn, appears to have arisen during the seventies as a characterization of Lisp.

Big Ball of Mud architectures often emerge from throwaway prototypes or Throwaway Code, because the prototype is kept or the disposable code is never disposed of. (One might call these "little balls of mud.")

They also can emerge as gradual maintenance, and Piecemeal Growth impinges upon the structure of a mature system. Once a system is working, a good way to encourage its growth is to Keep It Working. When the Shearing Layers that emerge as change drives the system's evolution run against the existing grain of the system, its structure can be undermined and the result can be a Big Ball of Mud.

The Prototype Phase and Expansion Phase patterns in Foote and Opdyke [Foote+1995] both emphasize that it is often beneficial to have a period of exploration and experimentation before making enduring architectural commitments.

However, these activities, which can undermine a system's structure, should be interspersed with Consolidation Phases [Foote+1995], during which opportunities to refactor [Fowler1999] the system to enhance its structure are exploited. Proponents of Extreme Programming [Beck2000] also emphasize continuous coding and refactoring.

Brand [Brand1994] observes that buildings with large spaces punctuated with regular columns had the paradoxical effect of encouraging the innovative reuse of space precisely because they *constrained* the design space. Grandiose flights of architectural fancy weren't possible, which reduced the number of design alternatives that could be put on the table. Sometimes Freedom from Choice [Foote1988] is what we *really* want.

One of mud's most effective enemies is sunshine. Subjecting convoluted code to scrutiny can set the stage for its refactoring, repair, and rehabilitation. Code reviews are one mechanism one can use to expose code to daylight.

Another is the Extreme Programming practice of pair programming [Coplien1995], [Beck2000]. A pure pair programming approach requires that every line of code written be added to the system with two programmers present. One types, or "drives," while the other "rides shotgun" and looks on. In contrast to traditional solitary software production practices, pair programming subjects code to immediate scrutiny and provides a means by which knowledge about the system is rapidly disseminated.

Indeed, reviews and pair programming provide programmers with something their work would not otherwise have—an audience. It is said that sunlight is a powerful disinfectant. Pair practices add an element of performance to programming. An immediate audience of one's peers provides immediate incentives to programmers to keep their code clear and comprehensible as well as functional.

An additional benefit of pairing is that accumulated wisdom and best practices can be rapidly disseminated throughout an organization through successive pairings. This is, incidentally, the same benefit that sexual reproduction brought to the genome.

By contrast, if no one ever looks at code, everyone is free to think they are better than average at producing it. Programmers will, instead, respond to those relatively perverse incentives that do exist. Line of code metrics, design documents, and other indirect measurements of progress and quality can become central concerns.

There are three ways to deal with Big Balls of Mud. The first is to keep the system healthy. Conscientiously alternating periods of Expansion with periods of Consolidation, refactoring, and repair can maintain, and even enhance, a system's structure as it evolves. The second is to throw the system away and start over. The Reconstruction pattern explores this drastic, but frequently necessary alternative. The third is to simply surrender to entropy and wallow in the mire.

Since the time of Roman architect Marcus Vitruvius, architects have focused on his trinity of desirables: *firmitas* (strength), *utilitas* (utility), and *venustas* (beauty). A Big Ball of Mud usually represents a triumph of utility over aesthetics, given that workmanship is sacrificed for functionality. Structure and durability can be sacrificed as well, because an incomprehensible program defies attempts at maintenance. The frenzied, feature-driven "bloatware" phenomenon seen in many large consumer software products can be seen as evidence that designers allowed purely utilitarian concerns to dominate design.

Throwaway Code

Also Known As

Quick Hack, Kleenex Code, Disposable Code, Scripting, Killer Demo, Permanent Prototype, Boomtown

A homeowner might erect a temporary storage shed or carport, with every intention of quickly tearing it down and replacing it with something more permanent. Such structures have a way of enduring indefinitely. The money expected to replace them might not become available. Or, once the new structure is constructed, the temptation to continue to use the old one for "a while" might be hard to resist.

Likewise, when you are prototyping a system, you are not usually concerned with the elegance or efficiency of your code. You know that you will only use it to prove a concept. Once the prototype is done, the code will be thrown away and written properly. As the time nears to demonstrate the prototype, it can be hard to resist the temptation to load it with impressive but utterly inefficient realizations of the system's expected eventual functionality. Sometimes, this strategy can be a bit too successful. The client, rather than funding the next phase of the project, may slate the prototype itself for release.

You need an immediate fix for a small problem or a quick prototype or proof of concept.

Time, or a lack thereof, is frequently the decisive force that drives programmers to write Throwaway Code. Taking the time to write a proper, well-thought-out, well-documented program might take more time than is available to solve a problem or more time that the problem merits. Often, the programmer will make a frantic dash to construct a minimally functional program, all the while promising herself that a better factored, more elegant version will follow thereafter. She may know full well that building a reusable system will make it easier to solve similar problems in the future and that a more polished architecture would result in a system that was easier to maintain and extend.

Quick-and-dirty coding is often rationalized as being a stopgap measure. All too often, time is never found for this follow-up work. The code languishes, while the program flourishes.

Therefore:

Produce, by any means available, simple, expedient, disposable code that adequately addresses just the problem at hand.

Throwaway Code is often written as an alternative to reusing someone else's more complex code. When the deadline looms, the certainty that you can produce a sloppy program that works for yourself can outweigh the unknown cost of learning and mastering someone else's library or framework.

Programmers are usually not domain experts, especially at first. Use cases or CRC cards [Beck+1989] can help them to discover domain objects. However, nothing beats building a prototype to help a team learn its way around a domain.

When you build a prototype, there is always the risk that someone will say "that's good enough, ship it." One way to minimize the risk of a prototype going into production is to write the prototype in a language or tool that you couldn't possible use for a production version of your product.

Proponents of Extreme Programming [Beck2000] often construct quick, disposable prototypes called *spike solutions*. Prototypes help us learn our way around the problem space, but should never be mistaken for good designs [Johnson1988].

Not every program need be a palace. A simple Throwaway program is like a tent city or a mining boomtown and often has no need for 50-year solutions to its problems, given that it will give way to a ghost town in five.

The real problem with Throwaway Code comes when it isn't thrown away.

The production of Throwaway Code is a nearly universal practice. Any software developer, at any skill or experience level, can be expected to have had at least occasional first hand experience with this approach to software development. For example, in the patterns community, two examples of quick-and-dirty code that have endured are the PLoP online registration code and the Wiki-Wiki Web pages.

The original EuroPLoP/PLoP/UP online registration code was, in effect, a distributed Web-based application that ran on four different machines on two continents. Conference information was maintained on a machine in St. Louis, while registration records were kept on machines in Illinois and Germany. The system could generate Web-based reports of registration activity and even instantaneously maintain an online attendees list. It began life in 1995 as a quick-and-dirty collection of HTML, scavenged C demonstration code, and csh scripts. It was undertaken largely as an experiment in Web-based form processing prior to PLoP '95 and, like so many things on the Web, succeeded considerably beyond the expectations of its authors. Today, it is still essentially the same collection of HTML, scavenged C demonstration code, and csh scripts. As such, it showcases how quick-and-dirty code can, when successful, take on a life of its own.

The original C code and scripts probably contained fewer than three dozen original lines of code. Many lines were cut-and-paste jobs that differed only in the specific text they generated or fields that they checked.

Here's an example of one of the scripts that generated the attendance report:

```
echo "<H2>Registrations: <B>" `ls | wc -l` "</B></H2>"
echo "<CODE>"
echo "Authors: <B>" `grep 'Author = Yes' *  | wc -l` "</B>"
echo "<BR>"
echo "Non-Authors: <B>" `grep 'Author = No' *  | wc -l` "</B>"
echo "<BR><BR>"
```

This script was slow and inefficient, particularly as the number of registrations increased, but not least among its virtues is the fact that it *worked*. Were the number of attendees to exceed more than 100, this script would start to perform so badly as to be unusable. However, since hundreds of attendees would exceed the physical capacity of the conference site, we knew the number of registrations would have been limited long before the performance of this script became a significant problem. So while this approach was, in general, a lousy way to address this problem, it was perfectly satisfactory within the confines of the particular purpose for which the script was used. Such practical constraints are typical of Throwaway Code and are more often than not undocumented. For that matter, everything about Throwaway Code is more often than not undocumented. When documentation exists, it is frequently not current and often not accurate.

The Wiki-Wiki-Web code at www.c2.com also started as a Common Gateway Interface (CGI) experiment undertaken by Ward Cunningham succeeded beyond the author's expectations. The name "wiki" is one of Ward's personal jokes, having been taken from a Hawaiian word for "quick" that the author, when on vacation in Hawaii, had seen on an airport van. Ward has subsequently used the name for a number of quick-and-dirty projects. The Wiki Web is unusual in that *any* visitor may change indiscriminately anything that anyone else has written. This would seem like a recipe for vandalism, but in practice it has worked out well. In light of the system's success, the author has subsequently undertaken additional work to polish it up, but the same quick-and-dirty Perl CGI core remains at the heart of the system.

Both systems might be thought of as being on the verge of graduating from little balls of mud to Big Balls of Mud. The registration system's C code *metastasized* from one of the NCSA HTTPD server demos and still contains zombie code that testifies to its heritage. At each step, Keeping It Working is a premiere consideration in deciding whether to extend or enhance the system. Both systems might be good candidates for Reconstruction were the resources, interest, and audience present to justify such an undertaking. In the meantime, these systems, which are still sufficiently well suited to the particular tasks for which they were built, remain in service. Keeping them on the air takes far less energy than rewriting them. They continue to evolve, in a Piecemeal fashion, a little at a time.

You can ameliorate the architectural erosion caused by quick-and-dirty code by isolating it from other parts of your system, in its own objects, packages, or modules. To the extent that such code can be quarantined, its ability to affect the integrity of healthy parts of a system is reduced. This approach is discussed in the Sweeping It under the Rug pattern.

Once it becomes evident that a purportedly disposable artifact is going to be around for a while, one can turn one's attention to improving its structure, either through an iterative process of Piecemeal Growth, or via a fresh draft, as discussed in the Reconstruction pattern.

Piecemeal Growth

Also Known As

Urban Sprawl, Iterative-Incremental Development

Urban planning has an uneven history of success. For instance, Washington D.C. was laid out according to a master plan designed by the French architect L'Enfant. The capitals of Brazil (*Brasilia*) and Nigeria (*Abuja*) started as paper cities as well. Other cities, such as Houston, have grown without any overarching plan to guide them. Each approach has its problems. For instance, the radial street plans in

The Russian **Mir** *(Peace) Space Station Complex was designed for reconfiguration and modular growth. The core module was launched in 1986, and the* Kvant *(Quantum) and Kvant-2 modules joined the complex in 1987 and 1989. The* Kristall *(Crystal) module was added in 1990. The* Spektr *(Spectrum) and shuttle docking modules were added in 1995, the latter surely a development not anticipated in 1986. The station's final module,* Priroda *(Nature), was launched in 1996. The common core and independent maneuvering capabilities of several of the modules have allowed the complex to be rearranged several times as it has grown.*
Credit: *NASA.*

L'Enfant's master plan become awkward past a certain distance from the center. The lack of any plan at all, on the other hand, leads to a patchwork of residential, commercial, and industrial areas dictated by the capricious interaction of local forces such as land ownership, capital, and zoning. Since concerns such as recreation, shopping close to homes, and noise/pollution away from homes are not brought directly into the mix, they are not adequately addressed.

Most cities are more like Houston than Abuja. They may begin as settlements, subdivisions, docks, or railway stops. Maybe people were drawn by gold, or lumber, access to transportation, or empty land. As time goes on, certain settlements achieve a critical mass, and a positive feedback cycle ensues. The city's success draws tradespeople, merchants, doctors, and clergy. The growing population is able to support infrastructure, governmental institutions, and police protection. These, in turn, draw more people. Different sections of town develop distinct identities. With few exceptions (Salt Lake City comes to mind) the founders of these settlements never stopped to think that they were founding major cities. Their ambitions were usually more modest and immediate.

*   *   *

It has become fashionable over the last several years to take pot shots at the "traditional" waterfall process model. It may seem to the reader that attacking it is tantamount to flogging a dead horse. However, if it is a dead horse, it is a tenacious one. While the approach itself is seen by many as having been long since discredited, it has spawned a legacy of rigid, top-down, front-loaded processes and methodologies that endure, in various guises, to this day. We can do worse that examine the forces that led to its original development.

In the days before waterfall development, programming pioneers employed a simple, casual, relatively undisciplined "code-and-fix" approach to software development. Given the primitive nature of the problems of the day, this approach was frequently effective. However, the result of this lack of discipline was, all too often, a Big Ball of Mud.

The waterfall approach arose in response to this muddy morass. While the code-and-fix approach might have been suitable for small jobs, it did not scale well. As software became more complex, it would not do to simply gather a room full of programmers together and tell them to go forth and code. Larger projects demanded better planning and coordination. Why, it was asked, can't software be engineered like cars and bridges, with a careful analysis of the problem and a detailed up-front design prior to implementation? Indeed, an examination of software development costs showed that problems were many times more expensive to fix during maintenance than during design. Surely it was best to mobilize resources and talent up front to avoid maintenance expenses down the road. It's surely wiser to route the plumbing correctly now, before the walls are up, than to tear holes in them later. Measure twice, cut once.

One of the reasons that the waterfall approach was able to flourish a generation ago was that computers and business requirements changed at a more leisurely pace. Hardware was very expensive, often dwarfing the salaries of the programmers hired to tend it. User interfaces were primitive by today's standards. You could have any user interface you wanted, as long as it was an alphanumeric "green screen." Another reason for the popularity of the waterfall approach was its comfortable similarity to practices in more mature engineering and manufacturing disciplines.

Today's designers are confronted with a broad onslaught of changing requirements. It arises in part from the rapid growth of technology itself and partially from rapid changes in the business climate (some of which is driven by technology). Customers are used to more sophisticated software these days and demand more choice and flexibility. Products that were once built from the ground up by in-house programmers must now be integrated with third-party code and applications. User interfaces are complex, both externally and internally. Indeed, we often dedicate an entire tier of our system to their care and feeding. Change threatens to outpace our ability to cope with it.

Master plans are often rigid, misguided, and out-of-date. Users' needs change with time.

Change The fundamental problem with top-down design is that real-world requirements are inevitably moving targets. You can't simply aspire to solve the problem at hand once and for all, because, by the time you're done, the problem will have changed out from under you. You can't simply do what the customer wants, for quite often they don't know what they want. You can't simply plan, you have to plan to be able to adapt. If you can't fully anticipate what is going to happen, you must be prepared to be nimble.

Aesthetics The goal of up-front design is to be able to discern and specify the significant architectural elements of a system before ground is broken for it. A superior design, given this mind-set, is one that elegantly and completely specifies the system's structure before a single line of code has been written. Mismatches between these blueprints and reality are considered aberrations and are treated as mistakes on the part of the designer. A better design would have anticipated these oversights. In the presence of volatile requirements, aspirations toward such design perfection are as vain as the desire for a hole in one on every hole.

To avoid such embarrassment, the designer may attempt to cover him or herself by specifying a more complicated and more general solution to certain problems, secure in the knowledge that others will bear the burden of constructing these artifacts. When such predictions about where complexity is needed are correct, they can be a source of power and satisfaction. This is part of the allure of *venustas*. However, the anticipated contingencies sometimes never arise, and the designer and implementers wind up having wasted effort solving a problem that no one ever actually had. Other times, not only is the anticipated problem never encountered, but also its solution introduces complexity in a part of the system that needs to evolve in another direction. In such cases, speculative complexity can be an unnecessary obstacle to subsequent adaptation. It is ironic that the impulse toward elegance can be an unintended source of complexity and clutter instead.

In its most virulent form, the desire to anticipate and head off change can lead to "analysis paralysis," as the thickening web of imagined contingencies grows to the point that the design space seems irreconcilably constrained.

Therefore:

Incrementally address forces that encourage change and growth. Allow opportunities for growth to be exploited locally, as they occur. Refactor unrelentingly.

Successful software attracts a wider audience, which can, in turn, place a broader range of requirements on it. These new requirements can be addressed frequently, but at the cost of cutting across the grain of existing architectural assumptions. Foote [Foote1988] called this architectural erosion *midlife generality loss*.

When designers are faced with a choice between building something elegant from the ground up, or undermining the architecture of the existing system to quickly address a problem, architecture usually loses. Indeed, this is a natural phase in a system's evolution [Foote+1995]. This might be thought of as a "messy kitchen" phase, during which pieces of the system are scattered across the counter, awaiting an eventual cleanup. The danger is that the cleanup is never done. With real kitchens, the board of health will eventually intervene. With software, alas, there is seldom any corresponding agency to police such squalor. Uncontrolled growth can ultimately be a malignant force. The result of such neglect can be a Big Ball of Mud.

In *How Buildings Learn*, Brand observed that what he called *high-road* architecture often resulted in buildings that were expensive and difficult to change, while vernacular, *low-road* buildings like bungalows and warehouses were, paradoxically, much more adaptable. Brand noted that *function melts form*, and low-road buildings are more amenable to such change. Similarly, with software, you may be reluctant to desecrate another programmer's cathedral. Expedient changes to a low road system that exhibits no discernable architectural pretensions to begin with are easier to rationalize.

In the Oregon Experiment [Alexander1988, Brand1994] Alexander noted:

Large-lump development is based on the idea of **replacement**. Piecemeal Growth is based on the idea of **repair**. . . . Large-lump development is based on the fallacy that it is possible to build perfect buildings. Piecemeal Growth is based on the healthier and more realistic view that mistakes are inevitable. . . . Unless money is available for repairing these mistakes, every building, once built, is condemned to be, to some extent unworkable. . . . Piecemeal Growth is based on the assumption that adaptation between buildings and their users is necessarily a slow and continuous business which cannot, under any circumstances, be achieved in a single leap.

Alexander has noted that our mortgage and capital expenditure policies make large sums of money available up front, but do nothing to provide resources for maintenance, improvement, and evolution [Alexander1988, Brand1994]. In the software world, we deploy our most skilled, experienced people early in the life cycle. Later on, maintenance is relegated to junior staff, and resources can be scarce. The so-called maintenance phase is the part of the life cycle in which the price of the fiction of master planning is really paid. It is maintenance programmers who are called upon to bear the burden of coping with the ever-widening divergence between fixed designs and a continuously changing world. If the hypothesis that architectural insight emerges late in the life cycle is correct, then this practice should be reconsidered.

Brand observed that *maintenance is learning*. He distinguishes three levels of learning in the context of systems. This first is habit, in which a system dutifully serves its function within the parameters for which it was designed. The second level comes into play when the system must adapt to change. Here, it usually must be modified, and its capacity to sustain such modification determines its degree of adaptability. The third level is the most interesting: *learning to learn*. With buildings, adding a raised floor is an example. Having had to sustain a major upheaval, the system adapts so that subsequent adaptations will be much less painful.

Piecemeal Growth can be undertaken in an opportunistic fashion, starting with the existing, living, breathing system and working outward, a step at a time, in such a way as not to undermine the system's viability. You enhance the program as you use it. Broad advances on all fronts are avoided. Instead, change is broken down into small, manageable chunks.

One of the most striking things about Piecemeal Growth is the role played by *feedback*. Herbert Simon [Simon1969] has observed that few of the adaptive systems that have been forged by evolution or shaped by humans depend on prediction as their main means of coping with the future. He notes that two complementary mechanisms, homeostasis and retrospective feedback, are often far more effective. Homeostasis insulates the system from short-range fluctuations in its environment, while feedback mechanisms respond to long-term discrepancies between a system's actual and desired behavior and adjust it accordingly. Alexander has written extensively on the roles that homeostasis and feedback play in adaptation as well [Alexander1964].

If you can adapt quickly to change, predicting it becomes far less crucial. Hindsight, as Brand observes, is better than foresight [Brand1994]. Such rapid adaptation is the basis of one of the mantras of Extreme Programming [Beck2000]: *You're not going to need it*.

Proponents of Extreme Programming or XP (as it is called) say to pretend you are not as smart as you think you are and wait until this clever idea of yours is actually required before you take the time to bring it into being. In the cases in which you were right, hey, you saw it coming, and you know what to do. In the cases in which you were wrong, you won't have wasted any effort solving a problem you've never had when the design heads in an unanticipated direction instead.

Extreme Programming relies heavily on feedback to keep requirements in sync with code by emphasizing short (three-week) iterations and extensive, continuous consultation with users on design and development priorities throughout the development process. Extreme Programmers do not engage in extensive up-front planning. Instead, they produce working code as quickly as possible and steer these prototypes toward what the users are looking for based on feedback.

Feedback also plays a role in determining coding assignments. Coders who miss a deadline are assigned a different task during the next iteration, regardless of how close they may have been to completing the task. This form of feedback resembles the stern justice meted out by the jungle to the fruit of uncompetitive pairings.

Extreme Programming also emphasizes testing as an integral part of the development process. Tests are developed, ideally, before the code itself. Code is continuously tested as it is developed.

There is a "back-to-the-future" quality to Extreme Programming. In many respects, it resembles the blind code-and-fix approach. The thing that distinguishes it is the central role played by feedback in driving the system's evolution. This evolution is abetted, in turn, by modern object-oriented languages and powerful refactoring tools.

Proponents of extreme programming portray it as placing minimal emphasis on planning and up-front design. They rely instead on feedback and continuous integration. We believe that a certain amount of up-front planning and design is not only important, but inevitable. No one really goes into any project blindly. The groundwork must be laid, the infrastructure must be decided upon, tools must be selected, and a general direction must be set. A focus on a shared architectural vision and strategy should be established early.

Unbridled, change can undermine structure. Orderly change can enhance it. Change can engender malignant sprawl or healthy, orderly growth.

* * *

A broad consensus that objects emerge from an *iterative incremental* evolutionary process has formed in the object-oriented community over the last decade (see, for instance, [Booch1994]). The Software Tectonics pattern [Foote+1996] examines how systems can incrementally cope with change.

The biggest risk associated with Piecemeal Growth is that it will gradually erode the overall structure of the system and inexorably turn it into a Big Ball of Mud. A strategy of Keeping It Working goes hand in hand with Piecemeal Growth. Both patterns emphasize acute, local concerns at the expense of chronic, architectural ones.

To counteract these forces, a permanent commitment to Consolidation and refactoring must be made. It is through such a process that local and global forces are reconciled over time. This life cycle perspective has been dubbed the *fractal model* [Foote+1995]. To quote Alexander [Alexander1988, Brand1994]:

An organic process of growth and repair must create a gradual sequence of changes, and these changes must be distributed evenly across all levels of scale. [In developing a college campus] there must be as much attention to the repair of details—rooms, wings of buildings, windows, paths—as to the creation of brand new buildings. Only then can the environment be balanced both as a whole, and in its parts, at every moment in its history.

Keep It Working

Also Known As

Vitality; Baby Steps; Daily Build; First, Do No Harm; Continuous Integration

> Probably the greatest factor that keeps us moving forward is that we use the system all the time, and we keep trying to do new things with it. It is this "living-with" which drives us to root out failures, to clean up inconsistencies, and which inspires our occasional innovation.
>
> —Daniel H.H. Ingalls [Ingalls1983]

Once a city establishes its infrastructure, it is imperative that it be kept working. For example, if the sewers break and aren't quickly repaired, the consequences can escalate from merely unpleasant to genuinely life threatening. People come to expect that they can rely on their public utilities 24 hours per day. They (rightfully) expect to be able to demand that an outage be treated as an emergency.

*   *   *

Software can be like this. Often a business becomes dependent upon the data driving it. Businesses have become critically dependent on their software and computing infrastructures. There are numerous mission critical systems that must be on-the-air 24 hours a day/seven days per week. If these systems go down, inventories cannot be checked, employees cannot be paid, aircraft cannot be routed, and so on.

There may be times where taking a system down for a major overhaul can be justified, but usually, doing so is fraught with peril. However, once the system is brought back up, it is difficult to tell from among a large collection of modifications which might have caused a new problem. Every change is suspect. This is why deferring such integration is a recipe for misery. Capers Jones [Jones1999] reported that the chance that a significant change might contain a new error—a phenomenon he ominously referred to as a *bad fix injection*—was about 7 percent in the United States. This may strike some readers as a low figure. Still, it's easy to see that compounding this possibility can lead to a situation in which multiple upgrades are increasingly likely to break a system.

Maintenance needs have accumulated, but an overhaul is unwise since you might break the system.

Workmanship   Architects who live in the house they are building have an obvious incentive to ensure that things are done properly, since they will directly reap the consequences when they do not. The idea of the architect-builder is a central theme of Alexander's work. Who better to resolve the forces impinging upon each design issue as it arises than the person who is going to have to live with these decisions? The architect-builder will be the direct beneficiary of her own workmanship and care. Mistakes and shortcuts will merely foul her own nest.

Dependability   These days, people rely on our software artifacts for their very livelihoods, and even, sometimes, for their very safety. It is imperative that ill-advised changes to elements of a system do not drag the entire system down. Modern software systems are intricate, elaborate webs of interdependent elements. When an essential element is broken, everyone who depends on it will be affected. Deadlines can be missed and tempers can flare. This problem is particularly acute in Big Balls of Mud, since a single failure can bring the entire system down like a house of cards.

Therefore:

Do what it takes to maintain the software and keep it going. Keep it working.

When you are living in the system you're building, you have an acute incentive not to break anything. A plumbing outage will be a direct inconvenience, and hence you have a powerful reason to keep it brief. You are, at times, working with live wires and must exhibit particular care. A major benefit of working with a live system is that feedback is direct and nearly immediate.

One of the strengths of this strategy is that modifications that break the system are rejected right away. There are always a large number of paths forward from any point in a system's evolution and most of them lead nowhere. By immediately selecting only those that do *not* undermine the system's viability, obvious dead-ends are avoided.

Of course, this sort of reactive approach, that of kicking the nearest, meanest wolf from your door, is not necessarily globally optimal. Yet, by eliminating obvious wrong turns, more insidiously incorrect paths are all that remain. While these are always harder to identify and correct, they are, fortunately, less numerous than those cases in which the best immediate choice is also the best overall choice.

It may seem that this approach only accommodates minor modifications. This is not necessarily so. Large new subsystems might be constructed off to the side, perhaps by separate teams, and integrated with the running system in such a way as to minimize disruption.

Design space might be thought of as a vast, dark, largely unexplored forest. Useful potential paths through it might be thought of as encompassing working programs. The space off to the sides of these paths is a much larger realm of nonworking programs. From any given point, a few small steps in most directions take you from a working to a nonworking program. From time to time, there are forks in the path, indicating a choice among working alternatives. In unexplored territory, the prudent strategy is never to stray too far from the path. Now, if one has a map, a shortcut through the trekless thicket that might save miles may be evident. Of course, pioneers, by definition, don't have maps. By taking small steps in any direction, they know that it is never more than a few steps back to a working system.

> Some years ago, Harlan Mills proposed that any software system should be grown by incremental development. That is, the system first be made to run, even though it does nothing useful except call the proper set of dummy subprograms. Then, bit by bit, it is fleshed out, with the subprograms in turn being developed into actions or calls to empty stubs in the level below.

*   *   *

> Nothing in the past decade has so radically changed my own practice, and its effectiveness.

*   *   *

> One always has, at every stage in the process, a working system. I find that teams can *grow* much more complex entities in four months than they can *build*.

> —From *No Silver Bullet* [Brooks1995]

Microsoft mandates that a Daily Build of each product be performed at the end of each working day. Nortel adheres to the slightly less demanding requirement that a working build be generated at the end of each week [Brooks1995, Cusumano+1995]. Indeed, this approach, and keeping the last working version around, are nearly universal practices among successful maintenance programmers.

Another vital factor in ensuring a system's continued vitality is a commitment to rigorous testing [Bach1994, Marick1995]. It's hard to keep a system working if you don't have a way to make sure it will work. Testing is one of Extreme Programming's pillars. Extreme Programming's practices call for the development of unit tests before a single line of code is written.

Always beginning with a working system helps to encourage Piecemeal Growth. Refactoring is the primary means by which programmers maintain order from inside the systems in which they are working. The goal of refactoring is to leave a system working as well after a refactoring as it was before the refactoring. Aggressive unit and integration testing can help to guarantee that this goal is met.

Shearing Layers

Hummingbirds and flowers are quick, redwood trees are slow, and whole redwood forests are even slower. Most interaction is within the same pace level—hummingbirds and flowers pay attention to each other, oblivious to redwoods, who are oblivious to them.

—R.V. O'Neill, *A Hierarchical Concept of Ecosystems* [O'Neill1996]

The notion of Shearing Layers is one of the centerpieces of Brand's *How Buildings Learn* [Brand1994]. Brand, in turn, synthesized his ideas from a variety of sources, including British designer Frank Duffy and ecologist R. V. O'Neill.

Brand quotes Duffy as saying: "Our basic argument is that there isn't any such thing as a building. A building properly conceived is several layers of longevity of built components."

Brand distilled Duffy's proposed layers into these six: Site, Structure, Skin, Services, Space Plan, and Stuff. Site is geographical setting. Structure is the load-bearing elements, such as the foundation and skeleton. Skin is the exterior surface, such as siding and windows. Services are the circulatory and nervous systems of a building, such as its heating plant, wiring, and plumbing. The Space Plan includes walls, flooring, and ceilings. Stuff includes lamps, chairs, appliances, bulletin boards, and paintings.

These layers change at different rates. Site, they say, is eternal. Structure may last from 30 to 300 years. Skin lasts for around 20 years, as it responds to the elements, and to the whims of fashion. Services succumb to wear and technical obsolescence more quickly, in 7 to 15 years. Commercial Space Plans may turn over every 3 years. Stuff, is, of course, subject to unrelenting flux [Brand1994].

*   *   *

Software systems cannot stand still. Software is often called upon to bear the brunt of changing requirements, because, being as it is made of bits, it *can* change.

Different artifacts change at different rates.

Adaptability   A system that can cope readily with a wide range of requirements, will, all other things being equal, have an advantage over one that cannot. Such a system can allow unexpected requirements to be met with little or no reengineering and allow its more skilled customers to rapidly address novel challenges.

Stability Systems succeed by doing what they were designed to do as well as they can do it. They earn their niches by bettering their competition along one or more dimensions such as cost, quality, features, and performance. See Foote and Roberts [Foote+1998] for a discussion of the occasionally fickle nature of such completion. Once they have found their niche, for whatever reason, it is essential that short-term concerns not be allowed to wash away the elements of the system that account for their mastery of their niche. Such victories are inevitably hard won, and fruits of such victories should not be squandered. Those parts of the system that do what the system does well must be protected from fads, whims, and other such spasms of poor judgment.

Adaptability and *stability* are forces that are in constant tension. On one hand, systems must be able to confront novelty without blinking. On the other, they should not squander their patrimony on spur-of-the-moment misadventures.

Therefore:

Factor your system so that artifacts that change at similar rates are together.

Most interactions in a system tend to be within layers or between adjacent layers. Individual layers tend to be about things that change at similar rates. Things that change at different rates diverge. Differential rates of change encourage layers to emerge. Brand notes as well that occupational specialties emerge along with these layers. The rate at which things change shapes our organizations as well. For instance, decorators and painters concern themselves with interiors, while architects dwell on site and skin. We expect to see things that evolve at different rates emerge as distinct concerns. This is "separate that which changes from that which doesn't" [Roberts+1998] writ large.

Can we identify such layers in software?

Well, at the bottom, there are data. Things that change most quickly migrate into the data, since this is the aspect of software that is most amenable to change. Data, in turn, interact with users themselves, who produce and consume them.

Code changes more slowly than data and is the realm of programmers, analysts, and designers. In object-oriented languages, things that will change quickly are cast as black-box polymorphic components. Elements that will change less often may employ white-box inheritance.

The abstract classes and components that constitute an object-oriented framework change more slowly than the applications that are built from them. Indeed, their role is to distill what is common, and enduring, from among the applications that seeded the framework.

As frameworks evolve, certain abstractions make their ways from individual applications into the frameworks and libraries that constitute the system's infrastructure [Foote1988]. Not all elements will make this journey. Not all should. Those that do are among the most valuable legacies of the projects that spawn them. Objects help Shearing Layers to emerge, because they provide places where the more fine-grained chunks of code and behavior that belong together can coalesce.

The Smalltalk programming language is built from a set of objects that have proven themselves to be of particular value to programmers. Languages change more slowly than frameworks. They are the purview of scholars and standards committees. One of the traditional functions of such bodies is to ensure that languages evolve at a suitably deliberate pace.

Artifacts that evolve quickly provide a system with dynamism and flexibility. They allow a system to be fast on its feet in the face of change.

Slowly evolving objects are bulwarks against change. They embody the wisdom that the system has accrued in its prior interactions with its environment. Like tenure, tradition, big corporations, and conservative politics, they maintain what has worked. They worked once, so they are kept around. They had a good idea once, so maybe they are a better than even bet to have another one.

Wide acceptance and deployment causes resistance to change. If changing something will break a lot of code, there is considerable incentive not to change it. For example, schema reorganization in large enterprise databases can be an expensive and time-consuming process. Database designers and administrators learn to resist change for this reason. Separate job descriptions, and separate hardware, together with distinct tiers, help to make these tiers distinct.

The phenomenon whereby distinct concerns emerge as distinct layers and tiers can be seen as well with graphical user interfaces.

Part of the impetus behind using Metadata [Foote+1998b] is the observation that pushing complexity and power into the data pushes that same power (and complexity) out of the realm of the programmer and into the realm of users themselves. Metadata are often used to model static facilities such as classes and schemas in order to allow them to change dynamically. The effect is analogous to that seen with modular office furniture, which allows office workers to easily, quickly, and cheaply move partitions without having to enlist architects and contractors in the effort.

Over time, our frameworks, abstract classes, and components come to embody what we've learned about the structure of the domains for which they are built. More enduring insights gravitate toward the primary structural elements of these systems. Things that find themselves in flux are spun out into the data, where users can interact with them. Software evolution becomes like a centrifuge stirred by change. The layers that result, over time, can come to a much truer accommodation with the forces that shaped them than any top-down agenda could have devised. Christopher Alexander writes:

> Things that are good have a certain kind of structure. You can't get that structure except dynamically. Period. In nature you've got continuous very-small-feedback-loop adaptation going on, which is why things get to be harmonious. That's why they

have the qualities we value. If it wasn't for the time dimension, it wouldn't happen. Yet here *we* are playing the major role creating the world, and we haven't figured this out. That is a very serious matter.

This pattern has much in common with the Hot Spots pattern discussed in Roberts and Johnson [Roberts+1998]. Indeed, separating things that change from those that do not is what drives the emergence of Shearing Layers. These layers are the result of such differential rates of change, while Hot Spots might be thought of as the rupture zones in the fault lines along which slippage between layers occurs. This tectonic slippage suggests also the Software Teconics pattern [Foote+1996] that recommends fine-grained iteration as a way to avoid catastrophic upheaval. Metadata and Active Object-Models allow systems to adapt more quickly to changing requirements by pushing power into the data and out onto users.

Sweeping It under the Rug

Also Known As

Potemkin Village, Housecleaning, Pretty Face, Quarantine, Hiding It under the Bed, Rehabilitation

One of the most spectacular examples of *sweeping a problem under the rug* is the concrete sarcophagus that Soviet engineers constructed to put a 10,000 year lid on the infamous reactor number four at Chernobyl, in what is now Ukraine.

If you can't make a mess go away, at least you can hide it. Urban renewal can begin by painting murals over graffiti and putting fences around abandoned property. Children often learn that a single heap in the closet is better than a scattered mess in the middle of the floor.

*   *   *

There are reasons, other than aesthetic concerns, professional pride, and guilt for trying to clean up messy code. A deadline may be nearing, and a colleague may want to call a chunk of your code—if you could only come up with an interface through which it could be called. If you don't come up with an easy-to-understand interface, they'll just use someone else's (perhaps inferior) code. You might be cowering during a code review, as your peers trudge through a particularly undistinguished example of your work. You know that there are good ideas buried in there, but that if you don't start to make them more evident, they may be lost.

There is a limit to how much chaos an individual can tolerate before being overwhelmed. At first glance, a Big Ball of Mud can inspire terror and despair in the hearts of those who try to tame it. The first step on the road to architectural

Credit: AP/Wide World Photos

integrity can be to identify the disordered parts of the system and to isolate them from the rest of it. Once the problem areas are identified and hemmed in, they can be gentrified using a divide and conquer strategy.

Overgrown, tangled, haphazard spaghetti code is hard to comprehend, repair, or extend and tends to grow even worse if it is not somehow brought under control.

Comprehensibility   It should go without saying that comprehensible, attractive, well-engineered code will be easier to maintain and extend than complicated, convoluted code. However, it takes time and money to overhaul sloppy code. Still, the cost of allowing it to fester and continue to decline should not be underestimated.

Morale   Indeed, the price of life with a Big Ball of Mud goes beyond the bottom line. Life in the muddy trenches can be a dispiriting fate. Making even minor modifications can lead to maintenance marathons. Programmers become timid, afraid that tugging at a loose thread may have unpredictable consequences. After a while, the myriad threads that couple every part of the system to every other come to tie the programmer down as surely as Gulliver among the Lilliputians. Talent may desert the project in the face of such bondage.

Therefore:

If you can't easily make a mess go away, at least cordon it off. This restricts the disorder to a fixed area, keeps it out of sight, and can set the stage for additional refactoring.

By getting the dirt into a single pile beneath the carpet, you at least know where it is and can move it around. You've still got a pile of dirt on your hands, but it is localized, and your guests can't see it. As the engineers who entombed reactor number four at Chernobyl demonstrated, sometimes you've got to get a lid on a problem before you can get serious about cleaning things up. Once the problem area is contained, you can decontaminate at a more leisurely pace.

To begin to get a handle on spaghetti code, find those sections of it that seem less tightly coupled and start to draw architectural boundaries there. Separate the global information into distinct data structures and enforce communication between these enclaves using well-defined interfaces. Such steps can be the first ones on the road to reestablishing the system's conceptual integrity and discerning nascent architectural landmarks.

Putting a fresh interface around a run-down region of the system can be the first step on the way to architectural rehabilitation. This is a long row to hoe, however. Distilling meaningful abstractions from a Big Ball of Mud is a difficult and demand task. It requires skill, insight, and persistence. At times, Reconstruction may seem like the less painful course. Still, it is not like unscrambling an egg. As with rehabilitation in the real world, restoring a system to architectural health requires resources as well as a sustained commitment on the part of the people who live there.

The UIMX user interface builder for UNIX and Motif and the various Smalltalk GUI builders both provide a means for programmers to cordon off complexity in this fashion.

One frequently constructs a Façade [Gamma+1995] to put a congenial "pretty face" on the unpleasantness that is Swept under the Rug. Once these messy chunks of code have been quarantined, you can expose their functionality using Intention Revealing Selectors [Beck1997].

This can be the first step on the road to Consolidation, since one can begin to hem in unregulated growth that may have occurred during Prototyping or Expansion [Foote+1995]. Foote and Yoder [Foote+1998] explores how, ironically, inscrutable code can persist *because* it is difficult to comprehend.

This chapter also examines how complexity can be hidden using suitable defaults (Works out of the Box and Programming-by-Differrence) and interfaces that gradually reveal additional capabilities as the client grows more sophisticated.

Reconstruction

Also Known As

Demolition, Total Rewrite, Throwaway the First One, Start Over

> *Plan to Throw One Away (You Will Anyway)*
>
> —Brooks [Brooks1995]

Extreme Programming [Beck2000] had its genesis in the Chrysler Comprehensive Compensation project (C3). It began with a cry for help from a foundering project and a decision to discard a year and a half's worth of work. The process they put in place after they started anew laid the foundation for XP, and the authors credit these approaches for the subsequent success of the C3 effort. However, less emphasis is given to value of the experience the team might have salvaged from their initial, unsuccessful draft. Could this first draft have been the unsung hero of this tale?

Your code has declined to the point where it is beyond repair or even comprehension.

Obsolescence Of course, one reason to abandon a system is that it is in fact technically or economically obsolete. These are distinct situations. A system that is no longer state of the art may still sell well, while a technically superior system may be overwhelmed by a more popular competitor for nontechnical reasons.

In the realm of concrete and steel, blight is the symptom, and a withdrawal of capital is the cause. Of course, once this process begins, it can feed on itself. On the other hand, given a steady infusion of resources, buildings can last indefinitely. It's not merely entropy, but an unwillingness to counteract it, that allows buildings to decline. In Europe neighborhoods have flourished for hundreds of years. They have avoided the boom/bust cycles that characterize some New World cities.

Change Even though software is a highly malleable medium, the new demands can, at times, cut across a system's architectural assumptions in such a way as to make accommodating them next to impossible. In such cases, a total rewrite might be the only answer.

Cost Writing off a system can be traumatic, both to those who have worked on it, and to those who have paid for it. Software is often treated as an asset by accountants and can be an expensive asset at that. Rewriting a system, of course, does not discard its conceptual design or its staff's experience. If it is truly the case that the value of these assets is in the design experience they embody, then accounting practices must recognize this.

Credit: UPI/Corbis

Organization Rebuilding a system from scratch is a high-profile undertaking that will demand considerable time and resources that, in turn, will make high-level management support essential.

   Therefore:

   Throw it away it and start over.

   Sometimes it's just easier to throw a system away and start over. Examples abound. Our shelves are littered with the discarded carcasses of obsolete software and its documentation. Starting over can be seen either as a defeat at the hands of the old code or a victory over it.

   One reason to start over might be that the previous system was written by people who are long gone. Doing a rewrite provides new personnel with a way to reestablish contact between the architecture and the implementation. Sometimes the only way to understand a system it is to write it yourself. Doing a fresh draft is a way to overcome neglect. Issues are revisited. A fresh draft adds vigor. You draw back to leap. The quagmire vanishes. The swamp is drained.

   Another motivation for building a new system might be that you feel that you've got the experience you need to do the job properly. One way to have gotten this experience is to have participated at some level in the unsuccessful development of a previous incarnation of the system.

Of course, the new system is not designed in a vacuum. Brooks' famous tar pit is excavated, and the fossils are examined to see what they can tell the living. It is essential that a thorough postmortem review be done of the old system, to see what it did well, and why it failed. Bad code can bog down a good design. A good design can isolate and contain bad code.

When a system becomes a Big Ball of Mud, its relative incomprehensibility may hasten its demise by making it difficult for it to adapt. It can persist, since it resists change, but cannot evolve, for the same reason. Instead, its inscrutability, even when it is to its short-term benefit, sows the seeds of its ultimate demise.

If this makes muddiness a frequently terminal condition, is this really a bad thing? Or is it a blessing that these sclerotic systems yield the stage to more agile successors? Certainly, the departure of these ramshackle relics can be a cause for celebration as well as sadness.

Discarding a system dispenses with its implementation and leaves only its conceptual design behind. Only the patterns that underlie the system remain, grinning like a Cheshire cat. It is their spirits that help to shape the next implementation. With luck, these architectural insights will be reincarnated as genuine reusable artifacts in the new system, such as abstract classes and frameworks. It is by finding these architectural nuggets that the promise of objects and reuse can finally be fulfilled.

There are alternatives to throwing your system away and starting over. One is to embark on a regimen of incremental refactoring to glean architectural elements and discernable abstractions from the mire. Indeed, you can begin by looking for coarse fissures along which to separate parts of the system, as was suggested in Sweeping It under the Rug. Of course, refactoring is more effective as a prophylactic measure that as a last-resort therapy. As with any edifice, it is a judgment call whether to rehabilitate or resort to the wrecking ball.

Another alternative is to reassess whether new components and frameworks have come along that can replace all or part of the system. When you can reuse and retrofit other existing components, you can spare yourself the time and expense involved in rebuilding, repairing, and maintaining the one you have.

The U.S. Commerce Department defines *durable goods* as those that are designed to last for three years or more. This category traditionally applied to goods such as furniture, appliances, automobiles, and business machines. Ironically, as computer equipment is depreciating ever more quickly, it is increasingly our software artifacts, and not our hardware, that fulfills this criterion. *Firmitas* has come to the realm of bits and bytes.

Apple's Lisa Toolkit and its successor, the Macintosh Toolbox, constitute one of the more intriguing examples of Reconstruction in the history of personal computing.

An architect's most useful tools are an eraser at the drafting board, and a wrecking bar at the site.

—Frank Lloyd Wright

The Software Tectonics pattern discussed in Foote and Yoder [Foote+1996] observes that if incremental change is deferred indefinitely, major upheaval may be the only alternative. Foote and Yoder [Foote+1998a] explore the Winning Team phenomenon, whereby otherwise superior technical solutions are overwhelmed by nontechnical exigencies.

Brooks has eloquently observed that the most dangerous system an architect will ever design is his second system [Brooks1995]. This is the notorious second-system effect. Reconstruction provides an opportunity for this misplaced hubris to exercise itself, so one must keep a wary eye open for it. Still, there are times when the best and only way to make a system better is to throw it away and start over.

CONCLUSIONS

In the end, software architecture is about how we distill experience into wisdom and disseminate it. We think the patterns herein stand alongside the other work on software architecture and evolution that we cited as we went along. Still, we do not consider these patterns to be antipatterns. There are good reasons that good programmers build Big Balls of Mud. It may well be that the economics of the software world are such that the market moves so fast that long-term architectural ambitions are foolhardy, and that expedient, slash-and-burn, disposable programming is, in fact, a state-of-the-art strategy. The success of these approaches, in any case, is undeniable, and seals their patternhood.

People build Big Balls of Mud because they *work*. In many domains, they are the only things that have been shown to work. Indeed, they work where loftier approaches have yet to demonstrate that they can compete.

It is not our purpose to condemn Big Balls of Mud. Casual architecture is natural during the early stages of a system's evolution. At the same time, our purpose is not to make some sentimental plea for wetlands preservation. The reader must surely suspect that our hope is that we can aspire to do better. By recognizing the forces and pressures that lead to architectural malaise, and how and when they might be confronted, we hope to set the stage for the emergence of truly durable artifacts that can put architects in dominant positions for years to come. The key is to ensure that the system, its programmers, and, indeed the entire organization, *learn* about the domain and the architectural opportunities looming within it as the system grows and matures.

Periods of moderate disorder are part of the ebb and flow of software evolution. As a master chef tolerates a messy kitchen, developers must not be afraid to get a

Credit: Bill Bachmann/Photo Researchers, Inc.

little mud on their shoes as they explore new territory for the first time. Architectural insight is not the product of master plans, but of hard-won experience. The software architects of yesteryear had little choice other than to apply the lessons they learned in successive drafts of their systems, since Reconstruction was often the only practical means they had of supplanting a mediocre system with a better one. Objects, frameworks, components, and refactoring tools provide us with another alternative. Objects present a medium for expressing our architectural ideas at a level between coarse-grained applications and components and low-level code. Refactoring tools and techniques finally give us the means to cultivate these artifacts as they evolve and to capture these insights.

The onion-domed Cathedral of the Intercession in Moscow is one of Russia's most famous landmarks. It was built by Ivan the Terrible just outside of the Kremlin walls in 1552 to commemorate Russia's victory over the Tatars at Kazan. It is better known by its nickname, St. Basil's. Legend has it that once the cathedral was completed, Ivan, ever true to his reputation, had the architects blinded, so that they could never build anything more beautiful. Alas, the state of software architecture today is such that few of us need to fear for our eyesight.

ACKNOWLEDGMENTS

A lot of people have striven to help us avoid turning this chapter into an unintentional example of its central theme.

We are grateful first of all to the members of the University of Illinois Software Architecture Group, John Brant, Ian Chai, Ralph Johnson, Lewis Muir, Dragos Manolescu, Brian Marick, Eiji Nabika, John (Zhijiang) Han, Kevin Scheufele, Tim Ryan, Girish Maiya, Weerasak Wittawaskul, Alejandra Garrido, Peter Hatch, and Don Roberts, who commented on several drafts of this work over the last three years.

We'd like to also thank our tireless shepherd, Bobby Woolf, who trudged through the muck of several earlier versions of this paper.

Naturally, we'd like to acknowledge the members of our PLoP '97 Conference Writer's Workshop, Norm Kerth, Hans Rohnert, Clark Evans, Shai Ben-Yehuda, Lorraine Boyd, Alejandra Garrido, Dragos Manolescu, Gerard Meszaros, Kyle Brown, Ralph Johnson, and Klaus Renzel. Lorrie Boyd provided some particularly poignant observations on scale and the human cost of projects that fail. UIUC Architecture professor Bill Rose provided some keen insights on the durability of housing stock and on the history of the estrangement of architects from builders. Thanks to Brad Appleton, Michael Beedle, Russ Hurlbut, Bob Haugen, Rich Wellner, Urvashi Kaul, Michael Rauchmann, Jim Hannula, and the Chicago Patterns Group for their time, suggestions, and ruminations on reuse and reincarnation. Thanks to Steve Berczuk and the members of the Boston Area Patterns Group for their review. Thanks, too, to Joshua Kerievsky and the Design Patterns Study Group of New York City for their comments.

We'd like to express our gratitude as well to Paolo Cantoni, Chris Olufson, Sid Wright, John Liu, Martin Cohen, John Potter, Richard Helm, and James Noble of the Sydney Patterns Group, who workshopped this chapter during the late winter, er, summer of early 1998. John Vlissides, Neil Harrison, Hans Rohnert, James Coplien, and Ralph Johnson provided some particularly candid, incisive and useful criticism of some of the later drafts of this chapter.

REFERENCES

[Alexander1964] C. Alexander. *Notes on the Synthesis of Form*. Cambridge, MA: Harvard University Press, 1964.

[Alexander1979] C. Alexander. *The Timeless Way of Building*. Oxford, UK: Oxford University Press, 1979. Available: http://www.oup-usa.org/.

[Alexander1988] C. Alexander. *The Oregon Experiment*. Oxford, UK: Oxford University Press, 1988. Available: http://www.oup-usa.org/.

[Alexander+1977] C. Alexander, S. Ishikawa, and M. Silverstein. *A Pattern Language*. Oxford, UK: Oxford University Press, 1977. Available: http://www.oup-usa.org/.

[Bach1997] J. Bach. "Good Enough Software: Beyond the Buzzword." *IEEE Computer* 30 (August 1997): 96–98.

[Beck1997] K. Beck. *Smalltalk Best Practice Patterns*. Upper Saddle River, NJ: Prentice-Hall, 1997.

[Beck+1989] K. Beck and W. Cunningham. "A Laboratory for Teaching Object-Oriented Thinking." In *OOPSLA '89 Proceedings*, pp. 1–6. New Orleans, LA, October 1989.

[Beck2000] K. Beck. *Embracing Change: Extreme Programming Explained*. Cambridge University Press, 2000.

[Booch1994] G. Booch. *Object-Oriented Analysis and Design with Applications*. Redwood City, CA: Benjamin/Cummings, 1994.

[Brand1994] S. Brand. *How Buildings Learn: What Happens After They're Built*. Viking Press, 1994.

[Brooks1995] F.P. Brooks Jr. *The Mythical Man-Month* (*Anniversary Edition*). Reading, MA: Addison-Wesley, 1995.

[Brown+1998] W.J. Brown, R.C. Malveau, H.W. McCormick III, and T.J. Mobray. *Antipatterns: Refactoring, Software Architectures, and Projects in Crisis*. Wiley Computer Publishing, New York: John Wiley & Sons, 1998.

[Buschmann+1996] F. Buschmann, R. Meunier, H. Rohnert, P. Sommerlad, and M. Stahl. *Pattern-Oriented Software Architecture: A System of Patterns*. New York: John Wiley & Sons, 1996.

[Coplien1995] J.O. Coplien. "A Generative Development-Process Pattern Language." In J.O. Coplien and D.C. Schmidt (eds.), *Pattern Languages of Program Design*. Reading, MA: Addison-Wesley, 1995.

[Cusumano+1995] M.A. Cusumano and R.W. Shelby. *Microsoft Secrets*. New York: The Free Press, 1995.

[Foote1988] B. Foote. *Designing to Facilitate Change with Object-Oriented Frameworks*. Master's Thesis, 1988, University of Illinois at Urbana-Champaign. Available: http://www.laputan.org/afc/discussion.html.

[Foote+1995] B. Foote and W.F. Opdyke. "Lifecycle and Refactoring Patterns that Support Evolution and Reuse." In J.O. Coplien and D.C. Schmidt (eds.), *Pattern Languages of Program Design*. Reading, MA: Addison-Wesley, 1995.

[Foote+1996] B. Foote and J.W. Yoder. "Evolution, Architecture, and Metamorphosis." In J.M. Vlissides, J.O. Coplien, and N.L. Kerth (eds.), *Pattern Languages of Program Design 2*. Reading, MA: Addison-Wesley, 1996.

[Foote+1998] B. Foote and D. Roberts. "Lingua Franca." *Fifth Conference on Patterns Languages of Programs (PLoP '98)*, Monticello, IL, August 1998. Washington University, Department of Computer Science. Technical Report WUCS-98-25 (PLoP '98/EuroPLoP '98), September 1998.

[Foote+1998a] B. Foote and J.W. Yoder. "The Selfish Class." In R. Martin, D. Riehle, and F. Buschmann (eds.), *Pattern Languages of Program Design 3*. Reading, MA: Addison-Wesley, 1998.

[Foote+1998b] B. Foote and J.W. Yoder. "Metadata." *Fifth Conference on Patterns Languages of Programs (PLoP '98)*, Monticello, IL, August 1998. Washington University, Department of Computer Science, Technical Report WUCS-98-25 (PLoP '98/EuroPLoP '98), September 1998.

[Fowler1999] M. Fowler. *Refactoring*. Reading, MA: Addison Wesley Longman, 1999.

[Francis1999] A. Francis. *Peter Principle of Programming*. In W. Cunningham, Portland Pattern Repository. Available: http://c2.com/coi/wiki?PeterPrincipleProgramming.

[Gabriel1991] R.P. Gabriel. "Lisp: Good News Bad News and How to Win Big." Available: http://www.laputan.org/gabriel/worse-is-better.html.

[Gabriel1996] R.P. Gabriel. *Patterns of Software: Tales from the Software Community*. Oxford, UK: Oxford University Press, 1996. Available: http://www.oup-usa.org/.

[Gamma+1995] E. Gamma, R. Helm, R. Johnson, and J. Vlissides. *Design Patterns: Elements of Reusable Object-Oriented Software*. Reading, MA: Addison Wesley Longman, 1995.

[Garlan+1993] D. Garlan and M. Shaw. "An Introduction to Software Architecture." In V. Ambriola and G. Totora (eds.), *Advances in Software Engineering and Knowledge Engineering*, vol. 2, pp. 1–39. Singapore: World Scientific Publishing, 1993.

[Ingalls1983] D.H.H. Ingalls. "The Evolution of the Smalltalk Virtual Machine." In G. Krasner (ed.), *Smalltalk-80: Bits of History, Words of Advice*. Reading, MA: Addison-Wesley, 1983.

[Johnson+1988] R.E. Johnson and B. Foote. "Designing Reusable Classes." *Journal of Object-Oriented Programming*, 1(2): 22–35, 1988.

[Jones1999] C. Jones. "The Euro, Y2K, and the US Software Labor Shortage." *IEEE Software*, May/June 1999.

[Marick1995] B. Marick. *The Craft of Software Testing*. Upper Saddle River, NJ: Prentice-Hall, 1995.

[Meszaros1997] G. Meszaros. "Archi-Patterns: A Process Pattern Language for Defining Architectures." *Fourth Conference on Pattern Languages of Programs (PLoP '97)*, Monticello, IL, September 1997.

[O'Neill1996] R.V. O'Neill. *A Hierarchical Concept of Ecosystems.* Princeton. NJ: Princeton University Press, 1996.

[Roberts+1998] D. Roberts and R.E. Johnson. "Patterns for Evolving Frameworks." In R. Martin, D. Riehle, and F. Buschmann (eds.), *Pattern Languages of Program Design 3.* Reading, MA: Addison-Wesley, 1998.

[Shaw1996] M. Shaw. "Some Patterns for Software Architectures." In J.M. Vlissides, J.O. Coplien, and N.L. Kerth (eds.), *Pattern Languages of Program Design 2.* Reading, MA: Addison-Wesley, 1996.

[Simon1969] H.A. Simon. *The Sciences of the Artificial.* Cambridge, MA: MIT Press, 1969.

Brian Foote may be reached at foote@cs.uiuc.edu.

Joseph Yoder may be reached at yoder@cs.uiuc.edu.

About the Authors

Hany H. Ammar is an associate professor of computer engineering in the Department of Computer Science and Electrical Engineering at West Virginia University. He is a senior associated Scientist at the Institute of Software Research at WVU. His areas of research interests include parallel and distributed computing, software systems specification and design, object-oriented techniques, real-time systems, and image processing. He has published over 54 articles in journals and conference proceedings. Recently he has been a principal investigator on a number of research projects funded by NASA, the Department of Defense, and Loral Federal Systems. He has served on the program committees of several international conferences and workshops.

Francis Anderson is a solutions architect with the Network Communications Business Unit of Tivoli Systems in Austin, Texas. He has been developing systems for over 20 years in the insurance, electric utility, and telecommunications industries. He is particularly interested in frameworks that implement a Dynamic Object Model through user-maintained meta-data. He hopes that his five years of Smalltalk will not be coming to an end any time soon.

Ken Auer is the president and founder of RoleModel Software, Inc. whose mission is to provide leadership in the development of robust, flexible software assets. In late 1998, RoleModel Software began building the first eXtreme Programming Software Studio based on Ken's vision. He has applied his skills and experience in object technology to a variety of real-world projects and organizations since 1985. He is well known for his expertise in object technology through many published materials and his frequent participation in industry conferences, panels, and workshops. Before founding RoleModel Software, Ken served as Director of Applied Technology at Knowledge Systems Corporation (KSC) in Cary, North Carolina.

Jeffrey Barcalow is a programmer analyst for Reuters' Object Technology Center in Oak Brook, Illinois, where he develops C++, Java, and COM API's for accessing Reuters' financial data. In 1995, he graduated from the University of Illinois at Urbana-Champaign with a B.S. in computer science, earning university honors. Two years later he completed his M.S. in computer science from the same institution. While completing his masters, he worked on the NCSA-Caterpillar team developing financial models in Smalltalk.

Dirk Bäumer works as senior software developer at Object Technology International in Zurich, Switzerland. From 1991 to 1997 he was the chief architect of the GEBOS system at RWG Stuttgart. Dirk received a Ph.D. in computer science from the University of Hamburg. His research focuses on object-oriented software development environments and software architecture for large framework-based applications.

Mike Beedle is a principle consultant at Framework Technologies Inc., a company he cofounded in 1996. He is also the president of the e-commerce startup e-Architects, Inc. He has worked primarily as a software architect for the last 14 years, consulting for many Fortune 500 companies around the United States. His main focus is in helping companies develop software using technical and organizational patterns. He has published many articles in trade magazines as well as contributing papers to several books that show how patterns can be applied to practice by organizations. He is the author of an upcoming book, *Enterprise Architecture Patterns*, to be published by SIGS/Cambridge University.

Alexandre M. Braga holds a bachelor's degree in computer science from the Federal University of Pará, Brazil. He is presently a master's degree candidate in computer science at the University of Campinas, Brazil. His research interests include applied cryptography, electronic commerce, object-orientation, patterns, and frameworks.

John Brent has been a member of the UIUC patterns group for the last six years and has been working in Smalltalk for over seven years. Over the past several years, he has worked on the freely available Refactoring Browser, a practical tool for restructuring real-world Smalltalk programs.

Andy Carlson works in the IP Technology Division of AT&T Labs in Redditch, England, where he leads a team of developers involved in architecture and piloting as part of AT&T's Common Open IP Platform project. Andy has been with AT&T since 1986 and has had a number of roles in the development of systems for finance, manufacturing, retail, telecommunications, and travel markets. Andy has been using object-oriented technology since 1991 and patterns since 1994. He graduated from Loughborough University of Technology, England, with a B.S. in engineering science and technology in 1986. Andy is a member of the British Computer Society, and a chartered engineer.

James B. Coplien is a member of the Software Production Research Department in Bell Laboratories. He holds a B.S. in electrical and computer engineering, and an M.S. in computer science, both from the University of Wisconsin at Madison. His early career work includes applied research in software development environments, version and configuration management models, and in object-oriented design and programming. He is currently studying organization communication patterns to help guide process evolution. This research has already created a generative pattern language that has successfully been used for business process engineering in corporations worldwide. His other research areas include multi-paradigm design and architectural patterns of telecommunication software. He is the author of C++ *Programming Styles and Idioms*, the foremost high-end C++ book in the industry, and of *Multi-Paradigm Design for C++*. He was co-editor of two volumes of *Pattern Language of Program Design*. He writes a patterns column for the *C++ Report*. He is a Member Emeritus of the Hillside Group, a small consortium of industry leaders providing industry-wide leadership and support in the pattern discipline. He was program chair of GOPSLA '96.

Jacob L. Cybulski is a senior lecturer in the Department of Information Systems at the University of Melbourne. His primary research interests are software reuse and requirements engineering. He also works as a consultant working with organizations willing to introduce novel approaches to their development methods, for example, oriented analysis and design, design patterns, and CASE. Jacob's past experience includes projects ranging from mechanical engineering and telecommunications applications to developing software productivity environments and toolkits. His current work focuses on the application of design education, and reusability patterns to multimedia authoring and reuse.

Ricardo Dahab holds a bachelor's and a master's degree in computer science from the University of Campinas, Brazil, and a Ph.D. in combinations and optimization from the University of Waterloo, Canada. His research interests include cryptographic algorithms and protocols, electronic commerce, and graph theory. His is presently an assistant professor at the Institute of Computing of the University of Campinas, in Brazil.

Marine Devos is a business planning consultant at EDS EMEA. She has been director of the IS department at Argo since 1992. She has worked as a teacher and as a technical consultant and project leader to the Belgian Minister of Education and the Belgian civil service. As IS manager she introduced objects and she initiated and coordinated the development of a framework and several applications. Her main focus is on the use of IS—and "softer software"—to support change programs and learning. Her special interests are framework development and the use of patterns in organizations and the human side of IS and facilitating workshops. She is conference chair of EuroPlop '99.

Jim Doble has been employed in the telecommunications industry for 18 years as a software developer, software development manager, and software architect. He worked initially with Bell-Northern Research (Nortel), with Allen Telecom Systems, and currently with Motorola. Jim's technical interests include the design of change-resilient, reusable, large-scale software frameworks and architectures, rapid prototyping, and software tool development. Jim has been actively involved in the creation of the telecom patterns community, which meets annually at the ChiliPLoP conference, held near Phoenix, Arizona. Jim received a B.S. degree (electrical engineering–computer option) from Queen's University, Kingston, Ontario, in 1982, and an M.E. (systems and computer engineering) degree from Carleton University, Ottawa, Ontario, in 1988.

Sharon Estepp is a business consultant for CYBERTEK, a wholly-owned subsidiary of Policy Management Systems Corporation. She is currently serving as a mentor and facilitator for object-oriented analysis and design software development efforts. Sharon has represented CYBERTEK in the ACORD OLifE initiative and at the Object Management Group (OMG). Prior to joining CYBERTEK in 1997, Sharon held various technical and managerial positions focused on developing and delivering high quality software applications. Former employers include The State of Ohio Bureau of Workers Compensation, Motorists Insurance, and the Federal Reserve Bank of Cleveland. Estepp received a B.S. in business administration from Capital University.

Brian Foote a co-editor for this book, has been writing programs professionally for over 20 years and has been doing research on object-oriented programming, languages, frameworks, architecture, evolution, and refactoring since the mid 1980's. He is also a writer and consultant and has been active in the patterns community since its inception. He was chair of the PLoP '96 conference.

Martin Fowler is an independent consultant who advises clients on object-oriented development of business information systems. His recent clients include IBM, Andersen Consulting, Dade Behring, and Sterling Software. He is the author of *Analysis Patterns* and *UML Distilled*.

Robert Hanmer is a Distinguished Member of Technical Staff at Lucent Technologies. He was program chair for the Pattern Languages of Programming Conference held in September, 1997, at Allerton Park. He is active in the TelePLoP group, which is an informal collection of pattern advocates and authors interested in the field of telecommunications. He is a co-author of a collection of patterns in the PLoPD2 book on reliable system design, which has been republished in *The Patterns Handbook: Techniques, Strategies, and Applications*. Within Lucent, he is active as a advocate and teacher of patterns and designing for reliability. He has been learning the patterns of the 4ESS Switch since 1987.

Neil Harrison, lead editor of this book, works at Lucent Technologies in telephony, software testing and simulation tools, domain engineering, and software process and organization. He was an early advocate of patterns and teaches courses on patterns. He has published patterns and articles on patterns in earlier PLoPD volumes, and in *Best Practices: A Patterns Handbook*. He has collaborated with James Coplien on software organizational studies and patterns, and they have published several articles on the subject. He is past program chair of ChiliPLop. He received a B.S. from Brigham Young University (with high honors and university scholar designations) and an M.S. from Purdue University, both in computer science.

Tim Harrison is a member of the technical staff at Hewlett Packard Laboratories in Palo Alto, California. He is currently doing research on distribution architectures for embedded systems. Tim completed his master's degree at Washington University in 1997.

Thomas D. Jordan is a software engineer currently working on medical imaging systems with Cambronics Medical Systems in Hartland, Wisconsin. His professional career has focused primarily on object-oriented, real-time, and networked applications. He has worked on a diverse set of applications including: autopilots, precision farming, transit authority dispatch stations, airborne weather radar, warehouse management systems, and high-speed medical imaging networks. Thomas received his B.S. in electrical engineering from Southern Illinois University at Carbondale in 1992.

Tanya Linden is a lecturer in the Department of Information Systems at the University of Melbourne. She received bachelor's and master's degrees in mathematics and education at Moscow State Pedagogical University. She is currently working on her Ph.D. at the University of Melbourne. Her research interests include object-oriented analysis and design, multimedia computing, and multimedia in education.

Fernando Lyardet is an advanced undergraduate student at La Plata University, Argentina. He has been working in patterns and pattern languages for hypermedia and Web applications and CASE tools for Web Information Systems. He is a research and teaching assistant at LIFIA in Argentina.

Dragos-Anton Manolescu is a member of Ralph Johnson's Software Architecture Group at the University of Illinois. He has earned a Dipl. Ing. in electrical engineering and an M.S. in computer science. Dragos has been in school for the past 20 years and has been interested in computers since the days of Z80. He has studied and worked in several research centers—Universitatea Politehnica Bucuresti in Romania; Interuniversity Micro-Electronic Center in Belgium; Centre National d'Etudes des Télécommunication and Institut de Mathématiques Appliquées de Grenoble in France; University of Illinois and the National Center for Supercomputer Applications in the United States. Dragos is currently pursuing his Ph.D. in computer science at the University of Illinois, where he is researching work flow and object-oriented frameworks.

José Alves Marques is a full professor at Instituto Superior Técnico, Technical University of Lisbon, Portugal (IST/UTL) and head of the Software Research Groups at INESC. José received a B.S. in computer science from the New University of Lisbon and a Ph.D. in computer science in 1980 from Intitut Nationale Polytechnique of Grenoble. He has published numerous articles and papers in the areas of distributed systems and platforms.

Oscar Nierstrasz is professor of computer science at the Institute of Computer Science and Applied Mathematics of the University of Bern where he leads the Software Composition Group. He is interested in all aspects component-oriented software technology. He has served on the program committees of ECOOP, OPPSLA, ESEC, and many other conferences and as the program chair of ECOOP '93 and ESEC '99.

James Noble is a research fellow in object-oriented design a the Microsoft Research Institute, at Macquarie University, Sydney, Australia. He has researched, taught, and built object-oriented systems for over a decade, has presented and published papers on design patterns in three continents, and has a Ph.D. in computer science from Victoria University of Wellington, New Zealand. He established the Sydney Patterns Group, the first patterns group in the Southern Hemisphere, and with Charles Weir, is writing a book of patterns for Designing Smaller Software.

João Pereira is a teaching assistant at Instituto Superior Téchnico, Technical University of Liston, Portugal (IST/UTL) and a researcher of the database group RODIN, at INRIA, in France. He received a B.S. in electrical engineering in 1990 and an M.S. in computer science in 1995, both from IST. Currently he is working on Ph.D. His research interests include active database rules, design patterns, and object-orientation.

Nat Pryce is a research associate in the Department of Computing of Imperial College, London, England. His main area of research is in the area of distributed systems configuration and management. His current project is focused on the provision of multimedia services over broadband, multiservice networks and has resulted in the development of languages, object-oriented frameworks, and graphical tools to support the development of component-based distributed systems.

Irfan Pyarali is a doctoral student in the Computer Science Department at Washington University in St. Louis, working in the Distributed Object Computing Laboratory headed by Douglas C. Schmidt. He joined the Distributed Object

Computing Laboratory in August of 1996, and his research focuses on the development of high-performance, real-time distributed object computing systems. His current project is the design and implementation of a real-time Object Request Broker (ORB). Other recent projects have involved designing high-performance Web servers and asynchronous I/O frameworks on Windows NT and UNIX systems. Irfan received his B.S. in 1995 and his M.S. in 1998 from Washington University in St. Louis.

Dirk Riehe works at Credit Suisse in data warehousing. Currently, his main interest is in the use of metadata for making applications, application integration, and business models increasingly flexible. Most of his work can be found at www.riehle.org.

Linda Rising is a member of the Software Technology Group at AG Communication Systems. She has written a number of publications, including "A Training Experience with Patterns" in the October 1996 issue of *Communications of the ACM*, "Patterns: Spreading the Word" in the December 1996 issue of *Object* magazine, "The Road: Christopher Alexander and Good Software Design" in the March 1997 issue of *Object* magazine, and a chapter on "Pattern Mining" in the *Handbook of Object Technology* published by CRC Press. She is the editor of *A Patterns Handbook*, published in 1998. She was also the feature editor for a special issue of IEEE Communications on Design Patterns in *Communications Software*, which appeared in April 1999.

Hans Rohnert, co-editor of this book, is senior software architect at Siemens AG, Munich, Germany, where he works on diverse aspects of software of communication devices. He is co-author of *Pattern-Oriented Software Architecture: A System of Patterns* and is currently spending his free time on the second volume of that series.

Gustova Rossi received his Ph.D. from PUC-RIO in 1996 and is now a full professor at La Plata University, Argentina. His research interests include design patterns and frameworks for hypermedia. He is one of the authors of the Object-Oriented Hypermedia Design Method (OOHDM) and is working on the application of design patterns in the hypermedia and Web fields. He is the head of LIFIA, a computer science research lab in Argentina.

Cecília Rubira holds a bachelor's and a master's degree in computer science from the University of Campinas, Brazil and a Ph.D. in computer science from the University of Newcastle upon Tyne, England. Her research interests include object-oriented software development, frameworks and patterns, and fault-tolerant systems with an emphasis in exception handling software fault tolerance. She is presently an assistant professor at the Institute of Computing of the University of Campinas, in Brazil.

Douglas C. Schmidt is an associate professor and director of the Center for Distributed Object Computing in the Department of Computer Science and in the Department of Radiology at Washington University in St. Louis, Missouri. His research focuses on design patterns, implementation, and experimental analysis of object-oriented techniques that facilitate the development of high-performance, real-time distributed object computing systems on parallel processing platforms running over high-speed ATM networks and embedded system interconnects. He has published widely in top IEEE, ACM, IFIP, and USENIX technical conferences and journals on topics related to high-performance communication software systems, parallel processing for high-speed networking protocols, real-time distributed object computing with CORBA, and object-oriented design patterns for concurrent and distributed systems.

Daniel Schwabe received his Ph.D. from the University of California, Los Angeles in 1981. He has been working on hypermedia design methods for the last ten years. He is one of the authors of HDM, the first authoring method for hypermedia, and of the Object-Oriented Hypermedia Design Method, one of the mature methods currently in use by academia and industry for hypermedia application design. Daniel is associate professor at the Department of Informatics of the Catholic University (PUC) in Rio de Janeiro, Brazil.

Ken Schwaber is president of Advanced Development Methods (ADM), a process research and development company in Lexington, Massachusetts. Ken was one of the formulators of the SCRUM development process. Through ADM, he supports organization's developing complex software with SCRUM and SCRUM tools for distributed team development. He has a background of developing complex telecommunications and operating system software at the University of Chicago, Arthur D. Little, Honeywell, and Wang Laboratories, until 1985 when he founded ADM.

Yonat Sharon is an independent software developer working in entrepreneurial ventures. After working for a large military contractor and then for a small Internet startup company, she decided to focus on prototype and early system development in new ventures. Yonat edits "Object Orientation Tips" at http://www.kinetica.com/ootips/, participates in the "Experts Exchange" at http://www.experts-exchange.com, and co-moderates the newsgroup comp.object.moderated.

Wolf Siberski works as consultant and architect at Touristik Union International, Hanover, Germany. He is interested in architecture, large business models, and distributed systems. He received a Dipl.Inform. degree from the University of Hamburg.

António Rito Silva is a researcher of the Software Engineering Group at INESC in Lisbon, Portugal. During his Ph.D. studies he developed the DASCo (Development of Distributed Applications with Separation of Concerns) approach, based on design patterns, pattern languages, and object-oriented frameworks (http://www. esw.inesc.pt/~ars/dasco). His research interests include design patterns and pattern languages for distribution and concurrency, object-oriented frameworks, software architectures, analysis of design methodologies, and multiuser object-oriented environments. Currently, António is starting the MOOSCo (MOO with Separation of Concerns) project that applies separation of concern in the design and development of multiuser object-oriented environments (http://www. esw.inesc.pt/~ars/moosco).

Greg Stymfal is a principal engineer at AG Communication Systems. He has a B.S. in electrical engineering from the University of Colorado. He has developed, tested, and managed software in the embedded telecommunications industry since 1979. His current activities focus on integrated development environments for large-scale software projects.

Jeff Sutherland is senior vice president of engineering and product development at IDX Systems Corporation, a leading provider of information systems to the health care industry. His work on reusable business object components for Internet applications through the Object Management Group Business Object Domain Task Force and the OOPSLA Business Object Workshop has been used to create new database products, software development environments, and CASE/OOAD tools. He has applied these technologies to large object-oriented implementations in banking, insurance, library systems, aerospace, airline and aircraft leasing, nuclear engineering, robotics, and health care. As one of the inventors of the SCRUM development process, his expertise in organizational development has repeatedly enabled high-octane development teams to deliver world-class software products.

Paul Taylor is a business and systems consultant, project manager, software engineer, and part-time writer with 15 years of industry experience in a range of business and engineering contexts. He has been a project manager for the development of corporate software products and has led many teams in their use of object technology—it is from this base of experience that he writes on the behaviors of productive individuals and the culture of productive teams. Paul holds honor's master's degrees in computer science and has led an object technology special interest group for five years.

Dwayne Towell is technology director for ImageBuilder Software in Portland, Oregon. He joined ImageBuilder in 1988 and is responsible for the architecture, design, development, and use of cross-platform frameworks for multimedia and interest development. The multimedia framework has been used in over 30 products for Disney, Microsoft, IBM, Hasbro, and other companies. He has 14 years experience in object-oriented design and programming.

Charles Weir is an independent consultant based in Cumbria, England. He specializes in object-oriented architecture, providing on-site training, mentoring, and design assistance to development teams. He has worked on o-o projects in telecommunications, information systems, manufacturing, statistical analysis, and banking. Charles was chief architect for the Psion Series 5 Web Browser, which inspired an interest in patterns for working with very restricted systems. Recently he has been helping define the architecture and implementation of two "smart" mobile phones, for which these techniques are widely used.

Bobby Woolf is a senior member of technical staff at Knowledge Systems Corp., a Smalltalk consulting company in Cary, North Carolina. He specializes in mentoring clients in VisualWorks Smalltalk, ENVY/Developer, and design patterns. He has published in all four PLoP books, as well as publishing several articles in *The Smalltalk Report*. He has presented tutorials at OOPSLA, Smalltalk Solutions, the ParcPlace-Digitalk International Users' Conference, and Software Development East. He is co-author *The Design Patterns Smalltalk Companion*, published by Addison-Wesley.

Martina Wulf currently works as software developer in an object-oriented banking project at UBS in Zurich, Switzerland. She studied computer science at the University of Hamburg where she graduated in 1995. She is interested in framework development and business modeling.

Sherif M. Yacoub is currently finishing a Ph.D. in computer engineering at West Virginia University. He is currently working as a research assistant for the Institute for Software Research (ISR) in West Virginia. Sherif's areas of research include design patterns, software reuse, software architecture, object-oriented analysis and design, and design quality. He received his M.S. in electrical engineering in 1997 and a B.S. in computer engineering in 1994 from Cairo University, Egypt, where he also lectured in software engineering. Sherif has participated in several industrial and academic research projects.

Joseph W. Yoder has been studying and developing software since 1985. Since 1990 his focus has been an object-oriented technology. He has developed frameworks, helped design several applications, and mentored many new developers. For the last few years Joe has been investigating "visual languages for business modeling" and "active object-models." He is designing them, using them, and implementing them. He is also studying and writing patterns for developing reusable software and domain-specific languages, including how to evolve more reusable fine-grained components from frameworks and on how to manage or promote reuse through component libraries. Joe has a B.S. in computer science and mathematics from the University of Iowa and an M.S. in computer science from the University of Illinois. He is currently pursuing a Ph.D. in computer science at the University of Illinois and consulting for The Refactory Inc., of which he is one of the founders.

Index

The number in parentheses beside the page number is the chapter number.

16-bit Windows API
Session pattern use, [Petzold1990]; 96(7)

A
abstract
Abstract Class pattern
  See Also class(es)
  "Abstract Class", (chapter title); 5(1)
  Role Object use; 17(2)
Abstract Factory pattern
  See Also "Design Patterns"
  Essence relationship to, [Gamma+1995];
    40(3)
  [Gamma+1995]; 40(3)
  Secure-Channel Communication pattern
    relationship to; 345(16)
  Virtual Constructor relationship to,
    [Gamma+1995]; 185(10)
Abstract Session pattern
  "Abstract Session: An Object Structural
    Pattern", (chapter title); 95(7)
  (reference description); 95(7)
  Session relationship to, [Pryce1999]; 319(15)
data types
  See Also data types
  vs. concrete data types; 187(10)
  multiple implementation support, in
    Envelope/Letter pattern; 182(10)
interfaces, abstract sessions advantages for
    per-client state management; 96(7)
syntax trees, as Role Object known use,
    [Mitsui+1993]; 28(2)
abstraction(s)
See Also interfaces; metadata
evolution in system architectures, different
    rates of change impact on; 654(29)
interoperability importance; 330(15)
object-oriented, scaling issues; 15(2)
pattern reference descriptions, Basic FSM;
    417(19)
of synchronization policies, as Object
    Synchronizer pattern advantage; 118(8)

Acceptor pattern
Abstract Session relationship to,
    [Schmidt1995]; 108(7)
reactive synchronous event handling,
    [Schmidt1995]; 137(9)
access
Access Verification pattern, as alternate name
    for Check Point pattern; 307(15)
Check Point pattern, Single Access Point
    relationship to; 304(15), 305(15)
Service Access Point (SAP) pattern, as
    alternate name for Abstract Session;
    95(7)
Single Access Point pattern
  Check Point relationship to; 309(15)
  concurrency use; 306(15)
  Session relationship to; 319(15)
single location for, as security policy, in Single
    Access Point pattern; 304(15)
spatial, SAM feature extraction issues;
    396(18)
access control
See Also security
encapsulation of, Secure Access Layer pattern;
    329(15)
in real-time network use, Snapshot pattern;
    261(13)
role-privilege relationship management with
    ACLs, [Silberschatz+1997]; 314(15)
role-related, Roles pattern; 312(15)
Secure Access Layer protection from; 330(15)
in secure applications, architecture
    considerations; 302(15)
Security Access Layer pattern, Secure-
    Channel Communication pattern
    relationship to; 345(16)
UNIX classifications, as Roles known use;
    315(15)
accessors
Artificial Accessors pattern
  Cached Extensibility relationship to;
    215(11)

accessors *(continued)*
(reference description); 204(11)
relationships with other Smalltalk
scaffolding patterns; 218(11)
attribute, [Auer1995]; 206(11)
Generated Accessors pattern
(reference description); 206(11)
relationships with other Smalltalk
scaffolding patterns; 218(11)
accounts
See Also Analysis patterns; business
management
Account pattern, Posting relationship to,
[Fowler1997a]; 280(14)
Account Transaction pattern, Posting
relationship to, [Fowler1997a]; 284(14)
Accounts framework, as Formula Objects
known use, [Keefer1994]; 386(17)
**ACE (Adaptive Communications Environment)
framework**
Abstract Session pattern use, [Schmidt1994];
107(7)
as Proactor pattern influence, [Schmidt1994];
147(9)
Proactor pattern use, [Schmidt1994]; 156(9)
Proactor Web server sample code based on,
[Schmidt1994]; 153(9)
ACL (access control lists)
See access control
acoustic data
See Also multimedia
content searching issues; 393(18)
activation
of finite state machines
Hybrid, (reference description); 433(19)
Meally, (reference description); 428(19)
Moore, (reference description); 430(19)
active
Active Object pattern
object concurrency policy, [Lavender+1996];
125(8)
Object Synchronizer pattern relationship to,
[Lavender+1996]; 129(8)
Proactor pattern relationship to,
[Lavender+1995]; 157(9)
Active Object-Model pattern
Limited View relationship to, [Foote+1998];
328(15)
Report Objects relationship to,
[Foote+1998b]; 378(17)
Active Reference pattern, (reference
description); 451(20)
Active Value pattern
"Basic Relationship Patterns", (reference
description); 82(6)
Relationship As Attribute relationship to;
78(6)

active *(continued)*
Relationship Object pattern relationship to;
80(6)
Actors pattern
as alternate name for Roles pattern; 312(15)
adaptability
See Also extensibility; flexibility; reusability
as Big Ball of Mud pattern language goal;
655(29)
as eXtreme Programming (XP) strength,
[Beck2000]; 673(29)
as high-performance Web server requirement;
134(9)
need for, as SCRUM motivation; 638(28)
as Shearing Layers force; 678(29)
Adapter pattern
See Also "Design Patterns"
Abstract Session relationship to,
[Gamma+1995]; 108(7)
Abstract Session use, [Gamma+1995]; 103(7)
Object Recursion relationship to,
[Gamma+95]; 50(4)
Prototype-Based Object System,
[Gamma+1995]; 61(5)
Prototype-Based Object System relationship
to, [Gamma+1995]; 68(5)
addition
See Also mathematics
pattern reference descriptions
Abstract Class; 5(1)
Homogeneous Addition; 189(10)
Non-Hierarchical Addition; 193(10)
Promote And Add; 190(10)
address space
shared, Session pattern use; 316(15)
ADT (abstract data types)
See Also data types
vs. concrete data types; 187(10)
multiple implementation support, in
Envelope/Letter pattern; 182(10)
adventure games
as Prototype-Based Object System known use,
[Lebling+1979]; 67(5)
aesthetics
as Piecemeal Growth force; 671(29)
AFS (Andrew File System)
See Also I/O (input/output); security
low-level issues and techniques
[ICSP1998]; 303(15)
[Schneier1995]; 303(15)
aggregation
See Also composite; composition
of multimedia artifacts; 461(21)
aging
as history pruning mechanism; 292(14)
AI (artificial intelligence)
See Also modeling

AI (artificial intelligence) *(continued)*
frame-based knowledge modeling, Prototype-Based Object System derived from; 67(5)

alarms
Alarm Grid pattern, (reference description); 527(23)
Audible Alarm pattern, (reference description); 525(23)
Don't Let Them Forget pattern, (reference description); 530(23)
Office Alarms pattern, (reference description); 529(23)

Alexander, Christopher
See Also architecture; patterns; structure
bibliographic references, [Alex1977]; 238(12)
pattern forms
[Alexander+1977]; 222(12)
in "High-Level and Process Patterns from the Memory Preservation Society: Patterns for Managing Limited Memory"; 222(12)
Quality Without A Name, as pattern writers' workshop goal; 562(25)
view of structure, relationship to OO inheritance hierarchy; 167(10)

algebra
See Also mathematics
Algebraic Hierarchy pattern
Concrete Data Type relationship to; 187(10)
Envelope/Letter relationship to; 184(10)
(reference description); 187(10)
algebraic types, inheritance hierarchy for, Algebraic Hierarchy pattern; 187(10)
algebraic types in C++, patterns dealing with; 167(10)
pattern reference descriptions
Algebraic Hierarchy; 187(10)
Homogeneous Addition; 189(10)
Non-Hierarchical Addition; 193(10)
Promote And Add; 190(10)
Promotion Ladder; 192(10)

algorithms
See Also patterns
Check Point, (example); 310(15)
combinatorial explosion, [Ingalls1986]; 190(10)
complex object comparison, as Object Recursion motivation; 43(4)
compression, feature extraction problems; 408(18)
of reusability, as Abstract Class advantage; 10(1)
searching, feature extraction compared with; 392(18)
serialization, as Object Recursion known use; 49(4)

allocation
See Also memory
memory size impact of; 227(12)

altruism
See Also human relationships
Captain Oates pattern; 234(12)

Ammar, Hany H.
"Finite State Machine Patterns"; 413(19)

Amulet
as Prototype-Based Object System known use, [McDaniel+1995]; 69(5)

"An Input and Output Pattern Language: Lessons from Telecommunications"
(chapter title); 503(23)

Analysis patterns
See Also organizational patterns
bibliographic references
[Fowler1997]; 249(13)
[Fowler1997a]; 297(14)

anchors
See Also hypermedia
(term description); 445(20)

Anderson, Francis
"A Collection of History Patterns"; 263(14)

anger
See Also human relationships
pattern reference descriptions, Take Your Licks; 603(26)

animations
See Also hypermedia
as multimedia component; 463(21)

antipatterns
Big Ball of Mud pattern differences; 654(29)

Any framework
as Prototype-Based Object System known use, [Matzel+1996]; 69(5)

Anything pattern
Prototype-Based Object System relationship to, [Sommerlad+1998b]; 57(5), 69(5)

APC (Asynchronous Procedure Calls)
in Windows NT, Proactor pattern use; 156(9)

applets
See Also Java
authentication/authorization process, Check Point example; 311(15)
as multimedia component; 463(21)

architecture
See Also Alexander, Christopher; patterns; structure
"Architectural Patterns for Enabling Application Security", (chapter title); 301(15)
immature, advantages of in a growing system; 656(29)
Layered Architecture of Information Systems pattern, Secure Access Layer relationship to, [Fowler1997a]; 331(15)

architecture *(continued)*
Layered Architecture pattern, as software
architecture pattern; 653(29)
MVC
changing objects, Display List pattern;
491(22)
[Krasner1988]; 491(22)
premature, disadvantages of in a growing
system; 656(29)
software
application security enablement; 301(15)
"Big Ball of Mud", (chapter title); 653(29)
improvement, as Big Ball of Mud pattern
language goal; 655(29)
patterns that characterize,
[Buschmann+1996]; 653(29)
patterns that characterize, [Garlan+1993];
653(29)
patterns that characterize, [Meszaros1997];
653(29)
patterns that characterize, [Shaw1996]; 653(29)
predominant, Big Ball of Mud; 653(29)
Tropyc pattern language; 337(16)
Arjuna
Object Synchronizer pattern use,
[Shrivastava+1991]; 129(8)
Arrangement Glue pattern
Glue relationship to; 471(21)
Arranging the Furniture pattern
(reference description); 632(27)
artifacts
See Also products
creation and use, idioms for, (table); 462(21)
(term description); 461(21)
artificial
Artificial Accessors pattern
Cached Extensibility relationship to; 215(11)
(reference description); 204(11)
relationships with other Smalltalk
scaffolding patterns; 218(11)
Artificial Delegation pattern
Cached Extensibility relationship to; 215(11)
(reference description); 211(11)
relationships with other Smalltalk
scaffolding patterns; 218(11)
intelligence, frame-based knowledge
modeling, Prototype-Based Object
System derived from; 67(5)
**Artisan (Automatic Retrieval of Trademark
Images by Shape ANalysis) project**
feature extraction use; 410(18)
Assertions pattern
Full View with Errors relationship to,
[Meyer1992]; 323(15)
AssigningPapersToReviewers pattern
Identify the Champion relationship to,
[Coplien1998]; 542(24)

assignment
See Also language(s), elements
in C++, Counted Body pattern handling;
173(10)
association
See Also relationship(s)
Association as Class pattern, time
representation relationship,
[Rum+1991]; 251(13)
Association Class pattern, Edition relationship
to; 270(14)
as Association Object pattern, as alternate
name for Relationship Object; 78(6)
Association Object pattern
[Boyd1997]; 261(13)
Temporal Association relationship to,
[Boyd1997]; 254(13)
Associative Type pattern, time representation
relationship, [Fowler1997]]; 251(13)
spatial, in multimedia presentations,
Components Layout; 471(21)
ASTs (abstract syntax trees)
syntax trees, as Role Object known use,
[Mitsui+1993]; 28(2)
asynchronous
See Also concurrency; synchronization
Asynchronous Completion Token pattern,
Proactor pattern relationship to,
[Pyarali+1997]; 152(9), 156(9)
event handling
advantages and disadvantages; 139(9)
Proactor pattern use; 133(9)
Web server, Proactor pattern use; 140(9)
ATM (automated teller machines)
finite state machine use, [Gamma+1995];
437(19)
atomic artifacts
(term description); 461(21)
attacks
See Also security
cryptographic; 369(16)
attitudes
See Also human relationships; organization
patterns
programmer, memory constraint handling,
Think Small pattern; 225(12)
attributes
See Also properties
change, tracking, in Temporal Property;
242(13)
extended, accessing, Artificial Accessors
pattern, (reference description); 204(11)
Extensible Attributes pattern, (reference
description); 202(11)
hypermedia nodes; 445(20)
many-to-many relationship representation
disadvantages

attributes *(continued)*
  [Booch+1994]; 78(6)
  [Rumbaugh+1991]; 78(6)
  one-to-one relationship representation with; 77(6)
  [Beck1997]; 78(6)
  relationship modeling; 73(6)
  specification
    bibliographic reference, [Gilb1988]; 238(12)
    as Memory Budget tool, [Gilb1988]; 229(12)
  validation, "Essence", (chapter title); 33(3)
Audible Alarm pattern
  See Also "An Input and Output Pattern
      Language: Lessons from
      Telecommunications"
  (reference description); 525(23)
audience
  as force in deciding whether to use
      Reconstruction; 668(29)
audiovisual properties
  See Also hypermedia
  pattern reference descriptions, Components
      Layout; 471(21)
audit information
  attaching to domain object, in Edition; 267(14)
Auer, Ken
  "Smalltalk Scaffolding Patterns"; 199(11)
authentication
  See Also security
  Authentication and Authorization pattern, as
      alternate name for Check Point pattern;
      307(15)
  real-time network use, Snapshot pattern; 261(13)
  with secrecy, as Secrecy with Sender
      Authentication pattern motivation;
      355(16)
  as Secrecy with Integrity pattern motivation,
      (reference description); 353(16)
  of sender, in "Tropyc: a pattern language for
      cryptographic object-oriented
      software"; 337(16)
  as Sender Authentication pattern motivation;
      349(16)
  of signature, as Signature pattern motivation;
      351(16)
  of signatures, as Secrecy with Signature
      pattern motivation; 355(16)
  (term description); 308(15)
authorization
  See Also security
  Early Authorization pattern, as alternate name
      for Limited View; 323(15)
  (term description); 308(15)
authors (PLoPD4)
  Ammar, Hany H., "Finite State Machine
      Patterns"; 413(19)
  Anderson, Francis, "A Collection of History
      Patterns"; 263(14)

authors (PLoPD4) *(continued)*
  Auer, Ken, "Smalltalk Scaffolding Patterns";
      199(11)
  Barcalow, Jeffrey, "Architectural Patterns for
      Enabling Application Security"; 301(15)
  Bäumer, Dirk, "Role Object"; 15(2)
  Beedle, Mike, "SCRUM: A Pattern Language
      for Hyperproductive Software
      Development"; 637(28)
  Braga, Alexandre, "Tropyc: a pattern language
      for cryptographic object-oriented
      software"; 337(16)
  Brant, John, "Creating Reports with Query
      Objects"; 375(17)
  Carlson, Andy
    "Essence"; 33(3)
    "Temporal Patterns"; 241(13)
  Coplien, James O.
    "A Pattern Language for Writers'
        Workshops"; 557(25)
    "C++ Idioms Patterns"; 167(10)
  Cybulski, Jacob L., "Composing Multimedia
      Artifacts for Reuse"; 461(21)
  Dahab, Ricardo, "Tropyc: a pattern language
      for cryptographic object-oriented
      software"; 337(16)
  Devos, Martine, "SCRUM: A Pattern
      Language for Hyperproductive
      Software Development"; 637(28)
  Doble, Jim, "Smalltalk Scaffolding Patterns";
      199(11)
  Estepp, Sharon, "Temporal Patterns"; 241(13)
  Foote, Brian, "Big Ball of Mud"; 653(29)
  Fowler, Martin, "Temporal Patterns"; 241(13)
  Hanmer, Robert, "An Input and Output
      Pattern Language: Lessons from
      Telecommunications"; 503(23)
  Harrison, Tim, "Proactor"; 133(9)
  Jordan, Thomas D., "Proactor"; 133(9)
  Linden, Tanya, "Composing Multimedia
      Artifacts for Reuse"; 461(21)
  Lyardet, Fernando, "Patterns for Designing
      Navigable Information Spaces";
      445(20)
  Manolescu, Dragos-Anton, "Feature
      Extraction: A Pattern for Information
      Retrieval"; 391(18)
  Marques, José Alves, "Object Synchronizer";
      111(8)
  Nierstrasz, Oscar, "Identify the Champion: An
      Organizational Pattern Language for
      Program Committees"; 539(24)
  Noble, James
    "Basic Relationship Patterns"; 73(6)
    "High-Level and Process Patterns from the
        Memory Preservation Society: Patterns
        for Managing Limited Memory"; 221(12)

authors (PLoPD4) *(continued)*
"Prototype-Based Object System"; 53(5)
Pereira, Joao, "Object Synchronizer"; 111(8)
Pryce, Nat, "Abstract Session: An Object
Structural Pattern"; 95(7)
Pyarali, Irfan, "Proactor"; 133(9)
Riehle, Dirk, "Role Object"; 15(2)
Rising, Linda, "Customer Interaction
Patterns"; 585(26)
Rossi, Gustavo, "Patterns for Designing
Navigable Information Spaces"; 445(20)
Rubira, Cecilia, "Tropyc: a pattern language
for cryptographic object-oriented
software"; 337(16)
Schmidt, Douglas C., "Proactor"; 133(9)
Schwabe, Daniel, "Patterns for Designing
Navigable Information Spaces";
445(20)
Schwaber, Ken, "SCRUM: A Pattern Language
for Hyperproductive Software
Development"; 637(28)
Sharon, Yonat, "SCRUM: A Pattern Language
for Hyperproductive Software
Development"; 637(28)
Siberski, Wolf, "Role Object"; 15(2)
Silva, Antonio Rito, "Object Synchronizer";
111(8)
Stymfal, Greg, "An Input and Output Pattern
Language: Lessons from
Telecommunications"; 503(23)
Sutherland, Jeff, "SCRUM: A Pattern
Language for Hyperproductive
Software Development"; 637(28)
Taylor, Paul, "Capable, Productive, and
Satisfied: Some Organizational Patterns
for Protecting Productive People";
611(27)
Towell, Dwayne, "Display Maintenance: A
Pattern Language"; 489(22)
Weir, Charles, "High-Level and Process
Patterns from the Memory Preservation
Society: Patterns for Managing Limited
Memory"; 221(12)
Woolf, Bobby
"A Pattern Language for Writers'
Workshops"; 557(25)
"Abstract Class"; 5(1)
"Object Recursion"; 41(4)
Wulf, Martina, "Role Object"; 15(2)
Yacoub, Sherif M., "Finite State Machine
Patterns"; 413(19)
Yoder, Joseph
"Architectural Patterns for Enabling
Application Security"; 301(15)
"Big Ball of Mud"; 653(29)
"Creating Reports with Query Objects";
375(17)

authors/authoring
See Also human relationships; reviewing
Author Asks for Clarification pattern
Authors' Circle pattern relationship to;
567(25)
(reference description); 575(25)
Author Reads Selection pattern
Authors' Circle pattern relationship to;
567(25)
(reference description); 569(25)
Authors Are Experts pattern
(reference description); 561(25)
Workshop Comprises Authors relationship
to; 563(25)
Authors' Circle pattern, (reference
description); 567(25)
environments
in "Composing Multimedia Artifacts for
Reuse", (reference description); 461(21)
multimedia, in "Composing Multimedia
Artifacts for Reuse"; 461(21)
MARPL (Multimedia Authoring and Reuse
Pattern Language), overview; 464(21)
multimedia
dimensions, (figure); 464(21)
issues and constraints; 463(21)
Thank the Author pattern
Author Reads Selection relationship to; 570(25)
Authors' Circle pattern relationship to;
567(25)
(reference description); 576(25)
Suggestions for Improvement relationship
to; 575(25)
Workshop Comprises Authors pattern
Authors' Circle pattern relationship to;
567(25)
(reference description); 563(25)
automatic
automated teller machines (ATM), finite state
machine use, [Gamma+1995]; 437(19)
indexing, as feature extraction function;
393(18)

B
Baby Steps pattern
as alternate name for Keep It Working; 675(29)
Backlog pattern
(reference description); 643(28)
backtracking
See Also time
program, as time issue; 239(12)
balancing
disintegrating vs. consolidating forces, in Big
Ball of Mud pattern language; 674(29)
Barcalow, Jeffrey
"Architectural Patterns for Enabling
Application Security"; 301(15)

barriers
physical, avoiding in a pattern writers'
workshop; 566(25)
Base Class pattern
as alternate name for Abstract Class,
[Auer1995]; 5(1)
Basic FSM pattern
See Also finite state machines (FSM)
(reference description); 417(19)
"Basic Relationship Patterns"
(chapter title); 73(6)
Basket pattern
(reference description); 457(20)
Bäumer, Dirk
"Role Object"; 15(2)
Be Aware of Boundaries pattern
See Also customers, "Customer Interaction
Patterns"
(reference description); 605(26)
Take Your Licks relationship to; 604(26)
Be Responsive pattern
See Also customers, "Customer Interaction
Patterns"
Build Trust relationship to; 592(26)
Know the Customer relationship to; 590(26)
(reference description); 597(26)
Beedle, Mike
"SCRUM: A Pattern Language for
Hyperproductive Software
Development"; 637(28)
behavior
See Also dynamic; events
decoupling from state transitions; 427(19)
determining, in pseudo-method rapid
prototyping systems; 214(11)
modeling, "Finite State Machine Patterns";
413(19)
pattern reference descriptions, Basic FSM;
417(19)
separation from events and states, in Basic
FSM; 418(19)
Works Out of the Box, Report Objects use of;
377(17)
Beltline Terminal pattern
See Also "An Input and Output Pattern
Language: Lessons from
Telecommunications"
(reference description); 524(23)
bibliographic references
[Adams+1996]; 536(23)
[Adams1995]; 238(12)
[Agrawal+1993]; 411(18)
[Alexander+1977]; 238(12), 579(25), 636(27),
690(29)
[Alexander1964]; 690(29)
[Alexander1979]; 690(29)
[Alexander1988]; 690(29)

bibliographic references *(continued)*
[Alpert+1998]; 296(14)
[Anderson1998]; 261(13)
[Armstrong1992]; 609(26)
[Asokan+1997]; 370(16)
[Auer+1995]; 238(12)
[Auer1995]; 14(1), 219(11)
[Bach1997]; 690(29)
[Bahrat+1994]; 69(5)
[Barcalow1997]; 335(15)
[Bartle1985]; 69(5)
[Bäumer+1997b]; 30(2)
[Bäumer+1998]; 30(2)
[Beck+1989]; 690(29)
[Beck1993]; 556(24)
[Beck1994]; 502(22)
[Beck1996]; 30(2), 219(11), 556(24)
[Beck1997]; 69(5), 88(6), 296(14), 335(15),
690(29)
[Beck2000]; 690(29)
[Beckmann+1990]; 411(18)
[Beedle1997]; 650(28)
[Behymer1997]; 609(26)
[Benson1992]; 389(17)
[Bick1997]; 609(26)
[Blank+1995]; 238(12)
[Bobrow+1977]; 69(5)
[Bodenstein1996]; 296(14)
[Booch+1994]; 88(6)
[Booch1994]; 690(29)
[Bounds+1998]; 609(26)
[Boyd1997]; 88(6), 261(13)
[Braga+1998]; 370(16)
[Brand1994]; 690(29)
[Brant+1996]; 335(15)
[Bronshtein+1997]; 411(18)
[Brooks1975]; 238(12)
[Brooks1995]; 636(27), 690(29)
[Brown+1995]; 390(17)
[Brown+1998]; 690(29)
[Budlong+1977]; 536(23)
[Buford1994]; 488(21)
[Buschmann+1996]; 69(5), 88(6), 335(15),
370(16), 690(29)
[Cardelli1994]; 69(5)
[Cargill1996]; 197(10)
[Carlson+1998]; 297(14)
[Carlson1998a]; 262(13)
[Carlson1998b]; 262(13)
[Cheng+1998]; 370(16)
[Clement+1977]; 536(23)
[Coldewey1997]; 88(6)
[Coplien+1995]; 30(2), 690(29)
[Coplien1992]; 197(10)
[Coplien1995]; 609(26), 636(27), 650(28)
[Coplien1996]; 579(25)
[Coplien1997]; 579(25)

bibliographic references *(continued)*
[Coplien1998a]; 556(24)
[Coplien1998b]; 556(24)
[Covey1989]; 609(26)
[CSS1997]; 370(16)
[Cunningham1991]; 390(17)
[Cunningham1995]; 335(15)
[Cunningham1999]; 690(29)
[Cusumano+1995]; 690(29)
[Cybulski+1997]; 488(21)
[Decouchant+1991]; 130(8)
[Dijkstra1968]; 130(8)
[Dijkstra1971]; 158(9)
[Dutoit+1996]; 70(5)
[Dyson+1998]; 437(19)
[Eakins+1998]; 411(18)
[Edler1995]; 609(26)
[Evans+1997]; 30(2)
[Faloutsos+1994]; 411(18)
[Faloutsos+1995a]; 411(18)
[Faloutsos+1995b]; 411(18)
[Fazzolare+1993]; 130(8)
[Ferreira+1998]; 370(16)
[Foote+1995]; 390(17), 691(29)
[Foote+1996]; 335(15), 390(17), 691(29)
[Foote+1998]; 335(15), 390(17), 691(29)
[Foote+1998a]; 691(29)
[Foote+1998b]; 691(29)
[Foote1988]; 219(11), 691(29)
[Foote1991]; 70(5)
[Fowler+1997]; 130(8), 412(18)
[Fowler1996]; 30(2)
[Fowler1997]; 30(2), 88(6), 262(13)
[Fowler1997a]; 297(14), 335(15)
[Fowler1997b]; 297(14), 335(15)
[Fowler1999]; 691(29)
[Freeman-Benson1993]; 88(6)
[Gabriel1991]; 691(29)
[Gabriel1996]; 691(29)
[Gamma+1995]
   Chapter 01; 14(1)
   Chapter 02; 30(2)
   Chapter 03; 40(3)
   Chapter 04; 51(4)
   Chapter 05; 70(5)
   Chapter 06; 88(6)
   Chapter 07; 108(7)
   Chapter 08; 130(8)
   Chapter 09; 158(9)
   Chapter 10; 197(10)
   Chapter 11; 219(11)
   Chapter 14; 297(14)
   Chapter 15; 335(15)
   Chapter 16; 370(16)
   Chapter 17; 390(17)
   Chapter 18; 412(18)
   Chapter 19; 437(19)

bibliographic references *(continued)*
   Chapter 22; 502(22)
   Chapter 23; 536(23)
   Chapter 29; 691(29)
[Gamma1998]; 30(2), 70(5), 412(18)
[Garlan+1993]; 691(29)
[Garrido1997]; 460(20)
[GemStone1996]; 335(15)
[German+1999]; 488(21)
[Gilb1988]; 238(12)
[Giunta+1977]; 536(23)
[Goldberg+1983]; 88(6)
[Goldratt1990]; 650(28)
[Gosling+1996]; 108(7)
[Graham+1997]; 88(6)
[Green+1977]; 536(23)
[Guaspari1998]; 609(26)
[Haskins1994]; 488(21)
[Helm+1993]; 88(6)
[Herfert1997]; 370(16)
[Herzberg+1997]; 370(16)
[Herzberg+1998]; 370(16)
[Hoare1974]; 130(8)
[Holland1995]; 650(28)
[Holland1998]; 650(28)
[Hu+1997]; 158(9)
[Hu+1998]; 158(9)
[Hunter1998]; 609(26)
[Hutchinson+1991]; 108(7)
[Huttenhoff+1977]; 536(23)
[IBM 97]; 390(17)
[ICSP]; 336(15)
[Ierusalimschy+1996]; 70(5)
[Imperato1999]; 609(26)
[Information Processing Systems1989]; 371(16)
[Information Technology1995]; 158(9)
[Information Technology1998]; 371(16)
[Ingalls1983]; 691(29)
[Ingalls1986]; 197(10)
[Inside1998]; 609(26)
[Java]; 40(3)
[Johnson+1988]; 691(29)
[Johnson+1997]; 336(15)
[Johnson+1998]; 30(2), 70(5), 297(14)
[Johnson1992]; 390(17), 502(22)
[Johnson1995]; 556(24)
[Johnson1996]; 70(5)
[Jones1999]; 691(29)
[Kaliski1995]; 371(16)
[Kantor+1994]; 412(18)
[Kay1986]; 412(18)
[Keefer1994]; 390(17)
[Keene1989]; 70(5)
[Kelly1994]; 412(18)
[Knudsen1998]; 371(16)
[Koenig1995]; 197(10)
[Kohn+1997]; 609(26)

bibliographic references *(continued)*
[Korn+1997]; 412(18)
[Krasner1988]; 502(22)
[Kristensen+1996]; 30(2)
[Lange1998]; 262(13)
[Lanzelotte1993]; 460(20)
[Lavender+1995]; 131(8), 158(9)
[Lea1995]; 108(7), 336(15)
[Lea1997]; 336(15)
[Lebling+1979]; 70(5)
[Lewine1991]; 108(7)
[Li+1996]; 89(6)
[Lieberman1986]; 70(5)
[Linden+1999]; 488(21)
[Linn1993]; 371(16)
[Lyardet1997]; 70(5)
[Lyardet1998]; 460(20)
[MacNeil1995]; 238(12)
[Maes1987]; 70(5)
[Marick1995]; 691(29)
[Martin+1997]; 371(16), 412(18)
[Martin+1998]; 30(2)
[Martin1995]; 197(10), 438(19)
[Martin1997]; 197(10)
[M‰tzel+1996]; 70(5)
[McCarthy1995]; 609(26)
[McDaniel+1995]; 70(5)
[McHale+1991]; 131(8)
[McKusick1996]; 158(9)
[Menezes+1996]; 371(16)
[Meszaros+1998]; 609(26)
[Meszaros1997]; 691(29)
[Metsker+1998]; 89(6)
[Meyer1992]; 336(15)
[Meyer1994]; 89(6)
[Microsoft1993]; 109(7)
[Microsoft1996]; 158(9)
[Mitsui+1993]; 30(2)
[Mogul1995]; 158(9)
[Myers+1990]; 70(5)
[NCSA1998]; 336(15)
[Nilson1995]; 238(12)
[Noble+1995]; 89(6)
[Noble+1998]; 238(12)
[Noble+1999]; 70(5)
[Noble1996]; 89(6)
[Noble1997]; 502(22)
[Noble1998]; 89(6)
[Nonaka1995]; 650(28)
[ObjectShare1995]; 336(15)
[OMG]; 40(3)
[OMG1995]; 109(7)
[OMG1998]; 336(15)
[Ortega+1997]; 412(18)
[Palfinger1997]; 219(11)
[ParcPlace Systems1994]; 390(17)
[ParcPlace Systems1995]; 390(17)

bibliographic references *(continued)*
[ParcPlace1994]; 89(6)
[Paulk+1995]; 650(28)
[Petrakis+1997]; 412(18)
[Petzold1990]; 109(7)
[Piaget1946]; 297(14)
[PLoPD1995]; 14(1)
[PLoPD3]; 51(4)
[Pryce1997]; 336(15)
[Pyarali+1997]; 158(9)
[Raymond+1993]; 70(5)
[Raymond1998]; 636(27)
[Riehle+1995a]; 30(2)
[Riehle+1995b]; 31(2)
[Riehle+1995c]; 31(2)
[Riehle+1997]; 297(14)
[Riehle+1998]; 31(2), 71(5)
[Riehle1997]; 30(2), 70(5)
[Roberts+1998]; 692(29)
[Roberts1999]; 390(17)
[Rogerson1997]; 109(7)
[Rossi+1996]; 488(21)
[Rossi1996]; 460(20)
[Roth1975]; 438(19)
[Rudraraju1995]; 390(17)
[Rumbaugh+1991]; 89(6), 262(13)
[Rumbaugh1987]; 89(6)
[Rumbaugh1996]; 89(6)
[RW]; 40(3)
[Salton+1988]; 412(18)
[Salton1969]; 412(18)
[Saltzer+1984]; 371(16)
[Schatz1997]; 412(18)
[Schmidt+1997]; 336(15)
[Schmidt1994]; 109(7), 158(9)
[Schmidt1995]; 158(9)
[Schmidt1997]; 109(7), 158(9)
[Schneier1995]; 336(15)
[Schneier1996]; 371(16)
[Schoenfeld1996]; 31(2)
[Schwaber1997]; 650(28)
[Senge1990]; 650(28)
[Shaw1996]; 692(29)
[Shrivastava+1991]; 131(8)
[Silberschatz+1997]; 336(15)
[Silva+1997]; 131(8)
[Silva1998]; 131(8)
[Silva1999]; 131(8)
[Simon1969]; 692(29)
[Smith1995]; 71(5)
[Sommerlad+1998a]; 71(5)
[Sommerlad+1998b]; 71(5)
[Sommerlad1998]; 412(18)
[SSH1998]; 336(15)
[SSL1998]; 336(15)
[Stefik+1986]; 89(6)
[Stevens1990]; 109(7)

bibliographic references (*continued*)
[Stinson1995]; 371(16)
[Stroustrup1994]; 40(3)
[Sutherland1997]; 650(28)
[Taivalsaari1993]; 71(5)
[Thomsett1997]; 609(26)
[Tidwell1998]; 488(21)
[Tulloch+1996]; 71(5)
[UML1999]; 438(19)
[Ungar+1991]; 71(5)
[VI1998]; 336(15)
[Vlissides+1990]; 89(6)
[Weihl1993]; 131(8)
[Weinberg1997]; 651(28)
[White+1996]; 412(18)
[Whitenack1995]; 609(26)
[Wiki1999]; 651(28)
[Wilkerson1995]; 89(6)
[Woolf1994]; 89(6)
[Woolf1997]; 14(1), 40(3), 336(15)
[Yacoub+1998]; 438(19)
[Yoder+1997]; 371(16)
[Yoder+1998]; 336(15)
[Yoder1997]; 219(11), 336(15), 390(17)
[Zhao1998]; 31(2)
[Zimmermann1995]; 371(16)
Big Ball of Mud pattern
"Big Ball of Mud", (chapter title); 653(29)
(reference description); 658(29)
solutions; 664(29)
See Also eXtreme programming; SCRUM
strengths of; 658(29)
binary operations
See Also mathematics
in Algebraic Hierarchy pattern; 187(10)
in Promote And Add pattern; 191(10)
binding
early, disadvantages of in a growing system;
656(29)
bitmaps
as multimedia component; 463(21)
blackboard approach
Big Ball of Mud compared with,
[Buschmann+1996]; 661(29)
blight
software, isolation as tool for controlling; 654(29)
Blinders pattern
as alternate name for Limited View; 323(15)
body
(term description); 171(10)
bookmark list
See Basket pattern
Boomtown pattern
as alternate name for Throwaway Code;
665(29)
Bootstrapping pattern
(reference description); 615(27)

Borland
Database Engine, as Query Objects known
use, [Rudraraju1995]; 380(17)
BOS (Basic Object System)
as Prototype-Based Object System known use,
[Dutoit+1996]; 67(5)
The Bottom Line pattern
See Also "An Input and Output Pattern
Language: Lessons from
Telecommunications"
(reference description); 518(23)
boundaries
human, Be Aware of Boundaries, (reference
description); 605(26)
software systems, as Big Ball of Mud pattern
language force, [Brand1994]; 658(29)
spatial, *See* spatial
structural, *See* structure
Braga, Alexandre
"Tropyc: a pattern language for cryptographic
object-oriented software"; 337(16)
Brant, John
"Creating Reports with Query Objects";
375(17)
Bridge pattern
See Also "Design Patterns"
Algebraic Hierarchy relationship to,
[Gamma+1995]; 189(10)
Handle/Body Hierarchy relationship to,
[Gamma+1995]; 182(10)
History on Self relationship to,
[Gamma+1995]; 289(14)
Secure-Channel Communication pattern
relationship to; 345(16)
bring-forward tool
as Display List pattern use; 492(22)
broadcasting
through data structures, as Object Recursion
known use; 49(4)
as Object Recursion use; 43(4)
Broker pattern
Prototype-Based Object System relationship
to, [Buschmann+1996]; 69(5)
buffering
See Also performance
display redraw impact
Double Buffer use; 500(22)
Page Flip use; 501(22)
Build Trust pattern
See Also customers, "Customer Interaction
Patterns"
(reference description); 592(26)
Builder pattern
See Also "Design Patterns"
Essence relationship to, [Gamma+1995]; 37(3)
Limited View relationship to, [Gamma+1995];
325(15), 327(15)

C

C++ language
See Also language(s)
Abstract Session implementation; 103(7)
"C++ Idioms Patterns", (chapter title); 167(10)
idioms, [Coplien1992]; 167(10)
Object Synchronizer pattern example code;
    125(8)
proactive asynchronous event dispatching,
    example code; 142(9)
reactive synchronous event dispatching,
    example code; 139(9)
synchronous multithreading Web server,
    example code; 135(9)

CA (Certification Authority)
(term description); 370(16)

Cached Extensibility pattern
Artificial Accessors relationship to; 205(11)
(reference description); 213(11)
relationships with other Smalltalk scaffolding
    patterns; 218(11)

capabilities
Capability Maturity Model, as SCRUM
    motivation, [Paulk+1995]; 637(28)
"Capable, Productive, and Satisfied: Some
    Organizational Patterns for Protecting
    Productive People", (chapter title);
    611(27)
software development team; 612(27)

Captain Oates pattern
See Also human relationships
(reference description); 234(12)

Carlson, Andy
"Essence"; 33(3)
"Temporal Patterns"; 241(13)

Caterpillar/NCSA Financial Model Framework
Check Point example; 311(15)
as Limited View known use, [Yoder1997];
    328(15)
as Report Objects known use, [Yoder1997];
    378(17)
Roles example; 314(15)
as Secure Access Layer known use,
    [Yoder1997]; 332(15)
Session example, [Yoder1997]; 318(15)
as Session known use, [Yoder1997]; 320(15)
[Yoder1997]; 302(15)

cathedral and bazaar
software development team; 612(27)

Certification Authority
See CA (Certification Authority)

Chain of Responsibility pattern
See Also "Design Patterns"
Clip Requests relationship to, [Gamma+1995];
    499(22)
Object Recursion relationship to,
    [Gamma+95]; 50(4)

Chain of Responsibility pattern *(continued)*
Painter's Algorithm relationship to,
    [Gamma+95]; 495(22)
Proactor pattern relationship to,
    [Gamma+1995]; 157(9)

chaining set methods
in Essence implementation, [Stroustrup1994];
    39(3)

champion
See Also human relationships; organization
    management
Champions Review Papers pattern, (reference
    description); 544(24)
Champions Speak First pattern, (reference
    description); 552(24)
as conference paper evaluation role; 539(24)
"Identify the Champion: An Organizational
    Pattern Language for Program
    Committees", (chapter title);
    539(24)

change
See Also dynamic; finite state machines (FSM);
    history; time
as Big Ball of Mud pattern language force;
    658(29)
Change Log pattern
    (reference description); 271(14)
    Temporal Property relationship to,
        [Anderson1999]; 250(13)
different rates of, as Shearing Layers force;
    678(29)
eXtreme Programming (XP) adaptability in the
    face of, [Beck2000]; 673(29)
isolating developer from, Secure Access Layer
    pattern; 330(15)
local, Keep It Working use; 676(29)
managing
    "Big Ball of Mud", (chapter title); 653(29)
    "SCRUM: A Pattern Language for
        Hyperproductive Software
        Development", (chapter title); 637(28)
modeling, Prototype-Based Object System
    pattern support of; 53(5)
of objects, preserving history of, in Memento
    Child; 290(14)
as Piecemeal Growth force; 671(29)
rate of, abstraction evolution aided by
    differences in; 654(29)
as Reconstruction force; 684(29)
in requirements
    as SCRUM motivation; 638(28)
    as software erosion force; 654(29)
Selective Changes pattern, (reference
    description); 577(25)
Show Changes pattern, as alternate name for
    George Washington is Still Dead
    pattern; 517(23)

change *(continued)*
   state, modeling, "Finite State Machine
      Patterns"; 413(19)
   over time, modeling, in "Temporal Patterns";
      241(13)
channels
   See Also communication; multimedia
   delivery, as Define and Run multimedia
      pattern dimension; 465(21)
   synchronization of, as Define and Run
      multimedia pattern dimension; 466(21)
chaos
   Sweeping It under the Rug handling of;
      681(29)
chapter titles
   "Abstract Class"; 5(1)
   "Abstract Session: An Object Structural
      Pattern"; 95(7)
   "Architectural Patterns for Enabling
      Application Security"; 301(15)
   "Basic Relationship Patterns"; 73(6)
   "Big Ball of Mud"; 653(29)
   "C++ Idioms Patterns"; 167(10)
   "Capable, Productive, and Satisfied: Some
      Organizational Patterns for Protecting
      Productive People"; 611(27)
   "A Collection of History Patterns"; 263(14)
   "Composing Multimedia Artifacts for Reuse";
      461(21)
   "Creating Reports with Query Objects";
      375(17)
   "Customer Interaction Patterns"; 585(26)
   "Display Maintenance: A Pattern Language";
      489(22)
   "Essence"; 33(3)
   "Feature Extraction: A Pattern for Information
      Retrieval"; 391(18)
   "Finite State Machine Patterns"; 413(19)
   "High-Level and Process Patterns from the
      Memory Preservation Society: Patterns
      for Managing Limited Memory";
      221(12)
   "Identify the Champion: An Organizational
      Pattern Language for Program
      Committees"; 539(24)
   "An Input and Output Pattern Language:
      Lessons from Telecommunications";
      503(23)
   "Object Recursion"; 41(4)
   "Object Synchronizer"; 111(8)
   "A Pattern Language for Writers'
      Workshops"; 557(25)
   "Patterns for Designing Navigable
      Information Spaces"; 445(20)
   "Proactor"; 133(9)
   "Prototype-Based Object System"; 53(5)
   "Role Object"; 15(2)

chapter titles *(continued)*
   "SCRUM: A Pattern Language for
      Hyperproductive Software
      Development"; 637(28)
   "Smalltalk Scaffolding Patterns"; 199(11)
   "Temporal Patterns"; 241(13)
   "Tropyc: a pattern language for cryptographic
      object-oriented software"; 337(16)
check
   Check Point pattern
      (reference description); 307(15)
      relationship to Single Access Point pattern;
         309(15)
      Roles relationship to; 315(15)
      Session relationship to; 319(15)
      Single Access Point relationship to; 304(15),
         305(15)
   Checks pattern
      Full View with Errors relationship to,
         [Cunningham1995]; 322(15)
      Limited View relationship to,
         [Cunningham1995]]; 328(15)
Child Proofing pattern
   as alternate name for Limited View; 323(15)
Chronology pattern
   bibliographic references, [Carlson1998a];
      262(13)
   Temporal Association relationship to,
      [Carlson1998a]; 254(13)
circle
   as communication facilitator, in a pattern
      writers' workshop; 566(25)
circular dependencies
   as Essence issue; 38(3)
civil engineering
   as Prototype-Based Object System known use;
      67(5)
clarity
   code, as pair programming side effect;
      665(29)
class(es)
   See Also polymorphism
   abstract
      "Abstract Class", (chapter title); 5(1)
      Abstract Class pattern; 5(1)
   class-based context, (term description);
      448(20)
   hierarchy, Abstract Class pattern; 5(1)
   polymorphic, as Abstract Class advantage;
      9(1)
Clearing the Palate pattern
   (reference description); 577(25)
   Suggestions for Improvement relationship to;
      575(25)
clients
   See Also architecture; distributed; Internet;
      servers

clients *(continued)*
    Client-Dispatcher-Server pattern, Secure-
        Channel Communication pattern
        relationship to; 345(16)
    context roles, patterns for, in "Role Object";
        15(2)
    server, sessions, patterns for, in "Abstract
        Session: An Object Structural Pattern";
        95(7)
    shared objects management, Object
        Synchronizer pattern; 112(8)
Clip Requests pattern
    See Also GUIs (graphical user interface)
    (reference description); 498(22)
    Request Update relationship to; 493(22)
cloning
    See Also copying
    in Prototype-Based Object System
        implementation; 62(5)
    two-step recursion, as Object Recursion
        known use; 48(4)
CLOS (Common Lisp Object System)
    See Also language(s)
    Prototype-Based Object System relationship to
        [Foote1991]; 63(5)
        [Keene1989]; 67(5)
CMM (Capability Maturity Model)
    limitations, as SCRUM motivation,
        [Paulk+1995]; 637(28)
code
    See Also language(s); programming
    features that impact memory size; 227(12)
    generating, in pseudo-method rapid
        prototyping systems; 214(11)
    quick and dirty
        persistence, as source of Big Ball of Mud;
            654(29)
        persistence, PLoP registration code as
            example of; 667(29)
    readability and clarity, as pair programming
        side effect; 665(29)
    reviews, role in solving Big Ball of Mud
        situations, [Foote+1995]; 664(29)
    source code control systems, history patterns
        collection; 265(14)
    working set, (term description); 225(12)
cohesion
    as force, in relationship patterns; 75(6)
collaborations
    See Also relationships
    Object Synchronizer pattern use; 111(8)
Collect Damage pattern
    as alternate name for Consolidate Requests,
        [Beck1994]; 497(22)
"A Collection of History Patterns"
    bibliographic references, [Anderson1999];
        261(13)

"A Collection of History Patterns" *(continued)*
    (chapter title); 263(14)
collection(s)
    See Also associations; composite; composition
    Collection Object pattern
        Display List relationship to, [Noble1999];
            492(22)
        Mutual Friends pattern relationship to; 87(6)
        (reference description); 80(6)
        Relationship As Attribute relationship to;
            78(6)
        Relationship Object pattern relationship to;
            80(6)
    Smalltalk
        [Beck1997]; 82(6)
        [Buschmann+1996]; 82(6)
        classes in; 201(11)
        Query Objects relationship to; 379(17)
collegiate
    (term description); 296(14)
combinatorial explosion
    of algorithms, [Ingalls1986]; 190(10)
communications
    See Also networks; telecommunications
    "Abstract Session: An Object Structural
        Pattern"; 95(7)
    human, Open Review pattern, (reference
        description); 559(25)
    network, Session pattern use; 97(7)
    pattern
        understanding, Fly on the Wall; 570(25)
        understanding, Volunteer Summarizes the
            Work pattern; 571(25)
    Positive Feedback First pattern, (reference
        description); 572(25)
    protocols, Abstract Session pattern use; 104(7)
    Sitting in a Circle pattern, (reference
        description); 566(25)
Community of Trust pattern
    Open Review relationship to; 560(25)
    (reference description); 564(25)
comparison
    of complex objects, as Object Recursion
        motivation; 41(4)
compilation
    features that impact memory size; 227(12)
    generated compilers, debugging difficulties;
        146(9)
complexity
    application domain, as Big Ball of Mud pattern
        language force; 657(29)
    as Big Ball of Mud pattern language force;
        657(29)
        [Coplien1995]; 663(29)
    essential, (term description), [Brooks1995];
        657(29)
    feature extraction handling of; 395(18)

complexity *(continued)*
  as force, in relationship patterns; 75(6)
  multimedia as complex data; 393(18)
  as Prototype-Based Object System issue; 59(5)
  as reactive synchronous event dispatching
      disadvantage; 139(9)
  reduction, with Formula Objects use; 385(17)
  as synchronous multithreading disadvantage;
      136(9)
components
  -based environments, attribute validation
      patterns, in "Essence"; 33(3)
  Components Layout pattern
    Glue relationship to; 471(21)
    (reference description); 471(21)
  multimedia, reuse; 461(21)
composite
  See Also composition; relationships
  artifacts
    Glue creation of; 466(21)
    (term description); 461(21)
  Composite pattern
    See Also "Design Patterns"
    Abstract Class relationship to,
        [Gamma+1995]; 13(1)
    Composable Query Objects relationship to,
        [Gamma+1995]; 384(17)
    Display List relationship to, [Gamma+1995];
        492(22)
    History on Tree relationship to,
        [Gamma+1995]; 295(14)
    Limited View relationship to,
        [Gamma+1995]; 325(15), 327(15)
    Mutual Friends pattern relationship to,
        [Gamma+1995]; 87(6)
    Object Recursion relationship to,
        [Gamma+1995]; 49(4)
    pay-per-click framework use; 338(16)
  CompositePart pattern, Mutual Friends use,
      [ParcPlace1994]; 87(6)
  multimedia artifacts, authoring tool reuse
      weaknesses; 463(21)
  recording of history, in History on Tree;
      293(14)
composition
  See Also inheritance; relationships
  Composable Query Objects pattern
    Formula Objects relationship to; 386(17)
    Query Objects relationship to; 379(17),
        380(17)
    (reference description); 381(17)
  "Composing Multimedia Artifacts for Reuse",
      (chapter title); 461(21)
  inheritance relationship to, in Layered
      Organization; 428(19)
  pattern reference descriptions, Glue; 466(21)
  of queries, Composable Query Objects; 381(17)

comprehensibility
  as Sweeping It under the Rug force; 682(29)
compression algorithms
  feature extraction problems; 408(18)
compromise
  need for, in software development; 660(29)
compulsory attributes
  handling, Essence; 33(3)
computer graphics
  display update issues; 489(22)
concepts
  See Also abstractions
  automatic indexing view of; 393(18)
concrete
  class, Abstract Class relationship to; 5(1)
  Concrete Data Type pattern, (reference
      description); 185(10)
concurrency
  See Also synchronization; time
  "Finite State Machine Patterns", (chapter title);
      413(19)
  as high-performance Web server requirement;
      134(9)
  object, management policies; 125(8)
  pattern reference descriptions, "Finite State
      Machine Patterns"; 413(19)
  Proactor pattern; 133(9)
  Single Access Point pattern use; 306(15)
  synchronous multithreading, advantages and
      disadvantages; 135(9)
conference committees
  "Identify the Champion: An Organizational
      Pattern Language for Program
      Committees", (chapter title); 539(24)
confidentiality
  See Also security
  data, in "Tropyc: a pattern language for
      cryptographic object-oriented
      software"; 337(16)
  as Information Secrecy pattern motivation;
      346(16)
  (term description); 367(16)
configurability
  See Also extensibility
  dynamic, as Prototype-Based Object System
      advantage; 58(5)
  ENVY configuration management tool, history
      patterns collection known use; 265(14)
  pattern reference descriptions, Report Objects;
      376(17)
  Prototype-Based Object System pattern; 53(5)
  PVCS software configuration management
      tool, as Change Log known use;
      276(14)
Connected Group pattern
  Active Value pattern relationship to,
      [Li+1996]; 84(6)

Connector pattern
  Abstract Session relationship to,
      [Schmidt1995]; 108(7)
conservation
  of memory, patterns for, in "High-Level and
      Process Patterns from the Memory
      Preservation Society: Patterns for
      Managing Limited Memory""; 221(12)
consistency
  as Mutual Friends force; 85(6)
  object, Object Synchronizer pattern use;
      114(8)
Consolidate Requests pattern
  See Also GUIs (graphical user interface)
  (reference description); 496(22)
  Request Update relationship to; 493(22)
Consolidation Phase pattern
  Big Ball of Mud pattern language relationship
      to
      [Coplien+1995]; 655(29)
      [Foote+1995]; 655(29)
  role in solving Big Ball of Mud situations,
      [Foote+1995]; 664(29)
constraints
  See Also encapsulation; isolation
  Constraint Observers pattern
      Formula Objects relationship to; 386(17)
      (reference description); 387(17)
  constraint-based systems, [Benson+1992];
      387(17)
  Constraints pattern, Constraint Observers
      relationship to, [Johnson1992]; 389(17)
  pattern reference descriptions, Constraint
      Observers; 387(17)
  role in effective design, [Brand1994]; 664(29)
construction
  See Also structure
  as Components Layout multimedia pattern
      dimension; 465(21)
  Constructor Methods pattern, Single Access
      Point pattern relationship to,
      [Beck1997]; 306(15)
  Constructor Parameter Method pattern, Single
      Access Point pattern relationship to,
      [Beck1997]; 306(15)
  as Glue multimedia pattern dimension;
      464(21)
  pattern reference descriptions, Components
      Layout; 471(21)
  as Template multimedia pattern dimension;
      465(21)
Constructive Feedback pattern
  as alternate name for Suggestions for
      Improvement pattern; 573(25)
containment
  See Also encapsulation; isolation
  as Glue known use; 469(21)

context
  See Also environment; views
  client, patterns for, in "Role Object"; 15(2)
  Context pattern, as alternate name for Abstract
      Session; 95(7)
  context-sensitive menus, as Limited View
      known use, [Yoder+1998]; 328(15)
  navigation, (term description); 447(20)
  Navigational Context patterns; 446(20)
  pattern reference descriptions, Nodes in
      Context; 448(20)
  perspective on, importance for good design;
      655(29)
  separation of navigational objects from;
      450(20)
  subtype characteristics selection from, in
      Virtual Constructor pattern; 185(10)
  text information retrieval issues; 445(20)
Continuous Integration pattern
  as alternate name for Keep It Working; 675(29)
control
  See Also access control
  elements, as multimedia component; 463(21)
  of software blight, isolation as tool for; 654(29)
  thread, reactive vs. proactive handling,
      (footnote); 143(9)
controlled chaos
  as system development stage; 655(29)
conversion
  See Also data types
  numeric, as Abstract Class motivation; 5(1)
  pattern reference descriptions
      Algebraic Hierarchy; 187(10)
      Homogeneous Addition; 189(10)
      Non-Hierarchical Addition; 193(10)
      Promote And Add; 190(10)
      Promotion Ladder; 192(10)
      Type Promotion; 195(10)
Conway's law
  as Big Ball of Mud pattern language force,
      [Coplien1995]; 657(29)
  system architecture impact, [Coplien1995];
      663(29)
Cooldraw
  Active Value use, [Freeman-Benson1993];
      83(6)
cooperation
  Object Synchronizer pattern use; 111(8)
Coplien, James O.
  "A Pattern Language for Writers'
      Workshops"; 557(25)
  "C++ Idioms Patterns"; 167(10)
copying
  See Also cloning
  in C++, Counted Body pattern handling;
      173(10)
  semantics

copying *(continued)*
  [Cargill1996]; 176(10)
  in Counted Body pattern; 176(10)
  two-step recursion, as Object Recursion
    known use; 48(4)
CORBA
  [OMG1995]; 102(7)
  Security Services, as Secure Access Layer
    known use, [OMG1998]; 332(15)
cost
  as Big Ball of Mud force; 661(29)
  as Big Ball of Mud pattern language force;
    656(29)
  of initial development, as Big Ball of Mud
    pattern strength; 658(29)
  as Reconstruction force; 684(29)
counting
  See Also garbage collection; memory
  Counted Body pattern
    Concrete Data Type relationship to; 187(10)
    (reference description); 173(10)
  counter synchronization, Guide use,
    [Decouchant+1991]; 123(8)
  Detached Counted Body pattern, (reference
    description); 176(10)
  reference
    [Cargill1996]; 179(10)
    in Counted Body pattern; 173(10)
    Detached Counted Body pattern; 176(10)
    [Koenig1995]; 179(10)
coupling
  as force, in relationship patterns; 75(6)
  threading policy with concurrency policy, as
    synchronous multithreading
    disadvantage; 136(9)
courtesy
  pattern reference descriptions, Mind Your
    Manners; 606(26)
CRC cards
  as domain knowledge capture tool,
    [Beck+1989]; 666(29)
CRC (Class Responsibility Collaboration)
  [Wilkerson1995]; 73(6)
creating
  "Creating Reports with Query Objects",
    (chapter title); 375(17)
  creator objects, Role Object relationship to,
    [Baumer+1998]; 26(2)
  as Glue multimedia pattern dimension;
    464(21)
  objects, in Virtual Constructor pattern; 185(10)
Crossing Chasms pattern language
  Query Objects relationship to, [Brown+1995];
    380(17)
cryptography
  See Also security
  basic concepts; 367(16)

cryptography *(continued)*
  cryptographic hash function, (term
    description); 369(16)
  in "Tropyc: a pattern language for
    cryptographic object-oriented
    software"; 337(16)
  "Tropyc: a pattern language for cryptographic
    object-oriented software", (chapter
    title); 337(16)
  Tropyc pattern language; 337(16)
culture
  preservation and dissemination, as pair
    programming side effect; 665(29)
customer(s)
  See Also human relationships
  "Customer Interaction Patterns", (chapter
    title); 585(26)
  Customer Meetings: Go Early, Stay Late
    pattern
    See Also customers, "Customer Interaction
      Patterns"
    Build Trust relationship to; 592(26)
    Know the Customer relationship to; 590(26)
    (reference description); 600(26)
  Customer Rapport pattern, It's a Relationship,
    Not a Sale relationship to,
    [Whitenack1995]; 587(26)
  interaction guidelines, [McCarthy1995];
    585(26)
  pattern reference descriptions, Know the
    Customer; 589(26)
  software release timing; 627(27)
cut-and-paste
  as Component Layout known use; 474(21)
Cybulski, Jacob L.
  "Composing Multimedia Artifacts for Reuse";
    461(21)
cycles
  closure, handling, with History on Tree; 293(14)
  as Constraint Observers issue; 388(17)

                    D
daemons
  Prototype-Based Object System
    implementation use, [McDaniel+1995];
    61(5)
Dahab, Ricardo
  "Tropyc: a pattern language for cryptographic
    object-oriented software"; 337(16)
Daily Build pattern
  as alternate name for Keep It Working; 675(29)
dance
  See Also teams
  customer relationships as; 588(26)
data
  acoustic, Feature Extraction: A Pattern for
    Information Retrieval; 393(18)

data *(continued)*
confidentiality, in "Tropyc: a pattern language for cryptographic object-oriented software"; 337(16)
generation data group
bibliographic references, [Bodenstein1996]; 296(14)
as known use for History on Self, [Bodenstein1996]; 289(14)
global, Big Ball of Mud characterized by; 661(29)
image
Artisan (Automatic Retrieval of Trademark Images by Shape ANalysis) project, feature extraction use; 410(18)
content searching issues; 393(18)
Feature Extraction: A Pattern for Information Retrieval; 393(18)
memory size impact of; 227(12)
similarity searches, feature extraction use; 409(18)
integrity
See Also security
(term description); 367(16)
in "Tropyc: a pattern language for cryptographic object-oriented software"; 337(16)
legacy, translating into a relational database format, "Creating Reports with Query Objects"; 375(17)
quantity, Feature Extraction: A Pattern for Information Retrieval; 393(18)
structures
broadcasting messages through, as Object Recursion known use; 49(4)
of graphical components, Display List pattern; 491(22)
memory size impact of; 227(12)
Variable Sized Data Structure pattern, Make the User Worry relationship to, [Noblet1998]; 232(12)
data types
built-in vs. user-defined, semantics of; 196(10)
Concrete Data Type pattern, (reference description); 185(10)
pattern reference descriptions
Algebraic Hierarchy; 187(10)
Concrete Data Type; 186(10)
Detached Counted Body; 176(10)
Envelope/Letter; 182(10)
Handle/Body pattern; 171(10)
Homogeneous Addition; 189(10)
Non-Hierarchical Addition; 193(10)
Promote And Add; 190(10)
Promotion Ladder; 192(10)
Type Promotion; 195(10)
Virtual Constructor; 184(10)
user, behavior determination; 171(10)

databases
See Also information retrieval
"Creating Reports with Query Objects", (chapter title); 375(17)
management systems
history patterns collection relationship to; 265(14)
Posting relationship to; 284(14)
object-oriented
GemStone OODB, as Roles known use; 315(15)
Mutual Friends pattern, [Graham+1997]; 88(6)
real-time network use, Snapshot pattern; 261(13)
relational
"Creating Reports with Query Objects"; 375(17)
Mutual Friends pattern use; 88(6)
DBTools.h++ class library
as Essence known use, [RW]; 40(3)
DCOM
[Rogerson1997]; 102(7)
deadlock
See Also concurrency; race
as Proactor pattern implementation issue, [Dijkstra1971]; 152(9)
debugging difficulties
with Composable Query Objects pattern; 384(17)
as Proactor pattern disadvantage; 142(9), 146(9)
decay
in system architectures, counteracting; 654(29)
decentralization
of complex processing, in Object Recursion; 45(4)
Decorator pattern
See Also "Design Patterns"
bibliographic references, [Gamma+1995]; 30(2)
Composable Query Objects relationship to, [Gamma+1995]; 384(17)
decorators, (term description); 381(17)
Edition relationship to; 269(14)
Mutual Friends pattern relationship to, [Gamma+1995]; 87(6)
Nodes in Context relationship to, [Gamma+1995]; 450(20)
Object Recursion relationship to, [Gamma+95]; 49(4)
Posting relationship to, [Gamma+1995]; 284(14)
Role Object relationship to, [Gamma+1995]; 21(2), 29(2)
decoupling
See separation

deferred checks
as Check Point design consideration; 309(15)
Define and Run Presentation pattern
Component Layout relationship to; 475(21)
Glue relationship to; 471(21)
(reference description); 482(21)
Synchronous Channels relationship to; 486(21)
delegation
See Also inheritance
Artificial Delegation pattern, (reference description); 211(11)
of complex processing, in Object Recursion; 45(4)
Self Delegation pattern, Mutual Friends pattern relationship to, [Beck1997]; 87(6)
Deliverables to Go pattern
(reference description); 625(27)
delivery channels
as Define and Run multimedia pattern dimension; 465(21)
Demolition pattern
as alternate name for Rehabilitation; 684(29)
dependability
as Keep It Working force; 676(29)
DependentsCollection
many-to-many relationship representation, [ParcPlace1994]; 80(6)
depth cues
management, Display List pattern use; 491(22)
design
See Also architecture; methodology; software, development
decisions, in feature extraction pattern application; 396(18)
engineering, Prototype-Based Object System pattern support of; 53(5)
features that impact memory size; 227(12)
interface, separating navigation design from; 445(20)
methodologies
See Also UML
as issues and limitations, as Prototype-Based Object System motivation; 54(5)
models, Basic FSM, (reference description); 417(19)
of navigable information spaces; 445(20)
navigational, separating interface design from; 445(20)
"Patterns for Designing Navigable Information Spaces", (chapter title); 445(20)
of review forms, as program committee meeting tool; 546(24)
software, "Big Ball of Mud", (chapter title); 653(29)
space, characteristics; 677(29)
top-down, problems with; 662(29)

"Design Patterns", [Gamma+1995]
Chapter 01; 14(1)
Chapter 02; 30(2)
Chapter 03; 40(3)
Chapter 04; 51(4)
Chapter 05; 70(5)
Chapter 06; 88(6)
Chapter 07; 108(7)
Chapter 08; 130(8)
Chapter 09; 158(9)
Chapter 10; 197(10)
Chapter 11; 219(11)
Chapter 14; 297(14)
Chapter 15; 335(15)
Chapter 16; 370(16)
Chapter 17; 390(17)
Chapter 18; 412(18)
Chapter 19; 437(19)
Chapter 22; 502(22)
Chapter 23; 536(23)
Chapter 29; 691(29)
"Design Patterns", *See*
abstract, Abstract Factory pattern
Adapter pattern
Bridge pattern
Builder pattern
Chain of Responsibility pattern
composite, Composite pattern
Decorator pattern
Facade pattern
Factory Method pattern
Flyweight pattern
Interpreter pattern
Iterator pattern
Mediator pattern
Memento pattern
Observer pattern
prototyping, Prototype pattern
Proxy pattern
Singleton pattern
state, State pattern
Strategy pattern
desktop environments
Display List pattern use; 492(22)
Detached Counted Body pattern
(reference description); 176(10)
Devos, Martine
"SCRUM: A Pattern Language for Hyperproductive Software Development"; 637(28)
DFA (Deterministic Finite Automata)
generated, debugging difficulties; 146(9)
DFT (Discrete Fourier Transform)
feature extraction use; 409(18)
dictionary
(term description); 265(14)

Different Chairs pattern
Sitting in a Circle pattern relationship to, [Alexander+1997]; 567(25)

digital
libraries, characteristics and information retrieval demands; 392(18)
signatures
Signature pattern; 353(16)
Signature with Appendix pattern use; 358(16)
(term description); 369(16)

dignity
See Also human relationships
Safe Setting pattern, (reference description); 560(25)

dining philosophers problem
as Proactor pattern implementation issue, [Dijkstra1971]; 152(9)

Director pattern
Relationship Object pattern relationship to, [Coldewey1997]; 80(6)

discrete
value change, tracking, in Temporal Property; 242(13)

displays
See Also GUIs (graphical user interface); hypermedia; multimedia
Display List pattern
Clip Requests relationship to; 499(22)
Painter's Algorithm relationship to; 495(22)
(reference description); 491(22)
display lists, Display List pattern, (reference description); 491(22)
"Display Maintenance: A Pattern Language" (chapter title); 489(22)
pattern relationships, (figure); 490(22)
updating, Request Update; 492(22)

Disposable Code pattern
as alternate name for Throwaway Code; 665(29)

distributed
environments, attribute validation patterns, in "Essence Pattern"; 33(3)
request processing, Object Recursion pattern; 41(4)
systems, Object Synchronizer pattern use; 129(8)

divide and conquer strategy
limitations of; 658(29)

Do What I Say Not What I Do
See Big Ball of Mud

Doble, Jim
"Smalltalk Scaffolding Patterns"; 199(11)

documentation
lack of, as Big Ball of Mud characteristic; 662(29)

domain
experience, importance for software development; 662(29)
immature understanding of, as system development stage; 655(29)
knowledge, as Big Ball of Mud pattern language force; 656(29)
mapping, feature extraction use; 395(18)
understanding, as early phase life cycle task, [Foote1995]; 663(29)

Don't Leave Your Customer Hanging pattern
as alternative name for Be Responsive; 597(26)

Don't Let Them Forget pattern
See Also "An Input and Output Pattern Language: Lessons from Telecommunications"
(reference description); 530(23)

Double Buffer pattern
See Also displays; GUIs (graphical user interface); performance
Page Flip relationship to; 501(22)
Painter's Algorithm relationship to; 495(22)
(reference description); 500(22)

Double-Checked Locking pattern
Session relationship to, [Schmidt+1997]; 319(15)

Dual Hierarchy pattern
Promote And Add relationship to, [Martin1997]; 192(10)

duration
See Also time
(term description), [Fowler1997a]; 267(14)

dynamic
See Also extensibility; runtime
behavior, finite state machine modeling; 413(19)
context, (term description); 448(20)
database programming, Composable Query Objects support of; 383(17)
database reporting patterns, in "Creating Reports with Query Objects"; 375(17)
Dynamic State Instantiation pattern, (reference description); 435(19)
Dynamic Template pattern, Prototype-Based Object System relationship to, [Lyardet1997]; 68(5)
extensible object representation, in Prototype-Based Object System pattern; 53(5)
object manipulation, Role Object; 18(2), 20(2)
object modification and extension, as Prototype-Based Object System motivation; 54(5)
query creation, in Query Objects; 379(17)
report generation
Formula Objects use; 386(17)
Report Objects; 376(17)
retyping, patterns that address; 182(10)

E

Early Authorization pattern
as alternate name for Limited View; 323(15)
ease
of reading, as force in relationship patterns; 75(6)
of writing, as force in relationship patterns; 75(6)
ecology
of Big Ball of Mud; 654(29)
Captain Oates pattern; 234(12)
edition
Edition pattern, (reference description); 267(14)
history representation by; 264(14)
Effective Handover pattern
(reference description); 630(27)
effectiveness
as Identify the Champion goal; 539(24)
efficiency
See Also performance
as Abstract Session pattern force; 95(7)
design, as force in relationship patterns; 75(6)
as high-performance Web server requirement; 134(9)
of programmer time, Think Small impact on; 227(12)
as Prototype-Based Object System issue; 59(5)
runtime, vs. type safety, in Session pattern implementation; 97(7)
Ego object system
Prototype-Based Object System sample code; 63(5)
electronic commerce
See Also security
navigation aids for; 457(20)
emergent structure
See Also prototyping
in pattern mining; 585(26)
empathy
See Also human relationships
for customers
[Armstrong1992]; 597(26)
[Covey1989]; 593(26), 596(26)
[Endler1995]; 593(26), 596(26)
[Guaspari1998]; 591(26)
[Hunter1998]; 593(26)
[Thomsett1997]; 591(26)
pattern reference descriptions
Build Trust; 592(26)
Know the Customer; 589(26)
Listen, Listen, Listen; 595(26)
encapsulation
See Also separation
of compulsory properties, in Essence; 35(3)
of concurrency mechanism, as Proactor pattern advantage; 145(9)

encapsulation *(continued)*
as Edition force; 268(14)
Encapsulated State pattern
(reference description); 434(19)
State-Driven Transitions relationship to; 423(19)
of formulas as objects, Formula Objects use; 385(17)
lack of, Big Ball of Mud characterized by; 661(29)
as Object Synchronizer pattern force; 113(8)
pattern reference descriptions
Encapsulated State; 434(19)
Interface Organization; 423(19)
Role Object; 15(2)
Piecemeal Growth use; 672(29)
of security policies
algorithm, Check Point pattern; 308(15)
Secure Access Layer pattern; 329(15)
of state
client, Abstract Session pattern; 95(7)
Encapsulated State pattern, (reference description); 434(19)
encryption
See Also security
authentication, Secrecy with Integrity pattern motivation; 353(16)
low-level issues and techniques
[ICSP1998]; 303(15)
[Schneier1995]; 303(15)
as security issue; 301(15)
Engage Customers pattern
It's a Relationship, Not a Sale relationship to, [Coplien1995]; 587(26)
engineering
design, Prototype-Based Object System pattern support of; 53(5)
entropy
in system architectures, counteracting; 654(29)
Entry pattern
as alternative name for Posting, [Fowler1997a]; 280(14)
enumerated
context, Prototype-Based Object System implementation use; 448(20)
types, (term description), [McDaniel+1995]; 61(5)
Envelope/Letter pattern
Handle/Body Hierarchy relationship to; 182(10)
Virtual Constructor relationship to; 185(10)
environments
See Also context
component-based, attribute validation patterns, in "Essence"; 33(3)
distributed, attribute validation patterns, in "Essence Pattern"; 33(3)
multimedia, (term description); 461(21)

ENVY configuration management tool
as known use, of history patterns collection;
265(14)

equality
relationship of identifier/object association to;
173(10)
testing of complex objects, as Object Recursion
motivation; 41(4)

erosion
of system architectures, forces that drive;
654(29)

errors
See Also security
user
handling, Full View with Errors pattern;
321(15)
handling, Limited View pattern; 323(15)

Essence pattern
"Essence", (chapter title); 33(3)
(reference description); 33(3)

Estepp, Sharon
"Temporal Patterns"; 241(13)

estimating
Temporal Property issues; 250(13)

evaluation
balancing, pattern workshop moderator role;
566(25)
out-of-memory conditions, Exhaustion Test
pattern; 235(12)

events
See Also behavior
asynchronous, Proactor pattern use; 133(9)
finite state machine activation by
Hybrid; 433(19)
Meally; 429(19)
handling, *See Also* finite state machines (FSM)
proactive asynchronous dispatching,
advantages and disadvantages; 139(9)
reactive synchronous dispatching, as
concurrency strategy, advantages and
disadvantages; 137(9)
separation from states and actions, in Basic
FSM; 418(19)
(term description); 266(14)

evolution
of architecture, advantages of; 662(29)
development, Prototype-Based Object System
pattern support of; 53(5)
in Piecemeal Growth; 674(29)

execution time
Prototype-Based Object System pattern impact
on; 53(5)

Exhaustion Test pattern
(reference description); 235(12)

Expansion Phase pattern
Big Ball of Mud pattern language relationship
to

Expansion Phase pattern *(continued)*
[Coplien+1995]; 655(29)
[Foote+1995]; 655(29)
role in solving Big Ball of Mud situations,
[Foote+1995]; 664(29)
tasks appropriate to, [Foote+1995]; 663(29)

experience
as Big Ball of Mud pattern language force;
656(29)

Experts Review Papers pattern
(reference description); 543(24)

exploratory
database programming, Composable Query
Objects support of; 383(17)

Exposed State pattern
Encapsulated State relationship to,
[Dyson+1998]; 434(19)
Finite State Machine pattern language
relationship to
[Dyson+1998]; 416(19)
(figure); 415(19)

expressiveness
as Object Synchronizer pattern force; 113(8)

extensibility
See Also reusability
Abstract Class pattern use, [Auer1995]; 14(1)
as Abstract Session advantage; 102(7)
Cached Extensibility pattern, (reference
description); 213(11)
database reporting patterns, in "Creating
Reports with Query Objects"; 375(17)
Extensible Attributes pattern
(reference description); 202(11)
relationships with other Smalltalk
scaffolding patterns; 218(11)
Extension Object pattern
Feature Extraction relationship to; 410(18)
[Gamma1998]; 30(2)
Prototype-Based Object System relationship
to, [Gamma1998]; 57(5), 69(5)
Role Object relationship to, [Gamma1998];
29(2)
Role Object relationship to,
[Schoenfeld1996]; 29(2)
Role Object relationship to, [Zhao+1998];
29(2)
as motivation for Abstract Class use; 8(1)
as Prototype-Based Object System advantage;
59(5)
Prototype-Based Object System pattern; 53(5)

eXtreme Programming (XP)
change adaptability, [Beck2000]; 673(29)
feedback use, [Beck2000]; 674(29)
history of; 684(29)
role in solving Big Ball of Mud situations
[Beck2000]; 664(29)
[Coplien1995]; 664(29)

eXtreme Programming (XP) *(continued)*
  as spike solutions, [Beck2000]; 666(29)
  testing importance; 677(29)

F

Facade pattern
  See Also "Design Patterns"
  Abstract Session relationship to,
      [Gamma+1995]; 107(7)
  Sweeping It under the Rug relationship to;
      683(29)
Factory Method pattern
  See Also "Design Patterns"
  Abstract Session relationship to,
      [Gamma+1995]; 107(7)
  State-Driven Transitions relationship to,
      [Gamma+1995]; 423(19)
failure
  actions, as Check Point design consideration;
      309(15)
  due to memory limits
    Graceful Degradation pattern handling;
        232(12)
    user control, in Make the User Worry
        pattern; 230(12)
false positives
  feature extraction strategies for handling;
      396(18)
fault lines
  system architecture benefits, different rates of
      change impact on; 654(29)
feature extraction
  in "Feature Extraction: A Pattern for
      Information Retrieval", (chapter title);
      391(18)
  Feature Extraction pattern, characteristics and
      components; 393(18)
feedback
  See Also SCRUM (from Rugby term
      scrummage); teams
  Author Asks for Clarification pattern,
      (reference description); 575(25)
  -driven development, as Big Ball of Mud
      pattern language goal; 655(29)
  effective
    Fly on the Wall pattern; 570(25)
    Volunteer Summarizes the Work pattern;
        571(25)
  encouraging, Author Reads Selection pattern;
      569(25)
  eXtreme Programming use, [Beck2000]; 674(29)
  as Piecemeal Growth force, [Simon1969];
      673(29)
  Positive Feedback First pattern, (reference
      description); 572(25)
  Suggestions for Improvement pattern,
      (reference description); 573(25)

finite state machines (FSM)
  See Also concurrency; events, handling; state
      activation; 429(19)
  Finite State Machine pattern language,
      concepts; 414(19)
  "Finite State Machine Patterns", (chapter title);
      413(19)
  pattern language for, "Finite State Machine
      Patterns"; 413(19)
  pattern reference descriptions
    Basic FSM; 417(19)
    Dynamic State Instantiation; 435(19)
    Encapsulated State; 434(19)
    Hybrid; 433(19)
    Interface Organization; 423(19)
    Layered Organization; 426(19)
    Meally; 428(19)
    Moore; 430(19)
    State-Driven Transitions; 421(19)
  patterns for
    [Dyson+1998]; 413(19)
    [Martin1995]; 413(19)
firewalls
  See Also security
  as Limited View known use; 328(15)
  low-level issues and techniques
    [ICSP1998]; 303(15)
    [Schneier1995]; 303(15)
First, Do No Harm pattern
  as alternate name for Keep It Working; 675(29)
first-class
  See Also software, development
  modeling concepts, roles as, [Riehle+1998];
      21(2)
  navigation strategy, Set-Based Navigation as;
      447(20)
  objects
    events as, in Command, [Gamma+1995];
        267(14)
    need for, as reason not to use Temporal
        Property; 246(13)
    relationship representation, Temporal
        Association pattern; 251(13)
    (term description); 54(5)
Five Minutes of No Escalation Messages pattern
  See Also "An Input and Output Pattern
      Language: Lessons from
      Telecommunications"
  (reference description); 520(23)
Fixed Size Data Structure pattern
  Make the User Worry relationship to,
      [Noblet1998]; 232(12)
flexibility
  See Also extensibility; reusability
  as Abstract Session advantage; 102(7)
  as Big Ball of Mud pattern language goal;
      655(29)

flexibility *(continued)*
as both strength and weakness, in software
development, [Brooks1995]; 660(29)
in memory constraint enforcement, Memory
Overdraft pattern; 229(12)
need for, as SCRUM motivation; 638(28)
as Prototype-Based Object System advantage;
58(5)
as Prototype-Based Object System issue; 59(5)
Report Objects characteristics that result in;
378(17)
role, as Object Recursion advantage; 46(4)
as Secure-Channel Communication pattern
motivation; 342(16)
security policy algorithm encapsulation
support of, Check Point pattern; 308(15)
user control of memory use, Make the User
Worry pattern; 230(12)
flicker
See Also GUIs (graphical user interfaces)
avoiding, Double Buffer use; 500(22)
Fly on the Wall pattern
Author Reads Selection relationship to; 569(25)
Authors' Circle pattern relationship to; 567(25)
(reference description); 570(25)
Flyweight pattern
See Also "Design Patterns"
Prototype-Based Object System relationship
to, [Gamma+1995]; 68(5)
Foote, Brian
"Big Ball of Mud"; 653(29)
forces
abstraction of synchronization policies, Object
Synchronizer; 118(8)
acoustic data, Feature Extraction: A Pattern for
Information Retrieval; 393(18)
attribute validation, Essence; 35(3)
Big Ball of Mud pattern language; 655(29)
change, Big Ball of Mud pattern language;
658(29)
cohesion, in relationship patterns; 75(6)
complexity
Big Ball of Mud pattern language; 657(29)
Big Ball of Mud pattern language,
[Coplien1995]; 663(29)
as Big Ball of Mud pattern language force;
657(29)
in relationship patterns; 75(6)
configurability, Prototype-Based Object
System; 58(5)
consistency, Mutual Friends; 85(6)
Conway's law, Big Ball of Mud pattern
language force, [Coplien1995]; 657(29)
cost
Big Ball of Mud; 661(29)
Big Ball of Mud pattern language; 656(29)
coupling, in relationship patterns; 75(6)

forces *(continued)*
data quantity, Feature Extraction: A Pattern
for Information Retrieval; 393(18)
design quality, memory management
patterns; 223(12)
disintegrating vs. consolidating, balancing, in
Big Ball of Mud pattern language;
674(29)
domain ignorance, as Big Ball of Mud pattern
language force; 656(29)
domain knowledge, as Big Ball of Mud pattern
language force; 656(29)
driving the descent into a Big Ball of Mud;
654(29)
ease of reading and writing, as force in
relationship patterns; 75(6)
efficiency, Abstract Session pattern force; 95(7)
efficiency of design, as force in relationship
patterns; 75(6)
employee turnover, as Big Ball of Mud pattern
language force; 657(29)
encapsulation
Edition; 268(14)
Object Synchronizer pattern force; 113(8)
Proactor; 145(9)
experience, Big Ball of Mud pattern language;
656(29)
explicit representation, as force in relationship
patterns; 75(6)
expressiveness, Object Synchronizer pattern
force; 113(8)
extensibility
Abstract Session; 102(7)
Prototype-Based Object System; 59(5)
in Feature Extraction: A Pattern for
Information Retrieval; 393(18)
flexibility
Abstract Session; 102(7)
Object Recursion; 46(4)
Prototype-Based Object System; 58(5)
fragmentation, memory management
patterns; 223(12)
graphical data, Feature Extraction: A Pattern
for Information Retrieval; 393(18)
hardware and operating system cost, memory
management patterns; 223(12)
immature architecture, growing system;
656(29)
integration, Prototype-Based Object System;
58(5)
lack of infrastructure, as Big Ball of Mud force;
660(29)
local vs. global, memory management
patterns; 223(12)
memory management patterns
effects on each pattern, (table); 224(12)
(table); 223(12)

forces *(continued)*
    modularity
        Object Synchronizer pattern force; 113(8)
        reactive synchronous event dispatching;
            139(9)
    organization, Big Ball of Mud; 661(29)
    pecking order, Big Ball of Mud pattern
        language; 663(29)
    performance
        Abstract Session; 102(7)
        Feature Extraction: A Pattern for
            Information Retrieval; 393(18)
        Proactor; 146(9)
        Proactor pattern force; 134(9)
        reactive synchronous event dispatching;
            139(9)
    polymorphism, Abstract Class; 9(1)
    portability
        Proactor; 145(9)
        Prototype-Based Object System; 59(5)
        reactive synchronous event dispatching;
            139(9)
    predictability, memory management patterns;
        223(12)
    programmer
        discipline, memory management patterns;
            223(12)
        effort, memory management patterns;
            223(12)
        as mind set, Big Ball of Mud pattern
            language force; 656(29)
        as skills, Big Ball of Mud pattern language
            force; 656(29)
    requirements change, as software erosion
        force; 654(29)
    response times, Feature Extraction: A Pattern
        for Information Retrieval; 393(18)
    reusability
        Abstract Class; 10(1)
        Object Synchronizer pattern force; 113(8)
        strong system design; 309(15)
    scale, Big Ball of Mud pattern language; 658(29)
    separation of concerns
        Object Synchronizer; 118(8)
        Proactor; 142(9), 145(9)
    simplicity, Constraint Observers; 388(17)
    simplification, Proactor; 146(9)
    skill, Big Ball of Mud; 661(29)
    Smalltalk lack of type(s), as Generated
        Accessors force; 206(11)
    software systems boundaries, as Big Ball of
        Mud pattern language force,
        [Brand1994]; 658(29)
    space, Feature Extraction: A Pattern for
        Information Retrieval; 393(18)
    status protection, Big Ball of Mud pattern
        language; 663(29)

forces *(continued)*
    structural erosion, system architectures, forces
        that drive; 654(29)
    system architecture erosion, forces that drive;
        654(29)
    territoriality, Big Ball of Mud pattern
        language; 663(29)
    testing cost, memory management patterns;
        223(12)
    time
        Big Ball of Mud pattern language; 655(29)
        Throwaway Code pattern; 666(29)
    type safety, Abstract Session; 102(7)
    usability
        Limited View; 325(15)
        memory management patterns; 223(12)
    visibility, Big Ball of Mud patterns; 657(29)
forms
    pattern reference descriptions, Template; 475(21)
Formula Objects pattern
    Query Objects relationship to; 380(17)
    (reference description); 384(17)
    Report Objects relationship to; 378(17)
formulas
    See Also mathematics
    pattern reference descriptions
        Constraint Observers; 387(17)
        Formula Objects; 384(17)
Forwarder-Receiver pattern
    Secure-Channel Communication pattern
        relationship to; 345(16)
Fowler, Martin
    "Temporal Patterns"; 241(13)
fractal model
    life-cycle perspective as, [Foote+1995]; 674(29)
fragmentation
    dynamic memory allocation impact on; 237(12)
frame of reference
    maintaining, Active Reference; 451(20)
Frame System pattern
    as alternate name for Prototype-Based Object
        System; 53(5)
frame systems
    Prototype-Based Object System derived from,
        [Bobrow+1977]; 67(5)
frameworks
    See Also infrastructure; structure
    Accounts, as Formula Objects known use,
        [Keefer1994]; 386(17)
    ACE
        Abstract Session pattern use, [Schmidt1994];
            107(7)
        as Proactor pattern influence,
            [Schmidt1994]; 147(9)
        Proactor pattern use, [Schmidt1994]; 156(9)
        Proactor Web server sample code based on,
            [Schmidt1994]; 153(9)

frameworks *(continued)*
Any, as Prototype-Based Object System
known use, [Matzel+1996]; 69(5)
black-box, rapid prototyping support,
[Yoder1997]; 200(11)
Caterpillar/NCSA Financial Model
Check Point example; 311(15)
as Limited View known use, [Yoder1997];
328(15)
Report Objects known use, [Yoder1997];
378(17)
Roles example; 314(15)
as Secure Access Layer known use,
[Yoder1997]; 332(15)
Session example, [Yoder1997]; 318(15)
as Session known use, [Yoder1997]; 320(15)
[Yoder1997]; 302(15)
development patterns, Big Ball of Mud pattern
language relationship to,
[Roberts+1998]655; 655(29)
error-handling, in logging errors, Full View
with Errors pattern; 321(15)
ObjectLens, as Session known use; 319(15)
OLE, Abstract Session pattern use,
[Microsoft1993]; 107(7)
pay-per-click, as electronic payment tool;
338(16)
Tool and Materials
as Role Object known use, [Riehle+1995b];
28(2)
as Role Object known use, [Riehle+1995c];
28(2)
User Defined Product
bibliographic references, [Johnson+1998];
297(14)
as known use for History on Association,
[Johnson+1998]; 280(14)
ValueModel, Active Value use,
[ParcPlace1994]]; 83(6)
xkernel, Abstract Session pattern use,
[Hutchinson+1991]; 107(7)
Freedom from Choice pattern
role in solving Big Ball of Mud situations,
[Foote+1995]; 664(29)
FSM (finite state machines)
See finite state machines (FSM)
ftp
login, as Check Point example; 311(15)
UNIX, as Session known use; 320(15)
full
Full View with Errors pattern
vs. Limited View pattern tradeoffs; 332(15)
Limited View relationship to; 327(15)
(reference description); 320(15)
Full View with Exceptions pattern, as
alternate name for Full View with
Errors; 320(15)

full *(continued)*
text scanning, performance problems in digital
library searches; 393(18)
Functionality a la Carte pattern
bibliographic references, [Adams1995];
238(12)
Make the User Worry relationship to,
[Adams1995]; 232(12)
future
values, Temporal Property issues; 250(13)

G
games
Double Buffer use; 500(22)
Global Update use; 494(22)
as Prototype-Based Object System known use,
[Lebling+1979]; 67(5)
gap
component, Template use; 475(21)
between speech and practice, as Big Ball of
Mud investigation target; 654(29)
garbage collection
See Also memory
C++ Counted Body pattern use; 173(10)
pattern reference descriptions, Counted Body;
173(10)
techniques, out-of-memory condition testing
with, Exhaustion Test pattern; 236(12)
Garnet
as Prototype-Based Object System known use,
[Myers+1990]; 69(5)
Gatekeeper
IO Gatekeeper pattern
See Also "An Input and Output Pattern
Language: Lessons from
Telecommunications"
(reference description); 509(23)
GEBOS project
as Role Object known use, [Baumer+1997];
28(2)
GemStone OODB
as Roles known use; 315(15)
Generated Accessors pattern
Artificial Accessors relationship to; 205(11)
(reference description); 206(11)
relationships with other Smalltalk scaffolding
patterns; 218(11)
generation
of code, in pseudo-method rapid prototyping
systems; 214(11)
data group
bibliographic references, [Bodenstein1996];
296(14)
as known use for History on Self,
[Bodenstein1996]; 289(14)
gentrification
software, (term description); 654(29)

geometry
 See Also mathematics; spatial; structures
 inheritance hierarchy relationship to; 169(10)
George Washington is Still Dead pattern
 See Also "An Input and Output Pattern
  Language: Lessons from
  Telecommunications"
 (reference description); 517(23)
global
 data, Big Ball of Mud characterized by; 661(29)
 dictionary, many-to-many relationship
  representation, [Goldberg+1983]; 80(6)
 Global Update pattern
  See Also GUIs (graphical user interface)
  Page Flip relationship to; 501(22)
  (reference description); 493(22)
  Request Update relationship to; 493(22)
 information
  Session pattern management of; 302(15)
  tracking, Session pattern use; 316(15)
  vs. local perspective, balancing; 674(29)
 nature of forces, Big Ball of Mud pattern
  language; 655(29)
 navigation bar, as Landmark known use;
  457(20)
 one-to-one relationships, Active Value pattern;
  82(6)
Glue pattern
 Component Layout relationship to; 475(21)
 (reference description); 466(21)
graceful degradation
 Graceful Degradation pattern, as alternate
  name for Partial Failure; 232(12)
 user control of memory use, Make the User
  Worry pattern; 230(12)
graph
 See Also data, structures
 data structures, broadcasting messages
  through, as Object Recursion known
  use; 49(4)
graphical
 See Also GUIs (graphical user interface);
  multimedia
 components
  Artisan (Automatic Retrieval of Trademark
   Images by Shape ANalysis) project,
   feature extraction use; 410(18)
  content searching issues; 393(18)
  memory size impact of; 227(12)
  positioning, Component Layout pattern;
   473(21)
  similarity searches, feature extraction use;
   409(18)
gratitude
 See Also human relationships
 Thank the Author pattern, (reference
  description); 576(25)

grayed-out menu items
 as Limited View known use, [Yoder+1998];
  328(15)
grouping
 as Glue known use; 469(21)
Groups pattern
 as alternate name for Roles pattern; 312(15)
Guide concurrency OO language
 See Also language(s)
 synchronization counter use,
  [Decouchant+1991]; 123(8)
guidelines
 for pattern writers' workshops, "A Pattern
  Language for Writers' Workshops";
  557(25)
GUIs (graphical user interface)
 display update pattern language; 489(22)
 finite state machine use, [Gamma+1995]; 437(19)
 graphical components organization, Display
  List pattern; 491(22)
 memory size impact of; 227(12)
 pattern reference descriptions
  Clip Requests; 498(22)
  Consolidate Requests; 496(22)
  Display List pattern; 491(22)
  Double Buffer; 500(22)
  Global Update; 493(22)
  Lazy Redraw; 497(22)
  Page Flip; 501(22)
  Painter's Algorithm; 494(22)
  Request Update; 492(22)
 problem/solution pairs, (table); 490(22)
 Shearing Layers in; 680(29)
GUIs (graphical user interfaces)
 "Display Maintenance: A Pattern Language",
  (chapter title); 489(22)
GUIs(graphics user interfaces)
 dynamic creation of, as Limited View pattern
  implementation; 325(15)
 multiple data views, security issues; 320(15)

H
hackers
 See Also security
 shutting out, Check Point pattern; 307(15)
handles
 Handle/Body Hierarchy pattern
  Envelope/Letter relationship to; 182(10)
  (reference description); 179(10)
 Handle/Body pattern, (reference description);
  171(10)
 Session pattern use; 96(7)
 (term description); 171(10)
Hanmer, Robert
 "An Input and Output Pattern Language:
  Lessons from Telecommunications";
  503(23)

hardware
  memory
    importance for different systems, (table);
        227(12)
    (table); 226(12)
Harrison, Tim
  "Proactor"; 133(9)
hash function
  (term description); 368(16)
HCI (human-computer interface)
  "An Input and Output Pattern Language:
      Lessons from Telecommunications",
      (reference description); 503(23)
HCI (human-computer interfaces)
  "An Input and Output Pattern Language:
      Lessons from Telecommunications",
      (chapter title); 503(23)
Help systems
  Office '97, as Roles known use; 316(15)
Hermes/ST
  Object Synchronizer pattern use,
      [Fazzolare+1993]; 129(8)
hidden files
  as Limited View known use; 328(15)
Hiding It under the Bed pattern
  as alternate name for Sweeping It under the
      Rug; 681(29)
Hiding the Cookie Jars pattern
  as alternate name for Limited View; 323(15)
hierarchy
  See Also inheritance; structure
  class, Abstract Class pattern; 5(1)
  inheritance, for algebraic types, Algebraic
      Hierarchy pattern; 187(10)
  pattern reference descriptions, Define and Run
      Presentation; 482(21)
  single, as Abstract Class issue; 10(1)
**"High-Level and Process Patterns from the
    Memory Preservation Society: Patterns
    for Managing Limited Memory"**
  (chapter title); 221(12)
history
  See Also persistence; time
  Historic Mapping pattern
    as alternate name for History on
        Association, [Fowler1997a]; 276(14)
    as alternate name for Temporal Property;
        241(13)
    Edition relationship to; 268(14)
    event use; 267(14)
    history patterns collection use,
        [Fowler1997a]; 265(14)
    Temporal Property relationship to,
        [Fowler1997]; 249(13)
  History on Association pattern
    History on Self relationship to; 286(14)
    (reference description); 276(14)

history *(continued)*
  History on Self pattern
    History on Association relationship to;
        280(14)
    (reference description); 285(14)
    Temporal Property relationship to,
        [Anderson1999]; 250(13)
  History On Tree pattern
    History on Self relationship to; 289(14)
    (reference description); 293(14)
  History pattern, as alternate name for History
      on Association, [Johnson+1998]; 276(14)
  object state, saving, in History on Self; 285(14)
  patterns
    See Also History on Self; Memento Child;
        Posting
    in "A Collection of History Patterns";
        263(14)
Holding Off Hackers pattern
  as alternate name for Check Point pattern;
      307(15)
Homogeneous Addition pattern
  (reference description); 189(10)
honor
  See Also human relationships
  pattern reference descriptions, Show Personal
      Integrity; 602(26)
Hot Spots pattern
  Shearing Layers relationship to,
      [Roberts+1998]; 681(29)
Housecleaning pattern
  as alternate name for Sweeping It under the
      Rug; 681(29)
"How Buildings Learn"
  architectural quality differences, [Brand1994];
      672(29)
  Shearing Layers pattern in, [Brand1994];
      678(29)
HTTP protocol
  Version 1.1, [Mogul1995]; 134(9)
human relationships
  See Also design, methodologies; security;
      software, development methodologies;
      teams
  "A Pattern Language for Writers'
      Workshops"; 557(25)
    (chapter title); 557(25)
  "An Input and Output Pattern Language:
      Lessons from Telecommunications",
      (chapter title); 503(23)
  "Big Ball of Mud", (chapter title); 653(29)
  "Capable, Productive, and Satisfied: Some
      Organizational Patterns for Protecting
      Productive People"; 611(27)
    (chapter title); 611(27)
  "Customer Interaction Patterns", (chapter
      title); 585(26)

human relationships *(continued)*
customers
[Behymer1997]; 588(26)
[Kohn1997]; 588(26)
HCI (human-computer interface), "An Input
and Output Pattern Language: Lessons
from Telecommunications", (reference
description); 503(23)
hierarchy, as Role Object known use,
[Schoenfeld1996]; 28(2)
"Identify the Champion: An Organizational
Pattern Language for Program
Committees", (reference description);
539(24)
pattern language for, "Customer Interaction
Patterns"; 585(26)
pattern reference descriptions
Mind Your Manners; 606(26)
Show Personal Integrity; 602(26)
Take Your Licks; 603(26)
"SCRUM: A Pattern Language for
Hyperproductive Software
Development", (chapter title); 637(28)
security concerns, "Tropyc: a pattern language
for cryptographic object-oriented
software"; 337(16)
software development teams; 611(27)
huMan-Machine Language pattern
as alternate name for MML pattern; 507(23)
Hybrid machine type
Finite State Machine pattern language
relationship to, [Roth1975]; 414(19)
Hybrid pattern
Meally relationship to; 430(19)
Moore relationship to; 432(19)
(reference description); 433(19)
hypermedia
*See Also ACM Hypertext conferences proceedings
and ACM SigWeb - formerly SigLink;
multimedia; relationships; sets; spatial;
time*
electronic payment, pay-per-click tool; 338(16)
navigation, patterns for; 445(20)
pattern languages
[Garrido1997]; 446(20)
[Lyardet1998]; 446(20)
[Rossi1996]; 446(20)
pattern reference descriptions
Active Reference; 451(20)
Basket; 457(20)
Landmark; 455(20)
Navigational Context: Nodes in Context;
448(20)
Navigational Context: Set-Based
Navigation; 446(20)
News; 454(20)
Set-Based Navigation; 446(20)

hypermedia *(continued)*
"Patterns for Designing Navigable
Information Spaces", (chapter title);
445(20)

I
I/O (input/output)
"An Input and Output Pattern Language:
Lessons from Telecommunications"
(chapter title); 503(23)
(reference description); 503(23)
IO Gatekeeper pattern
See Also "An Input and Output Pattern
Language: Lessons from
Telecommunications"
(reference description); 509(23)
IO Triage pattern
See Also "An Input and Output Pattern
Language: Lessons from
Telecommunications"
(reference description); 512(23)
Pseudo-IO pattern, (reference description);
523(23)
Raw IO pattern, (reference description);
533(23)
UNIX AIO, Proactor pattern use; 155(9)
Windows NT, Proactor pattern use; 155(9)
identifiers
semantics, separation from object semantics;
182(10)
identify
Identify Missing Champions pattern,,
(reference description); 550(24)
"Identify the Champion: An Organizational
Pattern Language for Program
Committees", (chapter title); 539(24)
Identify the Champion pattern, (reference
description); 540(24)
Identify the Conflicts pattern, (reference
description); 548(24)
identity
relationship of identifier/object association to;
173(10)
ignorance
domain, as Big Ball of Mud pattern language
force; 656(29)
illegal operations
See Also security
handling
Full View with Errors pattern; 321(15)
Limited View; 323(15)
image data
Artisan (Automatic Retrieval of Trademark
Images by Shape ANalysis) project,
feature extraction use; 410(18)
content searching issues; 393(18)
memory size impact of; 227(12)

image data *(continued)*
similarity searches, feature extraction use; 409(18)

immature
architecture, advantages of in a growing system; 656(29)

immutability
attributes, handling, Essence; 33(3), 35(3)

implementation
inheritance, separation from representation inheritance; 179(10)
interface separation from, in Handle/Body pattern; 171(10)

indexing
See Also information, retrieval; navigation
automatic
as feature extraction function; 393(18)
feature extraction use; 393(18)

indirection
as fundamental computer science concept; 173(10)

inexperience
varieties of, as Big Ball of Mud pattern language force; 657(29)

infinite loops
as Constraint Observers issue; 388(17)

information
See Also databases
appliances, patterns for handling, in "High-Level and Process Patterns from the Memory Preservation Society: Patterns for Managing Limited Memory""; 221(12)
audit, attaching to domain object, in Edition; 267(27)
Information Secrecy pattern
(reference description); 346(16)
Secrecy with Integrity pattern relationship to; 353(16)
Secrecy with Signature pattern relationship to; 355(16)
retrieval
"Creating Reports with Query Objects", (chapter title); 375(17)
in "Feature Extraction: A Pattern for Information Retrieval", (chapter title); 391(18)
spaces, patterns for designing navigable; 445(20)

infrastructure
lack of, as Big Ball of Mud force; 660(29)

inheritance
See Also composition; delegation; relationships; structure
Alexander's view of structure relationship to; 167(10)
composition relationship to, in Layered Organization; 428(19)

inheritance *(continued)*
hierarchy
for algebraic types, Algebraic Hierarchy pattern; 187(10)
geometric structures of; 169(10)
implementation, separation from representation inheritance; 179(10)
multiple
composition use, [Gamma+1995]; 428(19)
not supported by Smalltalk; 211(11)
pattern reference descriptions
Abstract Class; 5(1)
Algebraic Hierarchy; 187(10)
Handle/Body Hierarchy; 179(10)
Promotion Ladder; 192(10)
in Prototype-Based Object System implementation; 62(5)

input
"An Input and Output Pattern Language: Lessons from Telecommunications", (reference description); 503(23)

insertion
feature extraction strategies and issues; 396(18)
as Glue known use; 469(21)

instantiation
pattern reference descriptions, Dynamic State Instantiation; 435(19)

integration
as Prototype-Based Object System advantage; 58(5)

integrity
See Also human relationships
in customer relationships, [Kohn1997]; 603(26)
data, in "Tropyc: a pattern language for cryptographic object-oriented software"; 337(16)
pattern reference descriptions, Show Personal Integrity; 602(26)
state, as Proactor pattern implementation issue; 152(9)

Intelligent Children pattern
Promotion Ladder relationship to; 193(10)

intended use
perspective on, importance for good design; 655(29)

Intention Revealing Selectors pattern
Sweeping It under the Rug relationship to, [Beck1997]; 683(29)

interaction
See Also dynamic
customer guidelines, [McCarthy1995]; 585(26), 589(26)
"Customer Interaction Patterns", (chapter title); 585(26)
customer relationship characteristics; 588(26)
diagram, "Architectural Patterns for Enabling Application Security"; 333(15)

interaction *(continued)*
multimedia, (term description); 461(21)
pattern reference descriptions, It's a
Relationship, Not a Sale; 587(26)
searches, information retrieval demands;
392(18)

interest
as force in deciding whether to use
Reconstruction; 668(29)

interface(s)
Abstract Class relationship to, [Gamma+1995];
13(1)
design, separating navigation design from;
445(20)
Interface on Demand pattern, Active
Reference relationship to,
[Garrido1997]; 454(20)
Interface Organization pattern, (reference
description); 423(19)
pattern reference descriptions, Interface
Organization; 423(19)
Role Object use; 17(2)
separation from implementation, in
Handle/Body pattern; 171(10)

Internet
See Also distributed; WWW (World-Wide
Web)
financial transactions, security issues; 302(15)
IP (Internet Protocol)
package authentication, Sender
Authentication pattern use; 351(16)
package security authentication, Secrecy
with Sender Authentication pattern use;
356(16)

interoperability
See Also usability
abstractions importance for; 330(15)

Interpreter pattern
See Also "Design Patterns"
Composable Query Objects relationship to,
[Gamma+1995]; 382(17), 384(17)
Formula Objects relationship to,
[Gamma+1995]; 386(17)
Object Recursion relationship to,
[Gamma+95]; 50(4)
Prototype-Based Object System relationship
to, [Gamma+1995]; 57(5), 68(5), 69(5)

INTERSOLV
PVCS software configuration management
tool, as Change Log known use;
276(14)

intrusion
detection and handling, Check Point pattern;
307(15)

inversion
performance problems in digital library
searches; 393(18)

Invisible Road Blocks pattern
as alternate name for Limited View; 323(15)

IP (Internet Protocol)
package authentication, Sender
Authentication pattern use; 351(16)
package security authentication, Secrecy with
Sender Authentication pattern use;
356(16)

isolation
See Also separation, of concerns
of blighted software, as decline control
measure; 654(29)
of changing from unchanging system
components; 679(29)
layer, as security tool, Secure Access Layer
pattern; 329(15)
of role/client pairs, in Role Object; 18(2), 20(2)

It's a Relationship, Not a Sale pattern
See Also customers, "Customer Interaction
Patterns"
(reference description); 587(26)

Item pattern
as alternative name for Posting; 280(14)

Iterative-Incremental Development pattern
as alternate name for Piecemeal Growth;
668(29)
in Piecemeal Growth, [Booch1994]; 674(29)

Iterator pattern
See Also "Design Patterns"
Object Recursion relationship to,
[Gamma+95]; 50(4)

J

Java
See Also language(s)
in "A Collection of History Patterns"; 265(14)
Abstract Session implementation; 103(7)
applet authentication/authorization process,
Check Point example; 311(15)
AWT, Abstract Session pattern use,
[Gosling+1996]; 107(7)
BorderLayout manager, as Template known
use; 479(21)
containers, as Glue known use; 469(21)
Essence implementation; 38(3)
exception handling model, as Full View with
Errors known use; 323(15)
GridLayout manager, as Template known use;
479(21)
layout managers, as Component Layout
known use; 474(21)
Object Recursion sample code; 47(4)
PERC Real-Time Java
bibliographic reference, [Nilson1995];
238(12)
Memory Budget use, [Nilson1995]; 229(12)
Principal class, as Roles known use; 316(15)

Java *(continued)*
Prototype-Based Object System sample code, [Taivalsaari1993]; 63(5)
relationship pattern use; 74(6)
Reuters SSL Developers Kit
Check Point example; 312(15)
Secure Access Layer example; 332(15)
as Session known use; 320(15)
'this' variable, as object state; 285(14)
Tropyc source code; 362(16)
URL and URLConnection classes, as Essence known use; 39(3)
jobs
job security routines, *See* Big Ball of Mud pattern
Jobs pattern, as alternate name for Roles pattern; 312(15)
join
as Glue known use; 469(21)
Jordan, Thomas D.
"Proactor"; 133(9)

K
Kay, Alan
"Good ideas don't always scale", Big Ball of Mud pattern language; 658(29)
keep
Keep It Working pattern
(reference description); 675(29)
as system decay counterforce; 654(29)
Keep Your Customer in the Picture pattern, as alternative name for Be Responsive; 597(26)
Keeping It Working pattern
Throwaway Code relationship to; 668(29)
Kerberos
See Also security
low-level issues and techniques
[ICSP1998]; 303(15)
[Schneier1995]; 303(15)
Kevo language
See Also language(s)
Prototype-Based Object System relationship to, [Taivalsaari1993]; 63(5)
key
(term description); 368(16)
Killer Demo pattern
as alternate name for Throwaway Code; 665(29)
Kleenex Code pattern
as alternate name for Throwaway Code; 665(29)
Know the Customer pattern
See Also customers, "Customer Interaction Patterns"
(reference description); 589(26)

Know the Customer's World pattern
as alternate name for Know the Customer; 589(26)
knowledge
modeling, Prototype-Based Object System known use; 67(5)

L
Landmark pattern
(reference description); 455(20)
language(s)
See C++ language; CLOS (Common Lisp Object System); Guide concurrency OO language; Java; Kevo; LOOPS language; MARPL (Multimedia Authoring and Reuse Pattern Language); scripting languages; Self; Smalltalk; UML (Unified Modeling Language)
elements, See
assignment
copying
data types
inheritance
reflection
features, memory size impact of; 227(12)
layering
See Also architecture; structure
isolation, as security tool, Secure Access Layer pattern; 329(15)
Layered Architecture of Information Systems pattern, Secure Access Layer relationship to, [Fowler1997a]; 331(15)
Layered Architecture pattern, as software architecture pattern; 653(29)
Layered Organization pattern, (reference description); 426(19)
Layers pattern, Secure Access Layer relationship to, [Buschmann+1996]; 331(15)
pattern reference descriptions, Layered Organization; 426(19)
Secure Access Layer pattern, in access control handling, insecure applications; 302(15)
in Shearing Layers pattern; 678(29)
lazy
Lazy Optimization pattern
[Auer+1995]; 238(12)
bibliographic references, [Auer+1995]; 238(12)
Memory Performance Assessment relationship to; 238(12)
Lazy Redraw pattern
(reference description); 497(22)
Request Update relationship to; 493(22)
See Also GUIs (graphical user interface)
leadership
See Also champion; shepherding

leadership *(continued)*
Champions Review Papers pattern, (reference description); 544(24)
Moderator Guides the Workshop pattern, (reference description); 565(25)
learning
as Piecemeal Growth force, [Brand1994]; 673(29)
as prototyping goal; 199(11)
legacy data
translating into a relational database format, in "Creating Reports with Query Objects"; 375(17)
lex lexical analyzer
debugging difficulties, compared with Proactor pattern debugging difficulties; 146(9)
libraries
digital, characteristics and information retrieval demands; 392(18)
Lieberman, Henry
response to Alan Kay's scaling remark, Big Ball of Mud pattern language; 658(29)
life-cycle
as Big Ball of Mud pattern language force; 663(29)
development process, Big Ball of Mud pattern language goals for; 655(29)
early stage characteristics; 656(29)
patterns, Big Ball of Mud pattern language relationship to; 655(29)
perspective, in Big Ball of Mud pattern language balancing of forces; 674(29)
lifetime
decoupling from scope, in Concrete Data Type pattern; 186(10)
limitations
See Also forces
memory, patterns for handling, in "High-Level and Process Patterns from the Memory Preservation Society: Patterns for Managing Limited Memory'"'; 221(12)
Limited View pattern
Full View with Errors relationship to; 322(15), 332(15)
(reference description); 323(15)
Roles relationship to; 314(15), 315(15)
Session relationship to; 317(15), 319(15)
Linden, Tanya
"Composing Multimedia Artifacts for Reuse"; 461(21)
link(ing)
Link Attribute pattern, time representation relationship, [Rum+1991]; 251(13)
link-and-embed, as Glue known use; 469(21)
link-based context, (term description); 448(20)

link(ing) *(continued)*
linked-list structures
broadcasting messages through, as Object Recursion known use; 49(4)
distributing behavior throughout, as Object Recursion motivation; 43(4)
semantics, navigation contexts complementation of; 448(20)
LISP
See CLOS (Common Lisp Object System)
listening
active, in pattern writers' workshops; 565(25)
effective, Positive Feedback First pattern; 572(25)
Listen, Listen, Listen pattern
See Also customers, "Customer Interaction Patterns"
Build Trust relationship to; 592(26)
Know the Customer relationship to; 590(26)
(reference description); 595(26)
Live with the Customer pattern
as alternate name for Know the Customer; 589(26)
local
changes, Keep It Working use; 676(29)
vs. global perspective, balancing; 674(29)
Localized Globals pattern
as alternate name for Session pattern; 316(15)
location
reference, Active Reference; 451(20)
significance for telecommunications management; 506(23)
logging errors
in error-handling framework, Full View with Errors pattern; 321(15)
login screens
as Single Access Point pattern; 304(15), 306(15)
LOOPS language
See Also language(s)
Active Value use, [Stefik+1986]; 83(6)
lost in hyperspace
avoiding, Active Reference; 451(20)
Lua
as Prototype-Based Object System known use, [Ierusalimschy+1996]; 67(5)
Lyardet, Fernando
"Patterns for Designing Navigable Information Spaces"; 445(20)

M
MAC (Message Authentication Code)
Sender Authentication pattern use; 350(16)
(term description); 369(16)
machine type
(term description), [Roth1975]; 414(19)
maintenance
needs, as Keep It Working force; 675(29)

maintenance *(continued)*
as Piecemeal Growth force, [Brand1994]; 673(29)

Make Champions Explicit pattern
(reference description); 546(24)

'Make it fast'
(term description), [Beck1997]; 662(29)

'Make it right'
(term description), [Beck1997]; 662(29)

'Make it work'
(term description), [Beck1997]; 662(29)

Make the Punishment Fit the Crime pattern
as alternate name for Check Point pattern; 307(15)

Make the User Worry pattern
(reference description); 230(12)

management patterns
See Also human relationships; manners
Manager pattern, Prototype-Based Object System relationship to, [Sommerlad+1998a]; 62(5)
pattern writers' workshops; 557(25)
software development teams
productive team culture; 611(27)
SCRUM; 637(28)
telecommunications maintenance teams; 503(23)

manners
pattern reference descriptions, Mind Your Manners; 606(26)

Manolescu, Dragos-Anton
"Feature Extraction: A Pattern for Information Retrieval"; 391(18)

many-to-many relationship
See Also relationships
designing, Relationship Object pattern; 78(6)
of transactions, recording in Posting pattern; 281(14), 282(14)

mapping
domain, feature extraction use; 395(18)
from problem space into feature space; 392(18)

MARPL (Multimedia Authoring and Reuse Pattern Language)
See Also language(s)
overview; 464(21)

Marques, Jose Alves
"Object Synchronizer"; 111(8)

mathematics
Algebraic Hierarchy pattern; 187(10)
algebraic types in C++, patterns dealing with; 167(10)
pattern reference descriptions
Abstract Class; 5(1)
Algebraic Hierarchy; 187(10)
Formula Objects; 384(17)
Homogeneous Addition; 189(10)
Non-Hierarchical Addition; 193(10)

mathematics *(continued)*
Promote And Add; 190(10)
Promotion Ladder; 192(10)

MDC (Modification Detection Code)
Information Secrecy pattern use; 348(16)
pay-per-click framework use; 338(16)
Secrecy with Integrity pattern use; 354(16)
(term description); 367(16)

Mealy machine type
characteristics, [Roth1975]; 429(19)
Finite State Machine pattern language relationship to, [Roth1975]; 414(19)
Mealy pattern
Hybrid relationship to; 433(19)
Moore relationship to; 432(19)
(reference description); 428(19)

Mediator pattern
See Also "Design Patterns"
Abstract Session relationship to, [Gamma+1995]; 107(7)
Relationship Object pattern relationship to, [Gamma+1995]; 80(6)

meeting management
"A Pattern Language for Writers' Workshops", (chapter title); 557(25)
effective program committee meetings, patterns for, Identify the Champion pattern language; 539(24)
"Identify the Champion: An Organizational Pattern Language for Program Committees", (chapter title); 539(24)
Meet to Greet pattern, as alternative name for Customer Meetings: Go Early, Stay Late; 600(26)

Memento Child pattern
History on Self relationship to; 289(14)
(reference description); 289(14)

Memento pattern
See Also "Design Patterns"
Edition relationship to; 268(14)
History on Association relationship to; 277(14)
History on Self relationship to, [Gamma+1995]; 289(14)
history patterns collection use, [Gamma+1995]; 265(14)

memory
See Also performance; software, development
conservation, patterns for, in "High-Level and Process Patterns from the Memory Preservation Society: Patterns for Managing Limited Memory""; 221(12)
constraints, importance for different systems, (table); 227(12)
dynamically allocated, Detached Counted Body pattern; 176(10)
garbage collection, C++ Counted Body pattern use; 173(10)

memory *(continued)*
hardware use, (table); 226(12)
limitations, patterns for handling, in "High-
Level and Process Patterns from the
Memory Preservation Society: Patterns
for Managing Limited Memory""";
221(12)
Memory Budget pattern, (reference
description); 228(12)
Memory Overdraft pattern, (reference
description); 229(12)
Memory Performance Assessment pattern,
(reference description); 237(12)
pattern reference descriptions
Captain Oates pattern; 234(12)
Exhaustion Test pattern; 235(12)
Make the User Worry pattern; 230(12)
Memory Budget pattern; 228(12)
Memory Overdraft pattern; 229(12)
Memory Performance Assessment; 237(12)
Partial Failure pattern; 232(12)
Think Small pattern; 225(12)
prioritization of, Captain Oates pattern; 234(12)
Prototype-Based Object System pattern impact
on; 53(5)
reduction
as Secrecy with Signature with Appendix
pattern motivation; 359(16)
as Signature with Appendix pattern
motivation; 358(16)
Message Integrity pattern
Secrecy with Integrity pattern relationship to;
353(16)
in Tropyc pattern language, ((reference
description); 347(16)
messy kitchen phase
as term for change impact on architectural
integrity, [Foote+1995]; 672(29)
meta
See Also abstractions; reflection
meta-reflexive systems, characteristics and
pattern use; 68(5)
Metadata pattern
Limited View relationship to, [Foote+1998];
325(15), 328(15)
Report Objects relationship to,
[Foote+1998b]; 378(17)
Metadata pattern
Shearing Layers role, [Foote+1998b]; 680(29)
methodology
conference paper reviewing, "Identify the
Champion: An Organizational Pattern
Language for Program Committees",
(chapter title); 539(24)
design, as issues and limitations, as Prototype-
Based Object System motivation; 54(5)
software development

methodology *(continued)*
"Big Ball of Mud", (chapter title); 653(29)
"Capable, Productive, and Satisfied: Some
Organizational Patterns for Protecting
Productive People", (chapter title);
611(27)
"SCRUM: A Pattern Language for
Hyperproductive Software
Development", (chapter title); 637(28)
UML
finite state machine representation,
[UML1999]; 420(19)
[Fowler+1997]; 115(8)
inheritance symbol, Finite State Machine
pattern use, [UML1999]; 414(19)
Multimedia Authoring and Reuse Pattern
Language use; 466(21)
Object Synchronizer pattern; 115(8)
in Proactor pattern; 142(9)
stereotype use, in Temporal Property;
245(13)
[UML1999]; 438(19)
writing development, "A Pattern Language
for Writers' Workshops", (chapter title);
557(25)
midlife erosion loss
as term for change impact on architectural
integrity, [Foote1988]; 672(29)
mind, Take Your Licks relationship to; 604(26)
Mind Your Manners pattern
See Also customers, "Customer Interaction
Patterns"
(reference description); 606(26)
Mind Your Own Business pattern
See Also "An Input and Output Pattern
Language: Lessons from
Telecommunications"
(reference description); 511(23)
programmer mind set, as Big Ball of Mud
pattern language force; 656(29)
mining
for customers, [Kohn1997]; 597(26)
pattern reference descriptions
Know the Customer; 589(26)
Listen, Listen, Listen; 595(26)
patterns, emergent structure in; 585(26)
MML (huMan-Machine Language) pattern
(reference description); 507(23)
modeling
See Also abstraction(s)
change over time, in "Temporal Patterns";
241(13)
dynamic behavior, "Finite State Machine
Patterns"; 413(19)
dynamically changing objects, Prototype-
Based Object System pattern support of;
53(5)

modeling *(continued)*

knowledge, Prototype-Based Object System known use; 67(5)

pattern reference descriptions, Role Object; 15(2)

real-world, vs. program abstractions; 186(10)

of relationships, OO programming deficiencies; 73(6)

relationships amount events, states, and behavior of an entity, in Basic FSM; 418(19)

role; 21(2)

time patterns role in; 296(14)

Moderator Guides the Workshop pattern

(reference description); 565(25)

modification avoidance

as Information Secrecy pattern motivation; 347(16)

Modification Detection Code

See MDC (Modification Detection Code)

modular growth

as positive application of Piecemeal Growth; 668(29)

modularity

as Object Synchronizer pattern force; 113(8)

as reactive synchronous event dispatching advantage; 139(9)

monitoring

memory resource use, in Memory Budget pattern; 228(12)

system operations, telephone network requirement for; 505(23)

monitors

[Dijkstra1968]; 112(8)

Object Synchronizer comparison; 112(8)

Moore machine type

characteristics, [Roth1975]; 430(19)

Finite State Machine pattern language relationship to, [Roth1975]; 414(19)

Moore pattern

Hybrid relationship to; 433(19)

Meally relationship to; 430(19)

(reference description); 430(19)

morale

as Sweeping It under the Rug force; 682(29)

MUDS (Multi-User Dungeons)

as Prototype-Based Object System known use, [Bartle1985]; 67(5)

multimedia

See Also hypermedia; spatial; time

artifact creation and use, idioms for, (table); 462(21)

"Composing Multimedia Artifacts for Reuse", (chapter title); 461(21)

content searching issues; 393(18)

development and delivery issues, [Haskins1994]; 461(21)

multimedia *(continued)*

environment, (term description); 461(21)

feature extraction use; 409(18)

Multimedia Authoring and Reuse Pattern Language (MARPL), overview; 464(21)

pattern reference descriptions

Components Layout; 471(21)

in "Composing Multimedia Artifacts for Reuse"; 461(21)

Define and Run Presentation; 482(21)

Glue; 466(21)

Synchronize Channels; 485(21)

Template; 475(21)

reuse, patterns for, in "Composing Multimedia Artifacts for Reuse"; 461(21)

reuse patterns

[German+1999]; 466(21)

[Linden+1999]; 466(21)

[Rossi+1996]; 466(21)

[Tidwell1998]; 466(21)

multiple object synchronization policies

Object Synchronizer pattern use; 114(8)

multithreading

lack of OS support for, as reactive synchronous event dispatching disadvantage; 139(9)

synchronous, advantages and disadvantages; 135(9)

multiway indexing

[Buford1994]; 486(21)

museums

spatial navigation references; 453(20)

mutex

See Also concurrency

as object concurrency policy, [Lavender+1996]; 125(8)

Mutual Friends pattern

See Also HTML

in "Basic Relationship Patterns"; 73(6)

"Basic Relationship Patterns", (reference description); 84(6)

Relationship As Attribute relationship to; 78(6)

MVC (Model-View-Controller) architecture

changing objects, Display List pattern; 491(22)

[Krasner1988]; 491(22)

N

name/value relationship

as fundamental computer science concept; 173(10)

namespaces

Namespace pattern, as alternate name for Session pattern; 316(15)

separate, as Abstract Session issue; 102(7)

naming conventions

lack of, Big Ball of Mud characterized by; 661(29)

navigation

See Also GUIs (graphical user interfaces); hypermedia; information, retrieval; queries

context, (term description); 447(20)

hypermedia, patterns for; 445(20)

Navigational Context patterns
Nodes in Context, (reference description);
448(20)
Set-Based Navigation, (reference
description); 446(20)

pattern reference descriptions
Active Reference; 451(20)
Basket; 457(20)
Landmark; 455(20)
Navigational Context: Nodes in Context;
448(20)
Navigational Context: Set-Based
Navigation; 446(20)
News; 454(20)
Nodes in Context; 448(20)
Set-Based Navigation; 446(20)
"Patterns for Designing Navigable Information
Spaces", (chapter title); 445(20)

separation of context from; 450(20)

need fullfilment

as Big Ball of Mud pattern strength; 658(29)

News pattern

(reference description); 454(20)

NewtonScript

as Prototype-Based Object System known use,
[Smith1995]; 67(5)

Nierstrasz, Oscar

"Identify the Champion: An Organizational
Pattern Language for Program
Committees"; 539(24)

Noble, James

"Basic Relationship Patterns"; 73(6)
"High-Level and Process Patterns from the
Memory Preservation Society: Patterns
for Managing Limited Memory";
221(12)
"Prototype-Based Object System"; 53(5)

Nodes in Context pattern

(reference description); 448(20)

Non-Hierarchical Addition pattern

(reference description); 193(10)

non-portability

as synchronous multithreading disadvantage;
136(9)

non-repudiation

of sender, in "Tropyc: a pattern language for
cryptographic object-oriented
software"; 337(16)

(term description); 367(16)

Notified View pattern

as alternate name for Full View with Errors;
320(15)

NT (Windows)

as Limited View known use; 328(15)

Proactor pattern use; 155(9)

Null Object pattern

Essence relationship to, [Woolf1997]; 33(3)

Limited View relationship to, [Woolf1997];
324(15), 327(15)

Object Recursion relationship to, [PLoPD3];
50(4)

Secure-Channel Communication pattern
relationship to; 345(16)

O

object(s)

See Also class(es); inheritance

client context, patterns for, in "Role Object";
15(2)

creating, in Virtual Constructor pattern;
185(10)

distributed request processing, Object
Recursion pattern; 41(4)

Object Concurrency Control pattern, as
alternate name for Object Synchronizer;
111(8)

Object Concurrency pattern, Object
Synchronizer pattern relationship to,
[Silva1999]; 129(8)

Object Recovery pattern
Object Synchronizer pattern relationship to,
[Silva1997]; 129(8), 130(8)
Object Synchronizer pattern use; 121(8)
[Silva+1997]; 121(8)

"Object Recursion", (chapter title); 41(4)

Object Recursion pattern, in "Object
Recursion"; 41(4)

Object Serialization pattern, as alternate name
for Object Synchronizer; 111(8)

"Object Synchronizer", (chapter title); 111(8)

Object Synchronizer pattern, (reference
description); 111(8)

Object System pattern, as alternate name
for Prototype-Based Object System;
53(5)

ObjectLens framework, as Session known use;
319(15)

"Prototype-Based Object System", (chapter
title); 53(5)

real-world, vs. program abstractions; 186(10)

representation, runtime modification of,
Prototype-Based Object System pattern;
53(5)

"Role Object", (chapter title); 15(2)

Role Object pattern; 15(2)

state, saving, in History on Self; 285(14)

Obliq

as Prototype-Based Object System known use,
[Cardelli1994]; 67(5)

Observer pattern
See Also "Design Patterns"
Active Value pattern relationship to,
     [Gamma+1995]; 84(6)
Change Log relationship to, [Gamma+1995];
     276(14)
Composable Query Objects relationship to,
     [Gamma+1995]; 382(17), 384(17)
Constraint Observers relationship to,
     [Gamma+1995]; 387(17), 389(17)
Proactor pattern relationship to,
     [Gamma+1995]; 157(9)
Relationship Object pattern relationship to,
     [Gamma+1995]; 80(6)
Secure-Channel Communication pattern
     relationship to; 345(16)
obsolescence
as Reconstruction force; 684(29)
occlusion
of graphical components, data structure
     management, Display List pattern;
     491(22)
pattern reference descriptions
     Clip Requests; 498(22)
     Painter's Algorithm; 494(22)
ODMG-93 object-oriented database
Mutual Friends pattern, [Graham+1997]; 88(6)
Office Alarms pattern
See Also "An Input and Output Pattern
     Language: Lessons from
     Telecommunications"
(reference description); 529(23)
OLE (Object Linking and Embedding)
     framework
Abstract Session pattern use, [Microsoft1993];
     107(7)
OMT
bibliographic references, [Rum+1991];
     262(13)
time representation relationship, [Rum+1991];
     251(13)
one-step recursion
as Object Recursion known use; 48(4)
one-to-many relationship
designing, Collection Object pattern; 80(6)
one-to-one relationship
designing, Relationship As Attribute pattern;
     76(6)
one-way function
hash, (term description); 367(16)
one-way functions
with trapdoors, (term description); 367(16)
Only as Strong as the Weakest Link pattern
as alternate name for Secure Access Layer;
     329(15)
Open Review pattern
(reference description); 559(25)

operating system
environments, event dispatching selection
     choices, (table); 151(9)
Operational Calendar pattern
events in, [Fowler 1997b]; 266(14)
operations
binary, in Promote And Add pattern;
     191(10)
optimization
See Also performance
pattern reference descriptions, Global Update;
     493(22)
performance
     Lazy Optimization pattern, [Auer+1995];
          238(12)
     in memory constraint handling,
          [Blank+1995]; 237(12)
     in memory constraint handling, Memory
          Performance Assessment; 237(12)
     Optimize the Right Place pattern,
          [Auer+1995]; 238(12)
Optimize the Right Place pattern
[Auer+1995]; 238(12)
bibliographic references, [Auer+1995];
     238(12)
Memory Performance Assessment
     relationship to; 238(12)
options
restricted
     handling, Full View with Errors pattern;
          321(15)
     handling, Limited View pattern; 323(15)
ordering
of graphical components, Display List pattern;
     491(22)
partial, multimedia artifacts, Define and Run
     Presentation use; 482(21)
pattern reference descriptions, Painter's
     Algorithm; 494(22)
organization
See Also structure
as Reconstruction force; 684(29)
organizational patterns
See Also human relationships; software,
     development methodologies
"Capable, Productive, and Satisfied: Some
     Organizational Patterns for Protecting
     Productive People"; 611(27)
"Customer Interaction Patterns", (reference
     description); 585(26)
"Identify the Champion: An Organizational
     Pattern Language for Program
     Committees"
     (chapter title); 539(24)
     (reference description); 539(24)
Layered Organization pattern, (reference
     description); 426(19)

organizational patterns *(continued)*
"SCRUM: A Pattern Language for
Hyperproductive Software
Development", (reference description);
637(28)
Set-Based Navigation; 446(20)
orientation
maintaining, Active Reference; 451(20)
OS/360 project use
bibliographic references, [Brooks1975];
238(12)
Memory Budget pattern, [Brooks1975];
229(12)
Memory Overdraft pattern, [Brooks1975];
230(12)
Out-Of-Memory Testing pattern
as alternate name for Exhaustion Test; 235(12)
Outdoor Room pattern
Sitting in a Circle pattern relationship to,
[Alexander+1997]; 567(25)
output
See Also I/O (input/output)
"An Input and Output Pattern Language:
Lessons from Telecommunications",
(reference description); 503(23)
finite state machine
activation of, Hybrid; 433(19)
activation of, Meally; 429(19)
activation of, Moore; 431(19)
overhead
as synchronous multithreading disadvantage;
136(9)
Owner-Driven Transitions pattern
Basic FSM relationship to, [Dyson+1998];
420(19)
Encapsulated State relationship to,
[Dyson+1998]; 434(19)
Finite State Machine pattern language
relationship to
[Dyson+1998]; 416(19)
(figure); 415(19)
State-Driven Transitions relationship to;
423(19)

P
Page Flip pattern
See Also GUIs (graphical user interface)
Global Update relationship to; 494(22)
(reference description); 501(22)
Painter's Algorithm pattern
See Also GUIs (graphical user interface)
Display List relationship to; 492(22)
(reference description); 494(22)
pair programming
benefits of; 665(29)
role in solving Big Ball of Mud situations,
[Foote+1995]; 664(29)

palmtops
memory limitations, patterns for handling, in
"High-Level and Process Patterns from
the Memory Preservation Society:
Patterns for Managing Limited
Memory""; 221(12)
PaperChampion pattern
Identify the Champion relationship to,
[Coplien1998]; 542(24)
parallelism
in hardware, reactive synchronous event
dispatching disadvantage; 139(9)
parent
change of, recording, in Memento Child;
289(14)
partial
ordering, multimedia artifacts, Define and
Run Presentation use; 482(21)
Partial Failure pattern, (reference description);
232(12)
Partial Order Glue pattern, Glue relationship
to; 471(21)
Pass-Through Host pattern
Single Access Point pattern use, [Lea1997];
306(15)
passwords
as security issue; 301(15)
pattern languages
"An Input and Output Pattern Language:
Lessons from Telecommunications"
(reference description); 503(23); 503(23)
Big Ball of Mud; 655(29)
"C++ Idioms Patterns"; 167(10)
"Customer Interaction Patterns"; 585(26)
database reporting, "Creating Reports with
Query Objects"; 375(17)
"Display Maintenance: A Pattern Language";
489(22)
finite state machine; 413(19)
hypermedia
[Garrido1997]; 446(20)
[Lyardet1998]; 446(20)
[Rossi1996]; 446(20)
Identify the Champion; 539(24)
Multimedia Authoring and Reuse Pattern
Language (MARPL), overview; 464(21)
"A Pattern Language for Writers'
Workshops", (chapter title); 557(25)
SCRUM; 637(28)
(term description); 167(10)
(footnote); 539(24)
Tropyc; 337(16)
writers' workshops, "A Pattern Language for
Writers' Workshops"; 557(25)
pattern(s)
See Also Alexander, Christopher; structure
format

pattern(s) *(continued)*
Alexander; 222(12), 559(25)
Alexander, description of the form; 579(25)
[Meszaros+1998]; 585(26)
Portland; 489(22)
Portland, modified; 76(6)
life-cycle, Big Ball of Mud pattern language
relationship to; 655(29)
mining, emergent structure in; 585(26)
"Patterns for Designing Navigable
Information Spaces", (chapter title);
445(20)
(reference description); 5(1)
pay-per-click framework
as electronic payment tool; 338(16)
PC (program committees)
task management patterns; 539(24)
pecking order
as Big Ball of Mud pattern language force;
663(29)
peer review
See Also human relationships; reviewing
technical papers
"Identify the Champion: An Organizational
Pattern Language for Program
Committees"; 539(24)
review form design; 546(24)
Pereira, João
"Object Synchronizer"; 111(8)
performance
See Also efficiency; optimization; speed
as Abstract Session advantage; 102(7)
as Constraint Observers issue; 388(17)
as dynamic query issue; 380(17)
human
"Capable, Productive, and Satisfied: Some
Organizational Patterns for Protecting
Productive People", (chapter title);
611(27)
"SCRUM: A Pattern Language for
Hyperproductive Software
Development", (chapter title); 637(28)
in information retrieval systems; 393(18)
memory constraint impact on; 229(12)
of optimization
Lazy Optimization pattern, [Auer+1995];
238(12)
Optimize the Right Place pattern,
[Auer+1995]; 238(12)
optimization, in memory constraint handling,
Memory Performance Assessment;
237(12)
as Painter's Algorithm issue; 495(22)
pattern reference descriptions
Clip Requests; 498(22)
Consolidate Requests; 496(22)
Double Buffer; 500(22)

performance *(continued)*
Global Update; 493(22)
Lazy Redraw; 497(22)
Page Flip; 501(22)
as Proactor pattern advantage; 146(9)
as Proactor pattern force; 134(9)
as Prototype-Based Object System issue; 59(5)
as reactive synchronous event dispatching
advantage; 139(9)
as Secrecy with Signature with Appendix
pattern motivation; 359(16)
separation of concerns impact on, in Request
Update; 493(22)
as Signature with Appendix pattern
motivation; 358(16)
in virtual environment, display update issues;
489(22)
Perfunctory (routine) Meetings pattern
as alternative name for Customer Meetings:
Go Early, Stay Late; 600(26)
Permanent Prototype pattern
as alternate name for Throwaway Code;
665(29)
permissions
See Also security
role-related, Roles pattern; 313(15)
persistence
See Also history
quick and dirty code, as a source of Big Ball of
Mud; 654(29)
store, hypermedia use; 457(20)
Throwaway Code issue, scalability as an issue
with; 667(29)
as Throwaway Code problem; 667(29)
perspective
on purpose, importance for good design;
655(29)
pervasiveness
as Big Ball of Mud pattern language force
characteristics; 655(29)
Peter Principle of Programming
system architecture impact, [Coplien1995];
663(29)
PGP (Pretty Good Privacy)
See Also security
PGP (Pretty Good Privacy)
Secrecy with Signature pattern use; 358(16)
Signature pattern use; 353(16)
Secrecy with Signature pattern use; 358(16)
Secrecy with Signature with Appendix pattern
use; 361(16)
Signature pattern use; 353(16)
Piaget, Jean
bibliographic references, [Piaget1946]; 297(14)
pattern language of time, [Piaget1946]; 264(14)
space-time relationships; 296(14)
analysis; 285(14)

pictures
  as multimedia component; 463(21)
Piecemeal Growth pattern
  (reference description); 668(29)
  role in solving Big Ball of Mud situations;
    664(29)
  Throwaway Code relationship to; 668(29)
Pipeline pattern
  as software architecture pattern; 653(29)
Plan pattern
  Temporal Property relationship to,
    [Fowler1997]; 250(13)
planning
  Limited View incorporation importance; 327(15)
  memory use, as memory constraint tool,
    Memory Budget pattern; 228(12)
  Secure Access Layer incorporation
    importance; 331(15)
  Session incorporation importance; 319(15)
  Temporal Property issues; 250(13)
PLoP online registration code
  1995 version, as example of Throwaway Code
    persistence; 667(29)
  1998 version
    Check Point example; 312(15)
    Limited View known use, [Yoder+1998];
      328(15)
    Roles known use; 316(15)
    Secure Access Layer use, [Yoder+1998];
      330(15), 332(15)
    Session known use, [Yoder+1998]; 320(15)
pointers
  untyped, Session pattern use; 96(7)
policies
  object concurrency; 125(8)
  object synchronization, Object Synchronizer
    pattern use; 114(8)
  security, incorporating into software
    architecture design; 301(15)
politeness
  See Also human relationships
  pattern reference descriptions, Mind Your
    Manners; 606(26)
polymorphism
  See Also class(es); inheritance
  Abstract Class pattern use; 5(1)
  addition operations, Promote And Add
    pattern; 191(10)
  in distributed request processing, Object
    Recursion pattern; 41(4)
  pattern reference descriptions, Abstract Class;
    5(1)
Pool of Light pattern
  Sitting in a Circle pattern relationship to,
    [Alexander+1997]; 567(25)
portability
  See Also interoperability; reusability

portability *(continued)*
  of application, as Proactor pattern advantage;
    145(9)
  as Prototype-Based Object System advantage;
    59(5)
  as reactive synchronous event dispatching
    advantage; 139(9)
Portinari Project
  as Nodes in Context known use,
    [Lanzelotte1993]; 451(20)
positive
  Positive Closure pattern, (reference
    description); 576(25)
  Positive Feedback First pattern, (reference
    description); 572(25)
post
  Post pattern
    bibliographic references, [Fowler1996]; 30(2)
    Role Object relationship to, [Fowler1996];
      29(2)
  Posting pattern
    (reference description); 280(14)
    Temporal Property relationship to,
      [Anderson1999]; 250(13)
  Posting Rule pattern, Posting relationship to,
    [Fowler1997a]; 281(14), 284(14)
Potemkin Village pattern
  as alternate name for Sweeping It under the
    Rug; 681(29)
preemption
  policy, as Proactor pattern implementation
    issue; 152(9)
preferences
  See Also UI (user interfaces)
  user control of memory use, Make the User
    Worry pattern; 230(12)
premature
  architecture, disadvantages of in a growing
    system; 656(29)
  production, ways to prevent; 666(29)
presentations
  See Also champion; SCRUM (from Rugby term
    scrummage)
  Define and Run Presentation pattern
    Component Layout relationship to; 475(21)
    Synchronous Channels relationship to;
      486(21)
  multimedia
    Define and Run Presentation; 482(21)
    spatial association, Components Layout;
      471(21)
  writers' workshops, Suggestions for
    Improvement; 574(25)
preserving
  values
    of complex variables, in a History object;
      277(14)

preserving *(continued)*
>   of simple variables, in a change log; 271(14)

Pretty Face pattern
>   as alternate name for Sweeping It under the Rug; 681(29)

prioritization
>   *See Also* ordering
>   as Big Ball of Mud solution; 661(29)
>   IO Triage pattern, (reference description); 512(23)
>   of memory demands, Captain Oates pattern; 234(12)
>   by pattern author, Author Reads Selection pattern; 570(25)
>   as telecommunications management task; 506(23)

privacy
>   *See Also* security
>   PGP (Pretty Good Privacy), Secrecy with Signature with Appendix pattern use; 361(16)
>   Privacy-Enhanced Mail pattern
>>   Message Integrity pattern relationship to; 349(16)
>>   Secrecy with Integrity pattern relationship to; 355(16)
>>   Secrecy with Signature pattern relationship to; 358(16)
>>   Secrecy with Signature with Appendix pattern relationship to; 361(16)
>>   Signature pattern relationship to; 353(16)

proactive
>   asynchronous event dispatching, advantages and disadvantages; 139(9)

Proactor pattern
>   "Proactor", (chapter title); 133(9)
>   (reference description); 133(9)

Problem-Oriented Team pattern
>   (reference description); 618(27)

"Proceedings of the Memory Preservation Society"
>   bibliographic references, [Noble+1998]; 222(12), 238(12)

process(es)
>   pattern writers workshop, list of patterns; 558(25)
>   technical paper reviewing, patterns for, Identify the Champion pattern language; 539(24)

Product Trader pattern
>   bibliographic references, [Baumer+1998]; 30(2)
>   Role Object relationship to, [Baumer+1998]; 21(2), 29(2)
>   specification object use, [Baumer+1998]; 22(2)

production
>   premature, ways to prevent; 666(29)

production *(continued)*
>   Production Potential pattern, (reference description); 612(27)

profiles
>   Profiles pattern, as alternate name for Roles pattern; 312(15)
>   security, access control use, Roles pattern; 312(15)

program committees (PC)
>   task management patterns; 539(24)

programming
>   *See Also* language(s), elements; software, development
>   code reviews, role in solving Big Ball of Mud situations, [Foote+1995]; 664(29)
>   eXtreme Programming (XP)
>>   change adaptability, [Beck2000]; 673(29)
>>   feedback use, [Beck2000]; 674(29)
>>   role in solving Big Ball of Mud situations, [Beck2000]; 664(29)
>>   role in solving Big Ball of Mud situations, [Coplien1995]; 664(29)
>>   as spike solutions, [Beck2000]; 666(29)
>   in pairs
>>   benefits of; 665(29)
>>   role in solving Big Ball of Mud situations, [Foote+1995]; 664(29)
>   Peter Principle of Programming, system architecture impact, [Coplien1995]; 663(29)
>   programmer attitudes, memory constraint handling, Think Small pattern; 225(12)

Programming-by-Difference pattern
>   Sweeping It under the Rug relationship to, [Foote+1998]; 683(29)

Prograph
>   bibliographic references, [MacNeil+1995]; 238(12)
>   Memory Overdraft pattern, [MacNeil+1995]; 230(12)

project
>   management; 663(29)
>   Projects pattern, as alternate name for Roles pattern; 312(15)

Promote And Add pattern
>   (reference description); 190(10)

promotion
>   *See Also* data types
>   pattern reference descriptions
>>   Promote And Add; 190(10)
>>   Promotion Ladder; 192(10)
>>   Type Promotion; 195(10)
>   Promotion Ladder pattern
>>   Envelope/Letter relationship to; 184(10)
>>   (reference description); 192(10)

properties
>   *See Also* attributes

properties *(continued)*
audiovisual, pattern reference descriptions, Components Layout; 471(21)
Properties pattern, Limited View relationship to, [Foote+1998]; 325(15)
Property List pattern
Prototype-Based Object System relationship to, [Riehle1997]; 56(5), 68(5)
Prototype-Based Object System relationship to, [Sommerlad+1998b]; 56(5), 68(5)
Role Object relationship to, [Riehle1997]; 23(2)
prototyping
See Also "Big Ball of Mud"; change, management; design; eXtreme Programming (XP); SCRUM (from Rugby term scrummage); software, development
based object systems, [Noble+1999]; 68(5)
as domain knowledge capture tool; 666(29)
Prototype pattern
See Also "Design Patterns"
Prototype-Based Object System relationship to, [Gamma+1995]; 56(5), 69(5)
Prototype Phase pattern
Big Ball of Mud pattern language relationship to, [Coplien+1995]; 655(29)
Big Ball of Mud pattern language relationship to, [Foote+1995]; 655(29)
role in solving Big Ball of Mud situations, [Foote+1995]; 664(29)
tasks appropriate to, [Foote+1995]; 663(29)
Prototype-Based Object System pattern
in "Prototype-Based Object System", (chapter title); 53(5)
(reference description); 53(5)
when to use; 56(5)
Prototype-Based System pattern, as alternate name for Prototype-Based Object System; 53(5)
Prototype-Instance System pattern, as alternate name for Prototype-Based Object System; 53(5)
rapid, patterns for, in "Smalltalk Scaffolding Patterns"; 199(11)
Prototyping or Expansion pattern
Sweeping It under the Rug relationship to, [Foote+1995]; 683(29)
Proxy pattern
See Also "Design Patterns"
Abstract Class relationship to, [Gamma+1995]; 13(1)
Abstract Session use, [Gamma+1995]; 102(7)
Object Recursion relationship to, [Gamma+95]; 50(4)
Object Synchronizer pattern relationship to, [Gamma+1995]; 130(8)

Proxy pattern *(continued)*
as related pattern to, Feature Extraction pattern; 410(18)
Secure-Channel Communication pattern relationship to; 345(16)
Pryce, Nat
"Abstract Session: An Object Structural Pattern"; 95(7)
Pseudo-IO pattern
See Also "An Input and Output Pattern Language: Lessons from Telecommunications" (reference description); 523(23)
Psion Series 5
memory constraints; 228(12)
public-key
See Also PGP (Pretty Good Privacy); security (term description); 368(16)
publish-and-subscribe
See link-and-embed
Pulse pattern
(reference description); 623(27)
purpose
perspective on, importance for good design; 655(29)
PVCS software configuration management tool
as Change Log known use; 276(14)
Pyarali, Irfan
"Proactor"; 133(9)

Q
QOCA
Active Value use
[Gamma+1995]; 84(6)
[Helm+1992]; 84(6)
quality
assurance, in out-of-memory conditions, Exhaustion Test pattern; 235(12)
Quality Without A Name, as pattern writers' workshop goal; 562(25)
as Template multimedia pattern dimension; 465(21)
quantity
significance for telecommunications management; 506(23)
quarantine
See Also encapsulation; isolation
of blighted software, as decline control measure; 654(29)
Quarantine pattern, as alternate name for Sweeping It under the Rug; 681(29)
queries
See Also databases; navigation
composition of, Composable Query Objects; 381(17)
"Creating Reports with Query Objects", (chapter title); 375(17)

queries *(continued)*
  database reporting patterns, in "Creating
      Reports with Query Objects"; 375(17)
  pattern reference descriptions
    Composable Query Objects; 381(17)
    Query Objects; 378(17)
  processing, feature extraction strategies and
      issues; 396(18)
  query by example, similarity search as;
      393(18)
  Query Objects pattern
    (reference description); 378(17)
    Report Objects relationship to; 378(17)
  runtime creation, in Query Objects; 379(17)
quick
  quick and dirty code
    persistence, as source of Big Ball of Mud;
        654(29)
    persistence, PLoP registration code as
        example of; 667(29)
    Quick Hack pattern, as alternate name for
        Throwaway Code; 665(29)
Quonset huts
  See Throwaway Code pattern
QWAN (Quality Without A Name)
  as pattern writers' workshop goal; 562(25)

R

race conditions
  See Also deadlock
  avoiding, in Request Update implementation;
      493(22)
Rainy Day pattern
  bibliographic references, [MacNeil+1995];
      238(12)
  [MacNeil+1995]; 230(12)
Range pattern
  Temporal Property relationship to,
      [Fowler1997]; 249(13)
rate of change
  differences in, abstraction evolution aided by;
      654(29)
Raw IO pattern
  See Also "An Input and Output Pattern
      Language: Lessons from
      Telecommunications"
  (reference description); 533(23)
Raymond, Eric
  cathedral and bazaar, software development
      team relationship to, [Raymond1998];
      612(27)
reactive
  Reactor pattern
    Proactor pattern relationship to,
        [Schmidt1995]; 157(9)
    reactive synchronous event handling,
        [Schmidt1995]; 137(9)

reactive *(continued)*
  synchronous event dispatching, as
      concurrency strategy, advantages and
      disadvantages; 137(9)
reading
  Author Reads Selection pattern
    Authors' Circle pattern relationship to;
        567(25)
    (reference description); 569(25)
  code readability, as pair programming side
      effect; 665(29)
  ease, as force in relationship patterns; 75(6)
  Reading Just before Reviewing pattern,
      (reference description); 568(25)
real-world
  representation, vs. program abstractions;
      186(10)
Reconstruction pattern
  (reference description); 684(29)
  Throwaway Code relationship to; 668(29)
recovery
  Object Recovery pattern, Object Synchronizer
      pattern relationship to, [Silva1997];
      130(8)
  policies, [Weihl1993]; 130(8)
recursion
  in distributed request processing, Object
      Recursion pattern; 41(4)
  "Object Recursion", (chapter title); 41(4)
  one-step, as Object Recursion known use; 48(4)
  in recording of composite history, in History
      on Tree; 293(14)
  Recursive Delegation pattern, as alternate
      name for Object Recursion; 41(4)
  two-step, as Object Recursion known use;
      48(4)
redrawing
  pattern reference descriptions
    Double Buffer; 500(22)
    Lazy Redraw; 497(22)
    Page Flip; 501(22)
refactoring
  as iterative development process, Big Ball of
      Mud pattern language goals for; 655(29)
  Piecemeal Growth use; 672(29)
  Shearing Layers solution use of; 679(29)
  of system architectures, as counterforce to
      system decay; 654(29)
  testing importance for success of; 678(29)
Refactoring Browser
  BrowserEnvironments, as Query Objects
      known use, [Roberts1999]; 381(17)
reference counting
  [Cargill1996]; 179(10)
  Counted Body pattern; 173(10)
  Detached Counted Body pattern; 176(10)
  [Koenig1995]; 179(10)

reference counting *(continued)*
pattern reference descriptions
Counted Body; 173(10)
Detached Counted Body; 176(10)
reflection
See Also Java; language(s), elements; Smalltalk
architectures, rapid prototyping support,
[Foote1988]; 200(11)
meta-reflexive systems, characteristics and
pattern use; 68(5)
Prototype-Based Object System
implementation use; 61(5)
Prototype-Based Object System pattern use of;
53(5)
Reflection pattern
Prototype-Based Object System relationship
to, [Buschmann+1996]; 57(5), 68(5), 69(5)
Secure-Channel Communication pattern
relationship to; 345(16)
weak, in Envelope/Letter pattern; 183(10)
regular expressions
performance problems in digital library
searches; 393(18)
Rehabilitation pattern
as alternate name for Sweeping It under the
Rug; 681(29)
Reified Variable pattern
as alternate name, for Active Value; 82(6)
relationships
See Also history; human relationships;
hypertext; sets; spatial; time
Active Value pattern; 73(6)
"Basic Relationship Patterns", (chapter title);
73(6)
change, tracking, in Temporal Property;
242(13)
change over time, Temporal Association
pattern; 250(13)
among classes; 179(10)
Collection Object pattern; 73(6)
among finite state machine patterns; 414(19)
known uses
[Booch+1994]; 74(6)
[Rumbaugh+1991]; 74(6)
many-to-many
Relationship Object pattern; 78(6)
of transactions, recording in Posting pattern;
281(14), 282(14)
Mutual Friends pattern; 73(6)
one-to-many, Collection Object pattern; 80(6)
one-to-one, Relationship As Attribute pattern;
76(6)
among patterns
defining, as pattern language development
task; 585(26)
exploring at a pattern writers' workshop;
262(13)

relationships *(continued)*
patterns for, in "Basic Relationship Patterns";
73(6)
Relationship As Attribute pattern; 73(6)
Mutual Friends pattern relationship to; 87(6)
(reference description); 76(6)
Relationship Object pattern relationship to;
80(6)
Relationship Object pattern; 73(6)
Active Value pattern relationship to; 84(6)
Collection Object relationship to; 82(6)
(reference description); 78(6)
Relationship As Attribute relationship to;
78(6)
Relationship Objects, [Fowler1997]; 80(6)
relationship pattern summary, (table); 74(6)
among the relationship patterns; 74(6)
role-privilege, ACL management,
[Silberschatz+1997]; 314(15)
spatial
Components Layout, (reference
description); 471(21)
in multimedia presentations, Components
Layout; 471(21)
temporal, as Synchronize Channels
multimedia pattern dimension; 466(21)
two-way, Mutual Friends pattern; 82(6)
whole-as-sum-of-parts, preserving, in History
on Tree; 293(14)
reliability
See Also security
as critical telecommunications attribute; 504(23)
as Keep It Working force; 676(29)
removing
objects, preserving history of, in Memento
Child; 290(14)
repair
as Piecemeal Growth force
[Alexander1988]; 672(29)
[Brand1994]; 672(29)
repeatability
as Check Point design consideration; 309(15)
reporting
database reporting patterns, in "Creating
Reports with Query Objects"; 375(17)
pattern reference descriptions
Query Objects; 378(17)
Report Objects; 376(17)
Report Objects pattern, (reference description);
376(17)
reports
"Creating Reports with Query Objects",
(chapter title); 375(17)
representation
See Also modeling
explicit
as force in relationship patterns; 75(6)

representation *(continued)*
Collection Object pattern use; 81(6)
Relationship Object pattern use; 79(6)
inheritance, separation from implementation
inheritance; 179(10)
object, runtime modification of, Prototype-
Based Object System pattern; 53(5)
pattern reference descriptions, Abstract Class;
5(1)
real-world, vs. program abstractions; 186(10)
of time
adding to models, Temporal Association
compared with Temporal Property;
250(13)
adding to models, Temporal Property
pattern; 241(13)
Request Update pattern
See Also GUIs (graphical user interface)
Clip Requests relationship to; 499(22)
Consolidate Requests relationship to; 497(22)
Display List relationship to; 492(22)
Global Update relationship to; 494(22)
Lazy Redraw relationship to; 498(22)
(reference description); 492(22)
resource
limitation, memory management patterns;
221(12)
management, as Proactor pattern
implementation issue; 152(9)
resources
as force in deciding whether to use
Reconstruction; 668(29)
respect
pattern reference descriptions, Mind Your
Manners; 606(26)
response
to attempted security violation, as Check Point
design consideration; 309(15)
issues, in information retrieval systems;
393(18)
pattern reference descriptions, Be Responsive;
597(26)
reusability
See Also extensibility; interoperability;
portability
Abstract Class pattern use, [Auer1995]; 14(1)
of algorithms, as Abstract Class advantage;
10(1)
authoring tool weaknesses; 463(21)
"Composing Multimedia Artifacts for Reuse",
(chapter title); 461(21)
multimedia
dimensions, (figure); 464(21)
patterns for, in "Composing Multimedia
Artifacts for Reuse"; 461(21)
as Object Synchronizer pattern force; 113(8)
pattern reference descriptions

reusability *(continued)*
Layered Organization; 426(19)
Template; 475(21)
as Secure-Channel Communication pattern
motivation; 342(16)
of security module, advantages for strong
system design; 309(15)
as Template multimedia pattern dimension;
465(21)
Reveal All and Handle Exceptions pattern
as alternate name for Full View with Errors;
320(15)
reviewing
See Also peer review
"A Pattern Language for Writers'
Workshops", (chapter title); 557(25)
code, role in solving Big Ball of Mud
situations, [Foote+1995]; 664(29)
Experts Review Papers pattern, (reference
description); 543(24)
"Identify the Champion: An Organizational
Pattern Language for Program
Committees", (chapter title); 539(24)
Open Review pattern, (reference description);
559(25)
patterns, Reading Just before Reviewing
pattern, (reference description);
568(25)
technical papers
patterns for, Identify the Champion pattern
language; 539(24)
review form design; 546(24)
Rialto suite
Repository, as Essence known use; 39(3)
as Snapshot pattern known use; 260(13)
as Temporal Association known use; 254(13)
temporal pattern use; 247(13)
Riehle, Dirk
"Role Object"; 15(2)
Rising, Linda
"Customer Interaction Patterns"; 585(26)
risks
of rewriting big balls of mud, as Keep It
Working force; 675(29)
roles
See Also security; views
champion, in conference paper evaluation
process; 539(24)
in client context, Role Object pattern; 15(2)
Decorator pattern use, [Kristensen+1996];
28(2)
design variations, [Fowler1997]; 18(2)
flexibility, as Object Recursion advantage;
46(4)
pattern reference descriptions, Role Object;
15(2)
"Role Object", (chapter title); 15(2)

roles *(continued)*
Role Object pattern, (reference description);
15(2)
Roles pattern
characteristics and implementation,
[Fowler1997b]; 314(15)
Check Point relationship to; 308(15), 311(15)
"Dealing with Roles", [Fowler1997b];
315(15)
Full View with Errors relationship to,
[Cunningham1995]; 322(15)
Limited View relationship to, [Woolf1997];
324(15), 327(15)
(reference description); 312(15)
Session relationship to; 317(15)
Single Access Point relationship to; 305(15)
user privilege association with, in secure
applications; 302(15)
Rossi, Gustavo
"Patterns for Designing Navigable
Information Spaces"; 445(20)
Round Pegs for Round Holes pattern
(reference description); 621(27)
RTTI (runtime type identification
in Promote And Add pattern; 191(10)
Rubira, Cecilia
"Tropyc: a pattern language for cryptographic
object-oriented software"; 337(16)
Rungs of a Dual Hierarchy pattern
Handle/Body Hierarchy relationship to,
[Martin1997]; 182(10)
runtime
See Also configurable; dynamic
database reporting patterns, in "Creating
Reports with Query Objects"; 375(17)
efficiency, vs. type safety, in Session pattern
implementation; 97(7)
information modification, Smalltalk facilities;
202(11)
modification of objects, Prototype-Based
Object System pattern; 53(5)
pattern reference descriptions, Query Objects;
378(17)
query creation, in Query Objects; 379(17)
retyping, patterns that address; 182(10)

S

safety
Authors' Circle pattern, (reference
description); 567(25)
Safe Setting pattern
Open Review relationship to; 560(25)
(reference description); 560(25)
Workshop Comprises Authors relationship
to; 563(25)
type
as Abstract Session advantage; 102(7)

safety *(continued)*
in Abstract Session pattern; 95(7)
vs. runtime efficiency, in Session pattern
implementation; 97(7)
Salton, Gerald
feature extraction use in SMART system;
408(18)
SAM (spatial access method)
feature extraction issues; 396(18)
Sandwich Feedback pattern
as alternate name for Positive Closure pattern;
576(25)
scaffolding
See Also structure
"Smalltalk Scaffolding Patterns", (chapter
title); 199(11)
scalability
as Big Ball of Mud pattern language force;
658(29)
object-oriented abstractions; 15(2)
as Throwaway Code issue; 667(29)
scheduling
conflicts, as reactive synchronous event
dispatching disadvantage; 139(9)
predicates, Object Synchronizer pattern
relationship, [McHale+1991]; 129(8)
Proactor pattern disadvantages; 146(9)
Schmidt, Douglas C.
"Proactor"; 133(9)
Schmooze! pattern
as alternative name for Customer Meetings:
Go Early, Stay Late; 600(26)
Schwabe, Daniel
"Patterns for Designing Navigable
Information Spaces"; 445(20)
Schwaber, Ken
"SCRUM: A Pattern Language for
Hyperproductive Software
Development"; 637(28)
scope
See Also identifiers
decoupling from lifetime, in Concrete Data
Type pattern; 186(10)
as fundamental computer science concept;
173(10)
scripting
See Also language(s)
languages
See Also language(s)
as limitations, as Prototype-Based Object
System motivation; 54(5)
Scripting pattern, as alternate name for
Throwaway Code; 665(29)
scriptlet, as multimedia component;
463(21)
SCRUM (from Rugby term scrummage)
See Also eXtreme Programming (XP)

SCRUM (from Rugby term scrummage) *(continued)*
   "SCRUM: A Pattern Language for
      Hyperproductive Software
      Development", (chapter title); 637(28)
   SCRUM Meetings pattern, (reference
      description); 644(28)
searching
   See Also navigation
   algorithms, feature extraction compared with;
      392(18)
   similarity, as feature extraction function; 394(18)
secrecy
   See Also security
   authentication with, as Secrecy with Sender
      Authentication pattern motivation;
      355(16)
   Secrecy with Integrity pattern
      (reference description); 353(16)
      related patterns, Information Secrecy
         pattern; 354(16)
      related patterns, Message Integrity pattern;
         354(16)
      related patterns, Privacy-Enhanced Mail
         pattern; 355(16)
   Secrecy with Sender Authentication pattern, in
      Tropyc pattern language, (reference
      description); 355(16)
   Secrecy with Signature pattern, in Tropyc
      pattern language, (reference
      description); 355(16)
   Secrecy with Signature with Appendix pattern
      (reference description); 358(16)
      in Tropyc pattern language, (reference
         description); 358(16)
   secret-key, (term description); 368(16)
security
   See Also access control; AFS (Andrew File
      System); attacks; authentication;
      authorization; confidentiality;
      cryptography; electronic commerce;
      encryption; errors; firewalls; hackers;
      human relationships; illegal operations;
      Kerberos; permissions; PGP (Pretty
      Good Privacy); privacy; public-key;
      reliability; roles; secrecy; validation
   architectural patterns, catalog, (table); 303(15)
   "Architectural Patterns for Enabling
      Application Security", (chapter title);
      301(15)
   checks, deferring, as Check Point design
      consideration; 309(15)
   low-level issues and techniques
      [ICSP1998]; 303(15)
      [Schneier1995]; 303(15)
   pattern reference descriptions
      "Architectural Patterns for Enabling
         Application Security"; 301(15)

security *(continued)*
   Check Point pattern; 307(15)
   Encapsulated State; 434(19)
   Limited View pattern; 323(15)
   Secure Access Layer pattern; 329(15)
   Session pattern; 316(15)
   Single Access Point pattern; 303(15)
   policies, incorporating into software
      architecture design; 301(15)
   profiles, access control use, Roles pattern;
      312(15)
   role-related access control, Roles pattern;
      312(15)
   Secure Access Layer pattern
      in access control handling, insecure
         applications; 302(15)
      Check Point relationship to; 311(15)
      (reference description); 329(15)
      Roles relationship to; 314(15)
   Secure Shell, as Secure Access Layer known
      use, [SSH1998]; 331(15)
   Secure Sockets Layer (SSL)
      as Secure Access Layer,; 330(15)
      as Secure Access Layer, known use,
         [SSL1998]; 331(15)
   Secure-Channel Communication pattern,
      (reference description); 342(16)
   Security Access Layer pattern, Secure-Channel
      Communication pattern relationship to;
      345(16)
   "Tropyc: a pattern language for cryptographic
      object-oriented software", (chapter
      title); 337(16)
   violation handling, encapsulation, secure
      applications; 302(15)
   violations, detection and handling, Check
      Point pattern; 307(15)
Selective Changes pattern
   (reference description); 577(25)
Selector Synthesis pattern
   (reference description); 217(11)
   relationships with other Smalltalk scaffolding
      patterns; 218(11)
self
   Self Delegation pattern, Mutual Friends
      pattern relationship to, [Beck1997];
      87(6)
   Self language
      See Also language(s)
      Prototype-Based Object System relationship
         to, [Ungar+1991]; 63(5)
   self problem, avoiding, in Prototype-Based
      Object System implementation,
      [Lieberman1986]; 62(5)
   'self' variable, as object state; 285(14)
semantics
   See Also modeling

semantics *(continued)*
of assignment in C++, Counted Body pattern
handling; 173(10)
built-in data types vs. user-defined data types;
196(10)
of copying, in Counted Body pattern; 176(10)
image, feature extraction use; 409(18)
links, navigation contexts complementation of;
448(20)
relationships, amount finite state machine
patterns; 414(19)
separation, of representation from
implementation hierarchies; 182(10)
of Smalltalk, Counted Body pattern
approximation of; 175(10)
semaphores
See Also concurrency
[Dijkstra1968]; 112(8)
Object Synchronizer comparison; 112(8)
sender
authentication
(term description); 367(16)
in "Tropyc: a pattern language for
cryptographic object-oriented
software"; 337(16)
non-repudiation, in "Tropyc: a pattern
language for cryptographic object-
oriented software"; 337(16)
Sender Authentication pattern, (reference
description); 349(16)
separation
See Also encapsulation; isolation
of behavior from state transitions, in Layered
Organization; 427(19)
of concerns
as Proactor pattern advantage; 145(9)
in Request Update; 493(22)
in software development process; 617(27)
of concurrency strategy from I/O model, as
Proactor pattern advantage; 142(9)
failure, as Captain Oates pattern issue; 235(12)
of inheritance hierarchies, in Handle/Body
Hierarchy pattern; 179(10)
of interfaces from implementation, in
Handle/Body pattern; 171(10)
of navigation design from interface design;
445(20)
of navigational objects from context; 450(20)
pattern reference descriptions, Layered
Organization; 426(19)
of scope from lifetime, in Concrete Data Type
pattern; 186(10)
of synchronization
from clients, as Object Synchronizer pattern
advantage; 118(8)
from functionality code, as Object
Synchronizer pattern advantage; 118(8)

Sequence of Sitting Spaces pattern
Sitting in a Circle pattern relationship to,
[Alexander+1997]; 567(25)
sequencing
multimedia artifacts, Define and Run
Presentation use; 482(21)
serialization
algorithms, as Object Recursion known use;
49(4)
Serializer pattern
bibliographic references, [Riehle+1997];
297(14)
Change Log relationship to, [Riehle+1997];
276(14)
Prototype-Based Object System relationship
to, [Riehle+1998]; 68(5)
servers
See Also architecture; clients; distributed;
Internet
client, sessions, patterns for, in "Abstract
Session: An Object Structural Pattern";
95(7)
secure web, Single Access Point pattern use;
306(15)
Web
asynchronous, Proactor pattern use; 140(9)
performance requirements, [Hu+1997]; 134(9)
performance requirements, [Hu+1998];
134(9)
Service Access Point (SAP) pattern
as alternate name for Abstract Session; 95(7)
Service Handler pattern
as alternate name for Abstract Session; 95(7)
sessions
See Also encapsulation; security
Abstract Session pattern
"Abstract Session: An Object Structural
Pattern", (chapter title); 95(7)
(reference description); 95(7)
client-server, patterns for, in "Abstract
Session: An Object Structural Pattern";
95(7)
Session pattern
Check Point relationship to; 311(15)
Limited View relationship to, [Woolf1997];
324(15), 327(15)
(reference description); 316(15)
relationship to Sessions, [Lea1995]; 319(15)
Roles relationship to; 315(15)
Single Access Point relationship to; 304(15),
305(15)
Sessions pattern
Abstract Session relationship to. [Lea1995];
107(7)
implementation issues; 96(7)
Session relationship to, [Lea1995]; 319(15)
three-phase protocol, [Lea1995]; 96(7)

Set-Based Navigation pattern
(reference description); 446(20)
setup patterns
for a pattern writers workshop, (list); 558(25)
Shadowing pattern
as alternate name for Know the Customer;
589(26)
shantytown
solutions; 664(29)
Shantytown pattern
as alternate name for Big Ball of Mud; 658(29)
shared
address space, Session pattern use; 316(15)
objects, Object Synchronizer pattern use;
111(8)
Sharon, Yonat
"SCRUM: A Pattern Language for
Hyperproductive Software
Development"; 637(28)
Shearing Layers pattern
(reference description); 678(29)
role in solving Big Ball of Mud situations;
664(29)
system abstraction development impact;
654(29)
shepherding
See Also leadership
in pattern writers' workshop process;
565(25)
(term description); 543(24)
shopping cart
as Basket known use; 457(20)
Show Changes pattern
as alternate name for George Washington is
Still Dead pattern; 517(23)
Show Personal Integrity pattern
See Also customers, "Customer Interaction
Patterns"
Be Responsive relationship to; 598(26)
(reference description); 602(26)
Shut Up and Listen pattern
See Also "An Input and Output Pattern
Language: Lessons from
Telecommunications"
(reference description); 522(23)
Siberski, Wolf
"Role Object"; 15(2)
signatures
See Also security
authentication, as Signature pattern
motivation; 351(16)
digital, Signature pattern; 353(16)
files, performance problems in digital library
searches; 393(18)
Secrecy with Signature pattern, in Tropyc
pattern language, (reference
description); 355(16)

signatures *(continued)*
Secrecy with Signature with Appendix
pattern, in Tropyc pattern language,
(reference description); 358(16)
Signature pattern
Secrecy with Signature pattern relationship
to; 355(16)
in Tropyc pattern language, (reference
description); 351(16), 358(16)
signed applets
Signature with Appendix pattern use; 359(16)
Silva, António Rito
"Object Synchronizer"; 111(8)
similarity searches
digital library use; 393(18)
feature extraction use of; 394(18)
in image data, feature extraction use; 409(18)
simplicity
as Constraint Observers advantage; 388(17)
difficulty in attaining, [Coplien1995]; 663(29)
of initial development, as Big Ball of Mud
pattern strength; 658(29)
simplification
of application synchronization, as Proactor
pattern advantage; 146(9)
Single Access Point pattern
Check Point relationship to; 309(15), 311(15)
(reference description); 303(15)
Session relationship to; 319(15)
Singleton pattern
See Also "Design Patterns"
Proactor pattern relationship to,
[Gamma+1995]; 157(9)
Session relationship to, [Gamma+1995];
316(15), 319(15)
Single Access Point relationship to,
[Gamma+1995]; 306(15)
site boundaries
in software systems, as Big Ball of Mud pattern
language force, [Brand1994]; 658(29)
sitting
Different Chairs pattern, Sitting in a Circle
pattern relationship to,
[Alexander+1997]; 567(25)
Sitting Circle pattern, Sitting in a Circle pattern
relationship to, [Alexander+1997];
567(25)
Sitting in a Circle pattern, (reference
description); 566(25)
skill
as Big Ball of Mud force; 661(29)
skill(s)
as Big Ball of Mud patterns force; 657(29)
low requirements, as Big Ball of Mud pattern
strength; 658(29)
programmer, as Big Ball of Mud pattern
language force; 657(29)

skills
  programmer, as Big Ball of Mud pattern
      language force; 656(29)
small computer systems
  memory limitations, patterns for handling, in
      "High-Level and Process Patterns from
      the Memory Preservation Society:
      Patterns for Managing Limited
      Memory""; 221(12)
Smalltalk
  See Also language(s)
  Abstract Class sample code; 11(1)
  concepts and facilities that support rapid
      prototyping; 201(11)
  database reporting patterns, in "Creating
      Reports with Query Objects"; 375(17)
  in history patterns collection use; 265(14)
  Mutual Friends use, [Goldberg+1983]; 87(6)
  rapid prototyping support; 200(11)
  recursion, as as Object Recursion known use;
      49(4)
  relationship pattern use; 74(6)
  'self' variable, as object state; 285(14)
  semantics approximation, in Counted Body
      pattern; 175(10)
  "Smalltalk Scaffolding Patterns", (chapter
      title); 199(11)
  VisualWorks
      as Session known use; 320(15)
      Single Access Point pattern use,
          [ObjectShare1995]; 306(15)
smart cards
  memory limitations, patterns for handling, in
      "High-Level and Process Patterns from
      the Memory Preservation Society:
      Patterns for Managing Limited
      Memory""; 221(12)
SMART system
  as feature extraction known use; 408(18)
Snapshot pattern
  bibliographic references, [Carlson1998b]; 262(13)
      [Carlson1998b]; 261(13)
  (reference description); 255(13)
  time-based pattern relationships
      [Anderson1999]; 261(13)
      [Lange1998]; 261(13)
sniffing
  See Also security
  Secure Access Layer protection from; 330(15)
Sockets
  UNIX, [Stevens1990]; 97(7)
software
  architecture
      application security enablement; 301(15)
      "Big Ball of Mud", (chapter title); 653(29)
      patterns that characterize,
          [Buschmann+1996]; 653(29)

software *(continued)*
      patterns that characterize, [Garlan+1993];
          653(29)
      patterns that characterize, [Meszaros1997];
          653(29)
      patterns that characterize, [Shaw1996];
          653(29)
      predominant, Big Ball of Mud; 653(29)
      Tropyc pattern language; 337(16)
  design issues, "Big Ball of Mud", (chapter
      title); 653(29)
  development; 663(29)
      See Also human relationships; organization
          management
      "Big Ball of Mud", (chapter title); 653(29)
      "Capable, Productive, and Satisfied:
          Some Organizational Patterns for
          Protecting Productive People";
          611(27)
      "Capable, Productive, and Satisfied: Some
          Organizational Patterns for Protecting
          Productive People", (chapter title);
          611(27)
      patterns for rapid prototyping, in "Smalltalk
          Scaffolding Patterns"; 199(11)
      rapid prototyping role; 199(11)
      "SCRUM: A Pattern Language for
          Hyperproductive Software
          Development", (chapter title); 637(28)
      SCRUM as a pattern language for
          managing; 637(29)
  gentrification, (term description); 654(29)
  release timing, customer impact and role;
      627(27)
  Software Tectonics pattern, Big Ball of Mud
      pattern language relationship to,
      [Foote+1996]; 655(29)
Software Tectonics pattern
  iterative incremental evolution in,
      [Foote+1996]; 674(29)
  Shearing Layers relationship to, [Foote+1996];
      681(29)
SortedPaperList pattern
  Identify the Champion relationship to,
      [Coplien1998]; 542(24)
sound
  as multimedia component; 462(21)
source code control systems
  history patterns collection relationship to,
      history patterns collection relationship
      to; 265(14)
spaghetti
  code, solutions; 664(29)
  Spaghetti Code pattern, as alternate name for
      Big Ball of Mud; 658(29)
  topology, avoiding in hypermedia design;
      456(20)

spatial
See Also navigation
access, SAM feature extraction issues; 396(18)
information, patterns for designing navigable; 445(20)
properties, of inheritance hierarchy; 169(10)
reference, as location orientation; 453(20)
relationships, Components Layout, (reference description); 471(21)
specifications
attribute
bibliographic reference, [Gilb1988]; 238(12)
as Memory Budget tool, [Gilb1988]; 229(12)
features that impact memory size; 227(12)
objects
[Evans1997]; 22(2)
[Riehle1995]; 22(2)
Role Object use; 22(2)
spike solutions
(term description), [Beck2000]; 666(29)
spreadsheets
limitations, as Prototype-Based Object System motivation; 54(5)
Sprint pattern
(reference description); 640(28)
stability
as Shearing Layers force; 678(29)
stages
of domain understanding, system development approaches; 655(29)
standardization
as Prototype-Based Object System issue; 60(5)
Start Over pattern
as alternate name for Rehabilitation; 684(29)
state
See Also finite state machines (FSM)
change
associating with causative event, in Edition; 268(14)
event role in; 266(14)
modeling, "Finite State Machine Patterns"; 413(19)
client, Abstract Session pattern encapsulation of; 95(7)
dependent objects, implementing, in rapid prototyping systems; 217(11)
encapsulation, Encapsulated State pattern, (reference description); 434(19)
finite state machine activation by
Hybrid; 433(19)
Moore; 431(19)
"Finite State Machine Patterns", (chapter title); 413(19)
implementation and representation inheritance separation issues; 179(10)
integrity, as Proactor pattern implementation issue; 152(9)

state *(continued)*
language relationship to, Finite State Machine pattern, (figure); 415(19)
in Memento pattern, [Fowler1997a]; 265(14)
object, saving, in History on Self pattern; 285(14)
pattern reference descriptions, State-Driven Transitions; 421(19)
separation from events and actions, in Basic FSM; 418(19)
State Action Mapper pattern, Selector Synthesis relationship to, [Palfinger1997]; 218(11)
State Object pattern
Finite State Machine pattern language relationship to, [Dyson+1998]; 414(19), 416(19)
Finite State Machine pattern language relationship to, (figure); 415(19)
State pattern
See Also "Design Patterns"
Algebraic Hierarchy relationship to, [Gamma+1995]; 189(10)
Envelope/Letter relationship to, [Gamma+1995]; 184(10)
Finite State Machine pattern language relationship to, [Gamma+1995]; 414(19)
Handle/Body Hierarchy relationship to, [Gamma+1995]; 182(10)
Limited View relationship to, [Gamma+1995]; 325(15)
Secure-Channel Communication pattern relationship to; 345(16)
Selector Synthesis relationship to, [Gamma+1995]; 217(11), 218(11)
Session relationship to, [Gamma+1995]; 317(15), 319(15)
State-Driven Transitions pattern
Basic FSM relationship to; 420(19)
Interface Organization relationship to; 426(19)
(reference description); 421(19)
Statechart patterns, Basic FSM relationship to, [Yacoub+1998]; 420(19)
statecharts, [Yacoub+1998]; 413(19)
Static State Instantiation pattern
Dynamic State Instantiation relationship to; 437(19)
Finite State Machine pattern language relationship to, [Martin1995]; 416(19)
temporal changes in, in "A Collection of History Patterns"; 263(14)
transition diagram, in finite state machine; 416(19)
transitions, decoupling from entity behavior; 427(19)

statecharts
    Statechart patterns, Basic FSM relationship to,
        [Yacoub+1998]; 420(19)
    [Yacoub+1998]; 413(19)
Static State Instantiation pattern
    Dynamic State Instantiation relationship to;
        437(19)
    Finite State Machine pattern language
        relationship to
        (figure); 415(19)
        [Martin1995]; 416(19)
status protection
    as Big Ball of Mud pattern language force;
        663(29)
Stay Within the Lines pattern
    as alternative name for Be Aware of
        Boundaries; 605(26)
stereotype
    UML
        not applicable to Temporal Association;
            253(13)
        in Temporal Property; 245(13)
storage
    in information retrieval systems; 393(18)
    persistent, hypermedia use; 457(20)
strategies
    for software decay reversal, Keeping It
        Working pattern; 654(29)
Strategy pattern
    See Also "Design Patterns"
    Check Point pattern relationship to,
        [Gamma+1995]; 308(15)
    Check Point relationship to; 311(15)
    Feature Extraction relationship to; 410(18)
    Limited View relationship to, [Gamma+1995];
        324(15), 325(15), 327(15)
    Object Synchronizer pattern relationship to,
        [Gamma+1995]; 130(8)
    Query Objects relationship to, [Gamma+1995];
        379(17), 380(17)
    Roles relationship to; 315(15)
    Secure-Channel Communication pattern
        relationship to; 345(16)
    Virtual Constructor relationship to,
        [Gamma+1995]; 185(10)
strengths
    of shantytowns; 658(29)
String A Wire pattern
    See Also "An Input and Output Pattern
        Language: Lessons from
        Telecommunications"
    (reference description); 531(23)
structure
    Alexander view of, relationship to OO
        inheritance hierarchy; 167(10)
    Authors' Circle pattern, (reference
        description); 567(25)

structure *(continued)*
    C++ idioms pattern language, (figure); 169(10)
    changes, Prototype-Based Object System
        handling; 62(5)
    as Components Layout multimedia pattern
        dimension; 465(21)
    dynamic evolution of, [Alexander1988];
        680(29)
    erosion, system architectures, forces that drive;
        654(29)
    functionality relationship to; 662(29)
    as Glue multimedia pattern dimension;
        464(21)
    haphazard, Big Ball of Mud characterized by;
        661(29)
    orderly change relationship to; 674(29)
    pattern reference descriptions
        Be Aware of Boundaries; 605(26)
        Components Layout; 471(21)
        Glue; 466(21)
        Set-Based Navigation; 446(20)
        Template; 475(21)
    Sitting in a Circle pattern, (reference
        description); 566(25)
    "Smalltalk Scaffolding Patterns", (chapter
        title); 199(11)
    Team Space pattern; 627(27)
    as Template multimedia pattern dimension;
        465(21)
Stymfal, Greg
    "An Input and Output Pattern Language:
        Lessons from Telecommunications";
        503(23)
subtypes
    See Also data types
    object creation issues, in Virtual Constructor
        pattern; 185(10)
Suggestions for Improvement pattern
    (reference description); 573(25)
suicide
    Captain Oates pattern; 234(12)
Sunny Place pattern
    Sitting in a Circle pattern relationship to,
        [Alexander+1997]; 567(25)
Sutherland, Jeff
    "SCRUM: A Pattern Language for
        Hyperproductive Software
        Development"; 637(28)
SVD (Singular Value Decomposition)
    feature extraction use with; 409(18)
swamps
    draining, as Big Ball of Mud pattern language
        goal; 655(29)
Sweeping It under the Rug pattern
    (reference description); 681(29)
    as software blight control tool; 654(29)
    Throwaway Code relationship to; 668(29)

symmetric key
(term description); 368(16)
Symmetrical Relationship pattern
as alternate name, for Mutual Friends; 84(6)
synchronization
See Also concurrency; time
counter, Guide use, [Decouchant+1991]; 123(8)
multithreading, advantages and
disadvantages; 135(9)
object, Object Synchronizer pattern use; 111(8)
"Object Synchronizer", (chapter title); 111(8)
pattern reference descriptions, Synchronize
Channels; 485(21)
Single Access Point pattern enforcement,
[Lea1997]; 306(15)
as Synchronize Channels multimedia pattern
dimension; 466(21)
Synchronize Channels pattern
Component Layout relationship to; 475(21)
(reference description); 485(21)
Template relationship to; 479(21)
synthesis
Selector Synthesis pattern, (reference
description); 217(11)

T

Take Your Licks pattern
See Also customers, "Customer Interaction
Patterns"
(reference description); 603(26)
Taylor, Paul
"A Pattern Language for Writers'
Workshops"; 611(27)
**Teacher's MATE (Multimedia-Assisted
Teaching Environment)**
[Cybulski+1997]; 461(21)
teams
See Also human relationships
building, in pattern writers' workshops;
564(25)
corporate, "Customer Interaction Patterns";
585(26)
development, in SCRUM process; 639(28)
pattern language for, "Customer Interaction
Patterns"; 585(26)
pattern writers' workshops, "A Pattern
Language for Writers' Workshops";
557(25)
Problem-Oriented Team pattern, (reference
description); 618(27)
program committee, "Identify the Champion:
An Organizational Pattern Language
for Program Committees"; 539(24)
software development, "Capable, Productive,
and Satisfied: Some Organizational
Patterns for Protecting Productive
People"; 611(27)

teams *(continued)*
Team Space pattern, (reference description);
627(27)
telecommunications
"An Input and Output Pattern Language:
Lessons from Telecommunications"
(chapter title); 503(23)
(reference description); 503(23)
Objectiva Architecture, as history patterns
collection known use; 265(14)
telecommuting
human relationship issues, Customer
Meetings: Go Early, Stay Late; 600(26)
telephone switching systems
"An Input and Output Pattern Language:
Lessons from Telecommunications",
(reference description); 503(23)
Telnet
UNIX, as Session known use; 320(15)
templates
in C++, (term description); 168(10)
Template Class pattern
Abstract Class relationship to; 10(1), 13(1)
as alternate name for Abstract Class.
[Woolf1997]; 5(1)
Template pattern
Component Layout relationship to;
475(21)
(reference description); 475(21)
(term description); 475(21)
temporal
See Also time
Temporal Association pattern
[Carlson+1998]; 297(14)
History on Association relationship to,
[Carlson+1998]; 277(14), 280(14)
(reference description); 250(13)
Temporal Property relationship to,
[Fowler1997]; 249(13)
"Temporal Patterns", (chapter title); 241(13)
Temporal Property pattern
(reference description); 241(13)
Temporal Association relationship to,
[Lange1998]; 254(13)
territoriality
as Big Ball of Mud pattern language force;
663(29)
testing
eXtreme Programming (XP) reliance on;
677(29)
Keep It Working reliance on
[Bach1994]; 677(29)
[Marick1995]; 677(29)
out-of-memory conditions, Exhaustion Test
pattern; 235(12)
Test Small pattern, as alternate name for
Exhaustion Test; 235(12)

text
  as multimedia component, formats and
     applications; 462(21)
  text editors, as Full View with Errors known
     use; 322(15)
Thank the Author pattern
  Author Reads Selection relationship to; 570(25)
  Authors' Circle pattern relationship to; 567(25)
  (reference description); 576(25)
  Suggestions for Improvement relationship to;
     575(25)
Think Small pattern
  (reference description); 225(12)
'this' variable
  See Also self
  as object state; 285(14)
thread
  See Also concurrency; synchronization
  policy decoupling from concurrency policy, as
     Proactor pattern advantage; 146(9)
  Thread-Specific Storage pattern, Session
     relationship to, [Schmidt+1997]; 319(15)
  Threaded-Based Singleton pattern, as alternate
     name for Session pattern; 316(15)
Three-Level FSM pattern
  See Also finite state machines (FSM)
  Dynamic State Instantiation relationship to,
     [Martin1995]; 435(19)
throwaway
  Throwaway Code pattern
    (reference description); 665(29)
    role in solving Big Ball of Mud situations;
      664(29)
  Throwaway the First One pattern, as alternate
     name for Rehabilitation; 684(29)
time
  See Also change; concurrency; distributed
     systems
  in "A Collection of History Patterns"; 263(14)
  basic concepts of; 266(14)
  as Big Ball of Mud pattern language force;
     655(29)
  capturing instants of, Snapshot pattern;
     257(13)
  as Define and Run Presentation issue; 484(21)
  execution, Prototype-Based Object System
     pattern impact on; 53(5)
  in Historic Mapping pattern, [Fowler1997a];
     265(14)
  interval, (term description); 267(14)
  in Memento pattern, [Fowler1997a]; 265(14)
  pattern reference descriptions
    Change Log pattern; 271(14)
    Concrete Data Type pattern; 186(10)
    Edition pattern; 267(14)
    History on Association pattern; 276(14)
    History on Self pattern; 285(14)

time *(continued)*
    History on Tree pattern; 293(14)
    Memento Child pattern; 289(14)
    Posting pattern; 280(14)
    Snapshot pattern; 255(13)
    Synchronize Channels; 485(21)
    Temporal Association pattern; 250(13)
    Temporal Property; 241(13)
  pattern writers group duration, in pattern
     writers' workshops; 564(25)
  Piaget's investigations, [Piaget1946]; 264(14)
  relationship span, Relationship Object pattern
     relationship to, [Boyd1998]; 80(6)
  role, in SCRUM process; 639(28)
  span, product market window vs. good
     architecture benefits, [Foote+1995];
     656(29)
  as Synchronize Channels multimedia pattern
     dimension; 466(21)
  "Temporal Patterns", (chapter title); 241(13)
  Temporal Property alternative approaches,
     [Anderson1999]; 250(13)
  as Throwaway Code pattern force; 666(29)
  Time Reference pattern, Temporal Association
     relationship to, [Lange1998]; 254(13)
  time-based pattern relationships, [Lange1998];
     262(13)
  time-series database, feature extraction use;
     409(18)
  Time-Value Pairs pattern
    as alternate name for Temporal Property;
      241(13)
    Temporal Property relationship to,
      [Lange1998]; 249(13)
  Timestamp pattern
    See Also "An Input and Output Pattern
      Language: Lessons from
      Telecommunications"
    (reference description); 514(23)
Tool and Materials framework
  as Role Object known use
    [Riehle+1995b]; 28(2)
    [Riehle+1995c]; 28(2)
tools
  impact on software development; 662(29)
top-down design
  problems with; 662(29)
topology
  See Also structure
  spaghetti, avoiding in hypermedia design;
     456(20)
Total Rewrite pattern
  as alternate name for Rehabilitation;
     684(29)
Towell, Dwayne
  "Display Maintenance: A Pattern Language";
     489(22)

tracking
change, in Temporal Property; 241(13)
tradeoffs
user control of memory use, Make the User
Worry pattern; 230(12)
transaction(s)
many-to-many relationships, recording, in
Posting pattern; 281(14), 282(14)
mechanism, (term description); 266(14)
Transaction pattern, Posting relationship to,
[Fowler1997a]; 281(14)
transformations
of state, representation of time using; 264(14)
transitions
See Also time
pattern reference descriptions
Interface Organization; 423(19)
State-Driven Transitions; 421(19)
state
decoupling from entity behavior; 427(19)
in finite state machine; 416(19)
translucency
impact on Clip Requests; 499(22)
impact on Painter's Algorithm; 495(22)
transparency
in Object Synchronizer pattern use; 124(8)
trees
See Also hierarchy; structure
change of parent in, recording, in Memento
Child; 290(14)
data structures, broadcasting messages
through, as Object Recursion known
use; 49(4)
preserving, in History on Tree; 293(14)
triage
IO Triage pattern, (reference description);
512(23)
Tropyc pattern language
(chapter); 337(16)
Information Secrecy pattern, (reference
description); 346(16)
Message Integrity pattern, (reference
description); 347(16)
Secrecy with Integrity pattern, (reference
description); 353(16)
Secrecy with Sender Authentication pattern,
(reference description); 355(16)
Secrecy with Signature pattern, (reference
description); 355(16)
Secrecy with Signature with Appendix
pattern, (reference description); 358(16)
Secure-Channel Communication pattern,
(reference description); 342(16)
Sender Authentication pattern, (reference
description); 349(16)
Signature pattern, (reference description);
351(16)

Tropyc pattern language *(continued)*
Signature with Appendix pattern, (reference
description); 358(16)
"Tropyc: a pattern language for cryptographic
object-oriented software", (chapter
title); 337(16)
trust
See Also human relationships
Community of Trust pattern, (reference
description); 564(25)
turnover
employee, as Big Ball of Mud pattern language
force; 657(29)
Two Dimensional History pattern pattern
Posting relationship to, [Fowler1997]; 284(14)
two-step recursion
as Object Recursion known use; 48(4)
two-way relationship
See Also relationships
[Fowler1997]; 87(6)
Mutual Friends pattern; 82(6)
[Rumbaugh1996]; 87(6)
type(s)
See Also data types
algebraic, inheritance hierarchy for, Algebraic
Hierarchy pattern; 187(10)
dynamic change, patterns that address; 182(10)
numeric, representation issues; 5(1)
safety
as Abstract Session advantage; 102(7)
in Abstract Session pattern; 95(7)
vs. runtime efficiency, in Session pattern
implementation; 97(7)
Smalltalk lack of, as Generated Accessors
force; 206(11)
Type Object pattern
Limited View relationship to,
[Johnson+1997]; 325(15)
Prototype-Based Object System relationship
to, [Johnson+1998]; 56(5), 62(5), 68(5)
Role Object relationship to, [Johnson+1998];
22(2)
Type Promotion pattern, (reference
description); 195(10)

U
UI (user interfaces)
See Also GUIs (graphical user interfaces)
"An Input and Output Pattern Language:
Lessons from Telecommunications",
(chapter title); 503(23)
as architectural component and Big Ball of
Mud pattern language force; 657(29)
user-configurable systems, in "Creating
Reports with Query Objects"; 375(17)
UML (Unified Modeling Language)
See Also language(s)

UML (Unified Modeling Language) *(continued)*
finite state machine representation,
[UML1999]; 420(19)
[Fowler+1997]; 115(8)
inheritance symbol, Finite State Machine
pattern use, [UML1999]; 414(19)
Multimedia Authoring and Reuse Pattern
Language use; 466(21)
Object Synchronizer pattern; 115(8)
in Proactor pattern; 142(9)
stereotype use, in Temporal Property; 245(13)
understanding
immature, as system development stage;
655(29)
Unidraw
Active Value use
[Gamma+1995]; 84(6)
[Vlissides1990]; 84(6)
UNIX
access classifications, as Roles known use;
315(15)
access security issues; 305(15)
AIO, Proactor pattern use; 155(9)
file API, Session pattern use, [Lewine1991];
96(7), 97(7)
ftp, as Session known use; 320(15)
Sockets, [Stevens1990]; 97(7)
Telnet, as Session known use; 320(15)
updating
See Also state
displays, Request Update; 492(22)
dynamic formula values, Constraint
Observers; 387(17)
pattern reference descriptions
Consolidate Requests; 496(22)
Global Update; 493(22)
Request Update; 492(22)
Update at User-Speed pattern, as alternate
name for Lazy Redraw, [Beck1994];
498(22)
Urban Sprawl pattern
as alternate name for Piecemeal Growth;
668(29)
usability
as Components Layout multimedia pattern
dimension; 465(21)
as Graceful Degradation pattern strength;
233(12)
Limited View advantage; 325(15)
as Template multimedia pattern dimension;
465(21)
use cases
as domain knowledge capture tool,
[Beck+1989]; 666(29)
user
See Also customer; human relationships
configurable reports, Report Objects; 376(17)

user *(continued)*
configurable systems, in "Creating Reports
with Query Objects"; 375(17)
control of memory use, Make the User Worry
pattern; 230(12)
errors
handling, Full View with Errors pattern;
321(15)
Limited View; 323(15)
privileges, as security issue; 301(15)
User Defined Product Framework
bibliographic references, [Johnson+1998];
297(14)
as known use for History on Association,
[Johnson+1998]; 280(14)
User Types pattern, as alternate name for
Roles pattern; 312(15)
User's Environment pattern, as alternate name
for Session pattern; 316(15)
Using Low-Level Security pattern
as alternate name for Secure Access Layer;
329(15)
Using Non-Application Security pattern
as alternate name for Secure Access Layer;
329(15)

V
validation
See Also security
of attributes
as Essence force; 35(3)
patterns for, in "Essence", (chapter title);
33(3)
Validation and Penalization pattern, as alternate
name for Check Point pattern; 307(15)
value(s)
saving
complex variables, in a History object;
277(14)
simple variable, in a change log; 271(14)
shared, Session pattern use; 316(15)
Value Holder pattern, as alternate name for
Active Value; 82(6)
ValueHolder object, Active Value use,
[ParcPlace1994]]; 83(6)
ValueModel framework, Active Value use,
[ParcPlace1994]]; 83(6)
variable(s)
saving values
of complex variables=complex variables, in
a History object; 277(14)
of simple variables, in a change log; 271(14)
Variable Object pattern, as alternate name for
Active Value; 82(6)
Variable Sized Data Structure pattern, Make
the User Worry relationship to,
[Noblet1998]; 232(12)

variable(s) *(continued)*
Variable State pattern
bibliographic references, [Beck1997]; 296(14)
Change Log relationship to, [Beck1997]; 276(14)
Extensible Attributes relationship to; 204(11)
Posting relationship to, [Beck1997]; 284(14)
Prototype-Based Object System relationship to, [Beck1997]; 69(5)
Role Object relationship to, [Beck1996]; 23(2)

versioning
See Also time
in "A Collection of History Patterns"; 263(14)
"A Collection of History Patterns", (chapter title); 263(14)
Versioned Object pattern, Temporal Property relationship to, [Lange1998]; 250(13)

vi text editor
as Full View with Errors known use, [VI1998]; 322(15)

video
as multimedia component; 463(21)

views
context-specific, Role Object use; 15(2)
role-defined, in secure applications; 302(15)

violations
security, detection and handling, Check Point pattern; 307(15)

virtual
See Also GUIs (graphical user interfaces)
environment, performance issues; 489(22)
Virtual Constructor pattern
Envelope/Letter relationship to; 184(10)
(reference description); 184(10)

visibility
as Big Ball of Mud patterns force; 657(29)

VisualAge
Smalltalk, as Formula Objects known use, [IBM1997]; 386(17)

VisualPart
Mutual Friends use, [ParcPlace1994]; 87(6)

VisualWave
as Session known use, [ObjectShare1995]; 320(15)

VisualWorks
Active Value pattern relationship to, [Woolf1994]; 84(6)
ReportWriter
as Formula Objects known use, [ParcPlace Systems1995]; 386(17)
as Query Objects known use, [ParcPlace Systems1995]; 380(17)
as Report Objects known use, [ParcPlace Systems1995]; 378(17)

Vitality pattern
as alternate name for Keep It Working; 675(29)

Vitruvius, Marcus
architectural goals; 665(29)

Volunteer Summarizes the Work pattern
(reference description); 571(25)

W
waterfall process model
strengths and weaknesses; 670(29)

"The Way Things Work"
as Nodes in Context known use, [MacAuley1997]; 451(20)

Web
See WWW (World-Wide Web)

Weir, Charles
"High-Level and Process Patterns from the Memory Preservation Society: Patterns for Managing Limited Memory"; 221(12)

"What's New" pattern
as alternate name for News; 454(20)

Where Am I pattern
as alternate name for Active Reference; 451(20)

white-box inheritance
advantages during early phase of a project; 663(29)

Who Asked? pattern
See Also "An Input and Output Pattern Language: Lessons from Telecommunications"
(reference description); 515(23)

Wiki-Wiki-Web
as example of Throwaway Code persistence; 668(29)
Mutual Friends pattern use, [Metsker+1998]; 87(6)
system architecture impact, [Coplien1995]; 663(29)

Windows
16-bit API, Session pattern use, [Petzold1990]; 96(7)
NT
access security issues; 305(15)
Proactor pattern use; 155(9)

Woolf, Bobby
"A Pattern Language for Writers' Workshops"; 557(25)
"Abstract Class"; 5(1)
"Object Recursion"; 41(4)

word processors
as Full View with Errors known use; 322(15)

working set
code, (term description); 225(12)

workmanship
as Keep It Working force; 676(29)

Works Out of the Box pattern
Report Objects relationship to, [Foote+1998a]; 377(17)

Works out of the Box pattern
Sweeping It under the Rug relationship to,
[Foote+1998]; 683(29)
Workshop Comprises Authors pattern
Authors' Circle pattern relationship to; 567(25)
(reference description); 563(25)
workshops
pattern writers', "A Pattern Language for
Writers' Workshops"; 557(25)
'worse is better'
Big Ball of Mud as illustration of,
[Gabriel1991]; 661(29)
wrappers
See Also adapters
historical, transaction recording, in Posting
pattern; 282(14)
(term description); 381(17)
writing
"A Pattern Language for Writers'
Workshops", (chapter title); 557(25)
ease, as force in relationship patterns; 75(6)
"Identify the Champion: An Organizational
Pattern Language for Program
Committees", (chapter title); 539(24)
pattern writers' workshops, "A Pattern
Language for Writers' Workshops";
557(25)
write-only code, *See* Throwaway Code pattern
Wulf, Martina
"Role Object"; 15(2)
WWW (World-Wide Web)
See Also distributed; hypermedia; Internet
ACE, Proactor Web server sample code based
on, [Schmidt1994]; 153(9)
.htaccess and .htgroups files, as Roles known
use; 315(15)

WWW (World-Wide Web) *(continued)*
as Limited View known use; 328(15)
secure servers, Single Access Point pattern use;
306(15)
server
asynchronous, Proactor pattern use; 140(9)
performance requirements, [Hu+1997];
134(9)
performance requirements, [Hu+1998];
134(9)
Wiki-WIki web, system architecture impact,
[Coplien1995]; 663(29)
WyCash Report Writer
as Formula Objects known use,
[Cunningham1991]; 386(17)

X
Xauth application
Check Point example; 311(15)
xkernel framework
Abstract Session pattern use,
[Hutchinson+1991]; 107(7)

Y
yacc compiler compiler
debugging difficulties, compared with
Proactor pattern debugging difficulties;
146(9)
Yacoub, Sherif M.
"Finite State Machine Patterns"; 413(19)
Yoder, Joseph
"Architectural Patterns for Enabling
Application Security"; 301(15)
"Big Ball of Mud"; 653(29)
"Creating Reports with Query Objects";
375(17)